David Silberklang

GATES OF TEARS

The Holocaust in the Lublin District

This publication was supported by
The Conference on Jewish Material Claims Against Germany

Claims Conference ועידת התביעות
The Conference on Jewish Material Claims Against Germany

David Silberklang

GATES OF TEARS

The Holocaust in the Lublin District

Yad Vashem
The International Institute for Holocaust Research
Center for Research on the Holocaust in Poland

David Silberklang

Gates of Tears
The Holocaust in the Lublin District

Language Editor: Leah Aharonov
Production Editor: Daniella Zaidman-Mauer

P.O.B. 3477, Jerusalem 91034, Israel
publications.marketing@yadvashem.org.il

ISBN 978-965-308-464-3

Typesetting: Judith Sternberg

Printed in Israel by Dfus Nathan Shlomo, Jerusalem

Dedicated to the memory of my parents,
Boruch and Rywka Silberklang,
Who lived through so much to preserve and give life and the promise of a better future

❖ ❖ ❖

And to the living joy of my family,
Bobbie, Yael and Mati, Hillel and Liron, Elisha, and Akiva,
who inspire every day anew

Table of Contents

Acknowledgements

This book could not have been researched and written without the help, interest and wisdom of many people. Those who had a helpful impact on my work towards this book are too numerous to name, and I apologize if I seem to overlook some. I do not forget them, but in the interests of brevity (this book is already long) I will name only several of those people.

My teacher, doctoral advisor, and friend, Yehuda Bauer, has provided unhesitating support over many years. Indeed, it was he who sparked the beginning of the doctoral work that resulted in this book with a well-placed comment: "You know, you can't remain *Mr.* David Silberklang forever." Yehuda was always available for questions and discussion and always read everything I showed him with remarkable speed and insight. His breadth and depth of knowledge, together with his singular ability to synthesize and make accessible the most complex historical matters, have been a constant source of inspiration.

My very good friend Robert Rozett read the entire original manuscript and made astute comments on both the large and small issues. Rob is an excellent and extremely knowledgeable historian who is always prepared for an in-depth discussion of the research issues that arise. His friendship, interest, and insight have been invaluable.

The insightful comments of David Engel and Omer Bartov, two readers of the first version of this book, were invaluable and I thank them for their careful reading. Richard I. Cohen was of great assistance in many ways, not least for his seemingly simple suggestion on how to organize time to reach the finish line, which made a world of difference, as did his other comments and suggestions.

I learned much from all these comments and took them all into account, but the final version, analysis and opinions are solely my responsibility.

During the course of the research, many people provided willing assistance to help me navigate archives and reach sources, including at times sources that had not yet been fully cataloged. In the Yad Vashem Archive, Hadassah Modlinger and Yehudit Kleiman helped me greatly during their consecutive tenures as heads of the Yad Vashem Archive reading room. Their familiarity with Yad Vashem's archive prior to and during the early stages of digitization was a boon to researchers. Mary Ginzburg gave of her time to help me with newly arrived archival material and in reading a number of sources in Russian. Nomi Halpern devoted much to help me find sources after they had been recataloged in the archive's reorganization a number of years ago. Similarly, the library staff at Yad Vashem was most helpful in providing everything I needed and in letting me retain materials beyond the time normally acceptable.

The late Yehoshua Büchler, director of the Moreshet Archive, helped me find important sources there, and discussed various topics at length, sharing his keen insight freely. My late friend Andrzej Nowodworski helped me in the beginning of my research by finding an expert who could help me in the Lublin State Archive and in many other ways. Robert Kuwałek was my original contact in the Lublin State Archive, and his invaluable assistance in the first stages of this research and ongoing friendship influence my work to this day. Michlean Amir of the United States Holocaust Memorial Museum Archive and her staff were most helpful in providing all the materials that I requested in an extremely efficient way, and in providing research space that enabled me to cover much ground.

I would also like to thank my friends and colleagues at the Yad Vashem International Institute for Holocaust Research for their interest and encouragement, and to Yad Vashem Publications, whose expert work and friendly encouragement helped me complete the job. And my friends on the staff of *Yad Vashem Studies*, Adina

Drechsler, Daniella Zaidman-Mauer, and Nathan Cohen, who were not only always interested and encouraging, but also graciously took upon themselves additional tasks as I became immersed in the writing and editing. Daniella also managed this book's production with the sure hand of an experienced professional. An author couldn't ask for more.

My language editor, Leah Aharonov, did her usual excellent job, tweaking where necessary, editing more extensively where needed, and asking numerous important questions that saved this book from lack of clarity in various places. The result is certainly a much better book thanks to her efforts.

This book has been a long time in the making, and it could never have happened without the support of my wife, Bobbie, who took many burdens upon herself with seeming effortlessness in order to help me find the time to research, write, and complete it. And she did it all with remarkable grace and always a smile. She and our children have not only stuck it out, so to speak, but also showed interest and even attended various lectures on the way to the book. Most importantly, they brighten the day and inspire the future.

Chapter 1

Introduction

In January 1942, according to the data prepared for the Wannsee Conference, the Nazis estimated that there were 2,284,000 Jews in the Generalgouvernement (GG) in Poland. One year later, according to SS statistician Dr. Richard Korherr, fewer than 298,000 were still alive.[1] The data are more staggering proportionally for the Lublin District of the GG. Whereas there were more than 300,000 Jews in the district in early 1942, there were only 20,000 (6.7 percent) still alive at the end of the year, according to Korherr. These statistics take on even more astonishing proportions considering the fact that the murder began only in mid-March of that year. Thus, nearly two million Jews had been murdered in this part of Poland in nine and a half months within the framework of "Operation Reinhard."

At center stage of this operation to murder all the Jews of the GG – and of a variety of earlier German anti-Jewish and demographic policies – were to be found Lublin and its SS chief, Odilo Globocnik. This district seemed to serve as an experimental area for anti-Jewish labor exploitation and residential policies, as well as for German colonization and demographic engineering policies. The Jews in this district faced large-scale refugee problems

1 Nuremberg Document NG-2586-G, minutes of the Wannsee Conference, January 20, 1942; Nuremberg Document NO-5194, Korherr Report, March 23, 1943. Both documents have been published in many sources. See, for example, Yitzhak Arad, Yisrael Gutman, Avraham Margaliot, eds., *Documents on the Holocaust* (Jerusalem: Yad Vashem, 1981), pp. 249–261, 332–334.

from the very beginning of the war, only to see these problems exacerbated extensively by Nazi anti-Jewish and demographic measures in 1939–1941. Similarly, these Jews faced large-scale round-ups for forced-labor camps at an early stage of the war (the summer of 1940), and Jews were still to be found in forced-labor camps as Red Army artillery thundered from the outskirts of Lublin in the summer of 1944. Thus, there was some level of apparent continuity in German policies toward Jews with regard to forced population movements and forced labor, and therefore some level of continuity in what the Jews in the district saw and confronted.

The policies and Jewish reactions that constitute this apparent continuity provide the connecting threads of this book. One of the underlying issues raised is the extent to which the Jews' early experience of the Germans' policies toward them influenced their later reactions to those policies.

A number of places and individuals have come to represent the Holocaust and the major axes of the "Final Solution" both in the historiography on the period and in the popular mind. Among the places Auschwitz-Birkenau stands out. The associations conjured up by the word "Auschwitz" are an encapsulation of the entire event. Indeed, Auschwitz-Birkenau was the place in which more Jews were murdered than any other site in the Nazi empire. It is also a place that was liberated and from which there emerged a relatively large number of survivors (albeit representing a tiny percentage of all the victims sent there) at the end of the war who could relate the story of the camp.

Of course, Auschwitz-Birkenau was not the only camp whose murderous credentials could help turn it into a symbol of the evil it embodied. It could be argued, for example, that Bełżec, with its lone known survivor – out of some 500,000 victims – was perhaps the place most representative of the totality and finality of the Nazi plans for the Jews. In fact, Bełżec was the only one of the death camps in which the assigned tasks were actually completed and therefore was shut down by the Nazis. This in itself symbolizes what the Nazis had intended for the "Final Solution." However, relatively little is known about this camp, which ceased operations and was dismantled nearly two years prior to the liberation of Auschwitz-Birkenau.[2]

The absolute finality of Bełżec and of the other "Operation Reinhard" death camps – Sobibór and Treblinka – is one of the major reasons that their awesome evil power did not assume the symbolic proportions of Auschwitz-Birkenau. Remote from the public eye and from eyewitness testimony, and remote in time and place from the liberation, none of the three death camps could be seen, photographed, or immediately investigated by the liberators. And even if these camps had been reached by liberators, there were few survivors to tell the story. As a result, these camps and the operation they served have until recently also remained far from the center of popular consciousness and scholarly interest. Just as the camps remained relatively obscure, so, too, did the events leading up to their establishment, as well as the people involved in those events. Those people, events, and places are at the heart of this book.

Among the individuals who have come to symbolize the murderers (in addition to Hitler himself) are Heinrich Himmler,

2 The memorial site at Bełżec, based on extensive research, refers to 500,000 Jews murdered there. Other recent research suggests that the number of Jews murdered at Bełżec was somewhat lower, around 434,000, whereas some research in the latter part of the 1990s suggested that the number of Jews murdered there may have been as high as 800,000. The United States Holocaust Memorial Museum has accepted the lower estimate, which is based on a British intelligence decode of a German radio message. Most historians have not accepted the higher estimate, which was based on excavations done at the site in advance of preparing the updated memorial center there. Regarding this research and the escapes from the camp, see Peter Witte and Stephen Tyas, "A New Document on the Deportation and Murder of Jews during 'Einsatz Reinhardt' 1942," *Holocaust and Genocide Studies*, vol. 15, no. 3 (Winter 2001), pp. 468–486; and the earlier reports of two of the active participants in the excavations and research at Bełżec in the late 1990s: Michael Tregenza, "Report on the Archeological Investigation at the Site of the Former Nazi Extermination Camp in Belzec, Poland, 1997–98" (Lublin, 1998); Robin O'Neil, "Belzec: A Reassessment: Resettlement Transports to Belzec, March-December 1942" (December 6, 1999). Both manuscripts can be found on www.jewishgen.org/Yizkor/belzec/belzec.html. The only available survivor account is Rudolf Reder, *Bełżec* (Kraków: Drukarnia Uniwersytetu Jagiełłonskiego, 1999, c1946). See also Dariusz Libionka, "The Life Story of Chaim Hirszman: Remembrance of the Holocaust and Reflections on Postwar Polish-Jewish Relations," *Yad Vashem Studies*, 34 (2006), pp. 219–247.

Reinhard Heydrich, and Adolf Eichmann. Whereas each of these men played a very important role in the murder of the Jews, they, too, symbolize more than they actually did. The Eichmann trial helped place Eichmann at the center of the Holocaust in the public mind. This extended even beyond his actual seminal role as Heydrich's organizer of deportations from western, central, and southern Europe to Auschwitz-Birkenau and other camps, and as a central player in the persecution and murder of the Jews in Hungary, Bohemia and Moravia, and other places.[3]

Himmler has been called "The Architect of Genocide" in Richard Breitman's book by that title, and other research has claimed this role for Heydrich. Breitman's argument, on the one hand, and that of Eberhard Jäckel and Charles Sydnor, on the other, have revolved around evidence of their respective protagonist's ability to read Hitler's intentions regarding the Jews and then offer operative plans to act upon them. This is what Sydnor refers to as "executive instinct." Jäckel highlights Heydrich's semi-independent position vis-à-vis Himmler, based on his appointments by Hitler as head of Jewish emigration (1939) and as "*Reichsprotektor*" for Bohemia and Moravia (1941), and by Göring as coordinator of the "Final Solution" (July 31, 1941). At the Wannsee Conference on January 20, 1942, Heydrich was clearly in charge, and one reason for convening the meeting was to present his credentials for the job and establish his preeminent position in Jewish affairs before all concerned.[4]

3 On Eichmann's activities and role in the Holocaust, see Yaacov Lozowick, *Hitler's Bureaucrats: The Nazi Security Police and the Banality of Evil* (New York: Continuum, 2002).

4 See Richard A. Breitman, *The Architect of Genocide: Himmler and the Final Solution* (New York: Knopf, 1992); Eberhard Jäckel, "From Barbarossa to Wannsee; The Role of Reinhard Heydrich," in Shmuel Almog, et al., eds., *The Holocaust, History and Memory: Essays Presented in Honor of Israel Gutman* (Jerusalem: Yad Vashem and Avraham Harman Institute of Contemporary Jewry, Hebrew University, 2001), pp. 1–9 ; Charles W. Sydnor, Jr., "Executive Instinct; Reinhard Heydrich and the Planning for the Final Solution," in Michael Berenbaum and Abraham J. Peck, eds., *The Holocaust and History; The Known, the Unknown, the Disputed, and the Reexamined* (Bloomington: Indiana University Press and the United States Holocaust Memorial Museum, 1999), pp. 159–186; Christian Gerlach, "The Wannsee Conference, the Fate of German Jews, and Hitler's Decision in Principle to Exterminate All European Jews,"

These arguments regarding these men raise a number of questions, reflecting the nature and role of symbols, as well as the approach of much of the research. All three of the above prominent figures were based in Berlin. We would expect to find evidence of regular visits to the scenes of the deportations and the death camps by the central figure in the entire operation of the murder of the Jews, or by his trusted subordinates. Jäckel notes in passing that Heydrich did not visit the GG (except one time in May 1940), whereas Himmler was there quite a number of times, as evidenced in his office diary and as Breitman discusses in detail.[5] Heydrich's authority lay in coordination of activities in Berlin and in deportations from across western, central, and southern Europe, mostly to Auschwitz-Birkenau. Eichmann was his expert at organizing these large-scale deportations. Both were committed mass murderers, but the foci of their murderous energies were Auschwitz-Birkenau, Chełmno, and the USSR, not the territories in between. In addition to the fact that Heydrich did not visit the GG, his chief subordinates, including Eichmann, were not seen there much either. This last point is not insignificant.

Heydrich's authority effectively stopped at the border of the GG. There, as in the Soviet Union, Himmler bypassed him and partially neutralized him with an alternative SS authority. The Einsatzgruppen (EG) were under Heydrich's authority, but Himmler stepped in to control or to circumvent much of their operations through other subordinates. In the Soviet Union, Himmler did this with an assortment of large units, such as the 18–25,000 SS and police soldiers of "Kommandostab Reichsführer-SS" and numerous police battalions. The local chain of command was answerable directly to Himmler and was headed by three regional *Höhere SS- und Polizeiführer* (HSSPF). The HSSPF apparatus was outside Heydrich's jurisdiction and superior in authority to his own appointments of Sicherheitspolizei (SIPO) and Sicherheitsdienst

The Journal of Modern History, 70 (December 1998), pp. 759–812, especially pp. 794–796.

5 See Peter Witte, et al., eds., *Himmlers Dienstkalender* (Hamburg: Christians, 1999), pp. 185–186, 203, 233–234, 379–380, 493–497, for some of Himmler's visits, summer 1941-summer 1942; Breitman, *Architect, passim.*

(SD) regional chiefs. In the GG the same sort of HSSPF apparatus functioned from late 1939 onward.[6]

Here Himmler went one step further. When it came to the murder of the Jews, he bypassed the very apparatus he had created to circumvent the hierarchy by giving Globocnik direct authority, independent of all other SS authorities, including his own immediate superior, HSSPF Friedrich Wilhelm Krüger. Although Heydrich was meant to oversee the transfer of many thousands of Jews from western, central, and southern Europe to death camps in the GG, his (and Eichmann's) authority ended once they arrived. The disposition of these Jews, as well as those within the GG, was in Globocnik's bailiwick. And Globocnik was Himmler's man.

Similarly, it is instructive to note that at the Wannsee Conference in January 1942, where Heydrich was the chairman and dominant figure, there were only two representatives of the GG, Josef Bühler and Eberhard Schöngarth, the deputy general governor and chief of the Sipo and SD, respectively. Schöngarth was Heydrich's man in the GG. Absent from the meeting were representatives of the Wehrmacht, the HSSPFs, and what was later called "Einsatzstab Reinhard," Globocnik's staff responsible for everything related to the murder of most of the Jews in the GG. Jäckel suggests that the absence of the armed forces is insignificant, since they would not have opposed any of the decisions reached in any event.

Assuming, for argument's sake, that Jäckel is correct regarding the armed forces, how can the absence of the HSSPFs and, most importantly, of Globocnik's team, be understood? Their absence demands explanation, since they, and not the civilian authorities or Heydrich's men, commanded and organized the murder of Polish Jewry in the GG. Schöngarth was not Globocnik's representative at

6 On the Kommandostab, see Yehoshua Büchler, "*Kommandostab Reichsführer-SS*: Himmler's Personal Murder Brigades in 1941," *Holocaust and Genocide Studies*, vol. 1, no. 1 (1986), pp. 11–25; Martin Cüppers, *Wegbereiter der Shoah: Die Waffen-SS, der Kommandostab Reichsführer-SS, und die Judenvernichtung 1939–1945* (Darmstadt: Wissenschaftliche Buchgesellschaft, 2005); Raul Hilberg, "The Kommandostab Revisited," *Yad Vashem Studies*, 34 (2006), pp. 355–367. On the HSSPF, see Ruth Bettina Birn, *Die Höhere SS- und Polizeiführer: Himmlers Vertreter im Reich und in den besetzten Gebieten* (Düsseldorf: Droste, 1986).

Wannsee. It is possible that they were not there because it was not necessary to gain their cooperation; they were already preparing the murder. However, it is also possible that the explanation for their absence is more straightforward: They were independent of Heydrich and Wannsee.

In order to understand the lives and deaths of more than two million Jews murdered in "Operation Reinhard" in 1942–1943, therefore, we must look elsewhere than Auschwitz and to people other than Heydrich and Eichmann. All the points mentioned above indicate the significance of Lublin in the Holocaust, at least from the German perspective.

The murder of most of Polish Jewry was planned in Lublin, and much of it was coordinated there. Yet only in recent years have Lublin and Globocnik begun to enter the historiography and the popular mind as symbols. Globocnik's influence was based to a great degree on his close personal relationship with Himmler, and perhaps this was one of the reasons that Himmler entrusted him with a mission as important as "Operation Reinhard." The location of the headquarters of "Operation Reinhard" in Lublin is also testimony to its centrality. Two death camps, Bełżec and Sobibór, were constructed in this district, and a third, Treblinka, also under "Reinhard" command, was built in the northern part of the Warsaw District. In addition, over a long period of time, Globocnik partially controlled the Majdanek camp adjacent to Lublin, as well as dozens of forced-labor camps, and a rather significant economic empire.

If the Lublin District was a center of Nazi anti-Jewish policy and murder, then its Jews are central to the story of the Holocaust and to our understanding of it. The approach taken to the Jews in this book reflects developments in perspectives regarding both the perpetrators and the Righteous Among the Nations.

Over the years perceptions about the perpetrators have changed considerably. Voluminous research has depicted the murderers as human beings who did monstrous things, rather than monsters in human guise. They were just like other people, with all their human strengths and weaknesses, with moral upbringings and modern education, yet they persisted in pursuing evil, mostly without apparent qualms of conscience. As such, despite their behavior, their socio-economic, political, and emotional profiles seem frighteningly close to those of ordinary people.[7]

Without entering into the debate regarding the origins of their motivations to participate in the persecution and murder of the Jews in their area, this book looks upon the German and Austrian perpetrators in the Lublin District as just such people and studies their attitudes toward Jews as they developed and put into effect anti-Jewish policies. What emerges is a picture of an apparently ideologically motivated, widespread consensus among the German and Austrian perpetrators, both uniformed and civilian, in the Lublin District regarding the murder of Jews in 1942–1943. This consensus and efficient collaboration emerged after more than two years of bickering, animosities, mutual recriminations, and mutual attempts by the civilian officials and the SS to undermine one another.

If in the past the perpetrators were the monsters among the non-Jews in the Holocaust, then the Righteous Among the Nations were the unequivocal heroes. They were deservedly placed on a pedestal and admired by all who approached the subject of those times. Since the late 1960s, attempts have been made to understand the motivations of these great heroes. The underlying premise of this research, most of it sociological, was a sort of *Tikkun Olam* ("mending the world"), to discover what motivated these rescuers, so that their superior moral behavior could be seen as a role model and replicated. In the pursuit of this aim, researchers tried to identify the particular shared characteristics in the rescuers' personalities, social environments, and upbringings that led to their actions. Although there are those who have claimed varying degrees of success in identifying these characteristics, it seems clear that there was no particular formula that produced a rescuer. An examination of the Righteous Among the Nations files in Yad Vashem reveals

7 On the "ordinariness" of the perpetrators, see, for example, Christopher R. Browning, *Ordinary Men: Reserve Police Battalion 101 and the Final Solution in Poland* (New York: HarperCollins, 1992); Raul Hilberg, *The Destruction of the European Jews*, Third Edition (New Haven: Yale University Press, 2003); Stanley Milgram, *Obedience to Authority* (New York: HarperCollins, 1974). See also Yehuda Bauer's reflections on the subject in his *Rethinking the Holocaust* (New Haven and London: Yale University Press, 2001), pp. 68–118.

the eminent normality and "ordinariness" of most of these people. Many of them had doubts, flares of temper, fears, temptations (to turn in Jews or exploit them), and so on. The key is that, with all their normal human strengths and weaknesses, they persisted in the pursuit of superior moral deeds, often over long periods of time, and at great risk.[8]

What about the Jews? When Polish underground figures or Nazi officials in World War II expressed dismay at one Jewish behavior or another (especially armed resistance), this can perhaps be attributed to their preconceived stereotypical image of the Jews. However, much of the historiography on Jewish responses to the Holocaust seems to be similarly based upon idealized images of Jews then and afterward. Nearly seventy years since the end of World War II, the Jews' reactions to the Holocaust often continue to be looked at (at least popularly) in mythic terms through the prism of "martyrs and heroes." That is, there were those who were killed, and there were those heroes who resisted before their death (or survival).

The search for a mythical heroism has at times been so overpowering that Jewish activities during the Holocaust have been examined largely from that vantage point – the extent to which Jews' activities in their efforts to survive were dangerous and heroic. The definition of heroism has evolved and expanded over the years to include not only those who engaged in organized armed resistance, but also what has been termed in Hebrew *amidah* – unarmed resistance and attempts to survive, including illegal activities, in the face of the Nazi onslaught. This is similar in many ways to what some

8 On the character of the Righteous Among the Nations, see, for example, David Gushee, "Many Paths to Righteousness: An Assessment of Research on Why Righteous Gentiles Helped Jews," *Holocaust and Genocide Studies*, vol. 7, no. 3 (1993), pp. 372–401; Mordecai Paldiel, "The Altruism of the Righteous Gentiles," *Holocaust and Genocide Studies*, vol. 3, no. 2 (1988), pp. 187–196; *idem*, *The Path of the Righteous: Gentile Rescuers of Jews during the Holocaust* (Hoboken, NJ: KTAV, 1993); Nechama Tec, *When Light Pierced the Darkness* (New York: Oxford University Press, 1986); Samuel and Pearl Oliner, *The Altruistic Personality* (New York: Free Press, 1988). From 1962 to early 2013, Yad Vashem honored nearly 25,000 people as "Righteous Among the Nations," and many more are expected to be honored in the next few years.

might call "passive" resistance, but, in the case of the Jews during the Holocaust, it was anything but passive.[9] *Amidah* has sometimes been described as including nearly all Jews, in the sense that they all struggled to survive, and in this very struggle they displayed courage and resistance against the German plans for them. However, such an all-inclusive definition of heroism and resistance does not address the question of how Jews responded to the Holocaust so much as that of who resisted the Nazis. Most Jews, it may be assumed, did all they could to survive, which means that almost all Jews during the Holocaust might be included under the heading "hero."

There is merit to the argument that any Jew who struggled to stay alive under the Nazis was in effect engaging in resistance by dint of the fact that staying alive foiled Nazi intentions for that person. But could all Jews really have been heroes? What can such a perspective say about all the people who lived and died as ordinary mortals and not as heroes on pedestals? Yehuda Bauer has aptly cautioned against creating a nostalgic or "overdrawn" picture of resistance or *amidah*.[10]

When Jews' actions and reactions are examined in the Lublin District (as in other areas), we find that there are no clear-cut conclusions. Jewish leaders and Judenrat heads or members who are fondly remembered by some are remembered with scorn by others. Judenräte that obeyed Nazi commands, such as in Lublin, also engaged in illicit activities for the benefit of members of the community through illegal contacts, smuggling, protecting "illegal" Jews, and so on. Regarding *amidah* by Jewish individuals and communities, Bauer notes that the extent to which *amidah* existed was largely dependent on the possibilities, which were usually greater in the larger communities in Eastern Europe than in the small ones. Generally, where conditions were too difficult, there was less *amidah*.[11]

9 On *amidah*, see Bauer, *Rethinking*, pp. 119–137, 148–166; Meir Dworzecki, "The Day-to-Day Stand of the Jews," in *Jewish Resistance During the Holocaust*, Aryeh Tartakower, et al., eds. (Jerusalem: Yad Vashem, 1971), pp. 152–181, and the discussion that follows on pp. 181–190.

10 Bauer, *Rethinking*, pp. 127–128.

11 Ibid., pp. 165–166.

Yet in Lublin, and in the district overall, conditions were generally better than in Warsaw; the Jewish leadership was also more representative than in Warsaw. Still, the extent of cultural, educational, and underground political activities that were integral to *amidah* were evident much less than in Warsaw. In this book the Jews in the Lublin District and elsewhere during the Holocaust are regarded as normal people in dire straits; their responses to their plight, as expressed in their behavior and activities, are examined from this perspective. This book also points, especially in the final two chapters, to the precariousness of Jewish existence under the Nazis and to the difficulty of categorizing or assigning labels.

The Jews' responses to the Nazis were influenced by an inability to grasp what Nazi policy intended, disbelief, and German deception. No less significant in influencing Jewish reactions was the continuity in German policies. The deportations in 1942 were a repeat collective experience for the Jews of the Lublin District, as Jews had been transported in and transported out in large numbers between October 1939 and May 1941. The same organizational framework for trains was used in 1942 as in 1940 and 1941, and, no less significant, excessive brutality, which attended the round-ups in 1942 for transports to death camps, had already been experienced in 1940, for transports to forced-labor camps.

Geographically, the Lublin District discussed in this research is that demarcated by the Germans in the GG, and not the Lublin District of prewar Poland's administrative organization of the country. The German-created district was largely the same as the Polish, excluding two northern counties (Siedlce and Garwolin were attached to the Warsaw District) and with the addition of small pieces of territory from prewar Galicia in the south. This geographic definition is the relevant one here, because the wartime district was one unit, with competing German district authorities each trying to implement its own anti-Jewish policy across the entire district. The Jews in this district maintained contacts with one another, often moved back and forth among the various communities, and faced the same German authorities and personalities overall. Developments in the two detached counties followed a different pace, along with the rest of the Warsaw District. Similarly, the Jews in the strips of territory attached from prewar Galicia shared the experience of the rest of the Jews of the Lublin District of the GG and not that of the Jews of Galicia. The Jews of the Lublin District were also the first to face collectively the policies that later affected the Jews all across the GG.

The Jews of the Lublin District were a diverse group that shared a very long history. While it is not the purpose of this book to present a history of the Jewish communities of the Lublin area, some background comments are important for our understanding of events under the Nazis. The first Jewish communities in this area date back to the thirteenth or fourteenth century; by the middle of the fifteenth century, Lublin's Jewish community had become one of the most important in East-Central Europe both religiously and economically. The centrality and growth of Lublin brought with it increased Jewish settlement in the sixteenth and early seventeenth centuries, and many new communities were established. By the sixteenth century, the city had become a religious, cultural, political, and commercial center for Jews in Central and Eastern Europe. Its famous trading fairs in the sixteenth and seventeenth centuries made it one of the two main seats of the "Council of the Four Lands," together with Jarosław to the southwest, during that autonomous Jewish governing body's 200-year existence. Lublin also became a natural center around which numerous Jewish communities developed over the centuries, until the final partition of Poland at the end of the eighteenth century.[12]

Part of the Lublin region was annexed by Austria in the first partition of Poland in 1772 and much more in the third partition in 1795, and it was governed together with Austrian-controlled Galicia.

12 The brief historical survey of Lublin is based upon the *Yizkor* books in the bibliography, and the following: Nachman Blumental and Meir Korzen, eds., *Encyclopedia of the Jewish Diaspora*, Volume 5: *Lublin* (Hebrew) (Jerusalem, Tel Aviv: Encyclopedia of the Jewish Diaspora, 1957); *Dos Buch fun Lublin: Memories, Testimonies, and Materials on the the Struggle for Life and the Martyrdom of the Jewish Community of Lublin* (Yiddish) (Paris: C.A.P.N. Press, 1952); Meir Balaban, *Die Yidn-Stadt Lublin* (Yiddish) (Buenos Aires: Union Central Israelita Polaca en la Argentina, 1946); Abraham Wein, ed., *Pinkas Hakehillot: Encyclopedia of Jewish Communities, Poland*, Volume 7: *Districts Lublin.Kielce* (Hebrew) (Jerusalem: Yad Vashem, 1999).

Napoleon incorporated it into the Duchy of Warsaw in 1807, and it then became part of Congress Poland, ruled by Russia from 1815 until the end of World War I, when an independent Poland rose again. The Lublin region was devastated in the mid-1600s, first by the Khmielnicki Massacres in 1648–1649, and then by the Swedish wars several years later. The city and the area recovered by the early eighteenth century, but by then Poland was already in decline as a European power, and, with it, Lublin and the surrounding towns began to decline as well, both as economic centers and as Jewish religious centers.

The century of Russian rule was accompanied by industrialization, tremendous population growth, and the gradual development of a Jewish labor movement. In the southern part of the region and parts of the north, there were also quite a number of Jewish farmers. However, the Lublin region of Poland lagged behind other parts of the country in development, and, in 1939, it had only a primitive road infrastructure and was under-industrialized in comparison to areas west of the Wisła (Vistula) River.

The Jews of the Lublin region were influenced in internal Jewish cultural terms by the *Litvak Misnagdim* to the north and by the Hasidic movement that developed in the south. One of the most important Hasidic leaders of the late eighteenth and early nineteenth centuries was Rabbi Yaakov Yitzhak HaLevi Horowitz, the "Hozeh of Lublin." By the end of the second decade of the nineteenth century, the southern half of the Lublin District was largely Hasidic, whereas in the areas further north, from Włodawa to Biała-Podlaska, there was still strong Litvak Jewish influence.

Alongside these trends, as the nineteenth century progressed, the region began to be influenced by modern political and religious developments, so that, by the early twentieth century, all the Jewish political parties of Eastern Europe — the Bund, the various Zionist parties, the ultra-Orthodox Agudat Israel, and the secular Yiddishist Folkspartei, which was particularly influential in Lublin — were well represented in the region. One of the leading figures in Agudat Israel in Poland in the 1920s, and member of the Sejm (Polish parliament), Rabbi Meir Shapira, was Lublin's most prominent rabbi in the 1920s. He laid the foundation for what arguably became the leading *yeshivah* in Poland in the 1930s, Yeshivat Hakhmei Lublin. In some of the larger, more modern towns in the district, such as Zamość, the younger Jews went through extensive secularization during the interwar period.

Still, the backwardness of the region's economy also influenced the Jewish community. As a result, many Jews remained in small villages and towns, and the *shtetl* was characteristic of Jewish life there. There was only one significant city in the region, Lublin, and even it was only a medium-sized city. Its 40,000-strong Jewish community numbered only one-fifth of the Lodz community and only one-eighth of the Warsaw community. In fact, the city of Warsaw alone had more Jews than the entire Lublin District. The underdeveloped infrastructure of the region and the close familiarity of many of the local Jews with dirt back roads and forest paths played a role in the Nazi policies toward the Jews and in the variety of Jewish responses, as will be discussed in later chapters. By the time Germany invaded Poland, there were some 250–300,000 Jews in the areas included by the Nazi occupation regime in the Lublin District.

Against the background of Lublin's centrality, decline, secularization, and renewed religious and cultural significance in the 1930s, with the opening of Yeshivat Hakhmei Lublin, and Lublin's apparent importance to the Germans and "pioneering" status in mass murder, the first, basic question asked in this book is, "what happened, and how?" Although there has been some important research on a number of aspects of the Holocaust in the Lublin District, the gaps in our knowledge are still great. Basic elements of the Holocaust as it took place here are still unclear, and much of what is known has been researched largely from only one perspective – either the Germans' or the Jews'. Lublin's very centrality means that there are more issues to uncover, discuss, and analyze regarding the Holocaust in this district.

This book examines the events of the Holocaust in the Lublin District both from the perspective of the Germans and Austrians, and from the perspective of the Jews, while focusing on filling in some of the lacunae in this vast subject. Two central aspects of the Holocaust that have not been addressed extensively in connection to Lublin serve as the foci and connecting threads of the story of the Holocaust in this region: these are forced population movements (including ghettoization) and forced labor. These two subjects were at the heart of Nazi policy-making and of the Jewish experience in this district from the first day of German occupation to the last. Therefore, forced population movements and forced labor occupy a central place in this book.

Furthermore, what connections can be drawn between German anti-Jewish policies early in the war in this district and later in the war? Similarly, to what extent were Jewish reactions to the Germans in 1942–1944 based on what they had experienced and how they had reacted in 1939–1941? Whereas Lublin was central to various Nazi anti-Jewish policies (resettlement, labor, and murder), this research indicates that it differed from the rest of Poland in relation to others. For example, as I embarked on this research, I understood one subject that is discussed below to be "life in the ghettos." However, although Jewish people were constantly being moved in the Lublin District, there were actually very few ghettos there. In fact, although many Jews throughout the GG were not put into formal ghettos before 1942, in Lublin it was the large majority of the Jews who were not in ghettos even at this late stage. There were many Jews in numerous villages, *shtetls,* and medium-sized towns who continued to live in their own homes and were not confined to a Jewish neighborhood. Moreover, they continued to have contact with their neighbors, with Jews elsewhere in the GG, and even outside Poland. Communications continued in an area where ghettoization was very limited. Why was this so? And what impact did this have on the fate of the Jews of the Lublin District? As the overall picture of Jewish life under the Nazis here, until the end of 1941, is somewhat different than in other regions, so are the questions we must ask regarding ghettos.

These are among the many facets of the investigation of what happened and how. The framework of this book did not allow for an exhaustive discussion of all subjects, such as internal life in the Jewish communities, Judenräte and Jewish police, partisans, and events inside the death camps. Rather, this book seeks to contribute to laying the foundations for further research on aspects of the

Holocaust that have merited only limited discussion to date, while it more briefly addresses subjects that have already been researched (e.g., the operation of the death camps and partisan activity).

When this research was begun, there were very few scholarly works on the Holocaust in the Lublin District. Three publications reflected research on the city or district of Lublin. The earliest of these was Tatiana Berenstein's 1950 article on deportations in the Lublin District during World War II, and the tables are still particularly useful.[13] In 1967, Nachman Blumental published his very important book containing the annotated minutes of the Lublin Judenrat's meetings.[14] Blumental's annotations and introduction are very useful. His comments reflected some familiarity with additional Lublin Judenrat documents that he had probably seen when he still lived in Poland but whose whereabouts were hidden from researchers until the fall of communism in Poland. However, the book provides only one part of one aspect of the Holocaust in the Lublin District – the *official* minutes of the Lublin Judenrat's meetings. And, even here, Blumental's discussion and analysis are due for reevaluation and expansion. Following the fall of communism in Poland, the full, extant Lublin Judenrat archive became accessible again, and this author has made extensive use of this archive.[15]

Twenty years after Blumental's book, Yitzhak Arad published

13 Tatiana Brustin-Berenstein, "Deportations as a Stage in the German Annihilation Politics Regarding the Jewish Population" (Yiddish), *Bleter far Geschichte*, vol. 3, nos. 1–2, January-June 1950, pp. 51–77. See also her later article in Polish that addressed the same themes: "Martyrologia, opór i zagłada ludności żydowski w dystrykcie lubelskim," *Biuletin Żydowski Institut Historyczny*, 21 (1957), pp. 22–92.

14 Nachman Blumental, ed., *Documents from the Lublin Ghetto: Judenrat Without Direction* (Hebrew) (Jerusalem: Yad Vashem, 1967).

15 The collection is in Wojewódstwo Archiwum Państwowe w Lublinie (WAPL), record group Rada Żydowska w Lublinie (RZ). Another important record group is that of the German district government, Gouverneur des Distrikts Lublin (GDL). Copies of some of these files are also in the Yad Vashem Archives (YVA), and of the entire collection in the United States Holocaust Memorial Museum Archives (USHMMA). When such copies exist, the reference given in this book will be to the original in WAPL (unless the document was seen only at YVA or USHMMA), with the YVA and/or USHMMA copy in parentheses at the first mention of the file and in the Bibliography.

the first extensive research of the "Operation Reinhard" death camps. Most subsequent research relating to "Operation Reinhard" has relied extensively on that book.[16] To these we should add Shmuel Krakowski's 1977 work on Jewish armed resistance in Poland, approximately one-third of which is devoted to the Lublin District.[17] Together, these works provided an outline of events in the district and an in-depth look at several aspects.

Two important books, written by Dieter Pohl and by Bogdan Musial,[18] on the Germans and German policy in this district appeared during the course of this research. From them we can gain some understanding of the SS and the German civilian authorities in this district and their anti-Jewish policies. Both books are useful in discussing the flow of the deportations in 1942, and Musial adds important insight into the development of the civilian administration and its personnel.

Still, important lacunae remain. For example, neither Musial nor Pohl looks at the Jews of the district, or makes more than very scant use of the Lublin Judenrat's archive, leaving the Jews as objects of Nazi policies. They also do not discuss Jewish forced labor at length. Yet forced labor was a factor that affected the large majority of Jewish households in the district and was perhaps the longest lasting of all Nazi policies toward the Jews. The story that emerges, therefore, from the above very fine pieces of research remains limited. We now have information on some of the German policies in the area and on the Jews in the death camps and with the partisans. But we know much less about ghettoization, living conditions, forced labor, deportations, or the Jews' own perspectives on the events.

16 Yitzhak Arad, *Belzec, Sobibor, Treblinka: The Operation Reinhard Death Camps* (Bloomington: Indiana University Press, 1987).

17 Shmuel Krakowski, *Jewish Armed Resistance Against the Nazis in Poland, 1942–1944* (Hebrew) (Jerusalem: Yad Vashem, Institute of Contemporary Jewry, and Sifriat Hapoalim, 1977); published in English as *The War of the Doomed* (New York: Holmes and Meier, 1984).

18 Dieter Pohl, *Von der "Judenpolitik" zum Judenmord; Der Distrikt Lublin des Generalgouvernements 1939–1944* (Frankfurt am Main, Berlin: Peter Lang, 1993); Bogdan Musial, *Deutsche Zivilverwaltung und Judenverfolgung im Generalgouvernement; Eine Fallstudie zum Distrikt Lublin 1939–1944* (Wiesbaden: Harrassowitz Verlag, 1999).

How did these people understand and react to the Nazi policies that affected them? To what extent did they have any influence over the course of events? Why did Jewish forced labor in this district continue until so late in the war — the summer of 1944? Were the Jewish forced-laborers essential to the German war effort? Who were the Germans involved in this and why? Did forced labor affect Jewish survival?

This book looks upon the Jews as a subject of history and, as such, their thoughts, activities, and perspectives were relevant to the events then and are relevant to our understanding of these events today. It makes extensive use of both German and Jewish sources, and through them attempts to present a fuller picture of events through multiple perspectives.

Like Pohl, Musial, and other Holocaust study in recent years, this research examines events in the field, more than at the center of the Third Reich. This makes the Jewish perspective all the more important. As Jews and Germans had regular contact on the local level, did this contact have an effect on policies, or on the Jews' fate? In what way, if any, were the local, "ordinary" Germans and Austrians affected by this contact and familiarity with Jews? To what extent was policy locally determined? We might expect that personal interaction over a period of time might have given the Jews a more human face in the eyes of the local Germans. Was this so? And all this connects to the question of which Jews survived and why? That is, was there anything that the Jews did or could have done that could have affected their collective fate?

In a sense, this book looks for the face of the Holocaust in the Lublin District through its discussion and analysis of the events. Early in the research I came upon two documents that shed some light on this face. On the human face of the perpetrators, one Jewish doctor observed after the war: "These people found pleasure in tormenting their little victims [the children] in the most bestial manner and worked out special methods to prolong a single murder for hours."[19] On the Jews' struggle to grasp what the Germans planned for them and then to act on it, one Jew who escaped his

19 Testimony of Erich Mossbach, YVA, O.33/2149.

town's deportations but did not survive commented: "...an expulsion is like a funeral procession – when a funeral procession passes by, heaven forbid, everyone thinks it is not for him. That's how it was with us."[20]

Between the pleasure these very human murderers derived from torturing their child victims and the Jews' difficulty in understanding that they were condemned and the futility of their responses lies the face of the Holocaust in the Lublin District of Poland.

German soldier guarding in front of Yeshivat Hakhmei Lublin, Yad Vashem Photo Archive, 1605/762

20 Fiszelzon report, YVA, M.10.AR.I/946, June 6, 1942.

Courtesy of the Jewish Historical Institute, Warsaw, Poland

Chapter 2

The Structure of the Lublin District

From the first days of the war, the cities and towns of the Lublin District were bombed by German airplanes, striking terror from the skies. Buildings were destroyed or ablaze, and the roads were filled with people fleeing for their lives. Polish troops retreated into the towns of the district and then retreated out, and municipal defense committees were formed with active Jewish participation. Underground shelters were quickly organized, food was distributed, defensive trenches were dug – but all this was to no avail. The Germans reached the Bug River in two weeks and conquered the city of Lublin on September 18, 1939; many Jews in the Lublin District already spent Rosh Hashanah 5700 (September 14–15) under German occupation.

Based upon the provisions of the Ribbentrop-Molotov Pact of August 23, 1939, the German army then withdrew westward from much of the area between the Bug and Wisła rivers, including the eastern and southern parts of the Lublin District. Most of the area between these rivers had been assigned in that pact to the Soviet partition zone, and the Red Army entered as the Germans withdrew. However, based upon the September 28 amended agreement between Germany and the Soviet Union, the Red Army withdrew east of the Bug and south of the new demarcation line, and the German army returned to the region gradually between October 4 and October 10. The Wehrmacht rule of Poland lasted only a few weeks, before making way for civilian rule.[1]

On the eve of the war, there were approximately 250–300,000 Jews in the Lublin District, with some 40,000 living in Lublin itself. It is not clear how many there were when the last Soviet troops withdrew on October 10.

German Civilian Government

Occupied Poland was divided into three main sections beginning in October 1939. These included the western areas, which were soon annexed to Germany (Pomerania, Danzig, East Prussia, Upper Silesia, and the "Warthegau"); the GG, administered by a German civilian occupation regime; and the eastern areas annexed by the Soviet Union (Vilna area, Białystok, Western Belorussia, Volhynia, and Eastern Galicia). For the Nazis the GG was *the* occupied territory of Poland, while the annexed areas were considered to be integrally German.

On October 12, 1939, Hitler issued a decree, effective October 26, creating the *Generalgouvernement für die besetzten Polnischen Gebiete* (General Government for the Occupied Polish Territories, or GG). Nine months later, on July 24, 1940, the territory was re-named simply *Generalgouvernement*, as though to say it was now neither Polish nor occupied. The first civilian officials were already on the scene in Lublin on October 4, appointed by the military's temporary head of civil administration. However, as a result of the changing borders and authorities in Lublin in October 1939, the civilian administration was somewhat slow in organizing.

1 Martin Broszat, *Nationalsozialistische Polenpolitik 1939–1945* (Stuttgart: Deutsche Verlags-Anstalt, 1961), pp. 9, 26–31; Czeslaw Madajczyk, *Die Okkupationspolitik Nazideutschlands in Polen 1939–1945* (Köln, Berlin: Akademie-Verlag and Pahl-Rugenstein, 1988), pp. 1–29; Dieter Pohl, *Judenpolitik*, pp. 22–33; and Hans Umbreit, *Deutsche Militärverwaltungen 1938/39; Die militärische Besetzung der Tschechoslowakei und Polens* (Stuttgart: Deutsche Verlags-Anstalt, 1977), pp. 65–79, 85–119. See also Zygmunt Klukowski, *Diary from the Years of Occupation 1939–44* (Urbana and Chicago: University of Illinois Press, 1993), pp. 36–38.

The German administrative structure of the GG was similar to that of the Reich and was based geographically on the prewar Polish administrative units. But because of a lack of German manpower and a mistrust of Polish officials, the Germans' administrative units were larger than those of prewar Poland. The GG's administrative center was in the new capital, Kraków (Krakau in German), and it was divided into four districts: Krakau, Warschau (Warsaw), Radom, and Lublin. A fifth district, Galizien (Galicia), was added on August 1, 1941, following the conquests of Soviet territories in "Operation Barbarossa."[2]

The GG was ruled by a civilian general governor (*Generalgouverneur*), Dr. Hans Frank, who was personally appointed by Hitler. Frank was theoretically the supreme administrative authority, wielding absolute power. Each district was in turn ruled by a district chief (*Distriktchef*), later called governor (*Gouverneur*), who was meant to wield absolute power within his own jurisdiction. Frank's administration had twelve governmental departments (*Hauptabteilungen*), each headed by a high-ranking civil servant, a *Staatssekretär*. Frank's first deputy was Arthur Seyss-Inquart (until May 1940), and his chief civil servant was *Staatssekretär* Josef Bühler (promoted to Frank's deputy in June 1941). The districts were divided into counties (*Kreise*), each headed by a county chief (*Kreishauptmann*). In addition, large cities were ruled by a German mayor (*Stadthauptmann*), while large rural towns were ruled by a town executive (*Stadtkommissar*), and rural sub-counties were ruled by a sub-county executive (*Landkommissar*). Polish mayors and

2 Many sources relate the events leading up to the creation of the GG. See, for example, Hilberg, *Destruction*, pp. 196–206; Jan Tomasz Gross, *Polish Society under German Occupation; The Generalgouvernement, 1939–1944* (Princeton: Princeton University Press, 1979), pp. 42–47; Broszat, *Nationalsozialistische Polenpolitik*, pp. 26–31; Madajczyk, *Okkupationspolitik*, pp. 46–65; Horst Rohde, "Hitler's First Blitzkrieg and its Consequences for North-eastern Europe," in Klaus Maier, et al., *Germany and the Second World War*, Volume II: *Germany's Initial Conquests in Europe* (Oxford: Clarendon Press, 1991), pp. 130–132; Norman Rich, *Hitler's War Aims*, Volume 2: *The Establishment of the New Order* (New York: W. W. Norton and Co., 1974), pp. 70–71, 88; Musial, *Zivilverwaltung*, pp. 14–22. See also Anklageschrift gegen Wolfgang Hoffmann, Julius Wohlauf, u.a., StA Hamburg, 141 Js 1957/62, pp. 165–169 (copy in YVA, TR.10/764).

village elders were responsible to their respective civilian German overseers, and the Jewish Councils were officially responsible to a *Stadthauptmann* or *Kreishauptmann*.[3]

The Lublin District's first civilian chief was Dr. Friedrich Schmidt, who was appointed by Seyss-Inquart on October 26, 1939. On December 13, Schmidt appointed district SS head Odilo Globocnik (see below) as his deputy. Globocnik, in turn, wished to replace Schmidt as district chief and thereby aggrandize more power for himself. In light of the subsequent adversarial relations between Globocnik and the Lublin civilian administration, this appointment seems remarkable. Perhaps Schmidt's own high SS rank (*Brigadeführer*) led him to trust Globocnik. However, although Schmidt's tenure as governor was indeed very brief, Globocnik never achieved his goal.

Schmidt had attempted to hold down two jobs, maintaining his party functions in Germany while assuming the position of district chief. In late January, Frank demanded that Schmidt choose between his party and district duties. When, after some consideration, Schmidt chose his party functions, Frank, on February 21, 1940, appointed Ernst Zörner, the former mayor of Dresden and most recently of occupied Kraków, to be the new governor. Zörner was a veteran Nazi who had held high governmental and legislative positions and had very high connections (he counted Josef Goebbels and other prominent Nazis among his close friends). His base was in the city of Lublin, and his administrative bureaucracy eventually grew to some 700 people.[4]

3 Max Freiherr Du Prel, ed., *Das Deutsche Generalgouvernement Polen; Ein Überblick über Gebiet Gestaltung und Geschichte* (Krakau: Buchverlag Ost, 1940), pp. 11–14, 139–144, 170–177; *idem*, ed., *Das Generalgouvernement* (Wurzburg: Konrad Triltsch Verlag, 1942), pp. 297–324; Broszat, *National sozialistische Polenpolitik*, pp. 70–74; Madajczyk, *Okkupationspolitik*, pp. 64–66, 72; Hilberg, *Destruction*, pp. 196–199. On the change of title for the governors, see "'Gouverneur des Distrikts' anstatt 'Distriktschef,' " *Krakauer Zeitung*, October 10, 1941. This GG Nazi newspaper can be found in YV library, PFi-48 and C-148. This notice is also in YVA, JM/4231, f. 5313959. See also Musial, *Zivilverwaltung*, p. 34.

4 WAPL, GDL, file 882 (parts copied in YVA, O.53/82 and JM/2699), contains lists of civilian administration personnel. On Schmidt's appointment of Globocnik, see Schmidt, letter to all officials, December 13, 1939, WAPL, GDL 677; Musial,

The district encompassed ten counties: Lublin-Land; Puławy; Radzyń; Biała-Podlaska; Chełm (Cholm); Hrubieszów; Zamość; Biłgóraj; Janów-Lubelski; and Krasnystaw. Only Lublin and Chełm had a German mayor with the rank of *Stadthauptmann*.

Zörner resigned on April 10, 1943. Following six weeks of supervision over the district by Warsaw Governor Dr. Ludwig Fischer, his replacement was announced on May 26. Dr. Richard Wendler (Himmler's brother's brother-in-law and a *SS Gruppenführer*) was appointed to the position. Five county chiefs in the district were replaced in 1941 and 1942, prior to the major deportations of Jews. They included Janów-Lubelski (January 1942); Krasnystaw (August 26, 1941); Hrubieszów (March 12, 1941); Chełm (January 1942); and Radzyń (January 26, 1942). In addition, the *Stadthauptmann* of Lublin was replaced on April 21, 1942, following the main deportations from that city (see district map above and list of governors, county heads, and other major German civilians in Tables 2.1 and 2.2).[5]

Regarding the Jews (and other national groups), one of the most significant departments of the civilian administration was the *Bevölkerungswesen und Fürsorge* (Population and Welfare; BuF) office of the Interior Department, which was responsible for all welfare and population registry affairs. As such, the BuF was involved in many of the issues relating to Jews — food, housing, relocation, etc. Richard Türk was the head of this department until the spring of 1942, when he moved to a higher position in Kraków once the Lublin deportations had been completed and other deportations in the district were already well under way.

Zivilverwaltung, p. 35. On Zörner's assumption of the position, see *Krakauer Zeitung*, March 5, 1940, "Generalgouvernement" page; Musial, ibid., pp. 35–36. See also *Nationalzeitung*, March 5, 1940, reporting from Kraków, in YVA, JM/4210, f. 5284643. On Zörner's Nazi record, see *The Goebbels Diaries 1942–1943*, translated and edited by Louis Lochner (Garden City, NY: Doubleday, 1948), p. 396, editor's note; Broszat, *Nationalsozialistische Polenpolitik*, p. 73, n. 2; Musial, ibid., pp. 37, 399.

5 WAPL, GDL, 882; Edward Kossoy, *Handbuch zum Entschadigungsverfahren* (Munich: Oldenburg, 1958); YVA, TR.10/764, pp. 169–174; Musial, *Zivilverwaltung*, pp. 93–94 and *passim*.

Table 2.1: Lublin Central Government

Governors	Amtschefs	Other Significant Officials
Dr. Friedrich Schmidt (26.10.39–2.40)		Richard Türk BuF chief, 1.40–16.4.42
Ernst Otto Zörner (21.2.40–10.4.43)	Dr. Fritz Schmiege (15.2.40–8.40)	Dr. Fritz Heinecke BuF deputy, 1.4.40–30.6.41
	Dr. Hans Damrau (16.8.40–11.11.40)	Ernst (Fritz) Reuter BuF deputy, 1942
	Dr. (Alfred?) Kipke (acting, 11.11.40–15.1.41)	Georg Hartig BuF chief, 16.4.42–2.43
	Dr. Ludwig Losacker (15.1.41–1.8.41)	Regierungsrat Jache Abt. Arbeit
Dr. Ludwig Fischer (caretaker) (10.4.43–26.5.43)	Dr. Wilhelm Engler (18.8.41–5.43)	Oberregierungsrat Dr. Hans-Heinrich Hasse Abt. Finanzen
Dr. Richard Wendler (26.5.43–7.44)	Ernst Schlüter (6.43–22.7.44)	Dr. Georg Claus, Abt. Ernährung un Land-wirtschaft
		Muth, Abt. Strassen-bau
		Dr. Waizenegger Abt. Gesundheitswes-en
		Dr. Roland Seeberg-Elverfeldt chief archivist, 1.40–11.42

Table 2.2: Lublin Kreishauptleute

Biała-Podlaska	(Eberhard?) Godau (10–12.39)	**Krasnystaw**	Hartmut Gerstenhauer (10.39–9. 40)
	Herbert Kühl (12.39–12.42)		Hennig von Winterfeld (10.40–1.41)
	Friedrich (Fritz) Sauermann (5.43–7.44)		Claus Volkmann (4.41–7.41)
Biłgoraj	Dr. Werner Ansel (10.39–3.42)		Adolf Schmidt (8.41–2.44)
	Hans Augustin (4.42–11.42)		Claus Harms (5.44–7.44)
	Dr. Karl Adam (12.42–8.43)	**Lublin-Land**	Emil Ziegenmeyer (10.39–7.44)
	Lövner (9.43–6.44)	**Puławy**	Friedrich Trampedach (10.39–1.40)
Cholm (Chełm)	Werner Kalmus (10.39–2.40)		Alfred Brandt (1.40–7.44)
	Erhard Hager (5.40–7.41)	**Radzyń**	Hennig von Winterfeld (10.39–8.40)
	Hans Augustin (9.41–4.42)		Dr. Fritz Schmiege (8. 40–10.41)
	Dr. Werner Ansel (4.42–11.42)		Ludwig Stitzinger (12.41–7.44)
	Claus Harms (12.42–3.44)	**Zamość**	Helmuth Weihenmaier (10.39–7.44)
	Dr. Werner Ansel (7.44)	**Lublin Stadthaupt-Mannschaft**	Dr. Fritz Cuhorst (11.39–6.40)

Hrubieszów	Dr. Walter Behrend (10.39–6.40)	Fritz Sauermann (7. 40–2.42)
	Karl-Heinrich Franke (6.40–2.41)	Curt Englaender (4.42–11.43)
	Otto Busse (3.41–7.44)	Karl Vielweib (11.43–7.44)
Janów-Lubelski (Kraśnik)	Otto Stössenreuther (10.39–8.40)	
	Hennig von Winterfeld (8.40–10.40)	
	Hans Adolf Asbach (10.40–7.41)	
	Hans Lenk (8.41–7.44)	

The district government bureaucracies were subordinate to their respective governors and to the central GG administration in Kraków, and, theoretically, the *Führerprinzip* (the absolute authority of the leader) was the rule of administration. However, Frank "inspired neither confidence nor loyalty among his colleagues,"[6] and dynamic, powerful, and independent personalities on the district and local levels could chart a relatively independent course. Zörner and a number of his subordinates exercised such independence in several important areas, including ghettoization and the nature and extent of cooperation with the SS in forced labor and deportations.

In general, the Jews' most frequent contact with the German authorities in their day-to-day lives was with the civilian administration, from its establishment until early 1942. At that time the SS took over all the important aspects of dealings with the Jews

6 Quote from Rich, *Hitler's War Aims*, vol. 2, p. 85. See also Gross, *Polish Society*, pp. 52–53.

as part of the preparation and implementation of the "Final Solution" in the GG. This came to be called by the Germans "Operation Reinhard." Still, even in the early stages of the occupation, the SS could and often did assert its dominance in aspects of Jewish policy almost at will. The well-known, ongoing competition and rivalry between the civilian and SS authorities in the GG capital, Kraków, was not as prevalent on the district level, except for Lublin. There the sharp competition and rivalry between the two authorities reflected the unusual personalities at the head of the SS and within the Lublin civilian administration. The widespread personnel changes in the civilian and SS authorities in the spring and summer of 1943 can be traced in part, at least, to the struggles between these two forces. Ultimately, both Zörner and the head of the district SS, Odilo Globocnik, fell victim to each other's strength and to the success of their own machinations against each other.[7]

SSPF Apparatus

Ruth Bettina Birn has written about the institution of the *Höhere SS- und Polizeiführer* (HSSPF) in general, although she did not deal with their subordinate SSPFs in the GG.[8] The HSSPF was Himmler's representative in his assigned area, and, like Himmler, he was meant to oversee and direct *all* SS and police activities within the area of his jurisdiction. As one postwar German indictment put it, each HSSPF was "a mini-Himmler" ("*ein kleiner* Himmler") in his own area of jurisdiction. The HSSPF's actual authority vis-à-vis other SS, police, military, and civilian officials was dependent largely on a number of factors apart from his actual title or rank, such as personalities,

7 On the relations between Globocnik and Zörner, see, for example, the 1960 testimony of Dr. Fritz Schmiege, Zentralestelle für Landesjustizverwaltungen, Ludwigsburg (ZStL), Ludwigsburg, 208 AR-Z 268/59, YVA, TR.10/1146 Z, pp. III:577–578, and the 1960 testimony of Konrad Gallen, ibid., p. VIII:1615. Many sources relate the SS-civilian rivalry in the GG. See, for example, Hilberg, *Destruction*, pp. 200–206; Broszat, *Natinalsozialistische Polenpolitik*, pp. 80–84; Madajczyk, *Okkupationspolitik*, pp. 66–70; Rich, *Hitler's War Aims*, pp. 81–82, 93–95; Musial, *Zivilverwaltung*, pp. 35–39, and *passim*.

8 Birn, *Die Höhere SS- und Polizei Führer.*

personal connections to Himmler or other top Nazis, ruthlessness, and others.

In the GG the HSSPF, from October 4, 1939 to November 9, 1943, was *SS-Obergruppenführer* Friedrich Wilhelm Krüger. He was succeeded by *SS-Obergruppenführer* Wilhelm Koppe.[9] The new function of SSPF was introduced in the GG on a district level. The district SSPF had the same responsibilities and authority district-wide as did the HSSPF throughout the GG. He was subordinate to Krüger, who could also intervene in the district as he saw fit and who was responsible for coordinating and directing the activities of the five SSPFs.

The HSSPF and SSPF apparatus were not under Heydrich's command, but Himmler's. They received their orders directly from Himmler and were completely independent of Heydrich and the RSHA in all matters, especially and including Jewish policy.[10] Just as Himmler oversaw all SS and police activities, so, too, did the HSSPF and SSPF oversee all SS and police activities in the GG. Therefore,

9 See Himmler to Krüger, October 4, 1939; Himmler to von Herff, October 6, 1943; Himmler to Krüger, October 22, 1943, in Krüger's Berlin Document Center file (BDC, today part of Bundesarchiv [BA]-Berlin), YVA, O.68/714. See also Himmler's December 18, 1939, "Dienstanweisung für die Höheren SS-und Polizeiführer," where these responsibilities were spelled out, in YVA, TR.10/813, Hamburg, "Anklageschrift" and "Urteil" against Georg Michalsen, et al., 147 Js 24/72, 147 Ks 3/72, p. 53; and the August 8, 1969, indictment of Georg Lothar Hoffmann, Hermann Worthoff, Dr. Harry Sturm, Friedrich Schubert, Walter Hesz, and Bruno Meiert, StA Wiesbaden, 8 Js 1145/60, pp. 234–236, copy in YVA, TR.10/1061. The "mini-Himmler" quote is from the last source, p. 234. Norman Rich, *Hitler's War Aims*, pp. 98–99, says that when Himmler replaced Krüger on October 22, 1943, effective November 9, it was because Krüger began to feel strong enough to challenge Himmler, but there is no clear evidence of this.

10 One reflection of this is the otherwise probably self-serving 1960 testimony of Walter Huppenkothen, KdS (*Kommandeur des Sicherheitspolizei-und SD*) Lublin from February 1940 to July 1941. He claimed that in response to a report he had written to Heydrich regarding the Jewish forced-labor camp in Lublin (the Lipowa 7 camp) established by Globocnik, Heydrich visited Lublin in May or June 1940. Heydrich told Huppenkothen to leave Jewish matters to Globocnik. See YVA, TR.10/1146 Z, III:536. Although Huppenkothen may well have fabricated this story in order to remove any suspicion of his wrongdoing, it nonetheless corresponds to the known facts regarding the German authorities in Lublin. See also the testimony of Dr. Fritz Schmiege, ibid., III:577.

just as Himmler was superior to the RSHA and the police in Berlin, the HSSPF and SSPF were formally superior to all RSHA and ORPO (Ordnungspolizei) officials in the GG.[11] This is also reflected in the relative SS ranks of the HSSPF as opposed to the RSHA and police heads in the GG, as described below. The HSSPF and SSPF were always at least three ranks above these RSHA subordinates.

For "Operation Reinhard" the HSSPF and SSPF had the same coordinating responsibilities and authority over other SS and police personnel in the GG. Whereas Heydrich had responsibility for coordinating the "Final Solution" with regard to other parts of Europe, with other local SS and police personnel often subordinated to his representatives for these tasks, the supreme "Final Solution" authorities in the GG were the HSSPF and the Lublin SSPF. Ultimately, "Operation Reinhard" was a part of the "Final Solution" that was outside Heydrich's domain.

In Lublin, the SSPF was the notorious Odilo Globocnik. Just as Himmler had created the HSSPF in part in order to bypass other SS officers and bureaucracies when needed, so he used the Lublin SSPF Globocnik in that capacity in a number of important matters, especially deporting and murdering the Jews. Globocnik received his orders directly from Himmler in this and other policy matters, such as responsibility for evicting Poles from areas destined for German settlement, setting up SS colonies, and more. This direct line to Himmler in policy central to the SS and the Nazi regime made Globocnik largely independent of Krüger.[12]

11 See Himmler's December 18, 1939, "Dienstanweisung für die Höheren SS-und Polizeiführer," where these responsibilities were spelled out, YVA, TR.10/813, p. 58. See also Birn, *Höhere SS- und Polizeiführer*; Hilberg, *Destruction*, pp. 201–206; Staatsanwalt Zeug, summary for the Zentralestelle der Landesjustizverwaltungen Ludwigsburg (ZStL), January 16, 1961, for the investigations for cases 8 AR-Z 74/60, "Zusammenfassung des bisherigen Ergebnisses der Vermittlungen," pp. 2–3, in YVA, JM/1905.

12 See Globocnik's BDC file in YVA, O.68/654, which contains many documents reflecting this independence. See also YVA, TR.10/868, "Urteilausfertigung des Landgerichts Hamburg vom 26 Juli 1974 gegen Mohwinkel, Gröger, und Offermann, 147 Js 32/70, 147 Ks 2/72," pp. 26–29. YVA, TR.10/1146 Z, p. IX:1734, corroborates the close relationship with Himmler. See also Joseph Poprzeczny, *Odilo Globocnik: Hitler's Man in the East* (Jefferson, NC and London: McFarland, 2004), pp. 81–102.

Globocnik's actual SSPF staff was not large, numbering 190 men according to a July 1941 personnel list for Lublin, and 153 men according to his October 27, 1943 report to Himmler.[13] However, Globocnik was deft at raising much larger forces. In the same October report, he referred to an additional 186 SS men in Lublin whose services he called on for various projects.[14] For deporting the Jews in 1942, he also had the use of several battalions of mostly Ukrainian "Hiwis" (*Hilfswillige*; renegades from the Red Army) trained in Trawniki (see Chapter 6), a battalion of Lithuanians trained in Vilna, the KdS (*Kommandeur des Sicherheitspolizei-und SD*) Lublin forces (see below), the ORPO regiment in Lublin (see below), the Polish and Ukrainian police units in the Lublin District, the Selbstschutz and Sonderdienst composed of local *Volksdeutsche* (see below), and other groups passing through or temporarily stationed in the district.[15] The total number of men at his disposal in Lublin at any given time for these operations was approximately 8,000.

Globocnik was Himmler's personal friend, and he exploited that relationship in his ambitious and ruthless drive to accumulate power and create a personal empire based in Lublin. He was also beholden to Himmler for having rescued his career following Globocnik's removal as *Gauleiter* of Vienna in January 1939, because of illegal currency speculation.[16] The combination of personal friendship,

13 See Nuremberg documents NO-057- NO-064. The personnel list is in WAPL, GDL, 882. See also YVA, O.68/654, and YVA, TR.10/869, "Landgericht Hamburg, Schwurgericht, Urteil in der Strafsache gegen Karl Richard Josef Streibel u.a., 147 Ks 1/72," pp. I:10, II:103–104.

14 Nuremberg Documents, ibid.; YVA, O.68/654, ibid., and Streibel verdict, TR.10/869, II:109.

15 This is derived from a conglomeration of sources, including Streibel verdict, YVA, TR.10/869, II:116–193, III:289–309, 314–340; Georg Tessin, "Die Stäbe und Truppeneinheiten der Ordnungspolizei," in *Zur Geschichte der Ordnungspolizei 1936–1945* (Koblenz: n.p., 1957), pp. II:51–53, 87–109; Hilberg, *Destruction*; Browning, *Ordinary Men*.

16 See YVA, O.68/654, Globocnik file. For general background on Globocnik, see Poprzeczny, *Odilo Globocnik*, pp. 45–80; Peter Black, "Odilo Globocnik – Himmlers Vorposten im Osten," in Ronald Smelser, Enrico Syring, and Rainer Zittelmann, eds., *Die Braune Elite II* (Darmstadt: Wissenschaftliche Buchgesellschaft, 1994), pp. 103–115.

loyalty, ruthlessness, boundless ambition, unscrupulousness, daring, and a desire to accomplish as much as possible for his most powerful patron, together with Himmler's preparedness to exploit these traits, seems to have played a significant role in the development of Globocnik's power and centrality in Jewish policy in the GG. Eventually, his differences with many other powerful Germans in the GG, as well as the fact that he had already accomplished his most important task for Himmler, the murder of the Jews in Poland, led to his transfer to distant Trieste, his birthplace. It is also possible that Himmler sent Globocnik to Trieste to protect him from a renewed SS investigation into his financial dealings.[17] Globocnik's successor, from August 16, 1943, was Jakob Sporrenberg.[18]

RSHA Apparatus

The RSHA apparatus in the GG was ostensibly a direct subordinate of the parent body in Berlin headed by Heydrich. However, since in the GG it was operationally subordinate to the HSSPF (and SSPFs), who was Heydrich's peer and reported directly to Himmler, Heydrich could not exercise full control over his men in the GG in all matters.

The GG RSHA was based on the personnel of the five Einsatzgruppen (EG) that operated in September-October 1939, in what was to become GG territory (two other EGs operated solely in other parts of Poland). It was headed by a *Befehlshaber der Sicherheitspolizei-und SD*, or BdS, based in Kraków, and each district was headed by a *Kommandeur der Sicherheitspolizei-und SD*, or KdS.[19] Each KdS had a staff in the district capital, as well as *Aussenstellen* in county capitals, and a number of *Aussenposten*

17 Ibid. The correspondence between Himmler and von Herff on this in the summer and autumn of 1943 points in this direction.

18 Globocnik file, ibid. Globocnik's final deportation act in Poland was outside the GG–the removal of the last Białystok Jews in August 1943. He actually left Lublin only in September 1943.

19 The term KdS referred to both the person holding the position and to his apparatus, and this is how the term is used in this book.

within each county. These county units were also commonly known as Gestapo posts, probably because of Gestapo dominance within them. The BdS reported to Heydrich, but he and his entire apparatus were also subordinate to the HSSPF and his staff, especially for certain important matters, such as Jewish policy. Similarly, the KdS reported to the BdS, but he and his men were subordinate to the SSPF. In practice, the district-level subordination did not require BdS approval or knowledge. Thus, the KdS received orders along three chains of command:

> RSHA → BdS → KdS;
> Himmler → HSSPF → KdS;
> Himmler → HSSPF → SSPF → KdS.

The first chain of command was for routine SIPO/SD matters; the others for special matters. In Lublin, a fourth chain of command existed: Himmler→SSPF→KdS. The KdS men carried out deportations on SSPF orders.[20]

The first BdS was *SS-Brigadeführer* Bruno Streckenbach, who had commanded EG I during the invasion of Poland. Seven EGs had been formed in August and early September 1939, five of them for operations in Polish territories not destined for immediate annexation. Their official function was to deal with anti-German elements behind the lines, including spies, and arrest politically undesirable people. In October 1939, their orders added *Ausschaltung* ("elimination") of Jews and Polish intellectuals, and this reflected their actual function of terrorization and pacification of the population. In fact, the EGs, together with other formations, were engaged in extensive mass-murder operations from the beginning of the war. Streckenbach was followed, on March 30, 1940, by *SS-Brigadeführer* Dr. Karl Eberhard Schöngarth, who

20 See YVA, TR.10/764, indictment, pp. 174–176; Mohwinkel verdict, TR.10/868; TR.10/859, Landgericht Wiesbaden, Urteil gegen Josef Hermann Worthoff, 8 Ks 1/70; Streibel verdict, TR.10/869; Michalsen indictment, TR.10/813, pp. 55–56. KdS Johannes Müller's adjutant, Helmuth Schneider, added that, whereas the KdS took orders from Globocnik, the KdS's men could not take orders directly from Globocnik or his men. See TR.10/1146 Z, p. IX:1691.

was in turn succeeded, on June 15, 1943, by *SS-Brigadeführer* Dr. Walter Bierkamp (former commander of EG D in the Soviet Union). Schöngarth attended the Wannsee Conference, on January 20, 1942, as the RSHA's senior man in the GG.[21]

The KdS offices in Lublin were located on ul. Uniwersytecka 6, in a building known popularly as *pod Zegarem* (*unter dem Uhr*; "under the clock").[22] The basement was a notorious torture center. The first KdS Lublin was *SS-Sturmbannführer* Dr. Alfred Hasselberg, who had commanded Einsatzkommando (EK) I/3, one of the two EKs that entered Lublin in October 1939. The other EK was III/1, commanded by *SS-Sturmbannführer* Dr. Wilhelm Scharpwinkel.[23]

Hasselberg was extremely brutal and corrupt and was disliked by his men. A SS investigation following complaints by at least two of his men led to his removal amidst scandal in December 1939.[24] His replacement was *SS-Sturmbannführer* Walther Huppenkothen, who had been Streckenbach's deputy in EG-I. He was succeeded, in July 1941, by *SS-Sturmbannführer* Johannes Müller, who was in turn followed, in November 1943, by *SS-Sturmbannführer* Dr. Karl Pütz. Thus, Huppenkothen oversaw the ghettoization of the Jews of Lublin; Müller was intimately involved in the deportations to death camps in 1942; and Pütz and Müller overlapped in sending the KdS men to participate in the *Erntefest* mass murders in November 1943.

The BdS and KdS were organized along the same departmental lines as the RSHA. Thus, Department III was SD, IV was Gestapo,

21 Ibid. See also Alexander Rossino, *Hitler Strikes Poland: Blitzkrieg, Ideology, and Atrocity* (Lawrence: University of Kansas Press, 2003), pp. 29–57; Hilberg, *Destruction*, pp. 201–205; Christopher R. Browning, *The Origins of the Final Solution: The Evolution of Nazi Jewish Policy, September 1939-March 1942* (Jerusalem and Lincoln: Yad Vashem and University of Nebraska Press, 2004), pp. 16–19; Michalsen verdict, YVA, TR.10/813, pp. 55–57.

22 YVA, TR.10/859, p. 18.

23 See, for example, the Hasselberg report, YVA, O.51/44; Hilberg, *Destruction*, pp. 201–205. On the two EKs that went to Lublin: YVA, Indictment of Hugo Raschendorfer, 113 Js 17/66, January 5, 1965, Munich, and verdict, 113 Ks 3/67 & 1/68, October 24, 1968, in YVA, TR.10/655, pp. 10–16; TR.10/1146 Z, II:233, V:847–848 (statements by Georg Lothar Hoffmann); TR.10/1146 Z, VII:1258, 1273, 1279, 1388–1389, VIII:1459, 1540, XI:2254, 2268, XII:2407.

24 YVA, O.51/44, ibid.

and V KRIPO (Kriminalpolizei). Although organized like the parent RSHA, this bureaucratic apparatus did not report to the parallel departments in Berlin; that is, IVB4 in Lublin was not an Eichmann subordinate or appointment, but rather a KdS subordinate and appointment. As in Berlin, Department IVB4 in Lublin dealt with Jews, and, as such, its head was responsible for enforcing regulations regarding Jews, such as curfews, armbands, and gathering intelligence information about them. In 1942, it was this department, then headed by *SS-Hauptsturmführer* Hermann Worthoff, that coordinated the brutal deportations from Lublin in March and April.[25] At the same time the KdS and BdS themselves did report back to the RSHA on their activities, as well as sending copies of at least some of their correspondence. Thus, despite the absence of full authority over his subordinates in the GG, Heydrich was well informed of their activities.

There were approximately 100 men in the KdS staff in Lublin. In addition, there were ten KdS *Aussenstellen*, with fifteen to twenty men each, and several Gestapo *Aussenposten* and KRIPO *Aussendienststellen* per county, with two or three men each, and a larger staff of Polish and/or Ukrainian policemen. Thus, the total KdS manpower was approximately 400–500 in 1942. See Table 2.3 for a list of the relevant KdS personnel in the Lublin District.[26]

25 See YVA, TR.10/859, Worthoff verdict, pp. 17–23, 47–200, as well as the West German interrogations relevant to this, and the relevant TR-11 testimonies. See also TR.10/764, pp. 175–176. On the organizational aspects of the KdS, see also TR.10/1146 Z, V:853–857.

26 See YVA, TR.10/859, pp. 117–123; TR.10/1146 Z, pp. V:853–857; TR.10/764, p. 176. The table is based on these sources as well. See also the Lublin personnel list for July 1941, in WAPL, GDL, 882. There were 389 men in the KdS apparatus at that time. See also TR.10/1146 Z, IV:706–711, and III:515–520, 530–533, on the organization of the Lublin district Kripo.

Table 2.3: Major KdS Personnel in Lublin

KdS ul. Uniwersytecka 6	**III SD**	**IV Gestapo**	**IVB4 Jews**
Sturmbannführer Dr. Alfred Hasselberg (11–12.39)	*Hauptsturmführer* Josef Faulhaber (11.39–1.40)	*Kriminalkommissar* Johann Schmer (5–12.41)	*Untersturmführer* Karl Levermann
Sturmbannführer Walter Huppenkothen (2.40–6.41)	*Sturmbannführer* Dr. Friedrich Buchardt (1–12.40)	*Sturmbannführer* Walter Liska (12.41–?)	*Untersturmführer* Walther
Sturmbannführer Johannes Müller (7.41–11.43)	*Hauptsturmführer* Fritz Stöcker (1.41–9.42)	*Sturmbannführer* Max Müller (?–7.44)	*Hauptsturmführer* Hermann Josef Worthoff (10.41–7.44)
Sturmbannführer Dr. Karl Pütz (11.43–7.44)	*Hauptsturmführer* Ewald Heinrich Biegelmayer (9.42–7.44)		

ORPO Apparatus

Like the RSHA apparatus, the police in the GG were headed by a *Befehlshaber*, or BdO, based in Kraków: *Oberst d. Gendarmerie* Emil Höring (October 1, 1939); *Generalmajor d. ORPO* Herbert Becker (October 25, 1939); then *Generalleutnant d. ORPO* Paul Riege (October 1940); *Oberst d. Gendarmerie* Rudolf Müller-Boenick (temporary replacement, August 22, 1941); *Generalmajor d. ORPO* and *SS-Brigadeführer* Gerhard Winkler (December

1941); Herbert Becker again (May 1942); *Generalmajor d. ORPO* Hans-Dieter Grünwald (August 1943); and *Generalmajor d. ORPO* Fritz Sendel (March 8, 1944). The organizational structure also followed the structure of ORPO in Germany. Thus, each district had a *Kommandeur der ORPO* (KdO), whose command was divided into two parts — Schutzpolizei (Schupo) as urban police, and the Gendarmerie created as rural police — based on Himmler's order of June 5, 1940. At a later stage the Schutzmannschaften, non-German auxiliary units, were also subordinated to the BdO. Subordinate to each KdO was a KdSch (Schupo) and a KdGend (Gendarmerie). In 1942, the district Schupo troops were reorganized as police regiments based in the district capitals. By late 1942, there were 15,186 ORPO men in the GG, in addition to 14,297 Polish police under ORPO supervision. Of these, some 2,000 ORPO men and a similar number of Polish and Ukrainian policemen operated in the Lublin district.[27] Like the BdS and KdS, the ORPO was subordinate in all important matters to the HSSPF and SSPF.

In the Lublin district, the first KdO was Gerret Körsemann, followed by Walther Griphan in early 1941 (both *Oberst der Schupo* and *SS-Standartenführer*); then *SS-Obersturmbannführer* and *Oberstleutnant der Schupo* Walther Soosten; *SS-Oberführer* and *Oberstleutnant der Schupo* Hermann Kintrup in early 1942; and *Oberstleutnant der Schupo* and *Reserve Polizeioberst* Konrad Rheindorf in November 1943. Table 2.4 below lists the major police officials in the Lublin District.[28]

27 Browning, *Ordinary Men*, pp. 3–8; Tessin, "Stäbe und Truppeneinheiten," pp. II:51–53, 87; Wolfgang Curilla, *Der Judenmord in Polen und die deutschen Ordnungspolizei 1933–1945* (Paderborn: Ferdinand Schönnningh, 2011), p. 53; YVA, TR.10/764, pp. 176–178; Himmler's Gendarmerie orders for the GG, June 5 and 17, 1940, and the follow-up within the GG through August 1940, YVA, O.53/80. See also Hilberg, *Destruction*, p. 505, n. 8, for somewhat different numbers. On *Schutzmannschaften*, see Tessin, ibid., II:101–102; YVA, TR.10/869, III:1–2.

28 YVA, TR.10/764, pp. 176–78; TR.10/869, pp. III:4–6; TR.10/1146 Z, pp. XIII:2824–2834; Curilla, *Der Judenmord in Polen und die deutschen Ordnungspolizei*, p. 687. The Streibel trial verdict indicates that Kintrup was KdO until September 1943, and that Rheindorf took over in November 1943. No exact dates are given. Table 2.4 is based on TR.10/764, pp. 176–178 and Curilla, ibid.

Table 2.4: Major KdO Personnel in Lublin

KdO, ul. Chopina 5	**KdSch,** ul. Chopina 7	**KdGend**
Oberst der Schupo and *SS-Standartenführer* Gerret Körsemann (1940–41)	*SS-Obersturmbannführer* Otto Peter (1942–1.43)	Major Ferdinand Hahnzog (1.40–4.42)
Oberst der Schupo and *SS-Standartenführer* Walther Griphan (3.41–11.41)	*Oberstleutnant der Schupo* and *Polizeioberst i. R.* Konrad Rheindorf (2.43–8.43)	*Oberstleutnant* August Preyssl (4.42–?)
Oberstleutnant der Schupo and *SS-Obersturmbannführer* Walther Soosten (11.41–1.42)	*Polizeimajor* Gustav Wilhelm Melcher (8.43–7.44)	Georg Weinzierl (?–?)
Oberstleutnant der Schupo and *SS-Oberführer* Hermann Kintrup (1.42–8.43)		
Oberstleutnant der Schupo and *Polizeioberst i. R.* Konrad Rheindorf (8 or 11.43–7.44)		

The KdO also served as commander of the police reserve regiment in his district, which was based there from November 4, 1939. In Lublin it was first called "Polizeiregiment Lublin" and then became "Polizeiregiment 25," as of July 14, 1942. Other police regiments in the GG were 22 and 24. The KdGend, until April 1942, was *Oberstleutnant der Gendarmerie* Ferdinand Hahnzog, followed by *Oberstleutnant* August Preyssl. There were three *Gendarmeriehauptmannschaften* in the district: in Lublin, Radzyń, and Zamość. These units were composed of a number of *Gendarmeriezüge* (platoons), each with approximately fifty-five men, stationed one platoon per county, which in turn sent their men to *Gendarmerieposten*.

The KdSch in 1942 was *SS-Obersturmbannführer* Otto Peter, followed by Rheindorf from February to August 1943, and then *Polizeimajor* Gustav Wilhelm Melcher until the German retreat in July 1944. Peter and Rheindorf also served as deputy KdO.[29] The ORPO regiment in Lublin in 1942–1943 was composed of more than three police battalions (101, part of 41, 65, 67, and SS- und Polizeireiterabteilung III), responsible for the northern, central, and southern parts of the district. An additional battalion was created along the Bug River, effective September 2, 1942, including the counties of Biała-Podlaska, Chełm, and Hrubieszów, from SS- und Polizeireiterabteilung III.[30] Christopher Browning has written about the activities of one of these battalions in his book *Ordinary Men*.[31]

Parallel to his appointment as *Reichskommissar für die Festigung des deutschen Volkstums* (RKFdV; head of German resettlement) on October 7, 1939, Himmler ordered the creation of a Selbstschutz, police formations of local *Volksdeutsche*, in occupied Poland. Whereas in the annexed western Polish territories these formations were subordinate to ORPO, in the GG they were subordinate to the HSSPF. Like the other SS and police frameworks in the GG, the Selbstschutz was commanded by a *SS- und Selbstschutzführer* who was a high-ranking SS officer — Kurt Hintze, and then Gustav

29 Tessin, "Stäbe und Truppeneinheiten," p. II:51; YVA, TR.10/764, p. 178; TR.10/869, III:4–6; Gendarmerie organizational table, YVA, O.53/80. See also Melcher testimony in 1962, YVA, TR.10/1146 Z, XIII:2824–2834.

30 YVA, O.53/121-W, pp. 27–31, 127–128, Kintrup's July 9, 1942, Regimentsbefehl, and his August 27, 1942, Regimentsbefehl, respectively. In the Streibel verdict, the court indicated that the change in the regiment's name occurred in early August 1942. See also Curilla, *Der Judenmord in Polen und die deutschen Ordnungspolizei*, pp. 687–688, 757–765; Tessin, "Stäbe und Truppeneinheiten," II:51–53, 92–93.

31 Browning, *Ordinary Men*. See also Daniel J. Goldhagen, *Hitler's Willing Executioners: Ordinary Germans and the Holocaust* (New York: Alfred Knopf, 1996).

Stolle (both *SS-Oberführer*) – with district commanders serving under them.

In Lublin, Globocnik built up his Selbstschutz to more than battalion strength (at least 800 men), the largest such unit in the GG. He used the Selbstschutz to do some of his dirtier work, such as implementing forced marches of Jews over the Bug River to the USSR, or to death, and as a tool to exercise control over Jewish forced labor. Within the first year of occupation, the Lublin District had seen three Selbstschutz commanders: Walter Gunst, Ludolf von Alvensleben, and Willi Stemmler (all with the rank of *SS-Standartenführer*). The Selbstschutz commander also served as commandant of the forced-labor camp at 7 Lipowa Street in Lublin. *SS-Hauptsturmführer* Karl Streibel, who would later be commandant of the Trawniki camps, was a Selbstschutz company commander in January 1940, "*Stabsführer*" (operations officer) from August 26, 1940, and then adjutant. The Selbstschutz was then transferred to GG civilian control and moved to Kraków on January 2, 1941, with each *Kreishauptmann* receiving a unit. When Krüger became *Staatssekretär* for Security in the GG, on June 3, 1942, in addition to his HSSPF position, the unit, now called Sonderdienst, reverted to his control. It is not clear to what extent Globocnik could use such units afterward, but men who had been active in the Selbstschutz in 1940, were also active in the murder of the Jews in 1942–1943.[32]

As we see, the German regime in the GG and in the Lublin District consisted of many different chains of command, bureaucracies, and individuals. Therefore, when we say that the Germans did this or that to the Jews, the Germans to whom we are referring may be different in each case. The various German authorities were complementary to each other in the sense that they

32 Peter Black, "Rehearsal for 'Reinhard'?: Odilo Globocnik and the Lublin *Selbstschutz*," *Central European History*, 25:2 (1992), pp. 206–210; Streibel verdict, YVA, TR.10/869, 1976, II:11–16, 192–193; Staatsanwalt Hamburg, Anklageschrift gegen Karl Heinrich Wolfgang Mohwinkel u.a., 147 Js 32/70, January 28, 1972, pp. 97–100 (copy in YVA, TR.10/770). The trials cite the date of the order to form the Selbstschutz as November 1, 1939. This was probably the date on which the order was passed on to Krüger and Globocnik, who had just arrived at their new posts.

all persecuted Jews. However, they were in constant competition, with a break in 1942, during the deportations.

Which Germans had authority over the Jews? This is not entirely clear, because several authorities claimed supremacy in this respect. The chart at the end of this chapter shows each of the above German hierarchies. We could actually add an additional horizontal line at the bottom to represent the Jews. However, if so, the word "Jews" would have to appear across the page in order to indicate that they were, in reality, at the bottom of the heap. The Jews were persecuted from all sides of the Germans' internal conflicts. All the competing and even adversarial German authorities trampled them at every turn, and the Jews had no recourse.

The Jews

Against this background we can begin to understand the densely complex web of authorities that the Jews faced. The fact that different parts of the district fell under German rule at various times affected their initial fate to some extent. For example, Soviet troops never entered the westernmost counties of the district, particularly Puławy County and parts of Janów-Lubelski County. Here persecution and street violence, led by the SS, began at once and was widespread and sustained. At the same time some Judenräte were created, apparently by the SS, who were already on the scene in the form of an EG. In places where the occupation began later, as a result of the changing border with the USSR and the Soviet occupation of parts of the district, the SS did not have much of a head start on the German civilian administration in getting organized. Judenräte generally were created in these places in December 1939 or January 1940, often by the civilian authorities. The first order of business for these Judenräte was providing forced-laborers for the Germans (civilians, military, and SS) and aid to refugees. Everywhere the Jews faced multiple uniformed men who were trying to grab them for forced labor, beatings, or murderous sport.

When the war broke out, there were more than 115 organized Jewish communities with at least 100 Jews each in what became the

Lublin District of the GG, in addition to several hundred villages where small numbers of Jews lived.[33] The district's Jewish population of 250–300,000 remained steady or even increased during the first two years of the war. Many thousands of local Jews fled to the Soviet Union during the first weeks of the war, but many thousands more came into the district on their own, or were deported to it by the Germans in 1939–1941.

Two extant orders told German officials how initially to deal with Jews: Heydrich's September 21 *Schnellbrief*, which ordered the creation of Jewish councils by his SS commanders in Poland; and Hans Frank's November 28, 1939 order on the same issue.[34] Frank ordered that the Jews themselves create councils to be approved by the *Kreishauptmann* (or *Stadthauptmann*). The civilian authorities had an advantage over the SS, as they had the manpower and training to implement such a decree. In the Lublin District they seem to have had some success in taking the lead in the creation of Judenräte and in imposing their will to some degree over the day-to-day control of the Jews' lives.

As soon as the occupying Germans began settling in to their new functions in Poland, they sought the cooperation of the local populations. There was, in a very limited sense, a sort of meeting of interests between the Germans, especially the civilian authorities, and the Jews in that they both wanted local leaders kept in place – though for very different, even opposing, reasons. For the Germans, having such recognized leaders and public figures available was useful in their dealings with both the Jews and the occupied Poles and Ukrainians. The Germans, who did not have the manpower to implement all their programs effectively, wanted these people to help them run daily affairs for the benefit of Germany. The Jews

33 *Blackbook of Localities Whose Jewish Population Was Destroyed by the Nazis* (Jerusalem: Yad Vashem, 1965), pp. 58–131; Wein, ed., *Pinkas Hakehillot – Districts Lublin, Kielce.*

34 Heydrich's *Schnellbrief* is Nuremberg Document PS-3363; Frank's order can be found in *Verordnungsblatt für das Generalgouvernement (VBlGG)*, 1939, pp. 72–73. Both have been published in many sources. See, for example, Arad, et al., eds., *Documents on the Holocaust*, pp. 173–178, 191–192. See also Isaiah Trunk, *Judenrat: The Jewish Councils in Eastern Europe under Nazi Occupation* (New York and London: Macmillan, 1972), pp. 1–6.

(and the Poles) wanted their leaders to remain at their posts and serve their people by intervening on their behalf and guiding them through these difficult times. The Jews, who now witnessed the rash of kidnappings off the streets and the beatings and killings by the SS, Selbstschutz, and police, sought to put a stop to these acts and to mitigate the effects of the harsh occupation regime. In the Lublin District, many Jewish leaders stayed with their communities and did not take advantage of their proximity to the USSR to flee.

As a result of their own needs, the German civilian authorities left existing Polish and Ukrainian village leaders in their positions, gave local rural Polish authorities some measure of authority over Jews, allowed many Polish municipal bureaucrats to remain in their jobs, and told Jewish leaders in each community to elect a Judenrat. In this way recognized leaders would be seen by their respective communities to continue in leadership roles. In return for this cooperation, the German authorities were prepared sometimes to appear to grant some concessions.[35]

The Judenräte in the district saw themselves initially as a continuation of the prewar *kehillah* authority. Indeed, in most cases they were created out of the prewar Jewish leadership and, as such, tried to serve the community's interests. The Lublin Judenrat went so far as to protest to the German civilian officials that Frank's Judenrat order specified that taking care of the Jews' needs was their main function.[36] Of course, this was not the case.

It seems that most of the Judenräte in the Lublin District were appointed by or on the orders of the German civilian authorities. Of forty-four Judenräte for which we have dates of appointment, thirty-seven were appointed in December 1939 or later, after Frank's Judenrat decree, and after the civilian government had begun to function. Of the seven that were created in October or November 1939, all the towns already had a German civilian government. In Puławy County, the first Judenräte were organized after Friedrich

35 Trunk, ibid., pp. 14–17; Gross, *Generalgouvernement*, pp. 123–125.

36 Judenrat Memo to Lublin *Stadthauptmann*, September 13, 1940, WAPL, RZ 22 (copies in YVA, O.6/395 and USHMMA, RG-15.101M); also cited in Trunk, *Judenrat*, pp. 117–118.

Trampedach had become the first county chief in October 1939.[37]

The development of the Judenräte in the Lublin District was thus somewhat different from other parts of Poland. Dan Michman, in his excellent and thought-provoking work on Jewish "headships" under the Nazis, notes that, by the time Frank issued his Judenrat order, more than half the Jews of occupied Poland were already living under Judenräte. The SS had already installed these bodies almost as soon as each territory was occupied and before the civilian administration could get organized.[38] However, in much of the Lublin District things were different. The civilian authorities were assertive of their jurisdiction, appointed many Judenräte on their own, or had a hand in running those that they did not appoint, and generally tried to play an active and sustained role in policy toward the Jews.

Until early March 1942, the Jews and their leaders primarily faced the German civilian administration in most affairs of daily

37 The early Judenräte were in Annopol-Rachów and Kraśnik (Janów-Lubelski county), Biała-Podlaska, Markuszów, Puławy, and Ryki (Puławy county), and Tomaszów-Lubelski (Zamość county). The later Judenräte were in Bełżyce, Biłgoraj, Bychawa, Chełm, Dęblin-Irena, Dubienka, Firlej, Gorzków, Hrubieszów, Izbica, Kazimierz Dolny, Kock, Końskowola, Konstantynów, Krasnystaw, Kurów, Łęczna, Lublin, Łuków, Międzyrzec-Podlaski, Opole-Lubelski, Ostrow-Lubelski, Parczew, Piaski, Radzyń, Siedliszcze, Sławatycze, Stężyca, Szczebrzeszyn, Tarnogród, Tyszowce, Ulanów, Włodawa, Wojsławice, Zakrzówek, Zamość, and Żółkiewka. The Judenrat in Wąwolnica was created only in 1941, and in Frampol and Modliborzyce, there was no local Judenrat at all. The information is based on the *Yizkor* books for each town and city, as well as *Pinkas Hakehillot, Poland, vol. 7*, Guy Miron and Shlomit Shulhani, eds., *The Yad Vashem Encyclopedia of the Ghettos in the Holocaust* (Jerusalem: Yad Vashem, 2009), and Martin Dean, ed., *The United States Holocaust Memorial Museum Encyclopedia of Camps and Ghettos, 1933–1945, Volume II, Ghettos in German-Occupied Eastern Europe* (Bloomington and Indianapolis: Indiana University Press with the United States Holocaust Memorial Museum, 2012).

38 Dan Michman, "Jewish 'Headships' under Nazi Rule: The Evolution and Implementation of an Administrative Concept," in *idem*, *Holocaust Historiography, A Jewish Perspective: Conceptualizations, Terminology, and Fundamental Issues* (London: Vallentine Mitchell, 2003), pp. 166–168. Michman bases himself on the sociologist C. E. Gibb, who identifies a "headship" as a ruling body that draws its authority and has its goals defined by a power outside the group, ibid., p. 161.

life. Still, the SS intervened at all times and in all matters, and GG Interior Minister Siebert had to reiterate, on March 23, 1940, that the civilians held jurisdiction over Judenräte.[39] In much of the Lublin District, the civilians and SS continued to vie for authority over the Judenräte. For example, in mid-June 1940, the Selbstschutz, acting for Globocnik, relieved the Bełżyce Judenrat of its duties and appointed a refugee from Stettin in its place. *Kreishauptmann* Emil Ziegenmeyer intervened on June 18 to reinstate the original Judenrat. Three months later Ziegenmeyer himself replaced the Bychawa Judenrat because of its alleged incompetence – or reticence – to carry out all his orders.[40] Similarly, Ziegenmeyer appointed the deputy Judenrat head in Melgiew, Mendel Bergier, to replace Moszek Kornblitt as Judenrat head. In this case the SS had apparently grabbed Kornblitt for forced labor for the army on August 17. The person that informed the higher German authorities of this was the Polish town head (the *wójt*, or *vogt*), Burdzanowski. Four different authorities were involved here in the conscription for forced labor and in dealing with the Judenrat – the SS, the army, the Polish town head, and the German civilian authorities – and it took ten days for the *Kreishauptmann* to sort out the problem.[41] Which one, therefore, were the Jews to address in this regard?

In general the Jews needed to turn to the civilian authorities for ordinary matters and to the KdS for whatever might be considered security matters. This was true both for the Judenräte and for special instances. Thus, when a group of forty-four Jews in Parczew felt that their Judenrat was exploiting the Jews of the town financially, they wrote a letter of complaint to the governor of the district, whose office passed the letter on to BuF. In the end their complaint was rejected by the authorities, in a letter from the county Gendarmerie

39 Siebert to all Kreis- and Stadthauptleute, via the district governors, giving them jurisdiction over the Judenräte. He also ordered the Jews to deal with their own social welfare. WAPL, GDL 891 (copy in YVA, JM/10,458).

40 Ziegenmeyer to Zörner, June 18, 1940 and September 21, 1940. Ziegenmeyer also asked Zörner in June to assert the civilians' authority in this matter, as per Frank's November 28, 1939 order. WAPL, GDL 891.

41 Burdzanowski to Ziegenmeyer, August 17, 1940, and Ziegenmeyer to Türk, August 27, 1940, WAPL, GDL 891.

post, which was to some degree under the shared authority of the *Kreishauptmann* and the police.[42] For the Jews it was not always clear who the authority was in these matters.

Still, security issues were undisputedly the realm of the SS. Hence, when the Bychawa Judenrat requested a phone connection from the BuF in Lublin in July 1940, the latter passed on the request, on July 22, to the KdS office in Lublin, with a covering note supporting the request because other Judenräte had telephones. The KdS's approval came a week later.[43]

The Jewish communities in the Lublin District, as elsewhere in Poland, were faced with a crisis situation as soon as the war began. Even before the conquest of each community, the Jews had to deal with destruction from bombing, injuries and deaths, homeless local Jews, housing for the growing number of refugees, and, together with the population at large, civil defense and food distribution. Once the battles ended the communities faced massive German violence against the Jews, as well as two major problems that will be discussed in the following chapters: the ever-increasing refugee and housing needs; and German forced-labor demands.

The German constrictions imposed upon the Jewish communities and their leaders and the demands made of them quickly transformed the Jews into hostage communities with leaders who faced unprecedented, enormous tasks yet were stripped of the means with which to meet them. The Jews were faced with these urgent needs even before there were any clear German orders regarding Judenräte. The communities set up committees to deal with housing, refugees, and labor, and then, after a Judenrat was established, these committees became departments or offices of the local Judenrat.

42 Letter of complaint from forty-four Jews in Parczew to the District Governor, April 22, 1941; the transfer of the matter to the BuF, May 2, and the rejection of the complaint by the county Gendarmerie commander in Radzyn, May 31, 1941, YVA, O.6/393. See also an anonymous letter of complaint against the Ryki Judenrat to the Governor, November 10, 1941, ibid.

43 Dr. H[einecke], BuF Lublin, to KdS Lublin, July 22, 1940, together with Bychawa Judenrat request and endorsement, and KdS Lublin, Dep't III-A-3 response, July 29, WAPL, GDL 891.

The Jewish communities attempted to maintain a semblance of normal life amidst the rapid deterioration of the Jews' status and standard of living. Their leaders, and then the Judenräte, intervened with the German authorities via memoranda, requesting that Jewish schools continue to function, curfews be extended, arbitrary beatings and arrests halted, public parks be open to Jews, livelihoods be maintained, and so on.[44] Most of these interventions and pleas were to no avail, except when the Germans feared a public health hazard.[45]

All attempts to limit the effects of the occupation on the Jews and to equalize their status with that of the Poles were rebuffed by the German authorities. The Judenräte found themselves increasingly preoccupied with ongoing crises in housing, health, labor, etc., and with ensuring obedience to German orders. Thus, the Judenrat in Lublin, in 1940, repeatedly posted announcements warning the Jews to wear the white armband with blue Jewish star or risk arrest.[46]

In the area of Jewish social welfare, the German civilian authorities intervened in the spring of 1940 to create a parallel leadership group. The various Jewish communities in the GG dealt

44 See, for example, Lublin Judenrat memos to the Lublin governor's office, February 16, and early summer (date unclear) 1940, WAPL, RZ 26 (copies in YVA, O.6/47-1*); Judenrat report to BuF on welfare and public health, mid-April 1940 (no exact date), WAPL, GDL 891. See also Judenrat complaints to KdS regarding unwarranted shootings of Jews in the streets of Lublin, June 12 and 14, 1940, WAPL, RZ 26. Recently the Yad Vashem Archive changed many of the archival registry numbers for its files, especially those relating to Poland. The archive also divided some old files into various new files. However, no list was made for what old numbers parallel what new numbers, or where certain parts of files were refiled. I conducted an extensive search for the new numbers and was assisted by then deputy director of the archive, Ms. Nomi Halpern, to whom I am very grateful for her time and her efforts. I succeeded in finding nearly all the new numbers, but the archive's method of registration did not lend itself to tracing all of them. Therefore, the YVA numbers given in this book are the new numbers unless marked with an asterisk (*), which indicates that the number is the original number. This is the case with the YVA file cited in this note.

45 See, for example, Alten to KdS, March 20, 1940, requesting permission to quarantine one refugee center due to an outbreak of typhus there and to open an alternate center, and the affirmative KdS (Abt. III-A-3) response the next day, WAPL, RZ 26.

46 See, for example, the Judenrat announcement in Polish and Yiddish in this regard, April 12, 1940, in WAPL, RZ, 26.

with social welfare from the very beginning of the war, as did the Poles. The German authorities set up an organization that at one and the same time recognized these social-welfare organizations and brought them under German supervision. In May, the BuF in Kraków set up the Naczelna Rada Opiekuncza (NRO; Central Welfare Council), with Polish and Ukrainian branches, as the official social-welfare organization for the GG.

Parallel to this the Germans gradually recognized the existing Jüdische Soziale Selbsthilfe (Żydowski Samopomoc Społeczny; JSS or ŻSS) between the end of May and September 1940. The Polish organization allocated 17 percent of its food budget to JSS, but for the most part the Jews had to fend for themselves in dealing with the massive social-welfare crisis that was created by the Germans. All social welfare was supervised by the district and county BuF offices. The JSS became a central Jewish social-welfare organization, with a central office in Kraków, run by Michał Weichert, district offices in each district capital in the GG, and several branch offices within each district. The local JSS officials were supposed to be chosen jointly by the Judenräte and the central JSS office.

The centralized nature of the JSS meant that the organization was able to coordinate social-welfare aid to some degree, so that local needs could be identified, examined, and addressed within the very limited means at the disposal of the organization. It also meant that the JSS was privy to information regarding Jews from all across the GG and could perhaps develop an overall picture of the Jews' fate. This remained true for all stages of the war, including during the 1942 deportations.

Isaiah Trunk notes that relations between Judenräte and the JSS ranged from close cooperation to animosity, because the Judenrat feared that JSS was trying to take over all welfare work.[47] However,

47 Trunk, *Judenrat*, pp. 116, 336; Yehuda Bauer, *American Jewry and the Holocaust: The American Jewish Joint Distribution Committee, 1939–1945* (Detroit: Wayne State University Press, 1981), pp. 85–90. On the establishment of the JSS, see also Michael Weichert, *Jewish Mutual Assistance 1939–1945* (Yiddish) (Tel Aviv: Menora, 1962), pp. 12–24; Blumental, *Documents*, Protocol 42–47, September 15, 1940, p. 185; Bogdan Kroll, *Rada Główna Opiekuncza, 1939–1945* (Warsaw: Wydawnictwo "Książka i Wiedza," 1985), pp. 90–93.

in the Lublin District, where most of the main JSS officials were also members of the Judenrat, there was generally good cooperation between the two bodies. Marek Alten, deputy chairman of the Lublin Judenrat, was appointed by the central JSS to be head of the Lublin District JSS. Although the JSS in the Lublin District was officially set up in June 1940, it did not become fully functional until the autumn.[48]

Table 2.5: Major JSS Personnel in the Lublin District

Lublin	**Lublin-Land County**	**Izbica**
Marek Alten* (District Head); Izak Kerszman*; Maurycy Schlaf*; Leon Hufnagel*; Dawid Rechtman; Dawid Frajdenberg	Szmul Wolman; Josef Siegfried*; Wolf Wiener**; Mendel Polisecki (Piaski)*; Szmul Nissenbaum (Bychawa)	Jakob Neumann; Tanchem Cwekin*; Hersz Tau*; Szymon Szwarc*; Efraim Kutner*
Biała-Podlaska County	**Hrubieszów County**	**Radzyń County**
Symcha Rozen	Szmul Brand*	Szymon Kleinbaum*
Biłgoraj County	**Krasnystaw County**	**Zamość County**
Zvi Hersz Zylberberg	Michael Szolson	Mieczysław Garfinkel*
Chełm County		
Dr. Maurycy Kleinhaus; Dr. Eliahu Tisch		

* Member of the Judenrat

** Member of second Judenrat

48 Kraków JSS Presidium to Alten, November 2, 4 (two letters), 5 (two letters), 1940; Heinrich [Heinecke], BuF Lublin, to JSS Kraków, November 7, 1940, YVA, JM/1574–1575.

Some Judenräte, like the JSS, in some cases also had jurisdiction beyond their town or county, as will be shown in the following chapters. This was true to some degree for the Lublin and Chełm Judenräte, as well as for the Lublin JSS. In both groups there were many cases where the appointed "headship" figures, to use Michman's term, also displayed leadership and commanded the respect of many in their community.

In general, Jews assessed the leaders of the Judenrat (especially the first in each community), the JSS, and others as basically honest. But many leaders, especially of the Jewish police units, which were generally created at a later date, were also seen as following German orders too closely. Some, especially in later Judenräte, created during or after the 1942 deportations, were viewed as corrupt or worse. Bunim Mandelkorn and the Judenrat in Annopol-Rachów were accused by some of becoming cold and distant from the Jewish community, while Pesach Kawa, head of the Jewish police in Kraśnik, was considered to be much worse.[49] The Rejowiec Judenrat led by Kessler (a Czech Jewish refugee) was considered to be very helpful to refugees in 1942, while the four Slovakian Jewish women who served on the subsequent Judenrat there got mixed reviews.[50] The Biała-Podlaska Judenrat was popular among the Jews as a result of its courageous work, especially with regard to the strong hints they issued in June 1942 not to report for deportation.[51] The Lublin Judenrat, arguably the most consistent with the prewar leadership, is remembered as being legalistic and distant, though basically honest.

Finally, Lagerräte (camp councils) generally acquired a mixed reputation among the Jews. Noah Stockman in Budzyń and Roman

49 Daniel Freiberg, *Darkness Covered the Earth* (Hebrew) (Tel Aviv: Ghetto Fighters' House, 1970), pp. 66–68.

50 "Facts Reported by a Jew Deported from Slovakia, Who has since Escaped and Returned, August 1943," YVA, M.2/236. According to the report, Mrs. Forbath and Mrs. Femes were helpful to refugees, while Mrs. Kaufman and Mrs. Singer were not. The same report refers to Fraenkel of the Chełm Judenrat as "very honest and respectable."

51 Moshe Yosef Feigenbaum, ed., *The Biała-Podlaska Book* (Hebrew and Yiddish) (Tel Aviv: Charity Fund in Honor of the Biała-Podlaska Community, 1961), pp. 67, 72–73.

Fischer in Lipowa 7 are generally fondly remembered and respected, unlike some of their subordinates. Pesach Kawa from Kraśnik is remembered ambivalently as to what extent he tried to serve the interests of the Jewish public in the Kraśnik forced-labor camp. Hermann Wenkart gets similarly mixed reviews from survivors of Dęblin. In part, this division seems to fall on either side of a cultural and personal fault line; that is, German speakers found it easier to establish good working relations with him and remember him positively, whereas local Yiddish-speakers had more difficulty and remember him as aloof. The Bełżec Lagerrat in 1940, led by Wolf Fajgeles, is the only one of those with records that was uniformly criticized by those who remembered them. Here the Lagerrat's corruption was obvious, well-known, and all-encompassing.

The picture of the Lublin District, then, is one of a multi-faceted, strife-torn German power that attacked the Jews from many sides simultaneously. The Jews were not leaderless, but, as became apparent to many of them as time passed, they were helpless. This helplessness became especially apparent during the 1942–1943 deportations.

Table 2.6: Major Judenrat Officials in the Lublin District

Lublin (* also 2nd)	**Biała-Podlaska**	**Krasnystaw**	**Tomaszów-Lubelski**
Henryk Bekker (chair) Marek Alten* (Deputy; 2nd chair) Leon Hufnagel* (Sec'y) Dawid Hochgemein* Jakub Kelner* Izak Kerszman*	Icchak Pyższyc (chair) Ajzyk Szajnberg **Biłgoraj** Mordechai Hirszenhorn (chair) Hillel Janower (2nd chair)	Lipa Reichman (chair) **Łęczna** J. Grynbaum (chair) M.J. Fruchtman (2nd chair) Józef Dawid Rabinowicz (deputy)	Jehoszua Fiszelson (chair) **Włodawa** Jehoszua Zomer (chair) Awraham Kohen (deputy) Dr. Szpringer

Lublin
(* also 2nd)

Nachman Lerner*
Aron Bach (d. 17.11.40)
Josef Siegfried (for Bach)
Ajzyk Bursztyn
Urysz Cymerman
Dawid Dawidson
Dawid Edelsztajn
Abram Goldsobel
Józef Goldsztern (d. 22.12.41)
Szlomo Halbersztat
Aron Jankel Kantor
Szlomo Kerszenblum
Salomon Kestenberg
Aleksander Lewi
Icka Lewinsohn
Dawid Rechtman
Maurycy Schlaf (d. 24.12.41)
Bencion Tenenbaum
Józef Wajselfisz

Bychawa

Boruch Hirszman (chair)
Dr. Izrael Flater (2nd chair)

Chełm

J. Frenkel (chair)

Dęblin-Irena

Szymon Drabfisz (chair)
Lajzor Tajchman (2nd chair)
Wolf Szulman (3rd chair)
Izrael Wajnberg (4th chair)
Józef Kanarienfogel

Lubartów

Mosze Joel Feldman (chairman)
Mosze Lichtenfeld (deputy chair)

Łuków

Mosze Aron Wajntraub (chair)

Międzyrzec

Klauberg (chair)

Opole-Lubelski

Jakub Hochman (chair)
Rabbi Winkler

Zaklików

Zalman Kuperschmid (chair)
Jehoszua Zoberman (2nd chair)

Zamość

Bencion Lubliner (chair)
Mieczysław Garfinkel (2nd chair)
Eliahu Epstein
Azriel Szeps
Boruch Fiszelson
Aron Szlafrok

Lublin – 2nd, New Members	**Hrubieszów**	**Piaski**
Wolf Wiener Ajzyk Brodt Daniel Kupferminc Józef Rotrubin (d. 31.10.42) Szulim Tajkef Bołesław Tenenbojm (killed 7.4.42) Izrael Katzenellenbogen	Szmul Brand (chair) Joel Rabinowicz (2nd chair) Joel Brand Ajzyk Finger **Izbica** Szymon Szwarc (chair) Hersz Tau	Mendel Polisecki (chair) **Puławy** Henryk Adler (chair)
Annopol-Rachów	**Kazimierz Dolny**	**Radzyń-Podlaski**
Bunim Mandelkorn (chair) Fajwel Szuchman (deputy) Rabbi Szmarjahu Finsterbusz **Bełżyce** Dombrower (chair) Paul Bauchwitz Dr. Palter Stein	Jakub Halberstadt (chair) Chaim Feierstein (2nd chair) **Kraśnik** Fiszel Rabinowicz (chair) Dr. Józef Szapira (chair from 1940) Pesach Kawa (head of police)	Dawid Lichtenstein (chair) Szymon Kleinbaum **Rejowiec** Mrs. Forbath Mrs. Femesz Mrs. Kaufman Mrs. Singer

Lublin and the *Generalgouvernement*

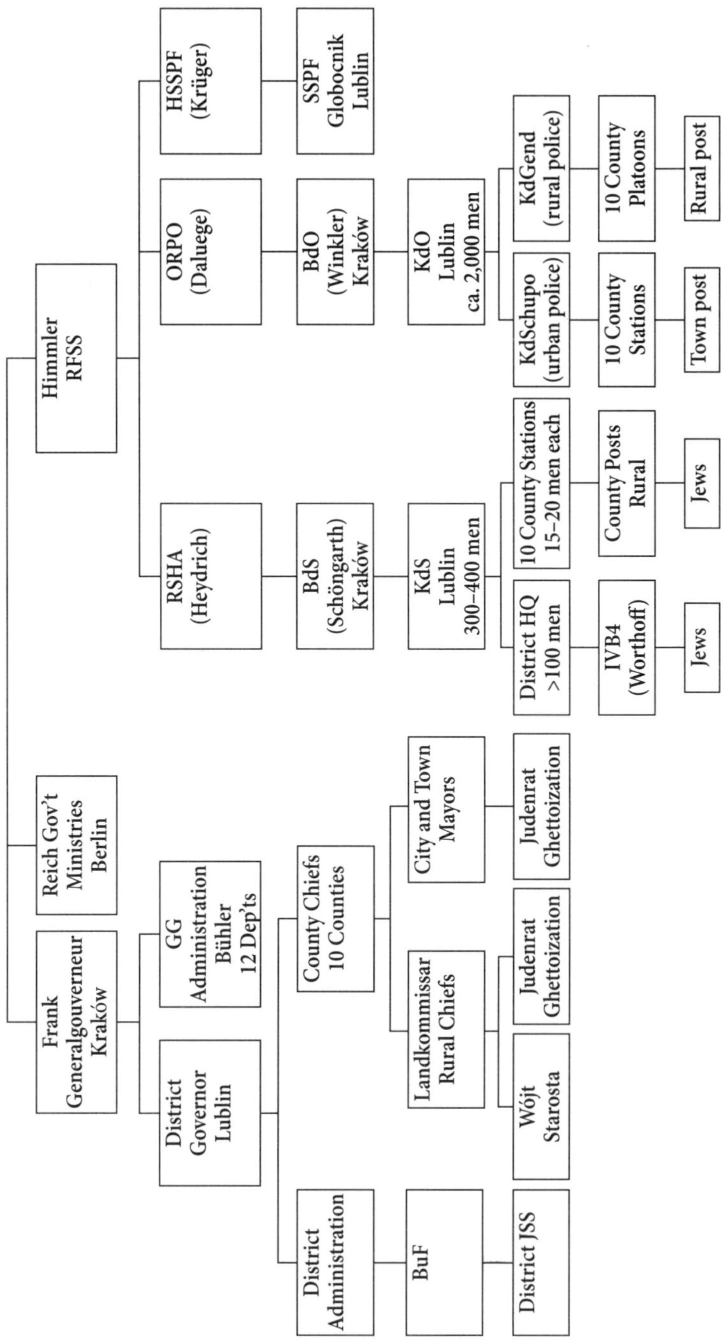

Chapter 3

Forced Population Movements, The First Year

Connecting Threads

Nazi terrorization was a permanent feature of the German occupation of Poland and became the daily bread of the Jews' existence there. Jews learned to adapt to the new circumstances and organize their lives as best they could both communally and individually. Two of the phenomena characteristic of this early terrorization – forced population movements and forced labor – later played a role both in the German planning of the first deportations to the death camps in 1942, and in how the Jews of the Lublin District perceived these deportations.

Both phenomena served as tools not only for terrorization, but also for radical demographic engineering and reorganization in various territories, while providing cheap labor for a wide variety of Nazi projects. They were implemented immediately after the Nazi conquest and attended nearly all Jewish suffering in the Lublin District until the very bitter end. The methods of round-ups in 1942 closely resembled those used in 1940–1941. In fact, the 1939–1941 deportations set the standards for the deportations to death in 1942–1943 – approximately 1,000 (or multiples thereof) people per train, crowded in tightly, at least fifty per freight car, on short notice, amidst extreme brutality. Similarly, some of the murder sites used in 1942, such as Bełżec, were associated in the Jews' memories with the earlier forced labor and deportations, as were many of the German murderers of 1942, such as Franz Bartetzko, Oskar Dirlewanger, Hermann Dolp, Reinhold Feiks, Odilo Globocnik, Otto Hantke, Georg Michalsen, Wolfgang Mohwinkel, Karl Streibl, Richard Türk, and many others.[1]

Having witnessed the absolute poverty and vulnerability forced upon so many of the thousands of refugees who constantly streamed into the cities, towns, and villages on their own or by force, native Jews in the Lublin District feared they might be reduced to the same

1 Bartetzko and Feiks, both *SS-Hauptshcarführer*, were labor overseers in Bełżec (Bartetzko served the same function at the Lipowa 7 camp) and later served in Trawniki, Bełżec (Feiks), Budzyń, and other camps where many Jews were murdered; see YVA, M.10.AR.1/423.

Hantke and Mohwinkel, also *SS-Hauptscharführer*, served in the Lipowa 7 camp in 1940, Hantke as a labor foreman and Mohwinkel as head of the technical department. Hantke served in Minsk with the EG, from the summer of 1941 to early 1942. He later helped set up the Poniatowa and Budzyń forced-labor camps (fall 1942) and then commanded the small camp at Puławy until the *Erntefest*. Mohwinkel became camp commandant of Lipowa 7 in December 1941, when he was promoted to *Untersturmführer*, and served in this capacity through the *Erntefest* murders in November 1943; see YVA, TR.10/770, pp. 33–36; TR.10/868, pp. 7–13; TR.10/813, pp. 38–42. On Mohwinkel and Hantke, see also Mark Lewis and Jacob Frank, *Himmler's Jewish Tailor: The Story of Holocaust Survivor Jacob Frank* (Syracuse: Syracuse University Press, 2000).

Michalsen, a *SS-Obersturmführer*, commanded the Płazów camp in the Bełżec complex, where he became ill with dysentery, was hospitalized, and given several months to recuperate. He was later sent by Globocnik to serve with EG A in the Soviet Union before returning to Lublin to become Höfle's deputy in "Operation Reinhard," when he was promoted to *Hauptsturmführer*; see YVA, TR.10/813, p. 32.

SS-Hauptsturmführer Streibl was a Selbstschutz commander who was sent to Bełżec on August 27, 1940, to serve as one of Dolp's junior officers. He later commanded the Trawniki camps. He was also apparently involved in several deportations from ghettos in 1942; see YVA, TR.10/869, I:14.

Dirlewanger commanded an infamous SS unit composed of convicted poachers and other criminals. He commanded the Dzików camp in the Bełżec complex and later served in the Lublin District under Globocnik in hunting Jews in the forests; see Hilberg, *Destruction*, pp. 255–259; Breitman, *Architect*, pp. 129–130.

Türk was the Lublin civilian government's Jewish expert from 1940 until his transfer to higher office in Kraków in the spring of 1942. He was intimately involved in Jewish policy throughout his term in Lublin. On Dolp, see Chapter 4.

Men of Leibstandarte SS Adolf Hitler cutting off the beard of an elderly Jewish man, Lublin, Yad Vashem Photo Archive, 1597/76

living standards. The possibility of becoming uprooted in the GG and thus plunged into such a precarious existence, always on the brink of death or beyond it, was itself sufficiently ominous to lead many Lublin District Jews to seek any and all ways to avoid forced relocation.

Similarly, as forced labor in many instances was carried out under such unimaginably difficult conditions, many Jews sought to evade being taken, especially to labor camps far away from their home communities. A large number of forced-laborers returned from these camps seriously ill or maimed – or did not return at all. By the time the deportations to the death camps began in March 1942, forced relocation or forced labor in a distant camp filled the Jews in the Lublin District with an evil foreboding, even though they could not know at first the actual meaning of these deportations. Ultimately, the fresh memory of other round-ups and forced-labor camps, reinforced by the presence of many of the same German persecutors, was more than enough to strike terror in the hearts of these Jews and led many to search for ways to avoid the deportations in 1942.[2]

2 On associating deportations in the spring of 1942 with memories of round-ups

Nazi Population Policy in Poland from September 1939

Massive population movements in occupied Poland were both "voluntary" – in the limited sense that people fled before they were evicted by the invading Germans – and involuntary. The population movements began immediately after the German invasion of Poland. As early as September 4, the roads in the Lublin District were already clogged with refugee traffic.[3]

Flight from an invading army is common in war, as is expulsion of civilian populations from "sensitive" areas, and Poland at the outbreak of World War II was no exception. Moreover, EG units operating in western Poland directed their attacks on Jews in order to instigate mass flight to the eastern parts of the country.[4] However, unlike victors in most other wars, the Germans in Poland quickly developed grandiose schemes for massive demographic engineering in Central and Eastern Europe.

It is not clear how well defined Nazi racial or Jewish policy was on September 1, 1939. However, it is clear that the availability of new territories in the East and the presence on these territories of many millions of people who were considered racially undesirable by the Nazis created the opportunity and need to define both a racial policy for Poland and a Jewish policy that included the territories and Jews of that country. The question is to what extent were Nazi racial or population policies and Jewish policies connected?

A number of scholars have suggested that, at least during the first year to eighteen months of the war, Nazi policy toward the Jews in Poland was part of the overall plans for the racial and demographic restructuring of Central and Eastern Europe. Heinrich Himmler and the SS were prime movers in these plans, which began to evolve in 1939.

Perhaps the first to suggest this close connection between Germany's early wartime Jewish policy and general population policy was Joseph B. Schechtman.[5] Nearly fifty years later Götz Aly

for forced labor-camps in 1940, see, for example, YVA, M.10.AR.1/259.

3 Klukowski, *Diary*, p. 6; Berenstein, "Deportations," p. 52.

4 Rossino, *Hitler Invades Poland*, pp. 90–115, *passim*.

5 Joseph B. Schechtman, *European Population Transfers 1939–1945* (New York:

was able to research the connections between these Nazi policies more extensively, taking advantage of archives that were unavailable to Schechtman, and arguing that these connections continued well into World War II.[6]

Schechtman contended that the Nazis' early population policies derived mainly from their desire to successfully annex western Polish territories. The motivation was largely economic, as they sought control over rich natural resources and industries. For the Nazis successful annexation also meant the racial Germanization of these territories. This required transferring both the agricultural and urban industries and trades to German hands and increasing the relatively low proportion of Germans in the prewar population there (8 percent). The result was a policy of deporting Poles and Jews from these territories into the GG and replacing them with ethnic German settlers brought in from the German minority groups in Eastern Europe, particularly from the Baltic countries and from the USSR.[7]

The idea developed in the upper echelons of the SS in September 1939 was to create three belts of settlement in Poland, from west to east, from Germany across Poland: German, Polish, and Jewish. Germans and ethnic Germans from the Baltic States and other parts of Europe would live in Germany and the territories annexed from Poland. Poles would live in most of the GG, and Jews would be confined to a salient in the easternmost corner of the GG and perhaps forced beyond it, into the USSR. This idea entailed of necessity massive expulsions of Poles into what was soon to become the Generalgouvernement, and of Jews from all territories considered German into the GG and beyond. It is in this context that Heydrich's well-known September 21, 1939 *Schnellbrief* to his

Oxford University Press and Institute of World Affairs, 1946).

6 Götz Aly, *"Final Solution": Nazi Population Policy and the Murder of the European Jews* (London: Arnold, 1999), originally published as *'Endlösung': Völkerverschiebung und der Mord an den europäischen Juden* (Frankfurt am Main: Fischer, 1995). Aly apparently was unaware of Schechtman's work. He does not mention Schechtman at all, neither in the text of the book nor in the bibliography.

7 Schechtman, *European Population Transfers*, pp. 258–268.

EG commanders in Poland can be understood. The document was a follow-up to a meeting of important Sipo, Kripo, SD, and Gestapo officers that day in which the settlement ideas were discussed. The territory indicated for Jewish settlement, the southeastern corner of the Kraków district, was moved further east to Lublin following the September 28 revision of the Nazi-Soviet pact for the division of Poland. However, the essence of the plan remained the same, and, in early October, deportations from within the prewar German borders had already begun, organized by Adolf Eichmann.[8]

The schedules of policy-making and German-organized population transfers are telling with regard to the connection between population policy and Jewish policy. In an October 6, 1939 speech before the Reichstag, Hitler discussed the importance of resettling the ethnic Germans. The following day Himmler was officially appointed *Reichskommissar für die Festigung des deutschen Volkstums*, based on the discussions that already had been underway for the previous three weeks and on the draft of his new appointment, which Himmler had already seen on September 29. On October 8, negotiations to transfer Germans began in Riga and Tallinn, and similar negotiations began in Moscow regarding the "repatriation" of ethnic Germans from the Soviet-occupied Polish territories. Treaties for population transfers were signed very quickly

8 Christopher R. Browning, "Nazi Resettlement Policy and the Search for a Solution to the Jewish Question, 1939–1941," in Michael Marrus, ed., *The Nazi Holocaust* (Westport, CT and London: Meckler, 1989), 3. *The "Final Solution": The Implementation of Mass Murder*, pp. 764–766; *idem*, *Origins*, pp. 25–26; Hilberg, *Destruction*, pp. 191–192, 206; Aly, *Final Solution*, pp. 14–15, 23, 34–35; *idem*, "'Jewish Resettlement': Reflections on the Political Prehistory of the Holocaust," in Ulrich Herbert, ed., *National Socialist Extermination Policies: Contemporary German Perspectives and Controversies* (New York: Berghahn, 2000), pp. 58–60. On the September 21, 1939 meeting, see the September 27, 1939 memo, "Protokoll SD-Hauptamt Stabskanzlei I11 v. 27.9.1939: Amtschef und Einsatzgruppenleiterbesprechung," YVA, Eichmann Trial Document TR.3/983, and the discussion of this period in Yehuda Bauer, "Who Was Responsible and When? Some Well-known Documents Revisited," *Holocaust and Genocide Studies*, 6:2 (1991), pp. 139–141. The document can also be found in Klaus-Michael Mallmann, Jochen Böhler, and Jürgen Matthäus, eds., *Einsatzgruppen in Polen: Darstellung und Dokumentation* (Darmstadt: Wissenschaftliche Buchgesellschaft with Deutsche Historische Institut Warschau and Forschungsstelle Ludwigsburg der Universität Stuttgart, 2008), pp. 144–145.

with all three countries – with Estonia on October 15, Latvia on October 30, and the USSR on November 3 – as well as with Italy regarding the transfer of Germans from the South Tyrol area (on October 21). According to Schechtman, it was the Italian treaty, which actually had begun to be implemented the previous July, well before its signing, that served as a sort of model for peaceful arrangements for transfers and exchanges of populations during the first months of the war. The German-Italian accord had been based on interwar population-exchange agreements, particularly that between Greece and Turkey. Thus, Schechtman proposed an interesting theory: The population transfers inaugurated by the Nazis in 1939 had primarily pro-German, rather than anti-Polish or anti-Jewish, motivations and were based upon both economic and racial considerations. These transfers, in turn, harked back to a great extent to the population-transfer agreements that had characterized the interwar period in Europe.[9]

With regard to the Jews, the first installment in this demographic engineering was the so-called "Nisko Plan." This was initiated on October 6, the same day as Hitler's above-mentioned speech, and when Gestapo chief Heinrich Müller authorized Eichmann to begin organizing expulsions of Jews from Eastern Upper Silesia. Both Müller and Eichmann had participated in the September 21 meeting with Heydrich, and the beginning of Nisko was connected to those discussions. Eichmann extended the expulsions to include Vienna and the Czech Protectorate, and, on October 18, the first transports of 901 evicted Jews from Moravská Ostrava, in Moravia, arrived at Zarzecze, near Nisko, in the GG. These Jews were marched to a swampy area near the small town of Nisko, on the border of the Kraków and Lublin Districts and bordering Soviet-held territory. The healthy among them were forced to construct barracks for a "transit camp," while the others were dispersed over the Lublin District. Four additional transports followed later that month,

9 Schechtman, *European Population Transfers*, pp. 3–22, 39–40, 48–65, 147–148, 482; Robert L. Koehl, *RKFDV: German Resettlement and Population Policy, 1939–1945* (Cambridge, MA: Harvard University Press, 1957), pp. 49–53, 92–94; Aly, *Final Solution*, pp. 34–37; Browning, "Nazi Resettlement Policy," pp. 764–766.

bringing 3,859 Jews from Katowice, Moravia, and Vienna, before the plan was scrapped by Himmler.

Each incoming group of expellees was treated similarly to the first group, with some being shoved into the San River and over into Soviet-held territory. During the winter months Nisko became a labor camp, until HSSPF Krüger ordered the release of the remaining 501 prisoners and they were allowed to return to their homes.[10]

The fact that Jews were being pushed over the border at this early stage reflects the direction of Nazi intentions; the planned Jewish belt of settlement at this time included both the eastern part of the GG and territories beyond Germany's control. As in October 1938, Jews were simply "dumped" over the border.

The next stage in the development of Nazi demographic policies, expanding upon the idea of three belts of settlement, looked to an overall "cleansing" of the annexed territories of Jews, Poles, and Gypsies, and settling ethnic Germans from the Baltic states and other parts of Europe in their place. According to this October 30 idea, 1,000,000 Poles and Jews from the annexed areas were to be deported into the GG by the end of February 1940, to be replaced by an undetermined number of hundreds of thousands of ethnic Germans, who would be "re-Germanized." The Jews would be confined to a "Reservation" in the Lublin District – in keeping with the September 21 discussions and Heydrich's *Schnellbrief* – which would ultimately be a repository for all Jews. The "Reservation" was no secret; Jews and Poles in Lublin and other places heard of it almost from the very beginning, and it was even reported in Western newspapers.[11] Other German officials also tried to take advantage

10 Se'ev Goshen, "Eichmann und die Nisko-Aktion im Oktober 1939," *Vierteljahrshefte für Zeitgeschichte*, 10 (1981), pp. 74–96; Jonny Moser, "Nisko, the First Experiment in Deportation," *Simon Wiesenthal Center Annual*, 2 (1985), pp. 1–30; Philip Friedman, "The Lublin Reservation and the Madagascar Plan: Two Aspects of Nazi Jewish Policy during the Second World War," in *idem*, *Roads to Extinction: Essays on the Holocaust* (Philadelphia: Jewish Publication Society of America, 1980), pp. 34–58; Bauer, "Some Well-known Documents," pp. 140–141; Zeev Goshen, "The Nisko Operation (1939–1940)" (Hebrew), *Dapim L'Heker Ha-Shoah*, 2 (1981), pp. 177–195; Browning, *Origins*, pp. 37–41.

11 Himmler's orders on resettling Jews from the annexed territories to the GG, October 30, 1939, and Baltic Germans to the annexed territories, November

of this plan in order to unload Jews on the Lublin District. For example, Warsaw Governor Ludwig Fischer suggested to Türk, on July 10, 1940, that since Lublin was taking in Jews, he would like to send 10,000 from his district as well.[12]

As with nearly all the Nazi deportations throughout the war, those related to the plans for massive demographic engineering were accompanied by an absolute disregard for the sensibilities and needs of Jewish deportees (and hardly more regard for the Poles). Nearly 88,000 Poles and Jews were deported into the GG by mid-December 1939, but the chaos and brutality that attended these swift deportations disturbed even a veteran, diehard Nazi like Frank.

Heydrich, Krüger, and their staffs met on January 30, 1940, to discuss further deportations into the GG. While recognizing Frank's objections to the way in which the deportations were carried out, they also noted that Frank did not have any objections in principle. Thus, they outlined plans for the relocation of an additional 40,000 Jews, 120,000 Poles, and 30,000 German Gypsies beginning in March 1940, thereby making room for ethnic Germans from the Baltic states and Volhynia. The civilian authorities in the GG were not interested in dealing with a rapid influx of starving, frozen, and impoverished people, literally dumped on them by the SS. On February 12, 1940, Frank won Göring's support to force a temporary halt to these

3, 1939, in YVA, O.53/68 (copies in Tatiana Berenstein, et al., eds., *Faschismus - Getto - Massenmord; Dokumentation über Ausrottung und Widerstand der Juden in Polen während des zweiten Weltkrieges* [Berlin: Rutten und Loening und Jüdischen Historischen Institut, Warschau, 1961], pp. 42–43, and Tatiana Berenstein, et al., eds., *Eksterminacja Żydów na ziemiach polskich w okresie okupacji hitlerowskiej; zbior dokumentów* [Warsaw: Jewish Historical Institute, 1957], p. 29); Browning, "Nazi Resettlement Policy," pp. 766–771; *idem*, *Origins*, pp. 43–54; Hilberg, *Destruction*, pp. 206–209; Broszat, *Nationalsozialistische Polenpolitik*, pp. 86–102; Madajczyk, *Okkupationspolitik*, pp. 233–260, *passim*; Aly, *Final Solution*, p. 18; *Faschismus*, Editors' Introduction, p. 15; Martin Gilbert, *Auschwitz and the Allies* (New York: Holt, 1981), pp. 13–14. See also Berenstein, "Deportations," pp. 52–53. On awareness of the "Reservation" plan, see, for example, Klukowski, *Diary*, November 1, 1939, p. 47; Emmanuel Ringelblum, *Diary and Notes from the Warsaw Ghetto: September 1939-December 1942* (Hebrew) (Jerusalem: Yad Vashem and Ghetto Fighters' House, 1992), entries for December 10–11 and 13–14, 1939, pp. 19, 21.

12 Fischer to Türk, July 10, 1940, and Türk's rejection of the idea, July 26, 1940, WAPL, GDL 891.

deportations until August, although Himmler managed to continue them for another month.[13] According to the 1946 estimate of Poland's Central Commission for the Investigation of German Crimes in Poland (Glówna Komisja Badania Zbrodni Niemieckich w Polsce), 330,000 people had been deported from the western Polish territories annexed to Germany into the GG through June 1940.[14]

It is noteworthy that the waves of deportations and of German settlement coincided closely. The major deportation periods were October 1939 to March 1940, and autumn 1940 to spring 1941, while the German settlement was concentrated in the periods mid-October 1939 to February 1940, September to November 1940, and January to March 1941. In these periods nearly 500,000 ethnic Germans from the Baltic states, former eastern Polish territories now under Soviet rule, and from Soviet-occupied Bessarabia and Bukovina replaced several hundred thousand Poles and Jews who had been deported from the German-annexed territories into the GG. Most of the ethnic German settlers were brought to the German-annexed territories, while a significant proportion of the displaced Jews from the western Polish territories were sent to Lublin. According to statistics compiled by Janina Kiełboń, some 47,000 Jews were deported into the Lublin District from outside the GG in 1939–1940. At the same time, more than 32,000 Poles from German-annexed territories were expelled to the Lublin District, and more than 24,000 ethnic Germans were settled in the district as well. In other words, the SS were indeed pushing Jews as far eastward

13 Browning, *Origins*, pp. 54–63; *idem*, "Nazi Resettlement Policy," pp. 766–771; Hilberg, *Destruction*, pp. 206–209; Broszat, *Nationalsozialistische Polenpolitik*, pp. 86–102; Madajczyk, *Okkupationspolitik*, pp. 233–260, *passim*; *Faschismus*, Editors' Introduction, p. 15; NO-5322, Memo on January 30, 1940 meeting of Heydrich, Krüger, et al., also in Klaus-Peter Friedrich, ed., *Die Verfolgung und Ermordung der europäischen Juden durch das nationalsozialistische Deutschland 1933–1945, Band 4, Polen September 1939—Juli 1941* (Munich: R. Oldenbourg, 2011), pp. 218–222; on the continuation of the deportations in March 1940, see also NG-2490, Lammers to Himmler, March 28, 1940. See also Heydrich's second short-range plan or "2. Nahplan," in Friedrich, ibid., pp. 190–193, and Browning's excellent discussion of this and other German deportations and resettlement for Jews in Browning, *Origins*, pp. 43–54.

14 Central Commission for the Investigation of German Crimes in Poland, *German Crimes in Poland* (New York: Howard Fertig, 1982, c1946–47), p. I:128.

as they could, while settling ethnic Germans as far westward as possible, and driving most displaced Poles to the center.[15]

Schechtman, Robert L. Koehl, and, most recently, Götz Aly see all the above as evidence that Aryan race notions and economic considerations stood behind the massive demographic engineering of this period. For them this is the best explanation for the coincidence of the deportations of both Jews and Poles with the settlement of ethnic Germans. In addition, the similarly brutal conditions under which the deportations were conducted for both Jews and Poles, and the fact that both groups were being sent to the same destination — the GG — making it a sort of Jewish and Polish "ghetto" during the first eighteen months of German occupation, also support their analysis.[16]

Aly emphasizes Nazi plans for racial and demographic engineering in Central and Eastern Europe, and he is the only one of these scholars who directly connects these early German actions with their later anti-Jewish policies. Significantly, he says the deportations and resettlements of Jews and Poles and the mass murder of German and Polish mental patients in 1939–1940 served as a prelude to the deportations to death in 1942–1943, in terms of German preparedness for murderous cruelty, organization, and personnel.[17]

Other interpretations regarding the deportations during this period place greater emphasis on Nazi ideology than economics.

15 Janina Kiełboń, *Migracja Ludności w Dystrikcie Lubelskim w latach 1939–1944* (Lublin: Państwowe Muzeum na Majdanku, 1995), pp. 28–33, 110–112, 127–140; Schechtman, *European Population Transfers*, pp. 145–173, 214–218, 267–271, 482–483; Koehl, *RKFdV*, pp. 100–101, 128–134; Aly, *Final Solution*, pp. 4–5, 9, 34–52, 59–81.

16 Schechtman, *European Population Transfers*, pp. 145–173, 214–218, 267–271, 482–483; Koehl, *RKFdV*, pp. 100–101, 128–134; Aly, *Final Solution*, pp. 14–148, *passim*. See also *idem*, "Erwiderung auf Dan Diner," *Vierteljahrshefte für Zeitgeschichte*, 41:4 (October 1993), pp. 621–635. Koehl actually uses the term "ghetto" in this connection. The exact number of Poles deported from these territories during this eighteen-month period is not clear. Schechtman cites Polish Historical Commission statistics referring to 1,500,000, whereas Madajczyk, *Okkupationspolitik*, pp. 429–433, says this number refers to all uprooted Poles in the annexed territories, most of whom remained there. He estimates the number of deportees into the GG as 460,000.

17 Aly, *Final Solution*, p. 76 and *passim*.

The contention is that radical demographic engineering was a major policy outgrowth of Nazi ideology. Thus, the economic realities that derived from the population composition of the annexed Polish territories might have influenced the choice of the first place where the engineering would be implemented, but not the fact of the engineering itself. Yet these explanations of Nazi population policies are not uniform in identifying the determining aspects of Nazi ideology. Martin Broszat and Czesław Madajczyk cite the sheer weight of the relative numbers of deported Poles and Jews and *Volksdeutsche* settled to point to general Nazi racial ideology as underpinning the early deportations. Other scholars, such as Raul Hilberg and Richard Breitman, see Nazi antisemitic ideology as the motivation behind the deportations of Jews at all stages, regardless of numbers.[18] The Nazis had long been hoping to rid Germany of Jews and had resorted to severe pressure on the Jewish population to leave and to outright deportations in late 1938 in their efforts to achieve this goal. This prewar desire continued naturally into the war, and the deportation of Jews from the annexed Polish territories was only one expression of the hope to "cleanse" Germany of Jews.

Christopher Browning also emphasizes the centrality of Nazi antisemitic ideology in these deportations, but he lends greater weight to the economic considerations than any of the above historians and agrees with the former group that, at this early stage, Jewish policy had not yet achieved the centrality it would later occupy.[19] Still, for Browning, as for Hilberg and Breitman, although economics and German reunion ideas clearly played a major role in choosing the annexed areas as the first site for major population transfers, anti-Jewish ideology and policy stood alone — sometimes in coordination with other policies, as with the Warthegau deportations, and other times operating under a dynamic all their own. Only in this way can the wide variety and long endurance of deportations of Jews be understood.

Alongside the radical population transfers revolving around

18 See Madajczyk, *Okkupationspolitik*, pp. 389–421; Broszat, *Nationalsozialistische Polenpolitik*, pp. 85–102; Hilberg, *Destruction*, pp. 206–216; Breitman, *Architect*, pp. 77–82.

19 Browning, "Nazi Resettlement Policy," pp. 764–766; *idem*, *Origins*, pp. 25–26.

the annexed Polish territories, which included Jews, Jews were also deported from other parts of the Reich, as well as from one place to another within the GG, and beyond the GG into the Soviet Union. These other deportations were primarily a result of Nazi antisemitic ideology mixed with local initiative, and they, too, reflect the evolving Nazi efforts to define a distinct Jewish policy for Poland and, ultimately, for Europe.

Forced Marches

The early deportations of Jews involving the Lublin District followed neither of the models suggested above. Whereas those from the Warthegau and other Reich territories were in some way connected to a grand scheme of demographic engineering in Eastern Europe, the brutal, murderous style of the deportations and the continued forced movements of the Jews once they reached the Lublin District were not clearly part of any Nazi population policy. Rather, the expulsions and other population movements in the Lublin District were often the result of local decisions, usually by SS personnel, based primarily on antisemitic ideology, together with a variety of other reasons. The death marches from Chełm and Hrubieszów discussed below were a local SS initiative, while most of the other expulsions and marches were within the GG, away from the border, and had no clear larger purpose beyond sheer cruelty and terrorization.

Just as the German civilian government had begun to establish itself only at the end of October 1939, so, too, did the EGs begin formally to function as the district SS and Police only around November 1. Even then it took the civilians, the SS, and the police many weeks to organize fully. The result of this relatively long interval was widespread local German freedom to implement independent anti-Jewish actions. Although there was as yet no apparent uniform policy for Jews, anti-Jewish measures were undertaken everywhere. This local autonomy was in many places manifested by a rash of expulsions of Jews into and within the Lublin District in November and December 1939. Though usually at local SS initiative, these expulsions followed the general pattern of pushing the Jews eastward and/or concentrating them.

Despite the distinction that the historian might be able to draw between the expulsions that were part of a grand strategy and those that were a local SS initiative, for the Jews they were all part of the same turmoil and upheaval, accompanied by extreme brutality and numerous deaths. This is validated by the fact that, despite the absence of central planning, the descriptions of the expulsions bear a close resemblance to one another. Perhaps the one unifying factor among all the expulsions and deportations during the first months of the war was the complete disregard for the humanity or lives of the Jewish deportees.

A characteristic feature of the early expulsions within the Lublin District was the long march on very short notice, often in the middle of the night. These late autumn and winter evictions took place in sub-zero temperatures, and many deportees died of exposure or of illnesses contracted on the march or on the train – if the SS and Selbstschutz guards did not murder them first. The evictions and marches affected local Jews and deportees into the district alike. Tables 3.1 and 3.2 below list many of the expulsions and deportations relating to the Lublin District during the first year of the occupation.

Among the very first expulsions was that from Lubartów in November 1939, when more than 2,500 Jews were evicted to Ostrów-Lubelski and Parczew. Some went from there to Sławatycze, Symjatycze, and Włodawa. Others sneaked across the Bug River into the USSR.[20] Similarly, on December 29, all the approximately 2,500 Jews of Puławy were evicted from their homes and marched to Opole-Lubelski. Somewhat earlier that month, fifty Jewish families from Kazimierz Dolny were evicted to the same destination.[21]

20 Kiełboń, *Migracja*, p. 158; Berenstein, "Martyrologia," p. 30; Adina (Elkin) Eichenbaum, "In a Snowstorm into the Unknown," and Mechl (Misha) Eckhaus, "[I] Survived Two World Wars," in *Ostrów-Lubelski Book*, edited by David Stokfisch (Yiddish) (Tel Aviv: Organization of Ostrów-Lubelski Immigrants in Israel, 1987), pp. 99, 260; Aryeh Barnea, *The Jews of Lubartów: Life, Holocaust, Remnants* (Hebrew) (Tel Aviv: Lubartów Immigrants' Committee, 1987), p. 13.

21 See, for example, testimony of Baruch and Sarah Roizman, YVA, O.3/3554; Mordechai W. Bernstein, ed., *Puławy Yizkor Book* (Yiddish) (New York: Pulawer Yizkor Book Committee, 1964), testimonies of Golda Pajek Kupfer, Etl Szabason-Briefman, and Golda Teich, pp. 387, 388, 393.

Table 3.1: Deportations to Lublin District, September 1939–May 1940 (more than 20,000)

Dates	From	To	Numbers
Nov.-Dec. 1939	*Annexed areas*	*Lublin*	*5,000*
Nov. 1939-Jan. 1940	*Annexed areas*	*throughout district*	*>7,400, including part of above 5,000*
Dec. 1939	Łódź, Kalisz, Suwalki...	Piszczac	200
Dec. 1939	Łódź, Kalisz, Włocławek	Tarnogród	371
Dec. 1939	Kalisz, Łódź	Annopol	63
Nov.-Dec. 1939	Łódź	Zakrzówek	350
Oct.-Dec.1939	Slupce, Konin, Szubin, Łódź	Gorzków	n.a.
Dec. 10, 1939	Koło	Izbica	1,139
Dec. 19, 1939	Łódź	Izbica, and then to Kraśniczyn, Gorzków, Wysokie, Turobin, Żółkiewka, Krasnystaw	1,900
Dec. 1939	Koło	Krasnystaw	62
Oct.-Dec. 1939	Łódź, Koło, Konin	Turobin	1,250
Dec. 1939	Posen	Ostrów-Lubelski	1,000
Dec. 1939	Rypin, Kalisz	Międzyrzec	n.a.
Oct.-Dec. 1939	Łódź, Koło, Głowno, Włocławek, Sierpiec	Komarów	200
Dec. 15, 1939	Koło	Zamość	175
Dec. 1939	Włocławek	Zamość	>250

Dates	From	To	Numbers
Dec. 18, 1939	Włocławek, Kolo	Szczebrzeszyń	100
Dec. 25, 1939	Łódź	Szczebrzeszyń	30
Jan. 1940	Łódź, Kalisz...	Włodawa	n.a.
Jan. 1940	Łódź	Wojsławice	260
early 1940	Łódź	Siennica Różana	56
early 1940	Kalisz, Koło	Żółkiewka	n.a.
Feb. 1940	Warthegau	Michów	400
Feb. 12, 1940	*Stettin*	*Lublin*	*1,200*
Feb. 25, 1940	Stettin	Bełżyce	>300
Feb. 1940	Stettin	Głusk	65
Feb. 1940	Stettin	Piaski	565
Mar. 12, 1940	*Schneidemühl (Piła)*	*Lublin*	*160*
Oct.-Dec. 1939	*Suwalki*	*Biała-Podlaska, Kock, Łuków, Międzyrzec*	*3,000*
Dec. 3, 1939	*Serock, Nasielsk*	*Biała-Podlaska*	*3,000*
Dec. 1939	Serock, Nasielsk	Łuków, Międzyrzec	n.a.
Sept. 1939	*Rozwadów, Rudnik, Nisko, Tarnobrzeg*	*Ulanów*	*609*
Dec. 1939	Nowy Dwór	Kock	n.a.
May 1, 1940	*POWs*	*Lublin*	*3,224*
Feb. 14, 1940	POWs (death march)	Lubartów, Parczew, Biała-Podlaska	ca. 800
Dec. 1939	*POWs (death march)*	*Włodawa*	*320*

Table 3.2: Intra-district Deportations, October 1939–February 1940 (approximately 15,000)

Dates	From	To	Numbers
Nov. 5, 1939	*Lubartów*	*Ostrów-Lubelski, Parczew, Kock...*	*2,616*
Dec. 3, 1939	Lubartów	Radzyń	10s
Aug.-Sept. 1940	Parczew, et al.	Lubartów	returnees
Oct. 1939; Dec. 6, 1939	*Radzyń*	*Sławatycze, Międzyrzec, Parczew, Kock, and more*	*n.a.*
Dec. 1939	Radzyń	Komarówka	70
Dec. 29, 1939	*Puławy*	*Opole-Lubelski*	*2,500*
Dec. 1939	Puławy	Chodel	n.a.
Dec. 1939	Puławy, Kurów, Markuszów	Nałęczów	46
Dec. 1939	Puławy	Końskowola	n.a.
Nov.-Dec. 1939	Puławy, Kurów	Ryki	92
Dec. 30, 1939	*Józefów n/Wisla*	*Opole-Lubelski*	*ca.300 (50 families)*
Dec. 1-2, 1939	*Chełm, Hrubieszów (death march)*	*Bug River, Belz, Sokal*	*4,000*
Nov. 20, 1939	*Łuków*	*Siedlce, Ostrów-Mazowiecki*	*2,000*
Dec. 1939	*Chełm*	*Lubomil*	*n.a.*
Dec. 1939-Feb. 14, 1940	*POWs*	*Lubartów, Parczew, Biała-Podlaska*	*3,544*

One of the most vicious and murderous expulsion marches began in Chełm on Friday, December 1, when approximately 1,000–2,000 Jewish men were marched to Hrubieszów, more than 50 kilometers to the south. Most were shot by their SS and Selbstschutz guards on the way, and the few hundred who reached Hrubieszów that night were chilled to the bone and completely exhausted. The next day an additional 1,000–2,000 Jewish men from Hrubieszów were gathered together, and they were ordered to march together with the surviving Chełm Jews along a circuitous route toward the Bug River. Very many were shot along the way, and others managed to flee, until there were only several hundred Jews remaining as they approached a crossroads. They were divided into two groups, one heading for Sokal, in Soviet-held territory, and the other for Belz. They were forced into the water at Sokal, but the Red Army guards on the other side opened fire on them to prevent them from crossing. In both groups, whoever reached the town alive received aid from the local community – from the Jewish community in Sokal, and from a local women's committee at the urging of the priest in Belz.[22]

Janina Kiełboń has estimated that the Germans deported

22 On Chelm and Hrubieszów, from YVA: M.2/235, testimony of Dr. J. L., Jerusalem, May 1942; Josef Rechtschaft testimony of October 27, 1960, TR.11/01121/V, affidavits taken by Israel police for West German investigation regarding suspected perpetrators in Hrubieszów; Abraham Dichter testimony, O.2/213; Avraham and Sheindl Goldfarb testimony, O.3/2140; Ahuva Shamai-Grossfeld, O.3/3135; O.12/46, unnamed sixteen-year-old, 1942; Anszel Krechman, M.1.E/1249; Benjamin Szporn, M.1.E/1463; Moshe Moskal, Avraham Zimmerman, Hersh Pachter, M.1.E/1536; Joel Ponczak testimony, O.33/243; Jakob Finkelstein testimony, M.9/576; "The Pogrom in Chełm," M.10.AR.1/1006; Zipora Hurwitz testimony, Moreshet Archive (MA), A.296; Ringelblum, *Diary and Notes,* December 12, 1939, p. 20; Shimon Kantz, ed., *Memorial Book for the Chełm Community* (Yiddish and Hebrew) (Tel Aviv: Chełm Immigrants' Association, 1981), testimonies of Ben-Zion Brucker, J. Feinsztok, Yitzhak Grojskopf, Haim Sobol, Manes Citrin, J. Hertz, Lazar Cohen, pp. 663, 689, 698, 699, 703–706, 710; Baruch Kaplinski, ed., *Pinkas Hrubieszów* (Hebrew and Yiddish) (Tel Aviv: Hrubieszów Immigrants' Association, 1969), testimonies of Moshe Moskal and Avraham Zimmerman, Eliahu Zylberberg, Reuven Katz, Zwi Pachter, Roza Zylbermintz, Avraham and Shaindl Goldfarb, pp. 613–614, 650, 693–695. See also Ariel Hurwitz, "The Death March of the Jews of Chełm and Hrubieszów to the Bug River, December 1939," graduate seminar paper, Hebrew University of Jerusalem, 1984; Martin Gilbert, *The Holocaust: A History of the Jews of Europe During the Second World War* (New York: Henry Holt and Co., 1985), p. 104; *idem, Atlas of the Holocaust* (London: Michael Joseph, 1982), pp. 33–34. Some testimonies say that the Belz clergyman was a Protestant minister.

15,000 Jews from the annexed territories to the Lublin District in 1939.[23] When the Jewish prisoners of war from the Polish army and the Jews from Stettin (now Szczecin) and Schneidemühl (now Piła) — all of whom were expelled to Lublin during the first months of 1940 — are taken into account, the total number of expellees from German territory exceeds 20,000. The Jews in the annexed territories would generally be brought from rural areas to urban centers; from there all the Jews would be transported in cattle cars to the GG. Transports came from Łódź, Kalisz, Koło, Włocławek, Poznan, Suwalki, and other places. The trains were sent to a number of reception centers in the district, such as Lublin (the Lipowa 7 camp), Zamość, and Biała-Podlaska, from which the refugees would be dispersed among various communities. The dispersal of the refugees would be carried out by a variety of transportation means, including horses and carts or sleds — if the local Jewish community could afford to hire these and the German authorities would allow it — or else by foot. The distances the refugees would have to travel could be dozens of kilometers.

A great many Jewish civilians were deported to Biała-Podlaska and its vicinity in December 1939, including more than 3,000 from Suwalki, near Lithuania, and a similar number from Serock and Nasielsk near Warsaw. The Serock Jews were marched 5 kilometers to the Nasielsk train station, where both towns' Jews were forced onto trains and shipped to Biała-Podlaska, Międzyrzec, and environs on December 3.[24]

Hundreds of Jews from Włocławek were deported to Szczebrzeszyń and Zamość in mid-December 1939. In the early winter a number of these refugees in Szczebrzeszyń were permitted by the local German civilian authorities to move to Zamość and

23 Kiełboń, *Migracja*, p. 132.

24 See M. J. Feigenbojm, "Destruction and Annihilation," in *Biała-Podlaska Book*, p. 49; Ringelblum, *Diary and Notes*, December 1–10, 1939, pp. 11–19; Zwi Kleinman, "Memories from a Persecuted Person, Biała-Podlaska," YVA, M.10. AR.1/1000 (JM/3489). See also Sarah Neshamit, "The Expulsion of the Jews of Suwalki and the Area, October-November 1939 and the Efforts to Save Them" (Hebrew), *Dapim L'Heker Ha-Shoah*, B (1981), pp. 202–216; Daniel Freiberg, *Darkness Covered the Earth*, pp. 41–43.

asked Judenrat head Mieczysław Garfinkel to obtain permission from the Germans for the other deportees to move as well. The German civilian authorities agreed, and the other Włocławek refugees set out for Zamość. But the SS cavalry unit at Janowice, three kilometers from Zamość, detained them there, forced them to undress, poured cold water over them, and then shot them all.[25] This was characteristic of the unorganized and chaotic violence that Polish Jews faced during the first months of the Nazi occupation.

Among those to suffer the worst during the early months of the occupation were Jewish prisoners of war from the Polish army whose homes were in the Soviet-occupied zone. When taken prisoner, the Jewish soldiers were generally separated from their Polish comrades and treated far more harshly. They were sent either to POW camps in Germany proper or to camps in East Prussia and western Poland. From these camps, many of those whose homes were in the GG were allowed to return home, while those whose homes were in the Soviet zone were sent to special SS-run camps in the GG, primarily in the Lublin District. They were often told that they were being returned to their homes in a prisoner exchange with the USSR.

Many thousands of Jewish POWs were deported into and out of Lublin, through the Lipowa 7 camp, between December 1939 and February 1941. These POWs were transferred from Wehrmacht to SS jurisdiction upon arrival in Lublin, which meant a considerable worsening of their conditions. The fact that the transfer of POWs out of Wehrmacht control to SS jurisdiction was contrary to the laws of war did not interest the Germans.

During the first months of the German occupation, more than 1,000 POWs were killed on death marches that had supposedly been aimed to send them to the Soviet zone. In December 1939, at least 320 Jewish POWs were deported by boxcar to Włodawa. More than half died en route, while the others were shot in the woods by the SS and Selbstschutz. When the Judenrat in Włodawa was told by local SS officials to send a delegation to the nearby woods (near

25 Tamari, *Zamość*, p. 103; Mieczysław Garfinkel testimony, YVA, O.33/322; Garfinkel testimony (Wiesbaden 1962), YVA, TR.10/1146Z, vol. 17, pp. 3729–3730; Klukowski, *Diary*, p. 62; Ringelblum, *Diary and Notes*, December 21, 1939, p. 31.

Sobibór) to receive a group of POWs, they found corpses in tattered uniforms. Only a few individuals survived this nightmare.

A similar and larger-scale murder of POWs occurred several weeks later, in February 1940. According to the Lublin Judenrat's annual report, 1,367 POWs reached the city in February (1,000 came during the second week of the month). Of these, the Judenrat reported that 864 whose homes were in the GG were soon let free. The Judenrat refused orders to feed the others, whose homes were in the Soviet zone, or to provide civilian clothing for them on the grounds that caring for POWs was the responsibility of the conquering power. Besides, the Judenrat did not have the means to care for additional refugees, as at that same time it was overwhelmed by trying to care for the needs of the 1,200 haggard deportees who had just arrived from Stettin (see below) and the several thousand refugees from other places.

The SS made an example of these POWs and marched them out toward Biała-Podlaska on Thursday, February 15, under heavy Selbstschutz guard, commanded by *SS-Sturmbannführer* Hermann Dolp (later of Bełżec notoriety). Dozens were shot the first day, on the way to Lubartów, and another 165 the following day. Most of the others were shot later during the four-day march. According to one survivor of the march, only 284 of the 862 POWs on the march reached Biała-Podlaska alive. Those who survived the 120-kilometer trek in deep snow, in temperatures that reached -30°C, according to some reports, were fed by the Jewish communities in Parczew and Biała-Podlaska and then housed in a POW camp in Biała-Podlaska.

The Lublin Judenrat report and the minutes of its meetings during that period relate the movement of these POWs in a sterile way, without mention of their true fate. However, numerous survivor statements make it clear that the Judenrat's records do not reflect the full story. Circumspection and caution in the face of prying German eyes probably precluded candor in the written record. Moreover, the Jews of Lublin learned a lesson from this tragedy and rarely challenged the SS on legalities after that.[26]

26 Lublin Judenrat Annual Report, WAPL, RZ 8 (copy in YVA, O.6/389; hereafter

The conditions in which the POWs and the other refugees lived were frequently difficult in the extreme. Those who did not have family, friends, or the community looking after them died of exposure, starvation, or disease — whichever came first. Fortunately for them, Lublin and other communities succeeded in providing sufficient food and housing to keep most of the refugees alive during the first year.

The POWs were often told by their Wehrmacht camp officers in Germany that they were being sent home to the USSR in a prisoner

cited by name only), pp. 21–25; Blumental, *Documents*, pp. 78–83, and Protocol 10, February 17, 1940, pp. 126–127; Roman Fischer testimony, Institute of Contemporary Jewry, Oral History Division (OHD), 1573; testimonies from YVA: M49.E/1016, Dr. Adam Szprynger; M.49.E/163, Yehezkel Brzezinski; O.3/2181, Arieh Leib Helfgot; O.3/2124, Roman Fischer; O.3/4056, Mottl Tuchweber; O.3/447, M.49.E/2791, O.3/6774, Josef Birger-Ezrahi; O.33/53, Yosef Grossfeld; M.1.E/649, Yeshayahu Weisfisz; M.1.E/925, Mietek Gruber; M.1.E/1249, Anszel Krechman; M.1.E/1563, Gedalje Erenberg; M.2/236, testimony of unnamed *chalutzah* from Lublin, Jerusalem, February 1943; M.10.AR.1/1073, AR.1/1174, AR.1/1372 (JM/3489); Ringelblum memo, M.10.AR.3/64a (JM/215/1); Samuel Gruber, *I Chose Life* (New York: Shengold, 1978), pp. 17–26; Ringelblum, *Diary and Notes*, March 6, 1940, p. 85; Mosze Josef Feigenbojm, *Podlosie in Its Downfall: Notes from the Destruction* (Yiddish) (Munich: Commission of the Liberated Jews in the American Zone in Germany, 1948), p. 7; Nachman Blumental, "On the Events of the Holocaust in Lublin," in *Encyclopedia of the Jewish Diaspora, Lublin*, pp. 672–676; Shmuel Krakowski, "The Fate of Jewish Prisoners of War in the September 1939 Campaign," *Yad Vashem Studies*, 12 (1977), pp. 315–318; *idem*, *War of the Doomed*, pp. 261–264; Krystyna Modrzewska, "Pamiętnik z Okresu Okupacji," *Biuletyn Żydowski Institut Historycznego*, nr. 31 (1959), pp. 63–64; Gilbert, *Holocaust*, pp. 110–111. The exact number of POWs on this death march is not entirely clear. The Judenrat report refers to 503 who were "transferred" to Biała-Podlaska, while one of the Oneg Shabbat sources (M.10AR.1/1073) and Ringelblum cite 627 and 287 survivors, Gilbert cites 880, and Mottl Tuchweber cites 1320. Yehezkel Brzezinski, who survived the death march and provided a very detailed report of it immediately after the war, says that 862 POWs set out on the march, but only 284 reached Biała-Podlaska alive. Kiełboń, *Migracja*, pp. 132–133, estimates that 5,000 POWs were brought to the Lublin District by the end of February 1941. However, the actual number seems higher. The Lublin Judenrat's statistics indicate that more than 3,000 had arrived in Lublin during the first five months of 1940. When this number is added to the 320 marched to Włodawa in December 1939, the 1,500 sent to Biała-Podlaska county in October-December 1940, and the 2,800 to Lublin in January-February 1941, not to mention other small groups sent to the district throughout this period, the total must have been closer to 8,000.

exchange. Exchanges between Germany and the USSR did take place, and the SS seems to have been willing to let POWs return to the Soviet zone at least at some point. An illustration of this is Globocnik's letter of March 19, 1940, to *Selbstschutzführer* von Alvensleben, saying that Jewish POWs in Lublin can go home if they live in the GG and relinquish their uniforms, or they can be included in "*Sammeltransporten*" connected with the Russian-German "*Flüchtlingsaustausch-Aktion*" (Refugee Exchange Operation).[27]

More POWs were brought to the Biała-Podlaska county in the autumn of 1940. On October 24, it was planned to send 1,500 POWs from Stalag IIB, Hammerstein (Pomerania; Czarne today), to Ryki and Biała-Podlaska for forced labor, and an undefined number from Stalag VIIIA, Görlitz, to Hrubieszów. Eight hundred of these had already arrived on October 23, of whom 250 were cripples who were unable to work. An additional 200 arrived from Hammerstein on November 8. On November 17, 1940, POWs arrived in Łuków and were assigned to the Luftwaffe construction project at Podladów, and nearly 400 were sent to Ryki in December.[28]

On the night of February 12, 1940, approximately 1,200 Jews of all ages in Stettin (Germany; Szczecin, Poland today) were given short notice (no more than eight hours) to be ready for "relocation" to the East. The deportees included residents of old-age homes, small

27 Lublin Judenrat Annual Report, pp. 10–15, 21–25; Blumental, *Documents*, pp. 78–83, and Protocol 10, February 17, 1940, p. 126; Josef Birger-Ezrahi, YVA, O.33/53, O.3/447, O.3/6774; Mietek Gruber; M.1.E/1249; *idem*, *I Chose Life*, p. 23; Yehezkel Brzezinski; O.3/2181; Globocnik to *Führer des SS- und Selbstschutzes*, Lublin, March 19, 1940, WAPL, GDL 891; Roman Fischer testimony, OHD, 1573; Bernard Schwartz testimony, *Dos Buch fun Lublin*, pp. 516–518; Krakowski, "The Fate of Jewish Prisoners of War," pp. 315–318.

28 Dr. Heineke, BuF Lublin, to Abteilung Arbeit, Lublin, October 24, 1940; Ramm to BuF Lublin, November 26, 1940; Arbeitsamt, Biala-Podlaska to Abteilung Arbeit, Lublin, October 28; Abteilung Arbeit, Lublin to BuF, Lublin, November 5; Arbeitsamt, Biala-Podlaska to Abteilung Arbeit, Lublin, November 11; Jache to BuF, Lublin, November 20; GG Labor Department, Kraków to Lublin Labor Department, November 13 and November 15; "Vermerk" (unclear signature, Lublin Labor Department), November 15; Jache to GG Labor Department, Kraków, November 20, all in YVA, JM/2700; Zörner report on Jewish forced labor, November 6, 1940, in *Faschismus*, p. 217, and *Eksterminacja*, p. 221; Krakowski, "The Fate of Jewish Prisoners of War," pp. 317–318.

children, prominent citizens, and a former city councilor. They were given permission to take one suitcase, but, in actuality, many were simply forced out in their nightshirts directly to the waiting trains, with no prior notice whatsoever. The train windows and doors were locked during the three-day trip, and the people were given no food or water. The Stettin deportees arrived in Lublin frozen, filthy, and terrified – several dozen died on the way – only to be met by Selbstschutz soldiers who rained beatings on them and shot several people. Many were brought to the hospital, and six died the first night. The deportees were housed for a day or two in the stables and barracks at Lipowa 7 in Lublin until their transfer by foot and sled, more than 26 kilometers, in temperatures that dipped to -22^{0}C, to Piaski, Bełżyce, Głusk, and a number of smaller communities in Lublin-Land county. A number of the oldest among them were brought to the Jewish old-age home in Lublin.

The death rate among the Stettin deportees was very high: seventy-two were reported to have died on the march to the nearby towns, and 230 died within a month.[29] Some of the Stettin deportees were able to receive packages from the Reichsvereinigung der Juden in Deutschland in Berlin and from the Munich Jewish community. In many cases, however, posting these packages and their contents was illegal and put the senders at risk. These packages also caused some tension vis-à-vis the local Jews, and the Lublin Judenrat decided to set aside a part of the packages for the Jewish hospital in

29 Lublin Judenrat Annual Report, pp. 36, 67–68; Nuremberg Document NG-2490, letter, Lammers to Himmler, March 28, 1940, including a March 14, 1940, report, "Die Deportation wird fortgesetzt, Der Todesmarsch vom Lublin – Erfrierungstode"; lists of arrivals from Stettin and their ultimate relocation destinations, in WAPL, RZ 166; death records of Stettin Jews, WAPL, RZ 167; Nuremberg Document NO-5322, "Ausserungen des Chefs des Reichssicherheitshauptamtes...," January 30, 1940; YVA, testimonies of Manfred Heymann, O.2/794; Erich Mossbach, O.33/2149; Elsa Meyring, O.33/2212; Vera Beckhard, O.33/2426; and Moshe Zylberberg, M.1.E/1402; Modrzewska, "Pamiętnik," pp. 65–68; Else Rosenfeld and Gertrud Luckner, eds., *Lebenszeichen aus Piaski; Briefe Deportierter aus dem Distrikt Lublin 1940–1943* (Munich: Biederstein, 1968), pp. 7–25; Sarah Erlichman-Bank, *In Impure Hands* (Hebrew) (Tel Aviv: Ghetto Fighters' House and Hakibbutz Hameuhad, 1970), pp. 19–20; Browning, *Origins*, pp. 64–65.

Lublin.[30] A month later, on March 12, 160 Jews arrived in Lublin in a terrible state from Schneidemühl. They, too, were beaten viciously by Selbstschutz troops upon arrival and were then scattered by the Judenrat among several nearby communities.[31]

There were two major differences between these deportations and the others during this period. First, these were deportations from the *Altreich* – the pre-Nazi German borders. Therefore, these deportees were German nationals by definition of the Nuremberg Laws. This led to the second major difference between these two deportations and the others: these Jews retained certain limited rights as German Jews, even as they lost other rights. They lost all their property, but, from September 1940, they continued to receive their pensions for another year and a half, with Himmler's approval. Since a very large proportion of the Stettin deportees were elderly, this was quite significant. The pensions, together with the packages they received from Germany, helped alleviate the deportees' plight somewhat. Nevertheless, retention of rights was not self-evident to the Lublin authorities, and they inquired with Berlin in this regard.[32]

Death marches were not unique to the Lublin District. For example, thousands of Jews from Jarosław and Łancut were force-marched to the San River, where they were shoved onto rickety rafts

30 Rosenfeld and Luckner, eds., *Lebenszeichen aus Piaski, passim*; Elsa Meyring testimony, YVA, O.33/2212; Blumental, *Documents*, Protocols 42–47, September 11–16, 1940, pp. 182–186.

31 Nuremberg Document NG-2490. Jews were also deported from Konin in November and December 1939, to Warsaw and Lublin, prior to large-scale deportations from there to Lublin in 1941. See YVA, M.10.AR.1/674 (also on JM/3489); M.10.AR.1/924 (also on JM/3489/22), referring to deportations in 1941; M.1.E/1407, Avraham Obarzonek; WAPL, RZ 169.

32 Türk to BuF Kraków, June 15, 1940, and BuF Kraków response, July 17, 1940, WAPL, GDL 891; Dr. Beelitz, *Regierungspräsident* Stettin, to *Kreishauptmann* Lublin-Land, August 23, 1940, WAPL, GDL 891; Dr. Hecht, BuF Lublin, to Deutsche Gericht Lublin, March 6, 1941, WAPL, GDL 892 (copy in YVA, JM/10455); Dr. Frauendorfer, Interior Department Kraków, to BuF Lublin, March 25, 1941, YVA, O.53/84. See also September 1940 correspondence between Türk's office and the Lublin legal department and Stettin municipality regarding the Stettin Jews' property, WAPL, GDL 891.

to cross over to the Soviet side.[33] The Wehrmacht expelled Jews from Eastern Upper Silesia over the San River into Soviet territory in September and October 1939.[34] Similarly, Jews from the annexed territories who had been sent to the Radom District were meant to be forced to cross by foot into the Lublin District near Sandomierz, or else to be sent in "closed Jewish transports" into Soviet territory at Brest-Litovsk.[35]

Despite the commonality of death marches during the first year of the German occupation, there was no known central policy or order to treat Jewish deportees in this way. Still, forced marches were widespread and resulted in many deaths. In the Lublin District, they included essentially *all* deportee groups, as well as many thousands of local Jews. We can account for more than 20,000 Jews who were so marched by March 1940, from Łuków, Lubartów, Puławy, Józefów nad Wisła, Chełm, Hrubieszów, and elsewhere, as well as expellees to the district and POWs. Based on the Jewish sources cited above, more than 3,000 of these marchers were killed.

The USSR – Flight and Exchanges

In addition to forced population movements, there was massive Jewish and Polish flight eastward from the very beginning of the war. According to the Polish Central Commission, approximately 60,000 Jews fled from the annexed Polish territories eastward by the summer of 1940. According to the Lublin Judenrat Report, there were 5,633 registered civilian Jewish refugees in the city by August 1, 1940, representing nearly 15 percent of the total Jewish population. There were probably a great number of unregistered refugees as well, since those who were not registered might have believed they could avoid being sent to a forced-labor site.[36]

In some places the number of refugees matched or even

33 *German Crimes in Poland*, I:143; Rossino, *Hitler Strikes Poland*, pp. 92–101.

34 Pohl, "*Judenpolitik*," p. 28; Rossino, ibid.

35 Letter, Radom governor to county and town heads, December 4, 1939, *Eksterminacja*, p. 35; Rossino, ibid.

36 There are many sources that relate the general flight eastward. See, for example,

surpassed the local Jewish population, such as in Turobin, which received more than 1,200 refugees from German-annexed territories. Similarly, the population of Biskupice more than doubled; that of Opole-Lubelski increased by 40 percent by the end of 1939.[37] Moreover, these numbers reflect only an undetermined fraction of the total refugee flow, since there is no clear accounting of Jews who managed to cross the border into the USSR, or of those who moved from place to place within the Lublin District.

A significant part of this flight was through the Lublin District or from it into the USSR, which continued even after the Soviet Union closed the border with the GG in 1940. This depleted the Jewish communities of the Lublin District during the first months of the war. For example, the 12,000-strong Jewish community of Zamość numbered only 8,412 in the October 1939 census taken upon German orders, and many of these were refugees. There were communities from which half or more of the Jews fled eastward. Nearly all the Jews of Belz succeeded in fleeing to the USSR. In general, the flight into, through, and out of the Lublin District during the first year of occupation actually left its total Jewish population more or less stable. However, by the autumn of 1940, as many as one-third of these Jews were refugees. The generally accepted estimate for the number of Jews who fled from German-occupied Poland into the Soviet zone is 300,000, or some 15 percent of the entire Jewish population of these areas.[38]

Lublin Judenrat Annual Report, pp. 15, 57; *German Crimes in Poland*, p. I:128; Gedalje Erenberg testimony, YVA, M.1.E/1563.

37 Unsigned report in Oneg Shabbat archive, YVA, M.10.AR.I/924. The comments on Biskupice and Opole are based on WAPL, Rada Żydowska w Biskupicach 1, and prewar population statistics compared to deportee and refugee statistics as shown in Table 3.1 above.

38 Much literature, including many survivor memoirs, discusses the flight to the USSR. See, for example, Henry Orenstein, *I Shall Live; Surviving Against All Odds, 1939–1945* (New York: Beaufort, 1987), pp. 31–40; Harold Werner, *Fighting Back; A Memoir of Jewish Resistance in World War II* (New York: Columbia University Press, 1992), p. 19; Klukowski, *Diary*, pp. 6–47, *passim*; Joseph Schupack, *The Dead Years* (New York: Holocaust Library, 1986), pp. 14–16; Abraham Goldfarb testimony, February 20, 1968, YVA, TR.11/01121/V; Ahuva Shamai-Grossfeld testimony, YVA, O.3/3135; Mendel Korn testimony, YVA, O.3/2941; testimony of unnamed *Chalutzah*, Jerusalem, February 1943,

The terror, fear, and family unity reasons Jews had for attempting to flee into the USSR also encouraged thousands to seek legal means to cross into Soviet-held territory. German-Soviet negotiations regarding the transfer of ethnic Germans from Soviet-occupied Polish territories to German-held territories led to negotiations regarding population and prisoner exchanges. These were to involve sending Ukrainians, Belorussians, and Poles into Soviet-held territory. Agreements were reached allowing for the exchange of tens of thousands in March and April 1940. Based on these agreements, 70,000 Polish citizens whose homes or families were in Soviet-occupied territory were to cross the border on March 15, at three points – Biała-Podlaska, Chełm, and Przemyśl. In April, some 60,000 ethnic Germans from the Soviet side entered the GG at these same crossing points, while nearly 14,000 Poles (fewer than the agreement) went from the GG to Soviet territory.[39]

Such exchanges were meant to continue, and Jews were given reason to believe they could be included, too. Their hopes to emigrate legally to the USSR were not limited to the promises given to Jewish prisoners of war by their captors and SS overseers.[40] Rather, in mid-May 1940, the German civilian authorities in Lublin initiated a systematic registration of Jews wishing to be reunited with their families on the Soviet side. The registration was coordinated district-

YVA, M.2/236; Boruch Silberklang, "Memoir" (unpublished Yiddish manuscript in author's possession), pp. 3–6; Ida Rapoport-Glikstein, in *Dos Buch fun Lublin*, pp. 389–390; *idem*, in *Encyclopedia of the Jewish Diaspora, Lublin*, pp. 685–686. See also the Zamość Judenrat census in WAPL, Rada Żydowska w Zamościu, files 3 and 4 (copy in YVA, JM/3695). Adam Kopciowski believes that the Zamość census was conducted in the spring of 1940, but, based on the census data and the other documentation, October 1939 seems much more likely. See Adam Kopciowski, "Demographic Structure of the Jewish Population of Zamość," in *Everlasting Name: Zamość Ghetto Population List – 1940* (Tel Aviv: The Israeli Organization of Zamość Jewry, vicinity & their descendants, 2001), pp. 4–10.

39 From WAPL, GDL 891: letter, Abteilung Ernährung und Landwirtschaft, Kraków, to the same department in Lublin, March 6, 1940; memos relating to population exchange, among Gedob (the trains' authority in the GG), Krüger, Interior Minister Siebert, and the BuF in Kraków and Lublin, April 5, 6, 8, 9, 10, 12, 13, 20, 27, 1940. On the transfer of ethnic Germans from Soviet-held territory in general, see Schechtman, *European Population Transfers*, pp. 145–173.

40 See, for example, Globocnik to *Führer des SS- und Selbstschutzes*, Lublin, March 19, 1940, WAPL, GDL, 891; Roman Fischer testimony, OHD, 1573.

wide by the Lublin Judenrat, with the cooperation of local Judenräte. By early August, 2,412 questionnaires had been completed in forty-one localities, involving 6,929 people (2,877 from Biała-Podlaska alone). Of these, only eleven had actually lived in the Soviet zone before the war. All the others sought ways to escape German rule via family connections: 2,625 claimed nuclear family ties (spouses, parents, children, siblings), while 4,293 cited more distant relations (in-laws, uncles and aunts, cousins).[41] The fact that 62 percent of the applicants' family connections seemed dubious to the Nazis reflects the extent of the terror the Jews were experiencing. As a result, many Jews indeed sought to escape the Germans in 1940.

Jews in the Lublin District also had reason to believe that some of them might be able to get visas to the United Sates or other countries. On June 25, 1940, the Lublin Judenrat issued an announcement that, in light of the fact that the American embassy in Berlin was issuing visas to certain people with close family connections in the United States, those who had such family connections should register with the Judenrat's Emigration Department.[42] Applications continued to be filed during the following three months, and hope continued to burn in some people's hearts, even though nothing ever came of this.

Among the Germans, both SS and civilian officials expressed strong reservations on two levels regarding any Jewish emigration from Poland. First, they believed that the limits on immigration in the receiving countries meant that Jewish emigration from the GG

41 See the records of the Lublin Judenrat's Emigration Department, in WAPL, RZ 165, 166, 170, especially its report to the Flüchtlingswesen office of the Lublin civilian administration Lublin, August 2, 1940, RZ 170 (also in WAPL, GDL 891); Heinecke to *Kreishauptleute* in all counties, May 17, 1940, WAPL, GDL 891; Holst, of Flüchtlingswesen office, Lublin, to Lublin Judenrat, August 2, 1940, WAPL, ibid.; Lublin Judenrat Annual Report, pp. 56–58, 64–68; Blumental, *Documents*, Protocol 2(63), February 5, 1941, p. 213. German encouragement of Jewish emigration planning in late 1939 and early 1940 was not confined to the Lublin District and is an underresearched aspect of the first part of the war. See, for example, Artur Szyndler, "It's high time that the emigration problem will be solved finally": Leon Schönker and His Plan for Jewish Emigration from the Katowice District," *Yad Vashem Studies*, 39:1 (2011), pp. 71–115, regarding emigration negotiations in Oświęcim and the Katowice area at this time.

42 WAPL, RZ 170.

would be balanced by decreased emigration from Germany itself. This would be contrary to the priority that had to be given first to relieving the Reich of all its Jews. Second, Polish Jews would be a particular boon to the Jewish community in the United States, where they would not only regenerate that community, but would also use it as a "platform" to wage battle with Germany.[43]

For the Germans, the Jews always constituted a distinct issue, requiring a distinct solution. This was true even when the policy toward Jews was closely tied to the general demographic policy. Thus, in the demographic engineering plans entertained by the Germans, Jews were not only a separate question, but they were also subjected to the most extreme treatment. Murder of Jews was both massive and random. The Jews were to be resettled the furthest out, beaten the harshest and the most, deprived of food and property, and exploited extensively and freely for forced labor. In the distinction between Jews and others at every turn, and in the severity of the treatment meted out to them, Nazi policies toward Jews in this period were a prelude to their treatment in 1942–1943. At the same time, there was a fundamental difference between the anti-Jewish policy in 1940–1941 and in 1942–1943: whereas in the latter period there was central, coordinated planning for implementation of a uniform policy (the murder of the Jews), in the former, policy decisions were often local and regional, both theoretically and practically.

For the Jews, the results of Nazi population and anti-Jewish policies in this early period were widespread upheaval, terror, cruelty, and death – but no succor.

43 Memo, Dr. I. A. Eckhardt, Interior Department, Kraków, to Interior Department, Lublin, November 11, 1940, including within it a RSHA edict ("*Erlass*") of October 25, 1940, on the subject, WAPL, GDL 891 (copy in *Faschismus*, p. 59, *Eksterminacja*, pp. 55–56).

Chapter 4

Forced Labor – The Bridge to Death

The Beginnings of Jewish Forced Labor in the Lublin District

Jewish forced labor in the GG can be understood in part as a component of the basic Nazi approach to the occupation – absolute exploitation. In fact, the entire GG was regarded "solely as an object of booty and was to be ruthlessly exploited in the German interest." All raw materials, machines, (Polish) labor forces, etc., that could be of use to the German war economy were to be shipped off to Germany.[1] Göring, in his capacity as Plenipotentiary for the Four Year Plan, issued an order in this vein on October 13, 1939, with regard to raw materials, machines, and the like, leaving behind for the GG only what was necessary to maintain the population's meager existence.[2] With regard to the Jews, however, this exploitation included another important feature. The Jews of Poland constituted a very significant percentage of the skilled labor force. Given their large numbers and their skills and trades, these Jews were an important potential source of production.

1 Rich, *Hitler's War Aims*, p. II:86; Gross, *Polish Society*, *passim*.
2 For an incisive analysis of the Nazis' exploitation approach to the occupation of the GG, see Gross, ibid., pp. 42–91. The Göring directive is Nuremberg Document EC-410. See also Hilberg, *Destruction*, pp. 251–263, for a brief, interesting analysis of the development of Jewish forced labor in Poland.

Although forced labor for Jews in the GG began officially with Hans Frank's forced labor order of October 26, 1939,[3] the actual starting point can be traced to the moment each community was occupied by the German army. Immediately, kidnappings off the streets for a wide variety of jobs were carried out by all arms of the German occupation – military, civilian, police, and SS. In many parts of the Lublin District, this persecution began slightly later than in other areas of the GG, as a result of the delay caused by the Soviet occupation. The motivations for these seizures included the ideologically-based desire to humiliate the Jews, but also the real need to clear and repair the destruction left by the battles of September 1939. The Germans dealt with this need in the most brutal and often murderous fashion, especially with regard to Jewish men. As a result Jewish men quickly grew fearful of walking out into the streets lest they be seized without warning and without any opportunity to inform their families of what had happened to them.[4]

As in other cities and towns in Poland, some Jewish community leaderships in the Lublin District approached the German authorities early in the occupation with a request to organize Jewish forced labor and thereby put a stop to some of the terror on the streets. The Lublin Kehillah Council made this request of the armed forces and the SS in mid-October 1939, and a Labor Office was established in the Kehillah on October 24 to carry out its part of the arrangement – providing 100 laborers daily. The various German authorities, recognizing their opportunity for easy exploitation of very cheap labor, rapidly multiplied the numbers of laborers demanded to 200 daily in November, and 400 in December 1939. The total number of forced-laborers in Lublin per month rose from 7,771 men and 877 women in December 1939, to 22,134 men and 7,854 women in July 1940 – 1,000 people per day.[5]

3 VBIGG, 1939, Nr. 1, pp. 6–7, in *Eksterminacja*, pp. 100–102 and in Friedrich, ed., *Polen*, p. 115; also published in translation in Lucy S. Dawidowicz, ed., *A Holocaust Reader* (New York: Behrman House, 1976), p. 65.

4 For a vivid description of some of these seizures, persecutions, and rubble-clearing operations, see Klukowski, *Diary from the Years of Occupation*, October 10–23, 1939, pp. 39–45. See also Musial, *Zivilverwaltung*, pp. 115–116.

5 See Lublin Judenrat Annual Report, p. 47; Judenrat Labor Department report

In order to facilitate the conscription of Jewish forced labor, the Lublin Kehillah was first ordered, on October 20, 1939, to take a census of the Jewish community in Lublin, and to record especially all Jews over fifteen years of age and categorize them by profession. This was according to what Heydrich had ordered in his *Schnellbrief* to the EG, even though it was not always his SS functionaries who ordered the censuses. The census reported, on October 25, before the German civilian government was officially established, that there were 37,054 Jews; 12,244 men and 15,476 women were older than fifteen years of age. Of these, 4,739 were skilled craftsmen (tailors, shoemakers, carpenters, among others); they would soon be a prime target of conscription for forced labor in camps within Lublin.[6] On December 4, all Jewish males in Lublin were again registered by profession so that they could be sent to work where the Germans needed them.[7]

The same obligations fell on other Jewish communities in the Lublin District and in the GG in general. In Zamość, for example, a very well-organized and thorough census resulted in an exact, detailed, alphabetical list of all Jewish residents in the city in October.[8]

Pursuant to Frank's October 26, 1939 order, which put Krüger in charge of Jewish forced labor, Krüger issued his own order on December 8, obligating the district chiefs in the GG to register all

for October 24, 1939—August 31, 1940, WAPL, RZ 6 (copy in USHMMA, RG-15.101M). See also Józef Kasparek, "The Situation and Extermination of Jewish Population in Lublin during the Nazi Occupation (1939–1942)," paper presented before the International Scientific Session on Nazi Genocide in Poland and in Europe 1939–1945, Warsaw, April 14–17, 1983, p. 3. The Lublin Kehillah's Labor Office was directed at this time by Hirsch Goldfinger.

6 See Lublin Judenrat Annual Report, pp. 39–41; Nuremberg Document PS-3363.

7 Lublin Judenrat Annual Report, pp. 40–41.

8 See Zamość Judenrat census in WAPL, Rada Żydowska w Zamościu, files 3 and 4. For a perspective on the Jews' apprehension regarding German census-taking and its possible implications, see the comments of Pnina Weiss, wife of Warsaw Judenrat member Avraham Weiss, on the Jewish census ordered by the Gestapo there in October 1939, in Esther Farbstein, "A Close-up View of a Judenrat: The Memoirs of Pnina Weiss — Wife of a Member of the First Judenrat in Warsaw," *Yad Vashem Studies*, 33 (2005), pp. 85–86.

Jewish males aged fourteen to fifty, including their occupations.[9] Three days later Krüger issued a second order, effective January 1, 1940, forbidding all Jews in the GG to change their current towns of residence and obligating all Jews in the GG not living in their own homes (i.e., refugees) to register their residences with the authorities.[10] Of course, the German civilian authorities passed this obligation on to the Judenräte. Hence a second count of Jewish residents in Lublin was conducted on January 1 (39,157 Jews), followed by yet another on February 24 (40,535).[11] There were to be many counts taken during the next two and a half years of the communities' existence.

Many survivor testimonies recall the kidnappings off the streets and the beginnings of more organized, though no less brutal, forced labor in December 1939. The conscripted laborers would meet at a designated place early in the morning and march from there to the work site for that day. In Lublin, the Lipowa 7 location was the main meeting place as early as October 1939. The site of the old Lublin aircraft factory (Plage Łaśkiewicz) was also converted into such a meeting place.[12] Both these sites soon became labor camps in their

9 *Eksterminacja*, p. 202.

10 Krüger order, December 11, 1939, VBIGG, 1939, pp. 231–232. The document has also been published in *Eksterminacja*, pp. 202–203; Friedrich, ed., *Polen*, pp. 175–176; and in English in *Documents on the Holocaust*, pp. 179–180. See also Werner Präg and Wolfgang Jacobmeyer, eds., *Das Diensttagebuch das deutschen Generalgouverneurs in Polen, 1939–1945* (Stuttgart: Deutsche Verlags-Anstalt, 1975) (hereafter, Frank, *Diensttagebuch)*, p. 77.

11 See the Lublin Judenrat's memo of late February 1940, "Angaben über die jüdischen Bevölkerung in Lublin," in WAPL, GDL 891 (copies in YVA, O.51/10 and JM/10,458). See also Lublin Judenrat Annual Report, pp. 40–41. A census on July 1 recorded 41,856 Jews in Lublin, and another on September 1 recorded 42,130. For other census counts, see, for example, "Statistik der Juden im Kreise Zamosc," n.d., ca. May 1940, in WAPL, GDL 274 (copy in YVA, O.6/455), and "Zahl der jüdischen Bevölkerung im Distrikt Lublin," n.d., WAPL, RZ 149 (copies in YVA, O.6/403 and USHMMA, RG-15.101M).

12 See, for example, Erlichman-Bank, *In Impure Hands*, pp. 17, 23; Freiberg, *Darkness Covered the Earth*, p. 52; Ida Rapoport-Glikstein, "The Lublin and Majdan-Tatarski Ghettos," in *Encyclopedia of the Jewish Diaspora, Lublin*, pp. 679–685; *idem*, in *Dos Buch*, p. 389; Kasparek, "The Situation and Extermination," p. 3; Ewa Szek testimony, YVA, M.49.E/42; Hanka Spector-Burstein testimony, MA, A.195. See also Lublin Judenrat Annual Report, pp. 41–42.

own right, where craftsmen worked during the day and returned home at night.

The obligation to provide a quota of Jewish laborers officially fell on the Judenräte. In Lublin, the Judenrat decided it could meet German demands by having each able-bodied adult male work one day a week at forced labor. This was increased temporarily to two days, on March 4, 1940, for a two-week period, and then permanently from September.[13] Not every adult Jew was taken for forced labor — at least not during the first months of the occupation. For example, only those physically fit for labor were ostensibly to be sent work notices by the Judenrat (the Kehillah initially) and taken to work. Thus, TOZ (Towarzystwo Ochrony Zdrowia Ludności Żydowskiej; Society for Safeguarding the Health of the Jewish Population), the Polish Jewish public health organization, which had been established in 1921, carried out physical examinations of 28,805 people in Lublin and found only 18,476 (64 percent) fit for hard physical labor. However, since the seizures on the streets never stopped completely, the unfit were never really fully exempt as long as the SS was involved in the labor conscription. In addition, Lublin Jews could buy their way out of forced labor for fees that ranged from 15 złoty to more than 50 złoty in May 1940. Most of this money was officially intended to help pay the salaries and maintenance of those who did go to work. In some communities, however, Judenrat members were accused of enriching themselves through this practice. In general, survivors recall this arrangement with disdain.[14]

13 Krüger, "Dienstbefehl an die Judenräte für die Erfassung und Bestellung der Juden zur Zwangsarbeit," January 20, 1940, WAPL, GDL 271 (copy in YVA, JM/10,458); Lublin Judenrat announcement regarding weekly forced labor, January 26, 1940, WAPL, RZ 10 (copies in YVA, O.6/23ד*; USHMMA, RG-15.101M, reel 3). On the increase in hours, see Judenrat announcements, March 13 and 26, 1940, WAPL, RZ 10 (copy in USHMMA, ibid.); Blumental, *Documents*, pp. 119–192, *passim*.

14 Lublin Judenrat Annual Report, pp. 41–42. See also Erlichman-Bank, *In Impure Hands*, p. 23; Freiberg, *Darkness Covered the Earth*, p. 52; Rapoport-Glikstein, "The Lublin and Majdan-Tatarski Ghettos," pp. 679–685; *idem*, in *Dos Buch*, p. 389; Tamari, *Zamość*, p. 107; Kasparek, "Situation and Extermination," p. 3; Ewa Szek testimony, YVA, M.49.E/42.

The laborers were meant to be paid a minimal daily wage, which in Lublin ranged from 0.50 złoty (in Bełżec) to 5 złoty (for POWs) in 1940. The wages were almost always paid by the Judenrat, although the army sometimes paid a share of the wage for those working in army projects. Approximately one-third of the Lublin Judenrat's expenses through August 31, 1940, or some 550,000 złoty, and approximately 40 percent of the sum paid by people to avoid labor, or 225,000 złoty, went toward these wages.[15] This reflects hundreds of thousands of manhours of forced labor – and perhaps well over a million hours – by Lublin Jews alone through August 1940.

The Jews were engaged in various kinds of forced labor during the first months of the occupation, with an initial emphasis on repairing war damage. Such work included road and bridge repair, clearing rubble, renovating partially damaged buildings, and similar jobs. The *Krakauer Zeitung*, a Nazi daily newspaper that began to appear early in the occupation, reported that 2300 kilometers of road had been repaired in the GG by February 19, 1940, while more than 100 bridges over the Wisła River had been repaired and reopened. In Annopol, the bridge repair that this newspaper reported as a great achievement of the German occupation regime was recalled by survivors as an exhausting and violent day of feverish work without a break.[16]

Gradually, beginning in December 1939, forced labor for particular construction and infrastructure projects began to be introduced, together with providing services for the Germans. Several hundred Jews were sent from Lublin to Hrubieszów in

15 Lublin Judenrat Annual Report, pp. 5–6, 43, 49–50; Report of Lublin Judenrat's Extra-Urban Labor Camp Department, WAPL, RZ 46 (copy in YVA, O.6/323); "Sprawozdanie z działalności Gremium Bełżeckiego oraz Komitetu Pomocy dla pracujących w Obozach Pracy" (Report on the Activities of the Association for Bełżec of the Committee for Aid to Laborers in Labor Camps), WAPL, RZ 46 (hereafter, Gremium Report). See also Mordche Szwarcbard testimony on Warsaw Jews in Konskowola, YVA, M.10.AR.1/402 (also JM/2712, ff. 20–21).

16 *Krakauer Zeitung*, February 19, 1940. Clippings can also be found in YVA. The repair statistics are taken from the August 15, 1940 issue, JM/4210, f. 5284249. On Annopol, see in YVA: Eli Fishman testimony, M.1.E/714; Hillel Borenstein, M.1.E/595.

January, and fifty to Chełm on March 29, for particular local German projects. In each case the Judenrat sent money, food, and supplies for the forced-laborers, as well as emissaries to Chełm to get a first-hand impression of the workers' conditions and to intervene on their behalf if need be. Their conclusion that the Jews labored under harsh conditions contrasted sharply, of course, with the Nazis' conclusions throughout the occupation.[17]

These Judenrat emissaries set a precedent for the Lublin Judenrat to send emissaries to Lublin Jews at other work sites as well.[18] The major German projects included road-laying, swamp drainage, redirecting river flows, peat mining, agricultural work, and building permanent labor camps. The services included handicrafts and personal services as servants in German homes and offices. By late summer 1940, the massive projects, based in labor camps, were the primary employment for Jewish forced-laborers in the Lublin District.[19]

Who rounded up the Jews for forced labor? Which authority was responsible for organizing the exploitation of Jewish manpower, and whose projects took precedence in the conscription of Jewish labor? From the creation of the GG to the deportations to the death camps, this was the subject of protracted debate and bureaucratic

17 On Hrubieszów and Chełm, see the following 1940 Judenrat Protocols in Blumental, ed., *Documents*: 4 (January 20, p. 115), 8 (February 6, p. 123), 18 (April 13, p. 143), 21 (April 27, p. 148), 22 (May 4, p. 149), 24 (May 13, p. 152). See also the Lublin Judenrat Annual Report, pp. 43, 49. On the German attitude to the work conditions for Jews, see, for example, Ramm's memorandum on his mid-November 1940 visit to three Chełm area forced-labor sites, together with Holzheimer, the civilian labor director for the water works there. They believed the Jews were well fed, well clad, and looked generally healthy. Ramm, "Vermerk," November 19, 1940, YVA, JM/2700.

18 "Denkschrift," Judenrat to SSPF, July 29, 1940, WAPL, RZ 26.

19 On the various types of labor, see Lublin Judenrat Annual Report, pp. 41–55; Erlichman-Bank, *In Impure Hands*, pp. 17, 23; Freiberg, *Darkness Covered the Earth*, p. 52; Ida Rapoport-Glikstein, "The Lublin and Majdan-Tatarski Ghettos," in *Encyclopedia of the Jewish Diaspora, Lublin*, pp. 679–685; *idem*, in *Dos Buch*, p. 389; Ewa Szek testimony, YVA, M.49.E/42; Hanka Spector-Burstein testimony, MA, A.195; and *Krakauer Zeitung*, cf. n.16, *passim*. On the transition to larger projects and permanent labor camps, see Lublin Judenrat Annual Report, ibid. On personal services for German officials, see, for example, Josef Birger-Ezrahi, YVA, M.49.E/2791, O.3/447, O.3/6774.

jockeying for influence and power among three main authorities: the German civilian regime, the SS, and the Wehrmacht. The last tended to bow out of the competition, as long as it could realize its interests through one of the other parties. Thus, the Wehrmacht was willing to let the civilian authorities in Lublin take charge of the much-needed road-construction project (which was later to serve the invasion of the Soviet Union), while the SS organized the construction of defensive fortifications along the new border with the USSR, especially along the stretch of land between the San and Bug rivers in the south of the Lublin District. When the deportation of the Jews to death camps seemed about to impinge on war production in the GG in 1942, the Wehrmacht again entered the fray, but this was a short-lived protest.[20]

The real jurisdictional struggle, therefore, was between the civilians and the SS, who both saw themselves as the supreme authority in the GG. Frank and the civilians based their claim upon the *Führerprinzip*, which, they claimed, should have given Frank absolute rule in the GG, and upon the legal argument that the structure of a state demands that police authorities be subordinate to government authorities. The SS based its claim on its being the ideological vanguard of Nazi Germany, subordinate to no one but Himmler and Hitler. For both, raw power and avarice were significant motivations in the struggle. Jewish forced labor, as a potential source of industrial manpower, output, and income, was a particular sticking point.[21]

Therefore, although Frank's forced-labor decree placed the HSSPF, his theoretical subordinate, in charge of implementation, implying both hierarchical governmental organization and cooperation between the two authorities, there was no harmony

20 On the Wehrmacht's disinterest in running the day-to-day affairs of occupied Poland, see, for example, Browning, *Origins*, pp. 16–24; Pohl, *Judenpolitik*, p. 21.

21 For a brief, yet generally astute review and analysis of the competition among various German authorities in the GG over Jewish forced labor, see Felicja Karay, "The Confrontation Among the German Authorities Regarding the Forced Labor Camps for Jews in the Generalgouvernement" (Hebrew), *Yalkut Moreshet*, 52 (April 1992), pp. 107–122.

between the civilian bureaucracy and the SS. The centrality of Jewish policy to the Nazi regime made it a source of power and influence – and therefore of competition. Struggles over control of Jewish policy, or any aspect of it, were common both in Berlin and in other territories controlled by the Nazi regime, including the GG. Jewish forced labor became the major arena of SS-civilian competition over control of Jewish policy in the GG and the much coveted power and influence that could accompany such control.

From Frank's perspective, "delegating" certain organizational authority for Jewish forced labor to the HSSPF did not ipso facto relinquish all claims to Jewish forced labor or other aspects of Jewish policy to his domain. Therefore, both authorities appointed "*Judenreferenten*" (Jewish experts), both centrally and locally, to try to build a Jewish policy empire.

SS-Obersturmführer Dr. Karl Hofbauer, Globocnik's Nazi comrade from prewar Vienna, was officially installed as the first *Judenreferent* in Lublin by January 1940 – although Globocnik formally informed the District Chief (Schmidt) of this only on February 13. According to Globocnik, the SSPF's *Judenreferent* position was being created, "in order to centralize treatment of the entire Jewish question...with the Governor's consent."[22] Other branches of the district-level SS had Jewish experts as well, but just as Globocnik was the supreme SS authority in the district, his *Judenreferent* had the potential to become the main Jewish expert there, too.

Hofbauer immediately set about asserting his authority in Jewish affairs with a January 18 memo sent to all relevant Lublin District civilian officials, informing them that county and rural officials must report all plans for utilizing Jewish forced labor to him. The Lublin governor's Interior Department followed this with a February 8 request of all county officials to send reports of such plans within three weeks. However, compliance on the county and local levels was

22 See Globocnik to District Governor, February 13, 1940, in WAPL, GDL, 891. The exact date of Hofbauer's appointment is unclear. Blumental suggests it was December 1939, but this seems to be only an educated guess. See Blumental, *Documents*, p. 159, n.1. The January date given here is based on the first known document relating to Hofbauer, on January 18, 1940 (see note 140 below).

only partial. Perhaps one of the reasons for only partial acceptance of Hofbauer's authority was that, on March 4, the new District Chief Ernst Zörner assumed office.[23] His rich and well-established Nazi record and high connections, combined with his tough and independent personality, gave him a strong base from which to exercise his own authority in competition with Globocnik.

The apparent SS-civilian collaboration with regard to Jewish policy, in February 1940, was merely a facade hiding bitter competition. Frank issued an order on March 2 for the elevation of the "Judenwesen" desk within the BuF office of the Interior Department to a *Referat*. This referat had four functions: registering Jews and determining who is Jewish; Jewish Councils of Elders (Judenräte); regulations for Jews; and general affairs regarding Jews. All county and town heads were to send reports about the establishment of Jewish councils and other Jewish matters to their governors for forwarding to the central government in Kraków.[24]

On the face of it, the HSSPF, and through him Hofbauer in Lublin, was responsible only for Jewish forced labor. Thus, Hofbauer's January 18 memorandum was limited to this topic, while Frank's March 2 instructions covered other aspects of Jewish policy. However, just as the concept of forced labor was flexible enough for Globocnik to use it as leverage to try to gain control over all Jewish policy in his memo to the governor, so, too, was Frank's vague reference to "general affairs regarding Jews" an opening to expand his authority in this realm.

Frank's *Judenreferent* was Dr. Heinrich Gottong, a Nazi racial researcher; Zörner's, for the following two years, was Richard Türk (of BuF), a career civil servant and a Nazi party member. Türk was the Lublin civilian government's power in Jewish affairs even when the job was formally held briefly in the spring of 1940 by Türk's colleague, Dr. Fritz Heinecke. He was also the bureaucratic superior to the Jewish experts who were appointed at lower levels

23 Hofbauer's January 18, 1940 memo and the Interior Department's follow-up request of February 8 in WAPL, GDL 891. See also Hofbauer's reminder of March 2 and Interior's April 6 response, ibid. Zörner assumed his position on March 4, based on his February 21 appointment by Frank.

24 Frank order through BuF in Kraków, March 2, 1940, in WAPL, GDL 891.

of the civilian bureaucracy, both as city and county experts and as departmental experts in the district administrations. Thus, for example, Götzlaff was the *Judenreferent* for the city of Lublin.

Like Hofbauer in Lublin, Gottong set out to assert his authority as soon as he was appointed in April 1940. He sent a memo to all Jewish experts in the civilian government in the GG laying out ground rules for operation.[25] He did not include forced labor in his job description to the other experts, but this was to arise as a point of friction between the SS and the civilian authorities very soon.

The competition between the SS and the German civilian authorities in the GG over control of Jewish policy and Jewish forced labor continued throughout the next two years. In late March 1940, Globocnik ordered that all requests for Jewish laborers must be channeled through one of the organs under his control: those requesting large numbers of forced-laborers should address requests to the SSPF; those requesting small numbers for work within the county should address their requests to the county Sipo office (or Gendarmerie outpost in some cases). Requests for laborers for jobs within the city of Lublin or Lublin-Land county should be made to *Selbstschutzführer* Dolp.[26] On April 25, 1940, Frank stipulated that all orders to the Jews, save for forced labor, must be channeled through the *Kreishauptmann* of each county. He followed this with a similar order, on June 7, regarding the *Stadthauptmann*'s authority over the Jews in the cities.[27]

The SS was not content with this division of authority over the Jews. At a May 30 meeting of top GG officials, Bruno Streckenbach, the BdS, made a long speech, attempting to cajole the civilians into yielding full authority for Jewish affairs to the Sipo and SD in order to make Jewish policy and forced labor more efficient for the benefit

25 Memo by Dr. Gottong to all Jewish experts in BuF departments in GG and to all district governors, April 6, 1940, in WAPL, GDL 891 (copies in YVA, JM/10,458, *Eksterminacja*, pp. 48–50, *Faschismus*, pp. 55–56, Friedrich, ed., *Polen*, pp. 266–267). On Heinecke's temporary appointment, see Türk to Heinecke, May 5, 1940, in WAPL, GDL 891. On Götzlaff, see Ida Glickstein's testimonies in *Encyclopedia of the Jewish Diaspora*, pp. 681–682, and in *Dos Buch*, pp. 387–388. See also Götzlaff to HSSPF, May 20, 1940, in WAPL, GDL 891.

26 Globocnik order, n.d., late March or early April 1940, in WAPL, GDL 891.

27 For a brief discussion of these orders, see Trunk, *Judenrat*, p. 5.

of all German authorities. Zörner tried to deflect this ploy by arguing that Sipo did not have the manpower to handle the Judenräte, while Otto Wächter, district governor for Kraków, emphasized that the two authorities needed each other and should work together. Frank rejected Streckenbach's suggestions on the grounds that the police were the armed force of the civilian government and did not have a purpose independent of this.[28]

Frank and Krüger met on June 6 and 7 to iron out their differences regarding the Jews. They reached an accord whereby Krüger agreed that Jews were needed for labor in other aspects of the economy, outside the forced-labor projects controlled by the HSSPF.[29] However, Globocnik ignored all such accords that implied any yielding of authority on the part of Krüger or presumption to supremacy by Frank.

In an attempt to take firm control over Jewish forced labor, the civilian authorities established a "Judeneinsatzstelle" (Jewish labor office) within the district level "Arbeitsamt" (Labor Department) in July 1940. This office for Jewish labor was meant to act as a counterbalance to the SS, in part by taking over many of the functions of the labor offices of the Judenräte. The presence of a Judenrat official in the Judeneinsatzstelle would facilitate this, and the SS would then be forced to channel its labor needs as requests to the civilian authorities. However, Globocnik saw the Arbeitsamt's role as purely bureaucratic (registering Jews for labor), and in subordination to himself. The Judenrat's labor office was caught between the two, but learned relatively early where the real authority lay. As will be seen below, the Lublin Judenrat turned most often to SS officers with requests relating to work conditions or other forced-labor issues.[30]

28 A summary of the meeting is in Frank, *Diensttagebuch*, pp. 214–218; and Friedrich, *Polen*, pp. 301–304. See also Trunk, ibid.; Hilberg, *Destruction*, pp. 220–221; Browning, *Origins*, p. 143.

29 Trunk, ibid., p. 267; Browning, ibid., pp. 143–144; Tatiana Berenstein, "O Podolozu Gospodarczym Sporów Między Władzami Administracyjnymi A Policyjnymi w Generalne Guberni (1939–44)," *Biuletyn Żydowski Instytut Historycznego*, no. 53 (January.-March 1965), pp. 51–56.

30 See Lublin Judenrat Annual Report, pp. 47–55; Lublin Judenrat minutes,

The Lipowa 7 and Bełżec Camps

On February 8, 1940, Heinrich Himmler wrote a stern note to *SS-Sturmbannführer* Hermann Dolp, warning him that failure to abide by the SS court-martial decision against him (a two-year ban on alcohol intake) would result in his eviction from the SS and all attendant punishment implied therein. A humbled Dolp responded the following day, recognizing his probation status.[31] Six days later Dolp arrived at his new posting, Lublin, where he was to distinguish himself during the next twenty-seven months as arguably one of the most brutal, bloodthirsty SS men on Globocnik's staff.

Dolp was an aging *Altekämpfer* and early member of the SS, having joined the Nazi party and SS in 1928. He rose quickly, reaching the rank of *Standartenführer* by 1931, but then his drinking problem contributed to the halt in his career. His first assignment in occupied Poland was to establish and command the Selbstschutz in German-annexed Kalisz. On November 1, 1939, he was involved in a drunken altercation in which he tried to rape a young Polish woman who was a friend of a German official. Dolp pulled a gun on the official, and this resulted in numerous complaints against him by fellow Germans who witnessed the scene. He was immediately removed from his post, and a SS investigation followed. On February 4, 1940, he was court-martialed, demoted by two ranks, and reassigned to the staff of HSSPF Krüger. His immediate superior was instructed to write semi-annual reports about him until Himmler decided otherwise. Dolp, a short, squat man, was fifty-one years old, married, and the father of four when he reported to Krüger, who immediately assigned him to Globocnik's staff.[32]

Dolp was first assigned to the Selbstschutz in Lublin, and his

Protocol 52, November 2, 1940, in Blumental, *Documents*, pp. 193–194; Pohl, *Judenpolitik*, pp. 82–83.

31 Himmler to Dolp, February 8, 1940, and Dolp to Himmler, February 9, 1940, YVA, O.68/28, Hermann Dolp file from the Berlin Document Center (BDC).

32 All biographical data on Dolp taken from Dolp file, ibid. His SS number was 1293. See also YVA, M.9/576, the Jewish Agency Political Department's Records of War Criminals, file A/74, June 5, 1945. Dolp was approximately 1.58 meters tall (5'2"). The Jewish testimonies recall him as short and vicious.

first task was to lead the above-mentioned (Chapter 3) forced march of Jewish POWs from Lublin northward toward Biała-Podlaska. At that time he already displayed extreme cruelty and brutality.[33] He was then to assume command of a forced-labor camp on the grounds of several horse stables at 5–7 Lipowa Street. In late spring he was given responsibility for supervising the digging of defensive trenches along the border with the Soviet Union, especially along the stretch of border in the south of the GG between the Bug and San rivers. He was sent to Bełżec to set up a series of forced-labor camps for this purpose, but his authority also extended to many other forced-labor camps in the district, such as Sawin and Ruda-Opalin, near Włodawa.[34]

Dolp was very successful at his tasks. Regarding Bełżec, Globocnik praised Dolp's good work under difficult conditions and with "poor human material" – referring to the Jews and Gypsies.[35] The viciously evil way that he ran the camps left an indelible mark on the memories of the Jewish inmates, especially in Bełżec.[36] Perhaps he was trying exceedingly hard to please his superiors and thereby redeem himself. His promotion to *Obersturmbannführer*, in April 1944, indicates that he succeeded in this endeavor.[37]

Lipowa 7

The camp at 5–7 Lipowa Street existed longer than any other labor camp in the Lublin District, from the autumn of 1939 to November 3, 1943. It served several purposes, both successively

33 See the anonymous testimony of one of these POWs in the Ringelblum archive, YVA, M.10.AR.1/1073 (also in JM/3489). For a vivid survivor description of Dolp, see Moshe Zylberberg Caspi testimony, YVA, M.1.E/1402.

34 See *SS-und Selbstschutzführer* [Dolp] to Piaski Judenrat, June 8, 1940, demanding 500 Jews for these two camps by June 11. WAPL, RZ 26.

35 Globocnik to Krüger, "Halbjährige Berichterstattung" (on Dolp), August 13, 1940, YVA, O.68/28, Dolp file.

36 See, for example, on the Lipowa 7 camp: YVA, Moshe Zylberberg Caspi, M.1.E/1402; Avraham Lewin's report on Lipowa 7, based on discussions with an escaped POW, March 2, 1942, M.10.AR.1/377 (copy in JM/3489).

37 Promotion notification to Dolp, April 9, 1944, YVA, O.68/28, Dolp file.

and simultaneously: as a gathering place for Jewish forced-laborers in Lublin from as early as October 1939, and for the next two and a half years;[38] as a first repository for Jews deported from the West; as a prisoner-of-war camp for Polish Jewish POWs whose homes were in Soviet-occupied Poland; as a labor camp; as a way station for forced-laborers from other districts returning home and for POWs from the GG returning to their homes; and as a labor camp of the Deutsche Ausrüstungswerke (German Equipment Works; DAW).

The DAW was established in May 1939 by the SS as a central control over its production plants that exploited concentration-camp labor. The Lipowa 7 camp was the first DAW branch established in occupied Poland, and it was to be followed by additional camps in Lublin, Puławy, Lwow (Janowska), and other places. In 1943, more than 15,000 forced-laborers were working for DAW. The Lipowa 7 camp was the first instance in which POWs were brought under DAW control. Nachman Blumental correctly notes that Lublin was the first city in the GG that actually implemented organized Jewish forced labor, and it was done through this camp.[39]

38 It served as the meeting point for forced-laborers going off to forced labor each morning, beginning on December 4, 1939, according to German postwar trial records, YVA, TR.10/770, p. 97. However, Jewish testimony indicates that it served this purpose as early as October 1939 (see note 12). Even after the labor camps were established, the SS continued to kidnap Jews and bring them to this site. See, for example, two memos by Hecht, each headed "Vermerk" and dated October 21, 1940, in YVA, JM/2700. The camp has been under-examined by historians. Perhaps the most extensive study of it is by Wojciech Lenarczyk, "Obóz Pracy przymusowej dla Żydów przyul. Lipowej w Lublinie (1939–1943)," in idem and Dariusz Libionka, eds., *Erntefest: Zapomniany epizod* Zagłady (Lublin: Muzeum Państwowe na Majdanku, 2009), pp. 37–71. The camp's creation and early functioning receive brief mention in Goldhagen, *Willing Executioners*, pp. 295–296, and its later functioning is discussed by him on pp. 296–300. However, Goldhagen relied solely on German trial material and did not make use of the extensive Judenrat documentation or Jewish survivor accounts.

39 Blumental, *Documents*, p. 115, n. 4. On DAW, see Nuremberg Document NO-1216, Dr. May's report to Oswald Pohl, chief of the SS-WVHA, "Bericht über die Dienstreise vom 1.-8.6.42 nach Butschowitz, Auschwitz, Lemberg, Lublin und Posen"; Michael Thad Allen, *The Business of Genocide: The SS, Slave Labor, and the Concentration Camps* (Chapel Hill and London: University of North Carolina Press, 2002), pp. 95, 140; Jan Erik Schulte, *Zwangsarbeit und Vernichtung: Das Wirtschaftsimperium der SS; Oswald Pohl und das*

At first the Lipowa 7 camp was an assembly point and a labor site, but there were no barracks to house the laborers. When Jews were being kidnapped off the streets by the Wehrmacht, SS, and Selbstschutz soldiers in October 1939 and afterward, they would be taken either directly to a labor site or to one of the two gathering points – the square at Lipowa 7, and the site of the Plage Łaśkiewicz airplane factory – and from there to whatever labor site was intended. During November or early December 1939, Jewish men were brought to Lipowa 7 in order to convert some of the stables there into workshops for various craftsmen, such as shoemakers, tailors, furriers, carpenters, etc.[40]

The site then became a labor camp in its own right, while continuing to serve as a converging point for forced-laborers going to other labor sites. It was a flat, rectangular camp, 100m wide x 300m long, bordered on the east by Lipowa Street, on the north by Sklodkowskiej-Curie Street (later renamed by the Germans "Reinhard Heydrich St."), and on the south by the mixed Christian cemetery.[41] Those who worked at Lipowa 7 would arrive in the morning, work in the various workshops, and then return home in the evening. Their food rations and meager wages were provided by the Judenrat until mid-February 1941. Work conditions were difficult, and the SS, Selbstschutz, and local Ukrainian guards were very violent. Therefore, many Jews would try to evade forced labor at Lipowa. This phenomenon became so widespread that the Judenrat issued repeated warnings, threatening dire consequences by Dolp if the evasions persisted. Random kidnappings off the streets also continued, despite Dolp's express agreement to take Jews only from Lipowa (and later other gathering points) and many Judenrat interventions to stop the kidnappings.[42]

SS-Wirtschafts-Verwaltungshauptamt 1933–1945 (Paderborn: Ferdinand Schöningh Verlag, 2001), pp. 126, 129–131.

40 Jacob Frank relates conscription for mending German uniforms; Lewis and Frank, *Himmler's Jewish Tailor*, pp. 32–36.

41 For the camp's physical description, see YVA, TR.10/868, p. 36. The cemetery still exists and has sections for Roman Catholics, Russian Orthodox, and Lutherans, as well as a mixed communal section that includes atheists, too.

42 Globocnik forced labor order, May 8, 1940, WAPL, GDL 891 (copy in YVA, O.53/85); Alten to *SS-und Selbstschutzführer*, June 21, 1940; "Bericht," Judenrat

Polish Jewish prisoners of war began to arrive between December 1939 and February 1940, and the terrible ordeals of these first POWs in Lublin reflected both the intra-German struggles and the limited accords regarding authority over Jewish forced labor. Their experiences also demonstrated for all the Jews – locals, refugees, and POWs – the extraordinary capacity of the SS and Selbstschutz for the most extreme and murderous brutality at the slightest "provocation." The Judenrat learned from the forced march and the murder of hundreds of POWs in February 1940 that it must actively take responsibility for *all* Jews in Lublin in order to prevent, or at least limit, further loss of life. Therefore, the Judenrat supplied the camp kitchen, and its own appointee, Ester Feldman, ran it. It also paid the forced-laborers a meager wage, as they received nothing from the Germans – neither from the officials, nor from the firms for which they performed some of the jobs. However, the Judenrat's severe shortage of funds made effectuating this responsibility increasingly difficult during the following year.[43] Thus, from February or March 1940, the camp was both the permanent home for Jewish POWs transferred by the Wehrmacht to SS control and a labor camp for some 1,000 Lublin Jews, who generally returned home in the evening. Both groups ultimately fell under the control of the SSPF.[44]

The civilian Arbeitsamt was responsible for organizing the forced labor, and the Selbstschutz was its official tool of enforcement. The Selbstschutz was also under the authority of the SSPF and was commanded by SS officers. Thus, the Selbstschutz was involved in both the death march of the POWs and the supervision of the

to Dolp, July 6, 1940; "Denkschrift," Judenrat to SSPF, July 29, 1940, WAPL, RZ 26; Lublin Judenrat Announcement, May 6, 1940, WAPL, RZ 10 (copies in YVA, O.6/23d*; USHMMA, RG-15.101M, reel 3); Hofbauer memo on Jewish forced labor, May 8, 1940, Friedrich, ed., *Polen*, pp. 288–290.

43 WAPL, RZ 43 (copies in YVA, O.6/392; USHMMA, RG-15.101M) contains much correspondence and Judenrat lists and reports regarding Judenrat expenses for the forced-laborers. See also Blumental, *Documents*, p. 86.

44 Lublin Judenrat Annual Report, pp. 41–42; "Denkschrift," Lublin Judenrat to *Stadthauptmann*, September 13, 1940, WAPL, RZ 43 (copy in USHMMA, RG-15.101M); Jache, "Vermerk," on discussion with Globocnik, July 17, 1940, WAPL, GDL 746 (copy in YVA, O.6/11a*).

civilians' forced labor. Since Globocnik controlled the Selbstschutz, he also used it as a tool to control the labor.

At first the Lublin Selbstschutz commander was officially the camp commandant, but he would run the camp through a deputy. When Dolp arrived in Lublin, *Selbstschutzführer* von Alvensleben put him in charge of the camp, commanding a staff of forty. His forced-labor jurisdiction also included the city and county of Lublin. When Dolp was assigned by Globocnik to Bełżec, *SS-Hauptscharführer* Franz Bartetzko temporarily assumed the day-to-day running of the camp. Globocnik then relieved Dolp of his post at Lipowa in order to free him for the larger job at Bełżec and, in the latter part of July 1940, appointed the first non-Selbstschutz officer as camp commandant, *SS-Untersturmführer* Horst Riedel.[45]

Riedel was a merchant by trade, and his appointment as Lipowa camp commandant in 1940, together with Globocnik's success in later having this DAW camp set up as an independent company, reflect Globocnik's plans to build an economic empire in Lublin through the Jewish forced-labor camps. Riedel is recalled by the survivors as having been aristocratic in his bearing yet brutal. His right-hand man, until July 1941, was Wolfgang Mohwinkel, an engineer. Riedel and Mohwinkel, as well as others on the camp staff, were part of the SSPF staff, and not part of the Selbstschutz. This meant that Globocnik had become more independent of the civilian authorities and strengthened his control over the camp in the summer of 1940. It became part of the Berlin-based Deutsche Ausrüstungswerke in mid-1941.

Throughout the personnel changes in the Lipowa 7 camp, Dolp retained authority over the various camp commanders and visited the site frequently. He also ran various labor projects. Mohwinkel's efficient cruelty won him a promotion by Himmler to *SS-Oberscharführer* on July 20, 1941, during Himmler's visit to

45 See YVA, TR.10/770, pp. 97–103 and TR.10/868, pp. 37–38; Globocnik order regarding forced labor, n.d. (probably late March or early April 1940), WAPL, GDL 891; Hecht, "Vermerk," July 23, 1940, WAPL, GDL 748 (copy in YVA, O.53/79). Von Alvensleben's predecessor as *Selbstschutzführer*, *SS-Standartenführer* Walter Gunst, ran the camp until early 1940 through Schega and Möhlmann.

Lublin. The same day Mohwinkel was sent to Lwow to set up a DAW branch camp there – the Janowska Road branch. He returned in late November 1941, and in December replaced Riedel, who had fallen out with Globocnik and several of his senior advisors (apparently because of Riedel's arrogance). Mohwinkel's energetic efforts to make Lipowa a model camp in Globocnik's terms "profitable and ruthless" won him a promotion to *Untersturmführer* in January 1942, and a decoration the following summer. He transformed the Lipowa 7 camp into the most profitable DAW enterprise outside Germany. Mohwinkel served effectively as camp commandant until after the *Erntefest* and lived there with his wife and newborn daughter (b. 1942) in an apartment adjoining the camp.[46]

The Jewish prisoners recall most of the Lipowa 7 camp staff as being viciously cruel. Among the guards there in 1940 were members of the infamous Dirlewanger SS unit, who later that year served in the Bełżec camps. Mohwinkel himself was called "Mordwinkel" ("death corner") by the POWs.[47]

The Lublin Judenrat set up a committee to aid POWs in mid-February 1940. The SS were willing to let a POW native to the GG go home if two conditions were met: a sponsor for him could be found among the Lublin Jews; and he left behind his uniform, and with it his POW status. The Judenrat was able to get 2,000 people to sign a declaration of willingness to sponsor a POW. They also collected civilian clothing for them; the aid committee collected 1,694 suits of clothing. According to the Lublin Judenrat Annual Report, 3,224 Jewish POWs were brought to Lublin in the period February-May 1940: 1,367 in February; 1,810 in March; nineteen in April; and twenty-eight in May. Of the first group, 864 were released in Lublin, while 503 were transferred to a camp in Biała-Podlaska. All the others were freed in Lublin, according to the Judenrat, but this does

46 YVA, TR.10/770, pp. 33–36, 105–06; TR.10/868, p. 109; Birger-Ezrahi testimony, YVA, M.49.E/2791. See also Globocnik's summary report on "Operation Reinhard," January 5, 1944, Nuremberg Documents, NO-057, and NO-064 (also PS-4024).

47 YVA, TR.10/770, p. 46. Josef Birger-Ezrahi confirms this nickname in all his statements: YVA, O.3/447, O.3/6774, M.49.E/2791; Blumental, *Documents*, pp. 83–84.

not jibe with other evidence – unless this was not the same group of POWs who were marched northward and shot on the way.[48]

The Judenrat appointed a camp supervisory committee headed by Dawid Edelsztajn to oversee work in the camp and to intervene on the laborers' behalf when necessary and possible. However, the POWs did not want the Lublin Judenrat to be responsible for them. If they would submit to that authority, it would mean sacrificing their special, legally-protected POW status and becoming "just Jews." Edelsztajn's committee developed a working arrangement with the Lipowa Lagerrat (camp council), headed by Professor Hans Walter David, but relations with the POWs were more difficult.[49]

Dolp granted the POWs a modicum of recognition, although he insisted that only the Judenrat was responsible for their food, not the German authorities. One reflection of this limited recognition of their POW status is the fact that sick POWs were hospitalized in the Polish St. Joseph's hospital, and not in the Jewish hospital, even though the Judenrat was forced to pay the hospital bills. The Judenrat also paid for all other health care for all the laborers in the camp, military and civilian. When the POWs were ordered by Dolp to wear armbands like all the Jews in the GG, they refused on the grounds of their POW status. They seem to have gotten away with that.[50]

48 See Lublin Judenrat Annual Report, pp. 21–25; report of the aid committee for POWs, WAPL, RZ 133 (copy in USHMMA, RG-15.101M); Globocnik to *Führer des SS-und des Selbstschutzes*, Lublin, March 19, 1940, WAPL, GDL 891; Blumental, *Documents*, pp. 78–81. See also the excerpt from the Judenrat's interim report covering the period through February 15, cited by Blumental, pp. 80–81.

49 WAPL, RZ 43, September 4, 1940, names the three-man Judenrat committee: David Edelsztajn, Nachman Lerner, and Maurycy Schlaf. This file (copies in YVA, O.6/392; USHMMA, RG-15.101M) contains much correspondence among the three groups: the Judenrat, Edelsztajn's committee, and Professor David's Lagerrat. It also contains lists of laborers in various jobs during the latter part of 1940, and Judenrat expenditures on their behalf. See also YVA, Gruber, O.16/610*, M.1.E/925; Birger-Ezrahi, O.3/447, O.3/6774; Fischer, O.3/2124; Gruber testimony in MA, A.578; Blumental, *Documents*, pp. 86–87.

50 See YVA, Gruber, O.16/610*, M.1.E/925; Birger-Ezrahi, O.3/447, O.3/6774; Fischer O.3/2124; Ringelblum, *Diary and Notes*, February 19, 1941, p. 237. WAPL, RZ 43 (USHMMA, RG-15.101M) contains extensive correspondence among St. Joseph's Hospital, the Judenrat, the Lagerrat, and the *Stadthauptmann*'s office,

Further complicating the Judenrat's ability to affect the running of the Lipowa 7 camp was the fact that the Germans made it responsible for certain problems in the camp without giving it the authority or means to change the conditions or management methods. If any damage was caused to raw materials or finished products by Jewish laborers in Lipowa 7, the Judenrat was ordered to pay. The Judenrat was thus faced with a dilemma. It could pay and thereby accept an impossible future financial obligation to pay for everything, or it could insist that any damages were a matter for the German authorities and the alleged culprits to address. The latter option clearly left Jewish laborers completely unprotected. Both tactics were attempted at different times.[51]

The Judenrat also had difficulty maintaining control over civilian forced labor in Lipowa 7 because of friction between Judenrat appointees to oversee camp affairs and some Jewish work foremen there. An example of this is the case of the brothers Zvi Hersz and Moshe (Mojżesz) Zylberberg. The former was a Judenrat employee who, despite many run-ins with the Judenrat, managed not only to hold his job but also to expand his position. In August 1940, he was one of the Judenrat employees accused of enriching himself by means of arranging bribes to German officials for Jews seeking to buy their way out of being sent to Bełżec. Both brothers were later work foremen at Lipowa 7, where Zvi Hersz physically attacked Judenrat member Josef Wajselfisz, apparently during the latter's working visit to the camp. The Judenrat issued a stiff warning to Zylberberg that a repeat of such behavior would result in a report to the German authorities and subsequent punishment. However, this warning proved meaningless, since the German authority that the Judenrat would have turned to was the *Stadthauptmann*, and Zylberberg had already associated himself with the SS at Lipowa 7, particularly Dolp.

regarding payment of bills for hospitalizations of Lipowa inmates, September 15, 1940 - February 16, 1942. The file also contains correspondence with the Jewish hospital regarding medical supplies for the camp. See also Blumental, *Documents*, pp. 86–87.

51 See, for example, an exchange of letters on such a case of damaged items between *SS-Scharführer* Eugen Lehnert in Lipowa 7 and Bekker, May 31 and June 6, 1941, WAPL, RZ 43 (copy in USHMMA, RG-15.101M).

Thus, Zvi Hersz Zylberberg became a Jewish policeman in March 1941, despite some Judenrat members' objections to his immorality, and he retained that position at least through December.

When an official of the Judenrat's Labor Office, Zyskind Dawidson, tried to discipline Moshe Zylberberg for dereliction in his duty in July 1941, the two Zylberberg brothers threatened to put "an end to you. This sore must burst. We are going to our own chief, Dolp, to teach you."[52] Zvi Hersz Zylberberg had made some very powerful friends during his tenure in the Judenrat Labor Office, Bełżec, Lipowa 7, and the Jewish police, and he may also have been an informer.

Conditions in the Lipowa 7 barracks were very overcrowded, and there were virtually no medical facilities available for months. By mid-summer 1940, the SS recognized that all the laborers there were infested with lice, and so it was determined that Jewish laborers should be checked for lice by Jewish doctors. Overwhelmed by the vastly increased social-welfare needs in Lublin, the reduction in available funds, and despairing of gaining any sympathy from Dolp or other SS officers, the Judenrat tried, in September 1940, to convince the German civilian authorities to assume responsibility for feeding and paying at least the civilian forced-laborers in Lipowa 7. This intervention met with some success when, five months later, on February 17, 1941, *Stadthauptmann* Sauermann ordered the Judenrat to cease all financial undertakings for the camp, including wages and food supplies. In light of its own dire financial straits, the Judenrat did not object to this order, and apparently did not inquire officially as to who was now to provide for these laborers.[53]

The main period of POW forced labor began with the arrival of

52 See Zyskind Dawidson to Judenrat Presidium, July 23, 1941, WAPL, RZ 22 (copy in USHMMA, RG-15.101M); Judenrat Protocols 37, 55, 57, 68, for August 10 and November 23 and 1940, and March 16, 1941, in Blumental, *Documents*, pp. 174, 197, 198, 201, 222–223.

53 Memo to Judenrat (signature illegible), August 24, 1940, WAPL, RZ 22 (copy in USHMMA, RG-15.101M); "Denkschrift," Judenrat to *Stadthauptmann*, September 13, 1940, WAPL, RZ 43 (copy in USHMMA, RG-15.101M); Blumental, *Documents*, Protocol 4(65), February 17, 1941, p. 217; "Protokoll über die Judeneinsatz besprechung vom 6. August 1940...," WAPL, GDL 748 (copy in YVA, JM/2700); Lublin Judenrat Annual Report, pp. 40–41.

some 2,800 Jewish POWs from German POW camps in late January 1941, bringing the total number of POWs to approximately 3,000, in addition to the handful of civilians then living in the camp and approximately 200 Polish "political" prisoners.[54] The new POWs were received by the SS with severe beatings. They were no longer under Wehrmacht jurisdiction, and, from the Nazis' point of view, they were not POWs. The POWs lived in five large stables, and a sixth served as their kitchen. They worked mainly outside the camp, while the camp workshops were manned primarily by Lublin Jews.[55]

The POWs were divided into thirteen or fourteen work companies, each headed by a Jewish foreman. The outside jobs included working at the airfield (150–200 people, under Dolp); Heeres Unterkunft Verwaltung (Army Lodgings Administration, fifty people); the army supply camp (about 200 people); loading ammunition onto rail wagons (fifteen people); hospitals (about 200 people); constructing the first barracks at Majdanek (about 200 people); assorted jobs at the railroad station (about 100 people); work for SS people (fifty people) and for the German police and administration. Approximately 250 POWs also worked in the camp workshops, which included auto repair, tailoring, hat-making, shoemaking, carpentry, glassworks, and what became a very profitable roofing factory (Dachpappenfabrik). The POWs referred to the airfield work site, where they took down buildings and put up new ones, as "Dolp-Platz," because Dolp was in charge and many were beaten or killed there at his command. Here and at

54 YVA, JM/10,670–10,672; WAPL, GDL 901 (copy in YVA, JM/10,454); Josef Birger-Ezrahi statements, YVA, M.49.E/2791, O.3/447, O.3/6774. According to a January 6, 1941 report on Lipowa 7, there were 518 POWs and fifteen civilians living and working in the camp at that time, as well as 192 Polish laborers. See "Stan ludzi skoszanowych w Obozie," Lublin, January 6, 1941, YVA, JM/217/3. See also Tatiana Berenstein, "Obozy Pracy przymusowej dla Żydów w dystrykcie Lubelskim," *Biuletyn Żydowski Instytut Historycznego*, 24 (1957), p. 10.

55 YVA, TR.10/868, pp. 41–42; Mieczysław/Samuel Gruber testimonies, in YVA, O.16/610* and M.1.E/925, and his memoir, *I Chose Life*, p. 24. See also Josef Cynowiec testimony, O.3/3009; Josef Birger-Ezrahi testimonies, O.3/447, O.3/6774, M.49.E/2791; Roman Fischer, O.3/2124.

the Majdanek construction site he would set his bloodhounds on the Jewish forced-laborers. He is recalled as a "crazy sadist."

The POWs working for Dolp were part of the construction teams that began to prepare ground in Rury Jezuicka, near the Lipowa camp, for a new camp for Soviet POWs. Zörner revoked the building license on August 29, 1941, as part of his jurisdictional battle with Globocnik. The SSPF then moved the planned camp to the Majdanek site, and the Jewish POWs at Lipowa built the first barracks, as well as the barbed wire around the camp, alongside Soviet POWs. The latter group of POWs were treated even worse than the Jews from Lipowa 7, and they died "like flies" from typhus. The SS then gave the Jews the dead soldiers' clothing, which caused a typhus epidemic in the Lipowa 7 camp. Estimates of how many POWs contracted the disease range as high as 70 percent (or about 2,000). Former POW Samuel Gruber estimates that 400–500 Jewish POWs became ill with the disease and at least 100 died.[56]

There were frequent escape attempts from the camp by POWs. Some succeeded, while others ended in the capture and death of the escapee and often of additional prisoners as a form of collective punishment.[57] Roman Fischer, one of the original 200 POWs in the camp from early 1940, became the head of the POWs following one such escape by several POWs on February 2, 1941, including the former POW head Brandel. As a result of the escape, the inmates were forced to stand outside in the snow on the night of February 4/5, barefoot and half-naked for several hours for roll call, while Globocnik oversaw as other SS men rained beatings, insults and threats on them.

56 Avraham Lewin's report on the POW camp, March 2, 1942, YVA, M.10.AR.1/377 (also JM/3489); Gruber, YVA, M.1.E/925, O.16/610*; Birger-Ezrahi, O.3/447, O.3/6774, M.49.E/2791; Josef Cynowiec, O.3/3009; YVA, M.9/576; TR.10/868, pp. 36, 42–44; Sol Holzman, O.33/1305; Blumental, *Documents*, pp. 87–88; Gruber, *I Chose Life*, pp. 32–34. The quotations are from Gruber, M.1.E/925. See also Józef Marszałek, *Majdanek: The Concentration Camp in Lublin* (Warsaw: Interpress, 1986), pp. 20–26.

57 For example, the Lipowa 7 *Lagerälteste*, David, reported to the Judenrat on October 25, 1940, that the prisoner Menachem Juda Zyskind was shot earlier that day while attempting to escape. David, Lagerrat, to Judenrat Presidium, WAPL, RZ 43 copy in USHMMA, RG-15.101M). An escaped POW reported to Avraham Lewin in the Warsaw ghetto in 1942 that every escape resulted in others being shot. See Avraham Lewin's report, YVA, M.10.AR.1/377.

Ten POWs died of pneumonia they contracted that night. Roman Fischer is remembered clearly, though sometimes with mixed reviews, by most of the surviving POWs who have recorded memoirs.[58]

The escapes were sometimes also connected to friction among the POWs and between the POWs and the Jews of the ghetto. According to some testimony, at times Fischer assisted the SS in hunting down escapees. This was apparently out of fear of the dire consequences that would befall the other POWs, based on their bitter experience with collective punishment.[59] The POWs also participated at times in rounding up Lublin Jews for forced labor, which naturally led to friction between the Jews of the ghetto and the POWs. They also were used by the SS on a number of occasions to dig mass graves for Poles who were to be shot in groups, and afterward they buried the victims.[60]

Some Jewish civilian prisoners lived in the camp with their families, such as the camp *Lagerälteste*, German music professor, Hans Walter David. He had been an officer in the German army in World War I and fled to the USSR when the Nazis came to power. The Soviets delivered him to the Germans early in the war, and he was imprisoned in the Lublin castle until May 1940. He was then transferred to Lipowa 7, where he was assisted by another German Jew, Simon. Both were informers, especially Simon.[61]

58 YVA, TR.10/868, pp. 42–44; Fischer, O.3/2124; Cynowiec, O.3/3009; Birger-Ezrahi, M.49.E/2791, O.3/447 and O.3/6774; Gruber, O.16/610*, M.1.E/925; Investigations in the case of Georg Michalsen, Ludwigsburg, 208 AR-Z 74/60, copy in YVA, TR.10/1291, testimonies by Jehoszua Zwiebak, July 1964, pp. 7150–7152, Pawel Oszerowski, 1965, pp. 7051–7052, Szlomo Frydman, January 10, 1966, pp. 7167–7168, Mieczysław Kliszczowski, 1966, pp. 7168–7169; Blumental, *Documents*, pp. 85–86. Birger-Ezrahi asserts that Fischer kowtowed to the Germans and helped them persecute the Jews until the camp underground prevailed upon him to change his ways in December 1941.

59 Birger-Ezrahi, YVA, M.49.E/2791, O.3/447, O.3/6774. See also Gruber, *I Chose Life*, pp. 27–28. Gruber generally has very kind words for Fischer in all his testimonies.

60 See Ramm, "Vermerk," December 23, 1941, in Nachman Blumental and Józef Kermisz, eds., *Dokumenty i Materiały do Dziejów Okupacji Niemieckiej w Polsce*, Volume 1: *Obozy* (Lodz and Warsaw: Centralna Żydowska Komisja Historyczna, 1946), pp. 136–137; Birger-Ezrahi testimony, YVA, M.49.E/2791.

61 YVA, Gruber, O.16/610*, M.1.E/925, O.33/1304; Birger-Ezrahi, M.49.E/2791, O.3/447, O.3/6774; Holzman, O.33/1305; Gruber, *I Chose Life*, p. 27; Lewis and

The POWs were able to have contact with the outside world – including receiving mail, packages, and money – until the invasion of the USSR and the entry of the United States into the war cut off this lifeline. For example, a check in the sum of $13 was sent from Chicago to the POW Benjamin Rogaczewski. Clearly, either Rogaczewski had been in contact with someone in Chicago, or else the interested party in Chicago had learned of Rogaczewski's whereabouts from other sources, such as the Red Cross. Moreover, the German civilian authorities, through the Deutsche Bank, were willing to give him the money, albeit in local currency.[62] However, contacts between the POWs and individual Jews in the Lublin ghetto were forbidden, and meeting women was considered a serious crime. This policy was enforced sporadically by Mohwinkel, and, in fact, there were actually frequent contacts, not all of them clandestine. Mohwinkel had one POW hanged in early 1942 for meeting with a woman outside the camp, while only a few months earlier he had allowed a camp inmate to marry a woman from the ghetto.[63]

Among the Jewish POWs at Lipowa 7 was an army chaplain, Rabbi Klein, who organized clandestine Yom Kippur services in 1941, in a barrack specially cleared for the purpose. They were discovered by Globocnik and some of his subordinates, who entered the barrack as the prayers were going on. However, the Jews were not beaten.[64]

Frank, *Himmler's Jewish Tailor*, p. 38. Frank says that David had been Worthoff's piano teacher, so Worthoff made sure that he had a good job in Lublin. Birger-Ezrahi adds that before the war both Simon and David were German spies in Russia. There were prisoner exchanges between Germany and the Soviet Union during the first months of the war, in 1939–1940. See, for example, Globocnik to *Führer des SS- und Selbstschutzes*, Lublin, March 19, 1943, WAPL, GDL, 891. See also Blumental, *Documents*, p. 86, n.36. He cites Aleksander Weisberg-Cybolski, "The Conspiracy of Silence" (Hebrew), pp. 513–514.

62 YVA, O.6/11b*, Deutsche Bank (Berlin) to Lublin Judenrat, June 5, 1941, Deutsche Bank to Judenrat, July 11, 1941, Judenrat to Lagerrat (Lipowa), July 16, 1941. On receiving packages from the USSR, see Avraham Lewin's report on the POW camp, March 2, 1942, YVA, M.10.AR.1/377 (JM/3489).

63 YVA, TR.10/868, pp. 130–132; Birger-Ezrahi, O.3/447, O.3/6774, M.49.E/2791; Cynowiec, O.3/3009. Birger-Ezrahi says there were quite a few such marriages, nearly all performed secretly.

64 Birger-Ezrahi, ibid. All his statements relate the prayers, but, in his 1992

There were also some cultural activities in the camp, such as an orchestra headed by the Lwow pianist, Segal. They played for the SS on Sundays and held a concert with songs on Pesach (1941). A prisoners' mutual-aid organization was run by Gruber. Part of the organization's supplies came from packages some of the POWs received from Lublin Jews.[65]

Although there was no serious underground movement in the Lublin ghetto, there was a very active one among the POWs in the Lipowa 7 camp. Roman Fischer himself became active in the underground. Two of its main functions were collecting information and acquiring arms via the POWs working in the Wehrmacht's armory and by bribing some local Ukrainian guards to turn a blind eye. The massing of German troops and military materiel in the Lublin District in the spring of 1941 made it clear to the POWs in Lipowa 7 that an invasion of the USSR was imminent, and this was connected to one of the underground's first acts. When Simon expressed enthusiastic joy at the advance of the German army into the Soviet Union in the summer, the underground had him beaten up severely. As in other places, the underground's first open act was against perceived collaborators from within. In 1942, this underground organized mass escapes from the camp, and those who survived the escape became the nucleus of Jewish armed resistance groups in the forests of the Lublin District.[66]

The camp's conditions worsened considerably in mid-1942, as did conditions for Jews in general, when it became a place of "liquidation through work." However, in contrast to the civilian Jews, most of whom were murdered in 1942, the POWs in the Lipowa camp were not subject to outright mass murder from the death

statement, Birger says that the Nazis reacted violently when they discovered the prayers.

65 YVA, Gruber, M.1.E/925, O.16/610*, O.33/1304; Fischer, O.3/2124; Cynowiec, O.3/3009.

66 All the surviving POWs from this camp discuss the underground. See, for example, Gruber, ibid., and *idem*, *I Chose Life*; Birger-Ezrahi, YVA, O.3/447, O.3/6774, M.49.E/2791; Cynowiec, O.3/3009; Fischer, O.3/2124; Holzman, O.33/1305. See also Krakowski, *War of the Doomed*, pp. 260–271. Birger-Ezrahi and Fischer relate Simon's joy and his being beaten up. Birger-Ezrahi recalls Simon calling out "*unsere Gruppen gehen forwerts*!"

march of February 1940 until the *Erntefest* action in November 1943. In this sense, being part of the Lipowa camp during 1942 represented a temporary stay of execution, akin to what in other ghettos was known as "survival through work." As a result, despite the very harsh conditions under which the Jewish prisoners of war and the civilian forced-laborers in the Lipowa Street camp functioned and labored, living in the camp was considered by the Jews of Lublin to be relatively safe and even somewhat of a privilege.

The Establishment of Bełżec

The first documented mention of the border fortification project was at a meeting held in Berlin on January 30, 1940, on mass deportations into the GG. Heydrich, chairing the session, suggested that several hundred thousand Jews could be housed in the forced-labor camps to be established in connection with the "construction of the wall" in the East. The context of the reference indicates that the high-ranking SS participants at this meeting were already familiar with this project.[67]

On February 2, the border fortifications were one of the items discussed during a three-hour meeting between Chief of the General Staff of the Army, General Franz Halder, and Himmler. As Halder noted in his diary three days later, Himmler's grandiose plan was to utilize 2.5 million Jews (more than all the Polish Jews then under German rule) as forced-laborers for the massive project, which the army was willing to consider.[68] However, by the time the subject came up again at an April meeting of Lublin District civilian and SS officials designed to coordinate Jewish forced labor, the project had been greatly reduced to more manageable proportions from a local

67 NO-5322. A copy can be found in YVA, O.53/68, pp. 649–658, and JM/3695. Excerpts of the document have also been published in various sources. See, for example, *Eksterminacja*, pp. 41–43; *Faschismus*, pp. 50–52; *Documents on the Holocaust*, pp. 183–185.

68 Halder referred to the project again on February 24 and July 27. Franz Halder, *Generaloberst Halder, Kriegstagebuch*, Hans-Adolf Jacobsen, ed. (Stuttgart: W. Kohlhammer Verlag, 1962), I:184, 206, II:38. See also NOKW-3140.

SS point of view. At this time Globocnik sought to set aside 5,000 of the estimated 45,000 Jewish forced-labor pool in the district for the *Grenzgraben* (border trenches).[69]

The Bełżec complex of labor camps was centered around the Bełżec camp itself, some 35 kilometers south of Zamość. The first group of 100 forced-laborers from Lublin was sent there on May 29, 1940, followed shortly thereafter by an additional ninety from Piaski. Marek Alten, deputy chairman of the Lublin Judenrat and head of the district's JSS affairs, had been informed by May 26, probably by Türk, of the German plans to establish a labor camp at Bełżec. A day or two later he and other Judenrat members discussed forced labor and Bełżec with Hofbauer, who was responsible for supplying the manpower. On June 1, the Judenrat created a department for labor camps outside the city, chaired by Judenrat head Bekker himself, in order to deal with the needs of the Jews being sent to Bełżec and other camps.

At the same time Globocnik ordered the creation of a Gremium dla obozu Bełżeckiego (Association for Bełżec Camp Affairs). The functions of this body included administration, health and sanitation, all care for the laborers, preparing additional camps, and financing the digging of six kilometers of border trenches. Whereas this Gremium was created by the SSPF, its functionaries were appointed by the Lublin Judenrat. For the Germans this was the easiest method to get the Jews to organize internal camp affairs themselves. For the Judenrat this was in keeping with its policy that it was responsible for the welfare of all Lublin Jews, wherever they may be. Appointing the Bełżec camp functionaries, who were in effect the Lagerrat (camp council), allowed the Judenrat to extend its jurisdiction and thereby its recognized authority to the Lublin Jews at Bełżec, while also facilitating contact with them and sending them aid and supplies. The Judenrat's two controversial appointments as heads of the camp, Dr. Wolf Fajgeles and Lejb Zylberajch, were sent there on June 13, together with Fajga Nożyk, to serve as camp cook.

69 "Protokoll über die am 22.4.40 beim SS- und Polizeiführer stattgefundene Besprechung betreffend den Einsatz jüdischer Zwangsarbeiter," WAPL GDL 891 (copies in YVA, JM/10,458). Excerpt in *Eksterminacja*, pp. 207–208. Hofbauer prepared and signed the minutes. The copy in WAPL was Türk's.

The terrible camp conditions that prevailed are reflected, in part, in the fact that no camp kitchen whatsoever existed until the arrival of these three.[70] We can only wonder what the original 190 inmates ate during their first sixteen days in the camp.

An additional 150 Lublin Jews were sent to Bełżec on July 8, to be followed the next day by Judenrat emissary Abram Gorzyczynski, who was sent to inspect the camp. Thirty more forced-laborers were then sent to the camp from Piaski, and they were followed on July 15 by three additional officials to help run internal Jewish affairs there.[71] By the time Jews from other districts reached Bełżec the following month, the Lublin Judenrat had already established itself as the Jewish authority for the border fortification project. This ultimately redounded to the benefit of the Lublin Jews vis-à-vis Jews from other places in terms of supplies available to them from home. It worked to the disadvantage of the other Jewish forced-laborers, whose Jewish Councils generally would not or could not get intricately involved in their welfare.

Meanwhile, 354 Lublin Jews were sent to Tyszowce, northeast of Bełżec, on June 13, to work on regulating river flow. The Judenrat subsequently sent a physician, two nurses, and three clerks to Tyszowce to care for them. They all returned to Lublin on September 5, to be replaced by Jews from Warsaw.[72] This was part of a large

70 Gremium Report (see n.15); "Sprawozdanie z działalności Centralnej Rady Obozowej w Belzcu za czas od 13 czerwca do 5 grudnia 1941 [1940] roku" (Report on the Activities of the Central Camp Council at Bełżec from 13 June to 5 December 1941 [1940]), WAPL, RZ 47 (copy in YVA, O.6/322; hereafter, Bełżec Report), pp. 25–26.

See also Lublin Judenrat Annual Report, p. 52; and the travel permit to Bełżec for the three, dated June 13, signed by Bekker, in WAPL, RZ 46. Fajgeles was to be the physician, Zylberajch the director, Nożyk the cook; Blumental, *Documents*, Protocols 27 and 28, May 27 and 28, 1940, pp. 158–159, and pp. 170–171, n.3.

71 Travel permits signed by Bekker for Abram Gorzyczynski, July 9, and for Chil Honigman, Josef Wajsfeld, and Israel Abram Blumenkranc, July 15, in WAPL, RZ 46. See also Gremium Report; Lublin Judenrat Annual Report, p. 52.

72 Lublin Judenrat Annual Report, p. 52; Blumental, *Documents*, Protocols 33 (June 29, 1940), 35 (July 13), and 36 (August 3), pp. 166, 169, 170. See also Lublin Judenrat announcement, June 12, 1940, regarding reporting for transport to labor at Tyszowce, WAPL, RZ 46 (copy in YVA, O.6/323); and YVA, M.10. AR.1/373 for a description of conditions in the camp.

water regulation project undertaken by the civilian government's Wasserwirtschaftsinspektion, which was ultimately to encompass more than 10,000 Jews in many labor camps throughout the district.[73] In addition, massive road-repair and construction operations were undertaken, contracted to private German firms and supervised by the SS. These roads would later serve the German troops converging in the GG in preparation for "Operation Barbarossa." All the above labor camps, too, fell under Dolp's rule.

The air of cooperation between the German civilian and SS forces in the Lublin District that emanates from the minutes of an April 22, 1940 meeting of German officials dealing with Jewish forced labor proved to be as illusory as the cooperation on the GG level. Globocnik dominated the meeting's discussions, and in the process he attempted to gain recognition for Dr. Hofbauer as the sole *Judenreferent* for the district. Although no opposition from the civilian authorities is recorded in the minutes, subsequent actions show that Zörner and his men had no intention of allowing Globocnik to take full control of Jewish affairs without a struggle.[74]

Ostensibly, the roles of the two authorities were clear. Jewish forced labor was a joint venture in which the civilian labor departments in each district kept records of the Jews, based on data requisitioned from the Judenräte, and categorized them by skill. They could also requisition forced-laborers for civilian projects. The SS and police were responsible for security, rounding up Jews for labor when more were needed, and for the forced-labor camps.[75] At a June 17 meeting in Lublin attended by Zörner, Türk, Globocnik, his adjutant Reinhold von Mohrenschildt, and Hofbauer, Zörner and Globocnik disagreed over who was to organize Jewish forced labor, each citing discussions with Krüger as his premise for supremacy

73 Blumental, *Documents*, Protocol 30, June 8, 1940, p. 162; Pohl, *Judenpolitik*, p. 85; Musial, *Deutsche Zivilverwaltung*, p. 167.

74 "Protokoll" of meeting on Jewish forced labor, April 22, 1940, WAPL, GDL 891 (see note 69 above).

75 See the report on the GG's Department Heads' meeting, Kraków, June 7, 1940, in *Faschismus*, p. 210, and *Eksterminacja*, pp. 210–211. See also Krüger's letter to Dr. Frauendorfer, head of Abteilung Arbeit in Kraków, June 13, 1940, in WAPL, GDL 748 (copy in YVA, O.53/79).

in Jewish affairs.[76] Globocnik promised to clarify the matter with Krüger, but this was never done to Zörner's satisfaction.[77]

Globocnik caught the civilian officials unprepared when he submitted his demand for Jewish manpower for construction of the border fortifications on July 15. He wanted 3,000 men sent to Bełżec in two days' time and another 5,000 the following week. By early August he would need 30,000 men. The intended forced-laborers included 10,000 from Warsaw.[78] In addition, he wanted 1,000 Jewish men to be placed in the Lipowa 7 forced-labor camp.[79] Globocnik did not wait long to act. Without informing any civilian authority, Hofbauer organized raids on the night of July 22/23, in which the SS rounded up 300 Jews in the old airfield in Lublin for forced labor at Lipowa Street. When Hecht and Wagner of the Lublin Labor Department went to the airfield to complain, Hofbauer and Horst Riedel, the new commandant of the Lipowa camp, asserted that they were operating based on arrangements made between Globocnik and Jache, then head of the Lublin Labor Department. Moreover, they insisted that the SS would conduct such round-ups whenever they felt it necessary. Civilian officials meeting with Hofbauer on July 23 at night had to concede defeat regarding the border digging, although they thought that the SS had agreed that all other SS operations would await the upcoming meeting between Frank and Krüger.[80]

Again Globocnik moved quickly to assert his supremacy and independence in Jewish affairs when he dispatched one of

76 "Niederschrift" of meeting among Zörner, Globocnik, von Mohrenschildt, Türk, and Hofbauer, June 17, 1940, WAPL, GDL 891.

77 See minutes of meeting of Lublin District officials, June 25, 1940, YVA, O.6/11a*.

78 Globocnik to Jache, Head of the Lublin Labor Department, July 15, 1940, YVA, O.53/79; Hofbauer to Lublin Labor Department, July 15, 1940, in Friedrich, *Polen*, pp. 319–320. See also Jache, "Vermerk über fernmündlichen Anruf des Herrn Gouverneurs," July 22, 1940, and *idem*, "Verfügung vom 19, Juli 1940," WAPL, GDL 746 (copy in YVA, O.6/11a*).

79 "Vermerk" by Jache on discussion with Globocnik, July 17, 1940, WAPL, GDL 746.

80 "Vermerk" by Hecht, July 23, 1940; "Vermerk" on discussion among Dr. Damrau, Sauermann, Jache, Hecht, Nemitz, Dr. Hofbauer, July 23, 1940; Minutes of July 23, 1940 meeting – Dr. Damrau, Sauermann, Jache, Hecht, Nemitz, Dr. Hofbauer participating, WAPL, GDL 748.

his subordinates to Kraków to arrange transferring 1,000 Jewish craftsmen from there to the border fortifications project.[81] Another meeting, on August 6, in Kraków, attended by eighteen GG civilian and SS officials, attempted to hammer out an agreement on guidelines and numbers of Jews to be taken by Globocnik's and Krüger's men in the coming days. Hofbauer demanded 30,000 Jews for the border fortifications project; the Lublin water works' department sought an additional 3,000 Jews for its projects; and the road works' department sought an immediate allocation of the same number for work in rock quarries, along with an additional 9,000 soon afterward. All the civilian district labor chiefs agreed to supply Jews for the border fortifications. The decisions taken at the meeting reduced the demands to 2,700 allocated to the water works and all others to be sent to the border fortifications. However, in recognition of the fact that there was no surplus of 36,000 able-bodied Jewish men available for forced labor, the decision to gather Jewish laborers from the entire GG for a forced-labor project in one area represented a radical change in the status of Jewish forced labor. This was the first instance of coordinated labor conscription on a GG-wide scale.[82]

It was agreed that the SS would conduct raids to round up the numbers of Jews needed, informing the district labor departments in advance so that they could properly record all the Jews taken. Jews working in Labor Department projects and showing the appropriate *Ausweis* (identification card) would not be taken. In Lublin, Hofbauer was in charge of the round-ups.[83] Cooperation

81 Globocnik to *Stadthauptmann* Schmidt, Kraków, July 30, 1940, in *Faschismus*, p. 213. According to a handwritten note at the bottom of the page, *SS-Hauptscharführer* Tiefental met with Major Ragger in Kraków on August 2. Major Johannes Ragger, of the BuF office in the GG Interior Department, was to play a significant liaison role in helping to organize the deportations to death in 1942.

82 "Protokoll über die Judeneinsatz besprechung vom 6. August 1940, 10 Uhr," WAPL, GDL 748 (copies in YVA, JM/2700; *Eksterminacja*, pp. 216–217; *Faschismus*, pp. 214–215).

83 "Protokoll über die Judeneinsatzbesprechung," ibid.; "Vermerk" by Hecht, August 6, 1940, on meeting that day in Kraków, and "Vermerk" by Ramm, August 9, 1940, on meeting the day before with Globocnik, Nemec, and

had been worked out for the "Grenzwall" project, but it was to be honored by Globocnik largely in the breach.

On the nights of August 12/13 and 13/14, SS troops swooped down on Jewish homes all across the GG and rounded up more than 10,000 Jews in a lightning operation. The Jews were caught completely by surprise, and many found themselves being shipped off to Bełżec in pajamas and barefoot.[84] In Lublin, six Judenrat members and ninety-six employees were among those seized and taken to Bełżec when they went to Lipowa 7 to register those Jews reporting daily for forced labor.[85] However, not only were the Jews surprised; the German civilian authorities were no less caught off guard. Labor Department and county officials received notification either just before the raids began, or not at all. Calls came streaming in to various civilian government offices in Lublin from the various counties. There were complaints about unexplained large concentrations of SS troops appearing in town, or of unannounced, indiscriminate raids for Jewish laborers, in complete disregard of Lublin Labor Department identification papers that should have exempted the bearers from seizure. The raids were sometimes so indiscriminate that the German labor chief in Biała-Podlaska complained that only forty of the 1,600 conscripted Jews did *not* have these exemptions.[86]

Hofbauer on the "Grossrazzien" that Globocnik planned to begin the following week, WAPL, GDL 748 (copy in YVA, O.53/79).

84 According to Hofbauer, Jews from twenty-one locations in the Lublin District were to be taken: Biała-Podlaska, Biłgóraj, Chełm, Hrubieszów, Izbica, Kraśnik, Krasnystaw, Lubartów, Lublin, Łuków, Międzyrzec-Podlaski, Parczew, Puławy, Radzyn, Tarnogród, Tomaszów-Lubelski, Werbkowice, Włodawa, Zaklików, Zamość, and Zwierzyniec. See Hofbauer to Lublin Labor Department, August 13, 1940, WAPL, GDL 748 (copy in YVA, O.53/79).

85 Lublin Judenrat letter to "Herrn Lagerkommandant Obersturmbannführer Dolp," August 16, 1940, WAPL, RZ 46; Judenrat minutes, 38, August 18, 1940, in Blumental, *Documents*, p. 176.

86 See "Vermerk," Ramm, August 12, 1940, on Radzyn; "Vermerk," Hecht, August 13, 1940, on phone call from Chelm Labor Office; "Vermerk," Hecht, August 13, 1940, on conversation between Lerch and Ramm regarding raids, Chełm, Zamość, Warsaw, Kielce, ordering trains; "Vermerk," Hecht, on phone conversation with Lerch, August 13, 1940; Hofbauer to Labor Department, August 13, 1940, on twenty-one round-up sites in Lublin District; "Vermerk," Ramm, August 15, on meeting with Drs. Damrau and Kipke, re: SS raids;

The civilian authorities in Lublin were furious at the behavior of Globocnik's people. Heinz Ramm, head of the Lublin Labor Department, brought his complaints before Dr. Damrau, Zörner's chief of staff, who in turn relayed them in a long, confidential letter to Frank on August 16. Damrau insisted that Globocnik receive clear instructions regarding his authority with regard to Jewish forced labor.[87] Copies of the letter were sent to Dr. Frauendorfer, head of the GG Labor Department, and his deputy, Dr. Geschlisser.[88] On that same day Ramm and Hecht met with Globocnik and his new *Judenreferent*, Ernst Lerch, to try to iron out their differences and halt the round-ups for at least a few days. This would give the Labor Department officials time to register all the conscripts and replace those among them who were its own Jewish forced-laborers. Globocnik agreed to halt the round-ups until August 20, but the Labor Department was unable to complete its work by then.[89] Brushing aside Labor Department pleas for a further postponement, Globocnik charged Ramm and his staff with incompetence and renewed the round-ups as scheduled. Ramm countercharged that Globocnik's men had caused damage to many German labor

Damrau to Frank, August 16, complaining about SS raids; report by Marwan, Zamość Labor Office, August 16; Biała-Podlaska Labor Office to Lublin Labor Department, August 17; Lublin Labor Department to Globocnik, August 20, on new raids in Zamość; "Vermerk," Ramm, August 20, on call from Zamość Labor Office. All the above can be found in WAPL, GDL 748 and 749 (many are in both files; copies are in YVA, O.53/79).

87 Ramm, "Vermerk," August 15, 1940; Damrau to Frank, August 16, 1940, ibid.

88 Ramm to Frauendorfer, August 20, 1940; Ramm to Geschlisser, August 20, WAPL, GDL 749 (copies in YVA, O.53/79). Ramm added that relations with Globocnik had deteriorated because of the SSPF's disregard for the agreements he had reached with Ramm. To Geschlisser he complained that he had no Jews left for road-construction or water-regulation projects. Frauendorfer also informed the armed forces stationed in the GG of the status of Jewish forced labor. See Frauendorfer to Oberstleutnant von Tschammer und Osten, Verbindungsoffizier des Oberbefehlhabers Ost, August 20, 1940, WAPL, RZ 43 (copy in USHMMA, RG-15.101M).

89 Ramm, "Vermerk," August 17, 1940, on an August 16 conversation with Globocnik; Ramm to Globocnik, August 19, 1940; Ramm, "Vermerk," August 20, on conversation with Lerch, all in WAPL, GDL 745 and 749 (copies in YVA, O.53/79).

projects.[90] Frank would have to decide, he said; as it turned out, Frank was powerless to intervene.

Zörner and his staff attempted several countermeasures to foil Globocnik's round-ups, such as halting all cooperation with the SSPF and rerouting a Bełżec-bound train of deportees from Warsaw and Radom to the civilian government's waterworks project in Chełm, but these proved ineffective.[91] Despite a subsequent agreement between Krüger and Frauendorfer, placing Frauendorfer in charge of Jewish forced labor and obligating Globocnik to submit his Jewish labor requirements in centralized requests,[92] Globocnik continued to do more or less what he wanted, when he wanted, in the realm of Jewish forced labor. Thus, surprise raids for additional Jewish forced-laborers continued without coordination with the civilian authorities.[93] Even with regard to the release of the forced-laborers from the Bełżec camps to their homes or to civilian government labor projects later in 1940 – once they were ostensibly no longer needed by the SS – Globocnik disregarded agreements with other authorities at a whim. Many were not released on the dates, in

90 Globocnik to Ramm, August 20, 1940; Ramm to Globocnik, August 24, WAPL, GDL 748 (copies in YVA, O.53/79).

91 On the ceased cooperation order, see Ramm to Labor Office Heads in the District, August 20, 1940; Hecht, "Vermerk" on Ramm's notification to all labor offices in the district of Zörner's order to cease all cooperation with the SS and police in rounding up able-bodied Jews, August 20, 1940; Ramm to Frauendorfer, August 20, all in WAPL, GDL 749 (copies in YVA, O.53/79). On the rerouted train, see Globocnik's complaint to Türk, August 24, 1940, and Türk's response, August 27, WAPL, GDL 891 (copies in YVA, JM/10,458 and O.51/10). See also Türk to Kommando des Durchgangslagers, August 25, 1940, asking that the 1,000 Jews just arrived from Warsaw and Radom be fed, in WAPL, RZ 43 (copy in USHMMA, RG-15.101M).

92 Krüger to Globocnik, September 3, 1940, WAPL, GDL 891. See also Frauendorfer to Lublin Labor Department, September 6, 1940, YVA, O.6/11b*.

93 More than 2,000 Jews were rounded up in Lublin on the night of October 20/21, another 250–300 in Lublin on November 14–15, and sixty in Radzyn on November 16. See Hecht's three memos headed "Vermerk" on October 21, 1940, and his other "Vermerk" memos on November 15 and 16, 1940, in YVA, JM/2700. Riedel, Lipowa 7 commandant, was involved in these round-ups. See also Zörner's "Aktenvermerk," dated November 28, 1940, regarding cooperation with the police on Jewish forced labor. He noted yet another agreement by the police to respect Labor Department work cards and to halt raids for forced-laborers, in *Faschismus*, p. 218.

the numbers, or to the destinations agreed upon. Instead, he had these people sent wherever he wanted, or needed.[94] Frank's relative weakness and Globocnik's independent, broad power, as they emerged from these episodes, were lessons the civilian authorities in the Lublin District learned well for their future relations with both the GG authorities in Kraków and the SS authorities at home.

The Bełżec Forced-Labor Camp Complex

The Bełżec complex consisted of eight camps spread over a 145 square kilometer expanse. Bełżec itself accounted for four of these camps: the central camp at Bełżec; Bełżec-Dwór (at a stable); Bełżec-Młyn (at a mill); and Bełżec-Parowozownia (at an engine house). The other camps were Cieszanów, Dzików, Lipsko-Narol, and Płazów. People arrived at the camps in various states of unpreparedness. Jews from Lublin and the district were generally surprised by the night raids and arrived without any clothing or provisions. Jews from Radom were surprised by the round-ups, but were given a few moments to gather together some underwear, a blanket, and some food before departing. In Warsaw, the first transports of Jews to the Lublin District were organized somewhat in advance, with quite a few Jews volunteering for the first transport, according to the Warsaw Judenrat's report. Some of these Jews were able to prepare some clothing and provisions, but others went barefoot. However, once word got back to Warsaw about conditions in the camps, very few volunteered, and larger numbers had to be seized by the SS.[95]

94 See Hecht, "Vermerk," October 14, 1940; Jache, "Vermerk," October 17; Jache to Frauendorfer, October 19, all in YVA, O.53/79; Türk to Dr. Föhl, October 21, 1940, WAPL, GDL 891; Hecht, "Vermerk," October 2, and Jache, "Vermerk," October 21, on Jews to be released from Bełżec on October 19–21, in YVA, JM/2700; and Zörner's report on Jewish forced labor in October 1940, November 6, 1940, in *Faschismus*, p. 217, and *Eksterminacja*, p. 221.

95 On Lublin, see Bełżec Report, pp. 1–2, 30. On Warsaw, see the Warsaw Judenrat's Report on the Warsaw District Jews in the Lublin camps in 1940, n.d., YVA, M.10.AR.2/128 (and JM/3488), pp. 1–2 (hereafter, Warsaw Judenrat Report). (A Yiddish version of this report can be found in *Bleter far Geschichte*, II:1–4 [Jan.–Dec. 1949], pp. 242–272.) Partial German translations can be found in

The SS did not take Jewish needs or feelings into consideration at all in organizing the forced labor. Jews of practically all ages, family status, and states of health were seized. They were given no opportunity to prepare for their stay in a camp or often even to take proper leave from their loved ones. Frequently, more than one working member of a family was taken, leaving no breadwinner at home. When they arrived in Bełżec, they were greeted by beatings and immediate hardships.

The Jews from outside the Lublin District were first transported in cattle cars to Lublin, where they were met by a SS detachment, often led by Mohwinkel. They were dealt with violently, marched through the streets to a temporary station, usually at Lipowa 7 or the old airfield, and then further transported to whichever camp and project the SS had decided to send them. Transports from a particular place were generally divided among a number of camps, according to the manpower needs of the SS at the moment. This practice made it difficult for the Judenrat in the home community to keep track of their laborers in the Lublin District and to send them aid. The 5,253 deportees from Warsaw and its environs, for example, were distributed among some thirty camps.[96]

Jews sent to the Bełżec complex via Lublin arrived in cattle cars with almost no prior warning to the Bełżec Lagerrat. Often the Lagerrat could not organize any food for the new arrivals for as much as a whole day. The camp council learned of the impending arrival of the first 3,000 laborers only half an hour in advance, leaving them no opportunity to buy or prepare food. Within three days in August, 10,000 people had reached Bełżec. Since food was

Faschismus, pp. 218–222, and *Eksterminacja*, pp. 221–224. See also Ringelblum, *Diary and Notes*, August 14, 1940, pp. 130–131. On Radom, see Shlomo Rakocz testimony, in *Jewish Radom in Its Destruction* (Yiddish) (Stuttgart: Radom Jews Committee, 1948), pp. 60–65. See also Yitzhak ("Antek") Zuckerman, *A Surplus of Memory: Chronicle of the Warsaw Ghetto Uprising* (Berkeley: University of California Press, 1993), pp. 127, 145, who emphasizes the German brutality and the high death rate and notes that he was also taken there (although he gives the incorrect year); Tamari, *Zamość*, p. 107; Chaim Szymonowicz, "Terror and Annihilation" (Yiddish), in *Sefer Częstochow* (Hebrew and Yiddish) (Jerusalem: Encyclopedia of the Jewish Diaspora, 1967), p. 60.

96 Warsaw Judenrat Report, pp. 242–243 (of Yiddish version).

the highest initial priority, the camp council did not address the problem of lodgings until the arrivals had been fed. This meant that the inadequate quarters that had been prepared earlier by the first inmates in Bełżec could not be expanded, repaired, cleaned, or outfitted with even the most primitive accessories before the laborers arrived.

The council itself was too small and ill-equipped to cope with the sudden expansion in numbers. Whereas a Jewish community of 10,000 in the GG had a twenty-four-member Judenrat, employees, and a pre-existing kehillah structure to draw from, the Bełżec Lagerrat consisted of only five men. They had no appreciable structure or resources when thousands of rounded-up Jews began to arrive in mid-August. The council was not expanded to meet the radically increased demand until some of these Jews had already departed for their final labor-camp destination.[97]

The expansion of the Bełżec Lagerrat was initiated by Lublin Judenrat Chairman Bekker. He visited the camp very soon after the sudden round-ups and disappearances of Judenrat members and employees among the deportees in order to assess the situation personally and to gain the release of the Judenrat people. The inadequacy of the original camp council established out of the "Gremium" was evident, and a new camp council structure was created to replace it as of August 21.[98]

The new structure had a central Lagerrat in Bełżec, headed by the current camp council leaders, Lejb Zylberajch and Wolf Fajgeles. The central council oversaw the activities of councils now created in Lipsko (headed by Abram Blumenkranc), Płazów (Chil Honigman), and Cieszanów (Pinchas Pajczer), while it also served as the council for the camps at Bełżec itself (Młyn, Dwór, Parowozownia). When the Dzików camp was opened in October, Olmer of Częstochowa was appointed by the German commandant, the infamous Oskar Dirlewanger, to be camp head.

The central Lagerrat had nineteen officials working for it, and

97 Bełżec Report, pp. 1–2, 30–31.

98 Lublin Judenrat minutes, Blumental, *Documents*, protocols 38, 39 (August 18 and 24, 1940), pp. 176–177; protocol of Bełżec camp committee meeting, August 21, 1940, WAPL, RZ 46.

each of the subordinate councils had a staff of four to twelve people. There were four departments in the central council that served all the camps: post; supplies; cash and bookkeeping; and storerooms. In addition, the central council had a main secretariat of seven people, a health department with four doctors, who also oversaw an infirmary, a pharmacy (one employee), and a laundry (one employee). Each sub-camp set up its own departments as well, especially for health, food distribution, and workshops for camp needs.[99]

There was an inherent contradiction in the structure and hierarchy of the central Lagerrat. At one and the same time the Lublin Judenrat sought to subordinate it to itself yet to have it represent and care for all the inmates from all the communities. In order to build a consensus for this image of the central camp council and to defray some of the enormous financial burden of supplying all the inmates' needs – the Germans refused to supply even the smallest items or minimum amount of food – the Lublin Judenrat contacted the fifty-seven Judenräte who represented Jews who had been sent to Bełżec. By means of written messages, telephone calls, and personal messengers, the Lublin Judenrat requested that the others contribute to the maintenance and care of the Jews at Bełżec. There was even a conference of Judenräte on this subject in Warsaw on September 7.

Only nine Judenräte responded to the Lublin Judenrat's appeals. In some cases the other Judenräte preferred to send aid completely independently of the Lublin Judenrat and the central Lagerrat. In most cases they simply did not respond to the pleas for help. The result was recriminations between the Lublin Judenrat and many other Judenräte.[100] In some cases this led the Lublin Judenrat to turn to the German civilian authorities to intercede with other Judenräte to pay their share for the maintenance of the forced-laborers.[101] The

99 Bełżec Report, pp. 10–22, 25–29; Lublin Judenrat minutes, Blumental, *Documents*, protocols 38, 39 (August 18 and 24, 1940), pp. 176–177; protocol of Bełżec camp committee meeting, ibid.

100 Bełżec Report, pp. 22–23; Gremium Report; Lublin Judenrat Annual Report, pp. 53–54; travel permit to Warsaw for Henryk Bekker for September 7, 1940, WAPL, RZ 46.

101 Bekker to Radzyn *Kreishauptmann*, August 31, 1940, WAPL, RZ 46. Bekker was asking that the Michów Judenrat send 1,000 złoty.

Judenrat was also forced by the SS and the civilians to pay for the transport of the Jews to and from the camps and for any care they received, such as delousing. The Judenrat tried to collect these debts from other Judenräte as well, but rarely succeeded.[102] The absence of cooperation among the Judenräte sometimes led to anomalous situations; once the Lublin Judenrat detained a group of several hundred Radom Jews returning home, pending payment by the Radom Judenrat for their transport.[103]

The central Lagerrat's relations with the Lublin Judenrat and other Judenräte were uneasy at best. As a result of the bad relations all around, the terrible conditions in the camps, and the Lublin Judenrat's wavering faith in the central camp council, the Judenrat felt compelled to increase its direct involvement in camp affairs from August 31. The existing aid committee for Bełżec was placed under the Judenrat's control with Globocnik's consent, and Judenrat members and employees were co-opted onto its presidium and executive committee. Extended visits to the camp by several Judenrat members at a time were commonplace during September, in addition to very regular visits by Judenrat employees who brought supplies and money.

It is not clear how effective these efforts were to gain more control. The Germans constituted one of the Judenrat's obstacles to increased jurisdiction over the Lagerrat. Although the central Lagerrat was technically an extension of the Lublin Judenrat, it was in fact responsible to only one authority, the Germans in Bełżec. The "generally satisfactory" relations that prevailed between the central Lagerrat and Dolp and his staff ultimately worked to the

102 See, for example, Lublin Judenrat to Radom Judenrat, August 30, 1940, WAPL, RZ 46; Arbeitsamt Chełm to Labor Department, Kraków, December 6, 1940, on the cost of transporting 950 men from Chełm to Bełżec and Hrubieszów in August. On delousing, see, for example, exchange of correspondence between Dr. Baldauf of the Lublin Public Health Department and the Lublin Judenrat regarding payment for the delousing of 900 out-of-town Jews on October 13, November 28, and December 9. See also an undated report (probably mid-December 1940) to the Judenrat Presidium by Kelman Trachtenberg and Abram Gorzyczynski on the return of out-of-town laborers via Lublin, WAPL, RZ 43 (copy in USHMMA, RG-15.101M).

103 See Shlomo Rakocz testimony in *Jewish Radom*, p. 65. See also Kelman Trachtenberg and Abram Gorzyczynski to Judenrat Presidium, n.d. [ca. December 12, 1940], WAPL, RZ 43 (copy in USHMMA, RG-15.101M).

benefit of only certain council members.[104] The central Lagerrat claimed, in its summation report in March 1941, that its initiative and good relations with the Germans enabled it to overcome many camp hardships satisfactorily for the benefit of the forced-laborers. Certainly these relations were a dubious distinction at best.

Eventually food distribution did become organized, but even then it was wholly inadequate. Daily rations at first consisted of 500 grams of bread, half a liter of an unsweetened coffee substitute, and half a liter of soup made from potatoes, barley, and a few scraps of meat. In time the Bełżec camp council was able to supplement these rations with a few vegetables, but, by November 1, the SS had reduced the bread ration to 350 grams. The food supplies for all the camps were purchased wholesale by the camp council in nearby Tomaszów-Lubelski. If food was unavailable there, the council's emissaries would buy in Zamość or Lublin. Certain items were often difficult to obtain because of food rationing.

Eleven bakeries received flour from the Bełżec camp council in order to bake bread for the camps: five in Tomaszów, two each in Lipsko and Cieszanów, and one each in Bełżec and Płazów. All other food was transported daily from Bełżec to the other camps – at first by horse and wagon rented from local peasants. The Germans later provided a truck, which reduced costs and sped delivery. Whereas the food was entirely inadequate, especially for people engaged in very strenuous physical labor, some 40 percent of the laborers managed to supplement the meager rations allowed by the Germans and doled out by the camp council with packages sent from home. The other 60 percent, who received only occasional packages, or none whatsoever, were in the greatest danger of contracting diseases or dying of starvation or exhaustion, whichever felled them first.[105]

104 Protocols of Lublin Judenrat meetings, 40–48, August 31, September 7, September 10–16, 1940, in Blumental, *Documents*, pp. 178–186; Bełżec Report, pp. 22–23; Gremium Report; Lublin Judenrat Annual Report, pp. 53–54; WAPL, RZ 46 contains many travel permits for Judenrat members and employees to Bełżec to bring supplies and money. See also Henryk Bekker to Radzyn *Kreishauptmann*, August 31, 1940, and Hersz Zylber to Judenrat Presidium, August 26, 1940, in WAPL, RZ 46.

105 Bełżec Report, pp. 5–7. See also Warsaw Judenrat Report, pp. 248–249. All survivor statements on these camps refer to the poor food. See also the

However, it was not food alone that threatened the laborers' lives. The lodgings prepared for the laborers were notoriously inadequate. Even the Bełżec Lagerrat, which many Jews accused of corruption and callousness, could not gloss over this hardship and addressed the inadequate lodgings at length in its self-serving summary report for the Lublin Judenrat. The forced-laborers lived in what can only be described as a grotesque mockery of housing. The broken-down, dark, damp, drafty, and filthy ruins into which they were crammed to triple capacity were not quite the improvisation the camp council made them out to be. They were a reflection of the SS's deliberate callousness and indifference to the welfare of the Jewish forced-laborers they had rounded up. Rooms that measured 5m x 6m slept seventy-five men, giving each person less than half a square meter of space. The quarters were so crowded that people slept up against each other on the floor, unable to undress or remove their shoes.[106]

At Bełżec itself, the 3,000 laborers were housed in stables, a hayloft, an unfinished mill, and an engine house at the station. Approximately 1,000 Gypsies from Hamburg, who had also been brought in for the fortification work, were housed in the mill. The Gypsies were treated better than the Jews by the German authorities at the camp with regard to both housing and work. They were given the ground floor of the mill, which was larger and intact, while the Jews were housed in the much smaller and unfinished upper storey. The Gypsies were also given lighter work. The survivors recall that all this was part of a successful Nazi attempt to create friction between the two groups.[107] Little is known about the fate of these German Gypsies.

report of Wehrmacht Major Braune-Krikau, Operations Officer of Chief Field Headquarters 379 in Lublin, September 23, 1940, on his inspection visit to Bełżec on September 22, 1940, in Raul Hilberg, ed., *Documents of Destruction; Germany and Jewry, 1939–1945* (Chicago: Quadrangle, 1971), pp. 42–45.

106 Bełżec Report, pp. 4–5, 25–29; Warsaw Judenrat Report, p. 247; Shlomo Rakocz testimony in *Jewish Radom*, p. 65.

107 Bełżec Report, ibid.; Warsaw Judenrat Report, ibid.; Shlomo Rakocz testimony, ibid.; YVA, M.10.AR.1/396 (JM/2712, ff. 4–6); M.10.AR.1/423 (JM/2713, ff. 128–137), Mittelman; Szymonowicz testimony, *Sefer Częstochow*, p. 60.

Forced laborers digging anti-tank trenches, Bełżec, 1940, Yad Vashem Photo Archive, 16FO5

The Lipsko quarters for 2,086 people consisted of thirteen small, partially destroyed, formerly Jewish houses, as well as at least two large stables at Lipie, half a kilometer away. The gaping holes where doors and windows should have been were covered with boards. At Płazów, the 1,250 Jews from Warsaw and environs were placed in two large sheds – one with seven rooms, the other with five – when they arrived on August 22. There was no housing at all for the 3,000 Jews from Radom, Częstochowa, and Warsaw who arrived at Cieszanów on August 20. They were eventually housed in two synagogues, the adjacent house of the rabbi, and several other nearby houses, but for several days there was no functioning kitchen, no pots, no food, no source of water, and no supplies. Whatever meager food the inmates ate was cold. The only well, which served all the laborers, was first dug several weeks after they arrived. When additional forced-laborers were brought in after several weeks, they were compelled to sleep in an open field, surrounded by barbed wire and armed guards. In early October, 1,000 laborers were moved to nearby Dzików, where conditions were very similar.[108]

108 Bełżec Report, ibid.; Warsaw Judenrat Report, ibid; Shlomo Rakocz testimony, ibid.; YVA, M.10.AR.1/396, ibid; Szymonowicz testimony, ibid.

The workday at the Bełżec camps began officially with wake-up at 5:30 A.M. — some report as early as 4 A.M. — roll call, and a drink of a coffee substitute. At 6 A.M. the laborers marched off in columns to work, which could be more than 10 kilometers away. Officially the workday extended from 7 A.M. to 5 P.M., with a one-hour midday break for "lunch" (a thin soup, sometimes with potatoes and meat). In fact, the hours were much longer and the break much shorter — so short that often many workers failed to get any lunch at all before the return-to-work call was sounded. They worked seven days a week, including holidays, digging long trenches, three to four meters deep, over a stretch of many kilometers. The forced-laborers were required to work rain or shine, in the heat or cold, in sickness or health. Beatings rained down upon them frequently during the course of the workday, and there were more than a few instances of shootings for the slightest "infraction," such as pausing to lean on a shovel for a moment, or relieving oneself. Of course, the dysentery, which was rampant by mid-September, meant that it was nearly impossible to obey these rules.

At the end of the workday, the workers lined up in columns and marched the distance back to their camp. After evening roll call they received more coffee substitute, were given a few moments to relieve themselves, and then confined to quarters until morning. This was the only time allotted the workers to take care of their bodily needs, and this was done under Selbstschutz guard and beatings. Those who did not manage to relieve themselves during this time had to wait until the next evening, or else risk their lives by sneaking off at some point during the night, hoping to evade detection.[109]

109 YVA, M.10.AR.1/395, 396, 403, 410 (Dr. Uryson), 423, 378, 380, 658, 671, 916 (also on JM/3489); Warsaw Judenrat Report, pp. 250, 265 (Appendix 5, Report of Medical Delegation to Bełżec camps, mid-September, 1940); Shlomo Rakocz testimony, ibid.; Report by Major Braune-Krikau, September 23, 1943, in Hilberg, ed., *Documents of Destruction*, pp. 42–45; Wilden, Church Division, Kraków, to Zörner, September 27, 1940, and Türk to BuF, Kraków, October 5, 1940, WAPL, GDL 891. It is remarkable that five different official sources from Lublin do not discuss the actual work at the Bełżec camps: the Summary Report of the Bełżec Central Camp Council; the Gremium Report; the report of the Judenrat's Extra-Urban Labor Camp Committee, WAPL, RZ 46; the Lublin Judenrat Annual Report; and the Protocols of the Lublin Judenrat for the period of the existence of these camps.

The inadequate housing and the impossibility of maintaining any semblance of hygiene may have been an even more serious problem than the food shortage. This was the impression recorded by Wehrmacht Major Braune-Krikau, who visited Bełżec on September 22.[110] Housing and hygiene were problems whose cumulative deleterious effects could not be mitigated by packages from home, connections, or money – save the possibility for a laborer with means to buy his way out of the camp and be replaced by someone without means. The lack of time, water, and washing facilities meant that most of the Jewish laborers in the Bełżec complex were unable to wash themselves. They could not change their underpants or clothing for months, nor were they given any work clothing. Since they walked very far to and from work each day and toiled at very hard physical labor under rough conditions, their clothing and shoes wore out completely within a few weeks.

The central camp council estimated that 20–30 percent of the laborers went to work barefoot and in rags within a short time of their arrival in Bełżec. Yet replacements or mendings were almost impossible to come by. The shoemaker workshop in Bełżec employed three shoemakers; they repaired 269 pairs of shoes during a four-week period in the fall, while a shoemaker shop in Lipsko repaired 237 pairs of shoes. One reason for this meager output was the fact that most of the shoemakers' and tailors' time was spent working for the camps' German staff. If we add these repairs to the clothing and shoes received from the Judenräte in Lublin, Warsaw, and several other places, and kept in the storerooms of the central Lagerrat, the number of pairs of shoes repaired or received was 567 by mid-October. These were meant for the 2–3,000 people who were already barefoot a month earlier, according to the central Lagerrat's estimate.[111]

The brief, uncomfortable sleep that the laborers could manage was complicated by the lack of bedding. There were no beds and, in most places, no boards; blankets were rare; and sheets and pillows were unknown. Jews slept on the floor, if there was one, or on the

110 Major Braune-Krikau's report, ibid.

111 Bełżec Report, pp. 19–22, 26–27. These records are incomplete, as was the camp council's estimate of the number of needy. The records regarding articles of clothing and blankets are similar.

ground. At first many of the lodgings were provided with straw strewn on the floor as bedding. But the straw became bug-infested, and the laborers were quickly covered with lice and worms. When the straw wore out, it was not replaced, and then the laborers had nothing at all to sleep on.[112]

The SS made no advance arrangements for medical care, and Dr. Fajgeles was the only physician until the end of August. Additional physicians were then sent from Częstochowa, Lublin, Warsaw, and Kraków, until there were eleven physicians serving 11,000 forced-laborers. There were also several dozen "sanitary workers" (orderlies), but they generally had no real qualifications. When the doctors arrived, they were distributed among the camps and immediately set out to open infirmaries. However, these were chilly, drafty, and overcrowded at best, and there were practically no medicines. Those who were seriously ill or had contagious diseases could be sent to the hospital in Tomaszów-Lubelski — at least theoretically. According to the central camp council's report, the doctors saw approximately 400 people each day and were able to get some twenty relieved from work each week due to illness. All the reports and survivor memoirs regarding the camps agree that disease was rampant. According to Major Braune-Krikau, dysentery prevailed by the time he visited the camp. Other accounts add typhus, gastroenteritis, and many other ailments. The Warsaw Judenrat's estimation that few sick laborers could get a day off from work is borne out by the above data and accounts.[113]

Clearly there was little the doctors could do to help the forced-laborers. Some of them charged the central Lagerrat in general and Dr. Fajgeles in particular with corruption. Fajgeles was called the "exemplary bribetaker" by one survivor of the Bełżec labor camp, who also claimed that the young doctor had never completed his medical studies. Another called him an "immoral degenerate." He would examine only those who paid him an "honorarium," and

112 Bełżec Report, pp. 4–5; Warsaw Judenrat Report, p. 247; Major Braune-Krikau's report. All the testimonies by survivors of these camps refer to the terrible sleeping conditions.

113 See, for example, Bełżec Report, pp. 8–9; Warsaw Judenrat Report, pp. 247–248; Major Braune-Krikau report, ibid.; YVA, M.10.AR.1/396, 423.

only a bribe could win an inmate the desired work-exemption note from Fajgeles.[114]

The camp council as a whole was accused of taking bribes, withholding food rations and other necessary supplies from the laborers, and serving the Germans more than the Jews. This alleged corruption was a cause of concern for the Lublin Judenrat and was a major impetus in its attempt to increase its involvement in the Bełżec camps' internal affairs. Certainly the Lagerrat's description of its reasons for discontinuing to provide straw for bedding – it would become bug-infested anyway – and for halting attempts to mend tattered clothing and worn shoes – they could not hope to repair everything – are dubious. Leaving 11,000 people to sleep on the bare ground and with no clothing or shoes does not reflect a great sense of public duty. When taken together with the Lagerrat's self-proclaimed good relations with Dolp and his men, and bad relations with the Judenräte, this absence of public responsibility seems to corroborate the suspicions and charges against the Lagerrat by its contemporaries.[115]

Many from outside Lublin felt discriminated against by the Lublin-dominated camp councils and the presence of many Lublin officials at almost all times, while, at the same time, feeling abandoned by their own Judenräte. It was true that the Lublin Jews were at least better shod than others.[116] The Judenräte were also accused of sending primarily the most helpless Jews – refugees and the poor – to the camps, with promises of salaries and conditions that were never kept.[117] Not surprisingly, neither the minutes of the meetings of the Lublin Judenrat, nor the summary report of the central Lagerrat at Bełżec relates to these last charges.

114 YVA, M.10.AR.1/396, 423.

115 YVA, M.10.AR.1/423, 396; Lublin Judenrat minutes, 42–47, September 10–16, 1940, in Blumental, *Documents*, pp. 182–186; Bełżec Report, pp. 5, 7–8, 22–25.

116 YVA, M.10.AR.1/423, 396; Lublin Judenrat minutes, ibid.; Ringelblum, *Diary and Notes*, October 5, 1940, p. 154.

117 YVA, M.10.AR.1/423, 396; Ewa Szek testimony, M.49.E/42; Gedalje Erenberg testimony, M.1.E/1563; Yitzchak Lederhendler testimony, in *Jewish Radom*, pp. 59–60; Ringelblum, *Diary and Notes*, September 6–9, 1940, p. 135; Tamari, *Zamość*, p. 107.

One of the remarkable aspects of life under the Nazis in the Lublin District is the apparently mundane detail of the ongoing functioning of the postal service. Although Jews were forbidden to use the regular postal service from January 1940, they continued to make use of the limited, censored, and segregated service for Jews. The continued functioning of some measure of postal service was quite marked in connection with the Bełżec camps, where the postal department had the largest staff (seven people) of any in the Lagerrat. It handled some 50,000 incoming letters, 28,342 packages, and 1,463 money transfers to the inmates from their families (22,000 złoty), as well as 40,000 outgoing letters from the inmates. The Lagerrat's summary report also refers to the "heroic women" who trekked over dozens, sometimes hundreds, of kilometers in order to bring food and supplies to their loved ones in the camps.[118] The mere fact that these women were able somehow to travel, despite the overwhelming hardships and obstacles they had to overcome, is worthy of note. Undoubtedly, the large volume of letters and packages, as well as visits from family members, helped maintain at least a significant number of the forced-laborers at Bełżec and contributed to limiting the death rate there.

When the combined effects of the living conditions, lack of nutrition, work conditions, and absence of medical care are considered, it is remarkable that the central camp council reported only some 300 deaths in the Bełżec camp complex during its entire existence. It is impossible to ascertain the exact number of deaths, but it is clear that the number registered by the doctors at the Bełżec camps does not fully reflect the effects of the camp conditions on the Jews. Some other contemporary sources and survivor accounts point to a much higher death rate in both the Bełżec and the Lublin District camps as a whole.[119]

The effect of the impossible conditions in these camps on the Jewish forced-laborers is also reflected in the Lublin Labor Department's recommendation that the Bełżec laborers be sent

118 Bełżec Report, pp. 14–18, 25; Gremium Report.

119 See Bełżec Report, p. 9; the 175 death notices signed by Dr. Fajgeles and the full list of these deaths, August 30—December 4, 1940, are in WAPL, RZ 48; Ringelblum, *Diary and Notes*, September 19—November 8, 1940, pp. 142, 180.

home rather than on to new work for the Water Works Department. The SS in Bełżec had exploited them to the utmost, and they could no longer be considered able-bodied.[120] One official visitor from the Warsaw Judenrat expected 15 percent of the laborers to contract incurable diseases.[121] The Warsaw Judenrat's report indicated that 2,898 of the 3,298 returnees from the Lublin camps needed medical care upon their return. One of the doctors who examined these returnees wrote of his patients' debilitated physical condition and death within days of their return.[122] Thus, the total number of Jews who died in the Bełżec camps or as a result of their stay there was probably considerably higher than the number officially reported. Similarly, the total number of Jews who died in all the Lublin labor camps in 1940 seems to have been in the thousands.

Neither the exact number of Jewish forced-laborers in the Lublin District nor the exact number of camps and other forced-labor sites can be determined, as both were always in flux. New sites were being opened constantly, and existing ones closed as jobs were completed. Similarly, the number of Jewish forced-laborers fluctuated with the demands of the SS and the civilian authorities. In the period from late August to late October 1940, organized forced labor in labor camps in the Lublin District reached a peak that set a standard for Nazi labor demands from the Jews until their murder.

The Bełżec camp complex, with approximately 11,000 Jewish forced-laborers and 1,000 Gypsies, was the largest group of a widespread network of dozens of forced-labor camps across the district, with tens of thousands of Jewish inmates.[123] Probably the

120 Jache, Lublin Labor Department, to Abteilung Arbeit, Kraków, November 20, 1940, YVA, JM/2700.

121 YVA, M.10.AR.1/396.

122 Warsaw Judenrat report, p. 254, and Appendix 3, p. 260; Dr. Uryson's report, YVA, M.10.AR.1/410.

123 Dieter Pohl, basing himself on Edward Dziadosz and Józef Marszalek, "Wiezienia i obozy w dystrykcie lubelskim w latach 1939–1944," *Zeszyty Majdanka*, 3 (1969), pp. 60–65, believes there were 50–70,000 Jews in forced-labor camps and an unknown number working for Germans outside the camp framework. Bogdan Musial argues that the number was closer to 20,000. Pohl's estimate seems more accurate, especially when the turnover is taken into account. See Pohl, *Judenpolitik*, p. 85; Musial, *Zivilverwaltung*, p. 168.

most reliable data for Bełżec and the district as a whole are to be found in a series of official Jewish reports by and for the Lublin and Warsaw Judenräte. These, together with Jewish testimonies and various German sources, show that there were at least fifty-eight camps in the Lublin District in this period. The records do not always indicate how the Jews of a particular round-up were distributed among the various German camps and projects; they are also least detailed and accurate regarding agricultural work. Moreover, thousands of additional forced-laborers were brought in constantly for all the projects during the late summer and autumn of 1940 (e.g., 1,000 from Warsaw and Radom on August 25; 1,192 from Warsaw, Radom, and Kielce on September 7; 800 POWs from Hammerstein to Biała-Podlaska, October 24), which further complicates the calculations. In some cases, at least, those brought to the camps in September and October were meant to replace other forced-laborers who had been released, were incapacitated, or had died. Officially, the SS were interested in using only able-bodied Jewish men in the border fortification work. If German records of the "able-bodied" are taken at face value, then no more than 12,094 were found to be fit for hard labor. However, it cannot be assumed that those deemed unfit were released to their homes. Their fate is unclear at best, tragic at worst.[124]

Table 4.1 contains a list of fifty-eight known camps, with

124 The data are derived from the following sources: Warsaw Judenrat Report; Lublin Judenrat Annual Report; Bełżec Report; Gremium Report; Report by the Lublin Judenrat's Department for Extra-Urban Labor Camps, WAPL, RZ 46; YVA, M.10.AR.1/396, 403, 423, 619, 671; "Wochentliche Meldungen über den Einsatz von Juden," August 17 to November 1940, WAPL, GDL 747; WAPL, GDL 749 includes lists with numbers of Jews deported from outside the Lublin District to the labor camps in the autumn of 1940; Lerch to Ramm, August 19, 1940, Ramm to Geschlisser, August 20, WAPL, GDL 745 (copies in YVA, O.53/79); Türk to Kommando des Durchgangslagers, August 25, 1940, WAPL, RZ 43 (copy in USHMMA, RG-15.101M); Hecht, "Vermerk" on discussion with Lerch, September 6, 1940, WAPL, GDL 749; Lublin Interior Department report on August 1940, September 7, 1940, in *Faschismus*, p. 216 (also in *Eksterminacja*, p. 219); "Vermerk," Ramm, September 19, 1940, YVA, JM/2700; *Pinkas Tyszowiec*, edited by Yaakov Zifer (Yiddish and Hebrew) (Tel Aviv: Tyszowiec Immigrants' Association, 1971), pp. 214–215. On the deportation of POWs to Biała-Podlaska for forced labor, see extensive correspondence among the BuF Lublin, the Lublin Arbeitsamt, the Biała-Podlaska Arbeitsamt, and the Kraków Arbeitsamt,

estimated numbers of forced-laborers in each (where such information is available). The actual number of camps, if all the agricultural sites are taken into account, may have been twice as high.[125] Similarly, the total number of forced-laborers in the special projects – fortifications, water regulation, road construction – was probably quite a few thousand higher, since a number of labor sites are either not listed, or no numbers were found for them. Many of the numbers reflect the count taken by the Warsaw Judenrat or one of its emissaries. Therefore, the actual goal of 30,000 laborers sought by the SS in the summer of 1940 was probably achieved, or even exceeded.

The Bełżec camp complex operated at full capacity for only two months. In mid-October, the first trainloads of Jews began to be released from the camps, and the excavation work was largely halted by November. The first 132 Jews were released from the camps even earlier, from late August to mid-September, but these were mostly people who were unable to work.[126] The Lublin Judenrat also tried to obtain releases for people who had been in the camps for a long period of time, but these requests were generally ignored by the SS in the camps.[127] On October 22, the Lublin Judenrat appointed Judenrat member Józef Wajselfisz to oversee the liquidation of the Bełżec camp. He spent some three weeks there, but there is no record of what he did.[128] It is safe to assume that he did not benefit from

between October 24 and November 20, 1940, in YVA, JM/2700. Of the 800 brought to Biala-Podlaska, 250 were cripples.

On the fate of the frail and elderly in the Bełżec camps, see, for example, the testimony of Shlomo Rakocz regarding the fate of 150 unfit elderly people in Cieszanów, *Jewish Radom*, pp. 60–65.

125 The Lublin Judenrat Annual Report, pp. 54–55, relates that 829 Lublin Jews were working on twenty-eight farms in the summer of 1940. Jews from other communities in the Lublin District also worked on farms, and they were moved from farm to farm as jobs were completed.

126 See Lublin Judenrat to Radom Judenrat, August 30, 1940, travel permits for returnees, August 29 to September 16, 1940, and memorandum by M. Zorkraut of Lublin's Aid Committee for forced-labor camps, September 8, 1940, WAPL, RZ 46.

127 See Bekker to Dolp, September 11, 1940, WAPL, RZ 46.

128 Bekker to Aid Committee for Laborers in the Bełżec Labor Camps, October 22, 1940, WAPL, RZ 46. The often sterile minutes of the Lublin Judenrat's meetings do not mention either the closing of the camps or Wajselfisz's

any greater cooperation from Dolp and his men in succeeding to send the broken Jewish forced-laborers home than had the German civilian authorities.

The first Jews were to begin leaving the Bełżec camps on October 14. According to a schedule agreed upon between the SS and the civilian authorities, the trains were to depart for Lublin almost daily during the following week, and the laborers were to continue from there either to a new labor camp or to their homes. The plan was that, by October 22, 6,760 were to have departed. However, Globocnik's men wreaked havoc with the departure schedule and destinations to such an extent that Lublin Labor Department officials were very soon complaining of the disruption in labor projects all through the GG. In his report on Jewish forced labor in October, Governor Zörner could account for only 4,331. The first train, with 1,250 Jews for Hrubieszów, departed a day late and with only 1,021. Of these only 519 reached the destination. The civilian authorities had no idea what had happened to the others. Similarly, of 1,500 expected by the civilian authorities to depart for Dębica and Tarnów on October 19, Dolp agreed to 1,000. Of these, only 590 actually left Bełżec for these destinations, and only on October 20. The October 16 train, which was to return 900 Radom Jews to their home city in order to be integrated into Labor Department projects there, actually carried mostly Lublin Jews.

This was the general pattern for the departures from the Bełżec camps, which Türk disparagingly called a "circus."[129] The civilian authorities in the Lublin District were unable to gain control over the situation in 1940; the Lublin SS had succeeded in asserting its dominance in Jewish policy even in regard to the Jews' release from the SS forced-labor camps. However, for the 1942 deportations,

appointment to this job and his activities. The Bełżec Report also makes no mention of the closing of the camps and the transport of the forced-laborers.

129 Lublin Labor Department to Zamość Labor Office, October 11, 1940; Hecht, "Vermerk," October 14; Hecht, "Vermerk," October 17; *SS-Bannführer* Maubach to Lublin Labor Department, October 18; Jache to Frauendorfer, October 19, all in YVA, O.53/79. Türk to Dr. Föhl, October 21, 1940, WAPL, GDL 891. Hecht, "Vermerk," October 21, 1940, and Jache, "Vermerk," October 21, both on the missing Jews from the transport to Dębica, YVA, JM/2700. Zörner report on Jewish forced labor in October 1940, November 6, 1940, in *Faschismus*, p. 217. Warsaw Judenrat Report, Appendix 2, p. 260.

Türk succeeded in maneuvering himself into joint control of train requisitions. He had learned his lesson well.

By mid-December, the camps were closed for all intents and purposes, save for a small group of forced-laborers left behind to clean up and perform various odd jobs. Less than a year later, Dolp was back at Bełżec — this time to construct a death camp. A number of the Jewish forced-laborers brought to construct the new camp had worked at digging the original trenches there, some of which now formed the northern perimeter of the death camp. These trenches subsequently served as burial and burning pits for the corpses of the murdered Jews.[130]

The story of Jewish forced labor in the Lublin District in 1939–1941 reflects the ideological and political centrality of Jews to the German authorities in the GG in general and in Lublin in particular. Jews were a fundamental part of Nazi ideology and policy-making for the officials in Lublin and the GG as much as for the leaders in Berlin. Jews and forced labor were also sources of power. Whichever German authority controlled Jewish policy and forced labor accrued power and influence. Thus, for ideological reasons and in order to gain power, many figures and offices within the various German bureaucracies in the Lublin District sought to control Jewish forced labor. The rivalry and animosity that resulted between Globocnik's SS and the German civilian officials was so intense that the civilian authorities became unwilling to cooperate with the SS, and each side denigrated and tried to undermine the other at every turn.

The forced labor was performed in many cases under extremely brutal conditions, resulting in the death or serious maiming of many Jews. The Jews vividly remembered their very bitter experience in these forced-labor projects many years later. Still, in 1940–1941, the forced labor was work that held some purpose for the Germans, such as defense, improving the district's infrastructure, production, harvesting crops, and so on. Indeed, these two points — SS-civilian rivalry and mutual animosity, and the bitter Jewish memories of the

130 On the proximity of the death camp to the labor camp, see United Nations War Crimes Commission, Case 1372, f. 1261, YVA, JM/10,156; Arad, *Bełżec, Treblinka, Sobibor*, pp. 23–24; Michael Tregenza, "Bełżec Death Camp," *Wiener Library Bulletin*, vol. XXX, nos. 41/42 (1977), pp. 15–16.

forced labor — became important factors in the way the deportations to death were conducted in 1942, and how the Jews reacted.

Table 4.1: Forced-Labor Camps for Jews in the Lublin District, 1940–early 1941

Camp	Number	Camp	Number
1. Józefów/Wisła	667	30. Frampol	???
2. Bełżec-Parowozownia	2,500	31. Staw	100s
3. Bełżec-Młyn	500	32. Biała-Podlaska	600
4. Bełżec-Dwór	1,000	33. Ortel Książecy	200
5. Cieszanów	3,000	34. Terespol	@100
6. Płazów	1,350	35. Leszno	200
7. Dzików*	1,000	36. Kołody	350
8. Lipsko/Narol	2,086	37. Dokudów	350
9. Zamość City	>400	38. Rossosz	200
10. Białobrzeg	>200	39. Rogóżnica	760
11. Tyszowce	530	40. Krzanów	10s
12. Witków	350	41. Czasnówka	300
13. Wereszyń	1,060	42. Helenowo	300
14. Dolhobyczów	1,500	43. Holeszów	280
15. Oszczów	1,000	44. Ulany	???
16. Mircze	750	45. Zarzecze	300
17. Wareż	???	46. Horodyszcze	100s
18. Obrowen	200	47. Łomazy	100s
19. Maryszinie	???	48. Dęblin	>140
20. Włodawa	150	49. Bełżyce	>360
21. Hańsk	100	50. Busznie	100
22. Sawin	250	51. Uchrynowie	???
23. Luta	200	52. Kamień	115
24. Ossowa	300	53. Żmudź	200
25. Ruda-Opalin	650	54. Końskowola	400
26. Krychów	ca.1,000	55. Milejowo	200
27. Dorohusk	150	56. Lipowa 7	2,500
28. Siedliszcze	200	57. Lublin airfield	>200
29. Sajczyce	???	58. Turkowice	250

CHAPTER 5

"Resettlements" and Ghettos, 1940–1941

"There is no clear Jewish policy in the *Generalgouvernement*," concluded Dr. Heinz Kloss of the Deutsche Auslands Institut following a March 20—April 1, 1941 visit to the GG. As he traveled around the GG, in the midst of the massive German troop concentrations in preparation for "Operation Barbarossa" and the ghettoization of the Jews in several major cities, Kloss was struck by the stark inconsistencies of German policy toward the Jews. Whereas in Warsaw, he noted, Jews had been removed from small towns and concentrated in the big city, in Kraków it was the opposite — Jews were dispersed from the city to small towns. Kloss noted two prevalent opinions among Germans in the GG regarding the direction of Jewish policy: either all the Jews would be shot, or they would be sent to Alaska.[1]

Kloss's observations reflect the nature of German policy toward the Jews in the GG from the autumn of 1940 to the summer of 1941. The anti-Jewish policy in the GG was not centrally planned in detail, and regional and local German officials were allowed much discretion. This resulted in the concentration of Jews in some places and their dispersal in others; ghettos in some places, and permission for Jews to continue to live in their own homes in others. These

1 "Reisebericht Dr. Kloss — 20. März bis 1. April 1941," Appendix E, "Die Judenfrage im Generalgouvernement," YVA, JM/4198 (original in National Archives, T-81/418). Kloss was a prominent linguist and a leading figure, author, and editor in the Deutsche Auslands Institut, tracking, among other things, the settlement of *Volksdeutsche* in German-controlled territories.

apparent contradictions, born of local decision-making in response to local needs and problems, were especially marked in the Lublin District.

In both popular and much of scholarly literature on the Holocaust, the dominant picture of Nazi policy toward Jews in Poland and Jewish life under the Germans there has been that of the two largest ghettos – Warsaw and Lodz (Łódź). These two ghettos have often come to represent Jewish life everywhere in Poland and Eastern Europe under the Nazis. They have been the most widely discussed in the literature and, for very clear reasons, have become the best known ghettos. First, they were by far the largest in terms of population – the Warsaw ghetto's Jewish population alone exceeded that of each of the Lublin, Radom, and Kraków districts. Second, Lodz existed longer than any other ghetto (May 1940—August 1944). Third, the dramatic and heroic Jewish uprising in Warsaw in 1943, and the resultant widespread postwar discussion it engendered prompted a discussion of the events and conditions preceding the uprising well before discussion of ghetto life was common in the historiography of the Holocaust. Fourth, there is relatively more documentation on Warsaw and Lodz than on other places, largely for the reasons stated above. In addition, the preservation of most of the Oneg Shabbat archives in Warsaw and extensive Jewish and German records from Lodz added greatly to the source material. Finally, the physical conditions in these ghettos were so horrendous that they have left their indelible mark on our collective consciousness – more than 20 percent of each Jewish community died solely as a result of the conditions in the ghetto. These two ghettos, therefore, have come to represent the paradigm for the conditions under which Jews in Eastern Europe lived under Nazi rule.[2]

However, this paradigm does not tell the full story – not even as a generalization. Whereas most Polish Jews may have been forced into ghettos by the end of 1941 (exact statistical research has yet to be done), it is not clear that a ghetto was created for most communities. Similarly, there was a wide range of physical

2 For example, see Leni Yahil's sub-chapter, "The Ghetto," where these two ghettos serve as the paradigm for Poland; Yahil, *The Holocaust*, pp. 164–171.

conditions forced upon the Jews both within ghettos and outside them. In the Lublin District, most Jews and most communities had not experienced full-fledged ghettoization by the end of 1941, and, in most communities, conditions did not approach those of Warsaw and Lodz, which had produced such enormously high death rates. In fact, the term ghetto seems to fit only a very small number of communities, perhaps four, in the Lublin District in the first half of 1941 – Lublin, Opole-Lubelski, Piaski, and Zamość. Only Piaski was enclosed with a fence, and, collectively, these four places housed barely 20 percent of the district's Jews. A few additional ghettos were established later in 1941 and in 1942, as part of the process of murdering the Jews, but earlier ghettos were generally not part of the anti-Jewish policies here.[3]

Historians have noted that the formation of ghettos in occupied Poland was a decentralized process. Although the idea of ghettos was indeed a topic of discussion among German officials (at least as early as November 1938),[4] there was no policy decision in the Reich, in the GG, or even on the district level in Lublin to confine the Jews to ghettos. Thus, there was no central order to create ghettos in the GG and no guidelines for their regimen. The Warsaw and Kraków ghettos were surrounded by walls; the Lublin ghetto was a defined, unfenced area of streets that could not house all of Lublin's Jews even by brutal Nazi housing standards; and the Jews of Zamość continued to live alongside Poles even in their defined neighborhood. As Raul Hilberg notes, "[t]he initiative [for ghetto formation] in each city and town was taken by the competent Kreishauptmann or Stadthauptmann, and in the case of major ghettos only, by a Gouverneur or by Frank

3 This has been confirmed by two new encyclopedias of the ghettos, which show that there were considerably fewer ghettos in the Lublin District than elsewhere in the GG in 1940–1941. See Guy Miron and Shlomit Shulhani, eds., *The Yad Vashem Encyclopedia of the Ghettos in the Holocaust* (Jerusalem: Yad Vashem, 2009); Martin Dean, ed., *The United States Holocaust Memorial Museum Encyclopedia of Camps and Ghettos, 1933–1945, Volume II, Ghettos in German-Occupied Eastern Europe* (Bloomington and Indianapolis: Indiana University Press with the United States Holocaust Memorial Museum, 2012).

4 See "Stenographic Report of the Meeting on the Jewish Question held under the Chairmanship of Field Marshal Göring in the Reich Air Ministry at 11 A.M. on November 12, 1938," Nuremberg Document PS-1816.

himself."[5] Bogdan Musial's research on the civilian administration in the Lublin District confirms this.[6] However, Hilberg's assertion that the ghetto formation process in the GG was largely completed by the end of 1941 is not entirely accurate, certainly in the Lublin District, unless he meant that the few ghettos that were to be created had already been created. This inaccuracy regarding the widespread character of ghettoization by the end of 1941 is both statistical and conceptual, especially in the Lublin District.

Ghettoization was influenced by different factors before and after "Operation Barbarossa" was underway. After the summer of 1941, ghettos and other new restrictions on Jews in the Lublin District were directly related to the "Final Solution" (see Chapter 6). Given this critical turning point in Nazi policy toward the Jews in general, in the GG, and in the Lublin District in particular, one subject that will be examined in this chapter is the ghettoization policy between the autumn of 1940 and the summer of 1941.

During this period German officials in the GG and in Lublin were caught between two policy trends regarding Jews. On the one hand, there was the general policy of concentrating Jews for security reasons (the Jews were officially dangerous), control, and as a preparation for future measures against them. On the other hand, some German officials pursued a policy of dispersing Jews from German areas, or from areas intended for some level of Germanization, for security or "aesthetic" reasons. Much of this dispersal was directed toward the smaller communities in the Lublin District. These contradictory trends in anti-Jewish policy led to what can best be described as ad hoc policy decisions designed to resolve

5 Hilberg, *Destruction*, p. 222. See also Christopher R. Browning, "Nazi Ghettoization Policy in Poland, 1939–41," *Central European History*, XIX (1986), p. 345. For a thorough discussion of the beginning of such discussions in Nazi Germany, see Dan Michman, *The Emergence of Jewish Ghettos during the Holocaust* (Cambridge: Cambridge University Press and Yad Vashem, 2011), pp. 31–44. For a good general discussion of ghettoization, see Yisrael Gutman, "Ghetto," in *Encyclopedia of the Holocaust* (London and New York: Macmillan and Yad Vashem, 1990), vol. 2, pp. 579–582.

6 Musial, *Zivilverwaltung*, pp. 130–141.

specific problems as they arose.[7] Thus, "resettlements" of Jews and ghettoization were closely connected in this period.

The relocations/resettlements into the Lublin District from October 1940 through June 1941 were linked to "cleansing" "German" areas of Jews. Jewish POWs were sent from POW camps in East Prussia and the Warthegau to camps in the Lublin District, while Jewish civilians from Mława and Konin in the German-annexed areas (Warthegau and Bezirk Zichenau), from Kraków (destined to become a German city), and from Vienna were resettled among the Jews of the Lublin District. More than 23,500 Jews were "resettled" into the Lublin District during this half-year period.[8] At the same time, some 15,000 Jews were relocated out of municipal Lublin and dispersed among many small communities, while 34,000 of the remaining Jews in Lublin were ordered into a ghetto (more than 2,000 continued to live outside the ghetto). Similarly, thousands of Jews from other communities (e.g., Biała-Podlaska, Biłgoraj, Izbica, Kazimierz Dolny, Kraśnik, Zamość) were relocated, while most of the remaining Jews of Zamość were forced into a ghetto in an impoverished part of the city in April 1941. Not all those forced into ghettos found themselves evicted from their homes. Still, even the lives of those whose homes were within the ghetto boundaries were disrupted by the arrival of new, unexpected roommates. Thus, a conservative estimate of the number of Jews in the Lublin District who were people newly uprooted from their homes by the Nazis during this half-year period would be 84,000, or more than one-fourth of the district's known Jewish residents.

The above numbers do not take into account those Jews who moved from place to place on their own accord (and under great danger). If the constant movement of individual people into and

7 See, for example, Pohl, *Judenpolitik*, p. 87. The deportations were reported outside Poland as well. The Polish government-in-exile speculated that the new deportations to the Lublin District represented a revival of the "Reservation" idea. See, for example, Simon Segal, *The New Order in Poland* (New York: Alfred A. Knopf, 1942), pp. 61–63; Jon Evans, *The Nazi New Order in Poland* (London: Victor Gollancz, 1941), pp. 150–151.

8 Musial, *Zivilverwaltung*, pp. 157–159, gives lower estimates — 23,000 in all for 1940–1941. However, he adds an estimate of 10,000 unregistered refugees, which would bring his estimate for the two years in line with the statistics herein. See also Pohl, *Judenpolitik*, p. 53.

within the district could be quantified, it would add many thousands to the above estimate and raise the proportion of newly uprooted Jews in the district to more than one-third.

Table 5.1: Overview of Population Movements in the Lublin District, October 1940–June 1941

A. Resettlements into District		**B. Resettlements within District**		**C. Ghettos**	
Kraków	9,000	Lublin	15,000	Lublin	34,000
Mława	3,000–3,140	Kraśnik	2,200	Zamość	7,000
Kalisz	245	Kazimierz	500	Piaski	5,000
Konin	3,141	Zamość	650	Opole	7,500
Vienna	3,112	Biała-Podlaska	1,000		
Częstochowa	78	Others	2,450		
POWs	4,928				
Sub-total	23,504–23,644	Sub-total	21,800	Sub-total	53,500
Total	98,804–98,944	(including up to 15,000 in their own homes, e.g., in Zamość)			

The above "cleansing" operations clogged the roads and hampered Wehrmacht preparations for "Barbarossa." On the grounds that troop movements and Wehrmacht needs took precedence, and in response to Wehrmacht pressure to free up space, Krüger, on March 25, 1941, ordered a temporary halt to all relocations.[9] By the time "resettlements" were restarted in the latter part of 1941, they were resettlements of a radically different nature – now they were linked to the "Final Solution."

"Resettlements" were the connecting thread in these inconsistent and contradictory policies. Whereas the "resettlement" operations into the Lublin District, within the district, and toward ghettoization in the district during this period may not have been

9 Excerpts from a meeting between Krüger and Frank, March 25, 1941, *Diensttagebuch*, pp. 336–338. See also Browning, *Origins*, pp. 136–137.

Deportation, Kraśnik, probably February 1941, Yad Vashem Photo Archive, 6470/5

linked in a causal or policy sense, their circumstantial connection spoke volumes to the Jews who experienced or witnessed these massive relocations simultaneously. For the Jews this was a period of renewed upheaval and crisis.

"Resettlements"

On January 8, 1941, Reinhard Heydrich spelled out his population movement plans for the next four months – 831,000 people from western Poland would be resettled into the GG in order to make room for 200,000 *Volksdeutsche*. Space would also be cleared for the Wehrmacht. The first stage of these resettlements into the GG should be completed by May 1, and would include 248,500 Poles, of whom 10,000 would be assigned to the Wehrmacht as laborers to prepare camps and training areas. In addition, 10,000 Viennese Jews would be deported to the GG. Frank told Bühler and Krüger that he favored this massive relocation because Hitler had told him in November that it had to be completed during the war.[10]

10 Westerkamp memo on January 8, 1941 meeting at the RSHA, Friedrich, ed.,

Bühler quickly informed the German district governors, county chiefs, and mayors that the "evacuations" would begin on February 1, at a rate of two trains daily, each carrying 2,000 people. He also assigned responsibilities and addressed the issues of housing, provisions, and labor as follows. The county chiefs and mayors were responsible for all logistics within their areas of jurisdiction. Deportees were to be housed in existing quarters, and barracks (for 300 people each) could be ordered from the BuF in Kraków. Polish crews should be on hand to clean up. The governors would receive schedules a week in advance; they should report on each arriving train and submit a full report by May 1. Transports would be arriving from Lodz, Soldau (Działdowo), Gotenhafen (Gdynia), Katowice, and Vienna. Each train was being provisioned for fourteen days at its embarkation point, but kitchens should be set up for the first meals at the destination. Bühler added that the GG had been promised that the deportees would be permitted to bring winter clothing.

The able-bodied should be put to work. The deportees would each be given 40 złoty. Bühler urged the civilian authorities to try to cooperate with the police in organizing and settling the deportees – a request not easily met, given the ongoing friction between the civilian authorities and the police and SS. Jewish deportees were to be kept separate from the Poles and would be dealt with by the Jewish aid committees. The Polish Red Cross was to be kept away from the deportees as much as possible, and the local German officials would determine where to settle these people, and whether to settle Poles among Ukrainians.[11]

Polen, pp. 481–484; "Protokoll der Regierungssitzung in Krakau vom 15.1.1941," meeting among Frank, Krüger, Bühler, and other senior GG officials regarding deportations of Poles and Jews into the GG. Krüger reported on the January 8 meeting at the RSHA in which he had participated and at which Heydrich had talked about these resettlements, ibid., pp. 495–506. Excerpts of the minutes can be found in *Faschismus*, pp. 60–61; *Eksterminacja*, pp. 58–59 (from Frank's *Diensttagebuch*, 1941, I, pp. 1–3); Aly, *Final Solution*, pp. 137–139; Browning, *Origins*, pp. 99–100.

11 Bühler to District Governors and Kreis and Stadthauptleute, regarding "Evakuierung von Polen und Juden ab 1.II.1941," January 17, 1941, WAPL, GDL 153 & 892 (copy in YVA, O.51/211; JM/10,455). See also Berenstein, "Deportations," pp. 56–57.

The Lublin civilian authorities organized quickly. On February 5, Türk informed Dr. Ludwig Losacker, then Zörner's chief of staff, that the BuF and the county authorities had already made all necessary preparations. The housing of the incoming deportees had been determined; arrangements had been made with the Labor Department for the disposition of forced-laborers from among the deportees; and contact with the police (who were not yet prepared) had been established. The county BuF officials had met the day before to discuss technical details regarding receiving, provisioning, and dividing the deportees, and the necessary barracks had been ordered. Türk had also ordered that the Polish deportees not be settled among Ukrainians in the Lublin District, where such mixing was problematic.[12]

This round of deportations from western Poland had actually begun even before Heydrich's January 8 presentation of his plan. On December 10, 1940, Dr. Heinecke of the BuF in Lublin informed the Lublin Labor Department of the imminent "*Litauen-Aktion*" (i.e., of "Litvak" Jews), in which 3,000 Jews from Mława would be divided equally among Biała-Podlaska, Lubartów, and Łuków, on December 12, 13, and 14, respectively. These Jews were ordered to report to a schoolyard early in the morning on December 6, were loaded onto trucks amidst beatings, and taken to the Działdowo transit camp near the edge of the town. After several days there, under very brutal conditions, they were sent by freight train to the Lublin District. Many took ill because of the harsh conditions in the transit camp and on the train, and dozens (some reports say hundreds) died within weeks. Rabbi Yehiel Moshe Segalowitz, the town rabbi since 1892, took ill on the trip, and soon died in the Lublin Jewish hospital. Others fled – some to localities in the Lublin District where they had acquaintances, and some back to Mława.[13]

12 Türk to Losacker, February 5, 1941, in response to Losacker's February 3 memo to Abteilung Innere Verwaltung, both letters in WAPL, GDL 153 (copies in YVA, O.51/211).

13 Heinecke, BuF Lublin to Labor Department Lublin, December 10, 1940, WAPL, GDL 891 (copy in YVA, JM/2700, 10,458); unsigned testimony on Mława and Konin in Oneg Shabbat archive, YVA, M.10.AR.1/674 (and JM/3489); Avraham Wein, ed., *Pinkas Hakehillot: Encyclopedia of Jewish Communities, Poland,*

At the same time the Wehrmacht rid itself of nearly 5,000 Polish Jewish POWs. They were transferred to the Lublin District, variously to the authority of the SS, the civilian labor departments, and the local Wehrmacht, between October 1940 and January 1941. Eight hundred of a promised 1,550 POWs were sent to Biała-Podlaska from Stalag IIB, Hammerstein, on October 23, 1940, to be utilized as forced-laborers by the Wehrmacht and by the civilian Labor Department. Jewish POWs from Stalag VIIIA, Görlitz (Zgorzelec today), were to be sent to Hrubieszów after completion of the fruit harvest. Most of these "resettled" POWs were destined to spend the following months at hard labor, constructing bases, airfields, and other military installations for the Wehrmacht in preparation for "Operation Barbarossa." An additional 793 POWs arrived during the following weeks: 200 reached Biała-Podlaska on November 11; 194 reached Łuków on November 17, for labor with the Luftwaffe construction unit in Podladów; and 399 reached Ryki in November and December 1940.

As it turned out, some 250 of the first group were cripples who were unable to work.[14] For the local labor departments this was a double problem: first, it meant that they were short-handed; and second, it meant that the Lublin civilian authorities now had 250 "useless" Jews to feed and house. Since these POWs were all soldiers

Volume IV: *Warsaw and Its Region* (Jerusalem: Yad Vashem, 1989), p. 284. *Pinkas Hakehillot* gives the rabbi's first name as Yitzhak, but other sources indicate that it was Yehiel. The exact number of deportees to the Lublin District from Mława on these three transports is not entirely clear. The transport lists received by the Jewish communities from the trains indicate that either 3,000 or 3,140 arrived in the Lublin District. See WAPL, RZ 169 and GDL 897, 898. Götz Aly, basing himself on the embarkation lists at the train station in Lodz, compiled by the Lodz Umwandererzentralstelle (Central Resettlement Office), believes that 3,259 were deported. In light of the very difficult conditions under which the Jews were deported, it is quite possible that 3,259 left, yet only 3,140 arrived. See Aly, *Final Solution*, pp. 117, 130, n. 40–42.

14 Dr. Heinecke, BuF Lublin to Abteilung Arbeit, Lublin, October 24, December 10, and December 14, 1940; Arbeitsamt Biała-Podlaska to Abteilung Arbeit, Lublin, October 28, November 11, and November 15, 1940; Abteilung Arbeit, Lublin to BuF Lublin, November 5, 1940; Abteilung Arbeit of GG to Abteilung Arbeit, Lublin, November 15, 1940; Arbeitsamt Łuków to BuF Lublin, November 26, 1940, all in WAPL, GDL 891 (copies in YVA, JM/2700).

whose homes were now in Soviet territory, they could also not be sent home. Yet neither the Wehrmacht nor the civilians wanted to be saddled with such a burden. The civilian authorities found a simple solution to the problem of caring for the basic needs of these POWs – the local Jewish aid committees would be given full responsibility for their welfare, thereby relieving the Germans of any obligation.[15]

During the first half of December, approximately 500 POWs were brought to Lublin and incarcerated in the POW camp at Lipowa 7. They were followed later that month and in January by 2,835 POWs who were sent from seven POW camps to Lipowa 7. These prisoners of war joined the POWs who had been in the camp since earlier in 1940, and were put to work at forced labor within the camp and outside it. This included the construction of what became the Majdanek camp (see Chapter 4).[16]

"Cleansing" the Reich of Jews included the deportation of Jews from Vienna to the GG. Beginning in February 1941, some 5,000 Jews were deported from Vienna to the Kielce area, and 3,112, in three transports, to the Lublin District. The overall coordination of the deportations was handled from Eichmann's office; it passed on instructions to the Sipo office in Vienna, which in turn dealt with the details on the ground. All Sipo outposts that needed to know of a deportation were informed shortly before it commenced.[17]

15 Abteilung Arbeit of GG to Abteilung Arbeit, Lublin, November 15, 1940, and Jache, Abteilung Arbeit, Lublin, to Abteilung Arbeit of GG, November 20, 1940, WAPL, GDL 891 (copy in YVA, JM/2700).

16 Lists of POWs sent to the Lipowa 7 camp, WAPL, GDL 891 and 901 (copies in YVA, JM/10454, 10,458, and 10670–10672). Copies of some of the lists can also be found in the Jewish Historical Institute in Warsaw. The camps from which the POWs were sent were: Stalags VIA, VIIA, IVB, IVA, Edelbach, XIIIA, XIA (Altengrabow), and Görlitz. See also the January 6, 1941 report on Lipowa 7 in the Oneg Shabbat archive, "Stan ludzi skoszanowych w Obozie," YVA, JM/217/3. The report indicated that there were 518 Jewish POWs in the camp in December 1940, along with fifteen civilian Jews and 192 Polish laborers. See also Benjamin Meirtchak, *Jewish Prisoners-of-War Murdered by Germans in the Lublin District 1939–1943* (Tel Aviv: Association of Jewish Veterans of Polish Armies in Israel, 1996), p. 6. His statistics are somewhat different, but he seems not to have had access to all the relevant Polish archival sources.

17 See, for example, *SS-Gruppenführer* Ernst Kaltenbrunner's February 12, 1941

The first deportation to the Lublin District left Vienna on February 15, 1941, with 1,000 people. Apparently at least eight died on the way, as 1,000 names were on the embarkation list, but only 992 were on the debarkation list. They were housed in Opole-Lubelski.[18] This was followed by a second deportation, on February 26, with 1,034 Jews from Vienna to Opole. At least thirteen died in transit.[19] The third transport went to Modliborzyce on March 5, bearing 1,035 Jews. Here, too, there seems to have been a number who died, as there is a discrepancy of more than 100 people between the embarkation list and the debarkation list (929 vs. 1,035).[20]

memo of a meeting that day regarding general guidelines for "Evakuierung der Juden aus Wien in das Generalgouvernement," YVA, O.30/84, and the telegram from Eichmann's office to all Stapostellen regarding the upcoming "evacuation" of Viennese Jews to the GG, sent February 13, 1941, two days in advance of the first deportation, YVA, TR.3/1634.

18 There are two lists of the deportees on this first transport. One is a non-alphabetical embarkation list bearing 1,000 names: "1. Transport von 1000 Juden am 15.2.1941," WAPL, RZ 168 (copies in YVA, JM/1476). Fourteen names are crossed off from this list and replaced by fourteen others written in following the number 1,000. It is not clear whether the crossed-out names were people removed from the transport, or people who died. The second is an alphabetical list containing 992 names – "Alle evakuiert aus Wien am 15-II-41 alle Wohnhaft in Opole" – and was composed by the Opole Judenrat; WAPL, GDL 892. See also Yad Vashem's research project: "Transports to Extinction: Shoah Deportations Database," http://db.yadvashem.org/deportation/transportDetails.html?language=en&itemId=6983149

19 The embarkation list contains 1,002 names, of whom thirteen died, and thirteen more were crossed off the list and replaced by thirteen names added after the number 1,002: "3. Transport mit 1000 Juden am 26.2.1941," WAPL, GDL 892. A non-alphabetical debarkation list contains 1,023 names – "Alle evakuiert aus Wien am 26-II-41 alle Wohnhaft in Opole"; WAPL, GDL 892. Yet the report by the deportee put in charge of the Jews on the second train discusses 1,034 Jews on the train: Transportleiters Wien to Alten, February 26, 1941, WAPL, RZ 168 and GDL 892 (copies in *Faschismus*, pp. 62–63, and *Eksterminacja*, p. 62). See also "Transports to Extinction," http://db.yadvashem.org/deportation/transportDetails.html?language=en&itemId=6991401.

20 See the non-alphabetical embarkation list: "4. Transport mit 1000 Juden am 5-3-41," WAPL, GDL 892. This list has 929 names, eight of which are crossed out. A second embarkation list in the Lublin Judenrat's possession contains 1,035 names; WAPL, RZ 168. The exact number of Viennese Jews deported to the Lublin District in these three transports is not completely clear, but it seems that Janina Kielboń's estimate of 2,990 is slightly low. See Kielboń, *Migracja*, p. 139. See also Alfred Gottwaldt and Diana Schulle, *Die "Judendeportationen" aus*

Primarily Viennese Jews incapable of working were deported to Lublin at this time; the able-bodied were kept for labor in the Reich for now. The available demographic information on the deportees from these three trains, along with the report by the deportee put in charge of the Jews on the second train, composed for Marek Alten (in his capacity as the district's JSS director) show the age of these deportees. Of the 1,034 Jews on the second train, 60 percent were women, and most were over the age of sixty.[21] Apparently, "cleansing" the Reich of Jews at this time meant first and foremost disposing of "useless" mouths.

These Jews did not fare well in these difficult transports, as both Jewish and German observers agreed. Many of those who survived the trip arrived ragged, frozen, and starved, much the same as the deportees from Stettin a year earlier. They had to be housed in community buildings, as there was nowhere else available in the overcrowded Jewish quarter. Alten reported this to the JSS presidium as part of his aid request for the deportees. The conditions for these deportees were so bad — but the payoffs so lucrative — that *Landkommissar* Horst Goede in Opole-Lubelski approved letting some of the Viennese deportees return home. The clandestine return of 200 Jews to Vienna over the course of the spring and summer, half of them from Opole-Lubelski, prompted a complaint from the Zentralstelle für jüdische Auswanderung in Vienna to Zörner. The returning Jews would be sent back.[22]

dem Deutschen Reich 1941–1945 (Wiesbaden: Marix Verlag, 2005), pp. 46–49, who say that the first Vienna deportation included 996 Jews, the second 1,049, and the third 981–999; Abt. V, *Kreishauptmann* Pulawy, to BuF Lublin, July 7, 1941, reporting on the resettlement of 10,330 Poles in twenty-four localities in the county in June, and 2,004 Jews in Opole, WAPL, GDL 153. These 2,004 Jews were likely to have been those who found housing in Opole in this period, rather than all the Jewish refugees in the town. A fourth, small group of forty-three Jews arrived in the village of Pysznica on April 1. See also "Transports to Extinction," http://db.yadvashem.org/deportation/transportDetails.html?language=en&itemId=6996699.

21 Transportleiters Wien to Alten, February 26, 1941, WAPL, RZ 168 and GDL 892 (copies in *Faschismus*, pp. 62–63, and *Eksterminacja*, p. 62).

22 Alten to JSS Presidium, February 28, 1941, YVA, JM/1574–1575; Zentralstelle für jüdische Auswanderung, Vienna to Governor, Lublin District, September 18, 1941, WAPL, GDL 892 (copies in YVA, O.53/84).

Immediately on the heels of the Vienna deportations, 3,141 Jews from Konin and environs were deported to the Lublin District in three transports, on March 10, 12, and 13, 1941, each bearing approximately 1,000 Jews. Most of these Jews had been conscripted for forced labor, and they were now collected in a camp in the town of Konin before being transported to the Lublin District via Lodz. They were sent to Izbica – which was to become a major dumping ground for deported Jews – Józefów Biłgorajski, and several other towns. Most of the Konin Jews who arrived in Józefów in March 1941 were shot by Reserve Police Battalion 101 on July 14, 1942, along with most of the other Jewish inhabitants of the town.[23]

Table 5.2:
Deportations from Outside GG, October 1940–June 1941

Dates	From	To	Numbers
Dec. 1940	Mława and area	Lublin District	3,000
Dec. 12	"	Biała-Podlaska	1,000
Dec. 13	"	Lubartów	1,000
Dec. 14–19	"	Łuków	1,000
Dec. 16	"	Wisznice	n.a.
Dec.	"	Kamionka	100
Dec.	"	Międzyrzec, Michów	n.a.

23 List of 1,001 Jews deported from Konin to Izbica, March 10, 1941, WAPL, RZ 169 and GDL 897, 898 (copy in YVA, JM/10454); "Judenaussiedlung Transport Nr. 15/41 10-3-1941, Konin," the deportee list signed by the commandant of Lager Flottwellstrasse 4, the transit camp from whence they departed, WAPL, GDL 897–898 (copy in YVA, JM/1477); list of 1,000 Jews sent from Konin to Izbica, March 12, 1941, WAPL, RZ 169 and GDL 897, 898 (copy in YVA, JM/10454). A summation list of Konin deportees compiled by the JSS in the Lublin District based on Judenrat reports from each place includes 3,141 Jews; WAPL, RZ 169 and GDL 897. See also Avraham Obarzonek testimony, YVA, M.1.E/1407; Gorzków Judenrat to Alten, March 28, 1941, requesting aid in order to deal with the 500 refugees from many places, including Konin, and fifty local poor families in this very small town, YVA, JM/1574; undated and unsigned report on Konin and Mlawa Jews who were deported to Ostrowiec and Józefów, YVA, M.10.AR.1/674 (& JM/3489).

Dates	From	To	Numbers
Dec.	"	Czemierniki	n.a.
Jan. 1941	"	Sosnowica	40
Dec. 1940	Blaszki (Kalisz)	Konstantynów	245
Mar. 10–13, 1941	Konin county	Lublin, Józefów, Izbica	3,141
Feb.–April 1941	Vienna	Lublin District	3,112
Feb. 15	"	Opole-Lubelski	1,000
Feb. 26	"	Opole-Lubelski	1,034
Mar. 7	"	Modliborzyce	1,035
April 1	"	Pysznica	43
May 1941	Częstochowa	Zamość	78
Oct. 1940–Jan. 1941	POWs	Lublin District	4,928
Oct. 23	"	Biała-Podlaska	800
Nov. 8	"	"	200
Oct.–Dec.	"	Ryki	399
Nov. 17	"	Łuków	194
Dec.	"	Lublin-Lipowa 7	500
Jan. 1941	"	"	2,835

The table above summarizes the deportations of approximately 14,500 Jews from outside the GG (except for the small Częstochowa deportation, which was within the GG) to the Lublin District during this period.

Within the GG deportations to the Lublin District during this period came primarily from Kraków, at Frank's initiative. The motivation was much the same as for the deportations from Austria and the Warthegau – to "cleanse" German territories of Jews. Frank sought to Germanize his capital, and the first evictions toward achieving this goal of a *Judenfrei* Kraków took place in May 1940. Some 32,000 Jews had been forced to leave the city between April and September 1940.[24] Between November 1940 and April

24 Hilberg, *Destruction*, p. 210; Avraham Wein and Aharon Weiss, eds., *Pinkas*

1941, more than 9,000 Jews were deported to the Lublin District in two waves: November 29—December 14, 1940; and January 24—April 2, 1941.[25] As will be shown below, the last wave of these expulsions from Kraków was closely connected to ghettoization and was influenced by military considerations.

Many of these deportations did not follow the format of those from outside the GG – far fewer than 1,000 Jews were deported in most instances, and the guards on the trains were often taken from the Sonderdienst, which was ostensibly under German civilian control. This reflects the extent to which the SS was kept outside the planning circle of these expulsions and ghettoizations. As with the Vienna deportations, the train ride was exceedingly long and the numbers expected did not always match the numbers that actually arrived. The Jews were received at a receiving station, cared for by the Judenrat, and housed temporarily until permanent housing could be arranged. Many deportees had to make at least one additional trip, by wagon, sled, or foot, before their wanderings temporarily ceased. For example, a train with 265 Kraków Jews reached Lublin at 11 A.M. on December 10. The German civilian authorities sent 120 each to Piaski and Biskupice, and the remaining twenty-five to Trawniki.[26] For some small towns the burden became particularly heavy, as in the cases of Biskupice and Podedwórze, where the number of refugees exceeded the number of local Jews.[27]

Hakehillot: Encyclopedia of Jewish Communities, Poland, Volume 3: *Western Galicia and Silesia* (Hebrew) (Jerusalem: Yad Vashem, 1984). See also Browning, *Origins*, pp. 131–135.

25 WAPL, GDL 891, contains lists of names of Kraków Jews deported to the Lublin District, November 29—December 9, 1940; WAPL, GDL 892 (copy in YVA, JM/10,455) contains lists of names of Kraków Jews deported to the Lublin District, January 24—April 2, 1941. See also Kilebon, *Migracja*, p. 139, whose estimate for the number of Kraków Jews deported to the Lublin District – 5,436 – is considerably and inexplicably lower. See also Heinecke, BuF Lublin to Labor Department, Lublin, December 10, 1940, listing the Kraków deportations to the Lublin District for November 29—December 9, 1940, and the seven central destinations, WAPL, GDL 891 (copy in YVA, JM/2700).

26 Ziegenmeyer to BuF Lublin, December 13, 1940, WAPL, GDL 891.

27 See, for example, P. Zloto, Podedwórze Judenrat (part of Opole Kehillah) to Lublin Judenrat, April 12, 1941, asking for help to deal with the 600 deportees from Kraków in the town, YVA, JM/1574; WAPL, Rada Żydowska w Biskupicach

Table 5.3: Deportations to Lublin District from Kraków, November 1940—April 1941[28]

Dates	From	To	Numbers
Dec. 1940	Mława and area	Lublin District	3,000
Nov. 12, 1940–Mar. 22, 1941	Kraków	Lublin district	9,000–10,000
Nov. 12	"	Zaklików	200
Nov. 12	"	Radomyśl	384
Nov. 16	"	Grabowiec	40
Nov. 16	"	Uchanie	90
Nov. 16	"	Dubienka	90
Nov. 16	"	Belz	50
Nov. 29	"	Międzyrzec	1,000
Dec. 9	"	Lublin	265
Dec. 10	"	Trawniki	51
Dec. 13	"	Chełm	2,000
Dec. 14	"	Rejowiec	140
Dec. 14	"	Sawin	130
Dec. 14	"	Uhrusk	75
Dec.	"	Świerże	80
Dec.	"	Włodawa	500

6, which gives details of Jewish refugees from Kraków in Biskupice and Trawniki (copy in YVA, JM/3695).

28 Sources for Tables 5.2 and 5.3 include: WAPL, GDL 891, 892 897, 898, 901, RZ 168, 169; YVA, JM/1476, 1477, 1574, 1575, 2700, 10454, 10455, 10458, 10670–10672, and testimonies of former POWs Roman Fischer, O.3/2124, Samuel Gruber, M.1.E/925 and O.16/610*, Josef Birger-Ezrahi, O.3/447, O.3/6774, and M.49.E/2791, and others; Berenstein, "Deportations"; *idem*, "Martyrologia." Kielboń, *Migracja*, pp. 137–140, refers to 3,436 Jews deported from Kraków to Lublin, November 29, 1940—April 2, 1941, and an additional 2,000 to Hrubieszów in November 1941. She cites thirty-seven deportations with dates and numbers, based largely on a variety of documents in WAPL and the Bühler trial. She also refers to 2,990 deported from Vienna in 1941. However, the numbers above, from GDL 892, indicate a total of 3,069 or 3,112 (depending on where the April 1 deportation to Pysznica originated). In general, Kielboń's sources seem incomplete, especially for Kraków.

Dates	From	To	Numbers
Dec. 10	"	Biskupice	120
Dec.	"	Bychawa	n.a.
Dec.	"	Głusk	200
Dec. 10	"	Piaski	120
Dec.	"	Puchaczów	51
Jan. 24 & 31	"	Lublin	n.a.
Feb. 3	"	Chełm	n.a.
Feb. 4	"	Rejowiec	71
Feb.	"	Bełżyce	360
Feb. 12 & 18	"	Lublin	n.a.
Feb. 13 & 19	"	Biskupice	43
Feb. 25 & 27	"	Lublin	n.a.
Feb. 26 & 28	"	Bychawa	101
Feb.	"	Piotrowice	107
Mar. 4	"	Bychawa	145
Mar. 5	"	Bełżyce	161
Mar. 7 & 8	"	Chodel	203
Mar. 10–19	"	Biała-Podlaska	1,000
Mar. 22	Biała (deportees)	Podedwórze-Opole	600
Mar. 16	Kraków	Piszczac	650
Mar. 16	"	Wisznice	n.a.
Mar. 20	"	Koden	105
Mar.–April	"	Siedliszcze	n.a.
Mar. 20–April 2	"	Międzyrzec; Parczew	438–1,000

Table 5.3 above shows the deportations from Kraków to the Lublin District during the half-year period in question. More than 9,000 Jews arrived on more than forty transports and were dispersed over more than thirty localities. It should be borne in mind that these 9,000 Jews arrived at the same time as the large influx of Jewish POWs, the Jews from Mława, Konin, and Vienna, and the Poles from the Warthegau. To all this must be added the deportations of

Elderly man and two children, Lublin ghetto, (summer) 1941, Yad Vashem Photo Archive, 4982/8

many thousands of Jews within the Lublin District, part of which was connected to the creation of the ghetto in Lublin.

Ghettos

"All night there was very heavy military traffic…I haven't seen such heavy traffic for a long time…People involved in studying political events are sure that something big will happen soon."[29] What Dr. Zygmunt Klukowski observed on January 15, 1941, was part of the Wehrmacht's preparations for the invasion of the Soviet Union. During the first months of 1941, large concentrations of German troops began to gather in the GG, and especially in the Lublin District. Klukowski recorded their intensive activity in his diary, including the laying and expanding of roads, building bridges

29 Klukowski, *Diary*, p. 132.

and airfields, etc. Parallel to this, on January 28, he noted German preparations for "new initiatives" regarding the Jews.[30]

The incoming German soldiers needed bases, living quarters, training spaces, and the like. The command staffs were based in the large cities, and a 25-kilometer swath along the Wisła and San rivers, along with the entire Bug River area and other parts of the Lublin District, were declared closed military areas. Whereas in April 1940 there were 400,000 German soldiers in the GG, on the eve of the invasion there were two million.[31]

The Wehrmacht's growing housing and office requirements conflicted with the civilian government's need to find space for the steady flow of deported Jews being brought into the Lublin District. As more Jews were deported to the Lublin District, there were ever fewer spaces available to house them. Thus, Wehrmacht housing and office requirements precluded bringing large numbers of additional Jews into the cities. Moreover, since Jews were considered a security risk, they could not be concentrated in large numbers near military installations (except for limited numbers of forced-laborers). The result was a contradictory anti-Jewish policy of simultaneous concentration and dispersion.

By the end of May 1941, a large part of the LV Army Corps, including infantry, artillery, and other units had bivouacked in the area south of Krasnystaw. *Kreishauptmann* Claus Volkmann attempted to meet the Wehrmacht's security and space needs in his county by evicting all 1,400 Jews from Krasnystaw to fifteen outlying small localities. Similar expulsions were undertaken in Kraśnik in February, Biłgoraj and Zamość in April, and elsewhere.[32]

Preparations for some sort of ghettoization in parts of the Lublin District began in January 1941. Parallel to the population movements into the district and the Wehrmacht build-up, the

30 Ibid., pp. 132–160 (quotation from p. 134).

31 Secret memo, Kipke to Westerkamp, March 12, 1941, WAPL, GDL 153; Madajczyk, *Okkupationspoltik*, p. 239; Pohl, *Judenpolitik*, pp. 86–87.

32 YVA, JM/5395; memo, Janów-Lubelski *Kreishauptmann* Asbach to BuF Lublin, February 11, 1941, regarding expulsions from Kraśnik, in Friedrich, ed., *Polen*, pp. 527–528; Musial, *Zivilverwaltung*, pp. 135–136; Berenstein, "Deportations," pp. 56, 68–69.

district's Housing Department head, Dr. Walter Bausenhardt, met with the Lublin Judenrat's five-man presidium on or before January 11, 1941, to discuss a "voluntary" transfer of Jewish population out of Lublin as part of the preparations for confining the remaining Jews in Lublin into a ghetto. It should be noted that the space to be allotted for the ghetto, in the old Jewish quarter, was in no way large enough to house all the Jews.[33]

On January 17, Zörner "recommended" that his county chiefs and mayors concentrate Jews into fewer communities in order to eliminate them from trade and to better control smuggling.[34] He followed this, on February 15, with a new "*Aufenthaltsbeschränkung*" for the district's Jews: as of July 1, no Jew could leave the Jewish quarter without special permission. Violators would be punished with three months in prison and a 1,000 złoty fine. On June 27, Zörner extended the deadline to October 1.[35]

The Lublin governor's behavior in this respect is a bit puzzling. On the one hand, it can be understood as being part of the larger picture of ghettoization and limitations on the Jews in concert with security interests and Wehrmacht needs. On the other hand, the delay in implementing the limit on the Jews' freedom of movement – from February 15 to July 1, and then to October 1 – seems to run counter to such interests. If the order were implemented as decreed, then Jews would not have been limited to the Jewish quarters until after the invasion of the USSR was underway. Moreover, the threatened punishment for violating the decree was very mild by Nazi standards. Ghettoization, apparently, was not yet urgent.

In March-April 1941, there was a flurry of ghettoization in the GG's district capitals and several other larger cities and towns. The timing was connected to the Wehrmacht's security and space considerations. Frank issued a ghettoization decree for Kraków on March 3, after most of the Jewish community there had already been expelled and more were about to be. In Lublin, Zörner decreed a ghetto on March 24, after 10,000 Jews had already been evicted from

33 Blumental, *Documents*, Protocol 1(62), January 11, 1941, p. 211.

34 Musial, *Zivilverwaltung*, p. 134.

35 Zörner, "Anordnung," June 27, 1941, WAPL, GDL 58 (copies in YVA, O.6/23d* and O.6/11b*); Musial, *Zivilverwaltung*, p. 134.

the city. Similarly, ghettos were set up in Radom (March 29), Kielce (March 31), Częstochowa (April 9), and Zamość (early April). In each case, in contrast to the earlier ghettoization in Warsaw, the Jewish population had been reduced by expulsion prior to the ghettoization order. The close timing and similarities of these ghettoizations reflect central planning, also in contrast to prior practice.[36] It would seem that the lack of urgency evident in Zörner's orders had been superseded, resulting in this rash of ghetto planning.

The same security and Wehrmacht considerations that had led to the internal district expulsions of Jews and to ghettoization in the larger cities led the GG to pressure the authorities in Berlin to halt the deportations of Poles and Jews into the GG. On March 12, Dr. Kipke, head of the Lublin District's Interior Department, sent a secret memo to Eberhard Westerkamp, head of the GG's Interior Department, asking him to intervene with the authorities in Berlin to postpone all further incoming transports. The memo was prepared for Kipke by Türk, and it detailed the problems that had been revealed with the arrival of the first contingents of Polish and Jewish deportees. The plethora of closed military areas had made it impossible to deal with housing more deportees in addition to housing those within the district who needed to be resettled.[37] The result was that the deportations into the GG and the Lublin District were halted by March 16.[38]

At a GG meeting on March 25, Zörner related to the interconnections between the expulsion of 10,000 Jews from Lublin earlier that month and the ghettoization of the remaining Jews and making room for the Wehrmacht.[39] The basic plan was to remove the Jews from sensitive security areas by scattering them in non-military

36 Pohl, *Judenpolitik*, pp. 86–87, says Frank ordered the creation of ghettos in several large towns and cities in the GG during a February 25–26, 1941, GG meeting, but he gives no documentary source. The secondary source that he cites (Helge Grabitz and Wolfgang Scheffler, eds., *Letzte Spuren: Ghetto Warschau, SS-Arbeitslager Trawniki, Aktion Erntefest, Fotos und Dokumente über Opfer des Endlösungswahns im Spiegel der historischen Ereignisse* [Berlin: Edition Hentrich, 1988], p. 283) does not mention this meeting.

37 Secret memo, Kipke to Westerkamp, March 12, 1941, WAPL, GDL 153.

38 Aly, *Final Solution*, p. 144.

39 Excerpts from a meeting between Krüger and Frank, March 25, 1941,

areas or by confining them to ghettos, to have Poles in Lublin move into the vacated Jewish residences, and the Wehrmacht expropriate the Poles' homes.

The "voluntary relocation" from Lublin, which resulted in more than 15,000 Jews leaving the city for other localities in the district, began in the midst of the arrival of the deportees from Konin, which aggravated the chaos and suffering. The Lublin expulsions can be divided into two stages: the brutal deportation that took place on March 10–13, sandwiched around the Purim holiday (March 11); and the less brutal stage that began during the latter part of March and continued over several months. More than 10,000 Jews were relocated into more than 100 locations in the first stage. Police Battalion 306, which was then stationed in Lublin, was in charge of security. German and auxiliary police surrounded Jewish areas and ordered the Jews out within minutes for relocation.

Ida Glikstein recalls the sudden appearance of green-uniformed Germans (probably police) and black-uniformed Ukrainians with dogs at 6 A.M. on March 11, taking up positions at houses to be evacuated and ordering everyone out in 10 minutes with up to 25 kg. of baggage. There was panic – many of the men were laborers who had slept in the workshops that night, and now the women and children were to be expelled without them. "There were cries and wails...People laden with packages were chased like sheep from street to street...It seemed as though no one in the street was sane; not those chasing old people and children, and not the prey."[40] Moreover, the Lublin Judenrat did not always know where the Jews had been taken, and their arrival at their new destinations was not always coordinated.[41] On the receiving end, the communities were often ill-equipped to deal with such large numbers of refugees.[42]

Diensttagebuch, pp. 336–338. See also *Faschismus*, p. 64; *Eksterminacja*, p. 65; Pohl, *Judenpolitik*, pp. 86–87.

40 Ida Glikstein, in *Encyclopedia of the Jewish Diaspora*, pp. 689–692 (quotation from p. 689); *idem*, *Dos Buch*, pp. 391–392.

41 Alten, "Vermerk des Vorstandes der JSS in Krakow," March 12, 1941, *Faschismus*, pp. 120–121.

42 See, for example, the letter from Erich and Clare Silbermann, deportees from Stettin who were now in Bełżyce, to Margarethe Lachmund in Berlin, on March 16, 1941, reporting the sudden arrival of hundreds of refugees from Lublin

In order to prevent looting of the expelled Jews' homes – which the Germans themselves intended to exploit, of course – on March 11, *Stadthauptmann* Sauermann forbade entry into the cleared areas. Police were instructed to use arms against plunderers.[43] The heightened importance of Jewish affairs led Zörner to promote the Jewish Affairs office in the BuF to a *Referat* on March 12. One of its first tasks was to plan the concentration of Jews in the district. This office's new status also better equipped it to compete with Globocnik's *Judenreferent*.[44]

The Lublin Judenrat appointed a committee of seven of its members – Ajzyk Bursztyn, Urysz Cymerman, Dawid Dawidson, Abram Goldsobel, Jakub Kelner, Icek Levinson, and Józef Wajselfisz – to coordinate the relocations. The Lublin JSS also tried to place an official at each end of the expulsion. Marek Alten himself, as JSS head for the district, tried to follow the routes of the deportees and arrange aid for them at their destinations as needed. However, it was difficult to trace all the expulsion routes. Nevertheless, this attempt at coordination also gave the Lublin Judenrat influence over internal Jewish affairs in many places in the district.

The police confiscated the identification cards of the departing Jews, and each family unit was issued a five-day travel permit – "*Judenaussiedlung. Sonderaktion Lublin. Umzugsbescheinigung.*" This travel permit also served as an ID for those five days, until the authorities in the expelled Jews' new place of residence issued new identification papers. The family would submit the paper to the Judenrat at its new home, or to the Judenrat of the nearest organized *kehillah*. That Judenrat would pass the form on to the local Polish, Ukrainian, or German authority, who would stamp it and send all the stamped forms to the *Kreishauptmann*. After collecting all the forms from a particular group, the *Kreishauptmann* would return them to the BuF in Lublin.

The Judenrat set up a special registration office near its regular

in the town and the difficulties in caring for them; Rosenfeld and Luckner, *Lebenszeichen aus Piaski*, p. 146.

43 Sauermann order no. 197, March 11, 1941, YVA, O.53/84.

44 Zörner to Türk, March 12, 1941, and Türk to Kipke, March 13, WAPL, GDL 892.

offices for those who wanted to volunteer to relocate. Many of those who agreed to leave Lublin had to be cajoled by the Judenrat, which was operating under threats and pressure from the German civilian authorities and Police Battalion 306. It was often the refugees, who were least rooted in the city, who agreed to go. The Lublin Judenrat then contacted the receiving Judenräte via courier, telephone, or a personal visit in order to ask them to convince the new arrivals not to try to return to Lublin. The Germans' threats to the Judenrat were quite convincing.

In the second stage of the relocations, concentrated in late March and April but to continue through November 1941, the civilian authorities permitted the Jews who were relocating to take much of their belongings and to hire wagons and Polish drivers to transport them to their new locations. The Jews who volunteered to move could choose any destination within the district, as long as it was not in a sealed military area. Yet even with this relative openness on the part of the German authorities, the expulsion was traumatic.

The goal of the German civilian administration was to have an additional 15,000 Jews leave, in order to have only 20,000 Jews left in the proposed ghetto. Zörner decided to apply pressure – either people would volunteer to leave Lublin, or there would be a forced resettlement. The Judenrat relayed this pressure to the Jewish population, posting announcements on April 1 in German, Polish, and Yiddish, calling on all those who did not need to remain in Lublin for professional reasons to leave the city for other places in the district within the next few days. However, Zörner's goal was not met, as only a small number beyond 15,000 Jews "voluntarily" relocated out of Lublin in 1941, most of them in March.[45] As the expulsions progressed, the Wehrmacht occupied additional buildings

45 The signed and stamped travel permits can be found in WAPL, GDL 894, 895 (copies of many in YVA, JM/1478, 1479, 10456, 10457). Lists of names of Jews who voluntarily relocated in March, together with their destinations, can also be found in WAPL, RZ 151, 153 (copies in YVA, O.6/403; USHMMA, RG-15.101M). See also Blumental, *Documents*, Protocols 7, 8, 9 (68, 69, 70), March 16, 20, 21, 1941, pp. 221–225. See also memo by Dr. Ziegenhirt, March 31, 1941, on a meeting that day among Zörner, Bausenhardt, Schmidt, and himself on the "*Judenaussiedlung. Sonderaktion Lublin*," WAPL, GDL 892 (copies in YVA, O.51/10, O.53/84). The Judenrat's trilingual announcement can be found in YVA, JM/213/4.

in Lublin, yet they continued to ask for more. With regard to the Jews of Lublin, the expulsions cleared the way for creating the ghetto.

The Lublin Judenrat was not surprised by Zörner's March 24 ghetto order. Not only had the idea of a ghetto been discussed since January, but the *Stadthauptmann*'s office had already informed the Judenrat of the ghetto's boundaries by mid-March. At its March 16 meeting, the Judenrat discussed what to do regarding the shops, businesses, and homes of Judenrat members that would be outside the planned ghetto.[46]

These relocations caused severe dislocation and suffering for all the individuals and communities involved. In order to trace where all the Jews had gone, Alten traveled all over the district recording them and marking down the needs in each place. However, this job proved to be too big for one person, especially with the ghettoization in Lublin also underway, so Alten obtained permission from the civilian authorities for Mordechai (Mordko) Goldfarb, a veteran JDC official and part of the JSS in Warsaw, to come to Lublin to help him. Goldfarb went from place to place to see where the Lublin Jews had gone and what their needs were. He found that 1,250 of the expelled Jews were mostly well off and had gone to Rejowiec; 2,300 mostly poor Jews had gone to Siedliszcze, where a public kitchen had been set up; and 3,200 had gone to Sosnowica. This was in addition to the large numbers who had gone to small towns and villages. Sosnowica had had only 412 Jews prior to this refugee influx, and this highlights the turmoil into which the deportations had thrust the Jews. Others had gone to other central distribution towns in smaller numbers.[47]

Ongoing forced population movements within the district further complicated Alten's attempts to trace expelled Jews, identify their needs, and help them. On April 17, 1941, 250 Jews were expelled from Izbica to Siennica Różana. Since there was no JSS representative there, he asked the JSS representative in Krasnystaw

46 Blumental, *Documents*, Protocol 7(68), March 16, 1941, p. 223.

47 Ibid., Protocol 9(70), March 21, 1941, pp. 224–225; Alten to BuF Lublin, requesting a travel permit for Goldfarb in the district, YVA, JM/1574–1575; WAPL, GDL 894, 895, RZ 153; YVA, JM/1479, 10,457, O.6/403.

to visit these refugees and report on their needs.[48] Yet less than three weeks later, the 1,400 Jews of Krasnystaw themselves joined the ranks of the refugees, as they were expelled from their town and sent to fifteen different locations in the county.[49]

In his capacity as district JSS head, Alten had been dealing with expulsions and refugees from the beginning of the year. In February, he went to Opole-Lubelski to assess the needs of the incoming Viennese refugees and to try to organize some measure of aid for them in addition to what the Opole Judenrat could provide. He had also intervened successfully (as he understood the results) with the district civilian administration in order to put a halt to the expulsions from Kraśnik to Radomyśl that month.[50]

Table 5.4:
Intra-district Deportations, October 1940–June 1941

Dates	From	To	Numbers
Mar. 10–April 30, 1941	Lublin	district	15,000
Mar. 10	"	Bełżyce	495
Mar. 10	"	Chodel	370
Mar. 13–14	"	Michów	n.a.
Mar. 14	"	Sosnowica	3,200
Mar. 17	"	Lubartów	470
Mar. 17	"	Rejowiec	930
Mar. 17 & 19	"	Wysokie	320
Mar. 18	"	Siedliszcze	1,822
Mar.	"	Fajsławice	100
Mar.	"	Turobin	400
Mar.	"	Żółkiewka	200
Mar.	"	Czemierniki	200

48 Alten to JSS Krasnystaw, April 20, 1941, YVA, JM/1574–1575.

49 Musial, *Zivilverwaltung*, p. 136.

50 Alten to JSS Presidium, Kraków, February 28, 1941, YVA, JM/1574–1575.

Dates	From	To	Numbers
Mar.	"	Ostrów-Lubelski	200
Mar.	"	Firlej, Izbica, Tyszowce	n.a.
Mar. 14–16—April	" (+Wąwolnica)	Kurów	ca. 200
April 17	"	Siennica Różana	250
April	"	Parczew, Zaklików	n.a.
Feb. 1, 1941	Kraśnik (deportees and poor)	Radomyśl	600
Feb.	Kraśnik	Trzydnik, Kosin	1,400
May	"	Zakrzówek	200
Mar. 10, 1941	Kazimierz (refugees)	Józefów	500
April	"	Kurów	n.a.
Mar.	Biała-Podlaska (Suwalki refugees)	Parczew	n.a.
April 5	Zamość	Komarów	400
April 8	" (deportees from Włocławek and Łódź)	Krasnobród	248
April 6	Biłgoraj	Goraj	800
April 17	Izbica	Siennica Różana	250
April	Wąwolnica	Kurów, Opole, Urzędów	n.a.
May	Krasnystaw	Gorzków, Kraśniczyn, Siennica Różana, Wysokie, Zakrzew, and more	1,400

The JSS Presidium in Kraków promised to send 30,000 złoty immediately to aid the deportees from Lublin, and the first 15,000 złoty arrived on March 16. This sum was allocated at once, and the second 15,000 złoty was allocated on March 26, after which an additional 30,000 złoty of aid was sent by the JSS in Kraków on March 31. Alten and his colleagues in the Lublin JSS, particularly Josef Siegfried (Alten's JSS deputy), Izak Kerszman, and Mordechai Goldfarb, contacted other Judenräte regularly by letter, telephone, or personal visit in order to gauge the needs and to allocate aid accordingly. But the means available to the JSS and to the Judenräte were paltry at best. Thus, on March 17, Alten allocated 14,000 złoty of aid to 15,050 refugees. The Lublin Judenrat gave an additional 1,500 złoty, for a total of 1.03 złoty per person. Such sums did not go far in wartime Poland.[51]

As the weeks wore on, Alten and his colleagues were able to provide additional aid, but this was never near sufficient. For example, in March, the JSS in Lublin received 1,695 kg. of marmalade and 750 pairs of shoes to distribute to what was then estimated by Alten to be more than 30,000 new refugees in the district.[52] Translated into individual allocations, this came to 56 grams of marmalade per person and one pair of shoes for every forty refugees. In late May, the Lublin JSS received 1,250 kg. of meat for the now estimated 55,000 refugees, most of whom were part of the 120,000 people in great need.[53] This came to 10 grams of meat for each needy person in the Lublin District. However, since the meat was smoked pig meat, the individual portions were probably much higher, since many of the needy Jews would not eat it. This, of course, increased the rate of starvation.

Even if we add all the financial aid from the JSS during the critical months of February-April 1941, when the flow of refugees

51 Alten to BuF Lublin, March 17, 1941 (two letters, cc: JSS Kraków); Alten to JSS Kraków, March 26 (two letters); Alten inquiries to local JSS officials in Modliborzyce, Biłgoraj, Gorzków, Krasnystaw, Turobin, Józefów, Radzyń, and Parczew, and responses from many of these, March 31—April 4; JSS Kraków to Alten, April 1; Alten to local JSS and Judenrat officials, May 19–31; all in YVA, JM/1574–1575; Blumental, *Documents*, Protocol 7(68), March 16, 1941, p. 222.

52 Alten to JSS Kraków, April 7, 1941, YVA, JM/1574–1575.

53 Alten to BuF Lublin and JSS Kraków, June 19, 1941, presenting the distribution plan for the 1,250 kg. smoked pig meat received on May 28, YVA, JM/1574–1575. See also JSS Kraków to Alten, June 14, 1941, regarding allocations of medications and bandages, and Alten's May 31 population report to JSS Kraków, YVA, JM/1574–1575.

Jews being moved into the Lublin ghetto, (March-April) 1941, Yad Vashem Photo Archive, 1869/544

Jews leaving Lublin as part of ghettoization, (March-April) 1941, Yad Vashem Photo Archive, 52GO9

was large and constant, it does not come to significant amounts. The central office in Kraków sent 225,000 złoty by early April, for what were then more than 30,000 estimated new refugees. This came to 7.5 złoty per person, barely enough for even a loaf of bread.[54]

The amount of aid sent from the central JSS office in Kraków was a source of friction between Alten and the JSS Presidium. He argued that the central office was discriminating against Lublin, sending very small amounts of aid, and reneging on promises for more assistance. Whereas an additional 230,000 złoty had been promised, only 75,000 złoty had arrived in the previous month of upheaval. The Lublin District, he argued, housed 30 percent of the Jewish population of the GG and suffered from intense local poverty. Therefore, the local Jews were unable to raise the necessary sums in order to help the refugees. For its part, the central office maintained that no such promises had been made. Indeed, they could not have been rendered, since such sums did not exist.[55] It is not clear if Alten's charge was well founded or not. Perhaps the pressure of the new crisis led him to make extreme accusations out of sheer frustration. However, it is clear that the German civilian authorities were not lending the Jews any assistance whatsoever.

As the expelled Jews were leaving Lublin, the German civilian authorities were busily preparing Governor Zörner's ghetto announcement. On March 24, Losacker sent Türk a draft of the announcement (including a map), which was to be backdated to March 20, for his comments.[56] By this time the Judenrat had already received the order and had discussed it at its March 21 meeting. The announcement was posted from March 24, and then appeared in the Polish-language *Nowy Głos Lubelski* and the German *Krakauer Zeitung.*[57]

54 JSS Kraków to Alten, April 4, 1941, YVA, JM/1574–1575. On the prices of food in the Lublin District at this time, see Musial, *Zivilverwaltung*, p. 172.

55 See exchange of letters between Alten and JSS Kraków, April 1–5, 1941, YVA, JM/1574–1575.

56 Chef des Amtes to Türk, March 24, 1941, with enclosure, "Bildung eines geschlossenen jüdischen Wohnbezirks in Lublin," WAPL, GDL 892 (copy in YVA, JM/10455, O.53/84).

57 See Zörner's ghetto order, WAPL, GDL 892, and in YVA, JM/213/4; also in Friedrich, *Polen*, pp. 556–557. See also Blumental, *Documents*, Protocol 9(70),

The Lublin ghetto was situated in the old Jewish quarter, where many of the Jews of the city were already living. As the area was quite small, the ghetto was intended for only 20,000 Jews. For this reason Zörner put pressure on the Judenrat to find an additional 15,000 Jews to "volunteer" to leave the city; the Judenrat was also wary lest many of the expelled Jews might return. Jews had to move into the ghetto by April 5, and non-Jews to move out by March 31. Non-Jewish enterprises had until April 20 to leave the ghetto. The Jews moving into the ghetto were permitted to take only 25 kg. of personal belongings, whereas Jews agreeing to leave Lublin were given the incentive of being allowed to take all their possessions. Yet by the end of March, only 650 families – 2,330 people – had registered to leave the city.[58]

The Judenrat created a new housing department to deal with the major upheaval caused by the ghetto order and to find housing for the estimated 5–6,000 people who would have to move into the ghetto from their current homes. However, since 15,000 volunteers were not found to leave Lublin, the number of Jews who needed new housing in the ghetto was, in fact, much larger. The result was that tensions ran high, to the extent that at the Judenrat meeting of April 13, a fistfight broke out between Bekker and Kerszman.

The Germans consented to increase the number of ghetto residents to 25,000 and to extend the deadline by a few days, to April 24. On that day Zörner issued a curfew order: as of May 1, Jews would be under curfew from 9:00 P.M. to 6:00 A.M. As a further incentive for Jews to move out of Lublin, additional areas in the district were opened up to them and the deadline to leave Lublin was extended.[59] But when the ghettoization officially went into effect, there were still far more Jews than the Germans had permitted.

Sauermann ordered a census to be taken on the night of April

March 21, 1941, p. 225; Bausenhardt to Losacker, March 26, 1941, WAPL, GDL 892.

58 Zörner's ghetto order, ibid.; memo by Ziegenhirt on a meeting that day with Bausenhardt, Schmidt, and Zörner, WAPL, GDL 892 (copies in YVA, O.51/10, O.53/84; *Faschismus*, pp. 123–124; *Eksterminacja*, pp. 109–110).

59 Blumental, *Documents*, Protocols 16–20 (77–18), April 1, 2, 5, 10, 13, 1941, pp. 229–234; Zörner's curfew order in YVA, JM/213/4.

24/25, with the results to be submitted immediately. The Judenrat posted announcements regarding the census on April 22, in German, Polish, and Yiddish; the census was conducted from 8:00 P.M. to 6:00 A.M. on the assigned night. Instead of 25,000 Jews, there were 34,149 in the ghetto, or 37 percent above the allotment. Of these, 18,751 – 55 percent – were women. In addition, 504 families, numbering approximately 2,220 people, continued to live outside the ghetto.[60] Thus, there were 16,000 more Jews in Lublin than the Germans had intended.

In terms of the ghetto, these numbers translated into more severe overcrowding, more starvation, and more suffering; the Judenrat had not even received food or food vouchers for all these people. In this regard Aron Kantor addressed difficult questions to his Judenrat colleagues at their June 14 meeting. Not only were there not enough food vouchers for all the people in the ghetto, but there were also more people coming into the ghetto all the time. Jews who had left Lublin "voluntarily" had secretly returned, and Jews from other districts continued to sneak into Lublin in search of better living conditions.[61]

Ghettoization in Zamość followed a similar pattern to Lublin in many ways. In March, Karl Voss, in the *Kreishauptmann*'s office, informed the Judenrat in advance of the ghettoization. The Jews were ordered into the ghetto in early April, with a May 1 deadline. The area set aside for the ghetto, the Nowa Osada neighborhood in the new city, was heavily Jewish before the war, which meant that many Jews did not have to leave their homes in order to find themselves in the ghetto. However, Jews who lived in the old city did have to leave their homes, as did many in the new city, under the watchful eyes of the German and Polish police. Poles moved into the vacated

60 The initial count, as reported to the BuF on April 26, was 33,411. However, when the records were re-tallied more carefully, the total Jewish population reached 34,149, and this was the final number reported on May 18. See the Judenrat's Jewish population office's report of May 18, as well as subsequent reports for the balance of 1941, WAPL, RZ 150 (copies of the reports in YVA, O.6/402). This file contains all the census records, including street-by-street breakdowns. See also the Judenrat announcement of April 22, 1941 in YVA, JM/213/4.

61 Blumental, *Documents*, Protocol 33(94), June 14, 1941, pp. 247–248.

Jewish homes in the old city – although here the process was far more gradual than in Lublin, lasting until the end of the year. Like in Lublin, the number of Jews in the ghetto (7,000) was smaller than the prewar Jewish population (12,000), with a small number of Jews receiving permission to remain in their homes outside the ghetto. Here, too – like in Lublin – this was an open ghetto. Jews could leave the area, which meant that they could go to the old city and to other places in order to trade with the local non-Jews. The crowding in the Zamość ghetto was somewhat less severe than in Lublin or in the towns that had absorbed large numbers of refugees but had no official ghetto.

Large German and Polish police and other forces gathered at 5 A.M. on May 1, in order to search for Jews who had not yet moved to the ghetto. Approximately 250 people were discovered that day and expelled to Komarów. Some days later several hundred Jews were grabbed in the new city and sent to nearby Krasnobród.[62]

The ghettoization in Opole-Lubelski and Piaski differed from both the above in that they housed more Jews than had lived in these communities before the war. The Opole ghetto was established in March by the *Kreishauptmann*, with at least 7,500 Jews, a majority of them refugees. The Piaski ghetto was established by the Lublin-Land *Kreishauptmann*, Ziegenmeyer, in two stages: a Jewish neighborhood in early 1940; and a fenced-in ghetto in June 1941, for which he requisitioned 2,500 meters of barbed wire and other material for building the fence on June 11. Here, too, the majority of the ghetto population was composed of refugees, and the crowding was very severe.[63] The above variations in conditions and ghettoization

62 Garfinkel testimony in Mordechai Bernstein, ed., *Pinkas Zamość: Yizkor Book* (Yiddish) (Buenos Aires: Central Committee for Pinkas Zamość, 1957), pp. 1126–1128; Moshe Frank, *To Survive and Testify* (Hebrew) (Tel Aviv: Ghetto Fighters House and Hakibbutz Hameuhad, 1993), p. 34; Grzygorz Pawlowski testimony, YVA, O.3/4816; Mieczysław Garwin (Garfinkel) testimony in Wiesbaden in June and July 1962, YVA, TR.10/1146Z, XVII:3724–3774.

63 Ziegenmeyer to Abteilung Wirtschaft, June 11, 1941, WAPL, *Kreishauptmann* Lublin-Land 8 (copy in *Faschismus*, pp. 126–127); Aleksander Verba, "One Righteous Person in Sodom," and Yosl and Hayaleh Goldreich, "In Ghettos and Camps," in *Opole-Lubelski Yizkor Book*, edited by David Shtokfisch (Yiddish) (Tel Aviv: Association of Opole Immigrants in Israel and the Diaspora, 1977),

patterns within the Lublin District are a further reflection of the decentralized decision-making regarding details of the anti-Jewish policy, even where the general trend was guided by some central planning.

Health and Food

The extremely harsh, overcrowded conditions that were created by the new refugee and ghettoization crisis bred yet another emergency throughout the district — the outbreak of epidemics. Prior to the ghettoization of the Jews in Lublin, no cases of typhus (*fleckfieber*) had been reported, and the rate of other contagious diseases was quite low as compared to other places in the GG. In fact, the Lublin Judenrat did not even have a health department, because they did not see it as a necessity. They relied on the TOZ organization to deal with various aspects of public health. And, indeed, TOZ organized quickly and efficiently in the first months of German rule, opening a variety of clinics, conducting nearly 29,000 physical examinations by the end of 1939, and more than 33,000 typhus inoculations by the summer of 1940. By the end of the summer of 1940, the public health situation in Lublin and the district was considered by the Judenrat to be under control, considering the harsh conditions.[64]

Most Jewish hospitals in the Lublin District that had existed prior to the war ceased to function, which placed a greater burden on the Jewish hospital in Lublin. This hospital was modern and still functional in September 1939, and therefore in a position to try to

pp. 68, 277. The exact number of Jews in the ghetto is not clear. German records indicate a ghetto with 7,500 Jews, whereas other sources refer to as many as 9,000. Perhaps the additional refugees sent there in April 1941 are the basis for the latter number and the lack of clarity.

64 Lublin Judenrat Annual Report, pp. 30–33; Lublin Judenrat Announcement, April 12, 1940, that all Jews aged two to seventy must be inoculated for stomach typhus between April 15 and June 30, at the TOZ clinic at ul. Królewska 15, WAPL, RZ 10 (copy in USHMMA, RG-15.101M); TOZ reports for 1940, WAPL, RZ 131; Judenrat memo to Governor's office, "Bericht über die Tätigkeit der jüdischen Wohlfahrts- und Gesundheitsinstitutsionen in der Stadt Lublin," n.d. [mid-April 1940], WAPL, GDL 891.

deal with the community's health needs. However, the closing of the other hospitals in the district and the closing of the non-Jewish hospitals to Jews, together with the severe refugee crisis and the generally worsening living conditions for Jews, greatly increased the burden on the Jewish hospital in Lublin. It was forced to become a district hospital for Jews and to continue to treat all Jews, including those who could not pay. In the first year it doubled its capacity to 200 beds, and even more in subsequent years. By the end of the summer of 1940, the hospital had treated 2,107 patients, of whom 1,110 (53 percent) were from outside Lublin; the unpaid bills and other debts had led to a deficit of more than 216,500 złoty.[65]

In February 1940, the German civilian authorities appointed Dr. Szloma (Salomon) Bromberg as the new head of the Jewish hospital in Lublin. He was very unpopular, both because of the source of his authority and because the Jews saw him as arrogant, plotting, and overly cooperative with the Germans. By the end of the summer of 1941, the Lublin Judenrat began investigating Bromberg's work performance and found it wanting and slipshod. Izak Kerszman went so far as to call Bromberg a "murderer." His unpopularity complicated the work of the hospital staff. As conditions worsened from the spring of 1941, and disease became rife, the hospital staff's workload increased steadily. By the summer of 1941, it was not unusual for medical staff to spend sixteen hours a day in the hospital.[66] The period of March-April 1941, with the mass expulsions and ghettoization, was a clear turning point for public health in the Lublin District.

The relatively satisfactory health conditions in Lublin on the eve of ghettoization led the Judenrat to reject Josef Wajselfisz's March 1, 1941, suggestion that the Judenrat establish a health department.[67] The Germans feared that Jews would spread disease, but they also

65 Judenrat Annual Report, ibid., pp. 34–36; Judenrat memo, ibid.; Gedalje Erenberg testimony, YVA, M.1.E/1563.

66 Annual Report, ibid.; Erlichman-Bank, *In Impure Hands*, pp. 24–25, 35; Rapoport-Glikstein in *Dos Buch*, p. 390; Blumental, *Documents*, Protocol 44(105), September 20, 1941, pp. 269–271.

67 Blumental, ibid., Protocol 5(66), March 1, 1941, p. 219.

saw positive signs regarding this. Not only were health conditions in Lublin reasonable from the German public health perspective at that time, but also the status of public health throughout the GG had improved. At a March 25 GG meeting, Frank noted that the rate of disease in the GG had been reduced by half in recent months. Zörner explained that the Poles of Lublin were less resistant to typhus than the Jews, and therefore a special disinfection team was brought in from Warsaw to disinfect the vacated homes of the Lublin Poles before the Wehrmacht set up its offices there.[68]

Yet the Germans' fears of health problems that would be created by expulsions and ghettoization were realized, and Zörner proved to be mistaken regarding the Jews' innate resistance to disease. Indeed, the question was not of resistance to disease, but rather of succumbing to the inhuman, disease-breeding conditions imposed on the Jews by the Germans.

The expulsions and ghettoizations promoted the spread of disease in the Lublin District. The influx of refugees, including illegal travelers carrying diseases from stricken localities, such as Warsaw, threatened their new refuges. The severe overcrowding, poor nutrition, and deteriorating hygienic conditions in the refugee centers and in Lublin itself, where the housing conditions ranged from five to ten people per room in the ghetto,[69] compounded the threat to public health. Moreover, the daring and initiative of many Jews, who were willing to risk illegal travel in order to reach family or better living conditions, coupled with the German civilian government's limited willingness to allow some travel by Jews, meant that Jews who had contracted diseases were spreading them among themselves and among the non-Jewish population. The public health profile in Lublin changed drastically.

On April 12, 1941, the military staff doctor in Międzyrzec, Dr. Zoninger, complained to the county SS chief in Radzyń, *SS-Obersturmführer* Fritz Fischer, that the influx of more than 1,000 Jews in the previous six weeks had brought with it a marked increase

68 *Diensttagebuch*, pp. 337–338.

69 Lublin ghetto population records are in WAPL, RZ 150. The density in the Jewish homes outside the ghetto averaged four per room.

in cases of typhus. There were now twenty-eight positive cases in the hospital, in addition to one German soldier. Since the soldiers could not be completely isolated from the Jews, he "most urgently" requested that the influx of Jews be halted. Fischer supported the request in an April 21 letter to KdS Huppenkothen in Lublin. His request was honored, but it was too late to prevent the worst typhus outbreak to date.[70]

In early May, the Lublin ghetto had already recorded its first cases of typhus, and six apartment buildings, housing 1,054 residents, were quarantined. The numbers increased to eighty-seven buildings (out of 348 in the ghetto), housing 11,300 Jews, in July. Thus, one-third of the Lublin Jews were under quarantine only three months after the creation of the ghetto.[71] On May 19, the Judenrat in Józefów informed Alten of an outbreak of typhus.[72] By summer the city of Lublin and many parts of the district were faced with an epidemic, though still not of the proportions evident in Warsaw and other parts of the GG.[73] In July, the small Lublin Jewish hospital for communicable diseases, which had been set up in February 1940, on German orders, was moved into the ghetto and expanded. As the epidemic spread that summer and the number of stricken people grew, the hospital capacity was overextended to the point that there were four patients to a bed. By October, this hospital had expanded to 380 beds, yet it was still inadequate to meet the need.[74] The Germans' order to expand the hospital for communicable

70 Dr. Zoninger to KdS office in Radzyń, April 12, 1941, *SS-Obersturmführer* Fischer to KdS Lublin, April 21, and *Kreishauptmann* Radzyń to Interior Department, Lublin, April 29, all in WAPL, GDL 273 (copies in YVA, O.6/352, O.53/82); Friedrich, ed., *Polen*, p. 579; Pohl, *Judenpolitik*, pp. 86–87.

71 WAPL, RZ 128, 150 (copy in USHMMA, RG-15.101M); Trunk, "Sanitary Conditions and the Death Rate in the Ghetto," in *Dos Buch*, pp. 358–360; Blumental, *Documents*, Protocol 32(93), 33 (94), May 28, 1941, June 14, 1941, pp. 246–247.

72 Józefów Judenrat to Alten, May 19, 1941 and Alten's response, May 26, YVA, JM/1574–1575.

73 WAPL, RZ 128 (copy in USHMMA, RG-15.101M); Trunk, "Sanitary Conditions, pp. 359–360.

74 Blumental, *Documents*, Protocol 10, February 17, 1940, Protocol 37(98), July 8, 1941, pp. 126, 259.

diseases was not prompted by an interest to cure Jews, but in order to try to save themselves from the epidemic.

Christopher Browning has noted that the widespread incidence of typhus and other epidemic diseases in the ghettos (especially Warsaw) led GG public health officials, in 1941, increasingly to advocate killing Jews. These doctors advocated limiting the Jews' movements and creating ghettos. Yet Lublin seems to have been different. Perhaps the relatively better conditions for Jews in this district helped limit the epidemic and concomitantly doused the Lublin public health officials' enthusiasm for ghettos.[75]

One of the serious problems faced by the Jews beginning in this period was food. During the first year of the German occupation, restrictions on contacts with the local non-Jewish population were not as strictly enforced here as elsewhere in the GG. This enabled the Jews to acquire additional food and avoid starvation, which led many, especially from the Warsaw area, to try to smuggle themselves into the Lublin District. The accessibility of food and the ability to have some limited contact with the local Poles and Ukrainians was particularly marked in the more rural areas. Jews there were able to move about less guardedly, have more contact with the local farmers, and acquire more food. The German authorities did not have enough manpower to keep a close watch on all places, which meant that SS and SD personnel were rarely seen in some rural areas. The local government was in the hands of the local Polish or Ukrainian village elders, under long-distance German supervision. Survivors from this area report regular contact with local farmers to procure food. Daniel Freiberg even tells of weekly boat trips across the Wisła River from Annopol-Rachów to Warsaw in 1940 to sell things, as well as taking his daughter for sled rides during the winter of 1940–1941.[76] Dov Finger relates going for weekly forays with his father by horse and wagon from Hrubieszów to the local farmers to buy food.[77]

75 Christopher R. Browning, "Genocide and Public Health: German Doctors and Polish Jews, 1939–1941," *Holocaust and Genocide Studies*, 3:1 (1988), pp. 21–36.

76 Freiberg, *Darkness Covered the Earth*, pp. 53–63. See also Werner, *Fighting Back*, pp. 23, 28–31, 59–67.

77 Dov Finger Video Testimony, Massuah Archive. See also, for example, Eli

This set of circumstances took a turn for the worse beginning in early 1941. The stricter restrictions on where the Jews could live and move hindered their contacts with the local non-Jewish population, as well as their access to food. This especially affected the Jews who had been concentrated in Jewish quarters or ghettos. Four types of Jewish communities developed in this period. One type included mostly rural areas, such as Stężyca near Dęblin, where the Jews' dispersal among small towns and villages and employment in officially sanctioned agricultural work helped them avoid contact with Germans and keep themselves and their families fed.[78] Some Jews report even having had access to meat.[79]

A second type included more urban, non-refugee areas, which had received relatively small numbers of refugees during this period and continued to live without a formal ghetto, such as Hrubieszów, Tomaszów-Lubelski, Dęblin-Irena, and others. Here Jews continued to have limited access to local farmers and therefore to food and information.[80]

A third type included small refugee centers, small localities that had received many refugees but had not been put under a ghetto regime, such as Siedliszcze. Here the increased numbers of Jews looking for contacts and food made the connections with the local farmers somewhat more difficult. The fact that many of the refugees were not local people, and those who had been deported from Austria and Germany did not even speak Polish or Ukrainian further hindered contacts and the acquisition of food.

The fourth type was the ghetto, such as in Lublin, where food access was now much more restricted. Strict food rations were imposed by the German civilian authorities in 1941, but these varied according

Fiszman, YVA, O.93/14967 (original in USC Shoah Visual History Archive [VHA]/14967), and Doris Feldstein, YVA, O.93 (VHA)/37405, on Annopol and Kraśnik respectively.

78 See, for example, Moshe Zylberszpan testimony, YVA, M.49.E/4137; Werner, *Fighting Back*, pp. 23, 28–31, 59–67.

79 See, for example, Freiberg, *Darkness Covered the Earth*, pp. 50–63; Esther Krinitz, YVA, O.93 (VHA)/38606.

80 See the entries on these towns and others in Abraham Wein, ed., *Pinkas Hakehillot: Encyclopedia of Jewish Communities, Poland*, Volume 7: *Districts Lublin. Kielce* (Hebrew) (Jerusalem: Yad Vashem, 1999), pp. 141, 241, and *passim*.

Jewish woman, Lublin ghetto, Yad Vashem Photo Archive, 3331/101

to supplies, crop yields, and the whim of the *Stadthauptmann*. Officially, the weekly ration in the Lublin ghetto included 700 grams of bread, 50 grams sugar, 40 grams grain-based coffee, 250 ml. milk, and 3600 grams of dark flour per month, as well as various other items. Jews from Lublin recall much smaller rations and widespread hunger, though not starvation. But even under such a ghetto regime, all but one of the ghettos were open, and this enabled some contact to continue. Compared to Warsaw, Lublin was still a better place to be, so refugees continued to sneak into the Lublin District.[81]

The direct result of the new difficulties in obtaining food, the increased overcrowded conditions, and the influx of disease-carrying refugees was greater hunger and disease after the spring of 1941, and a spiraling death rate by the summer.[82] The Lublin Judenrat's

81 Musial, *Zivilverwaltung*, pp. 160–161; Paula Klajnman-Fradkoff testimony, YVA, O.33/1134. Klajnman-Fradkoff recalls receiving 50 grams of bread daily (half the official ration) and 300 grams of dark flour per month (less than one-tenth the official ration).

82 See death records for Lublin, in WAPL, RZ 172, 179; Judenrat Health Department report on August 1941, WAPL, RZ 6 (copy in USHMMA, RG-15.101M).

new health department reported, on January 5, 1942, on the number of typhus cases in Lublin in 1941: there were 1,691 cases reported during the year, with a much higher incidence rate for those in the ghetto than for those still living outside the ghetto. Among those in the ghetto, 1,652 cases were reported during the year, or approximately 4.8 percent of the population. Among those outside the ghetto, only thirty-nine cases were reported, or approximately 1.8 percent of the population.[83]

Communications

A subtle yet significant factor in the Jews' ability to cope with the situation during the first two years of the Nazi occupation was the possibility of maintaining communication. Until mid-June 1941, the Jews in the GG were able to keep up limited contact with relatives and friends across the Soviet border, and, until December 7, 1941, they had contact with Jews in the United States. Throughout the war period there were Jews in the GG who were able to carry on limited contact with one another and with Jews outside occupied Europe.

The importance of these contacts was threefold: material, psychological, and informational. The contacts brought Jews in the GG limited material relief in the form of packages and money sent by friends and relatives, much of which (though not all) the Germans allowed to reach the addressee. The communications also provided contact with the outside world, thereby relieving the Jews' isolation to some degree. And finally, they were also sent information, even if in code or through self-censorship. Once the USSR and the United States entered the war, however, the legal contact with these countries and the hope that it brought were cut off. This is reflected poignantly in a tragic irony. The day of the invasion of the Soviet Union was also the day that mass shootings of Jews began there, in the former Polish territories; the day after the legal channels between occupied Poland and the United States were cut, the death camp at Chełmno began operations.

83 WAPL, RZ 128, 129 (copy in USHMMA, RG-15.101M).

Communications took several forms. Judenräte maintained official communications with one another via correspondence, telephone, and personal visits by Judenrat officials. From January 1940, Jews were forbidden to use the regular post offices in the GG, so the Judenräte were forced to create some sort of Jewish postal service. Private individuals maintained a measure of contact via letters sent through these Jewish postal systems, letters sent secretly with couriers, and telephone calls. The extent of all these forms of communications in the Lublin District is striking. If assessed quantitatively, the total number of communications of all sorts would be in the hundreds of thousands. The Lublin Judenrat's postal department reported in the autumn of 1940 that it had processed 135,274 pieces of postage in the first eight months of the year. Nearly 90 percent of this postage (120,350) was incoming, but nearly 15,000 outgoing pieces of post reflect an active correspondence.[84] The records of the Judenrat and its postal department for 1941 and the first months of 1942 indicate an even greater volume of correspondence – 19,000 civilian items per month – which continued until the deportations to Bełżec in March-April 1942.[85]

However, quantitative summaries can be misleading. There were many Jews whose contact with people outside their community was severely limited, and others who had no contacts at all. For example, Moshe Becher reports that the Jews in Krzeszów had no communications with the outside; they were isolated from the Poles and from other Jews, without letters and without telephones.[86] Dov Freiberg reports that, although there were contacts between Turobin and other localities, the fact there were no telephones, electricity, or paved roads in Turobin meant that they were completely cut off from the outside world during the winter.[87]

84 WAPL, RZ 21, 22, 52 (copies in USHMMA, RG-15.101M); Lublin Judenrat Annual Report; Blumental, *Documents*, Protocol 2(63), February 5, 1941, p. 213.

85 WAPL, ibid., especially RZ 6, 52. The Postal Department's monthly reports for 1941 indicate an average of an additional 6,000 items per month for the Lipowa 7 camp, WAPL, RZ 6 (copies in USHMMA, RG-15.101M, reel 2).

86 Moshe Becher testimony, YVA, O.3/8403.

87 Dov Freiberg, *To Survive Sobibor* (Jerusalem and New York: Gefen, 2007), p. 131.

The effects of this isolation are difficult to measure, but the fact that the seemingly large total volume of communications in the Lublin District constituted only a fraction of the communications engaged in during normal times must be borne in mind. Thus, the focus in the following pages on communications does not imply a "normal" situation. Even those Jews who managed to maintain contact with the outside world and thus derived some relief and some hope were still living under a harsh occupation regime that sought to persecute and exploit them in the extreme. Yet the communications maintained by Jews in the Lublin District did provide a glimmer of normality and optimism, and so this glimmer and the extent and variety of the communications merit our attention.

The Lublin Judenrat was in written correspondence with dozens of Judenräte within the district, in other districts of the GG, and outside the GG. One file alone in the Judenrat archive contains correspondence with fifty-three Judenräte in 1939–1941, of which nearly half were outside the district. Much of this correspondence dealt with tracing people, people transferring from one locale to another, and similar day-to-day affairs. Each deportation or expulsion to or within the district would be followed by a flurry of correspondence among Judenräte regarding numbers, names, and needs of the deportees. Thus, the postal clerk in the Bełżec forced labor camp wrote to the Judenrat in August 1940 on how to correspond with the forced-laborers, and the Bełżyce Judenrat wrote to the Lublin Judenrat on April 27, 1941, detailing the numbers (1,929) and needs of the refugees being cared for there.[88] The Mława Judenrat wrote to the Lublin Judenrat on January 3, 1941, asking that Rabbi Yehiel Moshe Segalowitz, Mława's rabbi, be informed that 500 złoty were being sent to him via a courier in Warsaw. The Mława Judenrat was concerned that they had not yet heard from the elderly rabbi since his deportation to Lublin three weeks earlier.[89]

88 Bełżec postal clerk to Lublin Judenrat, August 1940 (exact date not written), and Bełżyce Judenrat to Lublin Judenrat, April 27, 1941, WAPL, RZ 21 (copy in USHMMA, RG-15.101M).

89 Mława Judenrat to Lublin Judenrat, January 3, 1941, WAPL, RZ 22 (copy in USHMMA, RG-15.101M).

Unfortunately, the rabbi was hospitalized, too ill to correspond, and soon died (see the section on Resettlements above).

Individual Jews could also correspond via the Judenrat. On February 12, 1941, Paulina Priwe in Kraków wrote to her husband Naftali in Lublin, enclosing clothing for him, and expressing surprise that he had not received the 30 złoty that she had sent him earlier. Naftali Priwe was one of the recent deportees from Kraków to Lublin.[90]

The Jewish postal system operated under the close and threatening supervision of the German post. Jews would post their letters at the Judenrat's post office; the Judenrat's representative or postal service would send and receive all Jewish mail at the regular post office; and the sorting would be done at the Jewish post office. All Jewish correspondence needed to be written in Latin letters, in German or Polish. Many wrote in Yiddish in Latin letters. Private telephone calls could be made from telephones in the Judenrat or in the post office. Only selected officials were allowed telephones in their offices, and only with German permission. Still, within these constricted parameters, there were a number of telephones available to Jews in Lublin; most other communities had at least one. All phone calls went through an operator and could be easily listened to by the German authorities. Telegrams could be sent via the Jewish post office, and these, too, were easily tracked. This system allowed the Germans to monitor Jewish correspondence, or at least suspend the threat of prying eyes over the Jews, while distancing them from the post office and from direct contact with their Polish neighbors and with the outside world.

The extent of correspondence and other communication lines maintained by Jews in the Lublin District went hand in hand with the relatively better conditions the Jews experienced there in comparison with other parts of Poland. One reflection of this is the Lublin Judenrat's request of February 8, 1941, for its postal department to look into the possibilities for sending packages *to* the

90 Paulina Priwe, Kraków, to Naftali Priwe, Lublin, February 12, 1941, WAPL, RZ 21 (copy in USHMMA, RG-15.101M). See also the letters between Julius Aoram in Tel Aviv and his parents, refugees from Vienna in Opole-Lubelski, YVA, O.75/82.

Soviet Union.[91] The fact that this discussion was undertaken in the midst of the deportations into the city and district of Lublin puts the relatively "good" conditions in Lublin into even sharper relief.

The private correspondence among Jews under Nazi rule and between them and people outside occupied Europe dealt with a number of subjects. The predominant topics in the "legal" correspondence were to do with tracing family members and basic exchange of information and aid. The clandestine correspondence, which was generally sent via non-Jewish couriers, was far more candid in its contents and would often be in Yiddish (and at times even in Hebrew), and not in the prescribed German or Polish. On October 28 and 30, 1940, an unidentified man in Biłgoraj (his name was removed from the Oneg Shabbat archive's copy of the letters) wrote to his sister in Warsaw after returning from four and a half months in a forced-labor camp. He and his son had no money and no shoes, and he asked his sister to send both right away. The fact that the letters were written in Yiddish in Hebrew characters and that they discussed the harsh conditions of the forced labor indicate that they were sent by courier.[92] Krystyna Modrzewska was able to correspond from her hiding place in a village near Lublin with her aunt and a friend in the Warsaw ghetto by sending letters from the regular post office in Lublin but without a return address.[93]

One of the most important elements in the correspondence was the responses that came into the Lublin District. In the exchange of letters between Zionist youth activists in Poland and Natan Schwalb, the World He-Halutz representative in Switzerland, nearly every letter to him from the district expressed extreme gratitude for his letters, which they said gave them both encouragement and information.[94] This underground correspondence pipeline continued

91 Blumental, *Documents*, Protocol 3(64), February 8, 1941, p. 215.

92 Letters via courier from Biłgoraj to Warsaw, October 28 and 30, 1940, YVA, M.10.AR.1/592 (also in JM/3489).

93 Modrzewska, "Pamiętnik," p. 79.

94 Ruth Zariz, *Letters from Haluzim in Occupied Poland, 1940–1944* (Hebrew) (Tel Aviv: Yad Tabenkin and Beit Lohamei Haghetaot, 1994). See also the exchanges of letters between the POW Felyks Rzeczynski in an officers' POW camp in Germany and his family in Warsaw and Poniatowa, YVA, O.48.B/19–1.

during the deportations in 1942, when the contents from Poland changed to pleas and desperation.

Szmul Zitomirski, a He-Halutz activist, was the director of the Lublin Jewish post office, under the supervision of Judenrat member Izak Kerszman. From the spring of 1941, he and Zionist youth colleagues regularly took advantage of his position to maintain contact with Schwalb. Ruth Zariz's research has uncovered dozens of letters from *halutzim* to Schwalb, many of them via Zitomirski's postal service in Lublin. Letters from *halutzim* bore one additional element to those mentioned above – movement and ideological affairs. Thus, Rivka Glanc wrote to Schwalb on January 24, 1941, to introduce herself as the Dror coordinator in the Lublin District, who had been referred to him by Zivia Lubetkin in Warsaw.[95] Similarly, Bracha Kam wrote from Hrubieszów introducing herself as the coordinator in that area.[96]

The letters from the Zionist youth activists in the Lublin District in this period reported on conditions in the district in general, relations with the various Judenräte, and movement activities. Many Zionist youth from the various movements joined a training farm at the sawmill at Werbkowice, near Hrubieszów, beginning in May 1941. Twenty members of Dror from Lublin joined some thirty members from the Hrubieszów area that month, along with a small number from other pioneer movements and an unclear but large number of Betar members from all over the GG, who spread out over seven farms near Hrubieszów. The secretary of the Hrubieszów Judenrat, Joel Brand, helped the Betar groups set up their farms, in an instance where the interests of the German civilian authorities, the local Polish and Ukrainian farmers, and the Zionist youth converged momentarily. The Zionist youth wanted to pursue their Zionist training, stay together, avoid forced-labor camps, and escape the harsh conditions in some of the ghettos, especially those outside the district. The Germans wanted manpower in the farms and sawmills and to pacify the Poles.[97]

95 Rivka Glanc to Natan Schwalb, January 24, 1941, Zariz, ibid., p. 56.

96 Bracha Kam to Natan Schwalb, February 9, 1941, ibid., p. 61.

97 Rivka Glanc (Hrubieszów) to Natan Schwalb, May 11 and 21, 1941; Szmul Zitomirski to Schwalb, May 27, 1941, ibid., pp. 81–82, 85–88; Israel Gutman,

Internal Life

Internal life in the Jewish communities in the Lublin District revolved around the chronically urgent social-welfare needs and just staying alive and healthy. As a result, community education, cultural pursuits, and religious life virtually disappeared from most of the district. The Lublin Judenrat is perhaps the most striking example of this, and certainly the best documented. Of 182 files in the Lublin Judenrat archive, only one deals with education. There was no department for religious or cultural affairs; there were almost no underground newspapers available, although there was access to certain outside news until late May 1941;[98] there were few libraries, no theaters and few cafés and restaurants. In Lublin, the last time the Jews were permitted to pray in a synagogue was during the High Holidays in 1939, when the Germans humiliated them in public. After that Jews prayed only in secret.[99] Conditions were similar throughout the district. Schools were replaced by limited, clandestine private education; synagogues became refugee shelters or were expropriated by the Germans; and theaters were closed.

Kosher slaughter was forbidden, and although some slaughterers continued to slaughter animals clandestinely,[100] the risks proved too great and the supply and means too limited for this work

The Jews of Warsaw, 1939–1943 (Bloomington: Indiana University Press, 1982), p. 140; Abraham Lewin, *A Cup of Tears: A Diary of the Warsaw Ghetto* (Oxford: Blackwell, 1989), May 23, 1942, pp. 91–93; Yitzhak Zuckerman and Moshe Basok, eds., *The Wars of the Ghettos: Behind the Walls, in the Camps, in the Forests* (Hebrew) (Tel Aviv: Hakibbutz Hameuhad, 1954), p. 106. Some sources refer to 600 Betar people there, which seems a very high number considering the conditions in the GG and the difficulty of travel, while others (e.g., Lewin) refer to only thirty. See also Dariusz Libionka and Laurence Weinbaum, "A New Look at the Betar 'Idyll' in Hrubieszów," *Yad Vashem Studies*, 37:1 (2009), pp. 85–108.

98 According to the Judenrat meeting on May 24, 1941 (protocol 31[92]), Jews were henceforth limited to reading only the Nazi-supervised, Polish-language *Gazeta Żydowska*, Blumental, *Documents*, p. 244. This reflects the fact that, until then, they had had access to other newspapers. Rivka Glanc wrote to Natan Schwalb on May 22, thanking him for the packages that he had sent, including the newspaper. See Zariz, ibid., pp. 85–86.

99 Erlichman-Bank, *In Impure Hands*, p. 26.

100 Matla (Kleiner) Blender video testimony, Massuah Archive.

to continue. Indeed, in March 1941, all cows were confiscated from Jews.[101] Without synagogues, without a day of rest on the Sabbath or holidays, and without access to kosher food, Jewish religious life became increasingly limited and private.

Only one element of religious activity was officially permitted to a degree by the German authorities even as late as 1942 – the baking of *matzah* for Passover. It is not clear why this holiday was the one chosen by the German civilian authorities in Lublin for relative leniency. In 1940 and 1941, pressure by the JDC in New York to be allowed to supply *matzah* to Jews in the GG may be one explanation. Yet permission was granted not only to receive *matzah* from abroad, but also to bake *matzah* locally. Moreover, on the eve of the deportations to Bełżec in 1942, when JDC pressure was no longer a factor, the authorities again gave permission to bake *matzah*. In this case the permission to bake *matzah* may have been part of the Germans' deception.

In late February 1940, the German authorities in Lublin acceded to the Judenrat's request that they provide flour for the baking of *matzah* for the upcoming Pesach holiday. A Judenrat committee was set up to organize the project, including commissioning the bakeries and bakers who would do the work. On April 4, 1940, the Lublin Judenrat announced that it was providing 2 kilograms of flour per person for the baking of *matzah*.[102] On March 8, 1941, the Judenrat again set up a *matzah* committee to begin planning for the baking and distribution of *matzah*. Shortly thereafter, in the midst of the expulsions and the ghettoization, the BuF agreed to provide flour for baking *matzah*. The Judenrat's *matzah* committee gave the *matzah*-baking concession to Zadok Brokstein and Szlomo

101 Meyer Fiszman, Chana Fiszman, Ela Cang, Aron Lejb Cang, Zelman Bulc, Jankiel Goldstejn to Judenrat, March 6, 1941, responding to orders to turn over all cows to Germans; WAPL, RZ 22 (copy in USHMMA, RG-15.101M). Fifteen cows were confiscated from Jews in the city of Lublin alone. Esther Krinitz reports the confiscation of five cows from Jews in the village of Mniszek, near Annopol, in fall 1941. See her interview in YVA, O.93 (VHA)/38606.

102 Blumental, *Documents*, Protocols 11, 12, 14, 16, February 25, March 2, 16, 30, pp. 129, 130, 134, 139. Judenrat announcement, April 4, 1940, WAPL, RZ 10 (copies in USHMMA, RG-15.101M).

Edelman, who rented a bakery from Chana Helfman. As in the previous year, Jews with means purchased *matzah*, while poor Jews received it for free from the Judenrat. At the same time the SS gave the Jewish POWs at the Lipowa 7 camp permission to organize a *seder* on April 12. Therefore, at its April 5 meeting, the Judenrat appointed Leon Hufnagel to help the POWs organize their *seder*.[103]

In general, there was far less cultural activity in the Lublin District than in the Warsaw ghetto. Many of the Zionist and other movement leaders had fled to the USSR in 1939, and this left a serious gap. Logistically speaking, the houses in which the Jews in the district lived were generally smaller and more spread out than in Warsaw (the Lublin District was underdeveloped in comparison to Warsaw, and so there were fewer modern apartment buildings), which meant that after curfew in the Lublin ghetto or in any other community it was difficult for more than a few people to gather for any purpose. There was also little time available before curfew for people to gather, as everybody worked a long day or else spent their time scrounging for food and supplies. Moreover, the large number of very poor refugees in the district in 1941 forced the local Jewish communities to focus their energies and sorely limited resources on social welfare. These factors resulted in relatively little cultural activity in the Lublin District, despite the better physical conditions that prevailed in comparison with other districts.

Jewish schools were shut down by the German civilian authorities almost immediately after they took the reins of power from the Wehrmacht, and Jewish children were evicted from the Polish public schools. A series of Lublin Judenrat memos to the district governor's office, beginning in February 1940, filed a number

103 See Blumental, *Documents*, Protocols 6(67), 10–14(71–75), 18(79), March 8, 23–27, April 5, 1941, pp. 224, 226, 232; [Prof.] David to Lublin Judenrat, April 4 and 14, 1941, WAPL, RZ 43 (copy in USHMMA, RG-15.101M); Chana Helfman to Lublin Judenrat, March 25, April 6, and April 14, 1941, WAPL, RZ 22 (copies in USHMMA, RG-15.101M). Helfman complained that the two bakers had not adhered to their part of the contract regarding the dates on which they could use the bakery and how much they were to pay her. At its April 14 meeting (Blumental, ibid., Protocol 21[82], p. 235), the Judenrat decided to give the sum of 2,000 złoty from the *matzah* committee's money to the relocation fund meant to help those who volunteered to leave.

of requests, including permission to open Jewish schools. Like most of the issues raised in these memoranda, the school request was ignored.[104]

On September 11, 1940, however, Frank issued an order, backdated to August 31, announcing that the Judenräte in the GG could open primary schools and trade schools. These schools would have to be under the supervision of the education authorities of the district; their locations would be determined in consultation with the district governor's office; and their maintenance would be completely under the responsibility of the Judenräte.[105] Despite the hampering limitations included in the decree, it was soon followed by a flurry of organizational activity in Lublin.

A group of educators and intellectuals there met with Alten and castigated him and the Judenrat for not acting energetically enough to establish schools in Lublin. In response, the Judenrat appointed a committee, including Judenrat member Maurycy Schlaf and educator Nahman Korn, to negotiate with the civilian authorities to open a school and to secure an appropriate building. They counted 127 trained teachers and some 5,000 primary-school-age children in Lublin in January 1941, and searched for an appropriate building. Finally, they decided to reclaim the building that had housed the Bais Yaacov school before the war and that was now being used as a refugee center. However, the new influx of refugees in the first months of 1941 used up all available space. They therefore met with the GG's superintendent for schools, Professor Kindler, in January 1941, and he agreed to let them use the auditorium of the former Jewish public school in Lublin that was now serving as a Polish school. However, the Polish school superintendent, Krupczak, refused on the grounds that the Polish schools were overcrowded. Kindler also expressed a willingness to

104 See the Judenrat's sixteen-page memo to the governor's office on February 16, 1940, and its subsequent five-page memo (undated, but apparently from early spring 1940) reiterating the outstanding unanswered requests from the February memo, in WAPL, RZ 26 (copy in USHMMA, RG-15.101M).

105 Frank's Jewish schools order of August 31, 1940 is in WAPL, RZ 37, and YVA, O.6/11b*.

help them organize Jewish schools for the entire district, but this idea, too, was never pursued.

Parallel to this search they tried to develop a curriculum with the help of the Kraków Judenrat's school department. On January 24, 1941, the Kraków educators suggested three variations on curricula for grades 1–7; the most ambitious of them called for a thirty-six-hour school week for grades 3–7, half of it devoted to Jewish studies. Ultimately the efforts to open Jewish schools in Lublin failed, as the Judenrat was overwhelmed by the creation of the ghetto and the need to deal with the new large numbers of refugees. The German authorities did not make any serious effort to facilitate the opening of Jewish schools anywhere in the district. Nachman Blumental says that the Lublin Judenrat itself was not earnest in organizing schools. Although this assessment may be a bit harsh, it also seems basically accurate. However, given the attitude of the German authorities and the Polish school superintendent, there seems to have been little the Judenrat could have done in any event. Was their limited energy in pursuing schooling for Jewish children perhaps a reflection of their realization that the German authorities and Polish school officials would not allow such schools to open?[106]

Private, clandestine education continued in Lublin and the district, but it reached only a small fraction of the school-age children. Nahman Korn recalls the initiative of the Lublin teachers in finding children to teach, and a number of survivors recall receiving some form of private education, but this was a limited phenomenon.[107] Youth-movement activity was seriously curtailed in

106 Kraków Judenrat's School Department to Lublin Judenrat, January 24, 1941, WAPL, RZ 29; Blumental, *Documents*, Protocols 42–47, 49, 57, 61, 3(64), 6(67), September 11–16, 29, November 30, December 28, 1940, February 8, March 8, 1941, pp. 183. 189, 201, 208, 215–216, 220; Nahman Korn, "Education Problems and the Suffering of the Children in the Ghetto" (Hebrew), *Encyclopedia of the Jewish Diaspora, Lublin*, pp. 725–730. The Kraków educators' three suggestions each included twenty-four hours a week for grades 1–2 and more for the other grades. The implementation depended on space, resources, and the cooperation of the German civilian authorities.

107 Korn, ibid.; Ruth Tatarko testimony on Hrubieszów, March 31, 1992, in Professor Yehuda Bauer's research seminar; Ruth Tatarko video testimony, Massuah Archive; Matla (Kleiner) Blender video testimony, ibid. See also Garfinkel, *Pinkas Zamość*, pp. 1155–1156.

1939–1941, declining to almost non-existent at times in many parts of the district. Many of the remaining movement leaders had been conscripted for forced labor by the German civilian authorities or by the SS. Moreover, the very living conditions that made physical existence in the Lublin District better than in other districts of the GG also contributed to the dearth of youth-movement and political activity. As the Jews were less crammed together than in some other areas, they had less opportunity to meet after curfew. The result was that much of the activity in the Lublin District was dependent on movement leaders coming secretly from Warsaw to help organize, to encourage activity, or actually to set up activities, such as the training at Werbkowice for movement members from all over the GG.

Identifying the Ghettos

As the summer progressed, with the German invasion of the Soviet Union well under way and Nazi plans for European Jewry taking shape, GG policy toward the Jews began to change. On July 17, 1941, Frank told a GG meeting that ghetto building should be suspended, because the Jews of the GG would soon be removed and the GG would serve only as a transit camp for Jews.[108] This was passed on to the county chiefs in the Lublin District on August 25.[109] Still, as part of the developing plans for the Jews of the Reich, the Interior Department of the GG asked the Lublin civilian government to report on ghettos and *Judensammelorte* (gathering places for Jews) in the district and the availability of space for incoming Jews. This request was passed on to Türk in the BuF office in Lublin, who in turn forwarded it to the ten county chiefs and the Lublin *Stadthauptmann* in a secret letter dated September 9.[110]

The county chiefs were asked to report by September 27 on three matters: all ghettos that they had established or were planning; all other *Sammelorte* established or planned; Jewish population

108 Frank, *Diensttagebuch*, p. 386; Musial, *Zivilverwaltung*, p. 138.

109 Musial, ibid., pp. 138–139.

110 Türk to Kreishauptleute, "Verfügung – Judensammelorte," September 9. 1941, WAPL, GDL 270.

Two Jewish women, Lublin, March 10, 1941, Yad Vashem Photo Archive, 5032

estimates and estimates of the number of additional Jews each county could receive. All but two county heads responded by the deadline, but none was interested in receiving any significant number of additional Jews.[111] The responses indicated that there were few ghettos and few planned and that there was room for no

111 The responses came in as follows: Brandt, Puławy, September 12, 1941; Lenk, Janów-Lubelski, September 16; Ziegenmeyer, Lublin-Land, September 19; Schmidt, Krasnystaw, September 23; Augustin, Chelm, and Hoffmann, Polizeidirektor in *Stadthauptmann*'s office, Lublin, both on September 25; Schmiege, Radzyń, and Ansel, Biłgoraj, both on September 26; Busse, Hrubieszów, September 27; Weihenmeier, Zamość, October 1; Kühl, Biała-Podlaska, October 6. All are in WAPL, GDL 270 (copies in YVA, O.6/47-3*, JM/10,458; copies of Brandt and Schmiege also in O.53/82). The details of the reports are taken from these sources. Both Dieter Pohl and Bogdan Musial refer to some aspect of this survey, but neither one addressed the entire correspondence and therefore could not fully assess ghettoization in 1941. See Pohl, *Judenpolitik*, p. 93; Musial, *Zivilverwaltung*, pp. 137, 222–223.

more than approximately 2,550 additional Jews in the entire Lublin District (1,550 in Janów-Lubelski county, 1,000 in Biała-Podlaska county, and a few in Biłgoraj county). *Kreishauptmann* Lenk in Janów-Lubelski was considering ghettos in seven towns; Augustin was planning a ghetto in Chełm; and Busse was planning ghettos or camps for Hrubieszów and Grabowiec. According to these reports there were ghettos only in Lublin and Piaski. There was a Jewish *Stadtteil* in Opole-Lubelski, a *Judenbezirk* in Biała-Podlaska, and Jewish quarters in Dęblin-Irena, Zamość, and the cities of Radzyń county. Bełżyce, Chodel, and Bychawa had *Judensammelorte*. In Biłgoraj county there was no ghetto, quarter, or *sammelort*, but Jews in the town of Biłgoraj were restricted to certain streets.

The Nazi nomenclature in this correspondence can be confusing. Many terms were used to refer to the ways in which the Jews' housing and movement were being restricted, while the term ghetto was used only in reference to Lublin and Piaski. Did each term refer to a specific type of space or policy for Jews, or were they variations on a theme? Türk clearly distinguished in his September 9 letter between ghettos and other types of concentration of Jews, but it is not clear if all the county chiefs made the same distinction. Weihenmaier, in Zamość, seems to have used the terms quarter and ghetto interchangeably in his report. Similarly, the *Krakauer Zeitung* carried a report on May 16, 1941, on the *Judenghetto* in Opole.[112] Does this mean that all the various terms can be subsumed under the concept of a ghetto for purposes of understanding the policy? Yet Brandt clearly distinguished among terms: there were no ghettos in Puławy county; there was a Jewish quarter in Dęblin-Irena; and there was a *Stadtteil*, not a ghetto, in Opole.[113]

Other terms and ideas raised in some of these reports seem to deepen the confusion. Augustin said he had considered turning the places in Chełm county that were occupied primarily by Jews into a *Judenreservat*, but since there was no room for more Jews, the ghetto in Chełm was postponed and the reservation idea dropped.[114]

112 *Krakauer Zeitung*, May 16, 1941, p. 5 (available in Yad Vashem Library, Pfi 48).

113 Brandt, Pulawy, Chef des Amtes, Lublin, September 12, 1941, WAPL, GDL 270.

114 Augustin to Chef des Amtes, Lublin, September 25, 1941, WAPL, ibid.

Ziegenmeyer argued that the Piaski ghetto and the three *sammelorte* in Lublin-Land county were all severely overcrowded. Remarkably, he suggested evacuating Poles from their homes as a way of clearing out space for Jews.[115] Like Ziegenmeyer, most of the county chiefs as well as the Lublin *Stadthauptmann* argued that lack of space forced them to allow significant numbers of Jews to live outside the areas officially set aside for Jews. In fact, in Lublin, 5,000 Jews out of 39,000 (13 percent) were reported to be living outside the ghetto in September.[116]

Whether for lack of space (e.g., Lublin-Land, Radzyń, Krasnystaw), the outbreak of a typhus epidemic (e.g., Zamość), the fear of an epidemic (e.g., Puławy), or simple lack of interest in ghettos (e.g., Biłgoraj), two things are clear. From the point of view of the middle echelons in the civilian government in the Lublin District, there was little use for ghettos, and there was no room for additional Jews.

This serves to reiterate the fact of the decentralization of the details of the anti-Jewish policy until mid-1941. The mere need for such a survey points to the absence of any central planning for ghettos. Moreover, the generally uncooperative and sometimes even lackadaisical responses from the county heads in Lublin regarding ghettos and taking in additional Jews underscore the authority of the local officials over day-to-day Jewish affairs. Not even pressure from the Wehrmacht or from Frank's office in the spring of 1941 to create ghettos, or in late summer 1941 to desist from creating ghettos, changed this significantly. And the confusing inconsistency in the officials' terminology suggests that certain basic concepts regarding anti-Jewish policy had not yet reached a stage of common discourse among the Germans. In other words, for some officials "ghetto" meant a closed-off neighborhood where Jews must live and could not leave without permission, whereas for other officials the term referred more generally to the mix of residential and movement restrictions. The result of the lack of clarity, the lack of central ghetto planning,

115 Ziegenmeyer to Chef des Amtes, Lublin, September 19, 1941, ibid.

116 Ibid. Note the increase in the Jewish population since the first ghetto census on April 25, 1941, indicating that the expelled Jews were returning.

and the lack of interest in ghettos in Lublin was that the large majority of Jews in the Lublin District did not live in closed ghettos in 1941.

The Jewish testimonies from the Lublin District also reflect varying interpretations of ghettoization and other restrictive German policies. Jewish testimony refers to more ghettos than the number reflected in the German documents. For example, in addition to Lublin and Piaski, Jewish testimonies from the district relate that at least sixteen ghettos were created between November 1939 and the summer of 1941.[117] Many of these ghettos are called "open ghettos" in the testimonies. At the same time, Jewish testimony relates a measure of freedom of movement in places that might otherwise seem to have been ghettos. For example, in Tomaszów-Lubelski the Jews were restricted to two streets in early 1940; in Janów-Lubelski their residence was restricted to one part of town; and in Radzyń to three streets. In all three cases Jewish testimony reflects the relative freedom of movement until well into 1941.

In Radzyń, many of the testimonies use the term ghetto for the restricted residential area, whereas in Janów-Lubelski they generally do not. Testimonies on Łuków and Biłgoraj differ as to whether there was a ghetto, while regarding Opole they differ on the date and whether there was a fence. By comparison, Jews from many other places clearly recall that there was no ghetto at least as late as near the end of 1941 or even in 1942.[118]

117 These ghettos included: Puławy as early as November 1939; Biała-Podlaska, in December 1939; Kazimierz Dolny, spring 1940; Chelm, gradual ghettoization from October 1940 to the end of 1941; Dęblin-Irena, in November 1940; Ryki, by the end of 1940; Wisznice, Kraśnik, Radzyń and Konstantynów, in late 1940; Włodawa in January 1941; Bełżyce, mid or late 1941; Łukow, July 1941; Biłgoraj, in summer 1940; Opole-Lubelski, in March 1941; Zamość in April 1941. Miron and Shulhani, eds., *The Yad Vashem Encyclopedia of the Ghettos during the Holocaust*, refers to twenty-three ghettos created in this period, whereas Laura Cargo refers to twenty-six ghettos in the Lublin District by the end of September 1941 in her introduction to the "Lublin Region" in Dean, ed., *The United States Holocaust Memorial Museum Encyclopedia of Camps and Ghettos, 1933–1945*, Volume II, *Ghettos in German-Occupied Eastern Europe*, p. 605.

118 Among these localities were: Belz, Bełżec, Bełżyce, Biskupice, Dzików Stary, Głusk, Hrubieszów, Kock, Końskowola, Krzeszów, Lubartów, Międzyrzec-Podlaski, Rachów-Annopol, Stężyca, Turobin, and Ulanów. Three of

The criteria for defining a ghetto are also not clear from the testimonies. Some refer to residence restrictions as ghettos, while others define the ghetto by curfews and restrictions on freedom of movement. There are also contradictions between German records and Jewish memory. In places where German records refer to some form of residence restriction other than a ghetto, Jews often recall a ghetto – as in Dęblin-Irena, Opole-Lubelski, and Zamość. Similarly, in a number of places where the German records do not refer to any kind of ghetto or concentration of the Jewish population, Jewish records refer to a ghetto – as in Puławy, Włodawa, and Kraśnik. None of this is surprising, since the harsh conditions and brutality that Nazis might have considered "normal" for Jews could easily match Jewish memory of a ghetto existence. What is more surprising is the two cases – Bychawa and Chodel – where a German *Judensammelort* is not recalled by the Jews as a ghetto. Large numbers of refugees had been brought to both these little towns in 1939–1941, making living conditions more difficult than before. Yet the survivor testimonies that discuss this do not refer to these conditions as a ghetto.

In the final analysis, how many ghettos were there in the Lublin District in 1940–1941, and how many of the district's Jews were living in ghettos? Bogdan Musial and this author have identified four ghettos with approximately 53,500 Jews (approximately 18 percent of the district's Jews), whereas the encyclopedias of the ghettos published by Yad Vashem and the United States Holocaust Memorial Museum cite 23 or 26 (respectively) by the end of September 1941. This ghetto discussion is part of our effort to understand how the Jews lived during this period, what policies

these places did have ghettos by June 1941, according to the *Yad Vashem Encyclopedia of the Ghettos during the Holocaust*: Bełżyce, Hrubieszów, and Konskowola. According to *The United States Holocaust Memorial Museum Encyclopedia of Camps and Ghettos, 1933–1945*, Volume II, *Ghettos in German-Occupied Eastern Europe*, Bełżyce probably never had a formal ghetto, although it is included among their ghettos based on the conditions and Kreishauptmann Ziegenmeyer's September 19, 1941 response to Türk (p. 613); Hrubieszów may have had "a form of open ghetto" at this time (p. 635); Kock effectively had a ghetto from November 1939 (p. 648); and Końskowola had a ghetto by the end of 1941 (p. 655).

the German authorities pursued, and how all this can compare with other places under German rule. By what criteria do we determine if a locality had a ghetto? Should German contemporary documents be our guideline – was there a ghetto only where they said that they created one? Or should Jewish memory be our guide – there was a ghetto wherever Jews felt they had been restricted in one? Here we can make a cogent argument for Jewish memory taking preference, since Jewish memory recalls the *complexion and texture* of the conditions imposed upon them. One thing is clear – not only are the Jewish and German records inconsistent with each other, they do not even maintain internal consistency.

Historians, too, have not been consistent in their definitions of a ghetto. Dan Michman has addressed this question in his recent book, *The Emergence of the Jewish Ghettos during the Holocaust*.[119] For Raul Hilberg, the essence of ghettoization was the Jews' isolation from the surrounding population, whereas the creation of separate "Jewish districts, complete with walls" was added in Poland and the USSR.[120] This means that, for Germany, a ghetto was a social-political status and a state of mind more than a place. Yet elsewhere, relating specifically to Poland, Hilberg defined a ghetto as usually a tightly packed slum without parks or open spaces. A few ghettos had massive walls around them, while others were fenced in, and others could not be sealed at all. He concluded that, by the end of 1941, "almost all the Jews in the incorporated territories and the Generalgouvernement were living in the ghettos."[121] The ghettos in Poland, therefore, were defined by a physical space. An additional element was the changed nature of the Judenrat from organizer of forced labor and welfare and go-between with the authorities on behalf of the Jews to a municipality.[122]

Hilberg also does not distinguish among the variety of conditions under which Jews lived in ghettos, nor between ghettos established at different times – in 1940, in the spring of 1941, or after "Barbarossa." The criterion of the functions of the Judenrat can also be interpreted

119 Michman, *Emergence of Jewish Ghettos*, pp. 6–19, 90–93, and *passim*.

120 Hilberg, *Destruction*, p. 157.

121 Ibid., pp. 229–230.

122 Ibid., p. 232.

in more than one way. The conditions in which the Jews lived in the communities in the Lublin district and the limited extent of ghettoization at least until the end of 1941 indicate that the Lublin District does not match Hilberg's definitions for ghettos.

Yisrael Gutman says ghettos "were, in fact, camps where the Jews were held under duress, with their internal life and organization imposed on them and enforced, through violent means, from the outside, by the Nazi regime." He notes the difference between the closed ghettos in some of the large cities in Poland and the ghettos in medium-sized cities and towns. In the latter there were ghettos from which the Jews were permitted to leave at certain hours of the day to purchase food, and others that were more or less open and movement within and without was possible without special difficulty.[123] Thus, for Gutman, a ghetto is a physical place where duress is the basic criterion.

The Yad Vashem Encyclopedia of the Ghettos employs a functional definition, "based on the actual conditions in which the Jews lived…any part of a pre-existing settlement occupied by Nazi Germany where Jews were forcibly confined for at least a few weeks."[124] In this definition, three criteria define a ghetto: forced confinement; a pre-existing community, or settlement; and the actual conditions. The USHMM's *Encyclopedia of Ghettos and Camps* employs a different, less precise functional definition: "A ghetto is a place where the Germans concentrated the Jews," where only Jews were permitted to live, and where there were family units.[125] These last two definitions leave somewhat open how to define places where Jews were permitted to have contact with their neighbors and where Jewish and German sources are unclear regarding the existence of a ghetto.

Residence under duress and the extent of the restrictions imposed on the Jews are certainly basic criteria for defining a

123 Yisrael Gutman, ed., *Encyclopedia of the Holocaust* (New York: Macmillan, 1990), pp. 579–582.

124 Guy Miron with Shlomit Shulhani, "General Introduction," *Encyclopedia of the Ghettos*, p. XL.

125 Martin Dean, "Editor's Introduction," *Encyclopedia of the Ghettos and Camps*, p. XLIII.

ghetto, regardless of Nazi nomenclature. And Jewish memory is also fundamental, also regardless of the nomenclature. Whatever German officials may have said, or what terms they may have used, it is the complexion of the living conditions that determines the ghetto. And our access to that complexion is largely through Jewish records and memory. However, where a Jewish community had regular, if limited, contacts with non-Jewish neighbors, with access to enough food to avoid starvation and some information from the outside, the conditions were not those of a ghetto. A ghetto without a fence may have been an "open ghetto," but a community with food, contacts, and travel permits was not living in a ghetto. This does not mean that Jews who were not in a ghetto were living normal lives. The German occupation regime was vicious particularly toward Jews. But at least until the summer of 1941, most of the Jews in the Lublin District were not living in a ghetto.

Conclusions

Two enduring aspects of the resettlements and ghettos in the Lublin District in 1940–1941 are particularly striking: the absence of closed ghettos; and the concomitant relatively better living conditions for Jews in this district as compared to other parts of the GG. However, the absence of ghettos and the existence of better conditions should not be mistaken to indicate an absence of antisemitism or lack of agreement with Nazism among the German authorities. As Bogdan Musial has so effectively demonstrated, and as the German civilians' subsequent enthusiastic and diligent cooperation with the SS in carrying out the deportations to death camps in 1942 indicates, the German civilian authorities in the Lublin District were generally very antisemitic and in full agreement with the regime's anti-Jewish policies.

Why, then, were there so few ghettos in the Lublin District? Until the run-up to the deportations in 1942, in practice, ghettos were within the jurisdiction of the civilian authorities. But, although the civilians technically controlled the ghettos, the fact that the SS dominated most aspects of Jewish affairs meant that the SS also could be the ultimate arbiter of ghetto affairs. Whereas the creation of a ghetto by the civilian authorities might have served as an assertion of their authority in some places, in the Lublin District it seems that the *absence* of ghettos served the very same purpose. By not establishing ghettos, the civilian authorities in effect made the job of the SS more difficult and increased their own involvement in Jewish affairs. Without a ghetto the SS would need increasingly to turn to the civilian authorities, becoming dependent on them for the data on the Jews available in the population and labor offices in order to be able to requisition certain numbers of Jews for various SS jobs. Raids such as those in August 1940 wreaked havoc for the SS, who also needed a certain measure of organization. Finding that 25 percent of the yield from the August 13-14, 1940, raids were unfit even by SS standards could only have increased their efforts by forcing them to grab far more Jews than they actually needed. Some measure of cooperation with the civilian authorities could serve SS purposes much better. The Jews, then, were more useful to the civilian authorities if there were no ghetto.

It was also no accident that the civilian authorities did not establish ghettos. It was a conscious decision, taken apparently without the full knowledge of their superiors in Kraków. This was a further reflection of the decentralization of the day-to-day conduct of anti-Jewish policy.

The relatively extensive communications in the Lublin District among Judenräte and between individual Jews via letters, telegrams, telephone, and travel had many ramifications. From December 1939, Jews needed special permission to travel in the GG, but this permission seems to have been granted often, especially to Judenrat members and employees. With much information being shared among the Judenräte and among the Jewish communities, Jews often knew what was happening in each other's communities. When Jews fled from Warsaw to Lublin, Hrubieszów, and other communities in the Lublin District during 1941, they confirmed that conditions were better in Lublin. And herein lies one of the ironies of the Jews in the Lublin District during the spring and summer of 1941. They persistently disobeyed German regulations regarding movement and residence and thereby unwittingly worsened their own living conditions. In the space that Zörner and his subordinates had intended to house 20,000 Jews, the Jews themselves squeezed in more than 34,000, and that number grew during the following months.

Yet despite the resultant overcrowding, beyond even the Nazis' plans, and despite the presence of gnawing hunger, there was little starvation in 1940 and 1941, especially outside the city of Lublin. There were also very few ghettos. Whereas the rate of disease and death rose dramatically in the spring and summer of 1941, it still remained significantly lower than in Warsaw. Death was less pervasive in Lublin than in Warsaw. Jews died at home and were buried in individual graves throughout the district.

The Lublin District Jews' contacts with their non-Jewish neighbors (Poles, Ukrainians, Belorussians) meant the Jews could procure food, some income, information, and human contact. Thus, although the Jews in the Lublin District lived in constant fear and dread both in the present and with regard to what the future held in store for them, they were living in less fear and dread than Jews in Warsaw, Lodz, or other communities. And they knew this from their contacts with these communities. The mere fact that they had means of communication with their neighbors, to which the German authorities seem to have turned a blind eye fairly frequently, must have contributed to their own awareness of their relatively less debilitating and less dehumanizing conditions. At the same time, as Szmul Zitomirski reported in July 1941, aside from food and social welfare, conditions in Lublin were actually worse than in Warsaw in terms of the Jewish spirit. Just as there was less of a socio-economic gap in Lublin than in Warsaw, there were relatively fewer cafés and theaters frequented by a ghetto upper class, far less underground political activity, no education for the children, no underground newspaper, and so on. And perhaps most important, the less debilitating living conditions in the Lublin District had absolutely no effect on the Jews' survival rate in 1942–1943.

Chapter 6

Organizing the Deportations

Globocnik's Appointment

Between July 17 and 21, 1941, in conjunction with his visit to Lublin, Himmler gave Globocnik two new assignments: to coordinate the establishment of SS and police colonies in the East (the GG and the USSR); and to build a concentration camp in Lublin to house 25–50,000 prisoners who would be employed in SS economic enterprises.[1] Globocnik's preparatory work both in anticipation of receiving these appointments and subsequently, combined with the general planning of anti-Jewish policy in Berlin, culminated in his assignment to organize and implement the murder of the Jews of the GG.

Some of this preparatory work regarding manpower, planning methods of murder, and "preparing" the intended victims for the moment when they would be taken to their deaths was begun even

1 Globocnik memorandum on SS- und Polizei Stützpunkte, July 18, 1941, and Himmler "Vermerk," July 21, 1941, in Globocnik's personnel file in BDC, copy in YVA, O.68/654; Peter Witte, et al., eds., *Der Dienstkalender Heinrich Himmlers 1941/42* (Hamburg: Christians, 1999), pp. 185–186, 189. See also Józef Marszalek, *Majdanek; The Concentration Camp in Lublin* (Warsaw: Interpress, 1986), pp. 18–19; Tomasz Kranz, *Extermination of the Jews at the Majdanek Concentration Camp* (Lublin: Państwowe Muzeum na Majdanku, 2007), pp. 10–11; Arad, *Belzec, Sobibor, Treblinka*, pp. 14–15.

before Himmler's July visit to Lublin. Globocnik's appointment to plan the murder came apparently on or around October 13, 1941, when Globocnik and Krüger were in Berlin to meet with Himmler on these matters. The summer appointment to coordinate the establishment of SS and police colonies also marked Globocnik's independence from Krüger, his formal superior in the GG. In planning the colonies – and in planning the murder – Globocnik reported directly to Himmler.[2]

The SS colonies' appointment was formally only an expansion of a November 2, 1940, appointment to do the same in the GG. Approximately fifteen such sites were established, each manned by some ten Germans and worked by Polish and/or Jewish forced-laborers. The earlier appointment had been an outgrowth of Himmler's October 7, 1939, appointment as RKFdV, which included the authority to create new German colonies in the occupied eastern territories.[3] Now Globocnik was to seek out appropriate sites for colonization in Soviet territory as well. During the summer and fall

2 Evidence of the October appointment can be found in *Dienstkalender*, pp. 233–234. For a thorough discussion of this, see also Bogdan Musial, "The Origins of 'Operation Reinhard': The Decision-Making Process for the Mass Murder of the Jews in the *Generalgouvernement*," *Yad Vashem Studies*, 28 (2000), pp. 117, 128–133; *idem*, *Zivilverwaltung*, pp. 192–200. See also Pohl, *Judenpolitik*, p. 101. According to Richard Breitman, it was during Himmler's same July visit to Lublin, and in connection with the SS and police colonies appointment, that he assigned Globocnik to head the murder operation; Breitman, *Architect*, pp. 184–190. However, Breitman's insightful analysis could not benefit from documents that were not yet available then, in particular Himmler's office diary. Still, Globocnik's early preparations for a large and murderous operation, as discussed below, do seem to indicate possible preparations for the murder of the Jews of the GG even prior to the appointment and as early as Breitman surmised. See also Józef Marszałek, "System obozów śmierci w Generalnym Gubernatorstwie i jego funkcje (1942–1943)," *Zeszyty Majdanka* XVII (1996), pp. 17–38. On Globocnik's independence based on the colonies appointment, see, for example, the 1976 Hamburg court ruling in the trial of Karl Streibel, YVA, TR.10/869, pp. II:82–83. Himmler's visit was well remembered by other Germans in Lublin. For example, Wolfgang Mohwinkel, then deputy commander of the Lipowa 7 camp, recalled that Himmler and Globocnik visited the camp on July 20, 1941, at which time both Mohwinkel and his commander, Riedel, were promoted by Himmler. See Mohwinkel indictment, YVA, TR.10/770, pp. 34–35; and his May 1964 interrogation, in TR.10/1291, pp. 5156–5157.

3 Globocnik file, YVA, O.68/654; Koehl, *RKFDV*, pp. 49–53; YVA, TR.10-1291,

of 1941, Globocnik did send a number of his officers (e.g., Georg Michalsen and Richard Thomalla) to Riga, Pinsk, Kiev, and other locations in the USSR under the guise of this project; soon thereafter these men were actively involved in implementing "Operation Reinhard."[4] In addition, the Trawniki training camp for Red Army renegades who joined the SS as auxiliaries was formally subordinated to Globocnik's colonization function, which was independent of all other authorities in the GG.[5]

Robert Koehl and Götz Aly have argued that the RKFdV was at "the center of Himmler's empire" and that the murder of the Jews was integrally connected to this, whereas Richard Breitman believed that the colonization appointment might have been camouflage for the murder assignment.[6] Later research by Bogdan Musial, Dieter Pohl, and others has shown that Globocnik was probably appointed to the murder function only in October, and that Frank and others in the civilian government in the GG and in the Lublin District knew of this by October 17.[7] However, the extensive overlapping and intertwining of Globocnik's staffs for the colonization and murder operations seems more than coincidental.

The path to Globocnik's appointment as head of the murder of the Jews in the GG in October goes back to the summer and is paved with massive murder in the USSR and planning of the murder by Globocnik and his staff during the summer and early fall. Both the developments relating to the general context of the "Final Solution" and Globocnik's summer and fall 1941 preparations, which soon were connected to the murder of the Jews in Lublin and the GG,

testimony of Gustav Hanelt, April 8, 1963, pp. 3579–3580. See also Streibel Trial judgment, YVA, TR.10/869, ibid.

4 YVA, TR.10/813, Michalsen indictment, pp. 32–34, 38–39, 45–46; TR.10/859, Worthoff verdict, pp. 4–6; TR.10/869, Streibel verdict, II–III:83–84; TR.10/1146Z, Worthoff interrogation, VII:1350–51, Pechmann interrogation, IX:1674; TR.10/1291, Michalsen interrogation, XXVII:4631–4632.

5 See Streibel verdict, ibid., II:83–91.

6 Koehl, *RKFDV*, p. 31 and *passim*; Aly, *"Final Solution," passim*; Breitman, *Architect*, pp. 184–190.

7 See Musial, *Zivilverwaltung*, pp. 196–206; *idem*, "Origins of 'Operation Reinhard,' " pp. 117, 128–133; Pohl, *Judenpolitik*, pp. 99–102; *Dienstkalender*, pp. 233–234.

were part of the context in which the murder of the Jews in the GG was planned. In the broader context of developments leading toward the "Final Solution," the formal appointment of Heydrich as coordinator of the "Final Solution," on July 31, 1941,[8] the spread of the murder in the USSR to include women and children in August and September, and the subsequent experimental gassing at Auschwitz in September[9] are among the events that constitute the murder environment that included Globocnik's appointment. In the specific Lublin and GG context, the dispatch of a unit of the SS and police in the Lublin District, personally chosen by Globocnik, as part of a larger Einsatzgruppe raised in the GG by BdS Schöngarth, to work together with and parallel to the EG in their mass-murder duties in Soviet territory,[10] and the preparation activities for murder

8 Nuremberg Document PS-710; Yehuda Bauer, "Who Was Responsible and When? Some Well-Known Documents Revisited," *Holocaust and Genocide Studies*, 6:2 (1991), pp. 144–147; Christopher R. Browning, "The Decision Concerning the Final Solution," in *Fateful Months: Essays on the Emergence of the Final Solution* (New York: Holmes and Meier, 1985), pp. 21–22; Breitman, *Architect*, pp. 192–193; Hilberg, *Destruction*, pp. 418–419; Yaacov Lozowick, *Hitler's Bureaucrats: The Nazi Security Police and the Banality of Evil* (London and New York: Continuum, 2002), pp. 76–77.

9 Rudolf Höss testified at times that Himmler summoned him to Berlin in the summer of 1941 to inform him of the upcoming "Final Solution." The accuracy of Höss's testimony is open to question, and it is entirely possible that he confused the years. Whereas he may have been told by Himmler in Berlin in the summer of 1941 of the decision to kill the Jews, the order to transform Auschwitz-Birkenau into the main killing center was probably given only in the summer of 1942. See Rudolf Höss, *The Commandant of Auschwitz* (New York: Popular Library, 1959), pp. 135–202; Bauer, ibid., p. 147; Breitman, ibid., pp. 188–190; Browning, ibid., pp. 22–26; *idem*, "A Final Hitler Decision for the 'Final Solution'? The Riegner Telegram Reconsidered," *Holocaust and Genocide Studies*, 10:1 (Spring 1996), pp. 3–10.

10 See Franz Magill trial, Landgericht Braunschweig, 2 Ks 1/63, pp. 36–98 in verdict, and pp. 28–32 in indictment (copies in YVA, TR.10/897 — indictment, and TR.10/ 516 — verdict); Hermann Worthoff verdict, YVA, TR.10/859, pp. 4–6; Yehoshua Büchler, "*Kommandostab Reichsführer-SS*: Himmler's Personal Murder Brigades in 1941," *Holocaust and Genocide Studies*, 1:1 (1986), pp. 13–17; Pohl, *Judenpolitik*, p. 91; Hilberg, *Destruction*, pp. 302–305, 339.

The Lublin SS company commanded by Hermann Worthoff played a major role in the murder of the Pinsk Jews in August 1941, together with two companies from the SS Cavalry Regiment, commanded by Franz Magill, who had commanded the SS Cavalry Regiment stationed in Lublin in 1940.

undertaken by Globocnik soon after Himmler's Lublin visit were also part of this environment.[11]

In July, Globocnik began to develop Trawniki as a training camp for a personal army of murderers. In September and October, his intellectual think tank developed the framework of a murder plan. In mid-October, Globocnik was formally appointed by Himmler, and shortly after that the construction of the Bełżec death camp got underway. The close proximity of the commencement of the construction at Bełżec to Globocnik's October 13 meeting with Himmler indicates that the site and basic plan for the camp were prepared before that meeting took place.

It is not only the question of the timing of Globocnik's appointment to command the "Final Solution" in the GG that is of interest. So, too, is the question of why this important operation was based in Lublin. Was this merely coincidental, or were there specific reasons for the choice?

Various theories have been proposed for why Lublin was chosen as the center of the murder of the Jews of the GG, ranging from the ideological, to the geographic, to the personal. There is Nazi ideological literature contemporary to the events that puts some emphasis on Jewish Lublin, such as Hermann Erich Seifert's late 1941 book *Der Jude an der Ostgrenze,* or articles like Gustav Andraschko's, in the *Krakauer Zeitung,* May 31, 1942, "Die 'Lehranstalt der Weisen Lublins.'" These and other works identified Lublin as the major center

Hermann Fegelein, one of the senior SS murderers in the USSR, was overall commander of the two SS Cavalry Regiments and the other forces attached to them for these murder operations. It is not clear if this former Lublin connection played any role in bringing together these two units in Pinsk in August 1941. See YVA, TR.10/897 and TR.10/516, ibid.; YVA, TR.10/1163 Z, Magill interrogation, November 15, 1960 (original in ZStL, 204 AR-Z 296/60); Horst Riedel interrogation, in YVA, TR.10/1291, XLIV:8148; and Büchler, ibid.

11 On these preparations in general, see, for example, Pohl, *Judenpolitik*, pp. 92–106; Arad, *Belzec, Sobibor, Treblinka*, pp. 15–23; Musial, "Origins of 'Operation Reinhard,'" pp. 114–115, 142–143; Breitman, *Architect*, pp. 199–201; Frank, *Diensttagebuch*, pp. 424–459, *passim*; Shmuel Krakowski, *Chełmno A Small Village in Europe: The First Nazi Mass Extermination Camp* (Jerusalem: Yad Vashem, 2009), pp. 31–50. For an excellent discussion of the development of plans for the murder of the Jews in this period, see Browning, *Origins*, pp. 352–373.

of religious and secular Jewish leadership in the world. Andraschko referred to Yeshivat Hakhmei Lublin as the largest Talmud school in Europe and to its heads as "the uncrowned kings" of the Jews.[12] For a confirmed Nazi this would indicate that Lublin was at the heart of the imaginary evil international Jewish conspiracy.

If Nazi leaders believed Lublin was so important to the Jews, then this could explain the apparent use of Lublin as an experimental area for Jewish policy; for example, the Jewish "Reservation" scheme. However, this argument has at least two serious flaws. First, no such references to Lublin by Hitler, Himmler, or other top Nazi figures have been found. Nazi literature from the GG in the first two years of the occupation makes no such reference to Lublin.[13] Second, most such references are contemporary to the planning and implementation of "Operation Reinhard," leaving open the question of whether they expressed the ideological motivation for choosing Lublin as the murder center, or, rather, a post facto justification for that decision.

The geographic argument for the Lublin decision, as stated by Shmuel Spector, for example, is based on the district's eastern location in the GG. Prior to the invasion of the Soviet Union, this was the frontier, and, following that invasion, it remained the easternmost section of the largest Jewish population under Nazi rule, a section that also remained outside the murder operations of the EG. Spector suggests that the location of the three "Reinhard" death camps very near to the former Soviet border (Treblinka in the north, on the way to Białystok; Bełżec on the southern border,

12 Hermann Erich Seifert, *Der Jude an der Ostgrenze* (Berlin: Zentralverlag der NSDAP, 1941); Gustav Andraschko, "Die 'Lehranstalt der Weisen Lublins,'" *Krakauer Zeitung*, May 31, 1942, nr. 127, p. 5. See also Nachman Blumental, "On the Holocaust in Lublin" (Hebrew), in *Encyclopedia of the Jewish Diaspora, Lublin*, pp. 66–67.

13 See, for example, du Prel, *Das Deutsche Generalgouvernement Polen*, pp. 13–14, 141–143, 166–169. Du Prel was propaganda minister under Frank when he wrote the book. The *Krakauer Zeitung* also has no such references prior to 1942. Both sources are full of disparaging, ideological remarks about Polish Jews, but no particular importance is given to Lublin, save Du Prel's passing mention of the Jewish autonomy there centuries ago and of the world-famous *yeshivah* (p. 169).

near Rawa Ruska and on the road to Lwów; and Sobibór on the Bug River in the east) was meant to serve the Nazi claim that the deported Jews were being sent eastward for labor. According to this theory, this geography also explains why Lublin was at times an experimental area for Jewish and other policies.[14] Here, too, there is no clear documentary evidence to support the theory. The fact that only Sobibór was actually in the east of the GG, and not in the north or south, casts doubt on the argument. Still, the Nazi deception of "relocation to the East" was clearly part of their overall deportation strategy, lending credence to the theory at least post facto.

The personal theory, as expounded by Yitzhak Arad, suggests that Lublin was chosen because Globocnik was there, rather than the other way around. Globocnik was ruthless, ambitious, creative, and both in debt to and loyal to Himmler (unlike his immediate superior in the GG, Krüger). Himmler had sent Globocnik to Lublin in 1939, in part in order to give him an opportunity to reclaim his reputation, which had been seriously tarnished by the embezzlement scandal in Austria that ended in his dismissal from his post as *Gauleiter* in Vienna. Globocnik's independent, ambitious, creative and ruthless character was evidenced in the struggle over Jewish forced labor in 1940 (see Chapter 4). By this very ruthlessness, and his success in accomplishing his assigned tasks with the cold brutality that was the SS ideal, he won praise from Himmler, as well as a promotion and support. Thus, his appointment to head "Reinhard" was a natural consequence of his personality and of his relationship with Himmler.[15] Bogdan Musial carries the personal

14 Conversations with Dr. Shmuel Spector, August 1992.

15 Arad, *Belzec, Sobibór, Treblinka*, pp. 14–15. There is much SS correspondence and several reports on the financial scandal surrounding Globocnik in Austria in Globocnik file, YVA, O.68/654. For Himmler's praise, see, for example, Himmler to Wendler, August 4, 1943, where he praises Globocnik for his skill and dynamism in performing his duties, despite his faults, ibid. In the December 1973 indictment against Heinrich Birmes, Ernst Gollak, and Benno Winkler for their roles in "Operation Reinhard," the prosecution in Hamburg also cited Globocnik's "restless and insatiable aspiration for ever more power" and his excellent ideas for overcoming problems of masses of people as reasons for the large role he and his Lublin staff played in the murder of the Jews; Anklageschrift gegen Heinrich Birmes, Ernst Gollak, Benno Winkler wegen Mordes - Zwangsarbeitslager Alter Flugplatz, Lublin, 141 Js 573/60,

theory even further, arguing that Globocnik himself initiated his own appointment.[16] His energetic preparations even prior to his October meeting with Himmler lend some credence to this analysis. As with the other theories, there is no clear documentary evidence to support the personal theory, despite the evident logic on which it is based.

It is quite possible, too, that the decision to appoint Globocnik to head the murder of the Jews of the GG, based in Lublin, was the result of a combination of the above factors. The "Reservation" plan was indeed influenced by Lublin's proximity to the Soviet border, fueled by the hope to send all the Jews ultimately into the USSR. Once this region had been discussed as the possible center for a "solution" to the Nazis' Jewish "problem," it may have continued to be one of the main regions under discussion as further ideas for the Jews were proposed. This would be especially true once the "territorial final solution," the notion of evicting all the Jews from Europe (to Madagascar or some other location) proved unfeasible by late summer or early fall of 1940. Globocnik's success as SSPF was likely to have influenced Himmler's decision, and his nearly boundless ambition may well have led him to seek such an appointment. After all, control of a major element of Jewish policy meant power in the Nazi regime. Ultimately, what is most significant is not why Lublin, or why Globocnik, but rather the fact that all the above factors coincided in early 1942 to fuel the murder machine that began operating on March 16, 1942.

Organization and Manpower

Once he received his appointments regarding SS and police colonies and the construction of Majdanek, Globocnik began gradually to organize three main areas that were crucial to the later murder operation: manpower, the locations and methods of murder, and the

Staatsanwaltschaft Hamburg, December 11, 1973, copy in YVA, TR.10/815, p. 57.

16 Musial, "Origins of 'Operation Reinhard,' " pp. 118–122.

intended victims. The manpower that Globocnik commanded directly or indirectly during the two years following these appointments was vast. Those who were ultimately involved in "Operation Reinhard" included: a core staff of some 450 SS men specially recruited for the operation from among his own SSPF staff, the top secret T-4 ("euthanasia") operation, run out of Hitler's chancellery, which had just been halted temporarily with regard to killing adults, as well as other members of the SS and police; all of the approximately 2,000 German SS and police in the Lublin District; nearly all 4–5,000 Red Army renegades who had volunteered for the SS from their POW camps in the Lublin District (e.g., Chełm) or had been brought to the GG from POW camps in the USSR;[17] local Polish and Ukrainian police; Selbstschutz units in their various manifestations; and other assorted smaller groups. In addition, he could call on the remainder of the 15,000 SS and German police in the GG, the hundreds of Selbstschutz-type troops in other districts, the remainder of the approximately 14,000 local Polish and Ukrainian police, and other units passing through the GG or serving other functions there. All together, at any given moment, he had at his disposal a manpower pool of some 35,000 men from all across the GG, of whom perhaps 8,000 were based in his district.

"Einsatzstab Reinhard" and the Lublin SS. The nerve center of what came to be called "Operation Reinhard" was the 450-man staff of "Einsatzstab Reinhard" (the "Operation Reinhard" staff) that Globocnik put together in the latter months of 1941. This staff existed independently of other SS units in the district and was even housed in completely separate quarters.[18] The separate address

17 On the recruitment of the Trawniki men, see Peter Black, "Foot Soldiers of the Final Solution: The Trawniki Training Camp and Operation Reinhard," *Holocaust and Genocide Studies*, 25:1 (2011), pp. 6–7; *idem*, "Die Trawniki Männer und die 'Aktion Reinhard'," in Bogdan Musial, ed., *"Aktion Reinhardt": Der Völkermord an den Juden im Generalgouvernement 1941–1944* (Osnabrück: Fibre Verlag, 2004), pp. 315–316.

18 See Arad, *Belzec, Sobibór, Treblinka*, p. 19; Marszałek, *Majdanek*, pp. 54–55; *idem*, "Centralny Zarząd Budowlany SS i policji w Lublinie," *Zeszyty Majdanka*, VI (1972), pp. 22–23; Mohwinkel, et al., indictment, YVA, TR.10/770, pp. 75–76. See also the testimonies of Josef Birger-Ezrahi, YVA, M.49.E/2791, O.3/447,

facilitated secrecy and direct control by Globocnik. This specially selected staff, along with other Lublin SS men who developed an expertise in large ghetto-clearing operations, were Globocnik's front line in the murder of some two million Jews.

According to Globocnik's October 27, 1943, report to Himmler, as he began to sum up "Operation Reinhard," the main components of "Einsatzstab Reinhard" were 339 SS men from a variety of SS functions in the district (among them, forty-nine from the SSPF staff; forty-two from the intellectual SS-Mannschaftshaus; twenty-six from the Trawniki training camp), ninety-two men on loan from Hitler's chancellery (the T-4 operation), and nineteen men from the economic branch of the SS (WVHA) who were associated with the DAW in the district.[19] These last were, for all intents and purposes, under Globocnik's command in any event.

"Einsatzstab Reinhard" was fully organized by early 1942, although not yet by that name. The operation's organizational structure had three departmental divisions:

a. the Main Department, headed by *SS-Sturmbannführer* Hermann Höfle (promoted July 21, 1942), in charge of organization, manpower, and deportations;
b. the death camps, headed by *SS-Sturmbannführer* and Police Inspector Christian Wirth (promoted July 21, 1942);
c. the sorting of Jewish valuables, headed by *SS-Sturmbannführer* Georg Wippern (promoted January 30, 1942).

The above three SS officers were the central figures under Globocnik in organizing and coordinating "Operation Reinhard." A fourth aspect that Globocnik oversaw directly, apparently in order to

O.3/6774, where he refers to Globocnik's multiple addresses for his different functions. The address for the "Reinhard" headquarters was 11 Pieradzkiego Street, in the former Stefan Batory secondary school. The "Reinhard" name began to be used in the summer of 1942.

19 See Nuremberg documents NO-057, NO-064. See also YVA, TR.10/869, vol. I, p. 10, and vol. 2, pp. II:103–104. This October 27, 1943, letter by Globocnik to the chief of personnel in the SS, *SS-Obergruppenführer* Maximilian von Herff, can be found in several sources. The original is in Globocnik's BDC file.

maintain the secrecy of some matters from his competitors and superiors, was forced labor by the skilled Jews left behind following the main wave of murders.[20]

Hermann Höfle was one of the many Austrians among Globocnik's close advisors and deputies. Following a tour of duty as the Selbstschutz commander in Nowy Sącz in 1939, he was transferred to Globocnik's SSPF staff in the autumn of 1940, where he was assigned to work on stationing SS and police colonies in the GG. In July 1941, Globocnik assigned him to the same type of work in the newly-occupied Soviet territories, and this may have served as the initial cover for Höfle's "Operation Reinhard" assignment. In fact, he was not listed among the SSPF staff in the district's personnel lists in July 1941, or later, appearing as "without assignment" ("*Ohne Beruf*"), which may also have been part of the operation's camouflage. In "Reinhard" he served as Globocnik's operations' chief and second-in-command in the murder of the Jews. Höfle coordinated all incoming and outgoing transports of Jewish deportees and instructed all "Reinhard" personnel on their duties. He also personally commanded various deportation operations within the Lublin District, especially the larger ones, as well as the Warsaw deportations that began on July 22, 1942.[21]

20 The details of the organizational structure of "Einsatzstab Reinhard" are based on the following sources: Globocnik's reports to Himmler, January 5, 1944, Nuremberg documents NO-057, NO-064; YVA, JM/1905, January 16, 1961, pp. 7–14 (original in ZStL, 8 AR-Z 74/60); Georg Michalsen interrogations, February 14, 1961, YVA, TR.10/1146Z, X:1865–1869; Georg Lothar Hoffmann interrogations, January 20 and 21, 1960, May 5 to June 9, 1960, TR.10/1146Z, II:234–237, III:853–865; Max Runhof (Czichotzki) interrogation, TR.10/1146Z, XII:2499–2503; TR.10/1061, indictment of Hoffmann, Worthoff, Sturm, et al., pp. 254–418, *passim*; TR.10/813, Michalsen indictment, pp. 51–77; TR.10/859, Worthoff verdict, pp. 10–42; indictment of Ernst Lerch and Helmut Pohl, November 17, 1971, Vienna, 15 St 2.696/62, copy in YVA, TR.10/736 (also in Moreshet Archive [MA], D.1.5873), pp. 21–24; Anklageschrift gegen Karl Streibel u.a., Staatsanwaltschaft be idem Landgericht Hamburg, 147 Js 43/69, December 7, 1970, p. 69, in YVA, TR.10/756, and TR.10/869, II:19–23, 43–60, 65–68, III:279; Mohwinkel indictment, YVA, TR.10/770, pp. 75–77; Arad, *Belzec, Sobibor, Treblinka*, pp. 15–19.

21 See Höfle's SS personnel file, YVA, JM/3669, which includes his various assignments and his promotion recommendation by Globocnik, December 1941. See also Michalsen verdict, YVA, TR.10/813, pp. 81–82, 92–100; Worthoff

Georg Wippern came to the "Reinhard" staff from heading the SS-Standortverwaltung (supply administration) in Lublin. This department was a branch of the same in Warsaw until July 16, 1941, when the SS administration in Berlin, in coordination with Himmler's impending visit to Lublin, elevated it to an independent status. This facilitated secrecy, as well as Globocnik's utilizing Wippern's department in his various ventures that were independent of Krüger. For example, Wippern was Globocnik's deputy for planning SS and police colonies in the East during the latter part of 1941 and early 1942. He opened branches of his Standortverwaltung in at least seven other GG locations, in connection with his "Reinhard" and German colonization functions. The Trawniki branch supplied the Ukrainians in the Bełżec and Sobibór death camps. In anticipation of the deportation operations, he set up Abteilung IV, "Werterfassung," which was his vehicle for confiscating valuables and sorting the deported Jews' possessions. It was also the vehicle for selling some of these possessions for a profit for Globocnik and his cohorts. Thus, Wippern's staff served "Reinhard" in two important ways: processing the valuables of the dead Jews, and feeding their murderers.[22]

Christian Wirth was the senior T-4 man brought in for the operation. He arrived in Lublin in the autumn of 1941, along with a number of other T-4 personnel, and his initial tasks included

verdict, YVA, TR.10/859; YVA, JM/1905, January 16, 1961, pp. 7–14, and February 16, 1961, p. 8; Streibel verdict, YVA, TR.10/869, II:43–47; Lerch and Pohl indictment, YVA, TR.10/736, pp. 21–24; Arad, *Belzec, Sobibor, Treblinka*, pp. 18–19. The personnel lists are in WAPL, GDL 882. Copies of several of these lists are in YVA, O.53/82 and JM/2699, and in MA, D.1.5869, D.1.5869/1, D.1.5869/2. The interrogations of Höfle himself are full of lies and are unreliable. See YVA, O.4/34-3.

22 YVA, JM/1905, February 16, 1961, p. 30; Streibel verdict, YVA, TR.10/869, II:65–68, III:279; Michalsen verdict, TR.10/813, p. 83; Lerch and Pohl indictment, TR.10/736, p. 23; Birmes and Gollak indictment, TR.10/815, pp. 58–60. On the sale of Jewish belongings locally, see YVA, O.53/68, which contains dozens of orders and receipts from the sorting camp at Chopin St. 27, in Lublin. WAPL, SSPF 2, contains orders and receipts from Kraśnik (see Chapter 8). The seven known branches were in Lwów, Chełm, Zamość, Lubartów, Poniatowa, Rejowiec, and Trawniki. On Wippern see also Hilberg, *Destruction*, pp. 1014, 1025–1026. It is odd that Dieter Pohl, in *Judenpolitik*, makes no mention of Wippern.

overseeing the construction of the first death camp, Bełżec, and determining the method of murder. In mid-December 1941, he was appointed commandant of Bełżec, and later, in the summer of 1942, he moved his office to Lublin after becoming inspector of the "Einsatz Reinhard" death camps. Shortly thereafter he also took over command of the main sorting station for Jewish valuables at the forced-labor camp in the old airfield in Lublin.[23]

In addition to his main department heads in "Operation Reinhard," Globocnik needed planners, organizers, trainers, deportation and shooting staff, camp staff, and sorting staff. Among his leading planners were the intellectuals in the SS-Mannschaftshaus in Lublin, to whom Globocnik turned to develop ideas and methods, while others dealt with building manpower and garnering field experience. The Mannschaftshaus, under the leadership of *SS-Hauptsturmführer* Gustav Hanelt (promoted January 30, 1942), was a sort of fraternity and think tank of SS academics to whom Globocnik would turn when he wanted plans developed to support some of his grander ideas. It is no coincidence that forty-two members of this think tank, including Hanelt, representing virtually the entire unit, were coopted into "Einsatz Reinhard." They became intimately involved in planning all aspects of the operation with Globocnik and his chief deputies. Himmler approved these plans.[24]

23 YVA, JM/1905, Zeug memos, January 16, 1961, p. 12, and February 16, 1961, p. 30; Victor Brack memo to Himmler, June 23, 1942, Nuremberg Document NO-205; Michalsen verdict, YVA, TR.10/813, pp. 82–83; Streibel verdict, YVA, TR.10/869, II:9–60; Arad, *Belzec, Sobibor, Treblinka*, pp. 17–25; Hilberg, *Destruction*, pp. 959–962; Tregenza, "Belzec Death Camp," pp. 16–17. On Wirth and the beginning of the development of these camps, see also Michael Tregenza, "Christian Wirth a Pierwsza Faza 'Akcji Reinhard,' " *Zeszyty Majdanka*, XIV (1992), pp. 7–37; Browning, *Origins*, pp. 362–364, 371–372. Brack's memo has also been published in various sources, such as Adalbert Rückerl, ed., *Nationalsozialistische Vernichtungslager im Spiegel deutscher Strafprozesse; Belzec, Sobibor, Treblinka, Chełmno* (Munich: Deutsche Taschenbuch Verlag, 1977), pp. 120–121.

24 See YVA, JM/1905, "Vermerk," February 16, 1961, p. 8; Streibel judgment, YVA, TR.10/869, pp. 102–105; Simcha Turkeltaub statement, YVA, TR.3/1416; and Turkeltaub's testimony in *Encyclopedia of the Jewish Diaspora, Lublin*, pp. 729–731. See also Pohl, *Judenpolitik*, pp. 101–102; Bogdan Musial,

Experience in mass murder was also an important element in preparing "Operation Reinhard." The veterans of the euthanasia program came with extensive murder experience, and they brought with them the idea of using gas chambers. Similar experience was accrued by the SSPF and KdS men who were sent into the USSR either as part of EG ZbV, or as part of Globocnik's search for appropriate sites for SS colonies. All these men had played an active role in murder operations in the USSR using the EG mass-shooting method; some almost certainly had witnessed the use of gas vans. When these men returned to the GG, they were hardened, experienced mass murderers. Those from Lublin could then be quickly incorporated by Globocnik into the planning and perpetration of the murder operations, while those from other GG districts would be able to benefit from this experience when called upon to liquidate the Jewish communities in their own areas.

Most noteworthy of the SSPF men sent into the Soviet Union in the summer of 1941 was *SS-Obersturmführer* (*Hauptsturmführer* as of January 30, 1942) Georg Michalsen, who became one of Globocnik's most important and competent ghetto-clearing experts. Like so many of Globocnik's murder deputies, Michalsen's first GG assignment was as a Selbstschutz commander in 1940. He then served as commandant of the Jewish forced-labor camp at Płazów, under Dolp. Globocnik sent Michalsen to Riga in mid-July 1941, to select sites for SS colonies in occupied Soviet territory; there Michalsen participated in shootings of Jews, including the murder of 26,000 in Rumbuli (November 30—December 2, 1941). He was assigned to "Reinhard" upon returning to Lublin in May 1942, and went to Warsaw in July as Höfle's deputy in the Lublin SS and police unit sent there to organize the deportation to Treblinka – by far the largest deportation operation of "Operation Reinhard." Like most

"Ursprünge der 'Aktion Reinhardt'. Planung des Massenmordes an den Juden im Generalgouvernement," in *idem*, ed., *"Aktion Reinhardt": Der Völkermord an den Juden im Generalgouvernement 1941–1944* (Osnabrück: Fibre Verlag, 2004), pp. 62–64. Simcha Turkeltaub recalled that he learned of the murder plans when he delivered leather coats to Hanelt and his wife, apparently in late 1941 or early 1942. Hanelt's tongue was loosened by liquor and perhaps a guilty conscience.

of the senior players in "Operation Reinhard," he joined Globocnik in Trieste in the autumn of 1943.[25]

Two KdS men who were sent to the USSR in the summer of 1941 later played prominent roles in the deportations: *SS-Obersturmführer* Hermann Worthoff and *Untersturmführer* Dr. Harry Sturm. The two became fast friends during their service in the USSR, and this friendship helped them to murder together efficiently.

Worthoff came to the KdS Lublin from the Gestapo in June 1941, and commanded the Lublin company within EG ZbV. His unit saw action murdering Jews in many places and played a central role in the murder of the Jews of Pinsk in August 1941. He

25 After his long bout with dysentery, which he contracted in Płazów, Michalsen returned to the SSPF Lublin staff in mid-April 1941. In Warsaw, he was actually in command much of the time, since Höfle frequently returned to Lublin during that operation, although he, too, was pulled out temporarily in late August in order to command the deportation of 11,000 Jews from Międzyrzec to Treblinka (see Chapter 7). In August 1943, Globocnik assigned him to liquidate the Białystok ghetto. In late 1942, Michalsen was officially put in charge of the unrelated task of resettling Balkan ethnic Germans in the Lublin District, and, in early 1943, he oversaw the transfer of the Schultz and Többens factories from the Warsaw ghetto to Trawniki and Poniatowa (see Chapter 8). He was then involved in organizing forced-labor camps in the district. Throughout these various assignments Michalsen was repeatedly called upon to command deportations. See Michalsen indictment, pp. 31–35, 45–46, 92–120, 158–168, and verdict, 30, 87, in YVA TR.10/813; Michalsen interrogation, Hamburg, February 14, 1961, in ZStL, 208 AR-Z 268/59, investigations of Müller, Hoffmann, and others, in YVA, TR.10/1146Z, X:1867–68; Michalsen interrogations, Hamburg, cases 141 Js 573/60 and 141 Js 192/60, January 7 to March 10, 1964, April 19 to November 20, 1967, and February 9, 1970 (13 sessions), TR.10/1291, XXVII:4624–4751, XLIV:4468–70, LIII:10,295–10,305; Eugen Lehnert interrogation, Hamburg, February 12, 1970, LIII:10,306–10,313; YVA, JM/1905, January 16, 1961, pp. 14–21; Streibel verdict, TR.10/869, pp. 50–51; Browning, *Ordinary Men*, pp. 88–95.

Otto Hantke also served in the USSR and then in "Operation Reinhard," mainly in the area of Jewish forced labor. He was also a member of the Lublin unit that orchestrated the Warsaw deportations, where he was in charge of the *Umschlagplatz*. Hantke was then assigned to set up the Budzyń forced-labor camp in the autumn of 1942, and the Poniatowa camp shortly thereafter. In June 1943, he was given command of the small camp in Puławy, most of whose Jewish forced-laborers were killed in the *Erntefest* operation in November 1943 (see Chapter 8). See YVA, TR.10/813, indictment, pp. 38–42, 123–138, 168–180, and verdict, pp. 120–139, and TR.10/1291, Hantke interrogation, XLIV:8103–8104.

received a promotion upon his return to Lublin in mid-September, and in October he took over the IVB4 ("Jews") office in the KdS Lublin, which he headed until the end of 1942. This position put him effectively in charge of the ghetto. He and his staff were well known to Lublin's Jews. They were frequently in the ghetto and had contacts with Jewish officials, Jewish police, and informers. Alten reported to him at least once or twice a week. To the Jews in Lublin he was the all-powerful ghetto ruler. He was the field commander of the deportations from Lublin in March and April 1942, as well as of the ghetto liquidation in November, heading a unit of some forty KdS men and four companies (480 men) of Ukrainian Hiwis from Trawniki. He was also the number-three man in the Lublin contingent sent to Warsaw to organize the deportations from there to Treblinka (he accompanied Höfle and Michalsen to Adam Czerniakow's office on July 22, 1942).[26]

Harry Sturm was assigned to EG ZbV from his position in the SD division of the KdS apparatus in Lublin – he headed IIIB, the "Volkstum" department. Although Worthoff was formally his

26 Worthoff verdict, YVA, TR.10/859, *passim*; TR.10/1146Z, Worthoff interrogations, October 9–10, and November 18, 1960, VII:1350–63, and Heinrich Pechmann interrogation, January 19, 1961, IX:1674; Michalsen indictment, TR.10/813, p. 92–113; Georg Lothar Hoffmann interrogations, May 5—June 9, and November 18, 1960, and January 9–10, 1963, TR.10/1146Z, V:855–856, VIII:1436–1438, XVI:3442–3460; Harry Sturm interrogations, February-March 1961, TR.10/1146Z, X:1924–1929, and March 23, 1964, TR.10/1291, XXVII:4945–4952; Johannes Erich Kalich interrogations, March 23—April 22, 1965, XX:4255–4336; Ida Glikstein testimony, *Dos Büch*, pp. 402–404; *idem*, *Encyclopedia of the Jewish Diaspora, Lublin*, pp. 707–711; Mina Halberstadt-Kaplan testimony, ibid., pp. 486–488; Klajnman-Fradkoff testimony, YVA, O.33/1134; Moshe Zylberberg testimony, YVA, M.1.E/1402.

See also Raul Hilberg, Stanislaw Staron, and Josef Kermisz, eds., *The Warsaw Diary of Adam Czerniakow* (New York: Stein and Day, 1982), p. 385; Blumental, *Documents*, Protocols 16(140)–26(150), pp. 314–333.

It is noteworthy that, like Eichmann in IVB4 in the RSHA, he was independent of his formal superior (Lublin IVB head Georg Lothar Hoffmann). Jewish affairs, especially in late 1941 and 1942, brought power beyond the formal position in the chain of command. Like many young SS men in the Lublin District, Worthoff met his future wife during his GG service. They met in Lublin and married in Tomaszów-Mazowiecki on September 5, 1943. For the SS men involved in the murder, normal life continued.

superior officer, they worked closely together as equals in all their joint operations. In Lublin, Sturm accompanied Worthoff to the Judenrat offices to issue the deportation decrees of March 17 and March 31, 1942.[27]

In this constellation of personalities leading "Operation Reinhard," *SS-Sturmbannführer* Johannes Müller, the KdS in Lublin from the summer of 1941 to November 9, 1943, also played an important role. Müller was not part of the contingent sent to the USSR, but he was involved in choosing those who were sent (together with his predecessor, Huppenkothen), and he reassigned the men upon their return. His rapport with Globocnik facilitated developing close working relations with regard to the murder of the Jews. Together with Globocnik and Höfle, he and his top subordinates determined the size of the KdS units allocated to deportation operations. However, the specific individual assignments to these operations in the city and the district were his responsibility alone. It seems that Müller and Globocnik were somewhat kindred spirits in corruption as well. In the autumn of 1943 Müller was investigated for having taken money in return for allowing seventy to eighty Jews with supposed South American citizenship to leave. Ultimately, Müller was allowed to go to Trieste to join Globocnik's staff there, but he was nearly arrested and punished for taking bribes.[28]

27 Worthoff verdict, YVA, TR.10/859, *passim*; Georg Wenk interrogation, March 16, 1964, XXVIII:4882–83, YVA, TR.10/1291. See also Sturm's interrogation, March 24, 1964, TR.10/1291, XXVIII:4944–53. Nearly all the sources refer to Sturm as well, in connection with Worthoff and their joint activities. Note the irony of Sturm's 1964 address – Anne Frank Street in Frankfurt.

Regarding other KdS men sent to the USSR to murder Jews, see also Worthoff interrogation, October 9, 1960, TR.10/1146Z, VII:1350; Heinrich Pechmann interrogation, January 19, 1961, TR.10/1146Z, IX:1674–76; Max Stöbner interrogation, April 25, 1961, TR.10/1146Z, XI:2268–71.

28 The story of Müller's investigation is based on the testimony of SS investigator Kurt Nieding. Lublin SD head Biegelmeier and Gestapo head Liska confirmed the allegations. See YVA, TR.10/1146Z, II:333–336, V:954–55, VIII:1655, IX:1691; Hoffmann verdict, TR.10/1061, pp. 217–218.

When questioned by Nieding, Müller did not deny having left some Jews behind, but he did not admit to taking bribes. In November 1943, BdS Bierkamp ordered Nieding to arrest Müller, but Müller had already departed Lublin on his way to Trieste. Nieding caught up to Müller and his wife, but ultimately he let him go. It is possible that this case was connected to the Kraśnik camp,

Finally, three other SSPF figures coopted to "Reinhard" should be mentioned for their significant roles in developing the murder infrastructure: *SS-Hauptsturmführer* Richard Thomalla, *Obersturmführer* Helmut Pohl, and *Hauptsturmführer* Karl Streibel. Thomalla was the *Baumeister* (master builder) for "Operation Reinhard," working with Wirth on the construction of Bełżec, supervising the construction of Sobibór and Treblinka, and serving as Sobibór's first commandant. Pohl was another of Globocnik's Austrian subordinates, arriving in Lublin in early 1942, and serving as Höfle's deputy in charge of directing incoming trains of deportees from the Reich, the Protectorate, and Slovakia. Together with German civilian officials from the BuF department, he conducted selections for laborers among the arriving deportees.[29]

"Operation Reinhard" was well coordinated among "Einsatzstab Reinhard," the KdS men, and the ORPO. Generally, following the Lublin model, in March 1942, a man from Höfle's department briefed the local men and supervised and coordinated with Lublin. It was also the "Reinhard" staff representative who was responsible for contacting Trawniki in advance of or during each operation to requisition Hiwis commanded by Germans. The KdS men were in charge of the operation in the field in each place, and ORPO served as additional deportation manpower and guards on deportation trains. The city or county German police determined whether and to what extent to utilize Polish or Ukrainian police from the district in a "ghetto-clearing" operation.

Building manpower for "Reinhard" also involved increasing SS and police manpower in the Lublin District. One example of local manpower enhancement is the near doubling of the KdS's Jewish Affairs department (IV B 4) to some forty men during the last three months of 1941, making it by far the largest department of the KdS staff. Worthoff's appointment as commander of this

where prisoners had prepared false papers from foreign countries in order to escape (see Chapter 8).

29 See Streibel verdict, YVA, TR.10/869, II:47–48; Lerch and Pohl indictment, TR.10/736, pp. 12–13, 38; Michalsen interrogation, February 26, 1981, ZStL, 201 AR-Z 313/63, VI:1727–1733, case 147 Js 8/75, Landgericht Hamburg; Tregenza, "Belzec Death Camp," pp. 17–18.

department also reflected the preparations for murder. His higher rank than his predecessor, Walther, who now became his deputy, and his recent experience in Pinsk had prepared him for this job. A more serious job required more men, more experience, and a more senior officer.[30]

Police units. The German police constituted one of the main sources of manpower for deportations in "Operation Reinhard." They engaged in deportations, shootings, round-ups, anti-partisan warfare, and general security.

In early 1942, German police units in the Lublin District totaled approximately 1,000 men in three battalions. By early summer these numbers had grown by many hundreds of men to include the following units: Reserve Police Battalion 41; Reserve Police Battalion 67; Polizeireiterabteilung III; Polizei Reiterzüge Lublin und Zamość (i.e., two platoons); Reserve Police Company Frankfurt/Oder (on loan from the Warsaw district); Reserve Police Company Gleiwitz; and Reserve Police Battalion 101 (included in district police orders as of July 3, 1942). These units were augmented by more than 1,000 local Polish and Ukrainian police.[31]

July 1942 was a month of extensive reassignments involving the

30 Interrogations of Johannes Erich Kalich, March 23 to April 22, 1965 (11 sessions), YVA, TR.10/1146Z, XX:4254–55, 4292; Worthoff verdict, TR.10/859, pp. 20–22.

31 See notes and memoranda from the KdO Hermann Kintrup, and KdSchupo Peter, dated June 4—July 3, 1942, in YVA, O.53/121. Polizeireiterabteilung III was formed in November 1941, in Vienna and arrived in Lublin in late April or early May 1942, filling the void left by the cavalry battalion that had gone into the USSR at the start of "Operation Barbarossa." Battalion headquarters were in Chełm, and the commander was Schupo Major Alfred Eggert. The third company was based in Hrubieszów and took an active role in all deportations and shootings there, as well as in the *Erntefest* shootings in Majdanek, on November 3, 1943. Other units of the Reiterabteilung were involved in murder and anti-partisan operations in Chełm, Biała-Podlaska, and Janów-Lubelski counties. See TR.11/01121, Generaldirektion für die Öffentliche Sicherheit, Des Ministerium für Inneres, Republik Österreich, to Dr. Warbinek, Abteilung 11, Bundesministerium für Justiz, December 17, 1964. On Police Battalion 306, see the trial record of eighteen of its members, in YVA, TR.10/790. For details on the activities of these and other police units in the Lublin district, see Curilla, *Die Judenmord in Polen und die Deutsche Ordnungspolizei*, pp. 687–832.

German police in the GG. New units were brought in and integrated into the general police structure there, while other units were moved within the GG, or reassigned to other parts of Europe. The net result of these police movements and reassignments, which were part of the ordinary run of affairs, was a further increase in police manpower in the Lublin District. These transfers were influenced in part by the steady increase and spread of partisan activity in the Lublin District and elsewhere.[32]

In Lublin, the police reorganization and redeployment took effect on July 14, 1942, in response to the increase of partisan activity since June 1, and made possible by the replenishment of manpower. The district police was reorganized as Police Regiment 25, and the district was divided into three geographic zones (north, central, and south), each policed by a battalion to which were attached: a company ("Reiterschwadron") of Polizeireiterabteilung III; a Gendarmerie platoon ("Hauptmannschaftsbereich"); local Polish or Ukrainian police; signal corps staff (radio; communications). Recently-arrived Reserve Police Battalion 101 was now called "Sicherungsabschnitt Nord" (Northern Security Section), based in the Gendarmerie offices in Radzyń; Battalion 41 was now "Sicherungsabschnitt Mitte" (Central Security Section), based in Lublin; and recently-arrived Battalion 67 was now "Sicherungsabschnitt Süd" (Southern Security Section), based in the Gendarmerie offices in Zamość.

The reorganization order by KdO and Regiment Commander Hermann Kintrup was originally to take effect July 13, but was delayed by one day. This was probably in connection to Battalion 101's shooting operation in Józefów (in the south, near Bilgoraj) on July 13, in which some 1,500 Jews were shot in the woods outside the town. Battalion 101 moved north to its new posting on July 20. The order went on to specify the assignments of assorted auxiliary

32 See, for example, the instructions to policemen being transferred to France, Norway, and Riga, dated July 31—August 5, 1942, and "Regiments-Befehl Nr. 33" of the KdO Lublin, August 7, 1942, in YVA, O.53/121. The same file and others contain numerous documents on the increase in partisan activity at this time. See, for example, Globocnik's June 27 order regarding the policy for "*Sühnemassnahmen*" (retaliatory actions) against the local population for the killing of Germans; ibid.

units and staff, indicating a total German police manpower in the district at this time of more than 2,000.[33] The Lublin regiment was again reorganized, effective September 2, into four zones, with Polizeireiterabteilung III now serving as a battalion, responsible for the three counties bordering the Bug River – Biała-Podlaska, Chełm, and Hrubieszów – and renamed "Sicherungsabschnitt Bug."[34]

Trawniki. Globocnik's main source of camp guards and one of his most significant pools of murderers was Red Army POWs, especially the non-Russians among them. Of the estimated 650,000 Soviet POWs that had been brought to the GG by early 1942, nearly half died very quickly of exhaustion, exposure, and hunger, or by shooting, and most of the remainder were in camps in the Lublin District.[35] Hundreds of thousands of Soviet citizens joined the Germans in various auxiliary units from among the POWs and from among local, anti-communist armed units and civilians.[36] Many thousands of POWs were employed as shooters in mass killings of Jews and others, as round-up units in deportations from ghettos, or as guards in forced-labor camps, in concentration camps, and in all

33 See top secret "*Regimentsbefehl*" by Hermann Kintrup, July 9, 1942, YVA, O.53/121. See also various orders of Central Command, July 14–30, 1942. Dieter Pohl provides incomplete figures regarding police manpower in 1942. However, two bits of data are of interest: 441 German gendarmes in the district in late 1942, and 1,315 Polish police. On Battalion 101's activities in Józefów, see Browning, *Ordinary Men*, pp. 55–70.

34 *Regimentsbefehl* (no number), KdO Lublin, August 27, 1942, YVA, O.53/121.

35 Pohl, *Judenpolitik*, pp. 90–91; YVA, TR.10/1146Z, interrogations of: Gotthardt Schubert, XV:3068–3081; Bruno Meiert, XVI:3295–3305; Wilhelm Wagner, XVI:3368–3373; Klaus Hornig, XVI:3376–3393; Wilhelm Kaussen, XVI:3422–3426; Heinrich Zaun, XVII:3791–3793, XX:4505.

36 On German treatment of Soviet POWs in general and the extent to which Red Army soldiers joined the Germans, see Christian Streit, *Keine Kameraden: Die Wehrmacht und die sowjetischen Kriegsgefangenen 1941–1945* (Stuttgart: Deutsche Verlags-Anstalt, 1978), pp. 128–190, pp. 244ff; Alfred Streim, *Die Behandlung sowjetischer Kriegsgefangner im "Fall Barbarossa"* (Heidelberg: C. F. Müller Juristischer Verlag, 1981), *passim*; Richard Breitman, "Himmler's Police Auxiliaries in the Occupied Soviet Territories," *Simon Wiesenthal Center Annual*, 7 (1990), pp. 23–39; and Alexander Dallin, *German Rule in Russia, 1941–1945: A Study of Occupation Policies* (New York and London: Macmillan, 1957).

the death factories. There are records of Ukrainians, Lithuanians, Letts, Estonians, Belorussians, Armenians, Uzbeks, Turkmen, and members of other nationalities in the USSR who joined the German forces both at the front and in the murder operations. The first three groups mentioned above were particularly prominently represented in these German-trained but often self-initiated auxiliary units.[37] In the USSR, these auxiliary units fought alongside the SS, German police, and Wehrmacht on the front, in rearguard anti-partisan warfare, and in brutal operations against civilian populations, especially against civilians of opposing nationalities (e.g., Lithuanians or Ukrainians in operations against Poles).

Within the Lublin District, the most prominent group of Red Army renegades recruited by the Nazis were the Ukrainians. The reasons for the willful and active participation of members of these national groups in German forces are numerous and sometimes complex, and this aspect of the history of the Holocaust and of World War II has been the source of much historical discussion and acrimonious polemics. Most of this discussion is beyond the parameters of this book. What concerns us here is the fact that there were volunteers from among these groups who became an integral part of the murder of the Jews in general and of "Operation Reinhard" in particular.

Two of the important sources of information on these volunteers are the interrogations and trial records of collaborators, kept in archives in the former USSR, and West German interrogation and trial records of Germans who were involved in training and commanding these units. Clearly, Soviet interrogations alone are not reliable, objective reflections of reality. Nor can statements by German SS or policemen be accepted at face value without close scrutiny and care. However, the KGB records cannot be dismissed outright as the product of Communist kangaroo courts, full of forced confessions and phony convictions, as Peter Black has so ably demonstrated in his extensive research on the Trawniki men.[38]

37 Black, in his excellent article, "Foot Soldiers," has made extensive use of Soviet interrogation files in his analysis of the makeup and behavior of the Trawniki men.

38 Ibid.

Similarly, the German trial testimonies cannot be dismissed as purely self-serving. Moreover, the overlap and mutual corroboration between these two bodies of material is extensive. There is also much Jewish and German contemporary and oral history documentation detailing the role of these volunteers in perpetrating the Holocaust and in other criminal activities. When examined carefully, both the KGB archival documents and the German trial documents can provide valuable information or corroboration regarding aspects of the recruitment, training, and activities of these volunteer units.

In order to recruit and train volunteers from among Red Army POWs, Globocnik sent agents to comb the POW camps. He established a special training camp for the volunteers at the site of a former Polish beet-sugar factory in the town of Trawniki, some 45 kilometers southeast of Lublin, in the direction of Chełm. The candidates for SS training at Trawniki initially were recruited primarily from the POW camp in Chełm, although other POW camps in the Lublin District, as well as camps outside the district and even outside the GG, were also visited by recruiters (volunteers for auxiliary units in occupied Soviet territory were generally recruited in these areas). Globocnik's SS officers recruited in Chełm, while local SS officers, most likely in contact with Globocnik, recruited in camps outside the Lublin District.

The first Ukrainians and Russians brought to Trawniki in early July 1941 included both recruits and prisoners. Among these were Volga Germans, many of whom became the drill sergeants for the large numbers of recruits who began to arrive in September 1941. By July 9, 1941, there were already 675 people in the camp, including Jewish prisoners guarded by Cossacks, Russian political commissars, Polish prisoners, 141 Ukrainian volunteers, and an undefined number of Russian volunteers. The Ukrainians were expected to undergo further improvement measures (*Verbesserungsmassnahme*).[39]

39 MGB Ukraine Wachmann interrogation files for: Grigoriy Stepanovich Nesmyan (April 1949), Filial Otraslevogo Gosudarstvennogo Arkhiva Sluzhby Bezopasnosti Ukrainy v Rovenskoy Oblasti, in YVA, TR.18/83, includes interrogation material of Aleksander Aleksandrovitch Duchno (January 1947); Gavril Mikhailovitch Milyushko (May 1950), Filial Otraslevogo Gosudarstvennogo Arkhiva Sluzhby Bezopasnosti Ukrainy v Dnepropetrovskoy

The first camp commandants during the early organizational and construction period were *SS-Obersturmführer* Erwin Rokita and Schupo officer Albert Drechsel. *SS-Hauptsturmführer* Karl Streibel (promoted to *Sturmbannführer* on Hitler's birthday, April 20, 1942), one of Globocnik's trusted deputies from early 1940, took over as camp commandant on October 27, 1941, and his two predecessors continued to serve under him. Streibel came to this job based on his background as a company commander and battalion adjutant in the Selbstschutz in Lublin from January 5, 1940 to February 20, 1941. He continued in these capacities in the Sonderdienst when it was transferred to Kraków, until his appointment to the Trawniki job. During his first term in Lublin, on August 27, 1940, he was also assigned to serve under Dolp in the Bełżec forced-labor complex in the summer and autumn of 1940, replacing Michalsen as commander of the Płazów labor camp following the latter's departure as a result of dysentery. His experience and success with training and commanding non-German or vaguely German recruits (the Selbstschutz) recommended him well to Globocnik for this new position.[40]

The camp was directly subordinate to the SSPF Lublin and was called at first "SS-Ausbildungslager Trawniki," or "Beauftragter des Reichsführers-SS für die Errichtung der SS- und Polizeistützpunkte im neuen Ostraum - Ausbildungslager Trawniki." The significance of the latter assignation is that it put the Trawniki camp outside of all GG jurisdictions other than Globocnik's, since Globocnik was answerable only to Himmler for his SS colonies' functions. In

Oblasti, in YVA, TR.18/49, includes interrogation material of Ivan Andrevich Tarasov; Vladimir Aleksandrovitch Gadzitskiy (October-November 1948), Filial Otraslevogo Gosudarstvennogo Arkhiva Sluzhby Bezopasnosti Ukrainy v Rovenskoy Oblasti, in YVA, TR.18/82, includes interrogation material on Petr Petrovitch Yatsenyuk (June 1947). I would like to thank my friend and colleague Mary Ginzburg for helping me find and read these files; "Bericht über die Besichtigung des Auffanglagers in Trawnicki," July 9, 1941, and Türk to Kipke, July 14, 1941, YVA, O.53/84 and *Dokumenty*, pp. 258–259; TR.10/869, III:211–212, cites the testimony of SS man Ewald Mader to the effect that he was assigned to Trawniki as early as July 6, 1941; Stanislaw Jablonski, "Obóz pracy SS w Trawnikach," unpublished manuscript, YVA, O.6/472, p. 4; Black, "Rehearsal for 'Reinhard,'?" pp. 225–226.

40 Streibel trial, YVA, TR.10/756, pp. 45–52, and TR.10/869, I:14–18, II:11–15.

fact, the oath that the recruits signed was to Himmler's deputy for establishing SS colonies in the new eastern territories. There was also a shorter version of the oath, which vowed loyalty to the SSPF. In both cases this meant that Streibel and his camp were directly responsible to Globocnik alone, and not to Krüger or any other SS, police, military, or civilian authority in the GG.[41]

The Trawniki camp began to be organized in early July 1941. The sugar factory's buildings were used for the training camp, the sorting center established at Trawniki in April 1942, to sort Jewish belongings, and later the Schultz and Co. factory's Jewish forced-labor camp, transferred from Warsaw in 1943. There is evidence that there was a Ukrainian Wachmann unit from Trawniki serving at the Lipowa 7 Jewish POW camp as early as the autumn of 1941.[42] The Trawniki camp was inside the town, approximately one kilometer from the train station. A rail spur led directly into an inner courtyard inside the factory's main building. The factory was surrounded by a three-meter-high stone wall, and a road circled it. The factory was constructed in two parts; these lent themselves easily to creating a division between the trainees' camp on one side and the labor camp on the other. The two parts of the camp were separated by a double barbed-wire fence, with three to four meters between the fences.[43]

When they arrived at Trawniki, the recruits were first set to work building their own barracks, alongside Jewish forced-laborers from Piaski and Lublin who had been brought there earlier in the summer. This work continued during and after the volunteers' training as well. They were generally not asked to complete personal

41 Streibel verdict, YVA, TR.10/869, I:14–18, II:11–15, 82–91. The various oaths of allegiance are in YVA, O.51/170.

42 Streibel verdict, YVA, TR.10/869, III:211–217; interview with Josef Birger-Ezrahi, YVA, O.3/6774; Roman Fischer testimony, YVA, O.3/2124. Malka Zyskind testified at the Streibel trial that a Wachmann unit was in Lipowa 7 by the autumn of 1941, and surviving Jewish inmates from the camp recall the presence of uniformed Ukrainian guards there at the same time. Similarly, *SS-Hauptsturmführer* Georg Lothar Hoffmann recalled in his 1960 interrogations that the KdS Lublin had a "Kosakenkompanie" of approximately sixty former POWs at his disposal from late 1941; TR.10/1146Z, V:857. The camp is first mentioned in the minutes of the Lublin Judenrat on July 28, 1941. See Blumental, *Documents*, Protocol 41(102), July 28, 1941, p. 263.

43 Streibel verdict, YVA, TR.10/869, III:259–260; TR.18/49, 82, 83.

questionnaires for at least one or two weeks; this process, with the assistance of translators, could occur in stages, which might stretch over several weeks. Completing the forms was accompanied by photographing, fingerprinting, and swearing in the new recruits, and the Germans added a physical description to the forms to complete the registration. The recruits were then told that they were no longer POWs, but were now part of the German army.[44]

Training at Trawniki was geared toward three functions: guarding camps, rounding up Jews for ghetto deportations, and mass shootings. The incoming volunteers received green uniforms, black caps, and gray coats and were divided into companies of approximately 100 men; each group was commanded by German officers and German and ethnic-German drill sergeants. The training period lasted two to three months, though it was sometimes shortened on the basis of manpower needs. During this time they learned German commands, weapons parts in German, handling weapons, shooting, guarding ghettos and camps, cordoning off sections of ghettos and camps, guarding valuables, shooting escaping prisoners, some basic German vocabulary, marching, anti-Soviet propaganda, and songs in German and Ukrainian. They eventually did guard duty at Trawniki, but at first this was done together with Germans, because the Germans did not trust them. When they first received their rifles, the Ukrainians did not receive any bullets. After they were observed a while longer, they received five bullets each. After further observation by the Germans, they were allowed to guard Trawniki. They were also put to work guarding the forced-labor camp, as well as performing maintenance tasks in the camp.

The daily routine went from 6 A.M. to 10 P.M. and included eight hours of training as well as other tasks in off-hours. On Saturday, training lasted only half a day, followed by camp chores.

44 MGB Ukraine interrogation files for Grigoriy Stepanovich Nesmyan, with material from Aleksander Duchno interrogations, YVA, TR.18/83; Gavril Mikhailovitch Milyushko, with material from Ivan Tarasov interrogations, YVA, TR.18/49; Vladimir Aleksandrovitch Gadzitskiy (October-November 1948), YVA, with material from Petr Yatsenyuk interrogations, TR.18/82. See also Black, "Foot Soldiers," pp. 12–14, and *idem*, "Die Trawniki Männer," pp. 321–323.

Sunday was a day off. At the conclusion of their training, the recruits received the rank of Wachmann, and they were now deemed ready for duty at a death camp or another camp, or for duty in ghetto round-ups. They were also sent to perform mass shootings. Among the Germans they were also known as Trawniki-men, Askaris, and Hiwis (for *Hilfswillige*). The precise number of Ukrainians and others trained at Trawniki cannot be ascertained, but some surviving documentation indicates that, in early 1943, there were 3,354 such men at Trawniki, in addition to those already stationed in camps and ghettos, or assigned to police units. Therefore, we might estimate that the total number of Wachmänner at Globocnik's disposal was between 4,000 and 5,000.[45]

Construction of Camps

Various methods of mass murder in Nazi Germany had been utilized since the war began, including shooting, poison, and gassing in small gas chambers. The EG in Poland shot many thousands of Poles and Jews in 1939, and their successors in the Soviet Union embarked on the shooting of hundreds of thousands shortly before Globocnik's appointment. Gas vans were being developed during the autumn of 1941 for use by the EG and, shortly afterward, at the camp at Chełmno, just as the method of gassing in gas chambers used in the euthanasia program was being adapted experimentally at Auschwitz. Based upon the collective experience garnered in the euthanasia program and by the EG, Globocnik and his advisors developed a murder plan based on gas chambers utilizing carbon monoxide gas (from diesel engine exhaust) as the main murder method.

45 MGB Ukraine interrogation files for Grigoriy Stepanovich Nesmyan, with material from Aleksander Duchno interrogations, YVA, TR.18/83; Gavril Mikhailovitch Milyushko, with material from Ivan Tarasov interrogations, YVA, TR.18/49; Vladimir Aleksandrovitch Gadzitskiy (October-November 1948), YVA, with material from Petr Yatsenyuk interrogations, TR.18/82; Streibel verdict, TR.10/869, III:317–319; Black, "Foot Soldiers," p. 7; *idem*, "Die Trawniki Männer und die 'Aktion Reinhard,' " pp. 317–319.

The murder sites had to fulfill several needs simultaneously for Globocnik and his men: proximity to major rail lines (for transporting deportees); remoteness from major population centers (to maintain secrecy); geographical proximity to the Lublin headquarters of the operation (for efficient control); and geographical spread (in that shorter deportation distances could enhance murder efficiency). The needs for nearness and remoteness and for centralization and camp dispersion could be contradictory, but the three sites that were chosen between the autumn of 1941 and the spring of 1942 – Bełżec, Sobibór, and Treblinka – met all these requirements.

During the latter part of October or beginning of November 1941, construction of a death camp began at a site adjacent to the Bełżec forced-labor camp that had operated in 1940. It is not clear which SS unit was responsible for the construction. Adalbert Rückerl and Yitzhak Arad, basing themselves on the 1965 trial of Christian Wirth's adjutant, Josef Oberhauser, say that the Zentralbauleitung der Waffen-SS in Lublin was contracted to do the construction under Oberhauser's supervision.[46] This would make sense, since this organization was in charge of all SS construction in the district. However, Michael Tregenza believes that Richard Thomalla, who designed and oversaw the construction of the Sobibór and Treblinka camps, did the same for Bełżec.[47] This proposition is supported by the 1981 testimony of Georg Michalsen, who called Thomalla Globocnik's *Baureferent* (construction expert) and claimed that he was not part of the above-cited Zentralbauverwaltung, which did not have a central role in "Operation Reinhard."[48]

Globocnik's approach to preparing other aspects of "Reinhard" would support this hypothesis; he took great care to

46 Arad, *Belzec, Sobibor, Treblinka*, p. 24; Rückerl, *NS-Vernichtungslager*, pp. 72–76, 107, 132.

47 Tregenza, "Belzec Death Camp," pp. 17–18; Peter Witte, "Functioning of the Death Camps in Belzec and Sobibor," paper presented at the conference "'Aktion Reinhardt': Extermination of the Jews in the General Government," Lublin, November 7, 2002.

48 In his February 26, 1981, testimony, Michalsen said that it was out of his "Reinhard" construction authority that Thomalla built Bełżec, Sobibór, and Treblinka. ZStL, 201 AR-Z 313/63, Bd. VI:1727–33, case 147 Js 8/75, Landgericht Hamburg.

maintain secrecy, at first even from ostensible colleagues in Lublin. "Einsatzstab Reinhard" was a secret unit that included men from outside the Lublin SS, and Globocnik went to great lengths to maintain the secrecy of the camps and of the murder operation in general. Therefore, an architect brought in from the outside, such as Thomalla, would have fit this pattern.

Construction at Bełżec was begun by Ukrainian Hiwis supervised by Germans, and within days a team of Poles from the area was brought in to continue the job. There was some turnover among the Polish laborers during the following weeks, and they were replaced shortly before Christmas by Jews, apparently from the small town of Lubycza Królewska, just south of the camp. There may also have been Jewish forced-laborers involved during the earlier stage. Construction was completed by mid- or late February 1942, at which time experimental gassings of several hundred Jews were conducted on the laborers and on others from the same town and from the area.[49]

Camp construction continued at Bełżec even after large-scale gassings began on March 17, 1942. The construction of the other two "Reinhard" camps was staggered; a new camp was begun as a previous one began operating. Construction began at Sobibór at approximately the same time that the first transport of Jews arrived

49 Polish War Crimes Commission Report to the United Nations War Crimes Commission, January 28, 1948, Case No. 1372, p. 1261, in YVA, JM/10156; testimony of Tadeusz Misiewicz before Polish War Crimes Commission, October 15, 1945, in YVA, JM/3536a. The testimonies of thirty-five Poles who were involved in the construction of Bełżec are on the same microfilm reel. All refer to Jews brought in from the direction of Rawa Ruska in December 1941, to replace the Polish construction workers. Lubycza Królewska is on the road to Rawa Ruska. They also all clearly recall the "blacks"; that is, the Ukrainian volunteers. The Polish War Crimes Commission and the Polish testimonies date the beginning of Bełżec construction to late October 1941. See also Central Commission for Investigation of German Crimes in Poland, *German Crimes in Poland*, vol. II, pp. 89–90; Arad, *Belzec, Sobibor, Treblinka*, pp. 24–26; Rückerl, *NS-Vernichtungslager*, pp. 72–76; Tregenza, "Belzec Death Camp," p. 16; *idem*, "Bełżec – Okres Eksperymentalny, Listopad 1941 – Kwiecien 1942," *Zeszyty Majdanka*, vol. 21 (2001), pp. 165–206; Musial, "'Modelfall über die Judenvernichtung'"; Witte, "'Functioning of the Death Camps in Belzec and Sobibor'."

at Bełżec from Lublin, while construction at Treblinka began shortly after the first transports arrived at Sobibór.

Thomalla was in charge of camp construction at both sites, and Polish and Jewish slave laborers were utilized there as well. As in Bełżec, an experimental gassing was conducted at Sobibór prior to the opening of the camp. In mid-April 1942, some 250 Jewish forced-laborers, most of them women, were brought in from the nearby Krychów labor camp and gassed to death. At Treblinka there seems to have been no experimental gassing prior to the arrival of the first transports of Jews from Warsaw on July 22, 1942.[50]

Finally, mention must be made of the camp known as Majdanek. Unlike Bełżec, Sobibór, and Treblinka, this camp, on the southern outskirts of Lublin, was not formally part of "Operation Reinhard." However, because Globocnik was put in charge of the construction of this camp at the same time that he received his other new appointments from Himmler, he attempted to integrate it into his overall activities as the need arose.

Majdanek's distinction from the "Operation Reinhard" camps is reflected in many of its aspects and functions. Unlike the "Reinhard" camps, whose design, size, and location were determined by Globocnik and his men, Majdanek's features and functions were influenced by Himmler and the Concentration Camps Inspectorate, in addition to Globocnik. It received Polish prisoners, Soviet POWs, and others, in addition to Jews, and served simultaneously as a forced-labor camp and as a murder center. It was constructed by Jews and Soviet POWs (see Chapter 4) beginning in the summer of 1941, but its projected size and function were altered several times by Himmler. It variably was meant to serve as a forced-labor camp, a concentration camp, a POW camp, and a death camp. It was built by the Zentralbauleitung der Waffen SS in Lublin, and neither Thomalla nor Wirth played any role in its construction.[51]

50 See Arad, *Belzec, Sobibor, Treblinka*, pp. 30, 37; Rückerl, *NS-Vernichtungslager*, pp. 72, 76, 166; testimony of Sonia Guter, YVA, M.1.E/1255; Jules Schelvis, *Sobibor: A History of a Nazi Death Camp* (Oxford and New York: Berg, in association with the United States Holocaust Memorial Museum, 2007), pp. 25–29.

51 For background on Majdanek's construction and role, see Marszalek, *Majdanek*,

Since Majdanek was formally part of Nazi Germany's concentration-camp system, its commandant was appointed through the Concentration Camps Inspectorate in Berlin, which was outside Globocnik's jurisdiction. At the same time the camp was subordinate to Globocnik in his SSPF functions. This was a certain formula for competition between the camp's commandant and Globocnik, although it gave Globocnik quite a bit of influence over the camp's affairs. The rank and experience of its first commandant is also telling regarding the somewhat incidental connection of this camp to "Operation Reinhard." Karl Otto Koch held the SS rank of *Standartenführer*, as opposed to the much lower ranks of Globocnik's subordinates in Bełżec, Sobibór, and Treblinka. Koch also brought with him years of experience in concentration camps, most recently as commandant of Buchenwald. The camp in Lublin was constructed under Globocnik's authority, but his authority over the day-to-day affairs of the camp was not absolute. Koch and his successors posed a challenge to Globocnik's economic and political empire in Lublin.[52]

Despite all these limitations on his freedom of maneuver in Majdanek, Globocnik was able to integrate the camp into several elements of "Operation Reinhard," such as establishing it as a sorting point for Jewish deportees from Germany and Czechoslovakia, using it as a sorting station for Jewish valuables, and as a Jewish forced-labor camp within Globocnik's economic enterprises. Ultimately, Majdanek played a relatively secondary, though important, role in "Operation Reinhard," until the murder of 18,000 Jewish forced-laborers there in *Aktion Erntfest* in November 1943.

pp. 18–35; *Die Judenausrottung in Polen*, MA, A.466/5, pp. 12–20; Tomasz Kranz, "Das Konzentrationslager Majdanek und die 'Aktion Reinhardt,' " in Bogdan Musial, ed., *"Aktion Reinhardt": Der Völkermord an den Juden im Generalgouvernement 1941–1944* (Osnabrück: Fibre Verlag, 2004), pp. 233–255; Barbara Schwindt, *Das Konzentrations- und Vernichtungslager Madanek. Funktionswandel im Kontext der "Endlösung"* (Würzburg: Köningshausen & Neumann, 2005), pp. 59–72; and the sources cited in this connection in Chapter 4 of this book.

52 Marszalek, *Majdanek*, pp. 37–48.

Operation Reinhard Structure

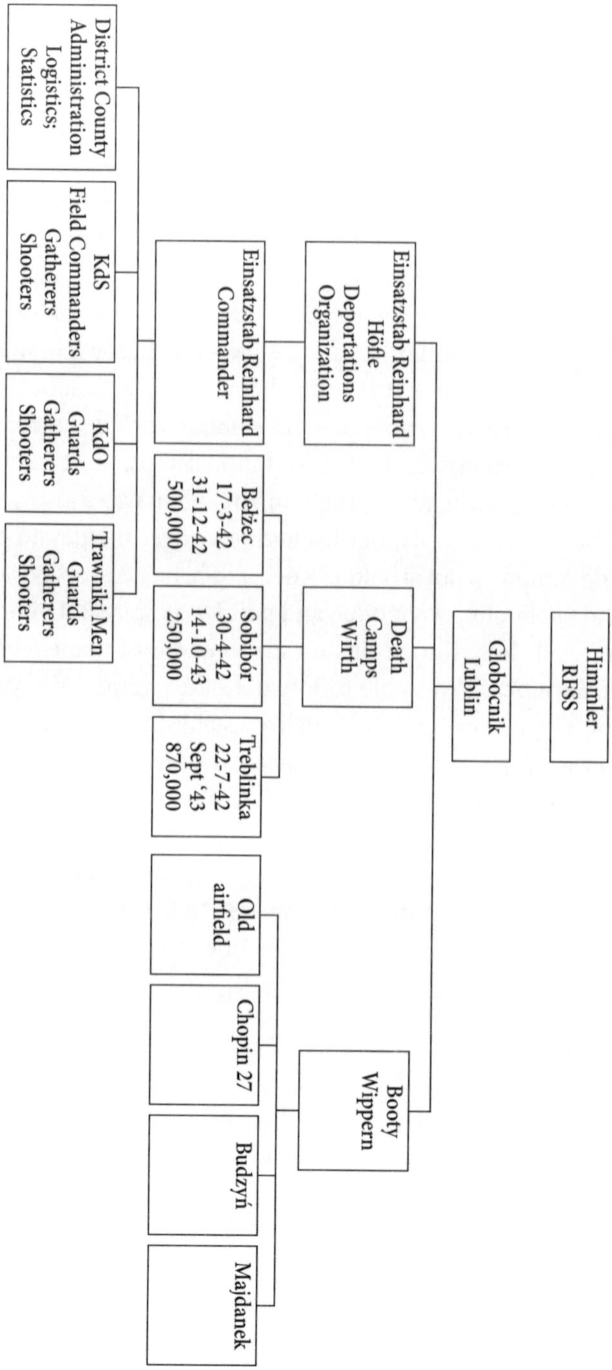

Cooperation Among the Various Authorities

Achieving cooperation among the various competing authorities in the GG in general and in Lublin in particular was essential to the smooth running of the murder operation. The hostility that attended the relations between Globocnik and Zörner, and between Krüger and Frank did not bode well for such cooperation. Globocnik's aggressive methods for getting his way and asserting superior authority over all others – as in the summer 1940 Jewish forced-labor disagreement – had earned him the enmity of Zörner and his staff.

The Wannsee Conference of January 20, 1942, chaired by Heydrich, has been interpreted by most historians as a coordinating conference meant to ensure maximum cooperation among the relevant authorities and to assert Heydrich's primacy as coordinator. The table of Jewish populations in Europe, prepared by Eichmann as background material for the participants, indicates that the conference's agenda included all Jews in Europe. The conference was attended by senior government bureaucrats and SS men; however, the absences from the conference are also significant. Among those not represented were the Wehrmacht, ORPO, Krüger as HSSPF (and most other HSSPFs), Globocnik and his "Einsatzstab Reinhard." In an attempt to promote cooperation between the civilians and the SS in the GG, Heydrich invited Frank's deputy, Josef Bühler, to the Wannsee Conference. The only SS figure from the GG was then BdS Eberhard Schöngarth, who was Heydrich's subordinate in the RSHA.[53]

Richard Breitman suggested that perhaps HSSPF Krüger was ultimately not invited (contrary to Heydrich's original intention) in order to avoid friction between him and Bühler and thereby increase the chances of winning over the civilian authorities in the

53 On Wannsee, see, for example, Hilberg, *Destruction*, pp. 419–423; Breitman, *Architect*, pp. 229–233; Christian Gerlach, "Wannsee Conference," p. 764; Browning, *Origins*, pp. 406–407, 410–414; and Yehoshua Büchler, "Document: A Preparatory Document for the Wannsee Conference," with additional remarks by Richard Breitman, *Holocaust and Genocide Studies*, 9:1 (Spring 1995), pp. 121–129.

GG to cooperate on the "Final Solution."[54] This is a logical analysis, although Krüger's sporting accident on December 30, 1941, which kept him bedbound through all of January, may also have been a factor in his not being invited to Wannsee.[55] However, Frank's enthusiasm regarding the upcoming "solution," as expressed in his well-known December 16, 1941, speech to GG officials, and Bühler's attendance at the conference, would indicate that the desired cooperation was a foregone conclusion. Indeed, an examination of the minutes of the Wannsee Conference reveals that the SS and the civilians were in agreement regarding the murder of the Jews. In fact, Bühler asked that the GG be given priority in having its Jews liquidated.[56] The absence of Globocnik or anyone else from his staff from the Wannsee Conference could not have helped cooperation. Perhaps, however, Globocnik's absence reflected his independence from Heydrich in the "Final Solution" more than Heydrich's desire to win over Frank. Nevertheless, it would seem that agreement on getting rid of the Jews was not difficult to achieve.

This was certainly true of the civilian administration and the SSPF apparatus in the Lublin District. They had little trouble achieving close cooperation in coordinating incoming and outgoing deportations of Jews. Each bureaucracy was informed through its chain of command in the GG, and the atmosphere was one of cooperation. Civilian officials in the GG were informed of the substance of the Wannsee Conference, while SS officials were informed of the plans for the Jews of the GG by Globocnik or members of his staff.[57] On March 4, 1942, as the SS preparations

54 See Büchler, "Preparatory Document," ibid., additional remarks by Richard Breitman, pp. 127–129.

55 Krüger's accident during his three-week holiday was reported to the SS Personnel Department by his adjutant on January 3, 1942. On February 2, Krüger wired Himmler at his personal train to inform him that he was now fully recovered and back at work. Krüger personnel file, YVA, O.68/714 (original in BDC); Gerlach, "Wannsee Conference," pp. 774–775.

56 Frank, *Diensttagebuch*, pp. 457–458. See also Pohl, *Judenpolitik*, pp. 104–111.

57 See, for example, testimony of Dr. Ludwig Losacker, former chief of staff of the Lublin District Government and head of the Interior Department in the GG, and of Oskar Reichwein, former SS "*Judenreferent*" in Zamość, both in the autumn of 1961, in YVA, TR.10/1146Z, XII:2603 and XIII:2681, respectively. See also Pohl, *Judenpolitik*, p. 109.

for the beginning of the murder were nearly complete in camp construction (at Bełżec) and manpower conscription (at Trawniki and elsewhere), Dr. Friedrich Siebert, head of the GG Interior Department, wired a request to BuF in Lublin to give Globocnik full assistance in his upcoming measures. This was followed three days later by the urgings of Major Johannes Ragger of BuF in Kraków. It was very important that an understanding be reached with Globocnik.[58]

Globocnik had kept the civilians uninformed regarding the details of the organization of the murder. Civilian officials in Lublin did not know at first that Globocnik had set up a special staff for the murder operation, separate from his regular SSPF staff. When Fritz Reuter, Türk's deputy at BuF in Lublin, in response to requests by Siebert and Ragger, sought the appropriate person in the SSPF apparatus to meet, he spent three days trying to find who turned out to be the wrong person – Globocnik's adjutant, *SS-Hauptsturmführer* Sepp Nemec. Reuter had sought Nemec because it was he who had represented Globocnik in working closely with Türk on the deportations from Mielec at the very same time that Siebert and Ragger were urging close cooperation for the murder operation. It turned out Nemec was on leave and, in any event, was not part of the special murder staff. Reuter did meet with *SS-Obersturmführer* Helmut Pohl on March 12, but he was also not in charge of deportations, so he referred Reuter to Hermann Höfle, Globocnik's deputy in the murder operation. Reuter and Höfle met at 5:30 P.M. on March 16, only hours before the first deportation from Lublin was to begin.[59]

Despite this inauspicious start, which gave the impression that Globocnik's men were uninterested in the cooperation of the civilian authorities, a close working relationship was soon achieved.

58 Reuter memo, March 17, 1942, WAPL, GDL 270 (copies in YVA, O.6/47-3*, O.51/10, O.53/82, M.9/256; *Dokumenty*, II:32–33; *Eksterminacja*, pp. 280–281). This detailed memorandum is one of the most important documents on the development of cooperation between the SS and the civilian authorities in Lublin regarding the murder of the Jews.

59 Ibid.; testimonies on Mielec deportations and forced labor, recorded by Israel Police, Department 06, February 1964—May 1967, in YVA, TR.11/01156.

Höfle was most interested in the civilians' assistance in dealing with incoming transports of Jews from the Reich and Slovakia, but they soon agreed on cooperation regarding the entire district as well. They concurred that the SSPF staff and the civilians together would select laborers from among the incoming transports at the station upon arrival. This limited number of able-bodied laborers would be sent where needed, with Piaski serving as the gathering point (*Sammelpunkt*) for the Reich Jews, after the town's own Jews were deported. The non-laborers would be sent to Bełżec, from whence they would cross the border, "never to be seen in the *Generalgouvernement* again."[60]

A superficial reading of the documents during the first week of the deportations could lead to the conclusion that Höfle and others were camouflaging the true nature of Bełżec from the civilians. However, a closer examination of the documents and the circumstances surrounding them points to the conclusion that this was a mutually understood coded language. Bühler's participation in the Wannsee Conference and Frank's December 16, 1941, speech before GG officials are two of the factors indicating that the murder plan was known at least to those civilians who needed to know, such as Türk. The same coded language prevailed in Türk's subsequent meetings, on March 19 and 23, with Helmut Pohl, who had been appointed by Höfle to be in charge of the incoming transports. They discussed the schedule for expulsions within the district, the priorities for localities in the southeastern part of the district to be "emptied" (*entleert*) of Jews, appropriate reception points for incoming Reich and Slovakian Jews, and the need to preserve the Jewish laborers employed by the Germans. Issues regarding specific places were dealt with in detail, such as the schedules and numbers of incoming and outgoing Jewish traffic from Izbica, Kraśniczyn, Piaski, Szczebrzeszyn, Krasnobród, Opole, and more. Pohl also agreed to consult county chiefs and county labor heads in order to keep them abreast of plans and schedules, and so as to avoid taking essential laborers.[61]

60 Reuter memo, March 17, 1942, WAPL, GDL 270.

61 Türk memos on meetings with Pohl, March 19 and 23, WAPL, GDL 273 (copies

It is interesting to note that, in this period, Globocnik's killing staff was hardly ever accused of taking Jews who were not scheduled for deportation. When such problems did arise, Türk and his staff did not make a great issue of it, but rather suggested that the local county officials take up the matter directly with Höfle or Pohl.[62] The Lublin civilians' attitude to such mishaps was one of disinterest. When BuF in Kraków wired Türk, on March 31, to complain that Dr. Josef Siegfried, an important JSS official and Judenrat member in Lublin, had been mistakenly taken to the gathering point for deportees, Türk did not even bother responding until it was much too late to save him.

In fact, Dr. Siegfried was among the Judenrat members removed by the SS authorities from the Judenrat on the morning of March 31, when the Lublin Judenrat was reorganized and reduced in size. He and former Judenrat chairman Bekker were assured by Worthoff and Sturm that day that they would be given administrative positions in their new location. This, of course, was a deliberate deception, and Türk and his staff were well aware of Siegfried's true fate. Türk responded to BuF in Kraków only on April 8, claiming that Dr. Siegfried had been deported before Türk could find any responsible SS person with whom to raise the issue. Since Türk and Reuter were then in daily contact and close coordination with Höfle and Pohl, this explanation is specious. It would seem that his closing comment to Kraków was more candid: "and perhaps there is nothing wrong with the resettlement having gone through."[63]

Alongside the disinterest of the German civilian authorities in Lublin regarding such supposed deportation errors, there was a certain eagerness on the part of many civilian officials, especially on the county level, to be rid of their Jews. For example, on March

in YVA, O.6/352, O.53/82, JM/10,458). Pohl was in charge of incoming and outgoing "*Judentransporten*" at the Lublin rail station from March to July 1942. See the Pohl and Lerch indictment, TR.10/736; Pohl, *Judenpolitik*, p. 119.

62 See, for example, Türk's memo of March 24, regarding a complaint by Meinecke of the Lublin Labor Department that 2,000 laborers had been deported from Piaski the day before; WAPL, GDL 273.

63 Telegram, Hensel, BuF Kraków, to Türk, March 31, 1942, and Türk letter to BuF Kraków, April 8, WAPL, GDL 273; Blumental, *Documents*, Protocol 16(140), March 31, 1942, pp. 314–318.

24, 1942, *Kreishauptmann* Brandt of Puławy county requested the speedy deportation of 2,700 Jews from two locations.[64] Similar requests were made by other county chiefs during the following weeks in what seems almost like a race to be the first county without Jews.[65] This eagerness was well reflected and summed up by Zörner's chief assistant, Amtschef Wilhelm Engler, at a government meeting in Kraków on May 31, where he expressed his pleasure that the "cleansing" of the district of Jews would soon be completed.[66]

For their part, Höfle and his men made a genuine effort to inform the local civilian authorities of their plans. The county chiefs of Krasnystaw and Zamość, Schmidt and Weihenmeier, reported to Reuter, on March 20, that they were well informed and that the deportations from their counties were proceeding well. Höfle had even come to inform Schmidt personally regarding plans and schedules.[67] On March 30, Pohl came to Türk's office to give him a progress report on the deportations: 24,550 had been deported to Bełżec, while 8,000 Reich Jews had been brought in, and approximately another 8,000 were on the way.[68]

All of the above stands in sharp contrast to the acrimony surrounding the round-ups of Jews for forced labor in the summer of 1940. Now the relations between Globocnik's men on the "Reinhard" staff and Zörner's men in BuF and in the counties appear to have been almost harmonious. Why was this so? The documents do not provide a clear answer, but several explanations suggest themselves. First, the "Final Solution" was understood as a Hitler order with

64 Türk to Höfle, and Türk to Brandt, March 24, 1942, WAPL, GDL 273.

65 See, for example, Lenk, *Kreishauptmann* Janów-Lubelski, to SSPF Lublin, May 9, 1942, requesting the deportation of 5,900 Jews from eight locations, YVA, O.51/10; Ziegenmeyer, *Kreishauptmann* Lublin-Land, to BuF Lublin, May 19, 1942, requesting the deportation of 19,735 Jews from six locations, YVA, O.51/10, O.53/83, JM/215/1; Busse, *Kreishauptmann* Hrubieszów, to BuF Lublin, May 22, 1942, requesting the deportation of 14,188 Jews from five locations, YVA, O.51/10, O.53/83, JM/215/1 (copies of all these documents in *Dokumenty*, II:53–55).

66 Frank, *Diensttagebuch*, p. 500.

67 Türk memo, March 20, 1942, WAPL, GDL 273.

68 Türk memo, March 30, 1942, WAPL, GDL 273. See also Türk's memo, "Zum Monatsbericht März 1942," April 7, 1942, WAPL, GDL 273 (copies also in *Eksterminacja*, pp. 282–283; *Faschismus*, p. 271).

which no official would contend. Second, there was general ideological consensus regarding the Jews. Christopher Browning, Götz Aly and Susanne Heim, Raul Hilberg, Bogdan Musial, and others have all noted the widespread willingness among civilian GG officials by late 1941 to participate in the murder of the Jews. To be sure, Browning and Aly and Heim disagree regarding the influence these officials had on the decision-making and planning processes, but the preparedness for large-scale murder of Jews was there.[69]

In addition, by early 1942, the SS in the GG was clearly the dominant force in Jewish policy. Himmler sealed this dominance when he cornered Frank on March 5, 1942, with several scandals within the civilian government in the GG and in his own family, leading to Frank's final retreat before SS authority. Based on the agreement extorted from Frank that day, Hitler decreed, on May 7, that Krüger become State Secretary for Security in the GG, in charge of all police and resettlement matters. This formally put the SS in charge of Jewish policy.[70] Although this retreat need not have implied a parallel withdrawal by district officials, it certainly influenced the extent to which the civilian government as a whole would object to SS policies regarding the Jews at that time.

One additional hypothesis may be suggested on the Lublin District level. That is, a strategic and tactical maneuver by leading

69 See, for example, Browning, "Genocide and Public Health," pp. 21–36; *idem*, "German Technocrats, Jewish Labor, and the Final Solution: A Reply to Götz Aly and Susanne Heim," *Remembering for the Future; The Impact of the Holocaust on the Contemporary World* (Oxford: Pergamon Press, 1988), II:2199–2208, and in revised form in *idem*, *The Path to Genocide* (Cambridge: Cambridge University Press, 1992), pp. 59–76; Aly, *"Final Solution,"* pp. 233–236; *idem* and Susanne Heim, "The Economics of the Final Solution: A Case Study from the General Government," *Simon Wiesenthal Center Annual*, 5 (1988), pp. 3–48; *idem*, "The Holocaust and Population Policy: Remarks on the Decision on the 'Final Solution,' " *Yad Vashem Studies*, XXIV (1994), pp. 45–70; Dan Diner, "Rationalization and Method: Critique of a New Approach in Understanding the 'Final Solution,' " ibid., pp. 71–108; David Bankier, "On Modernization and the Rationality of Extermination," ibid., pp. 109–129; Ulrich Herbert, "Racism and Rational Calculation: The Role of 'Utilitarian' Strategies of Legitimation in the National Socialist 'Weltanschauung,' " ibid., pp. 131–145; Götz Aly, "Erwiderung auf Dan Diner," pp. 621–635; Hilberg, *Destruction*, pp. 501–504.

70 Rich, *Hitler's War Aims*, pp. 95–96; Breitman, *Architect of Genocide*, p. 235.

civilian officials to help the SS remove one of its own major sources of power – the Jews. Globocnik had used control of Jewish policy in 1940 as a wedge to become the predominant Nazi figure in the Lublin District. Himmler transferred him to remote Trieste in late summer 1943, away from a looming financial scandal, once the bulk of the Jewish job was completed. In this way Himmler could protect his protégé and stunt his drive for power all at once. With the Jewish job completed, Globocnik became expendable.

The tension between the Lublin civilian authorities and the SSPF apparatus that resurfaced in early autumn of 1942, before the district murder operation was completed, indicates that the cooperation was forced and the competition had continued to simmer beneath the surface at least. If the close cooperation on murder had been influenced by such competitive considerations on the part of the civilian authorities, then their victory in seeing Globocnik removed from Lublin was pyrrhic at best. Zörner resigned as governor in April 1943, and several weeks later his permanent replacement was announced – Dr. Richard Wendler, a lawyer by profession, a veteran GG official and *SS-Brigadeführer*, and Himmler's brother-in-law. With that appointment Himmler's control over affairs in the Lublin District could be complete.

Preparing the Victims

In addition to preparing their own machinery of murder, the Germans needed to "prepare" the intended victims. This meant limiting and concentrating the Jews by decreeing yet tighter restrictions on their movements; concentrating rural Jews into larger communities in towns and cities; bringing in Jews from the Third Reich to be included in the murder operations; and sifting through the Jewish population to choose those who would not be murdered at first, such as essential laborers or those with foreign nationality. The close cooperation between the SS and the German civilian authorities in the deportations to death in 1942 originated in their frequent collaboration in further confining and circumscribing the Jews during the months leading up to those deportations.

Restrictions, Worsened Conditions, and Relocations. On October 15, 1941, Frank decreed the death penalty for any Jew found outside his/her ghetto or assigned residence area without prior approval. Permission to travel was limited even more severely than before, and ghettoization continued to varying degrees.[71] In the Lublin District, Zörner and his staff began implementing tighter restrictions even earlier. By late September 1941, Jews could travel only with the permission of the *Stadthauptmann* or *Kreishauptmann*, non-Jews were forbidden to support Jews in any way, and Jews were forbidden to travel on any public transportation.[72]

Supplies to the Jews also began to be reduced in many places – although there was an actual increase in some supplies in others. In February and March 1942, the civilian administrations in Janów-Lubelski and Radzyń counties ceased providing Jews with food altogether, whereas in Hrubieszów food rations were increased significantly between September 1941 and May 1942. These food ration decisions were a local German civilian government decision, in consort with the general policy environment at the time, but there is no clear explanation for the variations in implementation of certain details of policy.[73]

Nazi violence against the Jews grew, and increasing numbers of Jews were shot for various infractions. A major purpose of this violence is reflected in the comment of one Lublin official on the sentencing and execution of eleven Jews for leaving the Lublin ghetto without permission: "The names of the executed Jews should be posted as a deterrent..."[74]

Judenrat members were publicly humiliated by SS officials. The Gestapo attempted to tighten its control over the Jewish communities by various means, including imposing its informers and collaborators

71 Frank's decree can be found in *Faschismus*, pp. 128–129. See also Browning, "Genocide and Public Health," pp. 24–29; Pohl, *Judenpolitik*, pp. 92–93.

72 Zörner order, September 22, 1941; Engler announcement in Biała-Podlaska, September 25, 1941, MA, D.1.5868.

73 YVA, M.10.AR.1/814, "Hrubieszów – spichrz Polski," June 30, 1942; Pohl, *Judenpolitik*, pp. 70–71.

74 Memo from Dr. Hasse to the Lublin-Land *Kreishauptmann*, March 17, 1942, regarding a March 4 court verdict, WAPL, Kreishauptmannschaft Lublin-Land 75 (copy in YVA, O.53/82).

on the community. Curfew hours were lengthened, and exceptions to these rules were strictly limited. Various Jewish belongings were confiscated. Jews were barred from marketplaces in many counties, and poverty and hunger became much more widespread and visible. The JSS in Biała-Podlaska county found that nearly 7,000 Jews, approximately 40 percent of the Jewish population, were in need of assistance by December 1941. Of course, many of those not officially beneath this poverty line were also in dire straits.[75]

In the second half of 1941, the Jews in occupied Poland were cut off from contact with their brethren in the Soviet Union and the United States as a result of the developing war situation. Previously, these contacts had meant donations of supplies and money, as well as encouragement, and served for many Jews as a sort of lifeline to the free world and to hope.[76] Even after the invasion of the Soviet Union by Germany, the connection to the United States remained open for another half year. The case of the Jewish POW Benjamin Rogaczewski, mentioned in Chapter 4 above, illustrates this. In June and July 1941, the Deutsche Bank in Berlin was in contact with the Judenrat in Lublin regarding a $13 check for Rogaczewski that it had received from Liberty National Bank in Chicago, and expressed its willingness to forward the money to him in złoty from its Warsaw branch.[77] While the documents do not indicate the outcome of this

75 JSS in Biała-Podlaska, report for December 1941, January 9, 1942, WAPL, GDL 256 (copy in YVA, JM/2701). On poverty in the district in general, see Alten's reports to JSS in Kraków for May 1941 to February 1942, in YVA, JM/1574–1575. See also Manfred Heymann testimony, YVA, O.2/794; Rosenfeld and Luckner, *Lebenszeichen aus Piaski*, pp. 76–91; Klukowski, *Diary*, pp. 164–189, *passim*; "The Condition of the Jewish Population in Radzyń County" (Yiddish), anonymous testimony, YVA, M.10.AR.1/794; Nachman Korn testimony, *Encyclopedia of the Jewish Diaspora, Lublin*, p. 728; Dov Freiberg, *To Survive Sobibor*, pp. 170–172; Daniel Freiberg, *Darkness Covered the Earth*, pp. 75–76; Berenstein, "Deportations," p. 68 and Table 2.

76 See, for example, Josef Birger-Ezrahi testimonies, YVA, M.49.E/2791, O.3/447, O.3/6774; Roman Fischer testimonies, YVA, O.3/2124 and OHD (86)2; Shmuel Gruber testimonies, YVA, O.16/610* and M.1.E/925; Josef Cynowiec testimony, YVA, O.3/3009; Mieczysław Garfinkel testimony, YVA, O.33/322; Boruch Silberklang memoir, pp. 10–12; Bauer, *American Jewry and the Holocaust*, pp. 76–106, *passim*.

77 Deutsche Bank, Berlin, to Judenrat, Lublin, June 5, 1941; Deutsche Bank, Berlin,

episode — did Benjamin Rogaczewski ever receive the money? who sent the money? — what is clear is that someone in Chicago knew of Mr. Rogaczewski's whereabouts and had attempted to help him. The final lifeline to the United States was broken on December 7, 1941.

The significance of the loss of these contacts can be understood on two levels. First, just at the point when the murder of the Jews began, when the Jews most needed such links as a lifeline in the fullest sense of the term, these lines were cut. Whoever it was in Chicago who was able to discover the whereabouts and condition of Benjamin Rogaczewski and sent him thirteen dollars would no longer be able to do so. Mr. Rogaczewski was now all alone, facing the "Final Solution." And this brings us to the second level — a major source of hope had disappeared. The loss of supplies meant worse conditions, but the loss of contact meant the loss of a way to transmit information to the outside world and, therefore, of a channel of hope.

One of the most debilitating factors affecting the Jews both physically and morally at this time was one that the Germans had not specifically planned, but were prepared to exploit. During the summer of 1941, a typhus epidemic spread in Lublin and in many parts of the district. The epidemic was brought on by several factors: the continuing influx of refugees from the Warsaw area, many of whom were by now carrying the disease; the ongoing concentration of Jews in the district, which served as an incubator for spreading disease; and contact with Soviet POWs who had contracted this and other contagious diseases.

Thousands of Jews in the Lublin District died of typhus and other diseases during the following months, and the Lublin Judenrat, like others, tried to deal with the situation by expanding hospital space, improving hygiene, acquiring additional medications, and reorganizing health care. The JSS in Kraków sent aid to help deal with the epidemic that had hit the entire GG, but neither it nor the Judenräte could overcome the spread of disease under the conditions that the Nazis had imposed upon them. The German authorities reacted in ways that in effect prevented eradicating the epidemic,

to Judenrat, Lublin, July 11, 1941; Judenrat "Obmann" [Bekker] to Lagerrat in Lipowa 7, July 16, 1941, all in YVA, O.6/11b*.

even though they feared it would spread to them as well. On the one hand, they ordered many Judenräte to create or expand hospitals. On the other hand, rather than easing restrictions and overcrowding and providing more medications and other supplies, they continued to clamp down on the Jews and reduce their supplies of even basic necessities. For example, the Lublin Judenrat received permission, in June 1941, to open a new bathhouse in the ghetto. It then decided, on July 8, 1941, in an effort to limit the spread of the disease, to add showers to the public bath and to obligate all the Jews to bathe at least once a week. However, the *Stadthauptmann* confiscated the bathhouse ten days later, which now would be used by Poles, thereby increasing the danger of the disease spreading still faster.[78]

The infection of the POWs in the Lipowa 7 camp with typhus through their forced labor alongside Soviet POWs in constructing the Majdanek camp, during the fall and winter of 1941, was part of this epidemic. More than 400 Jewish POWs contracted the disease, which killed at least 100 of them (see Chapter 4). In Lublin, the Judenrat was granted additional burial space in the main Jewish cemetery in the autumn of 1941, to help them cope with the mounting death rate. Of approximately 1,000 Jews buried in Lublin's cemetery between mid-September 1941 and March 15, 1942, half died during the last six weeks before the deportations to Bełżec commenced. Similarly, Jews from all over Lublin county tell of the devastation left by the disease. By January 1942, at least six counties in the district had been seriously affected by typhus.[79] The German

78 Judenrat request to Lublin *Stadthauptmann*, June 18, 1941, the positive reply from the *Stadthauptmann*'s office, June 24, and the reversal of the permission to use the bathhouse, July 18, in WAPL, RZ 128 (copies in USHMMA, RG-15.101M, reel 21); Blumental, *Documents*, Protocol 37(98), July 8, 1941, p. 259; Trunk, in *Dos Buch*, p. 360; Memo, Bekker to *Kreishauptmann* Lublin-Land, July 16, 1941, YVA, O.6/11b*. On the spread of typhus in the district and Jewish efforts to deal with it, see the reports by Alten and the district JSS to JSS in Kraków for the months of May 1941 to February 1942, WAPL, RZ 129 and GDL 256, and YVA, JM/1574–1575.

79 Alten reports, ibid. The Lublin Judenrat discussed the health crisis many times during the second half of 1941 and early 1942. See Blumental, *Documents*, pp. 258–297. On the soldiers contracting the disease, see the testimonies by Josef Birger-Ezrahi, YVA, O.3/447, O.3/6771, M.49.E/2791; Roman Fischer, YVA, O.3/2124 and OHD (86)2; Samuel Gruber, *I Chose Life*, pp. 32–34; *idem*, YVA, O.16/610* and

authorities did not plan to infect the Jews with this disease, but once the epidemic spread they took advantage of the situation in order to exercise an additional measure of control over the Jews.

Gestapo agents were imposed on the Jews as powerful figures who could appear before the Jewish community as having the proper connections to get things done. Such was Shamai Grajer in Lublin, a professional barber and petty criminal before the war, who was imprisoned in the SS jail in the Lublin castle in late 1939 or early 1940 for beating up a *Volksdeutsche* who had been beating Jews. While in prison he befriended many influential SS men and emerged from his incarceration in mid-1941 as the proprietor of a café at 15 Lubartowska Street, which was frequented by some of the SS men. Grajer very quickly became a wealthy and influential figure, mistrusted and feared. He was able to acquire special privileges for those who paid him well, and he was correctly perceived by the ghetto community as a Gestapo informer. Nearly all survivors from Lublin remember him vividly. During the deportations in March 1942, he and his café were to play an important role.[80]

In December 1941, the Judenrat was ordered to create a disinfection unit of 140 people and a "sanitation police" numbering

M.1.E/925; Josef Cynowiec, YVA, O.3/3009; Sol Holzman, O.33/1305. See also Türk to BuF Kraków, January 26, 1942, on typhus in the district, YVA, O.53/83. Numerous testimonies discuss the epidemic. See, for example, Anszel Krechman, YVA, M.1.E/1249; Ewa Szek, YVA, M.49.E/42; "Hrubieszów – spichrz Polski," June 30, 1942, YVA, M.10.AR.1/814; "The Condition of the Jewish Population in Radzyń County," YVA, M.10.AR.1/794; Erlichman-Bank, *In Impure Hands*, p. 36. See also Marszalek, *Majdanek*, pp. 20–21; Trunk, in *Encyclopedia of the Jewish Diaspora, Lublin*, pp. 358–360; Rosenfeld and Luckner, *Lebenszeichen*, pp. 76–79; Klukowski, *Diary*, pp. 148–183, *passim*.

On the Lublin cemetery, see WAPL, RZ 177; WAPL, Gmina Żydowska 8 (copy in YVA, O.6/401).

80 Ida Glikstein testimony, *Dos Buch*, pp. 394–395; *idem*, *Encyclopedia of the Jewish Diaspora, Lublin*, pp. 693–694; Erlichman-Bank, *In Impure Hands*, pp. 38–39; Yeshayahu Weisfisch, YVA, M.1.E/649; Miriam Gryzolet, M.1.E/782; Shmuel Gruber, M.1.E/925; Anszel Krechman, M.1.E/1249; Moshe Zylberberg, M.1.E/1402; Gedalje Erenberg, M.1.E/1563; Nachman Krantz, M.1.E/2654. See also the mid-January 1942 report on Lublin in YVA, M.10.AR.1/1174 (on JM/3489). Based on the handwriting, this report seems to have been written by Rabbi Shimon Huberband. See also Grajer's business card, WAPL, RZ 9 (copy in USHMMA, RG-15.101M, reel 2).

fifty men. This was to be led by the young underworld figure and collaborator from Warsaw, Bołesław Tenenbojm, who was brought in specially by Worthoff. The Judenrat was forced to pay salaries and supply office space and housing for Tenenbojm and his men. Ostensibly, Tenenbojm's organization was meant to help fight the typhus epidemic, but in fact their function was to impose fear on the Judenrat and the Jewish community and to inform on the Jews.[81] The phenomenon of informers in the pay of the Gestapo spread in particular during the latter part of 1941 and early 1942. Since this timing coincided with the Nazi preparations for mass deportations to death and ultimately aided them in those deportations, it is possible that the Germans intended spreading the net of informers to help demoralize and undermine Jewish society.

Unlike the typhus epidemic, confiscation of various materials was a German-initiated idea designed to benefit the Germans and weaken the Jews all at the same time. In mid-1941, the civilian labor office created a large team of more than 500 Jewish "*Sammler*" (gatherers) all across the district. Their job was to comb the Jewish communities and other areas in search of metals, glass, paper, cloth, and other materials for industrial use. These people continued to work as *Sammler* until the spring of 1942. For those chosen for this job, it was a boon; it gave them relative freedom of movement and widespread contacts with other Jews and with Poles. In some cases it also could serve as a basis for underground activity. However, for the Jews forced to relinquish materials, this was yet another blow to their wellbeing.[82]

In another measure that cannot be causally connected with the impending "Final Solution," but in fact served the preparations

81 Blumental, *Documents*, Protocol 58(119), December 7, 1941, pp. 288–289; YVA, M.10.AR.2/305. Tenenbojm is clearly remembered by many Lublin survivors. Other Lublin informers recalled by many survivors are: Shalom "Lorba" Bober (or Bobe), Leib Moska (or Moshke), Avram Gemora, Sh. Mandelbojm, Perec Parech, and Reichenstein. See, for example, in YVA, Yeshayahu Weisfisch, M.1.E/649; Moshe Zylberberg, M.1.E/1402; Gedalje Erenberg, M.1.E/1563; Berenstein, "Martyrologia," pp. 33–34.

82 A list of 518 "*Sammler*," divided according to county and community, is in WAPL, GDL 896 (copy in YVA, JM/10454). See also the video testimony of Zvi (Finger) Naor, Massuah.

for murder, the Jews were ordered in December to hand over all their furs and wool clothing to the authorities. This confiscation was undertaken in order to supply the freezing German soldiers on the eastern front, but it also further debilitated the Jews during a particularly cold winter. The Jews were first given until December 28 to relinquish all furs and wool jackets, but when the response proved unsatisfactory to the SS (only 371 fur coats and sixty-nine fur hats were collected), Globocnik extended the deadline in Lublin until the end of the month. When that, too, proved insufficient for the Jews of Lublin to relinquish their winter clothing in the frost, Globocnik had five members of the Judenrat detained at the Lipowa 7 camp, while the deadline was extended for an additional day and a half. Thousands of coats and other apparel were collected in Lublin alone between December 31, 1941 and January 2, 1942.[83] The result of these confiscations and the failure of the German authorities to supply heating fuel that winter meant that the Jews froze. Through these measures, too, the German authorities were able to tighten their control and instill more fear over the Jews.

"Relocations" from the Third Reich to Lodz and then to Soviet territory began on October 14, 1941, and to the GG in March 1942.[84]

83 Schöngarth to SSPFs in GG, December 24, 1941, in *Eksterminacja*, pp. 167–168; Walther memo, December 25, 1941, Hörster memos on clothing received, December 29 and 31, 1941, list of items confiscated, January 2, 1942, and Worthoff memo on the need for additional items, January 12, 1942, all in WAPL, RZ 56 and 26 (copies in USHMMA, RG-15.101M). Blumental, *Documents*, Protocols 61–63(122-124), 1(125), December 25, 29, 31, 1941, and January 1, 1942, pp. 291–296.

WAPL, RZ 56 and 57 (copies in USHMMA, RG-15.101M), contain extensive records of the confiscated clothing (copies in USHMMA, RG-15.101M, reel 8). See also the testimonies of Dov Finger, YVA, O.3/2780; Moshe Zylberszpan, YVA, M.49.E/4137; Miriam Gryzolet, YVA, M.1.E/782; Klukowski, *Diary*, p. 182; Daniel Freiberg, *Darkness Covered the Earth*, p. 82.

84 Himmler to Arthur Greiser, president of the Warthegau, September 18, 1941, informing him that Hitler wanted all Jews in Germany and the "Protectorate" shipped to the GG and the USSR during the coming year, and that large numbers would first be sent to Lodz, and ongoing correspondence between Greiser and Himmler in October 1941, in YVA, JM/4372 (original in National Archives, RG 238, T 175/54); Hilberg, *Destruction*, pp. 213–216; Hans Günther Adler, *Der verwaltete Mensch. Studien zur Deportation der Juden aus Deutschland* (Tübingen: Mohr, 1974), pp. 172–186.

In the Lublin District, Nazi preparations to receive Jews from the Reich, as a stage toward murder, began in September 1941, with the inquiries regarding ghettos and available space for additional Jews in the district (see Chapter 5). Deportations from the Reich to the GG, and especially to this district, seemed imminent then, based on plans in Berlin.

No later than early January 1942, this issue arose again. Correspondence between the BuF in Lublin and the GG BuF in Kraków, beginning January 6, discussed the deportation of 4,500 Jews from Mielec, in the Kraków district, to the Lublin District later that month. The deportation was ultimately postponed to mid-March, when these Jews were distributed among the Jewish communities in four counties (see Chapter 7).[85] Among the reasons for the postponement was the fact that the Jewish social-welfare committees in Lublin, Chełm, and Hrubieszów learned of the impending deportations as early as January 18, and inquired with the German civilian authorities regarding details. Richard Türk believed that the Jews learned of the secret plans either by overhearing German conversations from the corridors, or through the regular contacts between BuF officials and the Judenrat and JSS in Chełm and Hrubieszów.[86]

Despite the increased efforts by all the German authorities to

85 See Türk telegrams to Major Ragger, January 6 and 21, 1942, in *Dokumenty*, II:10–14; BuF Lublin to BuF Cholm [Chełm], January 9, 1942, WAPL, GDL 893 (copy in YVA, O.51/10); Türk to BuF Hrubieszów, January 9, 1942, and Reuter, BuF Lublin to Ragger, January 23, 1942, WAPL, GDL 893 (copies in YVA, JM/10455 and O.53/83). See also correspondence between Weirauch in the GG Interior Department and the BuF in Chełm, Radzyń, Zamość, and Hrubieszów, February 9–10, 1942, in *Dokumenty*, II:15–19.

On the arrival of these deportations, see telephone message from Ragger to Türk, March 7; Türk response, March 9; Ragger's dispatch of the exact deportation schedule on March 10; Reuter's secret telegrams on these to BuF in Radzyń and in Chełm on March 11 and 12; Reuter to Nemec, in SSPF's office, March 12; Ragger's secret telegram to Türk on March 13; Reuter's memo of March 17; BuF Cholm to BuF Lublin, March 18. All documents may be found in WAPL, GDL 893, copies of most in *Dokumenty*, II:22–33. Several of these documents may also be found in WAPL, GDL 270, 273; YVA, JM/215/1 (Oneg Shabbat archive material), JM/10,455, O.51/10, O.53/82, O.53/83, O.6/352 and elsewhere.

86 Türk note on resettlement to Chełm and Hrubieszów, January 20, 1942, and Türk to Ragger, January 29, 1942, YVA, O.51/10.

maintain secrecy from the Jews, shreds of information and rumors continued to reach some Jews in the district, as did information regarding murders in Soviet territory. The latter information was brought by returning refugees from that area. As early as October 4, 1941, the Lublin Judenrat had heard rumors of impending drastic changes in the ghetto, a euphemism for liquidation.[87]

In order to facilitate the murder of the incoming Jews from the Reich, Josef Bühler asked Zörner to establish a transit camp (*Durchgangslager*) for the expected arrival of 14,000 Jews. In addition, space would have to be found for some 40,000 Jews from Slovakia who were also sent to the Lublin District during the spring and summer of 1942. As housing problems were under the domain of the civilian authorities, Türk's office suggested creating a sort of revolving door, or *Judenaustausch*, whereby incoming Jews would generally be sent to occupy the homes of recently deported local Jews. In this way no resources needed to be expended on constructing a new camp. In some cases the incoming Jews found unfinished meals still on the table. Jews not sent to the homes of deported Jews were generally transported directly either to Majdanek or to Sobibór.[88]

87 Blumental, *Documents*, Protocol 46(107), October 4, 1941, p. 272. See also Protocol 8(132), February 18, 1942, p. 303, note 3. Blumenthal's observation is apt: the brevity of the protocol regarding a meeting at which Alten related what he had learned while attending the JSS meeting in Kraków is telling.

88 Bühler to Zörner, March 3, 1942, WAPL, GDL 270; memo, Fritz Reuter, BuF Lublin, March 17, 1942, ibid.; Zörner to Wehrmacht officers in Lublin, April 1, YVA, O.53/82; Türk memo, March 19 (on meeting Helmut Pohl), WAPL, GDL 273; Türk memo, March 20 (on Reuter's meetings with *Kreishauptmann* Schmidt of Krasnystaw and Weihenmayer of Zamość), ibid.; Türk memo, March 20 (on call with *Kreishauptmann* Brandt of Puławy), ibid.; Arthur Liebehenschel, Concentration Camps Inspectorate, to Karl Koch, Kommandant at Majdanek, March 22 and 24, 1942, YVA, JM/3536א; BuF memos of March 14, 23, and 27, 1942 on the transport of 14,000 Czech Jews to Izbica and other destinations in the Lublin District, in WAPL, GDL 749. See also Miroslav Kryl, "Deportationen von Theresienstadt nach Majdanek," in Miroslav Karny, et al., eds., *Theresienstädter Studien und Dokumente 1994* (Prag: Nadace Terezinska iniciativa, 1994), pp. 74–76; Yehoshua Büchler, "The Deportation of Slovakian Jews to the Lublin District of Poland in 1942," *Holocaust and Genocide Studies*, 6:2 (1991), pp. 151–165; Livia Rothkirchen, *The Destruction of Slovak Jewry* (Hebrew and English) (Jerusalem: Yad Vashem, 1961), pp. 19–24, 57–101. The page numbers are from the Hebrew section.

Regarding "resettlements" within the GG, on December 16, 1941, Bühler ordered that every "resettlement" of more than fifty Jews must be reported to the BuF in Kraków. This was necessary in order to avoid clogging deportation routes, upsetting deportation schedules, or distracting resources from the central issue – which was to prepare the Jews for the impending "Final Solution."[89] One prominent resettlement of this sort was the march of some 2,000 Jews from Kazimierz Dolny to Opole-Lubelski in late March 1942 (see Chapter 7).[90]

In the meantime Jews who had fled to the USSR during the first months of the war began to return following the German invasion there.[91] From their perspective, the GG, with its harsh conditions, was now safer than the USSR, with its mass-murder actions. Although the German authorities had no direct hand in the decisions of most of these people, this return migration brought several thousand of them into the concentration areas in the Lublin District.

Not all the deportations at this time can be clearly connected to the impending "Final Solution" in the GG; they were, however, part of the deportation upswing with which the Jews had to contend. Civilian authorities throughout the GG initiated evicting Jews from their own areas of jurisdiction. In some cases these were relatively small-scale expulsions that seem to have been trial balloons for future attempts. For example, thirty-nine Jews from Sokolów-Podlaski, in the Warsaw District, arrived in Łuków in a German truck, on November 9, 1941. They were filthy, tattered, and ill, and the Judenrat's aid committee gave them assistance. However, what concerned the local German authorities, both civilian and police, was the fact that the arrival of these Jews had not been coordinated

89 See BuF Kraków to BuF Lublin, February 10, 1942, YVA, O.51/10 and O.53/83; Frank, *Diensttagebuch*, pp. 450–451; Worthoff verdict, YVA, TR.10/859, p. 33; Michalsen indictment, YVA, TR.10/813, pp. 60–64.

90 Letter, Pesach Goldblum, Opole, to Josek Goldblum, Warsaw, March 29, 1942, in YVA, M.10.AR.1/587 (and JM/3489); testimonies of Ester Kohen, and Baruch and Sarah Roizman, YVA, O.3/3057 and O.3/3554, respectively.

91 See, for example, Blumental, *Documents*, Protocol 45(106), September 26, 1941, p. 271; Orenstein, *I Shall Live*, pp. 70–73.

with them. Moreover, this was not the first such occurrence. Therefore, a complaint was filed with the Warsaw commissioner for Jewish affairs, Heinz Auerswald. Ultimately, most of these Jews remained in Łuków.[92] In other cases the expulsions were a result of local conditions, such as when the *Kreishauptmann* in Janów-Lubelski notified the Judenrat in Kraśnik, via the German mayor, on January 23, that 1,000 Jews would be deported to Radomyśl, on the San River, due to spreading illness in Kraśnik.[93]

Similarly, in Biała-Podlaska county, 149 Jews were evicted from their village homes on January 23, and brought to Sławatycze, while 138 Jews were evicted from their village homes to Wisznice on January 29. These evictions were carried out without notice, at the initiative of the German civilian commissioner of this rural area, Klemmer, in order to improve his control of the Jews – which is what he later told his superiors. The Wisznice Judenrat reported to the JSS in Kraków that the evicted Jews arrived half-naked and barefoot, while some twenty died from hunger and cold. The JSS complained to the BuF in Kraków, which forwarded the complaint to Türk in Lublin. He sent the complaint on to the Biała-Podlaska *Kreishauptmann*, who in turn inquired with Landkommissar Klemmer.

Several points are of particular interest in this tragic and brutal episode. First, although Klemmer's initiative in concentrating the Jews was ostensibly in concert with the implementation of the "Final Solution," he was reprimanded because all "resettlements" of Jews needed to be coordinated now, as per Bühler's December 16 orders. Of course, the brutality of this "resettlement" did not concern Klemmer's superiors. Therefore, this episode reflects the beginning of the coordination of activities toward the murder of the Jews in the GG. Second, this is another indication of the freedom of a local

92 Letter, Gendarmerie Łuków to *Kreishauptmann* Radzyń, November 12, 1941; Letter, *Kreishauptmann* Radzyń to BuF Lublin, November 19, 1941; Türk to BuF Warsaw, December 5, 1941; Türk to BuF Radzyń, December 6, 1941; BuF Warsaw to BuF Lublin, December 11, 1941; Auerswald to BuF Lublin, December 22, 1941, all in YVA, O.53/83.

93 *Kreishauptmann*, Janów-Lubelski to Bürgermeister in Kraśnik, for Kraśnik Judenrat, January 23, 1942, YVA, O.6/11b*.

initiative that was possible until that point in time. Third, this is yet another indication of the limited degree of ghettoization in the Lublin District until late 1941; these were just a few hundred of the thousands of village Jews who had continued to live in their own homes until then. Finally, this also demonstrates a certain measure of Jewish initiative, and perhaps the prior possibility for Jews to request redress from the civilian authorities – to a very limited degree – for brutality beyond the call of duty. Here the Wisznice Judenrat complained to the JSS in Kraków, who in turn complained to the BuF in Kraków. The Sławatycze Judenrat did not complain, probably because they saw no point in it. Of course, this case also reflects the futility of such complaints. The evicted Jews received no redress; they were murdered along with the other Jews of the area during the following summer and fall.[94]

There were numerous other "relocations" of Jews at local civilian Nazi initiative during this preparatory period for the "Final Solution." For example, 817 Jews were sent from Tomaszów-Lubelski to nearby Cieszanów, with luggage, on February 25, while 221 Jews were sent from Biłgoraj to Tarnogród on March 22. The JSS in Kraków asked the BuF for assistance for the former group, but there is no evidence of a German response.[95] In Hrubieszów county, the

94 JSS, Kraków to Interior Department, Kraków, February 8, 1942; BuF Kraków to BuF Lublin, February 10; Türk to BuF Kraków, February 23; Klemmer to *Kreishauptmann*, Biała-Podlaska, February 24; Biała-Podlaska *Kreishauptmann* to BuF Lublin, March 5; Türk to BuF Kraków, March 14, 1942. All documents in YVA, O.51/10 and in *Dokumenty*, II:5–7. The February 10 letter is also in YVA, O.53/83.

The Jews of Sławatycze and Wisznice were murdered in three ways: those deported from Sławatycze to Łomazy in June were shot together with those Jews in August; those deported from Sławatycze to Międzyrzec in late September were deported to Treblinka in October; and the last 120 Jews in Wisznice were shot in December. See Faigenbojm, *Podlasie in its Destruction*, pp. 116, 156; Berenstein, "Deportations," Tables 2, 10; Browning, *Ordinary Men*, pp. 80–89, 111–114.

95 Memo, BuF Kraków, February 26, 1942; telegram, BuF Kraków to BuF Lublin, February 26, 1942; Landkommissar Walter Panzer, Tomaszów-Lubelski, to BuF Lublin, March 6 and March 8, 1942; Türk to BuF Kraków, March 18, 1942; Türk telegram to Ragger, March 4, 1942; Ragger telegram to Türk, March 4; Zörner's office to BuF, Biłgoraj, March 5; Zörner's office to BuF Biłgoraj, April 17; BuF Biłgoraj to BuF Lublin, April 27, all in YVA, O.53/83 (also in *Dokumenty*, pp. 43–46); Klukowski, *Diary*, pp. 188–189.

Jews from all approximately 200 villages in the countryside were ordered in mid-April 1942 to liquidate their affairs and relocate to Hrubieszów by April 30. At the same time all 800 Jews from Horodło were ordered to move to Uchanie. All these Jews in the county were then deported together to Sobibór in June.[96]

For Jews in most places in the Lublin District, therefore, the period of late 1941 and early 1942 represented one of drastic decline in their living conditions and in the way in which the various German authorities related to them. Still, within the context of this general decline, there were local variations. For example, in general, the rural Jews suffered less from this trend than the urban Jews. Many rural Jews were still living in their homes, still rarely saw a German, and still had relatively more food than the average urban Jew in early 1942.[97]

It was a period of upheaval but also of contradictions. In Lublin, where conditions had deteriorated seriously during this period, the Judenrat still was making plans. Thirty days before the beginning of the deportations to Bełżec, and amongst rumors of impending drastic changes for the worse for Lublin's Jews, the Judenrat was concerned with the baking and distributing of *matzah* for the upcoming Pesach holiday (April 1942).[98] As Jews in most localities were increasingly constricted, others built a *sukkah* in the autumn of 1941, or continued uninterrupted public prayer well into 1942.[99]

These contradictions amidst a trend of general decline did not help the Jews in assessing their situation. The pace of turmoil had

96 YVA, M.10.AR1/814, "Hrubieszów – spichrz Polski," June 30, 1942.

97 See, for example, letter from Hanka to her girlfriends regarding Sosnowica, January 25, 1942, YVA, M.10.AR1/574; letters from Josef Kirszenfeld in Biłgoraj to Hersz Wasser, Warsaw, July 27, 1941, February 15, 1942, and March 15, 1942, YVA, M.10.AR1/584 (also in JM/3489); Werner, *Fighting Back*, pp. 23, 28–31, 59–67. Jürgen Matthäus comments on the same rural-urban distinctions in the occupied Soviet Union. See Matthäus, "What about the 'Ordinary Men'? The German Order Police and the Holocaust in the Occupied Soviet Union," *Holocaust and Genocide Studies*, 10:2 (1996), pp. 134–150.

98 Blumental, *Documents*, Protocol 7(132), February 14, 1942, p. 303.

99 See, for example, Rivka Dawidowicz testimony on Góraj, YVA, O.3/4478; Moshe Zylberszpan testimony on Stężyca, YVA, M.49.E/4137; Fiszelson testimony in June 1942 on Zamość, YVA, M.10.AR1/946.

quickened, but not all of these developments had been planned by the SS or the civilian authorities as part of the preparations for the "Final Solution." Nor did the Jews' two years of learning to cope with their very difficult circumstances and of their bitter experience with the Germans, in all its brutality, prepare them for what ultimately befell them, beginning on March 16, 1942. The reasons for this can be found in those very conditions and in the nature of that bitter experience, as well as in the one limited aspect of the war in the Soviet Union that they witnessed.

Even as living conditions for most Jews worsened considerably in the Lublin District, they were still relatively better off than many of their relatives and friends in other places. And they knew this, whether from the refugees who continued to come to the Lublin District during this time, from their correspondence with other Jews, or from their contacts with Poles.[100]

The death rate in Lublin had risen dramatically in the summer of 1941, but it still did not approach that of Warsaw, for example. Whereas approximately 4 percent of the Jews in the Lublin ghetto died in 1941 (most after the summer), nearly 10 percent of the Jews in the Warsaw ghetto died during the same period.[101] Conditions declined all over the district in every way — health, living standards, restrictions on movement, food rations, confiscations, and so on. Yet most Jews were still not in closed ghettos even in the spring of 1942, nor were they dying of starvation. Indeed, they could favorably compare their own conditions to those of friends and relatives elsewhere with whom they were in contact or about whom they heard, as well as to the Red Army POWs penned in camps in the Lublin District, in Chełm, Włodawa, Dęblin, Zamość, Majdanek, and other places. Jews were often put to work alongside or within sight of these POWs, and they

100 German officials complained of the continuing influx of refugees from the Warsaw District. See, for example, Gendarmerie Łuków to BuF Lublin, November 12, 1941, YVA, O.53/83.

101 The Lublin death records can be found in WAPL, RZ 172 and 179, and in WAPL, Gmina Żydowska (prewar community records) 8, burial records for September 1941—March 1942. See also Trunk, in *Dos Buch*, pp. 360–361; Blumental, in *Encyclopedia of the Jewish Diaspora, Lublin*, p. 670. On Warsaw, see Gutman, *The Jews of Warsaw*, pp. 63–65.

reported back to their communities the horrendous conditions under which these captured soldiers lived and died by the thousands.

On the one hand, the picture that emerged for Jews in the Lublin District was one of catastrophic upheaval. On the other hand, it was more of a change of degree, not of kind, when compared to the conditions of other Jews and of Red Army POWs. There were Jewish communities where Jews even led the way in trying to give food to the haggard, dying Red Army POWs in their vicinity.[102] If, amidst renewed warfare and massive death on all sides, they were still managing to hang on in a relatively better position than others, then they concluded that they were faced with more worrisome but not ominous circumstances. Thus, the change in March 1942 to massively violent deportations was sudden for them. In a sense this was just as sudden as the murderous wave that hit the Jews of the Soviet Union in the summer of 1941. In neither case did the Jews have any reason to expect what struck them like lightning on a clear day. They were caught completely unawares.

Sorting the Jews. "Sorting," or categorizing, the Jews involved a GG-wide census-taking of the Jews, counting and marking essential laborers, and identifying foreign Jews. A census of the Jews was ordered by the central BuF in Kraków on January 20, 1942 – the same day that the Wannsee Conference convened – in a letter sent to every district.[103] In the city of Lublin, the head of the municipal population department ordered the Judenrat, on January 30, 1942, to provide a list of Jews with American, British, or Palestinian nationality by February 5.[104]

On February 2, the municipal police ordered the Lublin ghetto divided into two – Ghetto A and Ghetto B – with a fence for each part. One ghetto would house most of the population, while the other would house those who worked for the Germans. The fence around the full ghetto was finally put up at the end of February

102 See, for example, Klukowski, *Diary*, p. 173.

103 Letter, BuF Kraków to BuF of each district regarding "Gettobildung und Angabe der Einwohnerzahl," January 20, 1942, WAPL, GDL 270.

104 Dr. Steinbach, Lublin *Stadthauptmann*'s office, to Judenrat, January 30, 1942, WAPL, RZ 24.

or early March. It ran along Lubartowska Street, whose eastern side was within the ghetto. At one end the gate was at Kowalska Street; at the other end it was at Cyrulnicza Street. The guard at the Kowalska Street gate was a German gendarme whom the Jews called "*Schiesser*," because he arbitrarily shot at Jewish passersby. Gradually, several parts of the ghetto around Grodzka Street were fenced off as Ghetto B for Jews who worked for the Germans and would not be among the first to be deported. The Judenrat was also ordered by the *Stadthauptmann* to assume full municipal duties. Although the members of the Judenrat seem not to have grasped the implications of this change, the separation of the ghetto from the municipality facilitated the deportations that soon followed.[105]

Another element of "sorting the Jews" involved increasing the relevant Jewish bureaucracy for round-ups; that is, the Jewish police. In January 1942, Worthoff's office ordered the Judenrat to increase the Lublin Jewish police to twenty men. This number was further increased, reaching 113 on the eve of the deportations. Developments followed much the same pattern elsewhere in the district. However, the Lublin Jewish police proved unsatisfactory for deportations from the SS point of view, as they were not aggressive enough. As a result, the SS and Ukrainians did nearly all the round-up work, and most of the Jewish police were also deported.[106]

Setting aside essential laborers was a fundamental part of the preparation for deportations and of the deportation process as a whole. Indeed, this was the reason for dividing the Lublin ghetto into two distinct sections, and part of the general purpose of ghettoization in other places in the district and elsewhere. There were certain skills

105 Hoffmann, Polizeidirektor in Lublin Municipality to Judenrat, February 2, 1942, YVA, O.6/11b*; *Amtsblatt des Gouverneurs des Distrikts Lublin*, February 28, 1942, including Zörner's February 4 order to set up a fenced-off "Sonderghetto" for Jews working for Germans, YVA, catalog number 8167* (also in MA, D.1.5868); Worthoff Verdict, YVA, TR.10/859, pp. 48–49; Blumental, *Documents*, Protocols 5–6(129–130), February 3 and 7, 1942, pp. 300–302. Fencing in the Lublin ghetto was first suggested by Amtschef Ludwig Losacker on June 3, 1941 but was not accepted then, WAPL, GDL 892 (copy in Friedrich, ed., *Polen*, pp. 649–650).

106 Streibel indictment, YVA, TR.10/756, p. 63; Blumental, *Documents*, Protocols 4(128), 17(141), January 31 and March 31, 1942, pp. 299, 319–320.

required by the German authorities for military production and local needs. Therefore, the goal was to leave a minimum number of Jewish skilled laborers alive temporarily, while all others would be deported.

The selection of necessary Jewish skilled laborers was a two-stage process, which took place from March to May 1942. First they set aside all Jews who worked for the Germans and later narrowed this pool to essential laborers. In Lublin, the KdS, *SS-Sturmbannführer* Johannes Müller, on March 7, 1942, ordered all Lublin Jews who were working for the Germans to report the next morning to KdS headquarters in order to receive a new SIPO stamp in their work identity cards. Beginning at 8:00 A.M. on March 8, the working Jews reported to Gestapo headquarters in order to have their place of employment confirmed and their work cards and families' identity cards stamped (in red) by SIPO. Müller oversaw the operation.[107] For many Jews this was a moment of great anxiety; they sensed it was better to have the new stamp for themselves and their families than not. Many suspected that a new expulsion, even larger than that in March 1941, was in the offing. In instances that they feared they would be unable to acquire the coveted stamp, some tried to find the right person to bribe. That person proved to be the well-connected informer Shamai Grajer, who apparently succeeded in providing the stamp to those who paid.[108]

When the deportation order was issued on the night of March 16/17, those with this stamp were permitted to remain in the ghetto together with their families. However, this regulation was changed again on March 31, when a new identity card was issued as the ticket to remaining alive — the "*J-Ausweis*." This further reduced the number of Jews permitted to remain temporarily in the ghetto to fewer than 3,000, or less than 10 percent of the population on March 16.[109]

107 Blumental, *Documents*, Protocol 12(136), March 7, 1942, pp. 63, 307–308; Klajnman-Fradkoff testimony, YVA, O.33/1134; Worthoff verdict, YVA, TR.10/859, p. 49; Pohl, *Judenpolitik*, pp. 110–111, 123–124.

108 Erlichman-Bank, *In Impure Hands*, pp. 36–37; Rapoport-Glikstein, in *Dos Buch*, p. 394; *idem*, in *Encyclopedia of the Jewish Diaspora, Lublin*, p. 694.

109 Blumental, *Documents*, Protocols 14(138), 16(140), 19(143), March 17 and 31, April 2, 1942, pp. 310–312, 314–317, 321. A full list of those who received a

The same sorting preparations were undertaken throughout the Lublin District and the GG during the following two months, leaving a small minority of the Jewish population marked for a temporary stay of execution (see Chapter 7). The types, numbers, and proportions of Jewish skilled and unskilled laborers to be left alive were not clear to the various German authorities at first. Thus, on the one hand, the BuF in Kraków and Lublin were canceling training courses for Jews in various crafts and in agriculture, which had been planned to begin in late March, while, on the other hand, the Lublin Labor Office was looking for ways to increase the number of Jews in agriculture to take the place of Poles who had been conscripted for labor in Germany.[110] Requests for lists of able-bodied Jews in April referred only to those working for the Germans; only in May were specific skills and crafts specified (see Chapter 7).[111]

Some civilian officials were impatient to be rid of their Jews and prepared statistical data before receiving a formal request from the BuF or Höfle to do so. Hans Lenk, *Kreishauptmann* for Janów-Lubelski county, having seen some 2,500 Jews deported from Kraśnik in April 1942, sent a list of 5,900 deportable Jews to Höfle on May 9. However, the BuF was responsible for coordinating population statistics for "Operation Reinhard," and they were not yet prepared to process this

"*J-Ausweis*" is in WAPL, RZ 164 (copy in USHMM, RG-15.101M, reel 24. The actual number of those who received this most sought-after identification card was 4,641, as the Judenrat had succeeded in increasing the number of recipients. See also YVA, TR.10/859, pp. 62–63, 68.

110 BuF, Kraków to District Governors, March 9, 1942; Türk to all BuF officials in district, March 18, 1942, YVA, O.53/82 (also in *Dokumenty*, II:42); Arbeitsamt Lublin to *Kreishauptmann* Lublin-Land, March 5, 1942, YVA, O.53/82; Meininger, Arbeitsamt Lublin, to Gemeindeverwaltung Biskupice, March 5, 1942, WAPL, RZ w Biskupicach (copy in YVA, JM/3695); Rundschreiben, Arbeitsamt Lublin, March 18, 1942, in *Eksterminacja*, pp. 234–235 (also in *Faschismus*).

111 Höfle to *Kreishauptmann* Lublin-Land, April 21, 1942; Ziegenmeyer to town and village heads in Lublin county, April 29, 1942; Ziegenmeyer to Höfle, 8-5-42, Arbeitsamt Lublin to *Kreishauptmann* Lublin-Land, March 5, 1942, all in YVA, O.53/82; Meininger, Arbeitsamt Lublin, to Gemeindeverwaltung Biskupice, March 5, 1942, WAPL, RZ w Biskupicach.

data, while Höfle's team was not yet ready for further deportations from this county. Lenk would have to wait until the fall.[112]

From all the above we can see that, from the perspective of the German authorities, everything was in place to begin the murder of the Jews of Lublin by the second week of March 1942. The deportation and killing manpower was trained and ready, and the gassing facilities at Bełżec were operational, with additional facilities at Sobibór already being planned. The cooperation of the German civilian authorities had been secured as well, while the necessary Jewish laborers had been specified in Lublin, as they soon would be in the rest of the district. While the Jews found themselves more constricted and more terrorized than they had been half a year earlier, they were still completely unaware of what awaited them. German deception and secrecy had succeeded so far.

Himmler arrived in the GG on March 14 for discussions with Globocnik, Krüger, and Schöngarth regarding the upcoming operation. He spent the night at Globocnik's home in Lublin. When he left for Berlin the next day, Globocnik had the go-ahead to begin what became the largest killing operation of the war and the Holocaust.[113]

112 Lenk to SSPF Lublin, May 9, 1942, YVA, O.51/10, and *Dokumenty*, II:54.
113 *Dienstkalender*, pp. 379–380.

CHAPTER 7

Deportations

The Deportations Begin

On March 15, 1942, Warsaw Zionist underground activist Zivia Lubetkin wrote in coded language to Nathan Schwalb in Switzerland that Vilna's Jews had been killed; only 10,000 remained. And now, she added, *shohet* (slaughterer) had arrived at Wilnicki (i.e., Lublin, where activist Moshe Wilnicki was at that time). She feared he would come to Warsaw and to the *hakhshara* training centers, too.[1]

What Lubetkin had surmised was that the concentration of Trawniki troops in Lublin was not merely an exercise. Two companies of Trawniki troops – some 200–250 men – had been assigned to Lublin in February and March 1942. On March 16, Hermann Höfle's office ordered Karl Streibel to provide an additional 200–250 men immediately for a "ghetto clearing" (*Räumung des Ghettos*). The new units arrived by truck after nightfall, and their officers were briefed by Höfle and several KdS officers.[2] Höfle oversaw the operation, which was to serve as the model for subsequent deportations in the GG. Shortly before his briefing, Lublin Gestapo head Walther Liska

1 Zariz, *Letters from Haluzim*, pp. 133–134. Lubetkin was one of the leaders of Dror in Poland and in the underground in the Warsaw ghetto, and Wilnicki was one of the Dror leaders in Lublin.

2 YVA, TR.10/756, pp. 71–76; TR.10/869, vol. III, pp. 325–327, V, pp. 5–19.

ran an operational meeting for the special KdS unit, commanded by Hermann Worthoff, which Globocnik had ordered to be set up for the deportation operation. Liska told the men that the Jews would be rounded up beginning early the next morning and sent across the Bug. Only working Jews or those with essential professions would be left behind, while the elderly, ill, and disabled were to be shot on the spot. Plundering was forbidden. Liska then passed on field command to Worthoff. In addition to the Trawniki men, Worthoff's unit, and the Lublin police, a Waffen-SS unit from Chełm and the Lublin Jewish police also played a role in the round-ups and deportations.[3]

As the deportation troops were positioning themselves, cordoning off the ghetto at 10:00 P.M., the Judenrat was summoned to a sudden meeting at which Worthoff read out the "resettlement" order. All those Jews who had received new SIPO stamps in their work cards on March 8 were to move into Ghetto B by March 19, while all Poles still in Ghetto B had until that date to move out. The daily "resettlement" quota was 1,400; each Jew could take 15 kilograms of personal belongings. Anyone who did not report when ordered would be summarily shot. The operation progressed systematically, from Cyrulnicza Street on one end of the ghetto until the other end, gradually reducing Ghetto A in size until it disappeared altogether. The order did not indicate where the deportees were going or what they would be doing there, but the fact that part of the order instructed them to bury the dead immediately was ominous.[4]

Worthoff set up his command post for the operation in Shamai Grajer's café. Grajer helped Worthoff and other SS officials select Jews for labor or deportation, and the telephone in his café, manned by *SS-Unterscharführer* Erich Kalich, facilitated coordination of the various facets of the round-up. Kalich also used runners to coordinate with the KdS, KdO, and SSPF offices. There was much

3 YVA, TR.10/859, pp. 50–78; TR.10/736, pp. 26–30; TR.10/756, pp. 63–72; Ida Rapoport-Glikstein in *Encyclopedia of the Jewish Diaspora, Lublin*, p. 694; *idem*, in *Dos Buch*, p. 395; Erlichman-Bank, *In Impure Hands*, p. 36.

4 Blumental, *Documents*, Protocol 14 (138), March 17, 1942, pp. 310–312; Pohl, *Judenpolitik*, p. 114.

hustle and bustle in the café during the deportation operation, with various commanders, including Globocnik himself, coming and going and messengers running in and out frequently, while Grajer's waitresses served them drinks.[5]

At 5:00 A.M. on March 17, the Jews were woken abruptly and given but a few minutes to leave their homes. The Trawniki men and Jewish police were assigned to remove the daily quota of Jews from their homes and escort them to the gathering point at the 375-year-old Maharshal synagogue on Jateczna Street, near the Zamek (castle). Whoever emerged slowly or tried to avoid joining the deportation was dragged out violently by the Trawniki men and beaten or shot.

SS-Untersturmführer Harry Sturm was in charge of containing the deportees at the synagogue and maintaining order there, as well as selecting out craftsmen whose skills might be needed. During the operation Alten often went to the synagogue to assist in this selection, in an apparent effort to keep more Jews in Lublin. The selected craftsmen were torn away from their families by SS men or Trawniki guards and escorted back to Ghetto B. The rest of the Jews were marched from the Maharshal synagogue, usually in the evening, 3 kilometers under ORPO guard to the freight rail station near the Majdan Tatarski neighborhood. The loading dock was at the slaughterhouse that belonged to a sausage factory — what macabre symbolism. Jews who did not fit onto the train were returned to the ghetto to await a subsequent round-up.

Early on the Germans found the Jewish police ineffective,

5 The account of the Lublin deportation is based on many sources, among them: YVA, TR.10/859, pp. 50–78; TR.10/869, V:8–9, 21–22; TR.10/1146Z, pp. 955–956, testimony of SS man Hellmuth Schneider, May 18, 1960 and January 21, 1961, pp. 1098 and 1614, testimony of Abwehr officer Konrad Gallen, September 12 and December 15, 1960, pp. 3523 and 3535, testimony of Fritz Stöcker, February 1–6, 1963, pp. 4255–4258, testimony of Johannes Erich Kalich, March–April, 1965; TR/10-1291, Georg Werk testimony, March 16, 1964 (Nuremberg), pp. 4882–4883; TR.10/736, pp. 26–30; TR.10/756, pp. 63–72; Daniel Lewkowicz letter to his sister, March 29, 1942, M.10.A.R.1/552 (also in JM.3489); Yeshayahu Wajsfisz testimony, YVA, M.1.E/649; Ida Rapoport-Glikstein in *Encyclopedia of the Jewish Diaspora, Lublin*, pp. 694–695; *idem*, in *Dos Buch*, p. 395; Sarah Erlichman-Bank, *In Impure Hands*, pp. 36–37; Hanka Spector-Burstein testimony, MA, A.195; Berenstein, "Martyrologia," pp. 35–38.

apparently because they were not brutal enough, so the Ukrainian Trawniki men were pressed into a greater role in the round-ups. The result was even more brutality and more blood flowing in the streets during the round-ups and the march to the station.

Shooting accompanied every stage of the operation. Jews were shot as they left their homes, as they marched toward the Maharshal synagogue, and as they were marched to the train. Once a section of the ghetto had been cleared, the Trawniki troops were sent back in to search for the Jews who were too ill to walk or were hiding. All these people were shot on the spot. At the end of each day, the special Jewish burial unit collected all the dead bodies from the ghetto and from along the deportation route and buried them in the Jewish cemetery. By the end of the first week, 10,564 Jews had been deported to Bełżec and 126 shot in the streets, according to official German police statistics; by March 29, 18,000 Jews had been deported and at least 1,000 had been shot, according to Jewish sources, in the course of the round-ups.

For the Jews the opening moments of the round-up were terrifying. The surprise, the shouting by the Germans and Ukrainians, the cries of the Jews, the beatings, and the shooting further increased the terror. The fear that the SS and Ukrainians imposed inside the ghetto was compounded by the fear imposed by the German civilian authorities should anyone try to get out. Just such a warning was the above-mentioned March 17 order by Dr. Hasse of the district Interior Department to the Lublin-Land *Kreishauptmann* to post in all Jewish quarters in his county the names of eleven Jews who were executed for leaving the ghetto without permission.[6]

The Germans felt that the first few days of the operation were not well organized. Many of the Trawniki men drank too much, and many Jews with SIPO stamps were taken by mistake.[7] For the Jews the relentless terror as the round-ups progressed led increasing numbers to try to hide or otherwise evade being taken. On March

6 Klajnman-Fradkoff testimony, YVA, O.33/1134; Yehoshua Kaniel testimony, O.3/10622; memo from Dr. Hasse to the Lublin-Land *Kreishauptmann*, March 17, 1942, regarding a March 4 court verdict, in WAPL, Kreishauptmannschaft Lublin-Land 75 (copy in YVA, O.53/82).

7 YVA, TR.10/859, pp. 50–78; TR.10/736, pp. 26–30; TR.10/756, pp. 63–72.

21, the Judenrat was forced to post an announcement that all Jews should report for relocation when ordered, "for their own good." The Jewish police would escort them to the synagogue, the announcement promised. The Germans hoped that a combination of threats and the offer to let the Jewish police serve as escort would ease their own job. When this failed, the Judenrat was then forced by the Germans to post an announcement in Ghetto B on March 23, calling on the Jews to search cellars and attics for those in hiding. They were to report such people to the Germans, or else risk deportation of all the Jews.[8]

The orphanage at Grodzka 11 (in Ghetto B), with approximately 200 children aged three to eighteen, was liquidated on March 24. The day before, some twenty Jewish men were taken to a farm on the northern edge of Lublin and forced to dig one or two long, deep pits. Worthoff's unit rounded up the children and loaded them onto trucks. The orphanage's patrons – Aharon Shapiro and Szmul Wollmann – gave the children candy in order to keep them calm. The veteran and widely-respected director and chief educator, Ms. Henia (Hanna) Kuperberg, and the housemother, Mrs. Anna Taubenfeld, voluntarily accompanied the children in order not to abandon them in their last moments. The Germans and Ukrainians first shot the younger children on the mound of dirt that had been formed by digging the pits. Other Ukrainians then threw the bodies into the pits. After approximately an hour of shooting, the older children and the two women were brought to the pits and shot as well.[9]

Many Jews tried to get into the Jewish hospital, hoping that the sick would be left alone. This hope reflects the people's difficulty in grasping just what the Germans intended. In reality, of course, not only did the Germans not respect the sanctity of a hospital,

8 WAPL, RZ 162 (copy in USHMMA, RG-15.101M); Blumental, *Documents*, p. 313.

9 YVA, TR.10/859, pp. 169–170; M.10.A.R.1/1172, report on the Lublin deportations, March 1942; Klajnman-Fradkoff testimony, O.33/1134, pp. 24–25; Karol Mulak testimony, *Faschismus*, pp. 272–273; Nahman Korn in *Encyclopedia of the Jewish Diaspora, Lublin*, p. 730; Kasparek, "Situation and Extermination of Jewish Population," p. 9. The exact date of the shooting of the orphanage children is not clear. More sources point to March 24 than to any other date, but some refer to April 1 or 2.

but they also saw the ill and weak as prime targets for immediate liquidation. Thus, all the approximately 100 patients in the hospital for communicable diseases were shot on March 24, along with the hospital staff; approximately ninety elderly in the old-age home were shot at the same time in the building's courtyard.

On the night of March 26/27, the staff at the main Jewish hospital on Lubartowska Street were awakened by SS officers at 4:00 A.M. and ordered to have the patients ready for "relocation" by 7:00 A.M. The staff divided the 300 patients into ambulatory and non-ambulatory groups. Children who sensed the danger began screaming that they were well and they wanted to go home. The nurse Sarah Erlichman felt that the patients understood what awaited them better than did the medical staff. Perhaps illness and hospitalization had affected their perspective on their own imminent mortality. The Trawniki men surrounded the hospital and ordered the staff to bring the patients to waiting vehicles that took them away in the direction of Lubartów. They were shot into a mass grave that thirty Jewish prisoners had been forced to dig. Then the prisoners were shot.[10]

On March 29, the Germans suspended the operation in Lublin for Easter and for regrouping, while rumors spread among the Jews that the Germans would be willing to accept a huge ransom in place of deportations. The Judenrat quickly organized a large payment of

10 Erlichman-Bank, *In Impure Hands*, pp. 39–41; Glikstein-Rapoport, *Dos Buch*, p. 396; *idem*, *Encyclopedia of the Jewish Diaspora, Lublin*, p. 695; Klajnman-Fradkoff testimony, YVA, O.33-1134, p. 26; Janina Kucharska (Sara Zygielwaks) testimony, JM/3536A; M.10.A.R.1/1172, report on the deportations from Lublin, March 1942; M.10.A.R.1/144 (and JM.3489), "Gehenna Żydów Polskich Pod Okupacja Hitlerowska," July 1942; TR.10/859, pp. 50–78; TR.10/736, pp. 26–30; TR.10/756, pp. 63–72; Moshe Zylberberg testimony, YVA, M.1.E/1402; Kasparek, "Situation and Extermination of Jewish Population," p. 9. Sarah Erlichman-Bank, who worked as a nurse in the Jewish hospital at the time, dates the murder of the patients and staff to March 26, as does the wartime underground report, "Gehenna Żydów Polskich," while Janina Kucharska, who was a doctor there, dates it to March 27. The postwar trials in West Germany date the murder to March 28, while Ida Glikstein-Rapoport recalls that it occurred on April 1, the Catholic Easter. However, Easter Sunday was March 29 that year, a day on which all sources agree that the Germans took a break in the deportations from Lublin. The exact date of these murders, therefore, is difficult to determine. I have relied here on the contemporary account and on Erlichman-Bank and Kucharska, since they were eyewitnesses.

500,000 złotys in gold, jewelry, and cash, and dispatched Judenrat members Solomon Kestenberg and David Edelsztajn on March 29 or 30 to pay Worthoff and Sturm to stop the deportations. The Germans took the money and arrested the Judenrat members on charges of illegally possessing gold and other valuables. According to one source, they were shot in the Jewish cemetery.[11]

Two days later, at 2:00 P.M., Worthoff ordered a special meeting of the Judenrat. He invited six non-members: Ajzyk Brodt, Daniel Kupferminc, Józef Rotrubin, Szulim Tajkef, Bolesław Tenenbojm, and Wolf Wiener. Most of these were informers or worked in close cooperation with the Gestapo. Worthoff and Sturm announced to the Judenrat that the deportations would be renewed forthwith and that the SIPO stamp was no longer valid. Instead, those with a new, yellow Jewish identity card (J-*Ausweis*) issued by the *Stadthauptmann* during the deportation would be the only Jewish people left in Lublin. These documents were not applicable to dependents, which meant that families would be further torn apart. The Judenrat was reduced to twelve; half were the six new members. They were joined by six veteran Judenrat members: Marek Alten, the new chairman, Izak Kerszman, David Hochgemein, Leon Hufnagel, Jakub Kelner, and Nachman Lerner. The other Judenrat members and their families would be deported that day.[12]

When the second phase of the deportations began, the Germans found it much more difficult to meet their daily quota, as the Jews had gone into hiding. This brought on even more violence from the angry and frustrated Germans and Ukrainians. This phase of the deportations included Ghetto B. Everyone had to leave their homes, but those with the new ID could return when the day's operation was completed. The Jewish police was ordered to check the IDs, while Worthoff and Sturm, with Alten's input, dealt with separating the

11 YVA, TR.10/859, pp. 50–78; TR.10/756, p. 65; Glikstein-Rapaport, *Dos Buch*, p. 396; *idem*, *Encyclopedia of the Jewish Diaspora, Lublin*, p. 695; Blumental, ed., *Documents*, Protocol 16(140), March 31, 1942, p. 315. According to TR.10/756, Shamai Grajer accompanied Edelsztajn and Kestenberg to the Germans but was not harmed.

12 Blumental, *Documents*, Protocol 16 (140), March 31, 1942, pp. 314–318.

Jews gathered for deportation, Lublin, 1942, Yad Vashem Photo Archive, FA 16/10

Jews being loaded onto a freight train for deportation to Bełżec, Lublin, 1942, Yad Vashem Photo Archive, A4613/1116

"useful" Jews. Sometimes this meant that Jews without the proper ID were also allowed to stay if they had valuable trades.[13]

By April 14, when the deportation from Lublin to Bełżec ended, some 30,000 Jews had been deported to the camp, while several thousand had been shot. The remaining Jews were ordered to go to a new, fenced-in ghetto in the Majdan Tatarski neighborhood. It was a three-day move, and the Germans provided 200 wagons. They also implied that any Jews still in Lublin, whether legally or illegally, would be permitted to stay in the new ghetto. On April 16, Zörner ordered a fenced-in ghetto to be established, effective April 20, for all Jews who had the new ID card. On April 17, the Jewish police, the disinfection unit, Judenrat employees, and craftsmen working for the Germans moved there. The next day all those living outside the ghetto who were not in these groups moved into the ghetto, too. On April 19, the remainder of the ghetto inhabitants moved to the new ghetto. While it could accommodate perhaps 2,000 people, now it housed 7–8,000, half of whom did not have the necessary ID.[14]

While the Majdan Tatarski ghetto's severe housing shortage demanded the new Judenrat's immediate attention, its first task from Worthoff was to conduct a new census. The orders were given to the Judenrat on April 19; the census was to be completed that night. Officially, the census was meant to determine the number of barracks that needed to be constructed to house the Jews. Since there was no electricity in Majdan Tatarski and insufficient fuel, the Judenrat conducted the census by candlelight and worked through the night.[15]

At 5:00 A.M. on April 20, Trawniki men surrounded the Majdan Tatarski ghetto. SS men then checked the Jews and divided them into two groups – those with the new ID, and those without. New

13 YVA, TR.10/859, pp. 50–78.

14 Blumental, *Documents*, Protocol, 22(146), April 14, 1942, pp. 324–326; Zörner order, April 16, 1942, MA, D.1.5868; YVA, TR.10/859, pp. 194–195; Glikstein-Rapoport, *Encyclopedia of the Jewish Diaspora, Lublin*, pp. 701–702; *idem*, *Dos Buch*, pp. 399–400.

15 Blumental, *Documents*, Protocol 23(147), April 19, 1942, pp. 326–327; Glikstein-Rapoport, *Encyclopedia of the Jewish Diaspora, Lublin*, p. 707; *idem*, *Dos Buch*, p. 401.

identification papers were issued to 3,300 people, while approximately 4,000 "illegal" Jews who were caught were marched to Majdanek and kept in an open field there overnight. The next day they were driven south toward Piaski and then marched to the Krępiec woods and shot into mass graves that they themselves were forced to dig. Here, too, Worthoff was the field commander; this time Höfle supervised the operation while circling above in a small Fieseler Storch airplane.[16]

Following the deportations and the subsequent murder operation, Lublin's streets and environs were strewn with Jewish corpses. As with the earlier round-ups, a burial detail was assigned to collect the corpses and bury them in the Jewish cemetery. This job lasted many days after the deportations had ended.[17]

Incoming Deportations

While the Lublin deportations progressed, Globocnik's men also had to deal with the expansion of the operation. Incoming Jews from Mielec, Theresienstadt, Germany, and Slovakia (and soon thereafter Austria) needed to be temporarily housed and then killed, while the operation also needed to spread to encompass the entire district (and the entire GG).

Jews were deported to the Lublin District from March 11, when 1,001 were sent from Thresienstadt to Izbica, to June 20, when 201 Jews were sent from Germany to Majdanek and Sobibór. Approximately 85–90,000 Jews were deported in eighty-six trains, but, as with the murder operation in general, it is apparent that there were two stages to this deportation to Lublin in the spring of 1942. During the first forty-one days (until April 20), twenty-five trains had brought in approximately 25,000 Jews — an average of 610 deportees

16 YVA, TR.10/859, pp. 198–200; TR.10/736, pp. 33–35; TR.10/756, p. 68; TR.10/1146Z, Worthoff interrogation, September-November 1960, p. 1357; Glikstein-Rapoport, *Encyclopedia of the Jewish Diaspora, Lublin*, pp. 707–708; *idem*, *Dos Buch*, pp. 401–402.

17 See, for example, the authorization signed by Sturm for Salomon Epsztajn to go anywhere in Lublin except Krakowska Street in order to collect corpses during the period April 22–26; WAPL, RZ 22 (copy in USHMMA, RG-15.101M).

daily (three trains every five days). During the next sixty days (April 22–June 20), sixty-one trains brought in more than 61,000 Jews – 1,016 people and one train daily. In this latter period systematic countywide sweeps of Jews were also introduced (see below) as Sobibór began operations as a second death camp in the district for the murder of the Jews. The increased tempo of deportations into and out of the Lublin District became synchronized.

In January 1942, the German civilian authorities began discussing the deportation of Jews from Mielec, in the Kraków District, to the Lublin District.[18] Able-bodied male Jews were to be put to work in a Heinkel airplane factory near Mielec; 2,000 children and old people would be shot at Mielec; and the remaining 4,000 Jews would be sent to Lublin. Major Johannes Ragger of the BuF in Kraków called Lublin deputy BuF head Fritz Reuter on March 7 to inform him of the impending deportation and to urge him to coordinate with Globocnik's men. Clearly, these Jews were to be included in the murder operation, as were all other Jews deported into Lublin. The trains reached the Lublin District on March 13, 14, and 16 (two trains), and, according to Richard Türk, the Jews were distributed as follows: half in the north and east of the district – to Włodawa (800), Sosnowica (200), and Międzyrzec (750); and half in the south – to Dubienka (843), Belz, and Cieszanów (500 each). There is a discrepancy among the documents: the dispatch reports indicate that 4,000 Jews were deported, but Türk's April 7 report accounts for only 3,593. In other words, more than 400 people incapable of forced labor had died or were murdered during the intervening three weeks. A JSS report of April 12 accounts for only 3,432 Mielec Jews in these places. Another 161 had died in five days.[19]

18 See Türk telegrams to Major Ragger, January 6 and 21, 1942, in *Dokumenty*, vol. II, pp. 10–14; BuF Lublin to BuF Cholm, January 9, 1942, WAPL, GDL 893 (copy in YVA, O.51/10); Türk to BuF Hrubieszów, January 9, 1942, and Reuter, BuF Lublin to Ragger, January 23, 1942, WAPL, GDL 893 (copies in YVA, JM.10455 and O.53/83). See also correspondence between Weirauch in the GG Interior Department and the BuF in Chełm, Radzyń, Zamość, and Hrubieszów, February 9–10, 1942, in *Dokumenty*, vol. II, pp. 15–19.

19 Phone message from Ragger to Türk, March 7; Türk response, March 9; Ragger's dispatch of the exact deportation schedule on March 10; Reuter's

These deportations also sometimes produced anomalous situations. On June 16, 1942, a sanatorium in Kobierzyn wrote to the BuF in Lublin requesting the forwarding address for the Mielec Jews in order to collect outstanding medical bills totaling 2,226.80 złotys. The BuF passed this on to the KdS only on July 14; on July 28, Sturm replied that he did not know the whereabouts of the Mielec Jews and referred the BuF to the SSPF. The BuF wrote to the SSPF on August 28, and, on September 4, *SS-Oberscharführer* Franz Hoskowetz of Abteilung Reinhardt responded that the Mielec Jews had been resettled in Russia and there were no precise details regarding their current whereabouts. Finally, on October 16, the BuF forwarded this information to Kobierzyn.[20] Clearly, all the Lublin officials involved in this four-month exchange knew what had really happened to the Mielec Jews, as they were all directly involved in the murder operation. So why did the well-informed BuF in Lublin go through all this dilatory, months-long letter-writing and not simply send the untruthful response earlier? This remains a puzzle.

secret telegrams on these to BuF in Radzyń and in Cholm on March 11 and 12; Reuter to Nemec, in SSPF's office, March 12; Ragger's secret telegram to Türk on March 13; Reuter's memo of March 17; BuF Cholm to BuF Lublin, March 18; Türk, "Zum Monatsbericht März 1942," April 7, 1942, YVA, O.6/11a*; BuF Radzyń to BuF Lublin, April 9, 1942, on the arrival of 750 Jews in Międzyrzec on March 14; JSS Kraków memo, April 12, 1942, *Faschismus*, pp. 275–276. The originals of most of these documents may be found in WAPL, GDL 893; copies of most in *Dokumenty*, vol. II, pp. 22–33. Several of these documents may also be found in WAPL, GDL 270, 273; YVA, JM/215/1 (Oneg Shabbat archive material), JM/10,455, JM/10,458, O.51/10, O.53/82, O.53/83, O.6/352, and elsewhere. See also Rochelle G. Saidel, *Mielec, Poland: The Shetl That Became a Nazi Concentration Camp* (Jerusalem and New York: Gefen, 2012), pp. 40–58, 65–73; Musial, *Zivilverwaltung*, pp. 224–227; Christopher R. Browning, *Nazi Policy, Jewish Workers, German Killers* (Cambridge and New York: Cambridge University Press, 2000), p. 73. The April 12 JSS report shows 460 in Belz, 465 in Cieszanów, 787 in Dubienka, 210 in Sosnowica, 740 in Międzyrzec, and 770 in Włodawa.

20 Staatliche Heil- und Pflegeanstalt, Kobierzyn to BuF Lublin, June 16, 1942; BuF Lublin to KdS Lublin (III2b), July 14, 1942; Sturm to BuF Lublin, July 28, 1942; BuF to Abteilung Reinhardt, August 28, 1942; Franz Hoskowetz to BuF Lublin, September 4, 1942; BuF to Staatliche Heil- und Pflegeanstalt, October 16, 1942, *Dokumenty*, vol. II, pp. 35–39. Hoskowetz was part of Wippern's economic branch of "Operation Reinhard," at the goods' sorting camp on Chopin Street; see YVA, O.53/68.

Jews from Germany (the "*Altreich*") and the Protectorate began to be deported to the Lublin District at the same time as the Mielec Jews. On March 3, 1942, Bühler told Zörner to prepare for the resettlement of 14,000 Jews from the Reich to the Lublin District during the coming months, as part of "the total solution of the Jewish Problem in Europe" (*der Gesamtlösung des Judenproblems im Europäischen Raum*).[21] In fact, between March 11 and June 20, twenty-eight trains brought more than 25,000 Jews from Germany, and fourteen trains brought 14,000 Jews from the Protectorate (all but one of these came from Theresienstadt). The trip from Theresienstadt or Germany generally took two days. Until the end of May, most of these Jews were housed temporarily alongside or in place of local Jews, rather than being sent directly to the death camps. In his March 30 memorandum, Türk noted that 6,000 Jews from the Reich had already arrived in the Lublin District and 1,000 were on the way. Two thousand of these Jews had been sent to Piaski, and the coming 1,000 would also be sent there, replacing 3,400 Jews who had just been deported to Bełżec. Similarly, 2,200 Izbica Jews had been deported and 4,000 had been brought in, and so on.

The able-bodied among them (as well as among the Slovakian Jews) were generally used first for forced labor, especially in swamp drainage and in the construction and expansion of Majdanek. This meant the break-up of families, as in the case of the April 27 train from Theresienstadt. It arrived in Izbica on April 30, with 600 Jews; 400 had been dropped off in Lublin and taken to Majdanek for forced labor. The transport costs from the local train station to the ghetto, as well as housing and maintenance costs for all these deported Jews were borne by the local Jewish communities, even as they themselves were being liquidated.[22]

21 Bühler to Zörner, March 3, 1942, WAPL, GDL 270. The letter was received on March 6, and forwarded by Zörner to Türk personally ("*ihn persönlich*") on March 9, with Zörner's notation "*streng vertraulich!*" ("top secret").

22 Türk memo, March 30, 1942, WAPL, GDL 273; BuF memos of March 14, 23, and 27, 1942, on the transport of 14,000 Czech Jews to Izbica and other locations in the district, WAPL, GDL 749; YVA, M.8 (ITS)-GD, reels 1, 3, 4, 5, 6, on transports of German Jews to Izbica, Piaski, and Trawniki. See also Mendel Korn testimony, YVA, O.3/2941; Alten memo to JSS Kraków, April 12, 1942, *Faschismus*, pp. 275–276; Rosenfeld and Luckner, *Lebenszeichen*, p. 91; Izbica Judenrat to

The most extensive and most protracted of all the deportations to Lublin was the March 27—June 14 deportation of nearly 40,000 Jews from Slovakia. The initial Nazi-Slovak plan, based on discussions begun in late January, was to deport 20,000 able-bodied Jews from Slovakia to Poland, of which half were to be sent to Majdanek and half to Auschwitz. As early as March 12, a tentative timetable for the deportations was ready, with trains scheduled for March 26—April 24. In other words, these operative plans were drawn up at the same time as the plans for the deportations from Mielec, Germany, and the Protectorate.

On March 22 and 24, Artur Liebehenschel (Richard Glücks's deputy in the Concentration Camps Inspectorate) cabled Karl Koch, commandant of Majdanek, with information on the imminent transports from Slovakia: 10,000 Jews would begin leaving Slovakia March 27 in "special trains," each bearing 1,000 Jews. The trains would all depart via Zwardon at 8:30 A.M. on March 27, 30, and 31, and April 5. Each train should arrive in Lublin the next day at 6:30 A.M. The Schupo guards would be carrying a list of names of the deportees on the train. However, by the end of March, the plan had changed to include the deportation of entire families. But as there was still a need for young, able-bodied forced-laborers, the result was that the

Lublin Judenrat, May 4, 1942, YVA, O.53/83; JSS memo, Kraków, May 4, 1942, ibid; Ziegenmeyer memo to Interior Department, Lublin, October 5, 1942, YVA, O.53/84; Kielboń, *Migracja*, pp. 142, 145–146; Kryl, "Deportationen von Theresienstadt nach Majdanek," pp. 74–89; Tatiana Berenstein, "Martyrologia"; Dziadosz and Marszalek, "Wiezienia i obozy w dystrikcie lubelskim"; Musial, *Zivilverwaltung*, pp. 230–231; Arad, *Belzec, Sobibor, Treblinka*, pp. 138–143; Peter Witte, "Letzte Nachrichten aus Siedliszcze: Der Transport Ax aus Theresienstadt in den Distrikt Lublin," *Theresienstädter Studien und Dokumente*, III (1996), pp. 98–113; Robert Kuwałek, "Die Durchgangsghettos im Distrikt Lublin (u.a. Izbica, Piaski, Rejowiec, und Tawniki)," in Musial, ed., *"Aktion Reinhardt,"* pp. 197–232; *idem*, "Das Durchgangsghetto in Izbica," *Theresienstädter Studien und Dokumente* (2003), pp. 321–351; Arnold Hindls, *Eine Kehrte Zurück: Bericht Eines Deportierten* (Stuttgart: Deutsche Verlags-Anstalt, 1965), pp. 9–15. The trains from Germany came from the areas of Aachen, Berlin, Chemnitz, Darmstadt, Dortmund, Düsseldorf, Frankfurt am Main, Fürth, Kassel, Koblenz, Köln, Leipzig, Mainz, Munich, Nuremberg, Regensburg, Stuttgart, Weimar, and Würzburg. See Gottwaldt and Schulle, *Die "Judendeportationen,"* pp. 137–219, for additional very valuable information on the deportations from Germany, Austria, and the "Protectorate."

total number of deported Slovakian Jews was tripled to 60,000 from the original 20,000, and the number to Lublin was quadrupled from the original 10,000 to 40,000. Globocnik's men and Koch integrated them into both the murder operation and the slave labor.[23]

Until the end of May, the Jews from Slovakia generally were sent first to one of two distribution points – Lublin or Nałęczów. In Lublin they were met at the station by a SS officer representing Globocnik, usually Helmut Pohl, and a German civilian representing the BuF. However, at Nałęczów they were usually met by a local SS officer or representative of the *Kreishauptmann*. This distinction, and perhaps a lack of coordination among the Germans regarding the disposal of the incoming Jews, resulted in a difference in how they were handled at the dispersal station. Until the end of May, the Jews arriving in Lublin would be divided into a small group selected for a labor camp and a large group that would be concentrated in ghettos or communities along or near rail lines. For example, on April 16, the Lubartów Landkommissar, Wilhelm Holzhey, reported that 1,600 Jews had arrived in the previous three days and had been dispersed in four communities in the area. On May 9, Holzhey reported that 841 Slovakian Jews had arrived on May 7 – older men and women with children – while 199 able-bodied men had been left behind in Lublin (Majdanek) as laborers. Helmut Pohl had coordinated both the deportation of the local Jews on April 9, and the distribution and later re-transports of the Slovakian Jews. At Nałęczów the families were usually not divided and were sent together, either to the towns where forced labor was needed, such as

23 Telegrams, Liebehenschel to Koch, March 22 and 24, 1942, YVA, JM/3536a; telegram, Woltersdorf, IVB4 Kattowitz, to RSHA, IVB4 Berlin, March 27, 1942, ibid., reporting the arrival of the second train with 1,000 able-bodied Slovakian Jews at 6:52 A.M. and its departure for Lublin at 8:05. The train also carried 3,170 kg. of food supplies and 7,000 kg. of wood for the Germans in Lublin; transport schedule sent from Slovakian Transportation Ministry to Wisliceny, March 12, 1942, YVA, M.5/105(Ia). For the various changes in the deportation schedule and the expansion of the plan, see YVA, M.5/105. See also Gila Fatran, *Struggle for Surviving? The Leadership of Slovakian Jews in the Holocaust 1938–1944* (Hebrew) (Tel Aviv: Moreshet and Institute of Contemporary Jewry, 1992), pp. 107–112, 127–135; Büchler, "Deportation of Slovakian Jews," pp. 151–153; Rothkirchen, *Destruction of Slovak Jewry*, pp. 19, 194, 199.

Dęblin, or to ghettos, such as Opole-Lubelski. Generally, these Jews were sent on to death camps within a few days or weeks. However, in some cases they remained in the ghettos or forced-labor camps for some months. One group in Dęblin remained there from May 14, 1942 to July 23, 1944.[24]

The last ten trains bearing 10,000 Slovakian Jews were sent directly to Sobibór and Majdanek. Whatever slave labor was to be conducted was limited mainly to Majdanek, while the majority was sent to Sobibór for immediate killing by gas. This represented the last change in the March-June operation against Slovakian Jews: it was clear that all were to be killed; none were to be maintained temporarily in ghettos.

Although the sources provide very accurate approximations of the numbers of Jews deported, it is difficult to establish exact statistics for deportees, arrivals, places of dispersal, dates of subsequent deportation, etc. For example, utilizing mostly identical sources (embarkation lists compiled in Slovakia and some arrival records in Lublin), Yehoshua Büchler, Janina Kielboń, and Gila Fatran come to different numbers of deportees — 39,883, 39,899, and 39,875, respectively.[25] Moreover, there are discrepancies both within and among the various lists and records of embarkation and arrival. For example, on April 27, German Police Lieutenant Sparmann signed a receipt of transport for 1,179 Jews when he took over a deportation train at the Slovak-Polish (German) border. However, the embarkation lists show that 1,251 Jews had been deported.[26] In addition, there are

24 Holzhey to *Kreishauptmann* Lublin-Land, April 16, 1942, WAPL, *Kreishauptmann* Lublin-Land 6 (copy in *Dokumenty*, vol. 2, pp. 47–48); Holzhey to *Kreishauptmann* Lublin-Land, May 9, 1942, ibid. (copy in *Faschismus*, p. 276); Malka Templer testimony, YVA, O.3/4278; Büchler, "Deportation of Slovakian Jews," pp. 153–154, 158–159; "Testimony of an Anonymous Jew from Slovakia Who Fled from the Lublin-Majdanek Camp in June 1942," Rothkirchen, *Destruction of Slovak Jewry*, pp. 166–204; letters from Moses Rubin, a Slovakian Jewish deportee in Chełm, to his children in Prešov, May-September 1942, YVA, O.75/57; Hermann Wenkart, *Befehlsnotstand Anders Gesehen; Tatsachenbericht eines jüdischen Lagerfunktionärs* (Vienna: Privately published, 1969), pp. 33–78; Musial, *Zivilverwaltung*, pp. 230–231; Pohl, *Judenpolitik*, p. 119.

25 Büchler, ibid, p. 166; Kielboń, *Migracje*, pp. 143–144; Fatran, *Struggle for Surviving?*, pp. 146–147.

26 Büchler, ibid., pp. 153, 166; Kielboń, ibid.; Fatran, ibid.

multiple copies of the embarkation lists themselves. Some copies have names crossed off, while others show most names checked off and different dates recorded next to a number of names. The lists for April 27 show 1,382 Jews from Pieštany, Nove Mesto, and Hlohovec. However, one Nove Mesto list has forty-two names crossed off and a later date penciled in next to eleven names. Similarly, one Hlohovec list has five names crossed off and a later date penciled in. For both lists there is also a list showing names checked off in red, as the Slovaks or the Germans must have taken attendance down the line. On this copy of the lists, forty-eight people from Nove Mesto and forty from Hlohovec are not checked off.[27] No combination of numbers from all this yields either 1,251 deportees or 1,179. How then do we resolve these discrepancies among the sources? Did some Jews not board the deportation, or get off before departure? Were some taken off along the way? Did some die on the way? Similar discrepancies exist for other trains from Slovakia and from other places. However, as important as it is to trace every Jewish person, the overall picture does not change. In this case between 1,179 and 1,382 Jews were deported on April 27 to the Lublin District and integrated into the murder operation and forced labor there.

Similarly, whereas very close estimates of the numbers of Jews deported from Germany can be culled from the sources, exact numbers are difficult to ascertain. For example, 659 people are listed on a Berlin deportation train that departed for Trawniki on April 2. However, although nineteen people committed suicide before the train departed, their names had apparently not been crossed off the list.[28] The Gestapo officer in the small Krefeld post reported to his superior in the Düsseldorf Gestapo that four Jews scheduled for "evacuation" the day before "unfortunately... could not be evacuated," as three of them had committed suicide and one had disappeared.[29]

27 The original and carbon copies of all these lists are in YVA, M.5/109. Similar lists and discrepancies exist for practically all the deportations from Slovakia. The lists can be found in YVA, M.5.

28 Report from office IVC3 of the Berlin Gestapo to Oberfinanzpräsident, Berlin-Brandenburg, April 9, 1942, YVA, M.8 (ITS)-GD, reel 1.

29 Report from Gestapo Aussenstelle Krefeld to *SS-Obersturmbannführer* Dr. Albath, Gestapo Düsseldorf, April 23, 1942, YVA, ibid., reel 5.

Here, too, it is not clear where these deaths were figured in German deportation statistics.

Jews from Vienna were the last to be deported from outside Lublin in 1942, and theirs was both the smallest (6,000) and the most spread out of all the deportations. On March 20, 1942, the police chief of Vienna ordered the commander of the Schupo Reserve Battalion there to prepare for the imminent deportation eastward of Vienna's Jews by trainloads of 1,000, to be accompanied by a lieutenant and fifteen guards.[30] At the end of each deportation, the lieutenant wrote a report to his superiors. The trains departed April 9 and 27, May 12 and 15, and June 5 and 14. Four of the first five trains were sent to the Izbica transit center, and one to Włodawa. Like the deportations from Germany, the Protectorate, and Slovakia, the last Vienna transport went to a death camp. This represented a change in policy, as noted by Schupo Lieutenant Fischmann in his report on the June 14 transport. Contrary to earlier indications, he said, the train was sent to Sobibór and not to Izbica.

Fischmann's report reflected what he saw as an uneventful deportation. The loading went smoothly from 12:00 P.M. on June 14, under the command of *SS-Hauptsturmführer* Alois Brunner and *Hauptscharführer* Ernst Girzik, and was completed at 4:00 P.M.; the train left Vienna at 7:08 P.M. and arrived in Lublin on June 16 at 9:00 P.M. Helmut Pohl met the train at the Lublin station and took fifty-one able-bodied Jews to a labor camp. Pohl gave the officer in charge three freight cars of supplies and 100,000 złotys. The train left Lublin two hours later, dropped off the supplies at Trawniki, and arrived at Sobibór on June 17 at 8:15 A.M. The sixty-four hours that these Viennese Jews spent on the deportation train were typical of all the transports to the Lublin District. At Sobibór, camp commandant Franz Stangl took charge of the disembarkation of the 949 Jews at 9:15.[31] Left unsaid in Fischmann's report was an obvious detail that did not concern him, as it was beyond his jurisdiction and

30 Order from Franz Butenop, ORPO chief in Vienna, March 20, 1942, YVA, O.51/63.

31 Report by Schupo Lieutenant Fischmann, June 20, 1942, YVA, O.51/63. See also the May 4 report by Lieutenant Johann Peter II on the April 27 transport to Włodawa, ibid., and in O.30/83. See also Browning, *Ordinary Men*, pp. 28–31;

interest – the Jews whom he delivered to Sobibór after a grueling three-day trip were dead within an hour or two of their arrival.

Revolving Door

The incoming transports of deported Jews brought large numbers of people to several small localities in concentrated time periods. These incoming transports largely matched outgoing deportations to death camps (see Tables 7.1 and 7.2 below) – what Türk and his colleagues had called the *Judenaustausch* ("Jew Exchange"). Many of the small towns to which incoming Jews were sent in the spring of 1942 were already refugee centers for deported Jews. For example, 1,000 of Izbica's approximate prewar Jewish population of 3,000 had fled early in the war, while 3,000 refugees from Koło and Lodz arrived in December 1939. In eight days in March 1942, 4,000 additional Jews were deported to Izbica from Theresienstadt and Germany, while more than 2,000 local Jews were deported to Bełżec. Similarly, of Rejowiec's prewar Jewish population of 2,600, half fled early in the war, to be replaced by 1,300 refugees from Lublin and Kraków in the spring of 1941. Most of these Jews were deported to Bełżec on April 7, 1942, to be replaced in turn within two weeks by 2–3,000 Jews from Slovakia and Theresienstadt. These were deported in early May and replaced by 3,650 Slovakian Jews deported to Rejowiec on May 23–25. Thus, in the spring of 1942, Izbica and Rejowiec (and Opole and Piaski) had overwhelmingly large refugee populations. Most of these people were deported to Sobibór and Majdanek in mid-October. Piaski was used in the same way. According to German records, 28,000 Jews were deported from there to Bełżec and Sobibór, of whom only 5,000 were the original residents of the Piaski ghetto. This was the "revolving door" policy developed by Türk and his colleagues in cooperation with the SS.[32]

Kielboń, *Migracje*, pp. 144–145; Musial, *Zivilverwaltung*, pp. 230–231; Arad, *Belzec, Sobibor, Treblinka*, pp. 138–140.

32 On Rejowiec, see, for example, JSS Kraków memo, May 4, 1942, noting that the JSS representative in Rejowiec had written on April 25 regarding two

Jews' belongings left in the street following a deportation, Lublin, 1942, Yad Vashem Photo Archive, FA 16/28

Jews' household belongings following deportation, Lublin, 1942, Yad Vashem Photo Archive, FA 16/12

Izbica and Piaski were initially planned as the main receiving points for the incoming Jews in the Lublin District (*Hauptunterbringungs und Umschlagpunkte im Wechsel*), with Rejowiec meant only as a stopgap. Other places were also used as temporary reception points, such as Kraśniczyn, where 2,000 Jews deported in April were replaced by approximately the same number brought in from Germany between April 28 and May 3.[33]

The same train stations that served to deport Jews out of the Lublin District to the death camps also served to deport Jews into the district. Thus, in April and May, 4–5,000 Jews from the Protectorate and Slovakia were deported to Opole via Nałęczów, in conjunction with 6,500 deported out in March and May. Similarly, 2,000 Slovakian Jews sent to Dęblin in mid-May replaced the 6,500 local and village Jews deported via Dęblin's train station a week earlier.

The "revolving door" policy also facilitated the Nazi deception of the Jews. New arrivals were told that the Jews whose homes they were now occupying had been relocated to the East or to the Ukraine. The Germans used innocuous euphemisms for murder both among themselves and with the Jews, thereby reinforcing the deception. Puławy *Kreishauptmann* Brandt reported, in May 1942, that 16,822 Jews from his county had been sent "beyond the Bug." The Germans

transports that had arrived on April 17 from Slovakia and the Protectorate, YVA, O.53/83. See also the August 17, 1943, testimony of an unnamed male from Sabinov, Slovakia, who had been among 1,000 deportees to Rejowiec, arriving May 26. Two thousand more from Stropkov and Humenne arrived the next day. He reported that 3,000 of the 6,000 local Jews had been deported during the intermediate days of Passover, and the incoming Slovakian Jews were housed twenty-five to a room in the homes of the murdered Jews, YVA, M.2/236 (also in M.4/12). On Izbica and Piaski, see, for example, Türk memo of meeting with Pohl, March 23, 1942, WAPL, GDL 273; report by Mrs. Banhart, YVA, M.10.AR.2/304; letter from Max and Martha Bauchwitz to Luise-Lotte Hoyer-Bauchwitz, in Rosenfeld and Luckner, eds., *Lebenszeichen*, p. 91. The Bauchwitzes themselves were deported on April 5, according to an April 15 letter to Ms. Hoyer-Bauchwitz from E. Sch., Piaski, in ibid., pp. 95–96. On Opole, see, for example, testimony of Malka Vered Templer, YVA, O.3/4278; YVA, TR.10/869, vol. VI, pp. 34–36. See also Kuwałek, "Durchgangsghettos"; Hindls, *Eine Kehrte Zurück*.

33 Türk memo, March 23, 1942, ibid.

were interested in having the refugee Jews report this information to their families and friends back home in order to keep the deportees and the remaining Jews placid. Musial believes that the incoming Jews were housed temporarily in the homes of the deported Jews and not killed immediately precisely so that they could write home and thereby promote calm.[34] However, this would help explain only the deportations into the Lublin District through April. After that increasing numbers of deportees from outside Lublin were sent directly to the death camps. The increasing transports directly to the murder sites were probably also a function of the increased killing capacity and the experience gained in March and April in deporting Jews to their deaths.

Table 7.1: Deportations into the Lublin District, March-June 1942 (ca. 85,000–90,000 Jews)[35]

Date	Origin	Number	Destinations
March 11	Theresienstadt	1001 (1003)	Izbica
March 13	Mielec	1000	Włodawa, Sosnowica
March 13	Germany	1003	Izbica
March 14	Mielec	750	Międzyrzec-Podlaski
March 16	Mielec	1343	Dubienka, Belz
March 16	Mielec	500	Cieszanów
March 17	Theresienstadt	1000	Izbica
March 19	Germany	1000 (1871)	Izbica
March 23 (25)	Mainz, Worms, Darmstadt	1500 (1000)	Piaski

34 See Malka Vered Templer testimony, YVA, O.3/4278; Jan Bachrich testimony (unpublished; I thank the late Dr. Leopold Laufer for sharing his cousin's manuscript with me); Brandt report to BuF Lublin, May 12, 1942, YVA, O.53/83 (copy in *Faschismus*, p. 438); Musial, *Zivilverwaltung*, pp. 230–231; Büchler, "Deportation of Slovakian Jews."

35 Some of the dates indicate departure and others arrival, based on the sources. In instances that the sources do not agree with regard to a detail, such as a date or destination, additional information is provided in parentheses.

Date	Origin	Number	Destinations
March 24	Würzburg, Fürth, Nuremberg	985 (1000)	Piaski, Trawniki (Izbica)
March 25 (22)	Aachen, Koblenz, Kassel	1000 (955)	Izbica
March 27	Žilina	1000	Majdanek
March 27 (24)	Nuremberg, Würzburg, Fürth	1008	Izbica, Trawniki
March 28	Berlin	985	Izbica, Trawniki (Piaski)
March 30	Sered	1000	Majdanek
March 31	Novaky	1003	Majdanek
April 1	Theresienstadt	1000	Piaski
April 2	Berlin	659	Trawniki
April 3	Munich, Augsburg, Regensburg	989	Piaski, Trawniki
April 5	Žilina	1495	Majdanek
April 9	Vienna	998	Izbica
April 12	Trnava	1040	Lubartów, Majdanek, Kamionka (200), Firlej (80), Ostrów-Lubelski (300)
April 13	Breslau	1000	Izbica
April 16	Nitra	1048	Rejowiec, Majdanek, Trawniki
April 18	Theresienstadt, Berlin	1000	Rejowiec, Piaski, (Sobibór)
April 20	Nitra	1030	Rejowiec
April 22	Topolčany, Sered	1001	Opole-Lubelski (via Nałęczów)
April 22	Düsseldorf, Essen, Duisburg, Wuppertal	1800 (1051; 942)	Izbica
April 23	Theresienstadt	1000	Lublin, Piaski

Date	Origin	Number	Destinations
April 25	Nuremberg, Bamberg, Würzburg	941 (955)	Izbica, Krasnystaw
April 26	Stuttgart, Berlin, Würtemberg	628 (1000)	Izbica
April 27	Nove Mesto, Pieštany, Hlohovec	1251	Opole-Lubelski, Poniatowa (via Nałęczów)
April 27	Theresienstadt	1000	Lublin (400), Izbica (600)
April 27	Vienna	998	Włodawa
April 28	Theresienstadt	1000	Zamość
April 28 (30)	Aachen, Koblenz	955	Kraśniczyn
April 29	Würzburg, Nuremberg, Fürth	1000	Lublin, Izbica (23 to Kraśniczyn)
April 30	Theresienstadt	1000	Zamość
May 1	Düsseldorf (Dortmund)	1000	Zamość, Izbica
May 3	Koblenz	1000	Kraśniczyn
May 3	Breslau	1000	unknown destination
May 5	Trebišov	1040	Lubartów, Majdanek, Kamionka
May 6	Michalovce	1038	Łuków
May 7	Michalovce	1040	Łuków
May 8	Michalovce	1001	Międzyrzec-Podlaski
May 9	Theresienstadt	1000	Ossowa, Siedliszcze, Sobibór
May 9	Frankfurt/Main	938	Izbica, Majdanek, Sobibór
May 11	Humenne	1009	Chełm
May 12	Žilina	1002	Chełm
May 12	Vienna	1001	Izbica
May 12 (10)	Weimar, Leipzig	1000 (1002)	Bełżyce

Date	Origin	Number	Destinations
May 13	Prešov	1040	Dęblin, Końskowola
May 14	Prešov	1040	Dęblin, Poniatowa
May 14	Germany	800	Majdanek, Sobibór
May 15	Vienna	1006	Izbica
May 17	Bardejov	1028	Puławy
May 17	Theresienstadt	1000	Lublin
May 17	Germany	1000	Majdanek, Sobibór
May 18	Bardejov	1015	Opole-Lubelski, Poniatowa
May 19	Vranov	1005	Opole-Lubelski, Kazimierz Dolny
May 20	Medzilaborce	1001	Puławy
May 23	Sabinov	1630	Rejowiec
May 24	Stropkov/Bardejov	1022	Rejowiec
May 25	Poprad	1000	Rejowiec
May 25	Theresienstadt	1000	Lublin, Ujazdów
May 26	Žilina	1000	Opole-Lubelski
May 26	Frankfurt/Main, Wiesbaden	930 (957)	Izbica, Majdanek, Sobibór
May 29	Spišska Nová Ves	1032 (1052)	Izbica, Majdanek
May 30	Poprad	1000	Izbica, Majdanek
June 1	Poprad	1000	Sobibór, Majdanek
June 1	Kassel, Halle, Chemnitz	1000	Sobibór
June 2	Liptovsky, St. Mikulas	1014	Sobibór, Majdanek
June 5	Bratislava, Žilina	1000	Sobibór Majdanek
June 5	Vienna	1001	Izbica
June 6	Žilina	1001	Sobibór, Majdanek
June 7	Bratislava, Žilina	1000	Sobibór, Majdanek
June 9	Zvolen, Kremnica	1019	Sobibór, Majdanek
June 10	Prague	1000	Lublin, Ujazdów
June 11	Novaky	1000	Sobibór, Majdanek
June 12	Sered, Žilina	1000	Sobibór, Majdanek

Date	Origin	Number	Destinations
June 12	Theresienstadt	1000	Trawniki
June 13	Poprad	1000	Sobibór, Majdanek
June 13	Theresienstadt	1000	Majdanek
June 13	Berlin, Potsdam	1016 (1030)	Majdanek, Sobibór
June 14	Novaky, Žilina	1000	Sobibór, Majdanek
June 14	Vienna	1000 (996)	Sobibór (51 in forced labor, Lublin)
June 15	Düsseldorf area	1003	Izbica, Majdanek, Sobibór[36]
June 19 (11)	Frankfurt/Main, Wiesbaden	1066 (1253)	Majdanek, (Izbica,) Sobibór
June 20	Germany	201	Majdanek, Sobibór
July (June) 15	Koblenz, Düsseldorf	13	Izbica

Jews boarding a train for the Lublin District, Hanau, Germany, May or June 1942, Yad Vashem Photo Archive, 102CO3

36 Some sources indicate that the train with 1,066 Jewish deportees was from Düsseldorf and other areas, whereas the train from Frankfurt delivered 947 Jewish deportees. See, for example, Kuwałek, "Das Durchgangsghetto in Izbica," pp. 326–327, and notes 37, 38; and Gottwaldt and Schulle, *Die "Judendeportationen,"* pp. 216–217.

Honing the Operation

Parallel to dealing with the tens of thousands of Jews brought in from outside the district who were to be included in the murder operation, Globocnik's forces honed their methods and fanned out over the entire district. The deportations from other parts of the Lublin District generally followed the Lublin model – but more efficiently and often more brutally. Each *Aktion* was preceded by a briefing chaired by an officer from "Einsatzstab Reinhard" and attended by the local SS and police commanders, representatives of the *Kreis-* and *Stadthauptmann*, and the local BuF person. An "Eisatzstab Reinhard" commander was also responsible for requisitioning manpower from Trawniki. The various types of units generally performed the same roles as in Lublin, with local variations. The Trawniki men would cordon off the area where Jews were to be rounded up, while Trawniki troops, KdS men, ORPO troops, and Jewish police would round up the Jews.[37]

In Zamość, for example, the deportation schedule was coordinated between Höfle's and Türk's offices in Lublin and the local BuF and KdS heads in Zamość – Oskar Reichwein and Gotthardt Schubert, respectively. Several men from Höfle's office arrived in Zamość shortly before the scheduled Saturday, April 11, 1942, deportation, in order to coordinate activities in the field. Reichwein and Schubert summoned the Judenrat on the morning of the deportation and read them the deportation order. The 2,500 Jews scheduled for deportation were ordered to report to the square

37 This was the model used in Piaski, from which 3,400 Jews were deported to Bełżec on March 23, and 1,500 on April 7: Höfle was the overseer, a KdS man had field command, and ORPO and Trawniki men participated. See YVA, TR.10/869, vol. VI, pp. 3–15, 31–36; TR.10/813, pp. 69–71, 81–82; TR.10/736, p. 25; Mendel Korn testimony, O.3/2941; letter from Max and Martha Bauchwitz, deportees from Stettin in Piaski, to their daughter, Luise-Lotte Hoyer-Bauchwitz, in Munich, March 25, 1942, in Rosenfeld and Luckner, eds., *Lebenszeichen aus Piaski*, p. 91. See also Szulim Garen testimony on Kraśnik, YVA, M.49.E/4399; Tatiana Berenstein, "Jews in Kraśnik During the Hitlerite Occupation," in David Sztokfisz, ed., *Sefer Kraśnik* (Yiddish and Hebrew) (Tel Aviv: Society of Kraśnik Jews in Israel, 1973), pp. 304–307; Shalom (Szulim) Garen testimony, ibid., pp. 317–319; Motl Brafman testimony, ibid., pp. 353–356. See also Berenstein, "Martyrologia," pp. 38–40.

at Lwowska Street in the afternoon. The local KdS and ORPO forces, together with a mounted police platoon and the small sixteen-man Jewish police participated in the round-up. In this case the mounted police took the place of the Trawniki men, but this did not lower the level of brutality. One hundred and fifty-three people were shot and loaded onto the deportation trains on Schubert's orders, while an additional eighty-nine corpses were later recovered inside homes and buried by a small crew assigned by the Judenrat after the deportation. All had been shot, while many others had been beaten. Some 3,000 Jews had been loaded onto the twenty-one-car freight train awaiting them.[38]

Deportations from small communities that were situated far from railroad lines and, in some cases, even from paved roads were often conducted on foot, or partly on foot and partly by rail or truck. For example, in Puławy county, Nałęczów served as the main deportation railroad station for the southern half of the county, while Dęblin was the main station in the northern half. Jews from small communities were marched there to be loaded onto deportation trains. Thus, 2,000 Jews from Kazimierz Dolny were marched 22 km. south to Opole-Lubelski on March 25–28, followed by approximately 1,900 Jews marched southwest more than 25 km. from Wąwolnica on March 31. On the same day, 1,950 Jews from Opole, including some of the new deportees, were marched 30 km. north to the Nałęczów train station and deported to Bełżec. The same pattern was true for the subsequent deportations to Sobibór in May — more than 7,500 Jews from Michów, Kurów, Józefów n. Wisła, and Opole were marched to Nałęczów, while more than 4,000 Jews from Bobrowniki, Baranów, Lysobyki, Ryki, and Stężyca were marched to Dęblin and deported from there by train to Sobibór, along with 2,500 Jews from Dęblin itself.[39]

38 YVA, TR.10/1146Z: Reichwein interrogation, pp. 2679–2684; Schubert interrogations, pp. 3083–3089, 3751–3764, 3766–3774; Meiert interrogation, pp. 3325–3335; Kaussen interrogation, pp. 3426–3429; Garfinkel interrogation, pp. 3735–3757; Fiszelzon report, June 6, 1942, M.10.AR.1/946; Moshe Frank, *To Survive and Testify*, pp. 35–39.

39 Letter, Pesach Goldblum, Opole, to Josek Goldblum, Warsaw, March 29, 1942, YVA, M.10.AR.1/587 (and JM/3489); Türk memo, March 31, 1942, WAPL, GDL

Similarly, in Turobin (Krasnystaw county), the Jews from the nearby villages were marched into the town on May 10. Two days later they and the Turobin Jews were ordered to take a package of belongings and some provisions and to report to the town square. Dozens of people were shot at or near the square before the crowd was marched out 35 km. northeast toward Krasnystaw. On the way they were joined by Jews from Wysokie (200), Żółkiewka (1,000), and Gorzków (400), until some 4,000 Jews were marching, guarded by German police and Ukrainians from Trawniki. Stragglers and those who stumbled on the march were shot. The haggard Jews completed their long march to Krasnystaw at night and were pushed into a large courtyard adjacent to the railroad tracks, where they spent the night. The Krasnystaw Jewish community set up tables with coffee and bread for the exhausted deportees, who were forced onto freight trains and deported to Sobibór early the next morning (May 13 or 14).[40]

The May deportations from the Opole, Dęblin, and Turobin areas reflected a change in the deportation pattern; now there were systematic countywide sweeps. As the initial murder operations in the district were being concluded, Sobibór came on line as a second death camp. The murder was now reorganized along territorial concentrations, with round-ups encompassing entire counties at a time. Prior to this the only total round-up had been in the Lublin ghetto. The first countywide round-up was in Puławy, on May 6–12, 1942, at the urging of *Kreishauptmann* Karl Brandt, who was especially eager to be rid of his Jews. According to his subsequent report, 16,822 Jews were deported to Sobibór. This was followed by sweeps in Krasnystaw (May 12–15), Chełm (May 18–24), Zamość

273; testimonies in YVA: Ester Kohn, O.3/3057; Baruch and Sarah Roizman, O.3/3554; Moshe Zylberszpan, M.49.E/4137; report from *Kreishauptmann* Brandt to BuF Lublin, May 12, 1942, that 16,822 Jews had been sent from Pulawy county "beyond the Bug," WAPL, GDL 3 (copies in YVA, O.53/83 and *Faschismus*, p. 438).

40 Arad, *Belzec, Sobibor, Treblinka*, pp. 58–59; Dov Freiberg, *To Survive Sobibór*, pp. 176–184; testimonies in YVA: Jankiel Kleinman, M.49.E/11; Szmul Lerer, M.49.E/104; Icek Lichtman, M.49.E/1204; Moszek Merenstein, M.49.E/2785; Leon Feldhendler, O.16/619*.

(May 22–27), and Hrubieszów (June 1–10), as well as a limited sweep in Biała-Podlaska (June 10).[41]

The Hrubieszów county deportations were different from the rest in that *Kreishauptmann* Otto Busse was the main initiator and organizer.[42] His ideological eagerness and his officer's rank and military experience in World War I made him the right person for the job. He was both the senior Nazi and the ranking military man in the county. In April and May, many hundreds of Jews from the small towns and villages were concentrated in the larger towns. Between May 26 and June 2, the Jews from several villages and from Belz were marched to Hrubieszów. These transfers of Jewish population were the first step in the deportations that followed over the first ten days of June.[43] Busse's staff conducted a selection in the county and, on May 12, provided the selected workers with red identification cards. Within a few days of receiving Busse's May 22 report on the numbers of Jews in his county to be deported, Höfle's staff informed Busse and KdS Aussenstelle commander Max Stöbner that the deportations would begin on June 1.[44]

Busse requisitioned the freight cars for the transport to Sobibór and ordered the Judenrat to select those to be deported

41 On the general pattern, see Pohl, *Judenpolitik*, pp. 120–122; Musial, *Zivilverwaltung*, pp. 243–245; Kielbon, *Migracje*, pp. 170–175. For specific deportations see, for example, Berenstein, "Deportations," pp. 72–73, Tables 2–11; *idem*, "Martyrologia," pp. 38–40, Tables 2–11; Arad, *Belzec, Sobibor, Treblinka*, pp. 383–391; Indictment of Otto Busse, Maz Stöbner, et al., 9 Js 204/67, June 5, 1967, Hildesheim, *passim*, and Verdict, 9 Ks 2/67, May 3, 1968, *passim*, in YVA, TR.10/742; Indictment of Richard Nitschke, Anton Müller, et al., 2 Js 165/61, July 24, 1963, Hannover, and Verdict, 2 Ks 4/63, October 29, 1962, in TR.10/631, *passim*; Joel Ponczak testimony, O.33/243; "Hrubieszów – spichrz Polski," June 30, 1942, YVA, M.10.AR.1/914; Yehezkel Kesselbrener testimony, O.3/2089; Mosze Zylberszpan testimony, M.49E/4137; Avraham and Shaindl Goldfarb testimony, O.3/2140; Dov Finger testimony, O.3/2780; TR.10/655, *passim*.

42 YVA, TR.10/742, Indictment, pp. 41–42, 83–124, and Verdict, pp. 14–22; Musial, *Zivilverwaltung*, pp. 248–254.

43 YVA, TR.10/742, Verdict, pp. 14–15, Indictment, pp. 83–124; Nahman Blumental, "Jewish Hrubieszów in the Years 1939–1945," in *Pinkas Hrubieszów*, pp. 106–107; Musial, *Zivilverwaltung*, pp. 248–250.

44 Stöbner interrogation, April 25, 1961, YVA, TR.10/1146Z, XI:2271.

and have them report to the market square on June 1.[45] When the Judenrat did not meet the quota, Busse ordered the Sonderdienst, the Gendarmerie, the local SS unit, a unit of fifty Trawniki men, and the Jewish police to fill the quota of 2,000 to be sent to Sobibór. These forces were augmented by the 3rd company of the mounted police battalion, Polizei-Reiterabteilung III, which had arrived in Hrubieszów from Vienna the previous month. Many were shot on the way to the square, at the square, and on the way to the train. Busse ordered the Judenrat to bury the dead, and Judenrat chairman Joel Brand appointed Josef Rechtschaft, a local wagon-driver, to be in charge of the burial. On the same day Busse's staff began organizing the deportation of all the Jews from Dubienka and Belz to Sobibór. On June 8, Busse's deputy, Josef Fieback, organized the deportation of the 2,850 Jews of Grabowiec and Uchanie, marching them to the Miączyn train station 10 km. south of Grabowiec, from whence they were transported in freight cars to Sobibór under Hiwi guard. According to both Jewish and German testimony, innumerable children, women, and elderly, slow, or ill men were shot that day.

On June 8–10, Busse oversaw the second *Aktion*, the deportation of 3,000 Jews from Hrubieszów to Sobibór. In all of these deportations, the civilian authorities were both the initiators and the commanders. The SS and German police hunted for Jews in hiding and deported or summarily shot all those who were caught. A group of some thirty Jews from among those who had been selected for forced labor were taken to the Jewish cemetery, where they were ordered to help Rechtschaft and his team bury the corpses piled in a mound there.[46]

45 Many sources cite Busse's leading role. See the following testimonies from his pre-trial investigation, all in YVA, TR.11/01121/V: Abraham Goldfarb, February 20, 1968; Josef Rechtschaft, October 27, 1960 and January 19, 1965; Dawid Rottenberg, October 4, 1966. See also Busse's trial verdict, in YVA, TR.10/742; Musial, *Zivilverwaltung*, pp. 248–254.

46 The description of the Hrubieszów deportations is based on: testimonies in YVA – Avraham and Shaindl Goldfarb, O.3/2140; Gisela Perec, O.3/4237; Yitzhak Leibush Perec, O.3/4238; Ruth Tatarko, O.3/7158, 7613; Ziporah Nahir, O.3/10488; Ziporah Hurwitz, O.3/11783; Fajge Schechter, M.49.E/22; M.10.AR.1/810, 812, 814, 815; Abraham Goldfarb, Josef Rechtschaft, and David

This phase of the deportations within the district was concluded with the stalled deportation of 1,500 Jews from Sławatycze, in Biała-Podlaska county, and the surrounding towns and villages to Sobibór. The village Jews were brought to Sławatycze, and from there they were all taken to Łomazy for further transport to the death camp. However, the trains in the area had meanwhile been requisitioned for the Wehrmacht for its summer offensive on the eastern front. These Jews would have to wait until August 17, when Reserve Police Battalion 101 became available to shoot them all.[47] Additional trains coming in from the west brought 5,000 Jews to Sobibór during the following week (June 14–20). After this there was a lull in the murder in the Lublin District.

Based on the Germans' apparent shift in deportation policy in May, Dieter Pohl and Bogdan Musial have concluded that the murder of the Jews in the Lublin District had two distinct stages: March-April 1942, when there was no clear pattern to the sweeps and round-ups; and the May-November systematic, countywide sweeps.[48] However, the summer lull in deportations and its aftermath suggest that there were actually four stages to the deportation and murder of the Jews of the Lublin District. Following the initial, geographically spread deportations, there were two distinct periods of systematic county sweeps, bridged by the summer lull in Lublin and by Himmler's July 19, 1942, order to complete the murder in the GG by the end of 1942. Browning, Musial, and others have argued that Himmler's order marked a change in the totality of the murder. From that point on only a small number of essential Jewish workers were to be left alive.[49]

Rottenberg, Chana Levi, Jochewed Deutsch, Dora Ilani, Jakob Biskubicz, Arie Perec, YVA, TR.11/01121/V; Ben-Zion Fink, investigation in Israel relating to case 8 AR-Z 24/63 against Polizei Reiterabteilung III, TR.11/02138; TR.10/742 indictment and verdict, vol. I, pp. 14–22, vol. II, pp. 83–124; detailed twelve-page memo from Generaldirektion für die Öffentliche Sicherheit, Abt. 2c, Austrian Interior Ministry, to Dr. Warbinek, Austrian Justice Ministry, Abteilung 11, Vienna, December 17, 1964, in TR.11.01121/V; Yaakov Czechowicz testimony, "And I Alone Survived," *Pinkas Hrubieszów*, pp. 661–664 (the Goldfarbs' testimony can also be found in this book, on pp. 654–656); Musial, *Zivilverwaltung*, pp. 248–254.

47 See YVA, M.2/235; Browning, *Ordinary Men*, pp. 81–91.

48 Pohl, *Judenpolitik*, pp. 120–122; Musial, *Zivilverwaltung*, pp. 243–245.

49 Himmler order to Krüger, July 19, 1942, NO-5574 (original copy in YVA,

The distinction between the May-June county sweeps and the August-December sweeps lay not in their coming on either side of a lull, but rather in the totality of the operation in the last stage. All three "Operation Reinhard" death camps were operational for much of the last stage of murder, as was Majdanek. The sweeps now included reductions in the numbers of Jewish forced-laborers, return sweeps in counties from which Jews had already been deported, and more mass shootings.

Civilian Authorities. The German civilians played a major role in the deportations, including in the disposition of the incoming Jews from outside the district, as well as in the countywide sweeps (as illustrated above). As Dieter Pohl notes, the disposition of the incoming deportees promoted SS-civilian cooperation; the placement of incoming Jews in particular towns was a joint decision by the BuF and Globocnik's men.[50] In addition to their active participation in counting, marking, and moving the Jews, they also dealt with the Jews to be set aside for forced labor. These forced-laborers were separated from the others both in blocs – as in the case of the 4,000 Jews left in Majdan Tatarski – or as individuals. For example, on April 18, Lublin-Land *Kreishauptmann* Emil Ziegenmeyer requested *Ausweise* for eight Jewish shoemakers named on a list he submitted. They were to work at repairing shoes in Majdan Tatarski and Sławinek.[51] Similarly, the fishing director of the county wrote to BuF Lublin requesting an *Ausweis* for Iser Silbersztein of Łęczna, who was needed for his expertise in lake fishing.[52]

O.51/246). See also Browning, *Nazi Policy, Jewish Workers, German Killers*, pp. 79–80; Musial, *Zivilverwaltung*, pp. 284–285; Pohl, *Judenpolitik*, pp. 125–129.

50 Pohl, *Judenpolitik*, p. 119.

51 Ziegenmeyer to KdS Lublin, Abt. IIIB.2b, April 18, 1942, YVA, O.53/84. Subsequent requests for other individuals were denied. See Walther, KdS, Abt. IIIB2b to Ziegenmeyer, ibid. Musial makes a strong case for the active participation of the civilian authorities in the murder in general and in the county sweeps in particular in *Zivilverwaltung*, pp. 244–276.

52 Kommissar, Fischergenossenschaft Lublin, to BuF Lublin, April 21, 1942; BuF Lublin-Land to KdS Lublin, Abt. IIIB2b, May 1, 1942; Walther, KdS Lublin-Land, Abt. IIIB2b, to *Krieshauptmann* Lublin-Land, May 12, 1942; BuF Lublin-Land to Fischergenossenschaft Lublin, May 18, 1942, YVA, O.53.84.

Similar individual requests were made in April, while Höfle and his men embarked on an effort to organize the forced labor in coordination with the deportations. On April 21, Höfle asked Ziegenmeyer to provide a list of able-bodied Jews (and their families) working for the Germans.[53] The counting was very soon systematized across the district in May, as reflected in the May 9 request from Lothar Weirauch, head of the BuF in Kraków to the BuF in Lublin that all county and town chiefs prepare lists of Jewish men up to the age of fifty-five who were able to work in specific crafts and skills. They were to list essential skilled laborers in metalwork, textiles, leather, construction, woodwork and carpentry, glass, mechanics, and haircutting. They were to do this through the Judenräte and JSS officials.[54]

The contrast between the massive numbers of deportations mentioned in the Nazi correspondence – many thousands coming and going all the time, and then killed – and the tiny numbers in the county chiefs' requests for forced-laborers is striking. In Hrubieszów, 1,233 Jews fit these skills, but none were in essential German industries according to *Kreishauptmann* Otto Busse's report.[55] In Puławy, fewer than 2,000 Jews had been left behind in three factories and one Luftwaffe camp.[56] Zamość county sent a list of names that included 529 Jewish skilled laborers, of whom 75 percent worked in essential war-related jobs. Similar small numbers were reported by other counties.[57] On May 16, with all but two counties having sent in

53 Höfle to *Kreishauptmann* Lublin-Land, April 21, 1942; *Kreishauptmann* Lublin-Land to town and village heads in Lublin-Land county, April 29, 1942; Ziegenmeyer to Höfle, May 8, 1942, YVA, O.53/82.

54 Telegram, Weirauch to Interior Department, Lublin, May 9, 1942; telephone calls and letters, Hartig, BuF Lublin, to Kreishauptleute in Biłgoraj, Biała-Podlaska, Cholm, Hrubieszów, Janów-Lubelski, Krasnystaw, Radzyń, and Zamość, May 9, 1942, WAPL, GDL 893.

55 *Kreishauptmann* Hrubieszów to BuF Lublin, May 12, 1942, WAPL, GDL 893.

56 Brandt to BuF Lublin, May 12 and 13, 1942; BuF Lublin, memo on telephone call from *Kreishauptmann* Pulawy, May 12, 1942, WAPL, GDL 893.

57 BuF Zamość to BuF Lublin, May 12 and 13, 1942, the latter with attached "Liste der in Judenwohnbezirk in Zamość ansässigen jüdischen Handwerker und Facharbeiter"; Reuter to Helmut Pohl, May 13, 1942; *Kreishauptmann* Bilgoraj to BuF Lublin, May 15, 1942, with "Liste der im Kreise Bilgoraj befindlichen Handwerker" (936 laborers); *Kreishauptmann* Krasnystaw to BuF Lublin, May

their statistics, the BuF in Lublin reported 9,841 skilled workers in the fields itemized by Weirauch. Of these, only 4,225 were working in what the authorities deemed essential labor.[58]

When these numbers are compared to population reports and requests for Jews to be deported from the same counties, the totality of this stage of the murder plan becomes apparent. For example, Ziegenmeyer reported, on May 19, that there were 19,735 Jews who could be deported immediately from Lublin-Land county, while 1,402 were skilled laborers in essential industries.[59] Busse reported, on May 22, that 14,188 Jews in Hrubieszów county could be deported, while 1,233 could be kept as skilled laborers.[60] And Brandt's forced-labor statistic was connected to his report that 16,188 Jews had been deported from Puławy county. In other words, Brandt reported that only 10.8 percent of the Jews in his county had been left alive. In Hrubieszów, only 8 percent were deemed worthy of keeping alive temporarily, and in Lublin-Land, only 6.7 percent.

18, 1942; Ziegenmeyer to BuF Lublin, May 19, 1942; *Kreishauptmann* Bilgoraj to BuF Lublin, May 28, 1942, WAPL, GDL 893; Busse to BuF Lublin, May 22, 1942, ibid. (copies in YVA, O.53/83, O.51/10, JM.215/1; *Dokumenty*, vol. 2 II, p. 55).

58 Telegram, Hartig, BuF Lublin to BuF Krakow, May 16, 1942, and letter the same day with attached lists of skilled laborers; Hartig to BuF Kraków, May 18 and 19, 1942; telegram, Hartig to BuF Kraków, May 20, 1942, WAPL, GDL 893 (copies in O.53/83). Some of the lists and tallies were handwritten by Hartig. He included information from Lublin-Land and Krasnystaw in his later report to Kraków.

59 Ziegenmeyer to BuF Lublin, May 19, 1942, WAPL, GDL 893 (copies in YVA, O.53/83, O.51/10, JM.215/1; *Dokumenty*, II:55). Ziegenmeyer initially reported 4,107 skilled Jewish textile workers in his county, but this percentage (30 percent) was too high. See BuF Lublin-Land memo, "Jüdische Textilwerker im Distrikt Lublin," May 16, 1942, WAPL, GDL 893.

60 Busse to BuF Lublin, May 22, 1942, WAPL, GDL 893 (copies in YVA, O.53/83, O.51/10, JM.215/1; *Dokumenty*, vol. II, p. 55).

Table 7.2: Deportations from the Lublin District, March–June 1942

Date	Origin	Number	Destinations
March 17–March 28	Lublin	18,000	Bełżec (+1,000 shot)
March 23	Piaski	3,400	Bełżec
March 24	Izbica	2,200	Bełżec
March 24	Wąwolnica	80	Shot
March 25–27	Kazimierz Dolny	2,000	Opole-Lubelski
March 30	Kazimierz Dolny from Opole, Nałęczów	1,600	Bełżec
March 31	Wąwolnica via Opole, Nałęczów	1,900	Bełżec (+ 52 shot)
March 31	Opole-Lubelski	1,950	Bełżec
March (end)	Biskupice	600	Bełżec
March	Trawniki	250	Bełżec
March 31–April 14	Lublin	12,000	Bełżec (+1,000 shot)
March or April	Siennica Rózanna	272	Bełżec
April	Sosnowica (children)	10s–100s	Shot
April	Kraśniczyn	2,000	Bełżec
April 7	Piaski	1,500	Bełżec
April 7	Rejowiec	2,400	Bełżec (200 shot)
April 8	Izbica	100s	Bełżec
April 9–10	Lubartów	800	Bełżec
April 11	Zamość	3,150	Bełżec (242 shot)
April 12	Kraśnik	2,000	Bełżec
April 12	Krasnystaw	2,000	Bełżec
April 13	Chrzanów	400	Turobin

Date	Origin	Number	Destinations
April 13	Dubienka	100	Shot
April 16	Szczebrzeszyn	30	Shot
April 17–20	Lublin	4,000	Shot at Krępiec Woods
April–May	Cieszanów (817 from Tomaszów)	1,300	Bełżec
May (early)	Chodel	1,400	Shot and Opole
May 1	Izbica	500	Sobibór
May 1	Mołodziatycze	285	Grabowiec
May 2	Rejowiec	2,700	Sobibór (300 to Krychów Labor)
May 5–7	Łuków	4,000	Sobibór
May 6	Bobrowniki (via Dęblin)	200	Sobibór
May 6	Dęblin-Irena	2,500	Sobibór (+ 42 shot)
May 6	Józefów nad Wisła (via Opole, Nałęczów)	1,270	Sobibór
May 7	Ryki (via Dęblin)	1,800	Sobibór (+ 10s shot)
May 7	Stęzyca (via Dęblin)	125	Sobibór
May 8	Baranów (via Dęblin)	1,500	Sobibór
May 8	Lysobyki (via Dęblin)	500	Sobibór
May 8	Końskowola	1,580	Sobibór (+ 10s shot)
May 8	Szczebrzeszyn	280	Bełżec
May 8	Kurów (via Konskowola, Nałęczów)	2,000	Sobibór

Date	Origin	Number	Destinations
May 9	Markuszów (via Nałęczów)	1,500	Sobibór
May 6–10	Michów	2,500	Sobibór
May 12	Opole-Lubelski	2,000	Sobibór
May 12	Turobin (via Krasnystaw)	2,750	Sobibór (+ 50 shot)
May 12–15	Żółkiewka (via Krasnystaw)	1,000	Sobibór
May 13 or 14	Gorzków (via Krasnystaw)	1,200	Sobibór
May 13 or 14	Wysokie (via Krasnystaw)	200	Sobibór
May 14	Skierbieszów, Gorajec	28	Shot
May 14–15	Krasnystaw	3,400	Sobibór
May 17	Łaskarzew	1,000	Bełżec
May (mid)	Sawin, Ruda	2,000	Sobibór
May 18	Siedliszcze	630	Sobibór
May (mid)	Sielec (via Włodawa)	450	Sobibór
May 21–23	Chełm (incl. refugees)	4,300	Sobibór (+ 200 shot)
May 22	Bełżyce	3,000	Majdanek, Sobibór
May 22	Tyszowce	800	Sobibór (+ 200 shot)
May 22	Tomaszów	100s	Bełżec
May 22–23	Krasnobród	1,000	Bełżec
May 23–24	Włodawa	1,300	Sobibór (10s shot)
May 23	Komarów	1,500	Bełżec
May 25	Opole	2,000	Sobibór
May 25	Międzyrzec	800	Shot
May 24–27	Zamość	1,500	Sobibór
May 27	Łaszczów	350	Bełżec

Date	Origin	Number	Destinations
June	Gorzków	200	Sobibór
June	Podedworze-Opole	250	Łomazy
June 1–2	Hrubieszów	2,000	Sobibór (+ 150 shot)
June 2	Belz (via Hrubieszów)	1,500	Sobibór
June 2	Dubienka (via Hrubieszów)	2,670	Sobibór
June 6	Kraśniczyn	800	Sobibór
June 6–8	Michów	100s	Sobibór
June 8–10	Hrubieszów	3,000	Sobibór (+ 300 shot)
June 8	Grabowiec	1,200	Sobibór
June 10	Uchanie (incl. 680 from Horodlo)	1,650	Sobibór
June 10	Biała-Podlaska	3,000	Sobibór
June (end)	Chełm	600	Sobibór
June	Cyców	400	Sobibór
June 13	Rossosz	200	Łomazy
June 13	Sławatycze (incl. 149 from Dolhobrody, Holeszów, Hanna from 1/42)	1,300	Łomazy

The schedule of deportation and murder thereafter was also affected by several factors that came into play in June and July. First, the German summer offensive in the USSR required major rail support. The result was a slowdown in transports from the entire GG to Bełżec from late June to late July, and from the Lublin District to Bełżec and Sobibór by rail during this period. While deportation of Jews to Bełżec continued in July, primarily from Rzeszów county (Kraków District), the total daily numbers deported to Bełżec were considerably smaller than before. The schedule of deportation and murder was also affected by the construction of new gas chambers at

Bełżec between mid-June and mid-July. In addition, the timing was connected to the requisitioning of railroad cars for the Wehrmacht. Meanwhile, repair work on the rail link to Sobibór halted the deportations to that camp from the second half of July to mid-October. This period was then utilized to construct additional gas chambers there. However, the shutdown at Sobibór a month ahead of the track repairs was more a result of Wehrmacht needs and perhaps overload.[61]

As Tables 7.1 and 7.2 above show, more than 19,000 Jews from the Lublin District were deported to Sobibór on June 1–10, while fifteen trains brought approximately 10,000 Jews to the camp (June 1–20) from outside the district. With a gassing capacity of only approximately 600 at a time, Sobibór's effectiveness was sorely taxed by these simultaneous transports from inside and outside the Lublin District. This, too, seems to have contributed to stopping the murder there temporarily.

In addition, Frank's final yielding of his authority over the Jews to Krüger (June 3, 1942)[62] affected Globocnik's and the SS's ability to continue the deportations in the Lublin District on their own. Much of the organizational and paper work had been done until then by the civilian authorities, as full partners in the planning of the murder. While they did not cease to be involved after June 3, as evidenced by the Hrubieszów deportations, Globocnik's men were now the senior partners in planning the murder operations. In general, the civilian authorities played less of an initiating role in organizing murder after early June. The time needed by Globocnik's men to adjust to these circumstances, together with the other factors cited above, seem all to have contributed to the temporary shutdown of Sobibór.

The regional division of the murder operation in the GG was also an important factor affecting the pace and timing of the murder in the Lublin District. Once the second phase of the operation had begun,

61 On track repairs, see Ganzenmüller to Karl Wolff, July 28, 1942, YVA, JM/4372. See also Frank, *Diensttagebuch*, pp. 508–524; Musial, *Zivilverwaltung*, p. 270; Rückerl, *NS-Vernichtungslager*, p. 114; Arad, *Belzec, Sobibor, Treblinka*, p. 67.

62 Rich, *Hitler's War Aims*, pp. 95–96; Breitman, *Architect of Genocide*, p. 235; Musial, *Zivilverwaltung*, p. 276.

Jews rounded up for deportation to Bełżec, Zamość, April 11, 1942, Yad Vashem Photo Archive, 8677/561

each death camp in "Operation Reinhard" had a more or less regional murder assignment. Bełżec was meant to kill primarily Jews from the Galicia and Kraków Districts, as well as parts of the southern counties of the Lublin District. Treblinka was meant to kill first Warsaw Jews, and then Jews from the Radom District and the northern counties of the Lublin District. And Sobibór was intended primarily for Jews from the central (and parts of the southern) Lublin District, as well as Jews from other countries. Thus, when various external factors conspired to close Sobibór temporarily, the deportations from the Lublin District were also temporarily suspended.

The influence of regional considerations is reflected in the county sweeps in the Lublin District in the later months of 1942. With the opening of Treblinka on July 22, a quickened pace of deportations to death camps could be resumed. Once Treblinka became operational, it was also available to kill the Jews of the Radom and Lublin Districts. When Höfle returned to Lublin from Warsaw, after he oversaw the first days of the operation there (see below), he was free to begin reorganizing the deportations from the Lublin District as well. The result was the deportation of 42,000 Jews from the northern counties in the Lublin District — Radzyń, Biała-

Podlaska, and the northern part of Puławy county — to Treblinka from August 19 to November 7. In the center of the district, most of the last Jews of the city of Lublin and of Lublin-Land county were deported or shot in September–November 1942. For the city of Lublin, approximately 1,000 were shot on September 2, and the last 2,000 or so were sent to Majdanek or shot on October 22 and November 9. For Lublin-Land county, 6,000 Jews were deported from Lubartów and Łęczna to Sobibór in October. Several sweeps in October and November sent 16,500 Jews in Chełm county to Sobibór (by truck or foot), except for 650 Jews from Dubeczno, who were sent there only in December; 2,000 Jews were deported from Hrubieszów to Sobibór on October 28. And finally, more than 24,000 Jews were deported to Bełżec from the southern counties (Biłgoraj, Janów-Lubelski, and Zamość), mostly in October and November (some were deported in August and September).[63]

Mass Shootings

The end of the second phase of the murder in June also brought a heightened pace of mass shootings thereafter. These included Tyszowce on June 16, the well-known murder by Reserve Police Battalion 101 in Józefów on July 13, Łomazy on August 17, Serakomla on September 22, three mass shootings in Biała-Podlaska in September, and more, as well as the ongoing mass murder during the round-ups themselves, from their resumption in August.[64] During the August 19–26 deportations of 16,500 Jews from Międzyrzec and Parczew, more than 1,000 were shot on the spot.[65]

63 On the deportation pattern in this period, see Arad, *Belzec, Sobibor, Treblinka*, pp. 383–395; Pohl, *Judenpolitik*, pp. 131, 135–138; Musial, *Zivilvewrwaltung*, pp. 286–287; Berenstein, "Deportations," pp. 73–74; *idem*, "Martyrologia," pp. 41–44; Kielboń, *Migracje*, pp. 155–156. Although details in the data differ somewhat among the researchers, the pattern is the same for all of them.

64 Dieter Pohl estimates that 3,500 Jews were shot in the operations in Tyszowce, Józefów, Łomazy, Serakomla, and Biała-Podlaska, Pohl, *Judenpolitik*, pp. 131–132. However, this seems low, based on Browning, Goldhagen, and Jewish sources.

65 Pohl, *Judenpolitik*, pp. 132–133; Browning, *Ordinary Men*, pp. 57–73, 81–99.

Taken together with the shooting at Łomazy two days earlier, the shooting at Parczew earlier in the month, and in Józefów in July, these shootings marked a modification in the German approach to killing the Jews. From mid-summer systematic shooting became an integral part of the murder operation, as well as serving as a parallel though less common murder method. Shootings into mass graves, similar to the method used by German forces in the Soviet Union, was the murder method chosen in many places across the GG. In the Kraków District alone, perhaps as many as 70,000 Jews, or one-fourth of all the Jews there, were shot. Thousands of Jews from Tarnów were shot in the town and in the Zbilatowska Góra and Skrzyszów woods on June 11–19, 1942.[66]

Christopher Browning and Daniel Goldhagen have written extensively about the mass shootings in Józefów, Łomazy, and elsewhere in the Lublin District in July-December 1942. The Germans resorted to mass shooting for several reasons, including inaccessibility of railroads, or even proper roads, from certain localities, the lack of sufficient rolling stock at various times, and the temporary unavailability of Sobibór and Bełżec during the summer of 1942. The desire of local Nazi authorities to secure the victims' valuables for themselves was also a factor.

The shooting method differed from much of the EG activity in the USSR in that the shooting in the Lublin District was much more individual, as described in detail by Browning. Rather than firing squads shooting at a row of Jews from a distance of several meters, the method used in the Lublin District often involved rows of individual Germans shooting rows of individual Jews one-on-one in the nape of the neck at point-blank range.[67]

Not only did the KdS men serving in the USSR in the summer

66 Krakowski, *War of the Doomed*, pp. 141–142; *Pinkas Hakehillot, vol. 3, Western Galicia*, p. 167; Miron and Shulhani, eds., *Encyclopedia of the Ghettos*, p. 815.

67 Browning, *Ordinary Men*, pp. 57–73; Goldhagen, *Hitler's Willing Executioners*, pp. 212–219; Arad, *Belzec, Sobibor, Treblinka*, pp. 59–60; 141 Js 1957/62, indictment and verdict against Wolfgang Hoffmann, Julius Wohlauf, et al., Hamburg, 1966–1972 (copy in YVA, TR.10/764), pp. 193–204; AR-3297/1965, 8 Js 430/68, interrogations for Ganzenmüller case (copy in YVA, TR.10/1107), pp. 51–54.

and fall of 1941 garner mass-shooting experience, but so, too, did SS and policemen in the Lublin District who had shot Soviet prisoners of war during the fall and winter of 1941. As participants in one such operation in Zamość described it, the POWs were gathered into one area and forced to undress to their underwear. German police guarded them along the path to the murder site and brought them in small groups to a pit that was 3m x 8m x 2 m. SS men showed them where to lie face down in the pit, and SS and policemen standing in the pit shot them at point-blank range in the nape of the neck. In five hours 780 Soviet POWs were shot to death.[68]

The mass shootings were also connected to anti-partisan activity, mop-up operations in the wake of the deportations in the second half of 1942 and early 1943, and "Jew-hunts." These encompassed the entire district and all available SS, police, and Trawniki units. Forested areas, such as Parczew in the northeast of the district, were especially targeted because of the large concentration of partisans and Jews in hiding. From the summer of 1942 onward, police and SS troops were officially cautioned to travel on main roads and never to travel alone, for fear of partisan attacks. Thousands of Jews were killed in these operations, but the exact number cannot be ascertained. The nearly 25,000 accounted for in Tables 7.2 and 7.3, together with other sources, is certainly too low. In other words, well over 10 percent of the Jews killed in the Lublin District in 1942 were killed by shooting.[69]

68 See YVA, TR.10-1146Z, Schubert interrogation, pp. 3080–3083; Meiert interrogation, pp. 3296–3305; Wilhelm Wagner interrogation, pp. 3367–3373; Klaus Hornig interrogation, pp. 3377–3393; Wilhelm Kaussen interrogation, pp. 3422–3426; Heinrich Zaun interrogation, pp. 3790–3797 and 4505. It is interesting to note that most of the Germans who testified on this event referred to approximately 200 killed in this operation, as though the smaller number somehow was less criminal! Trawniki men did not participate. They were not yet trained, and they would not necessarily have been used to shoot their fellow Red Army soldiers at such an early stage of their collaboration.

69 Browning, *Ordinary Men*, pp. 128–139; Pohl, *Judenpolitik*, pp. 148–152; orders from KdO Kintrup, June 10, July 3, July 9, August 4, October 1, 1942, from Globocnik, June 27, 1942, from KdSchupo Major Peter, July 13, 1942, commander of Sicherungs-Abschnitt Mitte, July 15, 1942, as well as operations reports for January 27 and 28, 1943, of Sicherungsabschnitt Bug, YVA, O.53/121-W; report by 1st company of Police Regiment 22 to Police Regiment 25 on anti-partisan

According to Musial's statistical analysis, there were approximately 300–320,000 Jews in the Lublin District at the start of the operation.[70] When the 85–90,000 Jews brought into the district in March-June are added to these, the total number of Jews in the district with whom the Germans were dealing was perhaps close to 400,000. According to the Korherr report, approximately 20,000 Jews remained at the end of the year in forced-labor camps or rump ghettos.[71] Korherr's statistics did not take into account Jews who were hiding throughout the district. Yet even when we include these people, probably less than 10 percent of the Jews were still alive at the end of 1942. This, then, was a devastatingly thorough murder operation.

As the tables above and below show, there are data regarding approximately 320,000 Jews in the Lublin District murdered in camps or by shooting in 1942. At least 137,000 were killed by mid-June; nearly 150,000 were killed in the last stage; approximately 30,000 from outside the GG were sent directly to Sobibór or Majdanek; and many thousands were killed in July in Józefów and in the constant large and small shooting operations throughout the year.[72] Yet based on Musial's population estimate and Korherr's report, we are missing records for the fate of 60,000 additional Jews in the Lublin District in 1942. If we double Korherr's estimate of 20,000 Jews alive in the district at the end of 1942, in order to account for Jews who were in hiding, there are still 40,000 Jews missing. In light of the convincing

activities and hunts for Jews in the latter part of October 1942 in Janów-Lubelski county, November 11, 1942, and on anti-partisan activities and hunts for Jews in the Parczew Forest on December 3–4, 1942, December 4, 1942, in which 465 Jews and eighty-three "bandits" were shot, WAPL, KdGend, file 271 (copy in USHMMA, RG15.011M, reel 21).

70 Musial, *Zivilverwaltung*, pp. 102–103.

71 Nuremberg Document NO-5194.

72 Arad estimates that 92,000 Jews from the Lublin District had been deported to Bełżec and Sobibór by June 10, while Browning estimates that 100,000 Jews from the Lublin District had been murdered by June 18. See Arad, *Belzec, Sobibor, Treblinka*, pp. 383–391; Browning, *Ordinary Men*, p. 55. Table 7.2 accounts for approximately 10,000 shot between March 17 and June 10, 1942. Since Arad did not tally the numbers of Jews shot, this statistic makes Arad's and Browning's estimates very close. However, Table 7.2 shows that the number of Jews deported in this period was considerably higher.

nature of Musial's population statistics and the thoroughness and near-inescapability of the murder operation, we can assume that the 40,000 Jews unaccounted for in German records were murdered in 1942.[73]

Table 7.3: Deportations and Shootings in the Lublin District, Summer-December 1942

Date	Origin	Number	Destinations
Summer	Krylów	100s	Bełżec
July 13	Józefów n. Biłgoraj	1,400	Shot
July (late)	Chełm	100s	Sobibór
August (early)	Parczew	400	Shot
August 7	Włodawa	100	Shot
August 8	Szczebrzeszyn	400	Bełżec (+ 200 shot)
August 9	Biłgoraj	1,000	Bełżec
August 9	Tarnogród (incl. 221 from Biłgoraj, 22.3.42)	1,500	Bełżec
August 9	Zwierzyniec	300	Bełżec
August 9	Szczebrzeszyn	700	Bełżec; Chełm
August 11	Zamość	350	Majdanek (+ 70 shot)
Aug. 16–19	Kock	400	Parczew
August 17	Łomazy	1,700	Shot
Aug. 19–25	Parczew (incl. Kock)	5,500	Treblinka
August 21	Goraj	850	Bełżec

73 There are no reliable Jewish data, of course. With a population in great flux at that time, and the Jews unable to keep track of themselves, we cannot expect statistical accuracy from them. The JSS in Kraków tried to compile data on the numbers of Jews in the Lublin District based on records taken by Alten and his colleagues, but they found the task all but impossible. They recorded 183,367 Jews in the district as of April 30, when, according to German data, there should have been 100,000 more. See JSS statistical report on Jewish population in the Lublin District, April 30, 1942, YVA, O.6/394.

Date	Origin	Number	Destinations
Aug. 25–26	Międzyrzec	11,000	Treblinka (+ 960 shot)
August-September	Kock	2,500	Łuków
September (early)	Zamość	400	Bełżec
September	Tyszowce	49	Shot
September	Piaski	2,000	Bełżec
September 2	Lublin	1,000	Krępiec (shot) and labor
September 21	Goraj	700	Bełżec
September 21	Józefów n. Biłgoraj	70	Shot
September 22	Radzyń	200	Shot
September 22	Serakomla	300	Shot
September 23–24	Janów-Podlaski	1,800	Biała-Podlaska
September 26	Kock	180	Shot
September (end)	Janów Jews in Biała		Międzyrzec-Podlaksi
September	Konstantynów	700	Biała-Podlaska
September (end)	Same Jews in Biała		Międzyrzec-Podlaski
September (end)	Koden	200	Międzyrzec-Podlaski
September (end)	Piszczac	1,000	Międzyrzec-Podlaski
September (end)	Rossosz	250	Międzyrzec-Podlaski
September (end)	Sławatycze	100s	Międzyrzec-Podlaski
September (end)	Terespol	284	Międzyrzec-Podlaski
September (end)	Komarówka	610	Międzyrzec-Podlaski

Date	Origin	Number	Destinations
September (end)	Wisznice	900	Międzyrzec-Podlaski
	(incl. 120 from Rozwadówka, Motwica, Czeptuka from 1/42)		
September 29	Radecznicz, Goraj	400	Szczebrzeszyn
Sept. 26—Oct. 6	Biała-Podlaska	4,800	Treblinka
	(via Międzyrzec; some to labor camps)		
Sept.-Oct.	Czemerniki, Wohyn, Kock	2,500	Parczew or Międzyrzec
October	Piaski	4,000	Sobibór (via Trawniki)
October	Wojsławice	1,200	Sobibór
October (early)	Końskowola (Czech and other refugees)	1,100	Shot
October (early)	Końskowola, Puławy	500–1,000	Majdanek
October	Ulanów	1,100	Bełżec
October	Drzierzkowice	140	Kraśnik
October	Ostrow-Lubelski	3,000	Bełżec/Sobibór
October	Puchaczów	350	Sobibór (via Piaski)
October 1	Parczew (above)	2,500	Treblinka
October 1	Radzyń	2,000	Treblinka
October 2	Parczew	>100	Shot
October	Parczew Forests	>1,000	Shot
October (early)	Firlej	150	Lubartów (Oct. 11 Sobibór)
October 5	Chełm	1,000	Sobibór
October 4–7	Adamów, Stanin, Ulan, Wojciezków	2,843	Łuków (in Nov. Treblinka)
October 5–8	Łuków	7,000	Treblinka
October 6	Międzyrzec-Podlaski	150	Shot
October 6–9	Międzyrzec-Podlaski	>4,000	Treblinka

Date	Origin	Number	Destinations
October 8	Kamionka (incl. Mława and Slovakia refugees)	800	Treblinka
October 9–11	Piotrowice	500	Bełżec
October 10	Rejowiec (refugees)	2,400	Sobibór, Majdanek
October 11	Lubartów	3,000	Bełżec, Sobibór
October 11	Bychawa Same Jews from Bełżyce to Bełżec later	2,600	Bełżyce
October 14–16	Radzyń	2,000–3,000	Międzyrzec
October 14–16	Turobin (via Izbica)	100s	Bełżec
October 15	Dęblin-Irena (mostly refugees)	2,500	Treblinka
October 15	Zaklików	1,000	Bełżec
October 16	Zamość	3,500	Izbica (+ 200 shot)
October 17	Biała-Podlaska	231	Shot
October 17–18	Zakrzówek (via Kraśnik)	1,100	Bełżec (+50 shot)
October 21–24	Szczebrzeszyn	2,000	Bełżec (+500 shot)
October 25–30	Szczebrzeszyn And villages	100s	Shot
October 21	Zwierzyniec	300	Bełżec
October 21	Hrubieszów	3,000	Sobibór (+400 shot at Polegon)
October 22	Siedliszcze	1,400	Sobibór (800 to Staw labor camp)
October 22–30	Izbica	5,000	Sobibór, Bełżec
October 23	Łęczna	3,000	Sobibór
October 24–25	Włodawa (incl. local refugees)	5,400	Sobibór

Date	Origin	Number	Destinations
October 25	Lublin	1,800	Majdanek
October 26	Krasnobród	10s	Shot
October 27	Międzyrzec (incl. Komarówka, Koden, Konstantynów, Radzyń Jews and others)	2,000	Treblinka
October 27	Tomaszów-Lubelski	2,000	Bełżec
October 27–28	Chełm	3,300	Sobibór
October–November	Świerże (450), Cyców, Krzywowierzba (350), Olchowiec (230),Pawlow (230), Sawin (800), Uhrusk (340) (via Włodawa)	3,000	Sobibór
October–November	Annopol (via Kraśnik)	1,900	Bełżec
October–November	Modliborzyce (via Kraśnik)	1,300	Bełżec
November	Sosnowica (same group to Sobibór in April '43)	1,000	Włodawa
November	Janów-Lubelski (via Zaklików and Kraśnik)	900	Bełżec
November 1	Kraśnik (incl. local refugees)	2,700	Bełżec
November 2	Frampol	2,000	Bełżec
November 2	Krzeszów	500	Bełżec
November 2	Izbica	1,700	Sobibór, Bełżec, Majdanek
November 2	Tarnogród	1,000	Biłgoraj
November 3	same Jews in Biłgoraj	Bełżec	
November 2	Kraśnik	2,000	Zaklików

Date	Origin	Number	Destinations
November 3	Zaklików	2,000	Bełżec
November 3	Biłgoraj	2,000	Bełżec
November 6	Krzeszów	600	Bełżec
November 6	Włodawa	2,000	Sobibór
November 6–7	Chełm	7,000	Sobibór (3,000 shot)
November 6	Kock	700	Łuków
November 7	Łuków (incl. Adamów, Kock)	3,000	Treblinka (+ 40–50 shot)
November 7	Międzyrzec-Podlaski	2,000	Treblinka
November 7	Włodawa	800	Sobibór (+ 300 shot)
November 9	Lublin	2,000	Majdanek and Shot
November 11	Łęczna	1,000	Shot (+ 270 to Trawniki)
November 11	Łuków	500–600	Shot
November 14	Łuków	500	Shot
November 15	Tyszowce	70	Bełżec (+22 shot)
November 16–18	Hrubieszów	100s	Shot
November 20	Zamość	200	Shot
November 30	Goraj	30	Shot
December	Łuków	500–600	Shot
December	Dubeczno	650	Sobibór
December 17	Wisznice	120	Shot
December 27	Międzyrzec-Podlaski	523	Trawniki

Globocnik's men had garnered such extensive experience in the early deportations that they became the recognized deportation experts of the GG. Therefore, a SS unit from Lublin, led by Höfle, Michalsen, and Worthoff, took command of the deportations from the Warsaw ghetto that began on July 22, 1942. The Warsaw KdS personnel were initially responsible for organizational details, such as rail space and guarding.[74] These commanders from Lublin came to Adam Czerniakow on July 22, to inform him of the deportation that was about to commence.[75]

This is not the place to review in detail the deportations from Warsaw, which have been discussed and analyzed thoroughly in many sources.[76] However, two points should be noted: the centrality of Globocnik's staff and of Lublin to the murder of the Jews of the GG; and the extreme brutality that attended the deportations from the first moment – March 17, 1942, in Lublin. The cruelty was not confined only to the extent to which the German and German-run forces became brutal during the course of their activities, but also, and perhaps more important, the extent to which extreme brutality was integral to the plan for the deportations.

Brutality and violence served German purposes in many ways, particularly in terrifying the Jews into submission. Such premeditated violence and murder had been built into the occupation of Poland from its first days. But was there a more long-term utility to this violence in terms of the efficiency of the deportation and murder operation as a whole? If the round-up and deportation personnel spent their time beating and shooting Jews, then they were not spending that time getting the Jews onto the trains. Moreover, extended brutality meted out by the troops could dehumanize the troops themselves and make them less disciplined in the performance of their murderous tasks. That, after all, was one of the lessons drawn by German murder planners from the firing-squad murders in the USSR that began in the summer of 1941.

One way the Lublin German commanders dealt with this problem was to delegate some of the "dirtiest" work to the Trawniki men. However, as Browning has shown, these troops were not always reliable.[77] In Warsaw, Globocnik's men found that the

74 YVA, TR.10/813, 92–94; TR.10/869, pp. 5–19, 28–43; TR.10/756, pp. 106–127.

75 Adam Czerniakow, *The Warsaw Diary of Adam Czerniakow*, edited by Raul Hilberg, Stanislaw Staron, Josef Kermisz (New York: Stein and Day, 1982), pp. 384–385; YVA, TR.10/813, pp. 95–100.

76 See especially Gutman, *Jews of Warsaw*, pp. 203–213.

77 See Browning's discussion of the shooting murders in Łomazy on August

Latvian and Lithuanian Trawniki trainees under ORPO command were too brutal. They were replaced by Ukrainian Trawniki trainees, who apparently were cruel within the call of duty but not beyond it.[78]

The effects of extended brutality on these men can be illustrated in the events named by the Germans who were involved and by the Jews "The Cauldron" (*Kessel*). On September 5, after more than half the residents of the Warsaw ghetto had already been deported to Treblinka, the commanders from Lublin ordered all the remaining Jews to gather the next morning in a small area of the rump ghetto for a final selection. Approximately 35,000 Jews were given work permits during the next two days, while the remainder was herded through a narrow bottleneck to the *Umschlagplatz*. The selection, overseen by Michalsen, took a very long time. The conditions were very crowded and hot, and the Jews, as well as their guards, commanded by Otto Hantke, became increasingly restless. Ukrainian and German guards, including those who had come from Lublin, opened fire on the Jews periodically, seemingly venting their frustration. Emanuel Ringelblum estimated that 1,000 people were killed during those two days. According to Yisrael Gutman, nearly 36,000 Jews were deported during the "cauldron" operation, and some 48,000 overall in the last phase of the deportation operation (September 6–21).[79]

Thus, the deportations in the Lublin District were carried out in close cooperation among the various German authorities. They developed as an expanding spiral, from the city of Lublin in March and April 1942, to the inclusion of several towns near Lublin and in other counties in late March and April, to the entire district from May onward. Jews were deported into Lublin from Germany, the

17, 1942, in *Ordinary Men*, pp. 83–87; see also Goldhagen, *Hitler's Willing Executioners*, pp. 227–230.

78 YVA, TR.10/813, pp. 94–95.

79 See YVA, TR.10/813, Verdict, pp. 120–134, and Indictment, pp. 105–106, 115–118, 131–133; TR.10/869, vol. VII, pp. 26–35; TR.10/756, pp. 117–119; Emanuel Ringelblum, *Notes from the Warsaw Ghetto* (New York: Schocken, 1974), pp. 312–313 (not in the Hebrew edition); Stanislaw Adler, *In the Warsaw Ghetto 1940–1943; An Account of a Witness* (Jerusalem: Yad Vashem, 1982), pp. 273–274; Gutman, *Jews of Warsaw*, p. 211; *Pinkas HaKehillot, Poland, vol. 4, Warsaw*, p. 116.

Protectorate, and Slovakia as these deportations got underway. When the district deportations moved to systematic, countywide sweeps in May, once Sobibór was operational, the tempo of the deportations both into and out of the district picked up. Following the temporary shut-down of Bełżec and Sobibór in the summer, the systematic deportations resumed, integrated with deportations from all over the GG, and supplemented by numerous large and small shooting operations. The deportations were extremely brutal and left many thousands of dead Jews lying in the streets of the towns and cities of the Lublin District. The cruelty, along with scraps of information reaching other Jews regarding the fate of the deportees led increasing numbers to seek ways to avoid the deportations. But the German juggernaut swept the Jews up relentlessly, and, by the end of 1942, after nine and a half months of murder, approximately 90 percent of the Jews were dead.

The deportations also occasionally produced bizarre instances. In the aftermath of the deportations from Lublin, while thousands of "illegal" Jews were still hiding in Majdan Tatarski, unsure of their immediate fate, Shamai Grajer decided that he wanted to marry his pregnant mistress, the seventeen-year-old, blond, blue-eyed Stettin refugee, Mira Fishman. Grajer forced the well-known Rabbi Zvi

German police guarding Jews awaiting deportation, Międzyrzec-Podlaski, May 26, 1943, Yad Vashem Photo Archive, 77EO2

Elimelech Talmud to grant him a divorce from his wife Bella (against her will) and to perform the wedding. Grajer threw a big wedding party at his café and invited his SS friends, including Worthoff and Sturm, to attend. Sturm even sent a large bouquet of white roses. A day or two later the "illegals" were shot in the Krępiec woods, and on November 9, Sturm shot Grajer, his wife, and his baby.[80]

Confronting the Unbelievable

> People live in panic...Everyone talks about the evacuations but no one knows too much about them. People ask one another, Will we be evacuated, or maybe shot? No one knows anything for certain....We ask ourselves, Where are the Germans taking the fully loaded trains of evacuees?....We are in a complete state of collapse...Only a quick end to the war can save us. It is particularly difficult to watch as all...are evacuated, how the Germans move people in carloads.[81]

Dr. Zygmunt Klukowski's description of the reactions to the deportations was not referring to Jews; it was of Poles relating to the evacuation of Polish villages in the Zamość area in late 1942. The Germans used Polish policemen and firemen to round up their countrymen, just as the same types of units (along with Jewish policemen) had been used frequently to round up Jews. Uncertainty, fear, and panic prevailed, and, as the deportations of villagers continued, increasing numbers of Poles hid or fled to the forests. But Klukowski's description of the Poles' reactions to the deportations, from his vantage point in Szczebrzeszyn, closely resembles the descriptions of Jews' reactions to deportations shortly before the Polish deportations began. Jews were uncertain as to where their fellow Jews were being sent and were left trying to garner information from their own very limited resources. Of course, there

80 Rapoport-Glikstein testimony, *Dos Buch*, p. 402; *idem*, *Encyclopedia of the Jewish Diaspora, Lublin*, p. 709; YVA, TR.10/859, pp. 243–245.
81 Klukowski, *Diary*, December 7–14, 1942, pp. 229–231.

was one fundamental difference between the perceptions by Poles and Jews. Whereas the Poles could hope to encounter a friendly hinterland and support among the local population should they succeed in escaping, the Jews sensed that they could not count on widespread support. As Klukowski noted on November 26, 1942: "There are many people who see Jews not as human beings but as animals that must be destroyed."[82]

What did the Jews perceive as the deportations got underway? It is clear that the Jews of Lublin were taken by surprise. Less than three days before the deportations began, the Judenrat was still looking ahead to communal baking of *matzah* for the upcoming Passover holiday.[83] And whereas many Lublin Jews sought hiding places and other ways to evade the deportations from a very early stage, this does not mean that they understood the nature of the Nazi plans. Even as the evidence mounted regarding the murder, and increasing numbers of Jews in the Lublin District learned of the murder operations, Jews were often not conscious of what was in store for them, or unable to do anything about it – or both. As noted in Chapter 1, one Jew from Zamość commented in 1942, "...an expulsion is like a funeral procession – when a funeral procession passes by, heaven forbid, everyone thinks it is not for him. That's how it was with us."[84]

Rumors and news of the deportations from Lublin had begun to spread across the GG quickly and with varied impact. On March 24, 1942, Markus Hirsch, in the town of Rosulna, Stanisławów county, Galicia District, sent a letter to the Lublin Judenrat, together with a stamped, self-addressed response postcard, inquiring about the whereabouts of his wife, Ryfka Friede Hirsch. Some time earlier he had sent her 30 złoty, but he hadn't heard anything from her in reply.[85] Hirsch sent his inquiry one week into the mass deportations

82 Ibid., p. 227.

83 Blumental, *Documents*, Protocol 13 (137), March 14, 1942, p. 309.

84 Fiszelzon report, YVA, M.10.AR.I/946, June 6, 1942. The extensive familiarity with detail in this testimony would suggest that this was either Baruch Fiszelzon, who had been a member of the Judenrat in Zamość, or Berek Fiszelzon, a Jewish policeman.

85 Markus Hirsch to Judenrat in Lublin, March 24, 1942, in WAPL, RZ 22. This file in WAPL contains dozens of inquiries of this sort. See, for example, Klara Herschthal, Lemberg, to Judenrat in Majdan Tatarski, May 1, 1942, inquiring

from Lublin to Bełżec, and just as deportations from other localities, including the Galicia District, were beginning. Ironically, it was only six days before deportations from Stanisławów county were to begin as well.[86]

Did this inquiry mean that he knew of the deportations from Lublin and their ominous meaning? His letter can be interpreted in two ways. It might have been a naive inquiry by a worried husband, reflecting his lack of knowledge or information about the deportations then underway from Lublin to Bełżec. Alternatively, it might have been the carefully written inquiry of a worried husband who feared his wife had been sent away, based upon information Mr. Hirsch had received about deportations.

One thing this inquiry certainly reflects is the possibility that some Jews had at least to inquire and to correspond to a very limited degree with loved ones. The ability to inquire also meant the ability to inform. Correspondence among Jews continued during the deportations, both legally and illegally. This was one of the most significant elements in how information about the Holocaust was spread among the intended victims. In most cases we will never be able to know for certain what people like Mr. Hirsch, who inquired with Judenräte regarding the whereabouts or welfare of loved ones, had heard or knew about the deportations. However, through their correspondence, we can get a glimpse of their anxiety, anguish, and fear, and the attempts of many to get information out as a cry for help, or as a hope to rescue others.

The extent to which Jews in the Lublin District had no premonitions regarding the fate being planned for them by the Germans is reflected in the case of Therese Borger. In February 1942, she learned that her mother, sixty-five-year-old Bertha Langer, of Brünn (Brno) in Moravia (the "Protectorate"), was ill. Ms. Borger decided to bring her mother to Lublin in order to care for her. She

about her brother Marek Alten; and Necha Ejbuszyc, Warsaw, to Alten, June 11, 1942, inquiring about her mother, who disappeared in Lublin on April 3 or 4.

86 For deportation dates from various places in the GG, see Arad, *Belzec, Sobibór, Treblinka*, Appendix A, pp. 383–398. On Stanisławów, see Dieter Pohl, "Hans Krüger and the Murder of the Jews in the Stanisławów Region," *Yad Vashem Studies*, 26 (1998), pp. 239–264.

wrote the Judenrat requesting a letter of reference for the German authorities affirming that she had the financial means to support her mother. Then, on February 23, Ms. Borger submitted a written request, together with the Judenrat's reference, to the district BuF to bring her mother to Lublin. The next day Türk forwarded the request to the mayor of Brünn for his approval. The mayor's March 10 affirmative response reached Türk's office ten days later. Since the BuF was then very busy with the mass deportations of Jews to Bełżec and into the district from other areas, it took Türk another six days before he informed Therese Borger that the resettlement of her mother to Lublin had been approved. On March 31, Bertha Langer was indeed resettled, in the fullest Nazi sense of the term.[87]

At least some Jews in Lublin began to discover the fate of the deportees within days after the deportations began. An important source of information was from Poles, especially those who worked for the railroad or lived near Bełżec. On March 17, at 7:30 A.M., Josef Siegfried, Judenrat member and Alten's JSS deputy in the Lublin District, called the Kraków headquarters of JSS to inform them that mass deportations of the Lublin Jews had begun at midnight. The SD was running the deportations, he reported, in which all non-essential people (those without the SIPO red stamp that had been given to some on March 8) were to be resettled. Twenty thousand were to be deported at a rate of 1,400 daily. Two days later Siegfried called Kraków again to report that all the deportees were being sent to Bełżec (not to the USSR).[88]

87 See the Judenrat's endorsement of Therese Borger's financial means, signed by Bekker, February 21, 1942; Therese Borger to BuF Lublin, February 23; Türk to Bürgermeister, Brünn, February 24; Dr. Karafiat, Obermagistrat, Brünn, to Governor, District Lublin, March 10; Türk to Therese Borger, March 26; Zentralstelle für jüdischer Auswanderung Prag to Governor, Lublin, April 30, all in YVA, O.53/83. Bertha Langer was sent to Theresienstadt that day, and shortly afterward was in a deportation of 1,000 Jews from there to the Lublin District.

On the March 31 deportation see http://db.yadvashem.org/deportation/nameDetails.htm/?/anguage=en&itemId=4811942. The April 30 Prague report and other records at Yad Vashem do not agree on the date of Bertha Langer's deportation to Poland, whether in early April or October.

88 YVA, JM/1576, pp. 122, 123, 124. See also Blumental, *Documents*, pp. 65–67.

Although Siegfried did not refer to the fate of the deportees, at least part of the Nazi deception had been exposed within two days. And the mere fact that the destination was Bełżec was enough to strike terror in the hearts of all Jews, especially those in Lublin who recalled the brutal, murderous conditions of the labor camp there in 1940. At the same time, there is other evidence that within days at least some Jews in the Lublin area might have learned not only of the destination of the deportees, but also of their true fate. For example, Symcha Turkeltaub testified on numerous occasions that Jews in Lublin had heard of the fate of the deportees from Poles by March 20.[89] The former head of the Zamość Judenrat and head of the JSS there, Mieczysław Garfinkel, reported that in late March 1942, he received a telephone call from the Lublin Judenrat asking him to check where the Lublin Jews were being sent and what was being done with them. Since telephone calls by JSS officials were not highly suspect in German eyes, it is likely that such a call would have been made by Siegfried or Alten to Garfinkel in that capacity. Garfinkel called the Judenrat in Tomaszów-Lubelski, which is near Bełżec, asking them to check into the matter. The latter Judenrat sent messengers to Polish railroad workers in the area. From them they learned that all the Jews who entered the camp never left — they were being killed. This was reported by messenger to Garfinkel, who then informed the Lublin Judenrat.[90] Hava Goldminc reported that her family paid a Polish courier 20,000 złotys to follow the trains and discover where the Jews were being sent and what was their fate. By the eve of Passover (April 1), they knew what was happening to the deportees.[91] And we can add to this the SS testimony cited above that all the Jews in Lublin were hiding by March 31.[92]

The above illustrations of Jews in Lublin acquiring knowledge

89 Turkeltaub testimonies, in YVA, TR.10/756, p. 75; TR.10/1146Z, XX:4285.

90 See Garfinkel testimonies in YVA, JM/3536a, testimony on December 5, 1945, before the Polish War Crimes Commission in Lublin; YVA, TR.10/1146, XVII:3724–74 (he had moved to Rhodesia and changed his name to Garwin); O.33/322; TR.10/859, pp. 74–75; see also *Pinkas Zamość*, pp. 1117–1158.

91 Hava Goldminc (Kirszenblat) testimony, YVA, O.3/11397.

92 YVA, TR.10/859, pp. 61–65; see also the pre-trial interrogations in TR.10/1146Z.

about the fate of the deportees indicate both that there were various means to obtain information and that quite a few people exercised those means. Still, it cannot be concluded from this that large numbers of Jews had clear knowledge of what the Nazis were doing. Yet even without access to such information, the fact of the deportations was enough to send many Jews into hiding or some other evasive action. Both the memories of earlier violent round-ups in the middle of the night and the extreme brutality of the first round-ups in Lublin, in 1942, increased the fears and affected the actions of the Jews. While there was practically nothing the Lublin Jews could have done with the information about the fate of the deportees, a fairly widespread attempt to evade the deportations ensued.

In Markuszów (Puławy county), Judenrat head Shlomo Goldwasser had heard about the Lublin deportations, so when he received information about the impending deportation from his town, he warned the Jews. The result was mass flight to the nearby forest on the morning of May 9, as all the Jews were ordered to report to the town square. But here, as in Lublin and elsewhere, nearly all the Jews who had escaped and went into hiding were eventually caught.[93]

Those who knew and managed to survive the initial deportations also informed friends and relatives in other places of what was happening in Lublin. For example, a concerned Chaim Kaplan recorded the deportations in his diary as early as March 22, and, within less than four weeks, he was well informed by refugees from Lublin regarding the fate of these Jews.[94]

There were several types of motivations behind the letters sent to family and friends: communicating with loved ones and sharing their troubles with people close to them; seeking help; getting information out; sending warnings in order for others to save themselves. Many letters reflected multiple motivations. The

93 David Shtokfisz, ed., *Destruction and Heroism from the town Markuszów* (Tel Aviv: Markuszów Immigrants' Association, 1955), pp. 159–194, Krakowski, *War of the Doomed*, pp. 61–62.

94 Chaim Kaplan, *The Warsaw Diary of Chaim A. Kaplan* (New York: Collier, 1973), pp. 304–305, 312–314. This is a not quite complete translation from the original Hebrew, which can be found in MA, D.2.470, pp. 236, 249–252.

large volume of these letters is most striking, as is the mere fact that the Nazis allowed the official postal system to continue functioning. Many Jews exploited this. We do not know how many letters were intercepted by German postal censors and therefore never reached their destination. However, from the existing informative and warning letters, the creativity of many Jews in discovering ways to evade the postal censors stands out.

Informing. On March 29, 1942, Daniel Lewkowicz wrote to his sister in Warsaw from a cellar in Lublin, where he had been hiding with a cousin since the deportations began. By this time 15,000 Jews had been deported, and 1,000 had been shot in the city, he said.[95] When such information was sent to loved ones through the legal post, it would be couched in cryptic messages, such as "*Malach Hamowes is in die gass*" ("the Angel of Death is in the street").[96] The same was true of letters sent to the outside world, such as that by Zivia Lubetkin quoted above. Moshe Wilnicki reported to Natan Schwalb on "bad news" from Lublin on March 28, while Szmul Zitomirski wrote the next day from Hrubieszów (where he had fled from Lublin) that "Uncle *Gerush*" (expulsion) had visited the Jews in Lublin.[97]

On April 25, 1942, a brief report sent from Izbica to Warsaw told of the deportations from Izbica to Bełżec on March 24 and April 8 (when the operation was "chaotic").[98] Several officials in

95 Daniel Lewkowicz to sister, March 29, 1942, YVA, M.10.AR.1/552.

96 Postcard from Chelm to Warsaw, April 13, 1942, YVA, M.10.AR.1/568, on JM.3489. See also the May 27, 1942, postcard from Janina Szylska in Sosnowica (Chełm County) to Ludwik Hirszberg in Warsaw, ibid., M.10.AR.1/579, and the May 5 cryptic letter from M. Altman in Międzyrzec-Podlaski to J. Berkal in Warsaw, M.10.A.R.1/558. Hela Ferstman reported that in Bełżyce she received information about the Lublin deportations almost immediately; see Hela Ferstman diary, M.49.P/2.

97 Letters from Moshe Wilnicki, Częstochowa, to Natan Schwalb, March 28, 1942, and from Szmul Zitomirski, Hrubieszów, to Natan Schwalb, March 29, 1942, in Zariz, *Letters from Haluzim*, pp. 135–137. See also the letters from Moses Rubin, a Slovakian Jewish deportee in Chełm, to his children in Prešov, especially his last letter, September 3, 1942, YVA, O.75/57; letters between Julius Aoram in Tel Aviv and his parents in Opole-Lubelski, ibid., O.75/82.

98 Note from Izbica (no name), YVA, M.10.AR.1/949. The reference to April 8, when there was no deportation from Izbica, probably referred to the deportations

the Zamość Judenrat sent cryptic postcards to Hersh Wasser of the Oneg Shabbat underground group in Warsaw reporting on the deportations from various places in the Zamość and Lublin areas. Szlamek reported in April on the deportations to Bełżec, which was "*dos bajs olem*" (the cemetery).[99]

Isser Roizman wrote to Schwalb from Zamość on April 20: "Mr. *Kilayon* [annihilation], whom you know from Mr. Haim Nahman of Nemirov, visited us. He looks bad and meeting him cost me half my health." The report referred to the April 11 deportation from Zamość in which Roizman believed approximately half the Jews had been killed. The reference to Haim Nahman was to Bialik and his poem on the 1903 Kishinev pogroms, "In the City of Slaughter."[100]

Sharing Troubles and Requesting Aid. On March 29, 1942, Pesach Goldblum in Opole-Lubelski sent a letter to his brother Josek in Warsaw reporting on his forced march there from Kazimierz Dolny together with other Jews; they had reached Opole the day before. Conditions in Opole were terrible, and he was very anxious for his life. "Save me!" he pleaded.[101]

In mid-April, amidst spreading panic in Szczebrzeszyn at the

begun the day before from Rejowiec and Piaski. Both deportation trains passed through Izbica on their way to Bełżec. The next day, April 9, a train with 998 Jews left Vienna for Izbica.

99 Postcards from Fela Bajler, Szlamek Bajler (or Feiner, or Wiener), and others working for the Zamość Judenrat to Hersh Wasser, February-April 1942, YVA, M.10.AR.1/596. See also Samuel D. Kassow, *Who Will Write Our History? Rediscovering a Hidden Archive from the Warsaw Ghetto* (New York: Vintage, 2009), pp. 287–292, for a detailed discussion of Szlamek's identity, and Ruta Sakowska, "Two Forms of Resistance in the Warsaw Ghetto — Two Functions of the Ringelblum Archives," *Yad Vashem Studies*, 21 (1991), p. 202. Sakowska adds that this is the same Szlamek who had reported to Oneg Shabbat on Chełmno in February, when he carried a temporary identification card from Piotrków under the name Jakob Grojnowski. Kassow expands on this discussion significantly. Copies of the original letters can also be found in Ruta Sakowska, ed., *Archiwum Ringelbluma: Listy o Zagładzie* (Warsaw: Wydawnictwo Naukowe PWN, 1997), pp. 125–134. See also Tregenza, "Bełżec — Okres Eksperymentalny," pp. 200–202.

100 Letters from Isser Roizman, Zamość, to Natan Schwalb, April 20, 1942, in Zariz, *Letters from Haluzim*, p. 139.

101 YVA, M.10.AR.1/587; copy in Sakowska, ed., *Listy o Zagładzie*, p. 136.

news of the April 11 deportations from Zamość to Bełżec, Fiszel and Sara Fryd sent several postcards to Sara's brother Mosze Wulf in Warsaw pleading for help. Mosze had sent 222 złotys, but these were spent quickly in the family's effort to remain alive. On April 18, Fiszel and Sara, desperate and sensing the ominous fate awaiting them, wrote: "We have asked many times that you send some money and you ignore us. I will remember this, if we live."[102]

Josef Kirszenfeld in Biłgoraj wrote to his brother-in-law Hersh Wasser (secretary of Oneg Shabbat) on June 10, two months before the first large deportations from that town, about the very hard times that had befallen them. He pleaded for assistance. Several days later Kirszenfeld received 100 złotys from Wasser.[103]

On July 23, Szmul Zitomirski, now in Majdan Tatarski, wrote a despondent, melancholy letter to Schwalb. He pleaded for aid packages and bemoaned the fact that he was the last remaining member of his family and of his Zionist movement in Lublin: "In my loneliness I pin all my hopes on you."[104]

Sending Warnings. One of the most detailed and moving cryptic warnings was dated June 1, 1942. It was written in Yiddish and sent from Włodawa to Warsaw, probably by courier. The original was copied by someone in the Oneg Shabbat underground. The copy bears no name of an addressee or a signature (these would have been omitted to protect both). Approximately 1,300 Jews were deported from Włodawa to Sobibór in a very violent "action" on May 22–23; in the aftermath many of the remaining Jews fled the town.[105]

102 Seven postcards from Fiszel and Sara Fryd, Szczebrzeszyn, to Moszek Wulf, Warsaw, April 14–18, 1942, YVA, M.10.AR1/545; copies in *Listy o Zagładzie*, pp. 89–95. On the spreading panic, see Klukowski, *Diary*, April 11–13, pp. 191–192.

103 YVA, M.10.AR.1/584.

104 Letter Szmul Zitomirski, Majdan Tatarski, to Natan Schwalb, July 23, 1942, in Zariz, *Letters from Haluzim*, p. 147. See also the plea from Josef Szalavac, a refugee in Opole-Lubelski, to his family in Haifa, August 1942, YVA, O.75/375; Hanka Spector-Burstein testimony on telephoning her German employer in a theater and receiving help from him, MA, A.195.

105 For details regarding the May 1942 deportation from Włodawa to Sobibór, see YVA, TR.11/02118; TR.10/631; Leon Lemberger testimony, M.49.E/2766. Ruta Sakowska believes the letter was copied by Eliahu Gutkowski, the

> We are thank God healthy. We don't know what to do regarding going to the doctor. We can't decide ourselves, although we had already decided to be by the doctor. Since Uncle wants God forbid [ח"ו] to have his children's party by you God Forbid, because he's renting an apartment near you, very near to you. Perhaps you don't even know this.
>
> Therefore, I am writing to you now and we are sending you this information specially, so you should know. It is true that you, too, shall rent apartments out of town [מחוץ לעיר] for all our brothers the Children of Israel. He has already prepared a new apartment for everyone – the same one he had near us. In case you perhaps don't know of this, I am writing especially so you'll know because uncle wants And He Expelled Man [ויגרש את האדם], and then you will be together with Shlomo Velvel of blessed memory [ע"ה].
>
> We know this with certainty and Uncle will soon complete the apartment by you. You should know. Perhaps you can figure something out. It should be generally known that Uncle wants God Forbid to have a wedding reception soon by you and the apartment is already prepared very near to you.
>
> Remember, be in your apartments [outside town] at all costs, so that you won't be with Shlomo Velvel of blessed memory, and for sleeping the only good fortune [סגולה] is that of He who sits secretly [יושב בסתר]. Remember well that we are holy and that which is left for morning, etc. [קדושים והנותר ממנו עד בוקר וכו'][106]

The cryptic Biblical references and acronyms would have been clear

second secretary of Oneg Shabbat. See Sakowska, "Two Forms of Resistance," p. 206.

106 Letter from Włodawa to Warsaw, June 1, 1942, YVA, Oneg Shabbat, M.10. AR1/563 (on JM/3489). See also Sakowska, "Two Forms of Resistance," p. 206, where there is a partial and, at times, inexact translation. Samuel Kassow says that "Shlomo Velvel" is a reference to the Radzyner *Rebbe*, Shmuel Shlomo Leiner, who had fled to Włodawa early in the war, became famous among Jews for his leadership and resistance activities, and was murdered by the Nazis in May 1942. See Kassow, *Who Will Write Our History?*, p. 293.

to almost any Polish Jew at the time. The last reference, to the first Passover sacrifice by the Israelites in ancient Egypt, was incomplete: "shall be burned by fire" (Exodus 12:10) is the end of the verse. The writer was convinced that the murder would reach Warsaw as well, and, by implication, all of the Jews of Poland. Did the writer know of the construction of Treblinka? Did he/she/they assume that the Warsaw Jews, too, would be murdered in Sobibór? This is not clear, and we will probably never know. But the warning was clear: get out of town and hide because the Germans are planning to kill all of you, too.

Much information of this sort was collected in an organized fashion by underground groups in the Warsaw ghetto and can be found in the Oneg Shabbat archive. They compiled reports detailing events concerning various deportations, smuggled them out, and even published them, hoping in this way to inform the Polish underground, the world, and the other Jews in danger. The information was based on personal letters such as the ones cited above, on personal testimonies from escapees who reached Warsaw, and on information received through the Polish underground groups. Reports either related to events in individual localities, or were surveys of events based on collected accounts. One of the first communications to synthesize information from various sources appeared in early April 1942, reporting that the Jews of Lublin and the towns in the area had been deported to Bełżec, the notorious forced-labor camp known from 1940: The Jews are killed there "in the same way as in Chełmno, that is, they are poisoned by gas."[107]

Perhaps the best known of these accounts was the Bund Report, smuggled out to the Polish government-in-exile in May 1942, via Swedish businessmen. This same detailed report, referring to a Nazi plan being implemented to "exterminate" the Jews, which had already claimed the lives of 700,000 Polish Jews, was circulated to some extent within the Warsaw ghetto and the GG as well.[108] Numerous

107 "Reports for the underground press. 'Report nr. 1, The Jewish Population Marked for Physical Extermination' " (Yiddish), YVA, M.10.AR1/259.

108 The Bund Report can be found in YVA, M.10.AR.1/937. On the dispatch and receipt of the report see Yehuda Bauer, "When Did They Know?," *Midstream* (April 1968), pp. 51–58; David Engel, *In the Shadow of Auschwitz: The Polish*

reports of this nature were in the Oneg Shabbat archive by early July 1942, indicating that fairly extensive information about deportations was available to at least some people by then. Similar descriptions reached other communities, although it is impossible to know in what quantity or to what extent in most cases. The information regarding the fate of the deportees was scantier.

When looked at all together, the extent and details of information that reached Warsaw and other places were vast. Of course, almost none of the Jews ever became aware of such extensive information, but it is important to note to what extent the murder operation was not covert. By early summer 1942, detailed information had gotten out regarding deportations from dozens of communities in the GG. The information on the Lublin District alone acquired by Oneg Shabbat by mid-June referred to some thirty localities, 75,000 Jews deported to Bełżec and Sobibór, and several thousand shot. This information was generally detailed and quite up to date.[109] Yet the overall Nazi plan did remain shrouded in secrecy.

A Warsaw Jewish underground report of May 5 referred to deportations to Bełżec, while a July 18 report said that all

Government-in-Exile and the Jews, 1939–1942 (Chapel Hill and London: University of North Carolina Press, 1987), pp. 185–186.

109 See the following reports in the Oneg Shabbat Archive, in YVA, M.10, dated April 3 to July 18, 1942:

Letter, M. Altman, Międzyrzec-Podlaski, to J. Berkal, Warsaw, May 5, AR.1/558; Janina Szylska, Sosnowica, to Ludwik Hirszberg, Warsaw, May 27, AR.1/579; undated Report from Lublin (apparently early April), AR.1/948; Report on Lublin and Izbica, April 3, AR.1/262; Report on Izbica, April 25, AR.1/949; Report on Lublin, September 1939 to April 1942, AR.2/305; Report on Rejowiec, undated (apparently mid-May), AR.1/1215; Report on Hrubieszów, June 1942, AR/1/998; Report by Mr. Rotring on Tyszowiec, June 1942, AR/1/1061; Report on Lublin District, May 5, AR/3/27); "The Scroll of Agony and Destruction," report by Eliahu Gutkowski (Yiddish), May 29, AR.1/1062 (also M.10.38-1-2 and JM/1209/1); Reports on deportations, June 18, July 3, and July 18, AR.1/472; Reports of May 5 and June 18, AR.1/317, on JM/3489; June 25 report on GG, "z Kraju" and July report, "Service prasowy," AR.1/471 (also JM/2719); June 30 report, "z Kraju," AR.1/261; the Bund Report, May 1942, AR.1/937; undated report, probably July, "Gehenna Żydów Polskich pod Okupacja Hitlerowska," AR.1/144. Reports continued to arrive and to be circulated after July as well.

the Jews sent to Bełżec were being killed; another report in July told of murders by electrocution in Bełżec. Stories of murder by electrocution were passed on from mid-April, and although there is no record of such a murder method in that camp, the rumors to this effect became widespread.[110]

Several of the reports attempted to put all the individual accounts into a larger perspective. The result was that some people with access to extensive information concluded that the Nazis were engaged in the systematic, methodical murder of the Jews. In general, from a historical perspective, these reports were quite accurate. Inaccuracies, such as a May report of 1,500 Jews being gassed daily at Trawniki, might have confused the recipients of these reports, but, by the summer, a terrible – but unbelievable – picture of Nazi activities in the GG had been presented.

But to what extent did the information affect the reactions? Did warnings help the endangered communities? When the Red Army POWs were marched passed the Jews of Zamość in the autumn of 1941, the Jews pitied them and tried to give them food and water. When these POWs were shot, the Jews were disturbed. But when Jews were shot shortly thereafter, their own behavior was much the same as that of the POWs. Outwardly, with some exceptions, they were compliant right up to the killing pits.

Similarly, the correspondence between Lublin and Warsaw reveals that the knowledge of murder in one place generally did not help the Jewish community in another, nor did such information seriously affect communal behavior, even if there were warning signs. Individuals often drew conclusions from the reports of deportations that led them to act in ways to evade the round-up

110 YVA, M.10.AR.1/472; AR.1/317); AR.3/27; July 1942 report, "Gehenna Zydów Polskich," ibid. See also Kaplan, *Warsaw Diary*, April 17, 1942, p. 313; Klukowski, *Diary*, April 8, 1942, p. 191; Levin, *Cup of Tears*, June 3, 1942, p. 116; Diary of Yehoshua Wohlfuss, ca. April 1, 1942, *Memorial Book to Kehillat Rawa-Ruska and the Area* (Tel Aviv: Rava Ruska Immigrants' Society, 1973), pp. 236–239. Rawa Ruska was in the Galicia District of the GG, on the border of the Lublin District, very close to Bełżec. On March 20, 1,500 Jews from Rawa Ruska were deported to Bełżec. Trains bearing Jews from Lwow and Lwow county to Bełżec had passed through Rawa Ruska between March and early April.

when it reached their hometown, but this generally did not affect the fate of the community at large. Thus, in Zamość, like in Warsaw, the stricter decrees against Jews that were imposed by the German civilian administration in early 1942, together with the killing of several dozen Jews for leaving the ghetto without permission, caused great anxiety. It was heightened by the news of the deportations from Lublin, and many Jews began thinking about where to flee. However, like in Lublin, many hoped that the deportation would not be worse than the one a year earlier, when 500 Jews had been expelled from Zamość as part of the ghettoization.

When the deportation to Bełżec began on April 11, the Jews of Zamość seemed to have been as surprised as the Jews in Lublin had been.[111] Individuals like Jan Bachrich were able to reach their own conclusions based on the evidence before them. Having witnessed the April 11 deportation from Zamość, Bachrich and several of his friends, who, like him, were deportees from the Protectorate, hid in the cellar of a Polish acquaintance when the Germans ordered the Jews to assemble for the second deportation in late May 1942.[112]

In Annopol-Rachów, Jews learned of the deportations from Lublin by Passover (April 1) from a fugitive who reported on Bełżec as well. Yet until conditions changed for them in October, they did not believe it would happen to them, because they worked for the Germans.[113]

In Hrubieszów as well, the first news regarding the murder of the Jews in Lublin reached the town shortly after the killing began. But this news in and of itself made only a limited impression on the local Jews. It was the forced move into Hrubieszów of Jews from the local villages in March and April 1942 that shook the Jews' sense of security. Their peace of mind was further unnerved by news of the

111 Fiszelson report, June 6, 1942, YVA, M.10.AR.1/946; Garfinkel testimonies, YVA, JM/3536a, TR.10/1146Z, XVII:3724–74, O.33/322, *Pinkas Zamość*, pp. 1117–1158.

112 Jan Bachrich, testimony. See also Jan Osers, *Under Swastika and Hammer and Sickle: Persecutions in Two Dictatorships* (Prague: Unpublished manuscript, 2005; available in Yad Vashem Library).

113 Daniel Freiberg, *Darkness Covered the Earth*, pp. 87–88, 93; Eli Fishman interview, YVA, O.93 (VHA)/14967; Majer Rozenblatt interview, O.93 (VHA)/5113; Benny Kleiman interview, O.93 (VHA)/477.

first deportation from Zamość; the deportations were now getting geographically closer, like a noose tightening around them.

When news began to spread at the end of May of an impending seven-day deportation from Hrubieszów, panic struck the Jewish community, and many went into hiding. But here, as elsewhere, hiding was an individual or small group decision. And whereas some had managed to flee to safety or to hide, nearly all those who hid were caught and shot in the cemetery at the end of the deportation operation.[114] Moreover, those who fled faced two dire dilemmas, with no time to resolve them: they often needed outside assistance in order to hide; and hiding often meant leaving behind loved ones. When Yehezkel Kesselbrener was warned by a Polish communist friend of the impending liquidation of the Ryki ghetto, he was able to flee on the eve of the May 6 deportation. However, he left behind his wife and six children.[115]

Of course, once having fled, their lives were still very insecure. When Yitzhak Leibusz Perec was warned by Hrubieszów Judenrat head Joel Brand of the impending deportation, he fled with his wife to Warsaw, only to face deportations there later. Mischa Stahlhammer fled from Kraśnik to a nearby forced-labor camp, hardly a safe place, when the ghetto liquidation began.[116] Ahuva Shamai Grossfeld fled Hrubieszów on the eve of the first deportation in June 1942, assumed a Polish identity, and ended up as a Polish forced-laborer in Germany. But she lived constantly in fear of discovery, amidst the suspicions of some of her fellow forced-laborers.[117]

News of the deportations from the Warsaw ghetto reached the remaining Jews in Lublin almost immediately. Lublin Jews lined up at the Judenrat telephone to call their loved ones in Warsaw, only to discover, much to their dismay, that the Jews in Warsaw were going to the deportation trains apparently oblivious of the fate that awaited

114 "Hrubieszów – spichrz Polski," June 30, 1942, YVA, M.10.AR.1/814; Avraham and Shaindl Goldfarb testimony, O.3/2140; Ahuva Shamai Grossfeld testimony, O.3/3135; Yitzhak Leibusz Perec testimony, O.3/4328.

115 Yehezkel Kesselbrener testimony, YVA, O.3/2089.

116 Yitzhak Leibusz Perec testimony, YVA, O.3/4238; Mischa Stahlhammer testimony, O.3/4312.

117 Ahuva Shamai-Grossfeld testimony, YVA, O.3/3135.

them. Ida Glikstein reports that when one Jewish policeman urged his brother to hide their mother, the brother responded that the mother was safe, since she had a work card.[118]

In general, the Judenräte in the Lublin District seem to have been helpless in passing on information or warnings, or in finding ways to save significant parts of their communities. Thus, Garfinkel in Zamość complied with German orders on April 11, and afterward, without warning the Jews. Joel Brand in Hrubieszów succeeded in warning individuals, but found no way to save the entire community – nor did he warn the community. In Lublin, the remnant Judenrat of the last seven months of the ghetto's existence was debilitated by the early deportations, locked behind a fence in Majdan Tatarski, and riddled with dubious personalities imposed on it by the SS. Nevertheless some members of the Lublin Judenrat succeeded in expanding the number of Jews permitted to live in the remnant ghetto and apparently in smuggling "illegal" Jews into the ghetto and legalizing them in the eyes of the Nazis. The original allotment of 3,000 "*J-Ausweise*" was eventually expanded to more than 4,500 through the Judenrat's cajoling in April, May, and June 1942. Moreover, in June and July, the Judenrat distributed at least 130 such passes that had belonged to Jews who had died to Jews who had been living in Majdan Tatarski secretly.[119]

As the summer wore on and further information about the murder of the Jews spread more widely across the GG, there were some places where proportionally larger numbers of Jews hid or tried to escape, even if they were unsure of their fate. In Bełżyce, for example, many of the Polish Jews prepared hiding places in 1942, while the German Jews did not. The Polish Jews also set up a guard system on the Lublin road to warn of the approach of the SS. Yet for many these precautions were taken with no understanding of the

118 *Dos Buch*, p. 404; *Encyclopedia of the Jewish Diaspora, Lublin*, p. 711.

119 See requests from the Judenrat to the SS for additional *Ausweise*, May 5–11, 1942, in WAPL, RZ 159, pp. 17–110; handwritten list, dated June 12, 1942, of 130 names of people who received the *Ausweise* of people who had died or been killed, ibid., pp. 111–120; the September 1942 list of 4,641 Jews in Lublin who had received *Ausweise*, WAPL, RZ 164 (copies in USHMMA, RG-15.101M).

death camps. When two Warsaw Jews who had just escaped from a death camp arrived in the town and described the gassing in 1942, this was the first news about death camps for many. The SS caught these fugitives and shot and wounded them, but the refugee doctor, Erich Mossbach, saved their lives.

The pattern of the deportation operation was the same as had been established by the Germans in the spring months. The round-up was accompanied by much shooting, both as part of the round-up and as part of an organized shooting operation. There were mounds of prone bodies at the Jewish cemetery – the living and the dead intermingled. The hospital patients were shot in the head in their beds. As elsewhere, the survivors vividly recall the murderers' attitude toward the murder: "These people found pleasure in tormenting their little victims [the children] in the most bestial manner and worked out special methods to prolong a single murder for hours."[120]

Jews' responses to round-ups from late summer 1942 to the end of the year were much the same as earlier, except for the attempts to hide or flee. Their dilemmas and difficulties also remained much the same. Yisrael Schleien escaped ghettos and labor camps several times – breaking away from one deportation was not enough. He and his father were among the several hundred Jews selected for labor in July 1942 in Józefów prior to the shootings by Reserve Police Battalion 101. They were taken to the Lipowa 7 camp in Lublin. Two months later they were marched to Piaski; many of the Jews were shot on the way. Schleien and his father fled back to Józefów after one day in Piaski, but they were captured by Germans near Żółkiewka during a German hunt for partisans. All escaped Jews who were captured were shot, including Schleien's father. Schleien escaped again, but was caught, identified as a Jew, beaten senseless, and taken to Żółkiewka. When the Żółkiewka Jews were ordered to go to Izbica, Schleien fled again, this time to Turobin. From there he went to Izbica on his own and joined a group of Jewish forced-laborers. From there he fled again to Józefów, and then fled from

120 See the following testimonies in YVA: Erich Mossbach, O.33/2149; Vera Mossbach Beckhard, O.33/2426; Manfred Heyman, O.2/794.

there to join the partisans, where he barely escaped capture several times. It took five escapes for him to reach the precarious safety of the partisans in the forests.[121]

In Łuków, rumors spread on Saturday, October 3, in the evening, at the beginning of the *Simhat Torah* holiday, that sixty freight cars were waiting for the 10,000 Jews there. By this time most of the Jews knew what this meant; they also knew about Treblinka and its purpose. They prepared bunkers and assumed correctly that the deportation would not take place on Sunday. On Monday, October 5, the Jewish quarter was surrounded by German and Polish police, Ukrainian Hiwis, and SS men; the bulk of the German forces came from Reserve Police Battalion 101. The fact that many of the Jews had gone into hiding slowed down the operation, and the selection began only at 10:00 A.M. Still, mass hiding, like in Lublin and Bełżyce, proved only a small nuisance to the Germans, and 7,000 Jews were deported to Treblinka. On Thursday, October 8, the Germans announced via the Judenrat that all the remaining Jews, including those in hiding, should report to the Judenrat to receive new work stamps. Two thousand reported and were taken by Germans and Ukrainians to Treblinka.

A series of round-ups took place during the following weeks, and a young man named Finkelstein (first name not known) was taken at 4:00 A.M. on November 8, and loaded onto the last train from Łuków to Treblinka. Some of the younger people on the train broke the door of their freight wagon, and hundreds escaped, including Finkelstein. Many of the escapees were caught by local villagers, returned to Łuków, and shot by the Germans in the Jewish cemetery between November 8 and 11 by men from Battalion 101.

A twenty-man firing squad shot twenty Jews at a time, one-on-one. The Schupo man would stand between the victim's legs, put the rifle to the victim's head, and shoot. The first shot only singed Finkelstein's head. He was shot again, through the arm and neck, but not killed. After the Germans left, Poles came to loot the bodies. Finkelstein fled to a Polish friend and from there he made it to

121 Yisrael Schleien testimony, YVA, M.49.E/105.

Warsaw in two weeks to join his brother and two sisters.[122] In his case hiding and escape made a difference, at least temporarily, but for the large majority of the Jews in Łuków, hiding and attempted escape were futile. Indeed, for all the Jews in general, as we have seen, receiving information about the murder of the Jews might or might not have affected their reactions or preparations. In any event, the fates of the communities remained the same with or without reliable information.

In Lublin itself, even after most of the Jews of Lublin had been murdered and the remaining Jews learned about the deportations from Warsaw, their reactions to the subsequent murder operations in Lublin on September 2, October 22, and November 9, were largely the same as they had been in March and April. It was more difficult to hide among the fenced-in barracks of Majdan Tatarski or to escape from there than it had been in the original Lublin ghetto. Moreover, contacts with Poles were more difficult to maintain from the Jews' physical isolation in Majdan Tatarski, which made preparing a hiding place among Poles even more difficult than it had been. The result was that few could escape Majdan Tatarski – although some did succeed in doing so – and there was no possibility of physically resisting the Germans. Moreover, in each community in the district, the small group of Jews that had been left behind as forced-laborers sometimes came to the collective belief that they, at least, would be allowed to live as long as they were working for the Germans.

Amidst the horror, anxiety, and despair, there seems also to have been a glimmer of hope, at least among some of them. In Lublin one reflection of this was the production of Jewish calendars for the New Year 5703 (1942–1943), apparently at the initiative of Rabbi Talmud.[123] Preparing a calendar with the dates and candle-lighting times for the Sabbaths and holidays is a natural Jewish

122 Testimony of Finkelstein, together with his sister, "The Destruction of Łuków" (Yiddish), YVA, M.10.AR.2/306, late November 1942; Browning, *Ordinary Men*, pp. 110–112.

123 WAPL, RZ 32 (copy in USHMMA, RG 15.101M), contains ten such calendars, most handwritten by Jews in the ghetto, apparently by Rabbi Zvi Elimelech Talmud, whose signature appears on some. See also Symcha Turkeltaub testimony, *Encyclopedia of the Jewish Diaspora, Lublin*, p. 737.

activity, and perhaps reflected in part the Jews' efforts to cling to their humanity. It also reflects hope in living to see the coming year. Yet if we follow Rabbi Talmud's own thinking, we can see that he lived in deep despair and hopelessness. In letters written to Rabbi Haim Arieh Berglas on July 28 and in early October 1942, Talmud related the deaths of nearly everyone important to him, both in Lublin and elsewhere. He knew of the deportations from Warsaw to Treblinka as they were taking place. He despaired of the God who had unleashed His wrath on European Jewry: "it is difficult for me, I cannot accept under any circumstances the notion that we are all guilty, all sinners to such an extent that a deluge of blood and fire and belching smoke should wash us away in wrathful waters." However, he also reported that High Holiday services in Majdan Tatarski had been held without incident and were attended diligently even by the secular Jews.[124]

All was lost – "there is not even a spark of hope to survive." God was inexplicably killing off His people, but the remaining Jews of Lublin were attending holiday services and preparing Jewish calendars for the coming year. Less than two months into that new Jewish year, the remnants of the Jewish community of Lublin were gone.

124 Letter from Rabbi Zvi Elimelech Talmud to Rabbi Haim Arieh Berglas, ca. early October 1942, following the *Shemini Azeret* holiday, WAPL, ibid., (copy in USHMMA, RG-15.101M) See also Talmud's letter to an unnamed correspondent (n.d.), and his letter of the third day of *Parshat Ekev* 5742 (July 28, 1942) to Rabbi Haim Arieh Berglas, ibid.; and Symcha Turkeltaub's testimony, *Encyclopedia of the Jewish Diaspora, Lublin*, p. 737.

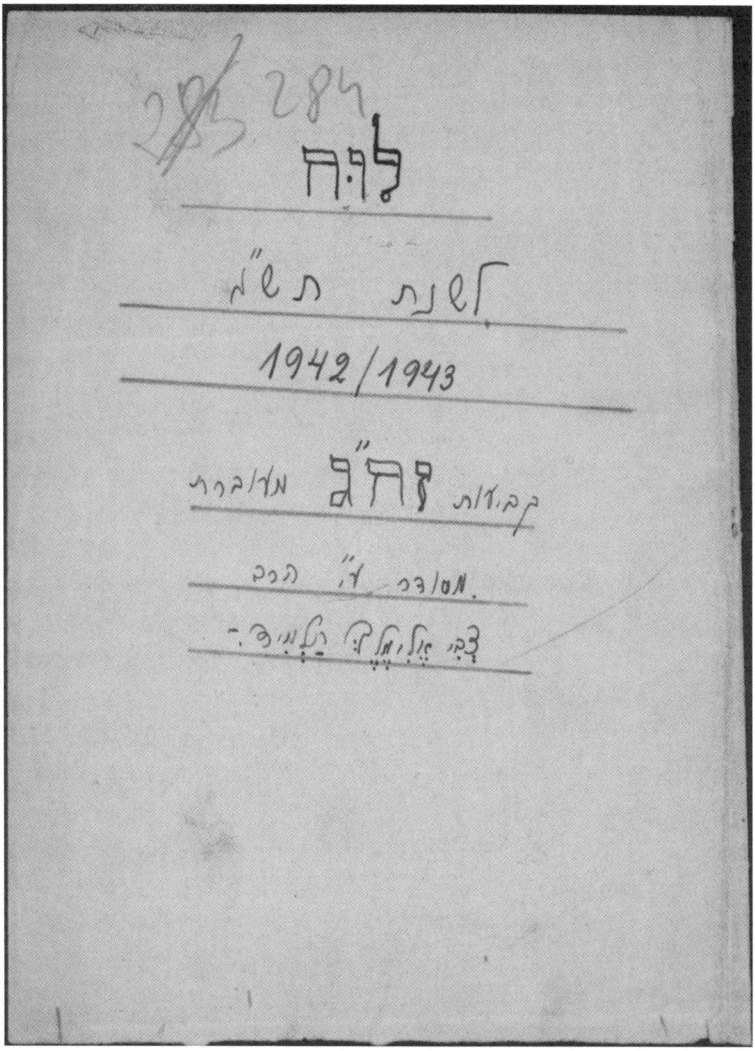

Cover of handwritten calendar for the year 5703 (1942/43), by Rabbi Zvi Elimelech Talmud, WAPL, RZ 32

Courtesy of Archiwum Państwowe w Lublinie

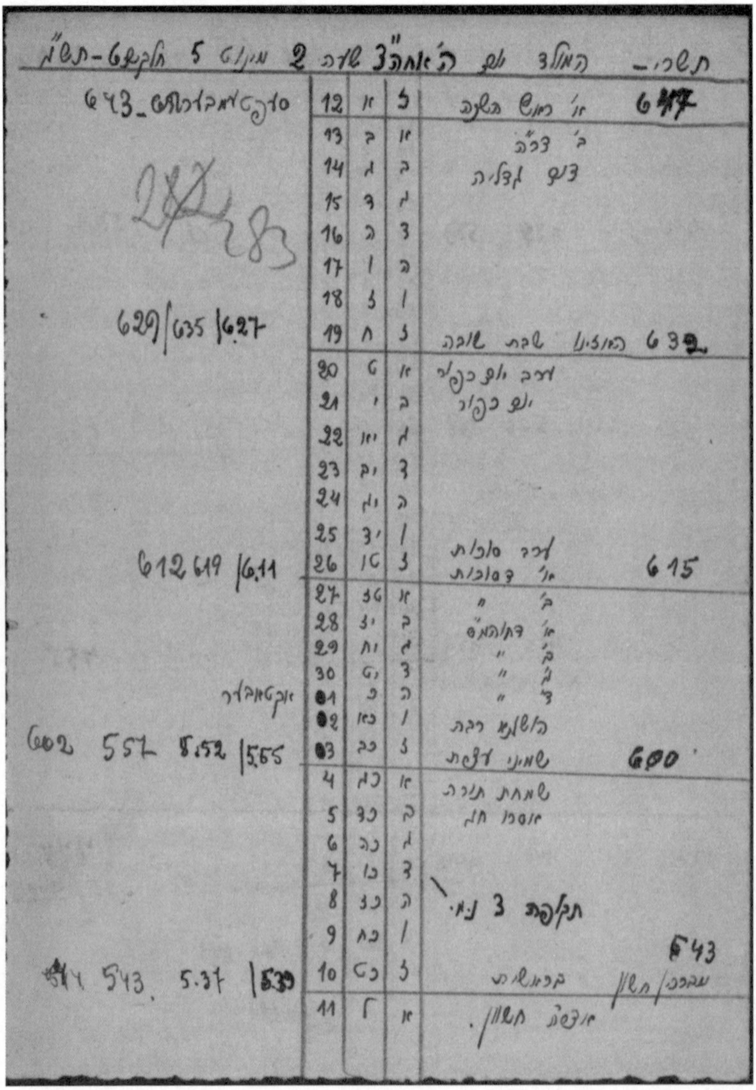

First page of handwritten calendar for the year 5703 (1942/43), by Rabbi Zvi Elimelech Talmud, WAPL, RZ 32

Courtesy of Archiwum Państwowe w Lublinie

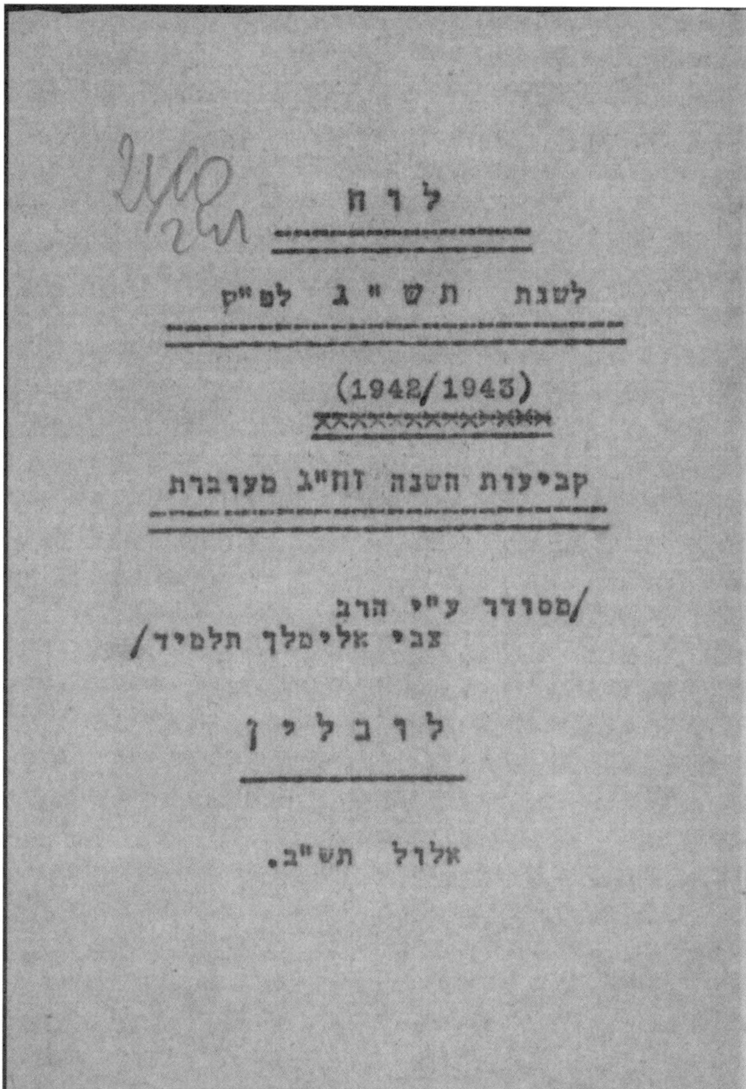
לוח

לשנת תש"ג לפ"ק

(1942/1943)

קביעות השנה זח"ג מעוברת

/מסודר ע"י הרב
צבי אלימלך תלמיד/

לובלין

אלול תש"ב.

Cover of printed calendar for the year 5703 (1942/43), by Rabbi Zvi Elimelech Talmud, WAPL, RZ 32

Courtesy of Archiwum Państwowe w Lublinie

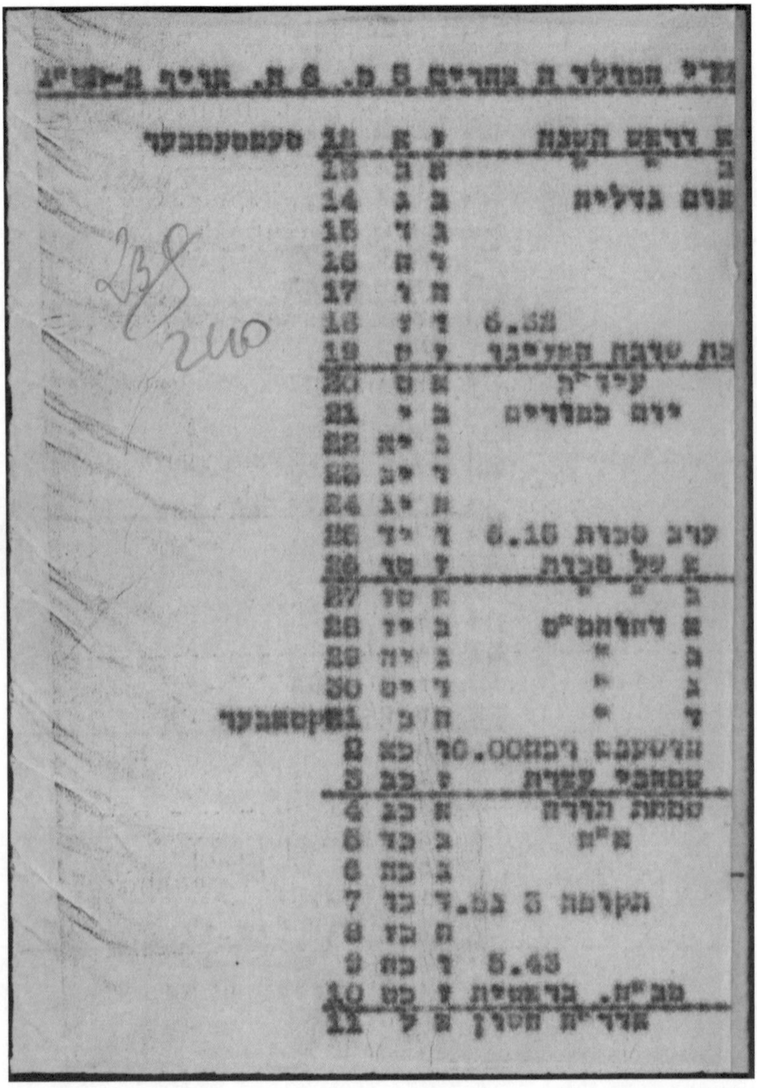

First page of printed calendar for the year 5703 (1942/43), by Rabbi Zvi Elimelech Talmud, WAPL, RZ 32

Courtesy of Archiwum Państwowe w Lublinie

Chapter 8

Working for Their Lives: The Last Jews in the Lublin District, 1942–1944

On Friday evening, November 6, 1942, at 6:00 P.M., when the 600 Jewish prisoners of the Janiszów forced-labor camp near Annopol-Rachów were already lying down in their barracks, eighteen partisans, most of them Jews, burst into the camp calling out "*Yidn, ratevet zikh*!" ("Jews, save yourselves!").[1] The partisans were led by Yehoshua Pintel, a former prisoner and Jewish policeman in Janiszów, who had escaped several weeks earlier, vowing revenge

1 The story of the liberation of the Janiszów camp is based on the following sources: P. Kristal, YVA, M.1.E/571; Hillel Borensztajn testimony, M.1.E/595; Eli Fiszman testimonies, M.1.E/714 and 715; Yaakov Farber testimony, M.1.E/716; Freiberg, *Darkness Covered the Earth*, pp. 107–113; *The Rachów/Annopol Book: Testimonies and Memoirs* (Hebrew and Yiddish) (Tel Aviv: Rachów Annopol Immigrants' Association, 1978), testimonies of B. Kleinman and Avrahamcze and Manis Brafman; conversation with Rabbi Eli Fishman (Freehold, New Jersey), August 2, 2002; Eli Fishman interview, YVA, O.93 (VHA)/14967; Majer Rozenblatt interview, O.93 (VHA)/5113; Hillel Borenstein interview, O.93 (VHA)/6998; Benny Kleiman interview, O.93 (VHA)/477; "Erfahrungs-Bericht über den Einsatz vom 1.11. – 8.11.42 in Kreis von Krasnik," WAPL, KDGend 276 (copy in USHMMA, RG 15.011M, microfilm reel 21, file 276); KdO Galicia, Hans Heitzinger, summary of KdO Lublin report on the Annopol escape, circulated to police in Galicia, November 13, 1942, USHMMA, RG 11.001, microfilm reel 82, Fond 1323, Opis 2, Folder 292b. I thank the late Professor Raul Hilberg for bringing this last KdO document to my attention. See also Krakowski, *War of the Doomed*, pp. 86–88.

on the vicious camp commandant, Peter Ignor, and his henchmen. As they stormed the camp, the partisans shot the non-Jewish guards and forced Ignor to hand over weapons, gold, and other valuables. Then they dragged him to the camp square, called on the inmates to take revenge, and killed him. On orders from their parent organization, the Gwardia Ludowa,[2] the partisans took only ten to fifteen prisoners with them to the forest, together with two horse-drawn wagons laden with supplies taken from the camp's storage rooms. As they left the camp at 8:30 P.M., they urged the remaining Jews to flee. Nearly 600 people were left standing there, unguarded, "free," and near a forest. How did they respond to their sudden liberation?

The Jewish prisoners reacted quickly. Local Jews who knew the area prepared to flee to Polish friends and acquaintances. Others began taking supplies from the storerooms to sustain themselves over the next days. It is not clear exactly how many Jews fled and how many remained,[3] but all the sources agree that all those who escaped, including the Jewish-led partisans themselves, were killed within a few months – most of them within days. They were hunted down by German police, by SS, and by local Poles. When local Poles found them, they either killed them or turned them over to the Germans.[4]

People fled in panic in the middle of the night, but many did not know where to go or what to do. Those prisoners who did not flee the camp were mostly non-local Jews. Finding themselves alone and unguarded in the camp, yet still trapped by their surroundings,

2 The Gwardia Ludowa was the communist-led Polish partisan movement that began operations in the spring of 1942. For a succinct overview of the Polish partisan movement, the Gwardia Ludowa, and Jewish relations with these groups, see Krakowski, ibid., pp. 3–25 *passim*, pp. 84–88. It is not clear who the camp guards were. The KdO report cited in note 1 indicates that there was one Polish guard, whereas the survivor testimonies differ regarding the identity (German or Polish) and number of guards, but most indicate that there were at least two. All agree that Jewish prisoners shared in the guarding.

3 Some sources refer to as few as 100–133 who fled, while others refer to as few as 100 who remained, or as many as a majority of the inmates.

4 Testimonies of Hillel Borensztajn, YVA, M.1.E/595, Eli Fiszman, M.1.E/714 and 715; B. Kleinman and Avraham and Manis Brafman, in *Rachów/Annopol Book*.

they decided to report the incident to the nearest police station, at Kosin, hoping for the best. The delegation elected to go to the police, led by the German-speaking Dr. Gross, was told to return to the camp and wait there. The Kosin gendarmerie post reported the incident to its superiors in Kraśnik shortly after midnight on November 7. Meanwhile, during the night a number of escapees also returned to the camp, bringing the number of prisoners there to approximately 160.

Some Jews tried to hide in other forced-labor camps. Between twenty and thirty-five arrived early on the morning of November 7, at the Gościeradów camp in the hope that the 100 Jewish forced-laborers there would be able to hide them. But those Jews had nowhere to conceal such a large increase of the camp prisoner population, so the Janiszów escapees turned to the sanctuary of the forest.

That same morning, at 7:00 A.M., a unit of SS men, accompanied by Polish firefighters and Ukrainian auxiliaries, surrounded Janiszów. They took the roll in the afternoon and then marched the Jews to Annopol. Whoever stumbled along the way was shot and his body loaded onto a cart. Some fifty Jews were killed, and the remaining Jews were loaded onto freight cars at Annopol and sent to Budzyń.

Among those who fled Janiszów that night was Leibl Muzykant, who, together with some thirty other people, hid in an underground bunker in the woods. One night Muzykant left on an errand for the group. When he returned the next morning, he found them all dead, stripped, and hacked to pieces. Based on the crude and seemingly uncalculated method of murder, he concluded that his comrades had been killed by local Poles. With nowhere to go, he made his way to the Budzyń forced-labor camp and turned himself in there, finding that the other Janiszów survivors were there as well. In the end Muzykant survived — but not because he escaped and became a partisan fighting in the forests, but because he gave himself up at a Nazi forced-labor camp and worked in the hope of surviving.[5]

5 Eli Fiszman testimony, YVA, M.1.E/714; Freiberg, *Darkness Covered the Earth*, pp. 104–105.

As one survivor commented, reflecting on the arrival in Budzyń of two other Janiszów escapees, "In their eyes we were free and they were imprisoned."[6]

Jewish existence at this time was extremely precarious, and the outcome of any action Jews might take in an effort to survive was completely unpredictable. Thus, in this case the 600 Jewish forced laborers in Janiszów reacted in one way or another, but the handful who survived were the ones who stayed, not the ones who tried to join the partisans.

The Jews After the Deportations

When the massive wave of deportations in the Lublin District ended in mid-December 1942, the remaining Jews found themselves in one of three types of circumstances: as forced-laborers, in hiding, or as partisans. According to German records, there were then approximately 20,000 forced-laborers in the district.[7] The year following the escape from Janiszów was marked by a steady increase in the number of Jews in the forced-labor camps alongside a consistent German hunt for those in hiding and in the forests.

The main influx of forced-laborers was brought in by the SS and German industrialists from the Warsaw ghetto, and, by the summer of 1943, there were more than 50,000 Jewish forced-laborers in the district. Meanwhile, whereas increasing numbers of Jews – tens of thousands – fled deportations during the summer and autumn of 1942, the number of partisans and Jews in hiding actually decreased during the following months, in 1943. The Germans, with local assistance, constantly hunted, captured and killed Jews.[8]

6 Freiberg, ibid., p. 104.

7 See Richard Korherr's statistical report to Himmler, March 23, 1943, covering the progress of the "Final Solution" in 1942, Nuremberg Document NO-5194. The actual number in the forced-labor camps seems to have been several thousand higher. In addition, there were perhaps 9,000 in remnant ghettos in Włodawa (2,000), Piaski (2,000), Łuków (3–4,000), Międzyrzec (1,200), Łęczna (200), and Izbica (300).

8 This aspect of the "Final Solution" has not yet been thoroughly researched. For astute observations, see Pohl, *Judenpolitik*, pp. 148–152; Browning, *Ordinary*

This chapter will examine the forced-labor camps for Jews in the Lublin District from the summer/fall of 1942 to the summer of 1944. This was the largest group of Jews in the district during most of this period. Their chances for survival depended in part on German need, and in part on the greed of local German officials, particularly Globocnik and a number of his associates. The more Jews who were killed elsewhere, the more the utility of these Jews seemed to stand out in the eyes of their German overseers. And as long as there was personal benefit to be had by German officials (SS and other), a particular camp might continue to exist. Many of these last Jews recognized and, with some measure of success, tried to exploit this unusual niche in which they found themselves in order to survive. In a sense the longer they survived, the better their living conditions became, despite diminishing German resources and what might have been expected to be — and what they expected to be — an ever-increasing threat to their lives.

There were two main types of forced-labor camps in 1943–1944: those that worked for the Wehrmacht; and those that served the SS, at times to satisfy the avarice of local SS officials. The camps that worked for the German civilian industries also fit into these categories. These camps stemmed back to the beginning of Jewish forced labor in late 1939 and 1940.

The continued exploitation of Jewish labor in these camps, even after more than 90 percent of the district's Jews were dead, represented an element of continuity in Nazi policy. Of course, the fact that Jews were still alive as forced-laborers did not mean that the various Nazi authorities did not intend to kill them. Rather, it was

Men, pp. 127–149 and *passim*. There has been some research done in recent years on other places regarding local Poles' participation in these hunts, including those undertaken at their initiative. See, for example, Jan Grabowski, "Rural Society and the Jews in Hiding: Elders, Night Watches, Firefighters, Hostages and Manhunts," *Yad Vashem Studies*, 40:1 (2012), pp. 49–74; *idem*, *Hunt for the Jews: Betrayal and Murder in German-Occupied Poland* (Bloomington and Indianapolis: Indiana University Press, 2013); Barbara Engelking, *"Jest taki piękny słoneczny dzień... Losy Żydów szukających ratunku na wsi polskiej 1942–1945"* (Warsaw: Centrum Badań nad Zagłada Żydów, 2011); Alina Skibińska and Jakub Petelewicz, "The Participation of Poles in Crimes against Jews in the Świętokrzyskie Region," *Yad Vashem Studies*, 35:1 (2007), pp. 5–48.

a reflection of the adaptability of certain Nazi policies to changing circumstances. The camps created or significantly expanded in the summer and fall of 1942 contained the seeds of the distinction between camps that survived "Operation *Erntefest*" in November 1943, and those that did not. The camps that had the best chance of survival were those that served the Wehrmacht (e.g., Dęblin), were of personal importance to well-connected Germans (e.g., Budzyń), or were created for the personal gain of well-connected SS officers. Objectively, all of these factors were beyond the Jews' control. Still, Jewish inmates in these camps sometimes intuitively understood this reality and tried to exploit these circumstances in order to survive.

The two-year period dealt with in this chapter was varied and can be divided into four sub-periods: (1) the spring of 1942, when Globocnik laid the foundations for his economic empire; (2) summer-fall 1942, when Globocnik negotiated with other Germans regarding Jewish forced labor, and the first new or expanded camps began to be established; (3) 1943, until "Operation *Erntefest*," when the forced-labor camps experienced relative calm and stability; (4) November 1943 to July 1944, when the last Jews in the district continued to work in forced labor. The summer to autumn in 1942 and the *Erntefest* were the decisive turning points in this period: the former marked the expansion of forced labor; and the latter marked the ostensible end of Jewish forced labor in the Lublin District.

The spring to fall in 1942 was a period during which Jews tried increasingly to insinuate themselves into the forced-labor facilities. This was a reaction to the systematic spread of deportations across the district, encompassing *all* the Jews, and to bits of information about the fate of the deportees that reached those still alive. The desire of many Jews to become part of the forced-labor complex in the district paralleled efforts by Globocnik and others to preserve and even to increase the number of Jewish forced-laborers, whether for the good of the Reich or for their personal interests.

The network of forced-labor camps in the Lublin District during this two-year period included camps adapted from their previous function, such as the Lublin airfield camps, Lipowa 7, Majdanek,

Trawniki, Dorohucza, Krychów, the Zamek (castle) in Lublin, and the military camps in Dęblin-Irena and Biała-Podlaska. For all intents and purposes others were new camps, such as the camp at 27 Chopin Street in Lublin, Budzyń, Kraśnik, and Poniatowa.

During 1943, when there were more than twenty camps in the Lublin District and a number of large farms with Jewish laborers, these camps settled into a routine. In most cases the Jewish forced-laborers experienced improvement in their daily living conditions in comparison to 1942, and the security measures surrounding them were somewhat eased. The main exceptions to this were Budzyń, the camps in Lublin, and Majdanek. In the spring of 1943, there was a consolidation of camps in the district, and a large influx of forced-laborers came from the Warsaw ghetto. Several camps in the Lublin District were shut down, portions of their prisoners were shot, and the rest were brought to Budzyń, Trawniki, or Majdanek.

The watershed date for Jewish forced labor in the Lublin District was November 3–4, 1943, when, in the course of "Operation *Erntefest*," most of the Jewish laborers there (42–43,000) were murdered. Yet even after this operation, there were still ten camps with more than 10,000 Jews. Most of these Jews remained until the July 1944 German retreat, always conscious of the *Erntefest* operation and looking for ways to avoid the same fate.

Conditions in these camps varied. They ranged from the extremely harsh, Auschwitz-like conditions in Majdanek, to the brutal but slightly better conditions in Budzyń, to the relatively livable conditions in Dęblin, to the relatively "free" conditions in Kraśnik. The reasons for the differing conditions were complex and cannot be attributed solely to the responsible German authority. That is, the conditions were not always worst in SS-run camps. Kraśnik, which had perhaps the best living conditions for Jews, was run by the SSPF, including people who had been intimately involved in "Operation Reinhard." Nor can the identity of the German authority in a camp, or the camp's conditions, serve as definite indicators of the Jews' chances for survival in each place. In some cases there are more survivors proportionally from some of the harsher camps (e.g., Budzyń) than from some of the less harsh camps (e.g., Poniatowa).

Why were thousands of Jews left alive until well into 1944? What were their chances for survival, and why?

Organizing Jewish Forced Labor for the Post-"Reinhard" Period

The March-May selection of Jews in the Lublin District to be exploited for forced labor was a major step in the adaptation of Jewish forced labor to the post-"Operation Reinhard" period. Many of these laborers were retained in forced labor through 1943. Alongside the county chiefs' selection of forced-laborers, Globocnik worked quickly to set up his own labor camp system. Georg Wippern's Abteilung IV "*Werterfassung*" (securing valuables), in what was later called "Einsatzstab Reinhard," was Globocnik's vehicle for confiscating valuables and sorting the deported Jews' possessions. It was also the means for selling some of these possessions for a profit for Globocnik and his cohorts.[9]

Globocnik proceeded to set up five camps for sorting Jewish belongings, while expanding other camps in the Lublin District and entering into business arrangements with *SS-Obergruppenführer* Oswald Pohl, head of the WVHA (SS-Wirtschafts-Verwaltungshauptamt; the Economic-Administrative Main Office). Pohl had consolidated his control over SS economic enterprises between January and May 1942, combining the various economic branches of the SS, together with the Concentration Camps Inspectorate, to turn the WVHA into a formidable economic power. By the summer of 1942, Pohl's authority included control of forced labor and jurisdiction over the sorting, packaging, and distribution of the valuables of murdered Jews.[10] The two men

9 YVA, JM/1905, February 16, 1961, p. 30; Streibel verdict, YVA, TR.10/869, II:65–68, III:279; Michalsen verdict, TR.10/813, p. 83; Lerch and Pohl indictment, TR.10/736, p. 23; Birmes and Gollak indictment, TR.10/815, pp. 58–60.

10 See Pohl report to Himmler, April 30, 1942, NO-719; Pohl memo on the utilization of Jewish valuables and clothing obtained in "Operation Reinhard," April 2, 1942, NO-2714; Brandt to Pohl, August 12, 1942, NO-3192. On Pohl and the development of the WVHA, see Hilberg, *Destruction*, pp. 865–870 and

reached an agreement whereby the concentration and forced-labor camps in the Lublin District were formally brought under WVHA control. But Globocnik retained functional control by being appointed the manager (or equivalent to CEO) of these camps, with his loyal subordinates holding key positions within them. In many cases his men simply continued to function in their previous camp positions.

These arrangements included negotiations with German businessmen who were already exploiting Jewish labor. As a result of these arrangements and his actions in the summer and fall to put them into effect, Globocnik accrued economic power through the control of tens of thousands of Jewish forced-laborers. This augmented the power and influence that he already had as a result of the murder operations. Working Jews could help maintain his power and influence after there were no more Jews to kill.

Jews who worked in the sorting of Jewish valuables confiscated in "Operation Reinhard," or in most of the other forced-labor enterprises set up in the last part of 1942, received a temporary reprieve from murder. With regard to the sorting, this was true for Jews working at each deportation site, Jews in the death camps, and those in the special sorting camps that Globocnik set up in Lublin.

In the spring and summer of 1942, various German authorities in the district were endeavoring to retain a Jewish labor pool. The Wehrmacht was interested in seeing its laborers remain in its bases and camps. In order to further this goal, they were even willing in some cases to allow the Jews some measure of family life.

Globocnik sought to build an economic empire and to turn a profit, which, together with a desire for power, was his motivation to negotiate with Oswald Pohl. Pohl needed to ensure SS economic interests; German industrialists, especially in Warsaw, sought to retain their lucrative enterprises based on cheap Jewish labor; and Globocnik sought to bring Jewish forced-laborers to the Lublin District in order to expand his power base and make money.

Allen, *The Business of Genocide*, pp. 154–158. For a brief overview of Pohl's entry into the control of Jewish forced labor and Jewish belongings, see Hilberg, *Destruction*, pp. 610–611.

Globocnik was phenomenally successful in these negotiations. By June 1943, he controlled or had his hand in at least fifteen camps in the district, as well as in several outside the district and numerous farms with Jewish forced-laborers. In the Lublin District alone, he controlled more than 50,000 Jewish forced-laborers by that time.

Apparently he did not report all of these activities in 1942 to his immediate superior, Krüger. In the midst of the deportations, on October 28, Krüger ordered that all remaining Jews in the Lublin District be confined to eight ghettos: Łuków, Parczew, Międzyrzec, Włodawa, Końskowola, Piaski, Zaklików, and Izbica. This was apparently meant as a follow-up to Himmler's July 19 order to complete the murder of the Jews by December 31.[11] Yet circumstances on the ground were different. No Jews in any significant numbers remained in Parczew, Zaklików, or Izbica by mid-January 1943, while Jews were still employed as forced-laborers in Kraśnik, Chełm, and Lublin itself. And in addition to remnant ghettos, there were numerous labor camps and farms where Jews worked, as well as camps that served the Wehrmacht. In Jewish forced labor, as in other matters, Globocnik often operated independently of his boss.

The Sorting Camps

The first camp that Globocnik set up in this context was the sorting camp at 27 Chopin Street, which was a huge warehouse for Jewish valuables. Other camps that followed and also played an important role in sorting Jewish belongings were the camp at the old airfield in Lublin, Budzyń, Kraśnik, Poniatowa, and Trawniki.

The Chopin Street camp began operating almost as soon as the deportations began, and before Himmler issued any orders regarding the disposal of Jewish belongings and valuables. From the very beginning Globocnik used the camp to sell Jewish belongings

11 Krüger order regarding "Judenwohnbezirken" in the Warsaw and Lublin Districts, October 28, 1942, in *Faschismus*, pp. 342–345. See also *Eksterminacja*, pp. 311–313; Musial, *Zivilverwaltung*, pp. 280–281.

locally to interested Germans, and the camp continued to serve as a warehouse for this retail and wholesale trade for two years. The camp had no clear official name, as though reflecting its gray economic and legal position. The documents from the camp refer to "Hauptlager Chopina 27"; "Materiallager Chopinstrasse 27"; "Judenlagerdepot Chopenstrasse 27"; "Materiallager Reinhard" (or, alternatively, "Reinhardt"). Correspondence to the camp was addressed to "SSPF Lublin, Einsatz Reinhardt"; "SS-Standortverwaltung, Abt. IVa"; "SS-Bekleidungslager." Still, the camp's function was obvious to any German who wished to know.

It is not clear how many Jews worked there; it seems to have been several hundred. The camp officially sorted Jewish clothing for shipping to Germany, but in fact the Jewish forced-laborers sorted a wide variety of Jewish belongings, much of it for sale locally to Germans. The proceeds would be deposited in a special account ("Einsatz R") in Lublin, or privately pocketed by Globocnik and his associates.[12] The camp existed as long as there were Jewish belongings to sort and sell and Germans to buy them – at least through April 1944.

Orders came in consistently from early in the murder operation until the German retreat from the area. The early orders for Jewish goods were made before the norms of secrecy had taken hold among the Germans. Hence they often referred to the nature or origin of the commodities to be supplied – "*aus dem jüdischen Magazin*" (from the Jewish warehouse), or "*aus dem Judennachlass*" (from the Jewish estate).[13] Some of the orders had an official application, such as the SS Kosaken Division that outfitted its field kitchen from the Chopin Street warehouse. However, the bulk of the orders were for personal items. Those happy to take advantage of the windfall of Jewish loot represented a broad swath of German society in and outside the Lublin District: the Hitlerjugend, forced-labor camps,

12 Documents from the camp at Chopin St. 27, in Lublin, including many orders and receipts, can be found in YVA, O.53/68.

13 See, for example, the orders by *SS-Hauptscharführer* Emil Lösch, in "Sonderlager Lublin" (Majdanek), for a suitcase and alarm clock, August 25, 1942, and the Kraków SS and Police Court VI order for various supplies, September 17, 1942, ibid.

KdS personnel, party personnel, policemen, and more. For example, Major Wilhelm Trapp, commander of Reserve Police Battalion 101, ordered shirts, linens, a lady's coat (for his wife), and more before returning home to Germany in September 1943. Orders came from as far away as the Hegewald camp near Zhitomir (for women's clothing for the troops' wives).[14]

As the deportations progressed in April 1942, and as Globocnik and Pohl began to arrange their economic and forced-labor cooperation, other camps began to be set up. Jurisdictions over Jewish forced labor were also consolidated. By the summer of 1942, only Globocnik and Pohl, for the SS, and the Wehrmacht had jurisdiction over Jewish labor and forced-labor camps. The civilian authorities were pushed out of the picture.

Perhaps the major site for Jewish forced labor in the city of Lublin was at and around the old Lublin airfield, on Fabryczna Street, approximately 1–2 km. north of Majdanek. The remnant ghetto at Majdan Tatarski that existed from April 20 to November 9, 1942 was effectively part of this complex, and most of the Jews in the ghetto worked here. The old airfield camp was first created in July 1940, and more Jews were brought there in late summer 1941 to work in Wehrmacht-related supply depots. During 1942–1943, huge warehouses for Jewish belongings were created inside hangars, and Jews, mainly women, were put to work sorting, cleaning, folding, and packing. By late summer 1942, there were 3,200 female forced-laborers here from Majdan Tatarski and nearby towns. The numbers increased steadily, as Jews were brought in from many liquidated ghettos and from other camps. By mid-1943, the airfield camps held approximately 5,000 men and 5–6,000 women.

Conditions in these camps were very severe — they lacked running water, a sewer system, and lights. Experienced, brutal SS overseers, among them the infamous Hermine Braunsteiner (-Ryan), were brought in from Ravensbrück. Among the camps in this complex were the supply camps for the southern Russian front and for the HSSPF for southern Russia and the Caucasus (Nachbaulager Russland-Süd and the Hauptnachschublager des Höheren SS- und

14 YVA, O.53/68.

Polizeiführer Russland-Süd und Kaukasien). In addition, clothing mending workshops were under the authority of Victor Kremin, who is the only labor supervisor here whom the forced-laborers recall as having treated them relatively decently.[15]

The other major Jewish forced-labor installations in or adjacent to Lublin in this period included Majdanek, Lipowa 7, and the castle. Majdanek's Jewish labor force expanded as Jews were brought in from Slovakia and the Protectorate in the spring of 1942. Many of these Jews had died by the end of 1942, but the total number of forced-laborers there was usually above 10,000.[16] The Lipowa 7 POW camp's 3,000 prisoners continued to work until the camp's liquidation in "Operation *Erntefest*." The castle was the main German prison in Lublin (as it had been for more than a century of Russian rule), under KdS authority, with many policemen working there as well. More than 1,000 Jews performed a variety of maintenance and craft functions there. Many of them were still alive in July 1944, constituting the very last Jews officially in the city of Lublin. There were also dozens of Jews in Lublin performing service functions for various German authorities.

The summer of 1942 was an important turning point in the development of Jewish forced labor in the Lublin District. As the massive killing in the GG resumed in late July (August in the Lublin District) and progressed at a very rapid pace, Globocnik just as rapidly put into place the pieces of his major economic conglomerate. He entered into negotiations with Walter Többens and Fritz Schultz

15 Birmes and Gollak trial, YVA, TR.10/815, pp. 84–94, 102–103; testimony of Mendel Korn, YVA, O.3/2941. The Jews called the camp Plage Łaśkiewicz, based on the prewar Polish firms that occupied the site, T. Plage and T. Łaśkiewicz. Some called it "*Mörderlager*" (murder camp), while the Germans referred to it simply as "*Alter Flughafen*" (or "*Flugplatz*"), "*Bekleidungswerke*" (clothing workshops), or "*Grosses Judenarbeitslager*" (large Jewish labor camp). The placement in Lublin of a supply camp for the HSSPF of the southern zone of the USSR is odd, yet the camp was never moved to the area that it served. It operated until the end of 1943.

16 Tomasz Kranz, "Das Konzentrationslager Majdanek und die 'Aktion Reinhardt,'" in Bogdan Musial, ed., *"Aktion Reinhardt": Der Völkermord an den Juden im Generalgouvernement 1941–1944* (Osnabrück: Fibre Verlag, 2004), pp. 233–255. See also Schwindt, *Das Konzentrations- und Vernichtungslager Majdanek*, pp. 171–194 and 220–228 *passim*.

to move their textile factories from the Warsaw ghetto to camps in the Lublin District, while also setting out to take control of the main private industry employer of forced labor in the district — the Heinkel Werke at Budzyń.

Budzyń

Globocnik began to work on establishing a forced-labor camp in Budzyń (6 km. from Kraśnik) in the summer of 1942. The Heinkel Werke had opened an airplane repair factory there on the grounds of an old Polish factory earlier in 1942, with Jews from Kraśnik brought in daily to work.[17] Globocnik planned the airplane factory to be the largest, but not the sole employer, in what he hoped would

17 The story and analysis of Budzyń is based on the following sources in YVA: the Michalsen and Hantke indictment and verdict, TR.10/813; testimony of Abraham Dichter, O.2/213; Manfred Heymann, O.2/794; Hertha Heymann, O.2/323; Mendel Korn, O.3/2941; Zipora Nahir, O.3/10488; E. Sigarus, O.2/1093; Yerahmiel Kojfman, O.3/1499; Yehiel Gutwein, O.3/5004; Zvia Steif, O.3/5224; Wladyslaw Friedhelm, O.33/637; Erich Mossbach, O.33/2149; Yashayahu Wajsfisz, M.1.E/649; Eli Fiszman, M.1.E/714; Hirsz Bojm, M.1.E/1608; Froim Krasnobrod, M.1.E/1715; Abram Erenberg, M.1.E/1755; Nahman Kranc, M.1.E/2654; Ber Twardagóra, M.49.E/1053 and 1195; Israel Hener, TR.10/1291; Israel Wein, ibid.; Chaskiel Bratman, TR.11/01113; Josef Korn, ibid.; Jakob Zukert, ibid.; Zeev Beck, ibid.; Jakob Ender, ibid.; Mosze Davidson, ibid.; Hermann Pinkus, ibid.; Arie Leib Rosenbusch, ibid.; Aharon Himelblau, ibid.; Jehoszua Szarason, ibid.; Otto Hantke, TR.10/1291. In addition, see the following: Freiberg, *Darkness Covered the Earth*, pp. 141–221; Morris Wyszogrod, *A Brush with Death* (Albany: State University of New York Press, 1999), pp. 115–180; Henry Orenstein, *I Shall Live*, pp. 134–166; Yehoshua Laks, *I Was There* (Hebrew) (Bnai Brak: Privately published, 1993), pp. 209–233; David Wdowinski testimony, June 6, 1961, *The Trial of Adolf Eichmann: Record of the Proceedings in the District Court of Jerusalem*, vol. 3 (Jerusalem: Ministry of Justice, 1993), pp. 1232–1237; *Sefer Kraśnik* , testimonies of Haim Meir Beck, pp. 225–232; Daniel Freiberg, pp. 233–292; Yaakov Arieh Ender, pp. 332–340 and 375–377; Motl Brafman, pp. 357–362; Jaakov Zukert, pp. 368–369; Nisan Zalc, pp. 371–373; Yehezkel Brotman, pp. 373–375; Hersz Zukerman, pp. 379–380; Yitzhak Lamhut, pp. 393–395; Yehoshua Hochrad, pp. 405–406; Yitzhak Kaftan, p. 423; Avraham Lichter, pp. 426–427, and "The Jews of Kraśnik in the Years of the Hitlerite Occupation" (Yiddish), pp. 308–314; Cipora Hurwitz, *Forbidden Strawberries* (New Rochelle, NY: Multi Educator, 2010), pp. 111–124; Wojciech Lenarczyk, "Obóz pracy przymusowej w Budzyniu (1942–1944)," in *idem* and Libionka,

be a lucrative and influential venture. He sent Otto Hantke there in September (after Hantke had completed his role in the Warsaw ghetto deportations) to plan and set up the camp. Hantke brought in Jewish POWs from the Lipowa 7 camp, where he had served prior to the Warsaw deportations, and from Końskowola, and appointed the POW Juliusz Gelbart to be the *Lagerälteste*. He then went to Kraśnik, selected craftsmen and laborers, and marched them to Budzyń to begin setting up a permanent camp there.

The Budzyń regime under Hantke was both "liberal" in some ways and brutal in others. On their first day at Budzyń, a number of Jews received permission to return to Kraśnik to get clothing and some personal effects. They were to spend the night in their homes in Kraśnik and return to Budzyń the next morning. Hantke took them to Kraśnik in a truck, and, as they arrived, one of the young men fell off the truck and was injured. Hantke had him carried to the woods and shot. Several days after Budzyń was erected, they were brought to the bathhouse in Kraśnik for delousing. During the liquidation of the Kraśnik community, Hantke returned to select additional forced-laborers. He sent approximately 100 women to the Lublin airfield camps and marched ninety-eight men to Budzyń. During the march a Ukrainian guard forced Baruch Krumholz to surrender his boots and exchange them for the Ukrainian's. The boots were too small for Krumholz, so he carried them in his hand, but had difficulty walking. Hantke pulled him out of line and shot him.[18] The "liberal" aspect of Hantke's treatment was expressed in a last night at home and a bath, but he would expend no energy to keep alive anyone who disrupted the smooth flow of affairs even in the slightest way.

Israel Hener was part of the first group of craftsmen that Hantke chose for Budzyń. Several weeks later, apparently in early December 1942, he asked the German guard Stoschik[19] to take him to Kraśnik

eds. *Erntefest*, pp. 261–286. Specific information and quotations will be cited from the relevant source.

18 See the testimonies of Israel Hener, Israel Wein, Chaskiel Brotman, Jacob Zukert, Jacob Arie Ender, Hermann Pinkus, and Arie Leib Rosenbusch, TR.10/1291; Ender in *Sefer Kraśnik*, p. 335.

19 The reference might be to *SS-Oberscharführer* Heinrich Stoschek, who briefly

to see his wife and four children. They were being held in a cellar together with other Jews who had been caught hiding. Stoschik agreed but refused Hener's subsequent request to take his oldest son (seven years old) back to Budzyń. He contended that *SS-Hauptscharführer* Reinhold Feiks – a Sudeten German who had meanwhile succeeded Hantke as Budzyń commandant – would discover them and shoot both father and son. Shortly afterward Hener's wife and children were shot in the Kraśnik Jewish cemetery along with most of the other Jews in the cellar.[20] Stoschik, who is remembered by Budzyń survivors as a murderer, here had been "kind." Not only did he take Hener to see his family, but he also ostensibly saved Hener's life, although Hener's family was taken out and shot.

In addition to the major waves of Jews brought to Budzyń by Hantke and then by Feiks, other Jews came to the camp individually or in small groups. Zeev Beck, who worked in the Gendarmerie offices in Kraśnik in the autumn of 1942, feared that the Ukrainian guard Georgi sought to kill him. Beck fled and sneaked into Budzyń, which seemed safer at the time.[21]

The Jewish forced-laborers constructed six wooden horse-stall-type barracks, like those at Majdanek, Międzyrzec, and other camps, plus a kitchen barrack and a toilet barrack. By the end of 1942, there were nearly 1,000 Jews in the camp, including 400 Polish Jewish POWs. The Jews' living compound was surrounded by a barbed-wire fence and four watchtowers guarded by Ukrainians trained at Trawniki. Over the gate a sign read: "*Jedem Das Seine*" ("to each his own").

Small numbers of Jews were brought to Budzyń during the following months, followed by large numbers from Warsaw and other places in the spring of 1943. By the summer of 1943, the number of Jewish forced-laborers had reached 3,000. The places that became feeder camps for Budzyń, in addition to the Warsaw

succeeded Hantke as commandant until Feiks arrived. It is possible that Stoschek remained in the camp as a subordinate commander after Feiks arrived.

20 Israel Hener testimony, ibid. On the shooting of the Jews held in the cellar in Kraśnik, apparently in early December 1942, see also the testimonies of Cipora Berger, Chaja Rotenberg Goldbaum, Asher Mandelblatt, YVA, TR.11/01113.

21 Zeev (Wolf) Beck testimony, YVA, TR.10/1291.

ghetto, included Gościeradów, Bełżyce, Krychów, and Hrubieszów. Each served as a forced-labor installation in its own right in the late months of 1942 and in 1943, prior to the Jews' transfer to Budzyń. Conditions varied in these places but were generally much better than in Budzyń. The Jews in these forced-labor sites lived in what was akin to the eye of a hurricane – a momentary relative calm following and preceding the worst of a terrible tempest.

Gościeradów. On October 15, 1942, when the Annopol-Rachów Jewish community was being liquidated, *SS-Obersturmführer* Lazarczyk and Winkler, the labor foreman for the Beikler Co., were permitted to spare their forced-laborers. One hundred men were chosen and taken to Gościeradów. Beikler chose sixty for labor in rock quarries and underground phosphorous mines in the area, and Lazarczyk chose forty for work on his nearby farmstead. Late the next morning these men saw their wives, children, and parents walking unguarded toward Kraśnik, from whence they were deported to Bełżec. That night two sixteen-year-old boys, Yitzhak Mojrenfeld and Shaulik from Popów, sneaked into the camp and asked to be taken in by the inmates. Despite the prisoners' fears that the two youths would be discovered and thereby endanger the entire group, they voted to let them stay. Both boys survived.

As at Budzyń under Hantke, the Jewish forced-laborers at Gościeradów were allowed to return home shortly after their arrival at the camp to get more clothing. Many found their homes had already been ransacked.

The Gościeradów Jews slept in one large shack on two-tiered bunks. Some recall the Jewish camp officials – Yaakov Apter, head of the Lagerrat; Yisrael Meleng, his deputy for labor; Yitzhak Hornfeld, in charge of camp administration; and Asher, the medic – as corrupt and interested only in money. For example, they had the camp's tailor and shoemaker workshop concentrate on jobs for local Poles rather than for the Jews, so that they could split handsome fees. The camp was unguarded, and the Jews could leave and return more or less freely, and the inmates could buy supplies in the adjacent, affluent village of Gościeradów. The Beikler Co. supervisors gave their laborers three meals a day, and generally did not interfere with the Jews' internal life in the camp. Moreover, the Jews in the camp were able to send food to other Jews hiding with farmers in the area. They also learned from local farmers and from Jews in the forests, who periodically sent messengers to the camp, that Jews hiding in the forests were being killed by Polish partisans and by local farmers. In contrast to the sufficient food and freedom of movement, the sanitary conditions in the camp were poor — no latrines and no changes of clothing. Still, there were no serious illnesses. There were no escapes from Gościeradów; sufficient food and fear of the forests made the camp seem safer than the alternative.[22]

Bełżyce had become a forced-labor camp following the spring 1942 deportations from the town. It was first under local German civilian supervision and then under Feiks's supervision on behalf of Globocnik. The number of Jews grew steadily from a few hundred to approximately 1,200 by early 1943, including women, children, and elderly. Dr. Erich Mossbach, a deportee from Stettin who ended up in Bełżyce in 1942, had hidden along with dozens of other Jews during the deportations. He then bribed the local German civilian authorities to allow him and the others in hiding with him to enter the camp. Many of the Jews worked at sorting the clothing and belongings of deported Jews from the area, while others worked in a stone quarry.[23]

Krychów was part of a complex of camps run by the Chełm county water works' director, Holzheimer. It was established in 1940, on

22 Eli Fiszman testimony, YVA, M.1.E/714; Hillel Borensztajn testimony, M.1.E/595; Eli Fishman interview, O.93 (VHA)/14967; Majer Rozenblatt interview, O.93 (VHA)/5113; Hillel Borenstein interview, O.93 (VHA)/6998; Benny Kleiman interview, O.93 (VHA)/477; Freiberg, *Darkness Covered the Earth*, pp. 104–113.

23 Mendel Korn testimony, YVA, O.3/2941; Erich Mossbach testimony, O.33/2149; Vera and Erich Mossbach testimony, O.33/2426; Marta Rubinsztajn testimony, M.1.E/205; Yeshayahu Wajsfisz testimony, M.1.E/649; Wladyslaw Friedhelm testimony, O.33/637; Manfred Heymann testimony, O.2/794; Freiberg, *Darkness Covered the Earth*, pp. 147–149; Yehezkel Brotman, *Sefer Kraśnik*, p. 374; Yitzhak Lamhut, ibid., p. 394. Similar to the cases of Jews sneaking into Budzyń for safety, Wajsfisz escaped from Majdanek in November 1942, and sneaked into Bełżyce. He then survived the liquidation of that camp and was sent to Budzyń.

the site of a Polish penal camp, for work at swamp drainage and river control. During the deportations from Rejowiec in 1942, Jews were sent to Krychów and the nearby camps – Hańsk, Luta, Osowa, Sajczyce, Sawin, and Ujazdów. By autumn there were 1,350 Jews in Krychów and more than 1,000 in the other camps – at least half of them deportees from Slovakia, Theresienstadt, and Germany. During the liquidation of Rejowiec, 105 men and fifty women working in swamp drainage were transferred to Krychów.

Conditions varied at these camps in the autumn of 1942. Whereas the 100 women at the Hańsk farm were relatively clean and well fed and usually not subject to beatings, the Jews at Krychów had meager rations (150 grams of bread daily, a thin cabbage-leaf soup, and black "coffee"), crowded conditions (200 per barrack; 1.2 sq. meters per person), and lived in filth, with no straw, no blankets, nothing to cover the dirt floor, and no washing accommodations. They developed swollen faces and feet from malnutrition, and many of them contracted typhus, dysentery, or both. Sixty of the 155 Jews brought to the camp from Rejowiec died by the end of the winter.

The work was difficult for them because of their weakened state. They had to work even when they were ill, with up to a 39-degree fever. Medications could be obtained only for large sums of money. Selections in these camps and consolidations of the camp populations reduced the Jews' numbers. On October 16, 1942, the elderly, weak, sick, and children were taken to Włodawa; four days later they were deported to Sobibór together with the local Jews.

After this deportation the inmates in the Ujazdów and Hańsk camps were brought to Krychów for the winter. On December 9, the prisoners at Krychów were informed of an imminent deportation, after which only 110 people would remain. Following the murder and contraction of the prisoner population, the conditions for the remaining prisoners improved. Their daily rations increased to 400–500 grams of bread and thick potato soup. They also received beds and washing accommodations. As a result, only three Jews died in the following months. The deputy camp commandant shot three others who were ill while the commandant was away.

In March 1943, the camp was expanded and the daily rations reduced again. In early 1943, more Polish Jews were brought to the camp, and in June the camps at Ossowa, Sawin, Sajczyce, and Luta were liquidated, many of the workers killed, and the survivors brought to Krychów. This further liquidation and consolidation reduced the number of prisoners in Krychów to 533. There were still approximately 115 in Hańsk (110 of them women). Unlike Gościeradów, there were repeated escape attempts from Krychów, especially by local Polish Jews. Surprisingly, the German reactions to these attempts mellowed with time. Whereas in 1942, escape attempts resulted in collective punishment, in 1943 only the escapees were punished.[24]

Hrubieszów. Similar to Bełżyce, the forced-labor camp in Hrubieszów was set up by the SS inside the town, on Jatkowa Street, following the June 10, 1942, deportation. Additional Jews were brought there during the liquidation of the ghetto in October. By the end of the year, there were 200 Jews in the camp and several dozen more hiding, including ten to fifteen children. In addition to those selected for the camp, others sneaked or bluffed their way in.

Josef Rechtszaft was deported from Hrubieszów in October. He knocked a hole in the cattle car together with forty other Jews and escaped. After hiding for two days, he returned to the town together with former Judenrat head Joel Brand and Joel Rabinowicz, telling the Germans the truth about their escape and adding that they had hidden gold and money. The ploy worked, and the Germans let them join the Jatkowa Street camp. Rechtschaft became the head of the burial detail.

24 "Facts Reported by a Jew Deported from Slovakia, Who Has Since Escaped and Returned," August 17, 1943, YVA, M.2/236 in English, and M.4/12 in Hebrew, on pp. 11–14 of the October-November 1943 Bulletin of the Rescue Committee of the Jewish Agency for Palestine; in German, "Tatsachenbericht eines aus der Slovakei deportierten und zurückgekehrten Juden," M.A., D.1.1266; Eli Fiszman testimony, YVA, M.1.E/714; Abraham Manes Citrin testimony, TR.11/02138; Freiberg, *Darkness Covered the Earth*, pp. 164, 177–178. For earlier background on Krychów, see, for example, Feiwel Kojfman testimony, YVA, M.10.AR.I/424. According to the Slovakian Jewish escapee, engineer Holzheimer, head of the water department in Chelm county, was in charge of all these camps, while his subordinates in the area were [Hugo] Raschendorf in Chelm, Johann Löffler in Krychów, Hilvert and Bajko in Ossowa, and Ondyk (a butcher) in Sawin.

Hannah Levi was the daughter of a laundry owner in Hrubieszów. She hid in a bunker together with her brother and thirty other people during the ghetto liquidation. Two Polish gendarmes discovered them a few weeks later, but one of them recognized her and let her and her brother go. With nowhere to turn, she and her brother decided to report to the Gestapo that evening. As they were walking, they saw Jews at Jatkowa Street. Joel Brand, now the *Judenälteste* in the camp, recognized them and took them in. When Gestapo man Johann Wagner heard that Hannah was the laundry man's daughter, he gave her his coat to wash. The next morning her entire work group of fifty people went out to work, only to be shot in the cemetery. Since she was left behind to finish the washing, she survived.

The Jews in Jatkowa sorted the belongings of the dead Jews and worked in various workshops for the Gestapo. Their difficult conditions improved when *SS-Untersturmführer* Adolf Waldner took over as Gestapo chief in January 1943, but, by June 1943, the Gestapo could find little work for the Jews to do.[25]

The Liquidation of the Budzyń Feeder Camps. Jews were transferred to Budzyń from Warsaw and the above camps in two periods: April-May 1943; and July 1943. These added more than 1,800 Jewish forced-laborers to the camp. Eight hundred were brought from Warsaw on April 29 and May 1, in the midst of the Warsaw ghetto uprising, and immediately became one of the prominent work forces in the camp.[26] In the other camps the prisoner population was generally reduced as

25 The story of Hrubieszów is based on: Orenstein, *I Shall Live*, pp. 105–137; Abraham Goldfarb testimonies, YVA, O.3/2140, TR.11/01121/V; Josef Rechtszaft testimony, TR.11/01121/V; Bencion Fink and Dawid Rottenberg testimonies, TR.11/01238; Dov Finger testimony, O.3/2780; Ruth Tatarko testimonies, O.3/7158, 7613; Hannah Levi, Jochewed Deutsch, Dora Ilani, Jakob Biskubicz, Arieh Perec testimonies, TR.11/01121/V; Gisela Perec testimony, O.3/4237; Yitzhak Perec testimony, O.3/4238; Zipora Nahir testimony, O.3/10488; Cipora Hurwitz testimonies, O.3/11783 and MA, A.296; Fajge Schechter testimony, YVA, M.49.E/22; *Pinkas Hrubieszów*, pp. 109–110; Hurwitz, *Forbidden Strawberries*, pp. 65–110.

26 Wyszogrod, *A Brush with Death*; Freiberg, *Darkness Covered the Earth*; David Wdowinski testimony, *The Eichmann Trial*, p. 1232; Yitzhak Lamhut, *Sefer Kraśnik*, p. 394; Yehoshua Hochrad, ibid., p. 405.

the Germans killed off part of the prisoners and consolidated the rest into one camp before they were sent on to Budzyń.

In the spring of 1943, the Gościeradów Jews were transferred to Lazarczyk's farm, and on April 29 Feiks came with a truck and took them to Budzyń. Seven escaped on the way.[27] Bełżyce was liquidated on May 8. Feiks and his Ukrainian adjutant Otto arrived in Bełżyce with a Ukrainian unit and ordered all the Jews out early in the morning. Three hundred men were sent to Poniatowa (17 kilometers west), and the Judenrat (which still existed) and Jewish police were taken to Budzyń (30 kilometers south). Other men were then ordered by Feiks to dig a large pit near the camp, at the synagogue, while the able-bodied men and some women were locked inside. Feiks ordered the remaining 300–400 women, children, and weaker men to undress, and his men shot them in groups of ten into the pit. All the elderly and ill were then shot in their beds. When the supply of bullets ran low, axes were used. Otto smashed the heads of small children against a wall. One five-year-old child (Kuropotowa or Kuropatwa) survived by playing dead and sneaking back to the camp later. The synagogue doors were then unlocked, and the surviving 400–500 Jews were marched to Budzyń. Many were shot on the way by Feiks and the Ukrainians. Upon arrival at Budzyń, Feiks selected an additional sixty-four Jews to be shot on the spot and then buried in a mass grave in the nearby woods.[28]

The last major influx of Jewish forced-laborers to Budzyń was

27 Eli Fiszman testimony, YVA, M.1.E/714; Hillel Borensztajn testimony, M.1.E/595; Eli Fishman interview, O.93 (VHA)/14967; Majer Rozenblatt interview, O.93 (VHA)/5113; Hillel Borenstein interview, O.93 (VHA)/6998; Benny Kleiman interview, O.93 (VHA)/477; Freiberg, *Darkness Covered the Earth*, pp. 104–113.

28 Mendel Korn testimony, YVA, O.3/2941; Erich Mossbach testimony, O.33/2149; Vera and Erich Mossbach testimony, O.33/2426; Marta Rubinsztajn testimony, M.1.E/205; Yeshayahu Wajsfisz testimony, M.1.E/649; Wladyslaw Friedhelm testimony, O.33/637; Manfred Heymann testimony, O.2/794; Freiberg, *Darkness Covered the Earth*, pp. 147–149; Yehezkel Brotman, *Sefer Kraśnik*, p. 374; Yitzhak Lamhut, ibid., p. 394. The survivor accounts differ on the number of Jews selected at Bełżyce for transfer to Budzyń and the number killed by Feiks upon arrival. It seems that the differences are based upon the reference point: those who refer to the number of Jews selected at Bełżyce tend to give a higher number, while those who refer to the number that actually worked at Budzyń cite a lower figure.

the 500–600 Jews from Krychów and the group of approximately 100 from Hrubieszów. When the Krychów Jews (mostly Czech and Slovakian) arrived in Budzyń in July 1943, they struck the other inmates as being relatively clean and healthy. The day after they arrived, Lazarczyk came and took a number of them to Annopol to enlarge his work force there. In mid-November, the 400 Jewish forced-laborers in Annopol, including the group from Krychów, were shot in a mine at Nowy Wieś. The mine was then sealed.[29]

On July 3, half the Jatkowa inmates were taken by train to Budzyń, followed by the other half a week later. Before the last group left Jatkowa, the Gestapo brought over some ten small children they had found hiding in the camp.[30]

> "Do these children belong to anyone here?" the chief asked. A couple in our group were the parents of two of the children. It was a tragic moment. They knew that if they admitted to having hidden the children from the Germans while they were living at the camp, they would be killed – and that nothing could save the children anyway. There was silence. No one claimed the children. Waldner ordered them taken away.[31]

With this closing memory of their homes, the last Jews of Hrubieszów boarded the train for Budzyń.

29 "Facts Reported by a Jew Deported from Slovakia, Who Has Since Escaped and Returned," August 17, 1943, YVA, M.2/236 in English (and M.4/12 in Hebrew); in German, "Tatsachenbericht eines aus der Slovakei deportierten und zurückgekehrten Juden," M.A., D.1.1266; Eli Fiszman testimony, YVA, M.1.E/714; Abraham Manes Citrin testimony, TR.11/02138; Freiberg, *Darkness Covered the Earth*, pp. 164, 177–178.

30 Orenstein, *I Shall Live*, pp. 105–137; Abraham Goldfarb testimonies, YVA, O.3/2140, TR.11/01121/V; Josef Rechtszaft testimony, TR.11/01121/V; Bencion Fink and Dawid Rottenberg testimonies, TR.11/01238; Dov Finger testimony, O.3/2780; Hannah Levi testimony, TR.11/01121/V; Gisela Perec testimony, O.3/4237; Yitzhak Perec testimony, O.3/4238; Ruth Tatarko testimonies, O.3/7158, 7613; Zipora Nahir testimony, O.3/10488; Cipora Hurwitz testimonies, O.3/11783, and MA, A.296; *Pinkas Hrubieszów*, pp. 109–110; Hurwitz, *Forbidden Strawberries*, pp. 108–110.

31 Orenstein, *I Shall Live*, pp. 136–137; the story of the children is corroborated by the other testimonies. Hannah Levi recalls that the children also refused to identify their parents. She estimates that there were eight to twelve children.

The Budzyń Regime. The SS regime in Budzyń was severe, especially under Reinhold Feiks, who came over from Bełżec to succeed Hantke and Stoschek in December 1942. If Hantke was Globocnik's expert in setting up camps, Feiks was his expert in camp brutality. Feiks was tall, young, blonde, and a vicious sadist; he tortured and killed people almost daily. He remained in the camp until mid-summer 1943, when he was succeeded by his deputy, Adolf Axmann, who was in turn followed by Werner Mohr, Fritz Tauscher, and Josef Leipold (or Leibhold).[32]

Noah Stockman was appointed *Lagerälteste* by Feiks after Gelbart fled Budzyń in December 1942. Stockman is generally remembered fondly by Budzyń survivors, unlike his deputy, Roman Szypiacki. His other deputies – Yehoshua Zoberman, who had been the head of the Zaklików Judenrat and was in charge of supplies for the prisoners in Budzyń, and Zvi Bruk, who was the office manager of the camp – get mixed reviews from survivors. The POWs held many of the leading positions in the camp, and received preferential treatment from Feiks and his men. As a result, the POWs were generally better dressed and healthier than the other Jews. Stockman was the dominant Jewish figure in Budzyń, known for his integrity, fairness, and efforts to protect the prisoners. He was tall and thin and always wore his Polish military uniform, which was clean and ironed. His integrity also influenced the camp *Ordnungsdienst*, who generally behaved well toward the Jewish prisoners. For all of this Stockman was widely respected among the Jews.

There were some exceptions to this caring behavior, such as Smoliar, who was responsible for the Jewish workers in the Heinkel factory. Szypiacki stands out in survivors' memories as a brutal Jewish official. But some brutality was a facade for protecting fellow Jewish prisoners. "*Roite Mordche*" ("Red Mordechai"; Mordechai Girszt) was a Jewish policeman in the camp who beat Jews in order to protect them from Feiks. He screamed at them and pretended to

32 The survivors' memory of Feiks's extreme cruelty is especially vivid. See, for example, Wyszogrod, *A Brush with Death*, pp. 115–163, *passim*; Abraham Dichter testimony, YVA, O.2/213; Mendel Korn, O.3/2941; Yerahmiel Kojfman, O.33/1499; Wladyslaw Friedhelm, O.33/637; Jeshajahu Wajsfisz, M.1.E/649; Nahman Kranc, M.1.E/2654; Pola Hirschmann, M.49.E/1476.

beat them, signaling them to fall. This kept the SS and Ukrainian guards away from these prisoners.[33]

In the camp's first fifteen months, the inmates lived in the closed compound that the first prisoners had built in the autumn of 1942, and were marched to their various places of employment. The prisoners' day began with a wake-up gong at 5:00 A.M. They had a half hour for the latrine, washing, and drinking a warm chicory drink as "breakfast." The washing area consisted of two long wooden troughs with pipes running across them in which there were faucets with cold water. The latrine was a long building with two parallel ditches and crossed wooden poles every few feet on which the prisoners sat while relieving themselves. They used leaves or bits of paper to clean themselves, or nothing at all. The time allotted for the latrines, which accommodated only fifty to sixty people at a time, averaged eighteen seconds per person (when the camp was at its capacity of 3,000 prisoners). Clearly, many never had the opportunity to use the latrine. Moreover, many of the prisoners suffered from diarrhea or dysentery and soiled themselves constantly.

The morning routine continued with an extended roll call, which could last as long as two hours. The prisoners were divided into work companies of 100, led by prisoner company leaders. Each company was divided into units of ten, each led by a prisoner foreman. Many of the companies were built around groups of Jews from specific places. The roll call was taken based on this structure of tens and hundreds, and was almost always accompanied by beatings or killing, especially under Feiks. The workday, including the march

33 Mendel Korn testimony, YVA, O.3/2941; Jacob Arie Ender testimony, YVA, TR.11/01113; Aharon Himmelblau testimony, TR.11/01113; Manfred Heymann testimony, O.2/794; Wladyslaw Friedhelm testimony, O.33/637; Eli Fiszman testimony, M.1.E/714; Freiberg, *Darkness Covered the Earth*, pp. 143–153, 160–161; Wyszogrod, *A Brush with Death*, pp. 129–131, 147–148; Hersz Zukerman, in *Sefer Kraśnik*, p. 379; Laks, *I Was There*, p. 230; Orenstein, *I Shall Live*, pp. 138–139. Wyszogrod calls Mordche "*Der Geyler Mordche*" ("Yellow Mordechai"), although he also describes him as a redhead. Regarding Stockman, Zukerman says, "He was like a father to us." Daniel Freiberg says that the local Jews were also in relatively good condition in the camp because they had lived in their own homes until shortly before the deportations and knew dependable Christian neighbors from whom they could supplement their supplies. The Warsaw Jews were in the worst shape of all; they were weaker, more starved, and deprived.

to and from the work site, lasted eleven to twelve hours. Lunch was made in the camp kitchen and served at the work site at noon; it was a thin soup made from "vegetable debris." The length of the march to and from work varied, depending on the distance to the work place; the 6 km. march to the Budzyń factory took one hour.

There was a second, protracted, and murderous roll call in the evening. If Feiks was in a good mood, he would order the prisoners to sing Polish, Yiddish, or Hasidic Hebrew songs. The prisoners were also often ordered to sing after executions. They were then given a supper of thin soup and bread that tasted of sawdust. On Sundays, they received a spoonful of marmalade or margarine in addition to this. After supper they had one to two hours free before the 9:00 P.M. lights-out curfew. It was then that Ukrainian guards would often come into the barracks and demand personal belongings from the Jews or a song to be played on a violin. They would beat the prisoners and threaten them if they revealed anything to the Germans. They also raped Jewish women in the women's barrack, using the same threats. The Jewish doctors would then secretly treat the women, and they performed abortions if necessary.[34]

The poor quality and insufficient amounts of food caused edema, starvation, disease, and deaths. Jews sought ways to supplement their rations, such as by bribing Ukrainian guards to sell them scraps at exorbitant rates. The local Jews sometimes received food from their Christian neighbors with whom they had entrusted their belongings. A number of local Poles were also employed in the factories, and some of them were willing to help the Jews with food. Conditions improved somewhat at the end of July, after Feiks left. Jews who worked in seasonal agricultural work sometimes were also able to bring food back to the camp.[35]

Under Feiks the brutality at the camp was so extreme that the forced-laborers dreaded the end of the workday and the return to

34 Wyszogrod, *A Brush with Death*, pp. 131–133, 139–141; Wladyslaw Friedhelm testimony, YVA, O.33/637; Erich Mossbach testimony, YVA, O.33/2149; Yitzhak Lamhut, in *Sefer Kraśnik*, p. 394. Wyszogrod recalls that Feiks was particularly fond of the Polish tango "Mariana" and the Hebrew song "*Yismehu*."

35 Mossbach and Friedhelm testimonies, ibid.; Freiberg, *Darkness Covered the Earth*, pp. 150, 163–164.

the camp. "Compared to staying in camp, work was a relief," recalls Morris Wyszogrod, and at the end of the workday, "a deep anxiety began to spread."[36] Feiks would go out of his way to torture and kill Jews at morning and evening roll call. He would ride into the square on his motorcycle, or on the white horse that he purchased in May 1943, with money that he had demanded as a "contribution" from the Jewish prisoners.[37] The Jews would stand at the camp square while Feiks selected prisoners for the day's treatment. They might be attacked by his German shepherd Rolf, or have their necks broken by Feiks as he tied the reins of his horse around a prisoner's neck and then made the horse rear up. "After the killing," relates Morris Wyszogrod, "you could feel a certain relief come over the *Appelplatz.*"[38]

Among those killed by Feiks was Paul Bauchwitz, a tall German Jew from Stettin; he was in his fifties, and his family had converted to Christianity when he was a child. Bauchwitz had been a lieutenant in the German army in World War I, and had been decorated with the Iron Cross First Class. In the camp he received certain special privileges, such as being allowed to live with his wife Mela in his own room. When two prisoners from the work company that he led fled one day in the summer of 1943, he covered for them by not informing the Germans, thus personally assuming the consequences. Deputy Commandant Axmann had him hanged, refusing him the privilege of a German war veteran to be shot. He did, however, grant him the right to say his last words, in which he condemned Hitler and asked the Jews to say *kaddish* for him.[39]

36 Wyszogrod, *A Brush with Death*, pp. 149–179, *passim.*

37 Ibid., pp. 132–136; Freiberg, *Darkness Covered the Earth*, pp. 147–148.

38 Wyszogrod, ibid., pp. 128, 133–136 (quotation from p. 128).

39 Ibid., pp. 162–164; David Wdowinski testimony, *The Eichmann Trial,* vol. 4, p. 1233–1234; Hertha Heymann testimony, YVA, O.2/323; Mendel Korn testimony, O.3/2941; Laks, *I Was There*, pp. 222–223. There are several differences in detail among these accounts. For example, whereas Wyszogrod and Wdowinski recall that Bauchwitz was hanged, Heymann says he was shot. Since Wyszogrod sketched the scene of the 1943 hanging shortly after the war, when his memory was still fresh, this version seems to be correct. This and other differences notwithstanding, the essence of the story is the same in all the accounts – Bauchwitz was a German Jew, who was publicly executed in the camp square.

One of the most gruesome stories from Budzyń, reflecting the sadism of Feiks and his staff, is that of the murder of the prisoner Bitter, a forty-year-old Warsaw Jew, at approximately the same time. Bitter had been caught by the Ukrainian guards Polakov, Popov, and Otto, while he was cooking potatoes in a tin can. Jews were forbidden to possess potatoes or to cook. One of the guards kicked the can off the fire and, feeling extra weight in the can, examined it and found some gold coins hidden in a false bottom. Bitter was dragged into the camp by Polakov and other Ukrainian guards with barbed wire tied around his neck. Feiks applied collective responsibility and ordered all the inmates to beat Bitter to death. They were forced to walk by him in groups of five and beat him. The Ukrainians then burned his eyes with cigarette lighters, forced a sharp wooden stake down his throat, and poured water into his mouth. Dr. Erich Mossbach was called in to declare him dead, and then he was buried in the forest.[40]

Illustrations of the camp's brutality have been detailed here not for the purpose of horrifying – though they are horrifying stories indeed – but rather to highlight the unpredictability of a Jew's existence in this framework. Although no exact statistics are available, it seems that, in comparison to other camps, a relatively high percentage of Jews who served as forced-laborers in Budzyń survived. Against the background of the terrible conditions and arbitrary, widespread torture and killing that characterized this camp, this is somewhat surprising.

The arbitrariness of life and death is further highlighted by examples of the relatively "liberal" camp regime in Budzyń. Mosze Schiff was periodically given permission to visit friends in the Kraśnik camp. He would go there unguarded, see his friends, and return to Budzyń the same day. On one of these Sunday visits

40 Wyszogrod, ibid., pp. 157–162; Mendel Korn testimony, YVA, O.3/2941; Wdowinski testimony, *The Eichmann Trial*, vol. 4, p. 1233; Laks, *I Was There*, pp. 225–226; Yehezkel Brotman, Hersz Zukerman, and Yitzhak Lamhut, in *Sefer Kraśnik*, pp. 375, 380, 395. All three of these guards are referred to as vicious sadists in survivor accounts, but Otto stands out. In addition to the above-mentioned sources, see, for example, Freiberg, *Darkness Covered the Earth*, p. 149; Marta Rubinsztajn testimony, YVA, M.1.E/649.

in the spring or summer of 1943, Schiff chanced upon Yitzhak Gerenreich, a forced-laborer at the Wifo camp, who was on his way (also unguarded) to the Kraśnik camp for the same purpose. As they approached the camp's perimeter fence, Gerenreich suddenly saw camp commandant Alois Gröger appear on the balcony of a building near the fence, above the camp barbershop, and pull out his pistol. Gerenreich and Schiff ran away, but Gröger shot Schiff in the chest. The barbers brought the body into the camp, and Schiff's close friend Moshe Graf carried him into a room, where prisoner Doctor Schapiro tried to save him. He was unsuccessful. Feiks came the next day with Dr. Förster, the chief prisoner doctor at Budzyń (he later performed an autopsy on Schiff), and shouted angrily at Gröger, "If you shoot my Jews, I'll shoot yours!"[41] Gröger was known to be a relatively calm and decent commandant, yet here he was the killer; whereas the vicious and sadistic Feiks had given Schiff permission to travel unguarded and then even "defended" his Jews.

At most of the work sites, German civilians were in charge. In general, they treated the Jews much better than did Feiks and his successors and generally did not turn Jews over to the SS. At times they even protested murders by Feiks and his aides.[42] The German civilian leaders of the Budzyń camp, Karl Jäger and Stefan Hentze, were somewhat decent at times.[43] Sometimes the civilians even went so far as to save Jews from Feiks. One day in the summer of 1943, a construction group from Annopol did not return from work. Feiks thought that they had escaped, but the German civilian administrators of the Beikler Company forced the German driver to admit that he had failed to pick up the workers that day.[44]

In the Heinkel factory the German civilians kept the SS and

41 Yitzhak Gerenreich testimony, YVA, TR.11/01113; Itzchak Rosenbusch testimony, ibid.; Asher Mandelblatt testimony, ibid.; trial of Gröger, et al., YVA, TR.10/868, pp. 287–300. Both Rosenbusch and Mandelblatt recalled Feiks's words (in almost identical form). Since Gröger killed Graf in May 1943, this event must have taken place before that. It may even have been connected. However, several Kraśnik survivors remember clearly that it was summer.

42 Freiberg, *Darkness Covered the Earth*, pp. 154–155, 173–174; Wyszogrod, *A Brush with Death*, pp. 149–179, *passim*.

43 Freiberg, Wyszogrod, Orenstein, and Israel Hener emphasize this point.

44 Freiberg, *Darkness Covered the Earth*, pp. 155–158.

Ukrainians outside. The only uniformed people there were the Werkschutz, who were not as brutal at Budzyń as the SS. This and the fact that German civilians and Poles also worked at the factory made conditions there seem better than in the camp.[45] Wyszogrod tells of Jäger inviting him to lunch at his home after Wyszogrod had completed a personal art project that Jäger had requested. They discussed art and Jäger's life before the war.[46]

One of the noteworthy points in the above story of the Annopol construction detail is that they did not attempt to escape when they found themselves forgotten by their driver and their supervisors. When the driver returned to fetch them the next day, they were still there. Feiks rewarded them with a better supper and cigarettes (which were usually forbidden), and allowed the Annopol group somewhat greater freedom of movement afterward. Yet as Daniel Freiberg notes, despite the relatively lax guarding at Budzyń, there were few escape attempts through the summer of 1943.[47]

Camp life included many cases of prisoner solidarity and mutual help, alongside incidents of corruption (e.g., Szypiacki) and informing. There were also limited cultural and religious activities, which helped maintain the prisoners' spirits. Zvia Steif peeled potatoes in the camp kitchen. In the summer of 1943, she became ill with typhus and was sent to the infirmary. Ewa, a forced-laborer in the infirmary, rescued her by transferring her to a new bed daily and telling Feiks each day that she was to be discharged the next day. Zvia was still ill when she returned to work, but her fellow workers covered for her, doing her quota while she rested among them and regained her strength.[48]

Morris Wyszogrod recalls, "In my experience, religious Jews were the best people in the camp." They were the most sensitive and trustworthy. He says they opposed escapes from the camp out of fear of the consequences to those left behind. Similarly, the poor and simple people also tended to display solidarity and sensitivity. In contrast, he adds, the assimilated intellectuals were the least

45 Ibid., pp. 173–174.

46 Wyszogrod, *A Brush with Death*, pp. 153–154.

47 Freiberg, *Darkness Covered the Earth*, pp. 155–158.

48 Zvia Steif testimony, YVA, O.3/5224.

exemplary group in the camp.[49] Wyszogrod's generalizations are neither corroborated nor contradicted by other survivor accounts. However, he provides specific examples to illustrate his points, and while these illustrations may or may not represent a phenomenon, they do reflect a level of solidarity and mutual aid in the camp. He tells of two poor Jews in the camp, Glatstein, the horse-cart driver, and Meyer Kociol. During the distribution of the warm breakfast drink, they would rush to the head of the line to collect portions for people who were too weak or ill to get up. They constantly encouraged these people to fight on for their lives.[50]

Szypiacki's brutality and corruption and the few informers – such as Smus, a fifty-year-old refugee from Danzig who had arrived with the Warsaw group in the spring of 1943 – stood in sharp contrast to the mutual aid and tone set by Stockman. Feiks appointed Smus to the camp *Ordnungsdienst*, and Smus became an informer. He accused Stockman and Zoberman of hoarding goods at the expense of the Germans and the camp inmates. The Germans searched their bunks and found goods and money belonging to Zoberman. Both were arrested and tortured for three days. Zoberman was killed, but Stockman was returned to his job. Zoberman had traveled to Kraśnik and Lublin as part of his camp supplies' job and had used these opportunities to acquire various things. When Stockman appeared at roll call after his release, all 3,000 inmates reacted with joy.[51]

There were also various religious and cultural activities that helped sustain the inmates. Henry Orenstein describes the camp show that Stockman arranged for the prisoners in January 1944, in which Orenstein's sister Hanka performed.[52] Wyszogrod tells of

49 Wyszogrod, *A Brush with Death*, pp. 145–147.

50 Ibid., pp. 146–147.

51 Freiberg, *Darkness Covered the Earth*, pp. 160–161; Laks, *I Was There*, pp. 225, 227. Freiberg recalls that the inmates sang "Hatikvah." It is difficult to imagine the Jewish inmates in Budzyń singing "Hatikvah" at roll call without being punished, but Stockman's punishment and Zoberman's death fit the picture of the camp, as does the prisoners' joyful reaction to Stockman's return.

52 Orenstein, *I Shall Live*, pp. 162–163. The periodic singing and musical performances that the inmates were forced by the Germans or the Ukrainians to put on were part of the persecution, not spiritual encouragement. See

regular evening prayers in his barrack, led by Yehuda Gram, who had a beautiful voice and knew the prayers by heart; Haim Meir Beck recalls daily morning prayers by some in his barrack.[53] Some also tell of Yom Kippur services held in 1943, led by Yoel Zintig.[54]

The Passover holiday in 1944 was unusual. Hoffmann, a Romanian *Volksdeutsche* SS man in charge of the bathhouse, suggested to two Warsaw rabbis, Szymszon Sztokhammer and David Szapira, that for a fee he would help them bake *matzot* for Pesach in the bathhouse oven. The rabbis seized the opportunity and informed Stockman, who had flour brought to the bathhouse. But the prisoners who brought the *matzot* into the camp were caught and arrested. Stockman went to Leipold and took full responsibility, insisting that the *matzot* were necessary so that those who would not eat bread would not starve. The result was that a *seder* was held in the barrack where the rabbis lived. The barrack was packed with people, and more stood outside. For Daniel Freiberg, a secular Jew, it was his first *seder* in fifteen years.[55] These stories point to Jewish initiative in maintaining a modicum of spiritual existence in Budzyń and to some level of flexibility on the part of the Germans after Feiks's replacement.

The WVHA-SSPF Camps, 1942–1943

The camps that held the most lucrative potential for Globocnik and others were the ones that resulted from the negotiations initiated

Wyszogrod, *A Brush with Death*, pp. 137–141; Mendel Korn testimony, YVA, O.3/2941.

53 Wyszogrod, *A Brush with Death*, p. 147; Haim Meir Beck, in *Sefer Kraśnik*, p. 229.

54 Haim Meir Beck and Yitzhak Kaftan, in *Sefer Kraśnik*, pp. 228, 423.

55 Freiberg, *Darkness Covered the Earth*, pp. 196–197; Wdowinski corroborates the story, *The Eichmann Trial*, vol. 4, p. 1237, as does Haim Meir Beck, in *Sefer Kraśnik*, p. 227; YVA, TR.10/813, pp. 171–172. On Sztokhammer's presence and influence in the camp, see also Wyszogrod, *A Brush with Death*, p. 145, and Wdowinski, ibid. On the identity of Rabbi Szapira, see Nehemiah Polen, *Holy Fire: The Teachings of Rabbi Kalonymos Kalman Shapiro, the Rebbe of the Warsaw Ghetto* (Northvale, NJ: Jason Aronson, 1994), pp. 185–186, n. 27.

with Többens and Schultz in the summer of 1942. These negotiations were within the framework of Globocnik's cooperation with Oswald Pohl and were connected particularly to the creation of the joint SSPF-WVHA enterprise, Ostindustrie GmbH. They resulted in the largest concentrations of Jewish forced labor in the Lublin District from the spring to autumn of 1943.

Parallel to the preparations for the transfer of the Warsaw enterprises, cooperation between Globocnik and the WVHA in the DAW was expanded. In 1943, there were five DAW camps. Four were in the Lublin District: Lipowa 7 (see Chapter 4) and its branches in Puławy, Końskowola, and the Lublin airfield; and there was Janowska in Lwow (set up by Lipowa 7 Commandant Wolfgang Mohwinkel in the autumn and winter of 1941–1942). The DAW camps were very profitable, especially Lipowa 7. The DAW in Lublin ran a tar-paper factory for roofs, as well as workshops that produced shoes, woven baskets, beds, chairs, couches, clothing, caps, and more. It also ran workshops in mechanics, electricity and radio, and glazing, as well as a smithy, and other crafts; it sold manufactured and repaired items to local Germans.[56] For example, on May 12, 1942, 323,000 kg. of raw materials was ordered in order to produce 10,000 rolls of tar roofing for one customer. The high volume of orders and the DAW's profitability made Jewish labor even more desirable for the SS; it also meant that these camps might offer Jews a chance for survival. Indeed, the number of Jewish forced-laborers in the DAW camps more than doubled by the summer of 1943, from 2,420 in the Lublin camps on December 31, 1942, to 5,448 on September 1, 1943. Lipowa 7 (DAW I) and the Lublin airfield camp (DAW II) each had 2,500 laborers, and the Puławy sawmill (DAW III), set up by Otto Hantke in June 1943, in a town whose Jews had long since been murdered, had more than 400.[57]

OSTI was created on March 12, 1943, following months of

56 YVA, JM/3696 includes production reports, prices, orders, etc., with lists of orders and production for 1942–1944. See also Mohwinkel indictment, YVA, TR.10/770, p. 106.

57 YVA, TR.10/770, pp. 106–109; Michalsen/Hantke indictment, YVA, TR.10/813, p. 42; Hantke interrogation, Hamburg, April 7, 9, 13, 1964, pp. 28:4964, in YVA, TR.10/1291.

negotiations and preparations. Himmler's anger at Krüger in January 1943, for not liquidating the Warsaw ghetto as ordered, served to spur on these discussions. Himmler insisted that the workshops be transferred as soon as possible to camps in the Lublin area.[58]

There were many issues to consider in the creation of the new enterprise, including the ownership of Jewish movable property, where to create or coopt camps, the availability of raw materials, prospects for orders from the new enterprise, adequate transport, jurisdiction, and so on. One fundamental issue was whether the utilization of Jewish forced labor by OSTI would be guided by politics, resulting in lower productivity and the killing of all the Jews, or by economics, resulting in higher productivity and perhaps tolerable conditions for the forced-laborers. The decision was to aim for both productivity and killing.[59]

Pohl assigned Dr. Maximilian Horn to do the groundwork and be his representative in the planning; Horn then became Globocnik's co-director of OSTI. The company's mandate was to utilize Jewish manpower and movable property in the GG, including machinery, tools, and material acquired in "Operation Reinhard." OSTI included eight factories, six of them in the Lublin District: the glassworks in Wolomin (Werk I, Warsaw district); the peat mine at Dorohucza (Werk II); the brush and basket workshops at the Lublin airfield (Werk III); a military textiles and equipment factory in Radom-Bliżyn (Werk IV); the ironworks at the Lublin airfield (Werk V); the Schultz fur factory at Trawniki (Werk VI); an earth and stonework factory in Lublin (Werk VII); and a pharmaceuticals factory in Lublin (Werk VIII). By the autumn of 1943, the factories employed some 15,000 Jewish forced-laborers, 650 Poles, and fewer than 100 Germans.[60]

58 Himmler to Krüger, January 1943, NO-1882.

59 Maximilian Horn memorandum on the proposed establishment of OSTI, February 13, 1943, NO-1270; Horn to Hohberg (Head of Staff W in WVHA), February 26, 1943, NO-1265; the notarized document creating OSTI, March 12, 1943, NO-1263. On the creation of OSTI and its operations, see Allen, *The Business of Genocide*, pp. 245–251; Schulte, *Zwangsarbeit und Vernichtung*, pp. 262–284, 316–317; Pohl, *Judenpolitik*, pp. 162–164.

60 Auditing Report on Ostindustrie G. m. b. H., June 21, 1944, for the period March 12, 1943—February 29, 1944, by *SS-Unterscharführer* Johann Sebastian

The company turned a handsome profit of 780,000 złotys during its brief existence, and disposed of tens of millions of złotys worth of machinery and property that were turned over to the WVHA on February 29, 1944.[61] However, like DAW, despite its profitability, OSTI was essentially liquidated in the *Erntefest*.

The camps at Trawniki and Poniatowa shared the rapid rise and fall of OSTI and DAW. Both camps had existed in some fashion prior to the beginning of "Operation Reinhard," and both underwent far-reaching changes in 1942. Trawniki had a small Jewish forced-labor camp in the summer of 1941, in the prewar sugar factory, next to the Hiwi training camp. The factory's main building was a quadrangle with an inner courtyard into which a rail spur led. Two sides of the quadrangle were for the training camp, and two sides were adapted, in 1942, for sorting Jewish belongings, especially textiles.

SS-Oberscharführer Franz Bartetzko, a brutal commander in the Bełżec camps in 1940, ran the forced-labor camp under Trawniki Commandant Karl Streibel. The Schultz workshops shared the space with other work that was not subsumed under OSTI. During the spring of 1942, Jewish forced-laborers were brought to Trawniki from Piaski, the Reich and Czechoslovakia. Although most of the last group was killed soon after their arrival, some continued to work in a variety of jobs both in the forced-labor camp and in the Hiwi training camp. In late 1942, the brush factory in Międzyrzec was transferred here, along with part of the forced-labor manpower. As the Schultz workshops were transferred to Trawniki in 1943, the sorting buildings were turned into the forced-labor camp.[62]

Fischer, NO-1271; Streibel Verdict, YVA, TR.10/869, II:23–24, 78–82; Birmes and Gollak indictment, TR.10/815, pp. 113–114. See also the September 30, 1943, OSTI personnel report, NO-1906; Maximilian Horn testimonies, Ulm, June 15 and 18, 1960, 208 AR-Z 74/60, vol. 52, pp. 1052–1072, in YVA, TR.10/1291. After Globocnik's departure from Lublin, Horn became the main director of OSTI.

61 OSTI Auditing Report, ibid.

62 See YVA, TR.10/869, III:259–260, XI:1; TR.10/756, pp. 147–149; Helge Grabitz and Wolfgang Scheffler, eds., *Letzte Spuren: Ghetto Warschau, SS-Arbeitslager Trawniki, Aktion Erntefest, Fotos und Dokumente über Opfer des Endlösungswahns im Spiegel der historischen Ereignisse* (Berlin: Edition Hentrich, 1988), pp. 318–323; Witold Mędykowski, "Obóz pracy dla Żydów w Trawnikach," in Lenarczyk and Libionka, eds., *Erntefest*, pp. 73–104; Stanislaw Jabloński, "Obóz pracy SS w Trawnikach," unpublished manuscript, YVA, O.6/472.

On February 1, 1943, Himmler formalized what Globocnik was already doing by appointing him to transfer the Warsaw firms and their Jewish laborers to the Lublin District. Globocnik quickly completed the negotiations with Schultz and Többens. Többens became the overseer of the transfer of the workshops, while Globocnik's trusted subordinate, Georg Michalsen, saw to the security aspects of the transfer in coordination with the Warsaw SSPF. The first 292 Jewish forced-laborers in the Schultz workshops were transferred to Trawniki on February 16, followed by 662 on March 16, and 448 on April 16. Each person was permitted to bring 15 kg. of personal belongings from Warsaw. Following this, more than 5,000 people were transferred by force during the uprising, in five groups, from April 21 to 30. More transports followed in May, and Jews from Białystok, Minsk, and Smolensk were brought in on September 16 and 19. By October 1, Schultz reported 6,296 Jews working for him in Trawniki, which is the last official estimate before the *Erntefest*. Officially, the prisoners worked sixty-two hours per week and had every other Sunday off.[63]

Until mid-summer 1943, conditions for the Jewish forced-laborers at Trawniki were relatively quiet and calm, with enough food and supplies. In August, Trawniki formally became a concentration camp under the WVHA, and this change brought harsher discipline and more arbitrary punishments. For example, in August, Bartetzko discovered white bread among four prisoners. He summoned all the forced-laborers to the camp square, decreed the death penalty for the "offenders," and thereupon shot them in the back of the head.[64]

63 See Horn and Feuchter, OSTI Lublin, to Grothe, Zentralbauabteilung of SS, March 31, 1943, YVA, O.53/82; the agreement with Többens, YVA, O.6/188; Michalsen and Hantke indictment, YVA, TR.10/813, pp. 34–35; Streibel verdict, TR.10-869, vol. IX, pp. 4, 54, 68–120, vol. XI, pp. 8–12; and indictment, TR.10/756, pp. 139–144; Birmes and Gollak indictment, TR.10/815, p. 113; Többens report on moving workshops to the Lublin area, April 21, 1943, *Eksterminacja*, pp. 250–251; Többens testimony, TR.10/26, pp. 53–61; Grabitz and Scheffler, eds., *Letzte Spuren*, pp. 179–210; Józef Marszalek, *Obozy Pracy w Generalnym Gubernatorstwie a Latach 1939–1945* (Lublin: Panstwowe Muzeum na Majdanku, 1998), pp. 111–114.

64 Grabitz and Scheffler, eds., *Letzte Spuren*, pp. 213–225; YVA, TR.10/756, pp. 147–149; TR.10/869, XI:1.

The peat mines at Dorohucza (6 km. from Trawniki) were made a sub-camp of Trawniki in 1942. The mines had been a seasonal forced-labor camp in the summer and fall of 1941, with Jewish forced-laborers from Lublin. In 1942–1943, the camp had a varying prisoner population of 600–1,000 Polish and Dutch Jews. The Germans used the peat for fuel, which lent the Jewish labor at Dorohucza military significance. In contrast to Trawniki, the conditions were severe, with inadequate food, difficult work conditions, insufficient bedding, constant beatings by the guards, and no medical care. The camp command did make some effort to clothe the Jews, such as with the June 1943 purchase of basic clothing from the Chopin Street sorting camp for newly arrived prisoners. Still, Dorohucza was one of the few forced-labor camps in the Lublin District at this time that could be said to have followed a "destruction through work" policy (*Vernichtung durch Arbeit*) consistently.[65]

The Jews brought to Dorohucza were usually taken in small groups from incoming transports of Jewish deportees and forced-laborers to the Lublin District. This was true for the deportations from Warsaw, as for those from Holland. For example, Jules Schelvis was deported from Westerbork on June 1, 1943, together with 3,000 other Dutch Jews. When the train arrived at Sobibor on June 4, Schelvis was among eighty-one chosen for work in Dorohucza. They were loaded onto two freight cars and transported for several hours to Trawniki, from where they were marched to Dorohucza. The prisoners at Dorohucza were soon starving and covered with lice. Their food rations consisted of small amounts of often-moldy black bread, a spoonful of "marmalade," and some "coffee" in the morning, and a small portion of thin soup in the afternoon. The veteran prisoners informed the Dutch newcomers of the nature of Sobibór and warned them that only the strongest had a chance to survive Dorohucza.[66]

65 Jules Schelvis, *Inside the Gates* (Tricht: Elzenhorst Tricht, 1990); *idem*, *Sobibor: A History of a Nazi Death Camp*, pp. 120–130; Marszalek, *Obozy Pracy*, pp. 86–87; Grabitz and Scheffler, eds., *Letzte Spuren*, p. 213; Bill #465 from Chopin Street camp to Ostindustrie, Dorohucza, June 30, 1943, for the delivery of clothing and blankets itemized in the bill, YVA, O.53/68.

66 Yehezkel Hering testimony, YVA, M.1.E/760; Schelvis, *Inside the Gates*, pp.

The function of Poniatowa (36 km. west of Lublin) underwent a radical change: from Stalag 359, where 24,000 POWs died during the last months of 1941, to a forced-labor camp under Globocnik, which Jews from Opole-Lubelski began constructing in October 1942. The Többens textile workshops were to be transferred here, and in early December Globocnik assigned Otto Hantke to set up the new camp. By January 1943, there were 1,500 Jews in the camp; the Többens forced-laborers were transferred from Warsaw from mid-March to early May 1943. By the time Hantke was transferred to Puławy in June, there were 16,000 Jewish forced-laborers in Poniatowa, of whom 10–12,000 worked for Többens.[67]

Conditions for the Jews in Poniatowa varied, depending on the jurisdiction under which they found themselves. Those who worked for Többens lived in relatively decent conditions, like the Jews in Trawniki who worked for Schultz; whereas those who worked for the SS were often treated far more brutally. The German camp administrator, *SS-Oberscharführer* Heinrich Gley, would beat and kill Jews and set his dog on them. Men and women were housed together in thirty 420 sq. meter barracks (35m x 12m), approximately 500 to a barrack), and there were a number of children there as well. The prisoners slept on multi-tiered bunk beds, and there were some reports of sexual activity among them.

Like in Budzyń, the camp routine began with a 5:00 A.M. wake-up, 6:00 A.M. roll call, a long workday, evening roll call, and a bit of free time before the evening curfew at 9:00 P.M. The camp had no fence until the summer of 1943. The prisoners could leave the camp for brief periods, and they exploited this privilege to maintain contact with local villagers and smuggle supplies into the camp. After the camp was fenced in, smugglers were summarily shot if caught. Gley and camp commandant *SS-Untersturmführer* Gottlieb Hering, who had served in the Bełżec death camp, established a Jewish camp

38–47; *idem*, *Sobibor: A History of a Nazi Death Camp*, pp. 120–130; Jabloński, "Obóz pracy SS w Trawnikach," pp. 20–21.

67 YVA, TR.10/813, p. 42; Hantke testimony (1967), TR.10/1291, vol. 44, pp. 8102–8103; Többens testimony, TR.10/26, pp. 53–61; Ryszard Gicewicz, "Obóz Pracy w Poniatowej (1941–1943)," *Zeszyty Majdanka*, 10 (1980), pp. 88–102; Marszalek, *Obozy Pracy*, pp. 112–114.

police. The survivors recall them as being very cooperative with the SS. During September and October 1943, hundreds of Jews were sent from Poniatowa to work in Luftwaffe airfields in Zamość and Biała-Podlaska. Nearly all the few Poniatowa survivors are from this group.[68]

Much of the agony of the struggle to survive the labor camps in this period is encapsulated in the story of Feliks (Efraim) Rzeczyński, a Polish Jewish lieutenant from Warsaw, who spent most of the war in an officers' POW camp in Germany — Offizierslager VIIa, in Murnau, Bavaria.[69] His wife, son, brothers, father, and brother-in-

68 Jerzy (Rosenberg) Ros testimony, YVA, O.3/3440; *idem*, in Józef Kermisz, ed., *Dokumenty i Materialy do Dziejów Okupacji Niemieckiej w Polsce*, Volume 1: *Obozy* (Warsaw: Jewish Historical Institute, 1946), pp. 260–261; *idem*, "The Labor Camp at Poniatowa" (Hebrew), *Yalkut* Moreshet, no. 13 (June 1971), pp. 17–27; Ester (Rubenstein) Winderbaum testimony, YVA, O.3/2314; Ludka Fischer-Chanesman testimony, ibid. (the Winderbaum and Chanesman testimonies are filed together); Ester Rubenstein, M.49.E/1013; Ludwika (Leah) Fischer testimony, *Opole-Lubelski Yizkor Book*, pp. 301–306; Hela Jaffe testimony, YVA, O.3/2911; Abram Goldman testimony, M.1.E/2289; letter from Szyja Hersz Feinzyberg to friends or family in Portugal, June 28, 1943, as reported to Ignacy Schwartzbart by Prof. O. Górka of the Department of Nationalities of the Polish Interior Ministry, in February 1944, YVA, M.2/240. Feinzyberg's letter had been posted from Berlin only on February 3, 1944, three months after he had been killed in the *Erntefest*. Therefore, it may be considered part of the Nazi deception. Yet it was written at a time when other testimonies confirm its contents, relating relatively good conditions in the camp.

69 The story of Feliks (Efraim) Rzeczynski is based upon a remarkable collection of more than fifty letters, which make up the correspondence between him and his family and others in August 1942—February 1945. He managed to preserve the correspondence, which he deposited together with a brief testimony in the Yad Vashem Archives in 1956, at the same time that he and his brother-in-law, Bernard Luxemberg, registered the same family members in Yad Vashem's Hall of Names. The collection is in YVA, O.48.B/19-1. For a similar story of wartime correspondence until the bitter end, see Nusia and Inia Szifman, *"My Life Is Still Before Me..."* (Yiddish) (Tel Aviv and Jerusalem: I.L. Peretz Verlag and Yad Vashem, 1962), edited by Nachman Blumental. Dr. Lejb Szifman was a physician in the Polish army, who was a POW in German hands. He, too, was able to correspond regularly with his family in Warsaw via the Red Cross. After his wife was deported to Treblinka in early September 1942, he continued to correspond with his daughters, eleven-year-old Inia (Irena) and fourteen-year-old Nusia (Anna). The girls worked in the Többens workshops and were transferred to Poniatowa in March 1943. The girls' letters were optimistic, and the correspondence continued until they were murdered in the *Erntefest*.

law were all in the Warsaw ghetto. As a recognized POW, he was permitted to correspond with them. His wife Ada (Adela) informed him on August 16, 1942, of the deportations from Warsaw, and, in October, she and his brother-in-law, Bernard Luxemberg, wrote him separately describing the deportations in detail. Luxemberg listed family members who had been taken, adding that all the deportees were dead. His family's condition soon became desperate. His wife wrote on March 27, 1943, and again on April 13, pleading with him to do all he could to get her and their fourteen-year-old son, Adam, out of the country on foreign papers. She despaired of ever seeing her husband again.

He did all he could from his POW status to get them out, and also sent them money (RM 590) between January 23 and October 21, 1943. He contacted people in Switzerland for help, and, on June 16, 1943, was informed by S. Fay in Zurich (it is not clear who this is) that a special messenger had been sent to rescue his wife and son from the ghetto. But it was too late; they were already in Poniatowa.

His first contact from his deported family came on August 5, from his father and his brother in Poniatowa, informing him that they had arrived safely in the camp on April 22, and were working in the laundry. In coded language they indicated that they wanted to try to get U.S. citizenship. He tried in vain to contact his wife and son. The Poniatowa camp informed him (on August 25) that his wife and son were not there, while Schultz and Többens each referred him to the other, and the SSPF's office offered no information. His father and brother wrote on September 12, in response to five letters from him (July 22—September 2), telling him, "Your son is healthy."

Rzeczyński was never able to corroborate this news. On September 22, his brother-in-law wrote him that he was now hiding in Warsaw under an assumed name and that his "life was hanging by a thread." In his efforts to obtain information about his wife and child, Rzeczyński wrote to Többens, Schultz, Hering, the *Stadthauptmann* in Lublin, Majdanek, the SSPF in Lublin, the Polish lawyer Szymański in Warsaw, the Polish Red Cross, his own commander in the Oflag, and more. He encountered lies and obfuscation from all the Germans, and helplessness from all the others. Only twice did he receive any real information from the Germans. Többens wrote to him on July 30, 1943, that his father and brother were in Poniatowa and were well, and Hering wrote on September 10, saying that he had still not received the 50 marks for them (it was cleared ten days later). When he could not find his wife and son, he wrote to the Population Registry in Warsaw on September 7, only to be told on October 2, that they had no record of a change of address. This was nearly half a year after they had been deported from Warsaw and the ghetto had been razed to the ground. Still, in the hope that perhaps they were indeed still in Warsaw, he wrote on October 2, to the Israelitische Flüchtlingshilfe (Jewish Refugee Board) in Basel asking for their assistance. But they had no contact with the GG. As late as May 17, 1944, German officials were still writing him that they did not know where his family was: the SS Standortverwaltung (garrison administration) in Lublin wrote that Hersz, Mosze, and Malka (Mosze's wife) had "left" Poniatowa, but Rzeczyński tried in vain to get a forwarding address. He had already received a letter from his friend Janina Komorowska in Warsaw (May 20) telling him of the fate of the Poniatowa Jews. Still, he tried desperately to get specific information in a last hope that perhaps they had indeed "moved."

Hering, Többens, Schultz, and the other German officials all knew that his family had indeed been moved. They had been shot to death more than half a year earlier in the *Erntefest* operation.

Military Camps

One other group of camps that provided Jewish forced-laborers with relatively decent conditions was those run by the German military. The two main sites with such camps in 1942–1943 were Dęblin-Irena and Biała-Podlaska.

Dęblin-Irena had several forced-labor camps prior to the May 1942 deportation. A prisoner-of-war camp for Red Army POWs was opened here on July 10, 1941. According to some estimates, 80,000

POWs were brought there, and within a few months they all died of starvation and exposure or of typhus.[70] Following the May 6 deportation from Dęblin, there were five forced-labor camps in and near the town: two in the old Polish air-force base and airfield, with approximately 1,000 Jews; one at the train station (300 Jews); one on Lipowa Street in the city (200 Poles and Jews); and one on the edge of town (300 Jews). When the ghetto was liquidated on October 15, 1942, some 280 women, 100 children, and more than 600 men were sent to the airfield camp, bringing the number of Jews there to approximately 2,000. German Luftwaffe soldiers ran this camp, which was surrounded by barbed wire. The men worked at laying landing strips, repairing airplane parts, construction, and various other maintenance jobs, while the women and children generally worked in the fields.

Families lived together in wooden barracks at the airfield camp, and the Jews were treated relatively tolerably by the Luftwaffe soldiers, even by those who were clearly antisemitic. Even the German SS man and engineer, Ringel, and the Wehrmacht camp administrator, Kattengel, and his successor, Duse, were generally decent.

The prisoners had enough food to subsist (1,700 calories per day), weekly baths, and were given coal to heat their barracks in winter. There was also a prisoner infirmary run by Drs. Kestenbaum

70 The story of the Deblin camp is based on: Yaakov Ahiezer testimony, YVA, O.3/2951; Hana Schildkraut Tupolski testimony, O.3/9295; Esther Neumann testimony, O.3/9077; Hersz Szerberg testimony, M.1.E/1327; Shlomo Welt testimony, M.1.E/1328; D. Cymerowicz testimony, M.1.E/1372; Moshe Mlawer testimony, M.1.E/1627; M.1.E/874, testimony with illegible signature; David Schtockfisch, ed., *Dęblin-Modzitz Book* (Hebrew and Yiddish) (Tel Aviv: Dęblin-Modzitz Immigrants' Association, 1969), testimonies of Staphian Fidelis, Zvi Eichenbrenner, Andzja (Hana) Tupolski, Aida Milgrojm-Citrinbojm, Devorah Reznik, Shloma Welt, S. Perlmutter, Kalman Paris, Yisrael (Ignatz) Bubis; Hermann Wenkart, *Befehlsnotstand anders gesehen; Tatsachenbericht eines jüdischen Lagerfunktionärs* (Vienna: Privately published, 1974), pp. 19–83; Stanley Hochman, *Mr. Fate: My Personal World War II Memoirs* (unpublished 1998 manuscript in Yad Vashem library), pp. 19–30; Ignatz Bubis, *Ich bin ein deutscher Staatsbürger jüdischen Glaubens; Ein autobiographisches Gespräch mit Edith Kohn* (Köln: Kiepenheuer and Witsch, 1993), pp. 51–64, 67; and the recent MA thesis by Talia Farkash, *The History of the Jews of Puławy District in the Province of Lublin during World War II and the Holocaust 1939–1944* (Hebrew), masters thesis, University of Haifa, February 2013, pp. 102–114.

and Rozenblüth. Hermann Wenkart, an Austrian Jew who had been deported to Opole-Lubelski from Vienna in February 1941, was sent by the Germans to the Dęblin airfield camp in May 1941, and soon was appointed *Lagerälteste.* Austrian Jews held many of the senior prisoner positions in the camp. These included Grossman, Wenkart's assistant; Poliak, who was in charge of supplies; Walter, who was in charge of the bath and the laundry; and Engel, who was the commander of the Jewish police.

Survivors have sharply differing memories of Wenkart. On the one hand, he is credited with exploiting his good relations with the Germans in the camp to bribe them in order to maintain reasonable conditions: "He saved us."[71] He also arranged to release Aida Milgrojm-Citrinbojm, a professional teacher, and several other women from labor so that they could care for the children. They were able to get a special diet prepared for the children in the camp kitchen and ran clandestine education. Here, too, bribery played an important role.[72] Similarly, the Jews purchased the right to conduct a Passover *seder* in 1943. Bribery won the Germans' consent, and 120 złotys per participant paid for the food and supplies. Eighty people paid and participated in the *seder*, including Wenkart himself.[73]

Other survivors of the Dęblin camp, however, remember Wenkart as cruel, loud, cunning, and sharp-tongued. Some accuse him of beating Jewish inmates. His good relations with the Germans were not used for the benefit of the Jews but rather in order to obtain positions for himself and his cronies. Stanley Hochman, who for a time was in charge of food distribution at the airfield camp, says that Wenkart demanded special favors, such as double rations for himself, his wife, and his little niece. Moreover, during the deportations in May and October 1942, he used his Jewish police to try to prevent Jews from sneaking into the airfield camp, where they would have been safe temporarily.[74]

71 Hana Tupolski testimony, YVA, O.3/9295; Yaakov Ahiezer testimony, O.3/2951.

72 Aida Milgrojm-Citrinbojm testimony, in *Dęblin-Modzitz Book.*

73 S. Perlmutter testimony, ibid.

74 Testimonies of Zvi Eichenbrenner, Devorah Reznik, and Yisrael Bubis, ibid.; Ignatz Bubis, *Ich bin ein deutscher Staatsbürger*, pp. 64–65.

Wenkart himself attributes the good conditions in the camp to the fact that in World War I he had saved the life of one of the Luftwaffe officers in the camp, Eduard Bromofsky. Wenkart claims that he always took initiatives on behalf of the Jews, using his good relations with some of the German and Austrian staff to protect the Jews in the camp and keep the children alive. He claims he kept out those trying to sneak into the camp because they endangered the existence of the camp and the survival of its Jews.[75]

It would seem, as with other Jewish officials under Nazi rule – Judenrat members and camp officials – that both versions about Wenkart are true. A person who seeks special conditions for himself while also working hard to preserve the camp may be remembered well for his hard work or poorly for his self-aggrandizement. The memory of Wenkart, as with other people in similar positions, would be affected by an individual's personal encounter with him. Thus, Hochman resented Wenkart's demands for additional rations, which Hochman refused, and what he believed were Wenkart's subsequent vengeful actions against him. Yet Tupolski is forever grateful for Wenkart saving her life when she was ill, and Citrinbojm remained impressed by his devotion to the children. Did he get along well with the German authorities in the camp in order to advance himself, or in order to preserve the camp and its Jews? Here, too, the answer would appear to be yes to both possibilities. Loud, crude, seeking position, and laboring to keep the Jews alive, Wenkart was in many ways a normal person with certain leadership qualities.

The train-station camp was closed in September 1943, and most of the Jews were sent to Poniatowa, where they shared the fate of the Jews in that camp during the *Erntefest* operation.

In *Biała-Podlaska* there were five forced-labor camps with several hundred Jews. They continued to function for a brief time after the October 1942 liquidation of the Jewish community, and included: the Battalion 34 camp; the Winete camp, where the prisoners worked at menial labor; the "Cid" camp, where they toiled at construction and sewer work; the airfield camp; and the Małaszewicz camp near

75 Wenkart, *Befehlsnotstand,* pp. 31–83, *passim.*

Terespol. Conditions in the camps were brutal, except for Battalion 34, which was bearable. The religious laborers there were even able to organize a daily *minyan* for *minha* and *maariv* (the afternoon and evening prayers).

Jews steadily trickled in from hiding places or were brought in by the Germans, so their numbers in each camp increased until December 1942. At the end of October, a group of young laborers from the Battalion 34 camp, led by Zilia Goldberg, stole some weapons and clothing and fled to the forests. They were later reported to be the ones who shot and killed *Kreishauptmann* Kühl on the Międzyrzec road.

There was a typhus outbreak in the Battalion 34 camp in December, and, on December 15, forty Jews were taken out of the Winete camp and shot. This caused all the other labor-camp inmates in Biała-Podlaska to worry. On December 17, 1942, the Jewish guards at the Battalion 34 camp notified the inmates at 4:30 A.M. that the camp was surrounded. All 231 Jews in the camp were rounded up and marched in rows of seven under the guard of five Gestapo men and ten soldiers. They heard shooting ahead and understood that the ill who had been taken out in trucks had been shot. As they reached a deep pit, Yisrael Rodzinek suddenly fled. The Germans shot and missed, and their commander's attack dog did not obey the attack command. Then the laborer Senjor yelled "Run!" and everyone fled, yelling "Hurrah!" Some were shot, while others made it to the Międzyrzec ghetto. Following this, additional Jews were brought in from other camps, such as Poniatowa, to supplement the manpower for the Luftwaffe.[76]

"Operation Erntefest"

Near the end of October 1943, Jewish forced-laborers in Majdanek, Trawniki, and Poniatowa were put to work digging zigzag trenches near the camp perimeter. Even though they were told that these

76 M. J. Feigenbaum, in *Biała-Podlaska Book*, pp. 68–74; Hela Jaffe testimony, YVA, O.3/2911.

were defensive trenches, the Jews sensed imminent danger. On October 28, fifty-one Jewish women were sent from Majdanek to the Milejowo jam factory, where some 150 men were working in a small Wehrmacht labor camp.

On November 2, 2–3,000 SS and police troops from Krakow, Warsaw, and the Lublin District gathered in Lublin. That night Sporrenberg met with the commanders of the various units, the commandants of the three camps, the new KdS, *SS-Sturmbannführer* Dr. Karl Pütz, and his own staff to discuss details of the two-day operation that was to commence at dawn – the murder of the Jewish labor force in the Trawniki, Poniatowa, and Lublin camps.[77] The reasons for this operation are not known definitively, but most historians agree that Himmler probably ordered it in reaction to the prisoner uprising and escape from Sobibór on October 14. Following the Warsaw ghetto uprising in April, and the Treblinka and Białystok uprisings in August, and with the ever-increasing partisan activity in the GG, especially in the Lublin District, Himmler sought to reduce the security risk and be finished with the Jews.[78] As a result, more than 50,000 Jewish forced-laborers in the Lublin District on November 2, 1943, were reduced to fewer than 10,000 by November 6.

The wake-up bell went off in the forced-labor camps as normal at 5:00 A.M. on a cloudy November 3, 1943. However, when the Jews in Trawniki, Dorohucza, Lipowa 7, the Lublin airfield, Majdanek, Milejowo, and Budzyń got up, they saw that their camp had been surrounded by masses of armed troops. In Poniatowa, following the

77 See Ester Winderbaum and Ludka Fischer-Chanesman testimonies, YVA, O.3/2314; Ester Rubenstein, M.49.E/1013; Ludwika (Leah) Fischer testimony, *Opole-Lubelski Yizkor Book*, pp. 306–308; Hava Halpern Brojtman testimony, YVA, M.1.E/2073; Werner Wehrheim testimony, TR.10/1291, pp. 51: 9858–9859; Browning, *Ordinary Men*, p. 144; Pohl, *Judenpolitik*, p. 171; Ester Rubenstein and Władysław Hobot testimonies, Edward Dziadosz, ed., *Juden Massen Exekutionen, 3. November 1943, Majdanek, Poniatowa, Trawniki; Erinnerungen* (Lublin: Panstwowe Muzeum na Majdanku and Uniwersytet Marii Curie-Skłodkowskiej, 1990), pp. 34–39; Grabitz and Scheffler, eds., *Letzte Spuren*, pp. 328–333.

78 For these suggestions by historians, see, for example, Grabitz and Scheffler, eds., *Letzte Spuren*, pp. 328–329; Browning, *Ordinary Men*, p. 144; Pohl, *Judenpolitik*, p. 171; Edward Dziadosz, Introduction, *Juden Massen Exekutionen*, p. 4.

usual roll call, the Jews were sent back to their barracks. There was no work that day.[79] At Trawniki and Majdanek, large loudspeakers had been set up near the trenches that the Jews had dug, and loud music was blaring. The Dorohucza Jews were loaded onto a train and brought to Trawniki, while the Trawniki Jews were ordered out of their barracks and marched in groups toward the trenches in the adjacent Hiwi training camp, guarded by the camp's Ukrainian Hiwis. By the time the Dorohucza Jews reached Trawniki at around 7:00 A.M., the shooting was already well under way. Each group of Jews was ordered to undress and place their clothing on what became a mountain of clothing. They were then ordered to lie face down on top of the previous victims, and the SS troops shot them at point-blank range in the nape of the neck. By approximately 3:00 P.M., 6,000 Jews were dead. Only a handful succeeded in hiding and, ultimately, surviving.[80]

At Majdanek the murder included Jewish forced-laborers in the airfield camp, in Majdanek, and in the Lipowa 7 POW camp. As the prisoners were being gathered by the SS guards, approximately 300 men and 300 women from the airfield camp were selected by the Germans in Majdanek for clean-up and exhumation and to burn the bodies. That morning the Jewish prisoners from Lipowa 7 and the airfield camp were marched under heavy guard toward Majdanek. At the camp itself, near Field 5, loudspeakers were already blaring loud music — tangos, waltzes, and marches. On the way to Majdanek, the Jewish POWs from Lipowa 7 rushed their guards, broke through the

79 Ester Winderbaum and Ludka Fischer-Chanesman testimonies, YVA, O.3/2314; Hava Halpern Brojtman testimony, M.1.E/2073; Werner Wehrheim testimony, YVA, TR.10/1291, pp. 51:9858–9859; Ester Rubenstein and Władysław Hobot testimonies, *Juden Massen Exekutionen*, pp. 34–39; Georg Klimanek testimonies, YVA, TR.10/1291, vol. 22, pp. 3833–3842; Zina Czapnik testimony, Grabitz and Scheffler, eds., *Letzte Spuren*, p. 269 (original in StA Hamburg, 147 Js 43/69, p. 13016).

80 Klimanek testimonies, YVA, TR.10/1291, vol. 22, pp. 3833–3842; Hobot testimony, *Juden Massen Exekutionen*, pp. 38–39; Grabitz and Scheffler, eds., *Letzte Spuren*, p. 262; Franz Skubinn testimony, pp. 267–268, ibid. (original in StA Hamburg 147 Js 43/69, pp. 7027ff.); Zina Czapnik testimony, ibid., pp. 269–270; Raja Mileczina testimony, ibid., p. 271; Streibel indictment, YVA, TR.10/756, pp. 173–179; Streibel verdict, TR.10/869, vol. 11, pp. 1–2, 41–54, 98–116, 147–180.

cordon, and began running away. Nearly all of them were shot by the police and SS guards before they could escape. The men and women from the airfield camp arrived at Majdanek during the morning. Waiting for them were firing squads of ten to twelve men each from the SS "Wiking" division or the police. The shooting began at around 7:30 A.M., as a steady stream of prisoners was marched into the camp and to the murder site all morning. The shooting progressed without pause. During the moments that the records were changed to play more music, the rat-a-tat-tat of the shooting could be heard by the other Majdanek prisoners and by Poles in Lublin (many of whom watched the scene from their rooftops). The shooting was conducted into three trenches simultaneously, and, by the time it was over, toward evening, 18,400 Jews had been shot dead in Majdanek.[81]

After the murder was completed in Majdanek, part of the murder troops proceeded to Poniatowa, where the shooting began early the next morning (November 4). Here, too, loudspeakers blared loud music to drown out the sound of the shooting. At morning roll call the Jews were surrounded by armed Ukrainians and Germans pointing guns at them. They were then squeezed into a few barracks. Some women thought that this was going to be a selection, so they tried to make themselves look better. The Jewish prisoners were taken out in groups and marched under armed guard to the trenches that they themselves had dug only a few days earlier. They placed their clothing and shoes in large piles that grew to be small mountains. Many tried to evade the round-up but were caught and returned to the killing pits. Others considered escaping, but stayed in order not to abandon loved ones. One men's barrack erupted in revolt. Consequently, the barrack was locked from the

81 *Juden Massen Exekutionen*, testimonies of Jerzy Kwiatkowski, Mieczyslaw Michalowicz, Feliks Siewa, Aleksander Zakoscielny, Ida Mazower, Stefania Perzanowska, Josef Reznik, Erich Muhsfeldt; YVA, TR.10/815, pp. 127–128; Wolf Antoni testimony, JM/3536b; Friedrich Ruppert testimony, NO-1903; Gotthardt Schubert interrogations, TR.10/1146Z, vol. 15, pp. 3094–3097; Georg Werk interrogation, TR.10/1291, vol. 28, pp. 4885–4887; Browning, *Ordinary Men*, pp. 145–147; Schwindt, *Das Konzentrations- und Vernichtungslager Majdanek*, pp. 268–286; Kranz, *Extermination of Jews*, pp. 64–69; Krakowski, *War of the Doomed*, pp. 270–271.

outside and torched, killing all the men inside. The operation lasted until 2:30 P.M.

Only three women survived the murder at Poniatowa. Ester Rubinstein (Winderbaum) covered her face and was uttering the "*Shma Yisrael*" prayer to herself when she was shot and fell into the pit. She had been shot in the leg, but the wound was not serious. She lost consciousness and awoke in the cold November evening. She saw bodies and heard moans of prisoners who had not yet died. Soon the Germans came to finish anyone who seemed to still be alive. One German lifted Rubinstein's head to check her, but apparently the blood of a corpse next to her had spread all over her head and led the German to think that she was dead. The Germans covered the pits with pine trees and left. Ester then crawled out of the pit and crossed a field. There she discovered Ludka Fischer (Chanesman), who had also survived and had crawled out of the pit naked. Fischer had refrained from trying to escape so that she could remain with her ten-year-old daughter. At the pit her daughter had asked her to cover her eyes so that she would not witness the horrible scene. The bullet that killed Fischer's daughter only wounded her arm. The two women wandered the woods and fields looking for help, but at first the sight of the two naked, bloody women frightened the local Poles who came upon them. As they continued to wander, some local farmers gave them bits of clothing. Soon they encountered Roza, a third woman who had escaped from the pits. The three began to wander together, with Ludka supporting them with money she had hidden in her vagina. Finally they encountered Maria Maciąg near Kazimierz Dolny. Maciąg was determined to help them in order to compensate for her failed effort to help the Jewish family for whom she had once worked. Ultimately Maciąg contacted the ŻEGOTA organization, which found hiding places for the three women until the end of the war.[82]

Following the shooting, special teams of Jews were put to work

82 Ester Rubinstein Winderbaum testimony and Ludka Fischer Chanesman testimony, YVA, O.3/2314; Ester Rubenstein, M.49.E/1013; Ludwika (Leah) Fischer testimony, *Opole-Lubelski Book*, pp. 308–320; Walter Többens testimonies, TR.10/26, pp. 65–68; August Bauch interrogation, pp. 13:2650–2659, in YVA, TR.10/1146Z; Heinrich Gley interrogation, ibid., pp. 14:2889–

sorting the clothing and belongings of the dead Jews and burning their bodies. At Poniatowa, 120 people were brought in from Majdanek to burn the bodies under SS and Ukrainian guard. Once the bodies were burned, 100 of the 120 were shot by the Germans. Those were burned by the remaining twenty. Then sixteen of these were shot by the SS and burned by the remaining four, who were then shot in turn and burned by the SS. The clean-up job of the 600 Jews who were left behind in Majdanek also included burning the bodies. When that job was done, they, too, were shot.[83]

The Jewish men and women forced-laborers in Milejowo were brought to Trawniki on November 5. Six women were put to work in the kitchen, while the men were assigned to burn the bodies on large pyres using railroad ties. The men had to pull gold teeth from the corpses and check the bodies for hidden valuables. The work was supervised by Ukrainian guards who constantly beat them. Men and women were housed together during this operation, and each day the men returned with horror stories from the crematory pyres. They worked around the clock in three eight-hour shifts and completed the work in eight days. On the last day, the second shift (8:00 P.M. to 4:00 A.M.) did not return. Bartetzko came with a group of Ukrainians and ordered all the men outside, while the women remained in the barrack. They were counted, and then a few days of quiet ensued. The women were moved to a separate barrack. When the shooting of the last men began, Yehezkel Hering succeeded in sneaking away and returned to the women's barrack. He put on women's clothing and hid among the women for two weeks before fleeing.

Another discovery by the women was five-year-old Moszek, who had succeeded in hiding in a barrack during the *Erntefest*. The Germans allowed him to stay with them until March 21, 1944, when he was taken by the Germans to Majdanek and killed. The women stayed in the camp sorting the victims' clothing and

2892; Gicewicz, "Obóz Pracy," pp. 102–104. Maria Maciąg was recognized as a Righteous Among the Nations in December 2012. See YVA, M.31/12474.

83 August Rudolf Bauch interrogation, YVA, TR.10/1146Z, pp. 13:2656–2659; Walter Többens testimony, TR.10/26, pp. 67–68; TR.10/815, pp. 127–128.

personal possessions until May 1944, at which time they were sent to Majdanek and from there to Auschwitz and other camps.[84]

The Last Forced-Laborers

Several camps were spared during "Operation *Erntefest*," leaving some 10,000 Jewish forced-laborers, primarily in the remnant camps in Lublin (Zamek, Chopin Street, and at maintenance work), in military camps (Dęblin, Biała-Podlaska, Zamość, and Wifo), and in the camps in the Kraśnik area (Budzyń, Kraśnik [and Wifo]). There were also Jews in the POW camp in Borki, near Chełm, until the end of 1943 or early 1944, and Jews remained working on German-run farms, such as the one run by Lazarczyk near Annopol.

The Military Camps. In Dęblin the prisoners were unaware of the *Erntefest*. Conditions worsened for them in early 1944, when Braun replaced Duse as commandant, but then improved again when the older and calmer NCO Rademacher took over shortly before the camp was dismantled. The airfield camp functioned until the German retreat from the area on July 22–23, 1944. The Jews were transferred to Częstochowa in three groups, on July 17, 20, and 23. The male workers were put to work in munitions factories there, while most of the women and children were killed in the Jewish cemetery in Dęblin or after their arrival in Częstochowa. Only the children on the last transport were spared.[85]

84 Hava Brotman testimony, YVA, M.1.E/2073; Yehezkel Hering testimony, M.1.E/760; TR.10/756, pp. 173–179; TR.10/869, vol. 11, pp. 147–180; Mirjam Blits, *Auschwitz 13917; Hoe ik de Duitse concentratiekampen overleefde* (Amsterdam and Brussels: Elsevier, 1961), pp. 54–116, *passim*.

85 Yaakov Ahiezer testimony, YVA, O.3/2951; Hana Schildkraut Tupolski testimony, O.3/9295; Esther Neumann testimony, O.3/9077; Hersz Szerberg testimony, M.1.E/1327; Shlomo Welt testimony, M.1.E/1328; D. Cymerowicz testimony, M.1.E/1372; Moshe Mlawer testimony, M.1.E/1627; M.1.E/874, testimony with illegible signature; testimonies in *Dęblin-Modzitz Book* — Staphian Fidelis, Zvi Eichenbrenner, Andzja (Hana) Tupolski, Aida Milgrojm-Citrinbojm, Devorah Reznik, Shloma Welt, S. Perlmutter, Kalman Paris, Yisrael (Ignatz) Bubis; Wenkart, *Befehlsnotstand*, pp. 19–83; Hochman, *Mr. Fate*, pp. 19–30; Farkash, *History of the Jews of Puławy District*, p. 114.

Many of the Jews working in the Biała-Podlaska airfield camp were shot in November 1943, but a small group of several dozen continued to work for the Luftwaffe and the Gestapo in Biała-Podlaska until April 1944, when they were transferred to Majdanek.[86] A third sizable Luftwaffe base outside Zamość also had a Jewish forced-labor camp that was set up in September 1943. Here 1,200 Jews – some from Poniatowa but most from outside the district – worked at construction and road-laying jobs. Their conditions were livable, and the *Erntefest* passed them by. Like Biała-Podlaska, the camp was liquidated in April 1944, and the prisoners sent to Majdanek, before being transferred to the Starachowice and Skarżysko-Kamienna camps further west.[87]

Whereas the survival of Jews working for the Luftwaffe may have made sense from a Nazi perspective in late 1943 and 1944, the survival of Budzyń seems odd indeed. As the stories of Trawniki, Poniatowa, and the DAW camps show, profitability was not a guarantee against destruction. Most of the Jews at the profitable Puławy sawmill were also shot during the *Erntefest* operation; only part of the camp was left until the German retreat in July 1944.[88] Yet unprofitable Budzyń survived.

The manifestation of relative decency toward the Jews at the Budzyń factories in spite of their low production level, as well as his own imminent departure and possible loss of lucrative camps, led Globocnik to attack the German civilians at Budzyń in a September

86 Feigenbaum, in *Biała-Podlaska Book*, pp. 68–74; Hela Jaffe testimony, YVA, O.3/2911.

87 Abram Goldman testimony, YVA, M.1.E/2289; Pohl, *Judenpolitik*, p. 166. Although Felicja Karay, in her excellent book *Death Comes in Yellow: Skarżysko-Kamienna Slave Labor Camp* (Amsterdam, et al.: Harwood, 1996) does not discuss a group of Jewish forced-laborers from Zamość that was brought to Skarżysko, Abram Goldman is very clear about this. Perhaps Karay included this group among other groups of forced-laborers brought to Skarżysko at that time. See also Christopher R. Browning's important account of the arrival of a group of Jews from these places in the Lublin District in Starachowice in spring 1944, in his *Remembering Survival: Inside a Nazi Slave-Labor Camp* (New York and London: W. W. Norton & Co., 2010), pp. 198–204.

88 YVA, TR.10/770, pp. 106–109; Michalsen/Hantke indictment, YVA, TR.10/813, p. 42; Hantke interrogation, Hamburg, April 7, 9, 13, 1964, YVA, TR.10/1291, vol. 28, p. 4964.

3, 1943, letter to Karl Brandt (for Himmler). Globocnik complained that the Heinkel factory that he had established at Budzyń was grossly under-productive. The large and well-staffed camp (about 15,000 sq. meters; 2,600 Jewish skilled laborers) had been ready for high-priority work on German warplanes by early 1943, yet the giant halls had remained empty. Heinkel never used them, he charged. Globocnik requested the intervention of Luftwaffe Field Marshal General Erhard Milch and suggested that the SS take over the whole operation, without the German industrialists, and produce war materiel.[89] This was followed by a flurry of correspondence between Brandt and various people, including Oswald Pohl, in an effort to utilize better the hangar warehouses at Budzyń.[90] However, although Budzyń was one of the camps that Pohl and the WVHA took over officially on October 22, making it a sub-camp of Majdanek, little changed in the camp until February 1944.[91] And despite its low production, which survivors confirm, and despite its connection to Majdanek, Budzyń was spared during the *Erntefest* operation. Unlike Dęblin, which really played a role in the German war effort, it seems that Budzyń may have been spared for other reasons entirely.

On November 3 or 4, at the morning roll call, Camp Commandant Tauscher told the prisoners to return to their barracks as there would be no work that day. Their barracks would be locked from the outside with heavy beams in order to protect them from possible attack by Polish partisans. Trucks arrived, and SS and

89 Globocnik to Brandt, September 3, 1943, NA (National Archives), T175/54, in YVA, JM/4372.

90 Brandt to Pohl, September 6, 1943; Rückenbauer, Bayernmotor, to Brandt, October 2, 1943, requesting use of the empty warehouses, and Brandt's October 16 response, referring him to Sporrenberg; Brandt to Sporrenberg, October 17, 1943, NA, T175/54, in YVA, JM/4372.

91 On the takeover of the district's forced-labor camps by Pohl and the WVHA, see Pohl's September 7, 1943, memo of a conference at the WVHA headquarters in Berlin, including himself, Globocnik, and others, Nuremberg Document, NO-599 (copies in: *Faschismus*, pp. 459–460; *Eksterminacja*, pp. 254–255); Globocnik's summary report on "Operation Reinhard," NO-060; YVA, Streibl verdict, TR.10/869, pp. II:167, XI:22–23; Birmes and Gollak indictment, TR.10/815, pp. 68–76, 120–124. For information on the roles of some of the WVHA participants at the meeting, see Allen, *The Business of Genocide*, pp. 181–189, 246–252.

Ukrainian troops poured out and surrounded the barracks. The prisoners realized that being locked in their barracks and surrounded by troops likely spelled their impending liquidation.

The no-work order apparently lasted three days. According to the survivors, Stockman meanwhile was able to telephone Jäger and Hintze and inform them of the danger. They then phoned their superiors in the Heinkel Company in Berlin, who in turn intervened with Göring (and/or other senior officials) in order to save the camp. They argued that the Jewish laborers were essential for the construction of an airfield and other war-related labor. The cordon around the Jews' barracks was then removed, and the Jews returned to work as usual.

They subsequently learned through various sources about the murder of the Jews at Trawniki and Poniatowa. A small group from Budzyń was taken one morning to Majdanek, returning in the evening with trucks full of clothing, some of it soaked in blood. These prisoners reported the murders at Majdanek, and some, at least, found cause for hope in the fact that the clothing was being transferred to them for sorting. This meant that they were not yet slated for death.[92]

No German sources have yet been uncovered to corroborate the details of this story, but it is clear that Budzyń should have been part of the *Erntefest* operation, like other Majdanek sub-camps, yet it was spared. Sparing Budzyń's Jews also meant sparing Budzyń's Germans from being sent to fight on the eastern front, allowing them instead to keep their comfortable jobs far from enemy lines. Was Himmler

92 Freiberg, *Darkness Covered the Earth*, pp. 176–177; Orenstein, *I Shall Live*, pp. 154–156; Wyszogrod, *A Brush with Death*, pp. 170–172; Władysław Friedhelm testimony, YVA, O.33/637; Eli Fiszman testimony, M.1.E/714; Dov Finger testimony, O.3/2780; Jehoszua Seweryn Szarason testimony, TR.11/01113; TR.10/869, pp. XI:28–29; Laks, *I Was There*, pp. 231–232; Wdowinski testimony, *The Eichmann Trial*, pp. 1234, 1236; *idem*, *And We Are Not Saved* (New York: Philosophical Library, 1963), p. 67, n.1; Yaakov Arieh Ender, Motl Brafman, and Yehoshua Hochrad, in *Sefer Kraśnik*, pp. 339, 361, 406; Hurwitz, *Forbidden Strawberries*, pp. 124–128. Wyszogrod recalls that the Jews were locked in their barracks following evening roll call and released at 7:00 A.M. the next morning, but most of the other testimonies relate a three-day confinement following the morning roll call. All the survivors relate there was German civilian intervention, and most attribute this to Stockman's initiative.

not aware of Budzyń's fraud, despite Globocnik's complaint only two months earlier? These questions remain unanswered, but the fact is that the camp was surrounded by troops apparently prepared to kill the Jews, only to have things return to normal shortly afterward.

Part of the Jewish labor force was put to work dismantling the Budzyń camp in December 1943, while another part began to level ground and to erect a new camp a few kilometers away, at the site of the factory. On the night of February 6/7 or 7/8, 1944, as people were returning from work, the Ukrainian guards opened fire from all sides. Everyone ran for cover; the shooting lasted about an hour and a half, killing several dozen Jews. Others were then selected by the Germans, stripped naked, and marched away to be shot.

Before dawn they were taken by groups for a quick cold shower and ordered to turn in their civilian clothing for striped concentration-camp clothing with red and yellow stars and prisoner numbers. At 3:00 A.M. they were then marched under SS and Ukrainian guard to the new Budzyń concentration camp. The new camp commandant was *SS-Scharführer* Josef Leipold; his deputy was *Unterscharführer* Wilhelm Kleist. Stockman was appointed *Lagerälteste*. The camp was surrounded by an electrified barbed-wire fence, and Leipold's regime included military discipline and stricter punishments than under the previous regime. But, in general, conditions at the camp actually improved now that it was a concentration camp. It was calmer and quieter for the Jews, and they had better food, easier work, less violence, a much shorter distance from roll call to work (several dozen meters), and better housing conditions – now they were 108 or 109 to a barrack instead of several hundred. Daniel Freiberg recalls that the Jewish inmates came to refer to the camp as a "rest home" relative to what had preceded and then followed it. The camp's transition to a concentration camp was finalized in the SS a week after the above events.

Among the new work that the prisoners performed was repair of tanks and of armored vehicles for the G.K. Mott Company. Many of the Jews shirked their work, but the German supervisors did not seem to mind. Jews found valuables and goods in the vehicles, which they began trading, with the Germans' tacit approval. The prisoners did not like Leipold because he was the severest of all the Germans, although he did not murder or beat anyone. Kleist, however, was well liked, and the more junior SS men, most of them Romanian *Volksdeutsche*, also behaved decently most of the time. The above-mentioned assistance with the Passover *seder* is one illustration of this.

Budzyń continued to function as a concentration camp and forced-labor camp until the spring of 1944. In March, the Germans (civilians and SS) began to send prisoners to other camps, and the camp was gradually liquidated during the following three months. The prisoners and staff were transferred to camps further west, such as the Heinkel factory in Mielec, the arms factories in Radom, and the camps at Wieliczka and Płaszów.[93]

The above account of the last months of the Budzyń camp is based to a large degree on survivor testimonies. There are slight differences among these testimonies, such as the exact date of the transfer to the new camp (the night of February 6/7 or 7/8) and the exact number of people per barrack (108 or 109). However, these insignificant differences only highlight the reliability of the testimony. They also reiterate the importance of survivor testimonies in obtaining an accurate account of the events. In German documents the formal change of Budzyń to a concentration camp was on February 15, 1944, but the survivors relate that the preparations for this began two or three months earlier, and the actual change preceded the formal document by a week.[94]

The Kraśnik Camps

The Kraśnik camp was in many ways perhaps the strangest of all the forced-labor camps in 1943–1944. It was a camp where life

93 Wladyslaw Friedhelm testimony, YVA, O.33/637; Freiberg, *Darkness Covered the Earth*, pp. 183–191; Laks, *I Was There*, pp. 232–233; Wyszogrod, *A Brush with Death*, pp. 173–175; Michalsen and Hantke indictment and verdict, YVA, TR.10/813, indictment, pp. 168–172, verdict, p. 42; Birmes and Gollak indictment, TR.10/815, p. 124; Mendel Korn testimony, O.3/2941; Yaakov Arieh Ender and Motl Brafman in *Sefer Kraśnik*, pp. 340, 361–362.

94 Friedhelm, ibid.; Freiberg, ibid.; *The Trial of Oswald Pohl*, Green Series, vol. IV (Washington: Government Press Office, 1948). Many of the documents cited in connection with WVHA can be found in the proceedings of this trial.

remained mostly peaceful and secure for the Jewish prisoners, who considered the commandant, *SS-Unterscharführer* Alois Gröger, a relatively decent fellow. There was a semblance of family life for some of the prisoners, and there were even a number of children. According to some accounts, the commandant's children and the Jewish children were actually permitted to play together. Yet Gröger periodically killed prisoners, and, in 1944, there was a series of escape attempts. For Globocnik and his men, the camp was a facade for a widespread Lublin SS conspiracy to reap personal profit from Jewish labor. As both Germans and Jews from the camp recall, the camp was "*Schwarz geführt*" (run "black"; i.e., as a black market), and its purpose was meant to be hidden from Himmler and the senior leaders of the SS. This unusual combination of factors kept the camp intact until the German withdrawal from the area in July 1944, and left the Jews there some room for maneuver in their struggle to survive. They had contacts with the outside, ate relatively well, were not physically debilitated, and prepared escape plans and false papers. In all but its longevity, the Kraśnik camp stood in sharp contrast to the Budzyń camp, even though both began with heavy SSPF influence.[95]

During the liquidation of the Kraśnik community and several nearby communities in October 1942, *Kreishauptmann* Hans Lenk had set aside 300 Jews — craftsmen, skilled laborers, some Judenrat

95 The story and analysis of the Kraśnik and Wifo camps is based on: WAPL, SSPF 2; YVA, O.51/211; YVA, O.53/82; YVA, JM/3506; the following testimonies in YVA, TR.11/01113: Itzchak Rosenbusch, Cipora Berger, Isak Gerenreich, Chaskiel Brotman, Pinchas Stein, Chaja Rotenberg Goldbaum, Moshe Dorn, Abraham Waks, Chaim Sztejnbok, Anczel Szteinberg, Salman Lederfein, Jecheskiel Rajndel, Reuven Feferkuchen, Szmuel Brand, Nahum Rozenel, Jehoshua Kron, Asher Mandelblatt; Mischa Stahlhammer testimony, YVA, O.3/4312; Ber Twardagóra testimonies, YVA, M.49.E/1053 and 1195; Shlomo Waks testimony, YVA, M.1.E/768; Chil Hener testimony, YVA, TR.10/1291, vol. 23, pp. 4002–4007; YVA, TR.10/770; YVA, TR.10/868; Alois Gröger interrogations, YVA, TR.10/1291, vol. 47, pp. 8791–8838; Johann Offermann interrogations, ibid., vol. 28, pp. 4820–4834, vol. 47, pp. 8839–8854, vol. 51, pp. 9798–9800, vol. 55, pp. 10679–10683; *Sefer Kraśnik*, testimonies of Shalom Garen, Shmuel Brand, and Yehiel Teper, pp. 317–331, 411–420, 428–430, the article by Tatiana Berenstein, pp. 293–316. Specific information and quotations will be cited from the relevant source.

members, Jewish policemen, and their families – to work for the civilian government. They were first kept in a school building, from which they could see the deportation of the other Jews. They were then transferred to the compound of the main synagogue, which had held refugee quarters and several workshops prior to the October deportation. Carpentry and upholstery workshops were quickly set up there. Pesach Kawa, the former head of the Jewish police in Kraśnik, became the *Lagerälteste* and head of the Jewish police in the camp. Initially the camp was guarded only by the Jewish police.

Approximately 200 of the Jews in the Kraśnik camp were put to work at various jobs for civilian officials, while the other 100 were sent to live and work at the Wifo camp some 2 km. down the road (see below), where they had worked prior to the October deportation. Globocnik took over the camp on November 23, and appointed Gröger commandant. Gröger's supervisor was *SS-Hauptsturmführer* Herbert Ulbrich, head of Globocnik's SSPF personnel department, who was succeeded, in September 1943, by *SS-Untersturmführer* Johann Offermann. The Kraśnik camp's official function was to make and repair school furniture for the German schools in the Lublin District, while the Wifo camp maintained a large gasoline depot and filling station for the Wehrmacht.

The Wifo camp – Wirtschaftliche Forschungsgesellschaft – had been operating since 1941, as Benzinabfüllkomando 974. The German firms Schmidt & Junk and Jucho had built a large gasoline depot and filling station there for the Wehrmacht. The initial laborers at Wifo included Jews from Kraśnik and some 300 Soviet POWs. The latter group all died within a few months. The gasoline was stored in two large tanks at a switchback on the road near the Kraśnik railroad station. When the Jews were brought here from the Kraśnik synagogue, they were moved to two barracks at the site. They worked in maintenance, construction, rail construction, and other jobs, and their food was sufficient for subsistence. A driver was sent weekly to Kraśnik with several inmates in order to buy bread. Not only were the quantities of food above starvation rations, but the Jews also maintained some contact with the outside world by means of these trips and were thus able to supplement their food supply. The Wehrmacht men at Wifo were mostly older, noncombatant soldiers, who treated the Jews decently. However, some of the German civilians at the camp, the SS, and the Ukrainians were far less benevolent. In late summer 1943, as Budzyń received Jewish forced-laborers from other camps, Ulbrich ordered Gröger to take over responsibility for the Wifo camp as well.[96]

On September 22, Offermann, Gröger and Ulbrich completed a report for Sporrenberg regarding the first period of the Kraśnik camp — "*Bericht über das Arbeitslager Krasnik*" — on the occasion of Offermann succeeding Ulbrich as the camp's supervisor in Lublin. Globocnik had allocated 63,826 złotys from confiscated Jewish money to set up the camp. The funds were deposited in a special account in Kraśnik in five unequal payments from December 1, 1942 to July 23, 1943. Of this, there were expenses of 24,398 złotys by September 15, 1943, leaving a balance of 39,428 złotys.[97] To maintain the camp and support the laborers, small workshops were set up on the side for county projects and to serve German SS and police for a fee. These workshops included tailor shops, shoemakers, watchmakers, gold-jewelers, dental technicians, furriers, metalworkers, saddlemakers, an automobile body shop, bookbinders, ropemakers, and tanners. The income from these jobs was meant to provision the camp and feed the workers. By September 15, 1943, the income reached 92,724.01 złotys, and expenses were 83,608.02 złotys, for a 9,116 złoty profit. There were 251 Jewish workers — 232 men and nineteen women.[98]

On the surface this was a standard interim report, reflecting a small profit that could be deposited in SS coffers or used to continue to run the camp. Yet this insignificant camp, which was turning over only modest sums of money, was spared during the *Erntefest*. Unlike Budzyń, it did not even have the facade of an essential war-related

96 Trial of Mohwinkel, Gröger, Offermann, et al., YVA TR.10/770, pp. 115–123, TR.10/868, pp. 246–247, 257–263; testimonies of Isak Gerenreich, Chaskiel Brotman, Moshe Dorn, Salman Lederfein, YVA, TR.11/01113; Mischa Stahlhammer testimony, YVA, O.3/4312; Tatiana Bernstein and Yehiel Teper, in *Sefer Kraśnik*, pp. 308–313, 428–430.

97 Although the numbers itemized in the report do not add up exactly to these sums, the gap is only 2,000 złotys and is not significant to this discussion.

98 "Bericht über das Arbeitslager Krasnik," WAPL, SSPF 2 (copy in YVA, O.51/211).

labor camp. An examination of records from the camp during the second half of its existence, following this report, reveals the true nature of the camp and the reasons for its longevity.

On February 22, 1944, handwritten German records showed that the camp had 24,810 złotys in cash and 407,199 złotys in two bank accounts. On the same day Sporrenberg ordered an additional 90,000 złotys of profits to be deposited into the Kraśnik account.[99] These 522,000 złotys are a truer reflection of the Kraśnik operation than Offermann's carefully crafted report on school furniture.

During the Christmas shopping period in 1943, the Kraśnik camp turned a huge profit for the SSPF conspirators. Between October 18 and December 24, 1943, Offermann forwarded 692 personal gift orders from SS personnel in and outside the Lublin District. The orders were all considered urgent, to be completed before Christmas, and, in many cases, before the particular SS client departed home for his Christmas furlough. Sporrenberg himself placed several orders during this period; he received the items gratis.[100] The German desire to keep this business going is what spared the Jews of Kraśnik until the end.

The Christmas orders included articles for use by SS personnel and their families, as well as items to be taken to family back home. On October 18 and November 2, Kurt Classen ordered a lamp for a children's room, a clothes' closet for the SSPF, four sewing boxes, a child's bed, kitchen buffet, radio table, and wardrobe, all for personal use. Gustav Hanelt ordered a child's bed and stuffing for a mattress (October 20). Richard Thomalla ordered a couch, a round table, and four stools (November 2). On November 22 and December 8, Sporrenberg ordered toys, two pairs of women's boots, and two pairs of children's shoes, all of which Offermann passed on as urgent and gratis. Sporrenberg also ordered twenty-two special SS rings (November 22), apparently as gifts to be given out at the SSPF Christmas party. On December 8, Offermann ordered 225 saucers for whiskey glasses and 225 plates for beer glasses for the SSPF Christmas party, along with

99 See handwritten ledgers for February 1944, and Offermann's memo to Kramme, February 28, 1944, WAPL, SSPF 2.

100 See the Christmas orders in WAPL, SSPF 2.

twelve dollhouses, twenty toy ships, fifteen toy automobiles, and many similar children's gifts to be ready by December 15. The party was scheduled for December 17, but many would be leaving on furlough before that date. Since Hermann Höfle would be leaving Lublin by the end of next week, Offermann wrote, his December 8 order for two pairs of children's slippers (sizes 29 and 31) and one pair of women's slippers (size 39) was also urgent.

Parallel to these private orders, orders for official use also continued to come in. For example, Abteilung Unterkunft (the lodgings' department) ordered a hat rack, a radio table, and a round table, while the Zentralkrankenrevier (central infirmary in Lublin) ordered 100 boxes for two sizes of medicine bottles. Streibel ordered a radio table, lamp, desk, desk chair, four Caucasian Walnut chairs, and more for his office. There were also orders for school furniture (e.g., two blackboards, on December 15), but the volume of official orders was far smaller than the rush for Christmas gifts.

So much was being ordered that there was a chance that there might not be enough raw materials in Kraśnik to meet the demand on time. Therefore, Offermann told Gröger and his staff to barter for missing raw materials for these orders. In other words, there was to be no record of purchase.[101] Thus, children's toys and furniture, shoes, slippers, beds, decorated egg holders and beer glasses, dressers, etc., kept the Jews of Kraśnik alive through Christmas of 1943.

After Christmas, however, the orders for personal items and gifts were still kept up, as the profits continued to roll in. These profits paid for the lavish Christmas party thrown by the SSPF staff. On February 28, 1944, Offermann sent a check for 22,662.95 złotys from the Kraśnik account to pay for the geese consumed at the Yuletide dinner.[102]

October and November 1943 were a turning point for Jewish forced labor in Kraśnik – although this is not apparent from the above account regarding the Christmas gifts. For the Jews news of the *Erntefest* operation was a cause for great concern and led many

101 Ibid.

102 Offermann memo, February 28, 1944, ibid. Exchange rates in 1943/44 were approximately 2 złotys = RM 1. So the geese cost approximately RM 11,331. In dollar terms ($1=RM 2.5), this was approximately $4,532.

in Kraśnik and Wifo to begin preparing escape plans. The *Erntefest* taught them that they could not rely on their labor to keep them alive. The SS, fearing partisan activity, tightened restrictions so as to prevent escapes and hook-ups with partisans. At the same time, with the conclusion of school-furniture production in the offing, Offermann and his colleagues sought a new facade behind which they could keep Kraśnik operating. Thus, it seems that the Kraśnik Jews' conclusions from the *Erntefest* operations may have been off the mark. Greed went a long way in Kraśnik.

Conditions of daily life in the Kraśnik and Wifo camps were remarkably livable in comparison to other forced-labor camps. Not only was there sufficient food and few beatings, but, in December 1942, Gröger informed the Jews that they could bring their families into the camp. This followed the killing of a Jewish policeman, in December 1942, by Ulbrich and Gröger, based on a mistaken impression that he was trying to escape. In fact, he had been going to get his wife, who was hiding nearby. Few Jews in the Kraśnik camp had any surviving family, but some whose family members were hiding in the vicinity acted on Gröger's offer. When other prisoners saw that these family members were integrated into the camp's operation, they decided to try to bring in their family members as well. For example, Itzchak Rosenbusch brought in his eleven-year-old daughter, who had been hiding with Poles. Nine-year-old Chaja Rotenberg was evicted by the Polish woman who had been hiding her in Kraśnik and who eventually turned her in to the Polish police. Chaja escaped and sneaked into the carpentry shop, where she was hidden together with two children whose fathers worked there. Eventually, because she said she was Pesach Kawa's niece, she was "legalized" and put to work in the camp kitchen.[103] There were eleven children in Kraśnik by the spring of 1943.

There was sufficient food in both camps. In February 1944, the

103 Itzchak Rosenbusch testimony, YVA, TR.11/01113; Chaja Rotenberg Goldbaum testimony, ibid.; Chaim Sztejnbok testimony, ibid.; Abraham Waks testimony, ibid; Mordechai Süssberg testimony, ibid.; Salman Lederfein testimony, ibid.; Shlomo Waks testimony, YVA, M.1.E/768; Shalom Garen testimony, *Sefer Kraśnik*, p. 321; Alois Gröger interrogation, YVA, TR.1291, pp. 8801–8804; TR.10/868, pp. 263–266.

prisoners in Kraśnik received 350 grams of bread daily, 49 grams of meat, 400 grams of fresh vegetables, and more.[104] Jews from both camps were given some degree of freedom of movement both inside the camp and out. They used this privilege to visit other camps. And when Gröger would send Jews on missions outside the camp — albeit guarded by Ukrainians — they could maintain contacts and trade with the local population.

There were also occasional theater performances in Kraśnik and Wifo, as well as small concerts and lectures. The performers would appear in both camps in the evenings, with the open approval of Gröger and his men. The prisoners were permitted to hold a Passover *seder* in April 1943, and to hold Rosh Hashanah and Yom Kippur services in October. The prisoners worked during the day on the holidays, but on Yom Kippur a number of them fasted until nightfall.[105] Both the fact that the *seder* and the services were held and the fact that at least some Jews felt strong enough to fast reflect the conditions in the camp.

Nevertheless, there were also deadly incidents that served to remind the Jews of where they were and limit any illusions they might have harbored. Such were the cases of the Jewish policeman who went to get his wife and of Mosze Schiff, whose May 1943 shooting has been discussed above. Shortly after the latter incident, Gröger shot his horse groomer, Mosze Graf, who was Schiff's close friend. Gröger became angry with Graf for poor work and marched him toward the Great Synagogue. Gröger then pulled out his pistol and shot Graf in the stomach, wounding him badly. Before Dr. Schapiro could treat Graf, the Ukrainian guard Vassili came over and shot Graf in the head.[106] There were several similar instances of

104 Receipt for delivery of food to Kraśnik to feed the prisoners of Kraśnik and Wifo, signed by Offermann, February 1, 1944, WAPL, SSPF 2. See also Shalom Garen testimony, *Sefer Kraśnik*, p. 323.

105 Nahum Rozenel testimony, YVA, TR.11/01113; Ber Twardagóra testimony, YVA, M.49.E/1053 and 1195; Shalom Garen testimony, *Sefer Kraśnik*, p. 323; Shmuel Brand testimony, ibid., pp. 419–420.

106 Itzchak Rosenbusch testimony, YVA, TR.11/01113; Salman Lederfein testimony, ibid.; Nahum Rozenel testimony, ibid.; Asher Mandelblatt testimony, ibid.; YVA, TR.10/868, pp. 310–320; Gröger interrogation, TR.10/1291, p. 8822.

killings or beatings, reminding the Jews of the volatility of their SS guards, even the calmest among them, and of the fragility of their situation. Still, in general, the Jews in Kraśnik and Wifo did their work, ate sufficiently to avoid starvation, saw that the few children who were still alive were left alone and fed, and lived in overall security.

During the autumn of 1943, these relatively liberal living conditions for Jews in the Kraśnik area camps began to raise security concerns for the SS. On October 12, KdS Müller ordered the Budzyń and Kraśnik camps to return prisoners from work before nightfall for security reasons.[107] On November 1, Offermann rebuked Gröger for lax security for an incident that had occurred on October 28. A *SS-Wachmann* from the Wifo camp escorted a Jewish camp inmate to Lublin to get materials; the prisoner was found to be carrying seven letters from Jews and 1,952 złotys. Schupo complaints at the time indicate that such events were not unusual.[108]

Yet this relative worsening of conditions for the Jews was not absolute. This was reflected in the Kraśnik SS request to Offermann, on November 11, 1943, for winter clothing for the Kraśnik and Wifo Jews. They asked for clothing from the *Sonderbehandlung* Jews and in order to prevent epidemics. Offermann was asked to raise the matter with Sporrenberg.

This, too, was an indication of SSPF intentions to leave the Kraśnik camps intact, as was the move to attach Kraśnik to Budzyń in labor as well as jurisdiction. Offermann wrote to Sporrenberg, on November 13, regarding a plan he had worked out the day before with the Heinkel Werke directors. With the completion of the school-furniture orders expected in January, Kraśnik would begin to get urgent Wehrmacht jobs so that production would be ensured.[109]

107 Müller order to Budzyń and Kraśnik, October 12, 1943, WAPL, SSPF 2.

108 Offermann to Gröger, November 1, 1943, ibid.; see also a series of correspondence regarding such security breaches, October 28–November 10, 1943, ibid.

109 Kraśnik camp to Offermann, November 11,1943, WAPL, SSPF 2; Offermann to Sporrenberg, November 13, 1943. See also Kraśnik camp to Offermann, November 4, 1943, regarding materials needed to complete school-furniture orders, and Offermann's November 17 letter to the Kraków supply offices, ibid.

Since the work at Budzyń had not been efficient or vigorous until this time, it would seem that the staffs of the two camps were now collaborating to hide the true nature of their enterprise.

At the same time, with the Jews of Trawniki murdered, Streibel formally transferred responsibility for the Kraśnik camp to Sporrenberg; that is, from the office of *Reichskommissar für die Festigung des deutschen Volkstums* to the SSPF. Streibel transferred a 116,569.77 złoty surplus for deposit in the Kraśnik special account. Much of the machinery connected to the Trawniki forced-labor camp was distributed to other camps in mid-November. Kraśnik received a sausage-making machine, which was soon sold for a profit, and other equipment and vehicles.[110] Clearly Kraśnik was not yet slated for liquidation, and Sporrenberg was a party to this.

In February and March 1944, there was a series of attempts and plots for escape from both Kraśnik and Wifo. During this period forty-one Jews actually did escape, of whom four were caught and shot or hanged; another ninety-four or ninety-five were shot as punishment for the escapes of others or for planning an escape.

Pesach Kawa and many others feared that all the Jews in Kraśnik would eventually be killed. These fears were heightened by Budzyń's transformation into a concentration camp. Thus, they began to plan an escape, hiding money and preparing false identification documents acquired through a Jew who had sneaked into the camp from Poniatowa when that camp was liquidated in November. One of the conspirators was the baker Shamai Greenwald, who had been in contact with a Polish woman in order to arrange a hiding place after the escape. The woman's husband revealed the plan to the IVB4 office in Kraśnik, who then arrested and interrogated Shamai. The local SS learned of the escape plan from other informers as well. Seven other Jews were arrested on February 13, and interrogated, and the informers' information was corroborated. When the Gestapo searched the rooms of Kawa and others, they found twelve false Polish identification documents and 21,490 złoty. As punishment,

110 Übergabeprotokoll, signed by Bartetzko, Offermann, and Klein, November 15, 1943, ibid.; Offermann to Sporrenberg, November 13, ibid.; Offermann memo to Kraśnik camp, November 27, 1943, ibid.; Offermann memo, "Notiz für das Arbeitslager Krasnik," December 6, 1943, ibid.

forty-four Jews (four from Wifo), including Kawa, were shot in two groups, on February 14 and 18. During the interrogations of the conspirators, two escaped – Jankel Ehrlich (February 14) and Chil Rolnik (February 16).[111]

While these investigations and punishments were under way, eighteen Jews fled the Wifo camp on February 17, at 4:00 P.M. (approximately sunset). Upon their return from work, they crawled through a corner of the perimeter fence. The Ukrainian guard Kiplok notified Gröger by telephone an hour later, and Gröger then notified Offermann by telephone. Offermann called the commander of the Kraśnik KdS post, Hans Augustin, who then took a SS unit to the Kraśnik camp. Gröger accompanied Augustin and his men to Wifo, where all the Jews were forced out of the barracks in whatever clothing they were wearing – some were barefoot – and a selection was conducted right there and then. A group of twenty close relatives of the escapees was selected and marched out in the direction of the fuel tanks. They were forced to lie down in the snow under the light of bright spotlights, and Gestapo troops and Ukrainian guards shot them in the nape of the neck.

While this was happening, a Schupo unit was dispatched from Kraśnik to check on the security needs of the Kraśnik camps and, if necessary, to reinforce them. A unit of five Schupo and fifteen SS arrived at Gröger's home just after 11:00 P.M., to find him in the midst of a party with seven guests. According to the Schupo commander, Gröger told him that everything was fine, no additional security was needed, and that the Schupo and SS unit should return to base quietly. However, the unit proceeded to Wifo, where three SS men told them that their forces were insufficient to guard the Jews and the various parts of the camp. The commander stayed the night at Wifo, supplementing the guard. He ordered the dead buried the next morning and left his men with Gröger to help guard the

111 Report by Wenk, IVB4, Kraśnik, to IVB4 Lublin, February 19, 1944, and memo from Liska, IVB4 Lublin to Sporrenberg, February 28, 1944, together with Wenk's report, WAPL, SSPF 2 (copies in YVA, O.51/211, O.53/82); Cipora Berger testimony, YVA, TR.11/01113; Ber Twardagóra testimonies, YVA, M.49.E/1053 and 1195; YVA, TR.10/868, pp. 321–330; Shalom Garen testimony, *Sefer Kraśnik*, pp. 328–330.

two camps. The commander concluded that the Kraśnik camp was chaotic and needed change immediately.[112]

Four of the escapees were caught and killed by the SS in the following days. Seventeen-year-old Moshe Dorn was spurned and harassed by the local farmers from whom he sought food and shelter. Two days after escaping he turned himself in at the Wifo camp and was locked up in the Kraśnik prison. There he learned that his father and brother had been among those shot in retaliation for his escape. The other prisoner in the cell was another escapee, Kuchczyk, who had developed a foot infection that hobbled him, and, consequently, the Gestapo had caught up with him. Gröger ordered both hanged, but the Wehrmacht men at Wifo were fond of Dorn and convinced Gröger to spare him. Two other escapees, Powroznik and Himmelblau, were captured on February 23, and hanged.[113]

It is noteworthy that very soon after suffering two serious security breaches and participating in the killing of twenty people at point-blank range, Gröger, the generally "decent" commandant, went on to party with friends and did not feel a need for added security. He and the camp were in the process of breaking down, and Offermann reacted by appointing the proven murderer of Bełżec and Trawniki notoriety, Franz Bartetzko, to take over command. Nevertheless, this change in command did not bring with it the liquidation of the camp, as might have been expected after such serious breaches. Moreover, the change did not result in any significant security modifications either. There were subsequent escapes and security breaches, as well as other lapses of discipline among the SS and the Ukrainians in the camp. Yet the Kraśnik camp kept operating right to the end, lining the pockets of the local SS.

Two Kraśnik prisoners escaped on March 28, and another

112 YVA, TR.10/868, pp. 333–338; Report by Schupo Zugwachtmeister (equivalent to sergeant) Menzel, Kraśnik, to Schupo Lublin, WAPL, GDL 153 (copies in YVA, O.51/211, O.51/82, JM/3506); Moshe Dorn testimony, YVA, TR.11/01113; Mordechai Süssberg testimony, ibid.; Avraham Waks testimony, ibid.; Yehiel Teper testimony, *Sefer Kraśnik*, p. 428.

113 YVA, TR.10/868, pp. 355–361; testimonies of Moshe Dorn, Mordechai Süssberg, and Avraham Waks, TR.11/01113.

sixteen two days later, after secretly making a copy of the key to the gate. On the evening of March 30, a sentry noticed that the gate was open and called the guard (the camp was guarded by three sentries and three guards at the gate). Police and SS forces began searching the area. The escape was reported to Offermann by phone on March 31, and in writing in an April 6 memo (by Gröger). A search of the camp on March 31, the day after the escape, uncovered $110 in paper money, gold dollars and rubles, and assorted jewelry. Twenty-eight Jews were arrested that day; they were shot on April 1 as punishment for those who had escaped.[114]

There were also individual escapes or captures during this period. On March 16, 1944, Bartetzko sent two guards and the Jewish prisoner Shmuel Hartbrot to the village of Owczarnia for supplies. At around 1:00 P.M. they were abducted by partisans. The local German police commander recorded the statement of village head Józef Wojtaszek with regard to the incident. Bartetzko went to the village himself to investigate when the three did not return, and he found the recorded testimony of the village head at the police office. Sporrenberg reprimanded Bartetzko for sending such a light unit on a mission. Yet on March 27, the Wifo camp's labor chief sent *Wachmann* Josef Scharen and two Jews to town to buy supplies. They came to the home of the Pole Jan Kozak and tried to buy personal things. While Scharen negotiated, one of the Jews escaped. The next day Bartetzko sent his report to Offermann, indicating that he now forbade the Wifo people to send Jews on purchase missions.[115] Despite these repeated security lapses, the camps were maintained.

During the last few months of their stay in the Lublin District, the SSPF personnel were busy cashing in on the loot and covering their tracks. Hundreds of thousands of złotys were involved. During

114 Gröger to Offermann, April 6, 1944 (two memos), WAPL, SSPF 2, pp. 271–275.

115 March 16, 1944, Claasen report on recording Wojtaszek's statement; Bartetzko's report, March 17; Offermann to Sporrenberg on above, March 20; Offermann to Bartetzko, passing on Sporrenberg's reprimand; Jan Kozak's affidavit, March 28; Bartetzko's report to Offermann, March 28, WAPL, SSPF 2.

this period the Kraśnik camp also became active in providing items that might be needed for the expected German retreat from the area for the local SS and for outside units. On February 28, 1944, on the same day that Offermann was trying to improve security at Kraśnik, he began to deal with Sporrenberg's desire to renovate the officers' club in Lublin. The Kraśnik camp was to provide 300,000 złotys for the project, toward which Offermann enclosed a check for 200,000 złotys.[116] This seems to be an odd decision by Sporrenberg, with the eastern front approaching and German dependants in the Lublin District returning to the Reich. Was this actually a way to launder large sums of money?

Perhaps some clues to this puzzle can be found in two developments. First, cash and valuables continued to be found among the Jews and sent for deposit in the Kraśnik account. On February 29, jewelry, four $20 gold pieces, and $25 in cash taken from Jews during the *Aktion* in the camp were sent for deposit. Similar finds were sent on March 31, upon completion of the investigation into the escape of the sixteen prisoners. On April 6, additional loot was sent along, as noted above.[117] On March 20, Offermann wrote to the Kraśnik camp command that in light of the current situation their work must continue uninterrupted.[118] What was the nature of that work that must continue? Certainly he was not referring to the renovation of the officers' club.

The necessary work referred to by Offermann was assistance to the SS in preparing for their retreat. For example, on March 20, Offermann sent a memo to Bartetzko and Gröger that he had received a telephone report that a cow and a pig had been slaughtered in the camp. While he was in full agreement, he cautioned that word of this should not get out. No meat or sausage products should be given to outsiders. As they had already discussed, they might be in great need of smoked sausage.[119] In other words, when they would begin their retreat, they would need food that would last a long time,

116 Offermann to Kramme, February 28, 1944, ibid.

117 Offermann to Kramme, February 29, 1944, and Gröger to Offermann, April 6, 1944, ibid.

118 Offermann to Kraśnik camp command, March 20, 1944, ibid.

119 Offermann to Bartetzko and Gröger, March 20, 1944, ibid.

such as smoked sausage, since they might be on the road without a proper kitchen.

This and the subsequent orders for trunks reflect their preparations for withdrawal. Amidst all this the intake of funds continued. In late March, more than 10,000 złotys were paid to Kraśnik for a canteen at one of the Budzyń work sites.[120] On March 27, Offermann sent a 6,015 złoty check to Kraśnik as payment from Richard Thomalla, representing the proceeds from destroying the Zamość ghetto.[121]

Discipline had become a problem in the Kraśnik camp, as reflected in a series of complaints in June 1944, about drinking parties among the SS men there and cavorting with Polish women. On June 14, Bartetzko denied the drinking parties, claiming that if occasionally some of the men shared a drink, there was no drunkenness. The result was that Claasen ordered Bartetzko to write weekly reports.[122] Bartetzko sent four such reports prior to the SS retreat from the area, noting the work that had been accomplished the previous week.

The Jews' labor related directly to the Germans' preparations for retreat from the area, including items that were needed for the retreat, such as trunks for packing their things, as well as personal gifts to bring to their loved ones. The items were made based on orders, as had been the case during the Christmas season. Offermann himself ordered twenty-two trunks. In his reports submitted on June 17 (for June 9–16), June 24, July 3, and July 10, Bartetzko reported on items made for various SS units, such as six field kitchens for the SS "Wiking" division and thirteen closets for trucks for a unit of Panzer Regiment 5, as well as dozens of trunks and many personal items (upholstered chairs, decorated beer glass plates; decorated egg dishes, etc.). Jews working in eighteen crafts had produced 1,896

120 See Flugzugwerk Budzyń to Siedler Wirtschschaftsgemeinschaft, Budzyń branch, March 20, 1944, informing it to pay its 10,292.65 złoty bill for a canteen directly to Kraśnik, since they handled these things, WAPL, SSPF 2.

121 Offermann to Kraśnik camp, March 27, 1944, WAPL, SSPF 2.

122 See Claasen to Bartetzko, June 8, 1944, Offermann to Augustin, June 12, 1944, Bartetzko to Claasen, June 14, 1944, in WAPL, SSPF 2.

items during this month, as the camp began to be dismantled for the German retreat.[123]

These reports, as well as other documents from the period, also note the number of Jews in the camp. Remarkably, this number increased during that month. Following the escapes and killings of February-April, there were fifty-eight Jews remaining in Wifo and 160–162 in Kraśnik, matching the numbers in Bartetzko's June 17 report (173 men, thirty-three women, and twelve children; i.e., 218 people). On June 24, there were 180 men (225 inmates); on July 3, 190 men; and on July 10, 192 men. In other words, the inmate population included thirty-three women and twelve children until the end, and nineteen men were added between June 17 and July 10.[124] It is not clear where the additional men came from, but it would be reasonable to guess that they were workers on local farms or small projects who were now being consolidated into one camp before the German retreat. It is also possible that they were Jews who had been in hiding and now found they could no longer remain where they were. In any event the camp regime under the notorious Bartetzko received them.

And through all this, camp secrecy was maintained. On June 28, 1944, Offermann sent a memo to the camp saying that in public it should not look like it is a SSPF camp. For the benefit of all outsiders, the camp should be referred to as: "Der Beauftragter des Reichskommissars f.d.F.d.V. – Arbeitslager Kraśnik"; that is, this was a camp that served German colonization needs. The SSPF letterhead for the camp should now be used only internally, and all letters to Lublin should be sent by Bartetzko. Offermann added that he would repeat and explain this orally at the next opportunity.[125] In other words, it was not to be known that the SSPF had been operating an illegal camp. And indeed, Bartetzko's weekly reports to Offermann were on SSPF stationery, whereas other correspondence during the last weeks was on "Beauftragter" stationery.

At Kraśnik, unlike Budzyń, Globocnik had had complete control. The camp's SS staff were his men, as were their overseers

123 See Bartetzko's reports of June 17, June 24, July 3, and July 10, 1944, ibid.

124 See Bartetzko's reports, ibid., and Goldberg's report, May 31, 1944, ibid., indicating that there were fifty-eight Jews in Wifo.

125 Offermann, Notiz, June 28, 1944, ibid.

in Lublin, and the Ukrainian guards were his trainees from Trawniki. The camp's growing reputation in 1943, as a place for Germans to get quality goods for low prices helped draw a wide circle of Germans into the camp's illegal activities. With so many implicated, it was unlikely that any of them would report the camp to Himmler. Thus, Globocnik succeeded both in making large sums of money and in keeping his operation going. And for the small group of Jews in the camp, his success made all the difference in the world.

In the summer of 1944, all the remaining forced-labor camps were evacuated westward, and most of the forced-laborers were put to work in new camps. For many of them this initiated a period of frequent moves from camp to camp. However, those Jews who had made it this far had entered a somewhat different phase of Nazi policy for Eastern Europe. As such they had in a sense increased their chances to survive until the end of the war. Still, we should not conclude that somehow these Jews had discovered the logic of the Nazi system and the path to survival within it.

On January 6, 1944, Szmul Zitomirski wrote to Zionist representatives in Istanbul from his hiding place in Lublin: "Every day brings new and terrible surprises...you have no idea how difficult and dangerous it is to live here...my most important goal now is to stay alive and to find out about my family. I cannot help [anyone] unfortunately."[126] Zitomirski did not survive, nor did most of those thousands of "last Jews" in the Lublin District.

Assessing Forced Labor

Did forced labor affect Jewish survival in the Lublin District in 1942–1944? This is a difficult question to answer, especially in light of the constant moving around of Jews by the Germans in deportations and mass killing operations. For the overwhelming majority of Jews in the district, there was no chance of survival. Fewer than 10 percent had been selected by the Germans to be left

126 Szmul Zitomirski, under the alias Misław Zitomirski, to Constantinople, January 6, 1944, in Zariz, *Letters from Haluzim*, p. 211.

behind temporarily as forced-laborers when all the others were killed. The available data indicate that there were well over 20,000 Jews in forced-labor camps in the Lublin District at the end of 1942, and perhaps an additional 9,000 in remnant ghettos. Perhaps one-third of these people were local Jews.[127]

In the spring and summer of 1943, the district's remnant Jewish population went through yet another upheaval, with the influx of large numbers of Jews from the Warsaw ghetto (and small numbers from Holland) and the consolidation of the forced-labor camps in the district. Thousands were killed, while tens of thousands were brought in. The result was that shortly before the *Erntefest* operation, there were officially more than 50,000 Jews in the district, but only perhaps 15 percent (7,500) were local. In the aftermath of *Erntefest*, there were some 10,000 Jews still working in the district, of whom perhaps 2–2,500 were local. Thus, by the end of 1943, the Jews still officially in the district represented only 3–4 percent of the Jewish population of more than 300,000 that had existed in early 1942. However, since most of these people were from outside the district, it was actually less than 1 percent of the original Jewish population of the Lublin District that was still alive. Even if we add to this the few hundred local Jews still alive in hiding or as part of partisan groups in the forests (where many were also not local), the percentage of surviving Lublin District Jews was negligible. The murder was complete.

Still, these statistics leave open an important question. Did forced-laborers indeed have a better chance for survival than others? The *Erntefest* operation provided conflicting evidence in this regard. More than 42,000 "productive" Jews were killed in two days, thereby effectively eliminating the Jews' contribution to the German war effort in the Lublin District. Yet thousands of Jews continued to be employed by the SS, civilian industrialists, and the Wehrmacht. If actually only the last group may have contributed to the German war effort, why were the Jews of Budzyń, Kraśnik, Chopin Street,

127 Nearly all the Jews in Majdanek and Lipowa 7 were not local, whereas nearly all those in the Lublin castle and at Chopin 27 were. In other places, such as Dęblin, there were mixed local and refugee populations.

and elsewhere still alive in 1944? The answers seem to lie in local German factors, including Globocnik himself.

While he was busy leading the killing of all the Jews in the district, Globocnik also began setting aside Jews who could help him build an economic empire and enrich himself and his colleagues. He set up sorting camps for profit before other German authorities even noticed. Then he negotiated with Oswald Pohl and the WVHA, as well as with Többens and Schultz to secure Jewish forced labor and a central economic role for himself. Parallel to this he opened his own camps and exerted his authority over others (e.g., Budzyń and Majdanek). His control seems to have continued even from Trieste. His men who remained in the Lublin District after his departure continued to be involved in the same forced-labor installations, and his successor, Sporrenberg, participated in what had become a conspiracy of graft and greed. Himmler's order to liquidate Jewish labor in November 1943 affected the camps that Himmler knew – Trawniki and Poniatowa – as well as the others that Globocnik had controlled in cooperation with Pohl and the WVHA. Of these camps, only Budzyń survived the *Erntefest* operation, which lends credence to survivors' stories regarding the high connections that Heinkel exercised in this regard. The other non-military camps were spared until the end because of their lucrative value locally – and probably because Himmler was not fully aware of their existence.

This can also explain why more Jews survived proportionally in a brutal camp like Budzyń than in a less harsh camp like Poniatowa. It was not necessarily the camp conditions that affected survival in the Lublin District, but rather German economic or personal interests. This might also be the reason why, in addition to the Luftwaffe camps, the camps that were among the new ones established in 1942 were the ones to survive the *Erntefest*. Earlier camps that continued to operate were known and already fit into a set categorization when it came to the German hierarchies. New camps, however, could be classified outside existing hierarchies and therefore out of view. This was especially true of Kraśnik. Thus, whereas earlier in this chapter there was a discussion of three types of forced-labor camps in the Lublin District – Wehrmacht, industrial, and SS – the functional dividing line in terms of a camp's survival was pure interest (military or personal). Jews who labored in Wehrmacht or personal-interest camps had a fair chance of surviving into the spring/summer of 1944, when these camps were liquidated and the prisoners were transferred westward to other camps. Jews who were still working at this late stage in the war had a chance to survive. Jews who sensed that working at jobs important to the Germans could save them were proved right in the Lublin District. What was unusual in this case was that this was true of jobs that served German individuals, such as Globocnik and the managers of the Heinkel airplane industry.

Thus, it is clear that many Jews in this period were indeed "working for their lives," but forced labor was not a formula for survival. The large majority of these Jews were killed, as were those in hiding or in the forests, and all the remaining Jews in the district saw this transpiring. Nevertheless, many Jews in forced labor tried to remain in these frameworks even when other opportunities presented themselves. Many did not escape from Janiszów even when they were "liberated." Jews visiting family and friends in Kraśnik returned to their camp despite the fact that they were lightly guarded or left unguarded altogether. They, too, generally did not exploit their "free" circumstances in order to escape.

Why was this so? The events at Janiszów and the generally bitter experience of Jews who had escaped indicated to at least part of the forced-laborers that escape did not improve their chances for survival. Thus, a number of Jews liberated from Janiszów turned themselves in (or sneaked in) to Budzyń. This does not mean that there were no escape attempts. Daniel Freiberg relates the successful escape of seven men from Budzyń in the summer of 1943. But in this case Noah Stockman succeeded in covering up for them by replacing them at roll call with fugitives who had been hiding in the camp.[128] It is a poignant reflection of the absolute uncertainty of Jewish life then that some who were in the camp sought freedom in escape, while others who had escaped sought safety in the camp.

Those still alive after the *Erntefest* had reason to believe that the factors that had kept them alive until then were still valid.

128 Freiberg, *Darkness Covered the Earth*, pp. 156–157.

So we can say that labor could help a Jew survive. On the other hand, if Jews survived it was a result of luck or the whims of their murderers or would-be rescuers. Jewish life hung by a thread in the most precarious form of existence imaginable. Their fate was determined by forces completely beyond their control.

Chapter 9

Lublin and the Holocaust — Some Conclusions

The Lublin District was a central piece in the persecution and murder of the Jews during the Holocaust. It served as a dumping ground for Jews deported from other areas in 1939–1941; as a center for Jewish forced labor; and as the center of the murder of the Jews of the GG and of all other Jews deported into that area. The methods for massive and ongoing deportations were developed and refined here, as were stationary gas chambers for large-scale murder. Approximately one million Jews were killed in the Lublin District within "Operation Reinhard," including 99 percent of the local Jews.[1]

The story of the Holocaust in the Lublin District is replete with paradoxes, even as it maintained elements of continuity with regard to certain aspects of both German policies and Jewish leadership. For the Germans this was true for their anti-Jewish policies as well as for the personnel implementing these policies, especially with regard to two areas – forced population movements and forced labor. This continuity was not necessarily premeditated. Still, it

1 The estimate of the number of Jewish people killed in the Lublin District is based on 500,000 Jews killed in Bełżec, 250,000 killed in Sobibór, at least 60,000 in Majdanek, in addition to the *Erntefest*, and many thousands killed during the round-ups in 1942–1943, and in subsequent murder operations and hunts for Jews in hiding. Nearly all the Majdanek victims were essentially part of "Operation Reinhard" as well (see Kranz, "Das Konzentrationslager Majdanek und die 'Aktion Reinhardt,'"). The estimate for the percentage of local Jews killed is based on the data that appear in Chapters 7 and 8 above, and in Krakowski, *War of the Doomed, passim*, regarding Jews in the forests.

facilitated a smooth German transition from brutal persecution to thorough, systematic murder. Important figures involved in the early persecution of the Jews – such as Karl Streibel, Georg Michalsen, and Franz Bartetzko in Bełżec in 1940, Otto Hantke and Wolfgang Mohwinkel in Lipowa 7 in 1939–1942, Richard Türk in BuF, and, of course, Odilo Globocnik – were later intimately involved in their murder.

The paradoxes lay in part in the contradictions in policy. Round-ups by the SS for forced labor in the summer of 1940 were indiscriminate, resulting in a large percentage of unqualified laborers, which hampered the effectiveness of the labor itself. Skilled forced-laborers were deported in 1942, despite a military need for them; and more than 42,000 were killed in November 1943, despite an even greater need. Yet thousands of other Jewish forced-laborers, many of them hardly essential to the German war effort, were left alive.

Large numbers of Jews were steadily deported to the Lublin District in a constant flow, in 1939–1941, from the Reich, western Poland, and other parts of the GG. The result was severe overcrowding in the Jewish communities in the district. Yet the German civilian administration in Lublin set up few closed ghettos – in part, paradoxically, to avoid excessive overcrowding. However, the seemingly "humane" concern for overcrowding in Lublin led to inhumane massive expulsions of Jews in March-April 1941, and excessive overcrowding in smaller communities in the district.

Although the German reasons for the deportations into the Lublin District and within it changed over time, the mere fact that these deportations and expulsions were constant features of life in the district spoke volumes to the Jews. Nearly 45,000 Jews were deported into the district in the first twenty months of the German occupation. In 1939 and early 1940, these deportations were connected to plans to "cleanse" the Reich of Jews and create some sort of "reservation" in the Lublin District. In 1941, they were connected to other resettlement ideas for Jews. Within the district nearly 10,000 Jews were marched from place to place in the first few months of the occupation; many thousands were kidnapped in the summer of 1940 for forced labor; and more than 75,000 were moved from place to place or put into ghettos in March-May 1941. The 1940 population movements were not undertaken for the same reasons as the ghettoizations and population movements in 1941. Still, the important point is that deportations of Jews were a constant feature in Nazi policy. The fact that almost every month Jews were brought into the district or moved around within it was significant to the Jews later as well.

The methods of round-ups by the SS in 1940, and of deportations to the district in February-March 1941, became models for the deportations to death in 1942. The similar elements included surprise in the middle of the night or early morning, extreme brutality, and trainloads of approximately 1,000 people each. Like the 1940 expulsions *to* Lublin, and the 1941 expulsions *from* Lublin, the 1942 deportations made use of forced marches, or, where access to trains was difficult, of local Poles with wagons. And if the indiscriminate seizures failed in terms of accomplishing labor goals in 1940, then, in 1942, the selection of laborers was more careful and discriminate, organized by the German civilian authorities. Thus, when the deportations got underway in March 1942, the Jews recognized a familiar though unwelcome phenomenon, coordinated by some well-known Germans using recognizable — though now more brutal — methods. The rumors they heard also spoke about familiar destinations. This alone was sufficient to frighten the Jews and press some of them to action.

For the Jews communal continuity was represented by the many prewar Jewish leaders who remained with their communities and then joined the Judenräte. This continuity of Jewish leadership was true not only in Lublin, where nineteen members of the Judenrat had been part of the prewar *kehillah* council or the expanded council of the first weeks of the war, but also in Biała-Podlaska, Zamość, Annopol, Żółkiewka, and many other places. Continuity of leadership played a major role in the ability of these communities to organize social-welfare facilities quickly and effectively in order to help refugees in 1939–1940 and afterward. They succeeded in curbing starvation, homelessness, and disease until the spring/summer of 1941. After that the effects of the limited spring ghettoization, together with labor in close proximity to Soviet

POWs, and contact with refugees from Warsaw and other starving communities combined to cause epidemic diseases in the district in the second half of 1941 and early 1942. Still, even then, the death rate in the Lublin District remained considerably lower than that in Warsaw, in part as a direct result of the efforts by Jewish leaders.

The better conditions and resultant lower death rate were also a result of German civilian government policies in the Lublin District. The civilian authorities decided not to put the Jews into closed ghettos, and this allowed many Jews to maintain contact with local Christians and to purchase food from them even after the spring of 1941. It also enabled Jews to maintain contact with family and friends in other places, thereby exchanging information and lending a small sense of continuity with their prewar world. However, herein lies another paradox in German policies toward Jews: better conditions were followed by near total death.

The continuity and contradictions in German policies regarding Jews were pronounced in forced labor during 1939–1943. Like forced population movements, there was hardly a moment when Jews in the Lublin District did not see or experience forced labor. Although German reasons and goals regarding forced labor changed with time, Jews saw some of the same policies repeated, albeit in changing magnitude. In 1942, there were fewer forced-laborers, working in fewer sites than in 1940–1941. Yet for many of them, if not most, their conditions improved, especially later, in 1943. Amidst massive, near total death and annihilation, and with their own demise looming ominously, many of them ate better and had access to better hygiene in 1943. They were often lightly guarded by the Germans and, in some cases, not guarded at all. It was as though the Germans knew that these Jewish forced-laborers had nowhere to flee. The Germans and the Jews shared a certain terrible knowledge – the chances for Jews to survive in hiding or in the forests were close to nil.

Among the Germans there were deep-seated animosities and rivalries between the SS and the civilians in the district. However, the Jews could not benefit from this in any significant way. When it came to murdering the Jews, all the Germans and Austrians cooperated closely. The widespread German-Austrian participation in the murder of the Jews was, in a sense, continuity with their earlier widespread participation in organizing and exploiting the forced labor. However, unlike the situation with regard to the forced labor in 1940–1941, and the constant fighting between Globocnik and Zörner and their respective subordinates, the murder was carried out in harmony. On the district level, the murder of the Jews was a microcosm of a national project.

Here the continuity in Jewish leadership and well-organized social-welfare institutions and communications did not help the Jews. Judenräte and camp leaderships were generally helpless when it came to saving Jewish lives. Shlomo Goldwasser in Markuszów urged his people to flee in May 1942, but only a few survived. Josef Siegfried in Lublin was able to acquire some information regarding the fate of the Lublin deportees in March, and he surely shared this with other members of the Judenrat, but both he and most of the Judenrat (like most of the Jews) were deported and killed nonetheless. Mieczysław Garfinkel and the Judenrat in Zamość received information early on about the deportations from Lublin, yet this did not help the Jews of Zamość when their turn came. And warnings sent from all over the Lublin District to Warsaw made no tangible difference there either. This might reflect the gap between information and knowledge that has been discussed extensively in connection to Allied responses to the Holocaust. It certainly reflects Jewish powerlessness, regardless of the awareness of the events.

Some of the murderers in the Lublin District, particularly German officials who had been in the area for some time, had had regular contact with particular Jews. Did this regular contact lend the Jews a human face in the eyes of the Germans? It would appear not. Thus, *SS-Untersturmführer* Dr. Harry Sturm could send a bouquet of flowers to Shamai Grajer for his wedding in April 1942, and then shoot him, his young wife, and his baby in the head in November. Similarly, Richard Türk, head of the BuF in Lublin, could have almost daily contact with Josef Siegfried, deputy head of JSS for the district, over a two-year period, and then nonchalantly include him in the March 31, 1942, deportation to Bełżec — even though this was against the wishes of the BuF in Kraków. And *SS-Unterscharführer* Alois Gröger could allow Jewish families to remain together in

Kraśnik and let his son play with the Jewish children in the camp while he killed Jews and their families individually and in groups.

When the persecution and deportations were impersonal, as for most of the round-up troops in 1942, they were extremely brutal. When the operations were up close and personal, as in the above examples (a few of many), they were generally equally brutal and cold-blooded. And the cold-blooded murderers included SS, police, and German civilians (e.g., Türk and Busse) alike. With very few exceptions, they all actively and eagerly participated. Moreover, they could be unpredictable. The Jews usually could not anticipate – even when using the experience they had acquired – which German official would be more decent and which more brutal. And there was often no correlation between "decency" and the extent of willingness to kill. Like the murderers, the "decent" ones could come from any part of the German hierarchies – Gröger was SS, Jäger in Budzyń was a civilian, and Hoffmann in Budzyń was a Romanian *Volksdeutsche* SS auxiliary. Similarly, the most vicious could have moments of "decency." Thus, the cruel, murderous Bartetzko could oversee a relatively peaceful last few weeks in the Kraśnik camp, and the sadistic Feiks could reward Jews who did not escape when they had the opportunity. Facing complete unpredictability on an individual level, alongside absolute murder on a group level, the Jews were at a loss.

One of the troubling questions about the Holocaust is was there anything that the Jews could have done that would have significantly affected their collective fate? In general, the events of the Holocaust in the Lublin District demonstrate Jewish helplessness and powerlessness. No Jewish action caused any significant difference for large groups of people in terms of survival, although certain actions could make a difference for individuals. When it came to survival, nothing was predictable or subject to rational analysis on the part of the Jews.

Escape offered limited hope for survival at best. Whereas some of the Lipowa 7 escapees survived as partisans, nearly all the Markuszów escapees were killed, and only one of the Janiszów escapees is known to have survived. At the same time, a relatively high percentage of Jews from the Gościeradów forced-labor camp did survive, though very few of them attempted escape. Escape and survival did not have a cause and effect relationship. Similarly, the conditions under which Jews lived did not necessarily affect their ultimate survival. Jews who lived in relatively calm and normal conditions in many of the smaller communities in the district until 1942, did not experience a higher survival rate than Jews who had lived under more difficult conditions in Lublin. Jews who had labored under relatively livable conditions in Poniatowa had a lower survival rate than Jews in the brutal Budzyń camp — and even than Jews who worked in Sobibór and Treblinka. Whereas escapes from these death camps succeeded in rescuing some lives, most were killed, and nearly all mass escapes from forced-labor camps were even less successful.

During the deportations the Jews were often deceived by their previous experience. "Resettlement" to them meant being forcibly moved to a new location, and being sent to forced-labor camps meant working under extremely brutal and often unlivable conditions. Round-ups by the Germans had always been accompanied by violence and death. When they saw the murderousness of the round-ups in 1942, many Jews sought to evade the deportations. Recent memories were enough to send Jews into hiding or flight. Thus, initially they often acted precisely because they were deceived regarding the purpose and destination of the deportations and despite the fact that hiding or fleeing meant an instant death sentence if caught. And herein lay two additional paradoxes — Jews acted with initiative based on a partial or total misunderstanding, and their communal death was nearly total death despite early action.

At the same time, quite a few Jews did grasp the meaning of various elements of Nazi policy toward them in 1942 sufficiently to consider ways to improve their chances of survival. Whether as a result of deception, misunderstanding, or partial understanding, many hid, fled, or tried to secure employment in German industries and forced-labor camps. According to Shmuel Krakowski, more than 50,000 Jews fled to the forests in the GG in 1942, half of them in the Lublin District. More than 25,000 of these people were subsequently killed by the Germans in the Lublin District. In other words, only a tiny percentage of the escapees in the Lublin District survived.[2] Many more thousands hid during the deportations, but nearly all of these, too, were caught. As we have seen in Chapter 8, the survival rate among Jews in forced-labor camps in the district was similar.

Communication among Jews was limited but widespread. Information traveled back and forth all through the German occupation, even during the murder operations. Jews in the Lublin District received information regarding ghettoization, forced labor, and other matters in other places. Some Jews in the Lublin District also picked up scraps of information on the deportations as they progressed, and if they could not save their own communities, they tried to warn others. Did this make a difference? We do not know to whom in Warsaw the June 1, 1942, Włodawa warning was sent, and we do not know what the recipient(s) did, or what his/her/their fate was. However, we do know that reports from Lublin and the Lublin District did not – and, indeed, could not – rescue the Jews of Warsaw or anywhere else. We know that some Jews in Majdan Tatarski learned, much to their chagrin, that their families and friends in Warsaw were being deported just as they had been.

The magnitude of the persecution and murder in the Lublin District – one million Jews killed in the district and another million Jews killed in other parts of the GG based on the murder operation run out of Lublin – raises the question as to the extent to which the events and players here can shed light on aspects of the Holocaust as a whole. With regard to the perpetrators, the broad participation in all aspects of the persecution and murder of the Jews was similar in the Lublin District to other parts of Poland and of Europe. The perpetrators included many firm antisemites and Nazi ideologues, alongside a variety of people whose motivations are more difficult to gauge. Regardless of the firmness of their ideological conviction, the perpetrators could disagree vehemently on policies and methods regarding the Jews, but there was no real disagreement on the essence of anti-Jewish policy. Significantly for the outcome

2 Krakowski, *War of the Doomed*, pp. 11, 59, 74, 80–100, and *passim*. On the relentless hunts for Jews in the forests, see also the KdO reports for September 1942—October 1943, in YVA, O.53/121; Browning, *Ordinary Men*, pp. 128–139.

regarding the Jews' fate, the perpetrators participated willfully and with determination.

At the same time, being a firm Nazi believer and confirmed participant in the persecution and murder of the Jews did not contradict being greedy. And this was true throughout the Holocaust. This encompassed local officials pocketing Jewish belongings, "contributions" exacted from Jews by individual Germans or local authorities, the personal aggrandizement of Majdanek Commandant Karl Koch, who was tried and sentenced to death by a SS tribunal, up to the organized corruption represented by Globocnik and his men.

They were not unique – neither in the Holocaust, nor in history in general. Certainly it is not unusual for occupation forces to pillage, plunder, and kill, even in disregard to explicit orders and regardless of ideology. Plunder and personal greed are common human features in war, occupation, and the wielding of power over people. The Lublin District was no different. Being a Nazi did not preclude being "normal" in these terms. In general, we know that there was no lack of corruption in the ranks of the SS and the civilian authorities. Himmler's infamous speech at Posen on October 4, 1943, in which he referred to the harsh punishment meted out to SS men who had enriched themselves from the victims, is a reflection of this.[3]

However, the Lublin District in particular and the Holocaust in general differ, of course, from other events at other times and in other places. Lublin stood at the center of the Holocaust, but this should not lead us to expect that normal human vices would be suspended there. In this sense the Lublin District is representative of the perpetration of the Holocaust in general. If the murderers were often "ordinary" people, as Christopher Browning has demonstrated, and if they were generally willful, as he and Daniel Goldhagen have shown, then they were also by and large "normal."[4] Türk, Sturm, Gröger, and the rest in the Lublin District were in a sense typically "normal" people in that they could often be contradictory. In the

3 Nuremberg Document PS-1919. For a published version, see Lucy S. Dawidowicz, *A Holocaust Reader* (New York: Behrman House, 1976), pp. 130–140.

4 Browning, *Ordinary Men*, pp. 45–48, 159–189, and *passim*; Goldhagen, *Willing Executioners*, pp. 181–406, *passim*.

broader picture of the events of the Holocaust in the Lublin District, contradictory was the norm.

Perhaps herein lies a sort of guide for the study of the Holocaust in general in many places, as well as for the study of perpetrators of genocide on the whole. What is most unusual in the story of the key perpetrators in Lublin, perhaps, is the fact that many of the perpetrators of the Holocaust did not always murder with a uniform single-mindedness and purity of conviction.

It has been suggested in this book that the Jews felt that they had no hinterland in the Lublin District on which they could rely. Although an analysis of the role of the local non-Jewish population in the fate of the Jews is beyond the scope of this research, it is clear that the Jews' perception of their neighbors' role played a part in their understanding of the events. Many survivor testimonies from the Lublin District and from the GG in general refer to the hostility that they sensed from their environment, even if that hostility was not uniform. Certainly many individuals turned to other individuals and, at times, to groups, and could hope to find assistance. An examination of the files of the Righteous Among the Nations at Yad Vashem reveals quite a number of such cases.[5] As most rescue stories in the GG indicate, such actions there involved great risk on the part of the rescuers. The danger often extended over long periods of time, even years, and was dependent, too, on the willingness of others at least to remain silent.

Yet as so many Jews sensed, it was not only the fear of the risk that led local Poles not to lend them a hand; it was an expression of open hostility. Polish courier Jan Karski's February 1940 report to the government-in-exile referred to the widespread antipathy toward Jews and the satisfaction with the Nazi persecution of them in the GG in late 1939 and early 1940.[6] Regarding the Lublin

5 These files are in YVA, M.31.

6 See David Engel, "An Early Account of Polish Jewry under Nazi and Soviet Occupation Presented to the Polish Government-in-Exile, February 1940," *Jewish Social Studies*, vol. 45, no. 1 (Winter 1983), pp. 1–16, especially p. 12; *idem, In the Shadow of Auschwitz: The Polish Government-in-Exile and the Jews, 1939–1942* (Chapel Hill and London: University of North Carolina Press, 1987), pp. 60–64.

District, Dariusz Libionka has shown that the Jews' impression of their neighbors' hostility was well founded. The general atmosphere in the Lublin District regarding the Jews ranged from apathetic disinterest to outright hostility. The Jews remained outside the local Poles' sense of moral responsibility.[7]

Emanuel Ringelblum noted the same for the Warsaw area and for the GG in general in his essay written while in hiding, *Polish-Jewish Relations During the Second World War.*[8] Alina Skibińska and Jakub Petelewicz, Jan Grabowski, Barbara Engelking, and, of course, Jan Tomasz Gross, and others have found the same with regard to rural areas in other parts of Poland.[9]

This situation was not unique to the Lublin District or to the GG. Martin Dean has shown that in the Soviet territories that were formerly eastern Poland, the voluntary participation of the local Ukrainians and Belorussians in German actions against Jews was widespread. Clearly, these territories differed significantly from the GG. The local population hated the Poles, the Russians, and the Soviet Union. They saw the Germans as their liberators from Soviet Russian rule, and the Germans, at least at first, encouraged their illusion that they would gain independence from the USSR in the new German-controlled Europe. Similar to the GG, there was also widespread and deeply rooted antisemitism among the local population in these areas, which the Nazis encouraged and exploited.[10]

7 Dariusz Libionka, "Polska Ludność chrześcijańska wobec eksterminacji Żydów—dystrykt lubelski," in *idem*, ed., *Akcja Reinhardt: Zagłada Żydów w Generalnym Gubernatorstwie* (Warsaw: Instytut Pamięci Narodowej, 2004), pp. 306–333.

8 Emmanuel Ringelblum, *Polish-Jewish Relations During the Second World War,* edited by Joseph Kermish and Shmuel Krakowski (Jerusalem: Yad Vashem, 1974).

9 Alina Skibińska and Jakub Petelewicz, "The Participation of Poles in Crimes against Jews in the Świętokrzyskie Region," *Yad Vashem Studies*, 35:1 (2007), pp. 5–48; Jan Grabowski, *Hunt for the Jews: Btrayal and Murder in German-Occupied Poland* (Bloomington and Indianapolis: Indiana University Press, 2013); *idem*, "Rural Society and the Jews in Hiding"; Barbara Engelking, *"Jest taki piękny słoneczny dzień... Losy Żydów szukających ratunku na wsi polskiej 1942–1945"* (Warsaw: Centrum Badań nad Zagłada Żydów, 2011); Jan Tomasz Gross, *Neighbors: The Destruction of the Jewish Community in Jedwabne, Poland* (Princeton: Princeton University Press, 2001).

10 Martin Dean, *Collaboration in the Holocaust: Crimes of the Local Police in Belorussia and Ukraine, 1941–44* (New York: Saint Martin's Press, 2000).

All of these factors proved to be an extremely lethal mix. Although the situation in the GG was quite different in that the Germans did not seek active Polish collaboration in the war, nor did they exploit Polish anti-Russian and anti-Soviet sentiments in their war against the USSR, hostility to Jews remained pervasive. The Poles were persecuted, oppressed, and repressed by the Germans. This certainly could have limited the extent of assistance individual Poles might have been willing to lend to Jews. Still, Dean's findings generally reflect attitudes toward Jews in Eastern Europe, and, at the same time, they make the Polish hostility that so many Jews sensed even more disturbing.

A look at other places in Europe during the Holocaust shows that things did not have to be this way. The reactions of the local non-Jewish population could have some impact on the fate of the Jews, as in parts of Western Europe (e.g., Italy). However, there was no area in occupied Europe where the circumstances were the same as in the Lublin District or the GG in general. The German occupation in Western Europe was less harsh than in the GG during the critical period of persecution and deportation of Jews. Moreover, in Western Europe the local population saw little mass murder in comparison to the GG. This could have allowed the local population more readily to consider assisting the Jews in their midst. The occupation in Hungary came at a much later stage; in Denmark the occupation was relatively benign; in Romania, Slovakia, and Croatia the governments themselves organized the deportations or murder of the Jews. In the final analysis, a comparison of the Lublin District to other places highlights the different circumstances in which the local population reacted to events. The Lublin District is most comparable to the rest of the GG.

Jewish powerlessness has been cited above as a major factor in determining the fate of the Jews in the Lublin District. The same could be said for the Jews in the Holocaust in general. Indeed, this is the significance of the role played by the Jews' neighbors. Without any power of their own and without any help from others, the Jews collectively could do little to affect their fate. To say that they were powerless to affect their fate substantially is not to say that they were passive, or that their actions had no meaning. In general, Jews constantly sought ways to help themselves, and many, including a large number of Jewish leaders, were always looking for ways to help others, and, ultimately, to survive. But as has been shown, neither rational analysis of their situation in an effort to deduce the best way to survive, nor intuition or a gut sense of their circumstances at any given time could provide the basis for any analysis or instinct in a subsequent situation. The Germans created a confusing and consistently unpredictable frame of reference, which in essence meant that the Jews had *no* frame of reference at all. The Germans held all the power; the Jews none. And despite this impossible situation, Jews in the Lublin District constantly and consistently tried to make sense of their situation and to create the means and circumstances that would help them survive. Many of them displayed great initiative, but when we draw the bottom line, it was the Germans who controlled the situation and therefore the Jews' fate.

This was true almost everywhere, of course. However, just as the reactions of the local non-Jewish population could have had some impact on the fate of the Jews, so, too, could the timing of the events. Indeed, timing was one of the key factors that led to the Jews' rapid demise in the Lublin District. When the Jews were being killed in 1942, partisans were not yet a serious element in the district, and the Allied forces were still very far away and not a factor in the Jews' fate. By the time the Allied forces could become a factor, in 1944, 99 percent of the Jews were already dead. The Jews had no role in causing their own death, and they had no chance of saving their collective lives. The communities were doomed — unless some outside force intervened on their behalf, or opened its heart and doors.

The classic illustration of a country where timing played a somewhat opposite role for large numbers of Jews is Hungary. The fact that the occupation began only in March 1944, and the deportations to death only in May, meant that Jews and others could think in terms of rescue by buying time until the war's end. The clear proximity of the end of the war lent weight to the rescue activities of the He-Halutz underground, the neutral consuls in Budapest, the Jewish negotiators with Eichmann, and the War Refugee Board, alongside the threats of the western Allies in the summer of 1944 to bomb Budapest.[11] But even here, in the end, the large majority of the Jews were killed. And none of these special factors was relevant to Lublin in 1942–1943. The Jews in the Lublin District were alone.

As the story of the Lublin District shows, for the Jews collectively there were no clear ways to assure survival during the Holocaust. In the Lublin District, some Jews survived by forced labor and some by hiding (or among partisans), but for most neither avenue represented a certain path to survival. Moshe Frank from Zamość perhaps epitomizes the role of chance as opposed to planned strategy in determining a Jew's fate during the Holocaust. At the age of nine and a half, in April 1942, he survived by not being discovered as he hid under the deportation train; during the children's deportation in July, he blended in with the Poles. He survived the deportation train to Bełżec when he was accidentally shoved by the heaving crowd through a crack in the freight car. He survived the fall and returned to Izbica, to which the last Zamość Jews had been deported. Finally, he survived the last deportation in November by hiding for two days beneath a huge mound of trash in a bend in the road.[12]

German actions regarding the Jews in the Lublin District were ideologically motivated, connected at times to grandiose plans for Europe, and tempered at times by infighting. This was true for the Holocaust in general. In 1942–1944, they were bent on murdering all the Jews they could get their hands on, save for the few who brought them temporary profit. The Germans' personal greed and corruption led to the survival of some Jews until the summer of 1944.

Jews in Lublin looked where they could for salvation from these murderers – to their leaders; to their neighbors and countrymen; to

11 On this issue in Hungary, see, for example, Robert Rozett, "Jewish Armed Resistance in Hungary: A Comparative View," in David Cesarani, ed., *Genocide and Rescue, The Holocaust in Hungary 1944* (Oxford: Berg, 1997), pp. 135–146.

12 Frank, *To Survive and Testify*, pp. 35–39, 42–45, 49–51, 55–68. Eventually he was taken in by Jan and Anna Huk, who managed to take care of him until the end of the war. The Huks had to convince their extended family and neighbors to keep their secret. See their Righteous Among the Nations file in YVA, M.31/4205.

their German employers; to the Polish and Russian partisans that had formed units in the woods after most of the Jews were already dead, but who often treated the surviving remnant with disdain; to their own initiative; to their God. From no quarter did more than a few find solace or salvation.

Knowing what the Germans were doing to the Jews did not help, and not knowing did not help. Attempting to flee did not help, and not fleeing did not help. Communicating with other Jews and warning them offered little solace and no survival. Indeed, their chances for survival were as slim as the answers that Rabbi Zvi Elimelech Talmud in Majdan Tatarski received from the God in whom he still believed.

> [God] make known among the nations and before our eyes your revenge for your servants' spilt blood. Let a savior arise for Israel and extricate us from the depths, for if not now, when? If not at this moment when we have reached 49 gates of destruction – when will the savior save and the rescuer rescue! Indeed all has come to an end and we are not saved[13]...I would wish that at least someone will remain to remember us...I would wish that there would remain some memory of my name and that of my forefathers, of my only son whom I have loved as all the world, and from whom I had high hopes and anticipated great things. I would wish that at least this letter should remain as an everlasting memory – and in that I would be consoled, but that, too, is denied us...Only the gates of tears have not been locked before us, and we are able and entitled to bemoan the destruction of our nation, to eulogize the rupture in our destroyed people, and to lead the river of our tears with us to the grave. This they cannot take from us.

13 Rabbi Talmud's writings are filled with Biblical and Talmudic references in every line. This one is based on the comment by Rav, in Tractate *Sanhedrin* 97:B of the Talmud, referring to the passing of all assigned dates for the coming of the Messiah. He concludes that salvation is now dependent on repentance and good deeds. Rabbi Talmud here has put this statement into a completely pessimistic context.

> And He who sits on high in heaven hid His face, and hidden will His soul weep, depressed and downtrodden.[14]

Rabbi Talmud's assessment was accurate. For nearly all the Jews in the Lublin District the only things about which they could be certain were that death sought them everywhere and their tears were all that was left to them. In the final analysis, it was not their initiative, flight, or communicated warnings that could save the Jewish people of the Lublin District, but sheer luck. What remain are their memory and a few records like Rabbi Talmud's letters. But luck – this was a scarce and very precious commodity.

14 Letter from Rabbi Zvi Elimelech Talmud to Rabbi Arieh Berglas, after the *Shemini Atzeret* holiday, October 1942, WAPL, RZ 32 (copy in USHMMA, RG-15.101M). A SD man in charge of propaganda, who was interested in his help with an antisemitic book, had kept Rabbi Talmud alive. He died in Majdanek.

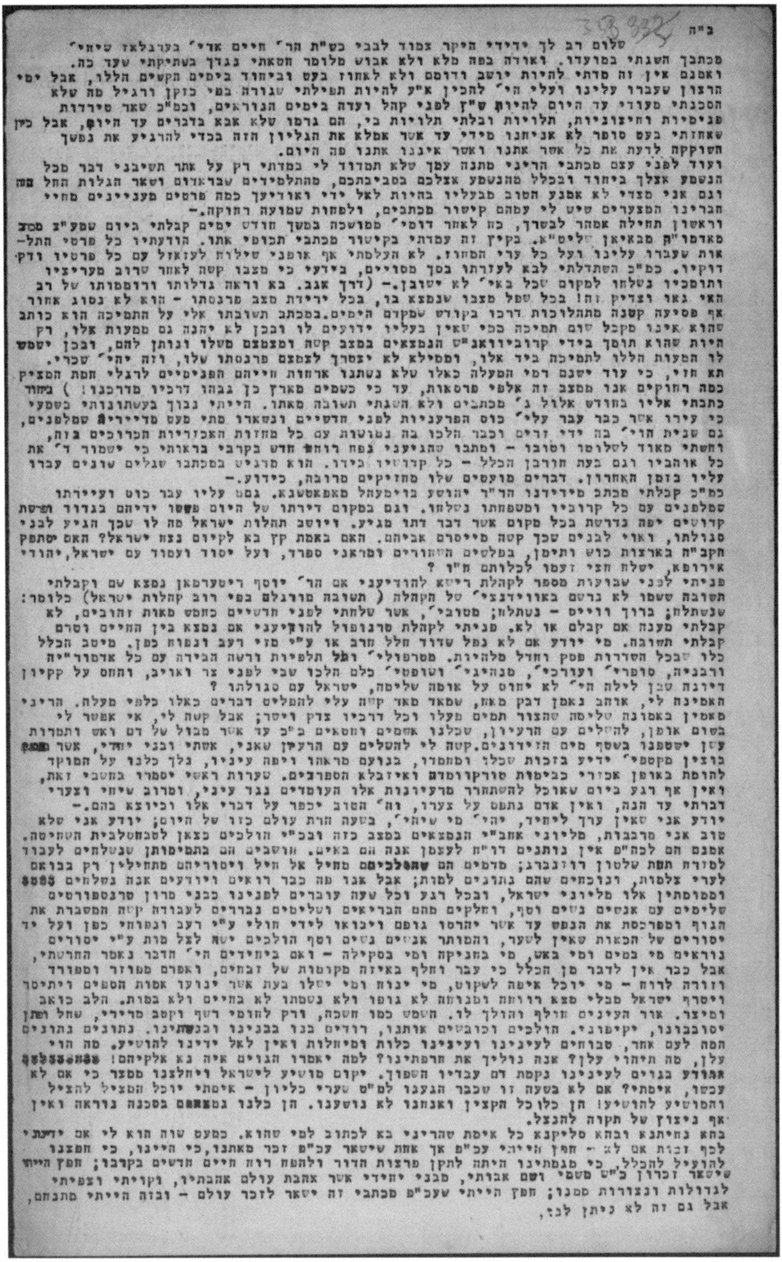

ב"ה

שלום רב לך ידידי היקר צמוד לבבי כש"ת הר' חיים ארי' בערגלאז שיחי'
מכתבך השגתי במועדו. ואודה בפה מלא ולא אבוש מלומר חטאתי נגדך בשתיקתי שעד כה.
ואמנם אין זה מדתי להיות יושב ודומם ולא לאחוז בעט וביחוד בימים הקשים הללו, אבל ימי
הרצון שעברו עלינו ועלי הי' להכין א"ע להיות תפילתי שגורה בפי כזקן ורגיל מה שלא
הסכנתי מעודי עד היום להיות ש"ץ לפני קהל ועדה בימים הנוראים, וכמ"כ שאר טירדות
פנימיות וחיצוניות, תלויות ובלתי תלויות בי, הם גרמו שלא אבא בדברים עד היום, אבל כיון
שאחזתי בעט סופר לא אניחנו מידי עד אשר אמלא את הגליון הזה בכדי להרגיע את נפשך
השוקקה לדעת את כל אשר אתנו ואשר איננו אתנו פה היום.
ועוד לפני עצם מכתבי הריני מתנה עמך שלא תמדוד לי במדתי רק על אתר תשיבני דבר מכל
הנשמע אצלך ביחוד ובכלל מהנשמע אצלכם בסביבתכם, מהתלמידים שבראדום ושאר הגלות החל מה
וגם אני מצדי לא אמנע הטוב מבעליו בהיות לאל ידי ואודיעך כמה פרטים מענינים מחיי
חברינו המצערים שיש לי עמהם קישור מכתבים, ולפחות שמועה רחוקה.-
וראשון תחילה אמהר לבשרך, כה לאחר דומי' ממושכה במשך חודש ימים קבלתי היום שמע"צ מכ
מאדמו"ר מבאיאן שליט"א. בקיץ זה עמדתי בקישור מכתבי תכופי אתו. הודעתיו כל פרטי התל-
אות שעברו עלינו ועל כל ערי המחוז. לא העלמתי אף אופני שילוח לעזאזל עם כל פרטיו ודק-
דוקיו. כמ"כ השתדלתי לבא לעזרתו בסך מסויים, בידעי כי מצבו קשה לאחר שרוב מעריציו
ותומכיו נשלחו למקום שכל באי' לא ישובן.- (דרך אגב. בא וראה גדלותו ורוממותו של רב
האי גאון וצדיק זה! בכל שפל מצבו שנמצא בו, בכל ירידת מצב פרנסתו - הוא לא נסוג אחור
אף פסיעה קטנה מתהלוכות דרכו בקודש שמקדם הימים. במכתב תשובתו אלי על התמיכה הוא כותב
שהוא אינו מקבל שום תמיכה ממי שאין בעליו ידועים לו ובכן לא יהנה גם ממעות אלו, רק
היות שהוא תומך בידי קרוביו־ואג"ש הנמצאים במצב קשה ומצמצם משלו ונותן להם, ובכן ישמש
לו המעות הללו לתמיכה ביד אלו, ומסילא לא יצטרך לצמצם פרנסתו שלו, וזה יהי' שכרי.
תא חזי, כי עוד ישנם דמי המעלה כאלו שלא נשתנו ארחות חייהם הפנימיים לרגלי חמת המציק
כמה רחוקים אנו ממצב זה אלפי פרסאות, עד כי כשמים מארץ כן גבהו דרכיו מדרכנו!) ביחוד
כתבתי אליו בחודש אלול ג' מכתבים ולא השגתי תשובה מאתו. הייתי נבוך בעשתונותי בשמעי
כי עירו אשר כבר עבר עלי' כוס הפרעניות לפני חדשיים ונשארו מתי מעט מדייריה שמלפנים,
גם שבית הוי' בה ידי זרים וכבר הלכו בה נטורות עם כל מחזות האכזריות המרוכים בזה,
וחשתי מאוד לשלומו וטובו - ומתבו שהגיעני נפח רוחי חדש בקרבי בראותי כי ישמור ד' את
כל אוהביו וגם בעת חורבן הכלל - כל קדושיו בידו. הוא מרגיש במכתבו שגלים שוגים עברו
עליו בזמן האחרון. דברים מועטים שלו מחזיקים מרובה, כידוע.-
כמ"כ קבלתי מכתב מידידנו הד"ר יהושע בוימעהל מאפאטשנא. גםמ עליו עבר כוס ועיירתו
שמלפנים עם כל קרוביו ומשפחתו נשלחו. וגם במקום דירתו של היום משו ידיהם בגדוד ופשת
קדושים יפה נדרשת בכל מקום אשר דבר דתו מגיע. ויושב תהלות ישראל מה לו שכך הגיע לבני
סגולתו, ואוי לבנים שכך קשה מייסרם אביהם. האם באמת קץ בא לקיום נצח ישראל? האם יסתפק
הקב"ה בארצות כוש ותימן, בפלשים השחורים ומראני ספרד, ועל יסוד ועמוד עם ישראל, יהודי
אירופא, ישלח חצי זעמו לכלותם ח"ו ?
פניתי לפני שבועות מספר לקהלת ריישא להודיעני אם הר' יוסף דיטערמאן נמצא שם וקבלתי
תשובה ששמו לא נרשם באווידענצי' של הקהלה (תשובה מורגלת בפי רוב קהלות ישראל) כלומר:
שנשתלח; ברוך ווייס - נשתלח; מסרבי', אשר שלחתי לפני חדשיים כחמש מאות זהובים, לא
קבלתי מענה אם קבלם או לא. פניתי לקהלת סרגופול להודיעני אם נמצא בין החיים וטרם
קבלתי תשובה. מי יודע אם לא נפל שדוד חלל חרב או ע"י מזי רעב ונפוח כפן. מיטב הכלל
כלו שבכל השדרות פסק וחדל מלהיות. מטרפולי' ותל תלפיות ודשה הבידה עם כל אדמור"יה
ורבניה, סופרי' ועורכי', מנהיגי' ושופטי' כלם הלכו שבי לפני צר ואויב, וחוס על קקיון
דירנה שבן לילה הי' לא יחוס על אומה שלימה, ישראל עם סגולתו ?
האמינה לי, אוהב נאמן דבק מאח, שמאד מאד קשה עלי להעליט דברים כאלו כלפי מעלה. הריני
מאמין באמונה שלימה שהצור תמים פעלו וכל דרכיו צדק וישר; אבל קשה לי, אי אפשר לי
בשום אופן, להשלים עם הרעיון, שכלנו אשמים וחטאים כ"כ עד אשר מבול של דם ואש ותמרות
עשן ישטפנו בשטף מים הזידונים. קשה לי להשלים עם הרעיון שאני, אשתי ובני יחידי, אשר נמצא
בוצין מקטפי' ידיע בזכות שכלו ומחמדו, בנועם מראהו ויפה עיניו, נלך כלנו על המוקד
להומת באופן אכזרי כבימות טורקוומדא ואיזבלא הספרדים. שערות ראשי יסמרו בחשבי זאת,
ואין אף רגע ביום שאוכל להשתחרר מרעיונות אלו העומדים נגד עיני, ומרוב שיחי וצערי
דברתי עד הנה, ואין אדם נתפס על צערו, וה' הטוב יכפר על דברי אלו וכיוצא בהם.-
יודע אני שאין ערך ליחיד, יהי' מי שיהי', בשעה הרת עולם כזו של היום; יודע אני שלא
טוב אני מרבבות, מליוני אחב"י הנמצאים במצב כזה ובכ"י הולכים כצאן לטבח ללבית השחיטה.
אמנם הם לכה"פ אין נותנים דו"ח לעצמן אנה הם באים. חושבים הם בתמימותן שנשלחים לעבוד
למזרח תחת שלטון רוזנברג; מדמים הם שמשלכים מחיל אל חיל ויסוריהם מתחילין רק בבואם
לערי צלמות, ובוכחים שהם נהרגים למות; אבל אנו מה כבר רואים ויודעים אנה נשלחים
ומפורסמין אלו מליוני ישראל, ובכל רגע וכל שעה עוברים לפנינו כבני מרון טרנספורטים
שלימים עם אנשים נשים וטף, וחלקים מהם הבריאים ושלימים נבררים לעבודה קשה המשברת את
הגוף ומפרכסת את הנפש עד אשר יהרסו גופם ויבואו לידי חולי ע"י רעב ונפוחי כפן ועל יד
יסורים של הכאות שאין לשער, והמותר אנשים נשים וטף הולכים ישר לצל מות ע"י יסורים
נוראים מי במים ומי באש, מי בחניקה ומי בסקילה - ואם ביחידים הי' הדבר נאמר החרשתי,
אבל כבר אין לדבר מן הכלל כי עבר וחלף באיזה מקוטות של זבחים, ואפרם מפוזר ומפורד
וזורה לרוח - מי יוכל איפה לשקוט, מי ינוח ומי ישלו בעת אשר ינוער אמות הספים ויתיסר
ויסרף ישראל מבלי מצא רווחה ומנוחה לא גופו ולא נשמתו לא בחיים ולא במות. הלב כואב
ומיצר. אור העינים חולף והולך לו. השמש כמו חשכה, ורק להומי רשף וקטב מרירי, שחל ופתן
יסובבונו, יקיפונו. הולכים וכובשים אותנו, רודים בנו בבנינו ובנשותינו. נתונים נתונים
המה לעם אחר, סבוחים לעינינו ועינינו כלות ומיחלות ואין לאל ידינו להושיע. מה הוי
עלן, מה תיהוי עלן? אנה נוליך את חרפתינו? למה יאמרו הגוים איה נא אלקיהם!
תודע בגוים לעינינו נקמת דם עבדיו השפוך. יקום מושיע לישראל ויחלצנו ממצר כי אם לא
עכשו, אימתי? אם לא בשעה זו שכבר הגענו למ"ט שערי כליון - אימתי יוכל המציל להציל
והמושיע להושיע! הן כלו כל הקצין ואנחנו לא נושענו. הן כלנו נמצאים בסכנה נוראה ואין
אף ניצוץ של תקוה להנצל.
בהא נחיתנא ובהא סליקנא כל אימת שהריני בא לכתוב למי שהוא. כמעט שוה הוא לי אם ידעתי
לכף זכות אם לא - חפץ הייתי עכ"פ אך אחת שישאר זכר מאתנו, כי היינו, כי חפצנו
להועיל להכלל, כי מגמתינו היתה לתקן פרצות הדור ולהפח רוח חיים חדשים בקרבו; חפץ הייתי
שישאר זכרון כ"ש משמי ושם אבותי, מבני יחידי אשר אהבת עולם אהבתיו, וקויתי וצפיתי
לגדולות ונצורות ממנו; חפץ הייתי שעכ"פ מכתבי זה ישאר לזכר עולם - ובזה הייתי מתנחם,
אבל גם זה לא ניתן לנו,

Letter from Rabbi Zvi Elimelech Talmud to Rabbi Arieh Berglas, October 1942, WAPL, RZ 32

Courtesy of Archiwum Państwowe w Lublinie

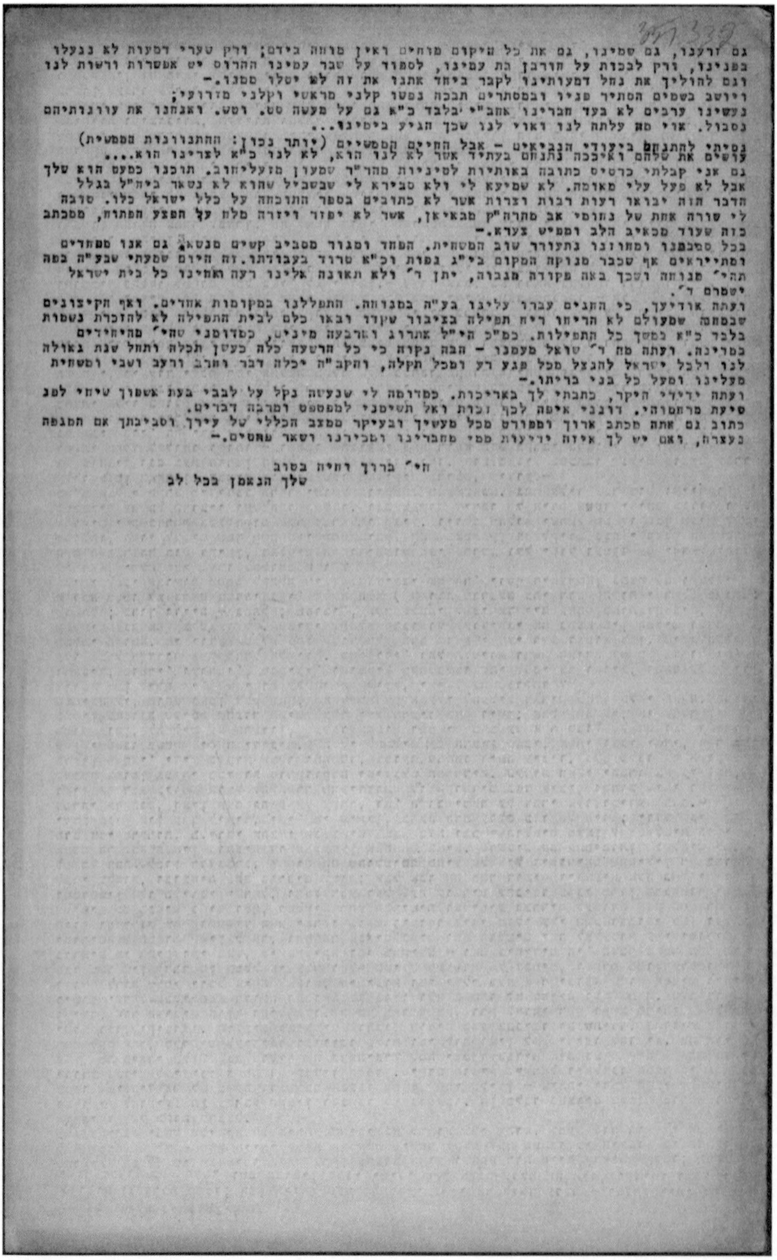

גם זרענו, גם שמינו, גם את כל מיקום מוחים ואין מושה בידם; ורק שערי דמעות לא ננעלו
בפנינו, ורק לבכות על חורבן בת עמינו, לספוד על שבר עמינו ההרוס יש אפשרות ורשות לנו
וגם להוליך את נחל דמעותינו לקבר ביחד אתנו את זה לא יטלו ממנו.—
ויושב בשמים הסתיר פניו ובמסתרים תבכה נפשו קלני מראשי וקלני מזרועי;
נעשינו ערבים לא בעד חברינו אחב"י בלבד כ"א גם על מעשה סט. וסט. ואנחנו את עוונותיהם
נסבול. אוי מה עלתה לנו ואוי לנו שכך הגיע בימינו..
נסיתי להתנחם ביעודי הנביאים — אבל החיים הממשיים (יותר נכון: ההתגוררות הממשית)
עושים את שלהם ואיככה נתנחם בעתיד אשר לא לנו הוא, לא לנו כ"א לצריכנו הוא...
גם אני קבלתי כרטיס כתובה באותיות לטיניות מהר"ר שמעון מזעליחוב. תוכנו כמעט הוא שלך
אבל לא פעל עלי מאומה. לא שמיעא לי ולא סבירא לי שבשביל שהוא לא נשאר ביה"ל בגלל
הדבר הזה יבואר רעות רבות וצרות אשר לא כתובים בספר התוכחה על כלל ישראל כלו. טובה
לי שורה אחת של נחומי אב מתרה"ק מבאיאן, אשר לא יפזר ויזרה מלח על הפצע הפתוח, ממכתב
כזה שעוד מכאיב הלב וממיש צערא.—
בכל סביבתנו ומחוזנו נתעורר שוב המשחית. הפחד ומגור מסביב קשים מנשא, גם אנו מפחדים
ומתייראים אף שכבר מנוקה המקום בי"ג נפות וכ"א טרוד בעבודתו. זה היום שמעתי שבע"ה בפה
תהי' מנוחה ושכך באה פקודה מגבוה, יתן ה' ולא תאונה אלינו רעה ואחינו כל בית ישראל
ישמרם ה'.
ועתה אודיעך, כי החגים עברו עלינו בע"ה במנוחה. התפללנו במקומות אחדים. ואף הקיצונים
שבסתה שמעולם לא הריחו ריח תפילה בציבור שקדו ובאו כלם לבית התפילה לא להזכרת נשמות
בלבד כ"א במשך כל התפילות. כמ"כ הי"ל אתרוג וארבעה מינים, כמדומני שהי' מהיחידים
במדינה. ועתה מה ה' שואל מעמנו — הבה נקוה כי כל הרשעה כלה כעשן תכלה ותחל שנת גאולה
לנו ולכל ישראל להנצל מכל פגע רע ומכל תקלה, והקב"ה יכלה דבר וחרב ורעב ושבי ומשחית
מעלינו ומעל כל בני בריתו.—
ועתה ידידי היקר, כתבתי לך באריכות. כמדומה לי שנעשה נקל על לבבי בעת אשפוך שיחי לפני
סיעת מרתמותי. ודובני איפה לכך זכות ואל תשימני למספט ומרבה דברים.
כתוב גם אתה מכתב ארוך ומפורט מכל מעשיך ובעיקר ממצב הכללי של עירך וסביבתך אם המגפה
נעצרה, ואם יש לך איזה ידיעות ממי מחברינו ומכירנו ושאר עסקים.—

הי' ברוך וחיה בטוב
שלך הנאמן בכל לב

Letter from Rabbi Zvi Elimelech Talmud to Rabbi Arieh Berglas, October 1942, WAPL, RZ 32

Courtesy of Archiwum Państwowe w Lublinie

Bibliography

Archives

Archiwum Państwowe w Lublinie

Record Groups:
Rada Żydowska w Lublinie
Gouverneur des Distrikts Lublin
Gmina Żydowska w Lublinie
SSPF Lublin
Rada Żydowska w Biskupicach
Rada Żydowska w Zamościu
WAPL, KdGend, file 276

Copies of some of these files can also be found in the Yad Vashem Archive (YVA), especially in microfilms JM/10,454-10,458, and Record Groups M.54 and O.6, and in the United States Holocaust Memorial Museum Archive (USHMMA), especially RG-15.101M and RG 15.011M. When such copies exist, the citation in the footnote cites the original (unless the document was examined only at Yad Vashem), while the copy in YVA and/or the USHMMA is cited in parentheses at the first mention of the file in the notes.

Yad Vashem Archives

Record Groups:

Recently, Yad Vashem's archive changed many of its archival registry numbers, especially those relating to Poland. The archive also divided some old files into various new files. However, no list was made for what old numbers parallel what new numbers, or where certain parts of files were refiled. I conducted an extensive search for the new numbers and was assisted by then deputy director of the archive, Ms. Nomi Halpern, to whom I am very grateful for her time and her efforts. I succeeded in finding nearly all the new numbers, but the archive's method of registration did not lend itself to tracing all of them. Therefore, the Yad Vashem Archive numbers given in this book are the new numbers unless marked with an asterisk (*), which indicates that the number is the original number. Much of the Polish State Archive material has been subsequently cataloged in record group M.54, but the previous record group and file number of microfilm cataloging remain, and this is what appears in the notes.

JM – The microfilm collection, containing documents from other archives. Many dozens of microfilms were examined, including documents from the following archives:
Archiwum Państwowe w Lublinie
Główna Komisja Badania Zbrodni Niemieckich w Polsce
Archiwum Państwowe na Majdanka
Żydowski Institut Historyczny
National Archives of the United States
United Nations War Crimes Commission Archives
YIVO
Bundesarchiv Berlin, Potsdam

M.1./E – Collection of survivor testimonies from the displaced persons camps in Germany.

M.1/Q – Questionnaires completed by survivors in displaced persons camps in Germany.

M.2 – Itzhak Schwartzbart archive

M.4 – Collection of the Rescue Committee of the Jewish Agency for Palestine

M.8 – Archive of the International Tracing Service (Arolsen)

M.9 – Simon Wiesenthal collection, war criminals investigation files

M.10 – Ringelblum Archive ("Oneg Shabbat")

M.21 – Archive of the [post-war] Jewish Historical Commission, Munich, war criminals investigation files

M.49.E – Testimonies from the Żydowski Institut Historyczny

archive in Warsaw, including testimonies formerly in record groups O.16 and OO.16
M.49.P – Memoirs collection from the Żydowski Institut Historyczny archive, Warsaw
M.54 – Polish State Archives Documents
O.2 – Collection of testimonies from the Wiener Library
O.3 – Testimonies collection
O.4 – Files on war criminals (original call numbers)
O.6 – Poland collection
O.12 – Collection of testimonies by Polish Jews, from the Jewish Agency
O.16 – Collection of testimonies from Poland. The record group is in the process of being dismantled and its files dispersed among other record groups. Most of the testimonies have received new call numbers in the M.49.E record group, but some still have their original call numbers.
O.22 – Collection of newspaper clippings, including articles and testimonies from the immediate post-war years, from the Yiddish daily, דער פֿאָרווערטס.
O.30 – Austria collection
O.33 – Collection of testimonies
O.48 – file B/19, Feliks (Efraim) Rzeczyński collection
O.51 – Collection of German documents
O.53 – Documents from the Zentralestelle des Landesjustizverwaltungen, Ludwigsburg (ZStL)
O.68 – Collection of SS personnel files from the former Berlin Document Center, today part of the Bundesarchiv Berlin
O.75 – Collection of letters and last letters
O.93 – Shoah Visual History Archive Interviews
TR.1, TR.2 – Nuremberg documents (cited in the book by their Nuremberg numbers)
TR.3 – Eichmann trial documents
TR.10 – Collection of indictments, verdicts, and pre-trial interrogations and investigations from Germany (and Austria), part from ZStL, and part from the courts themselves.
TR.11 – Collection of testimonies recorded in Israel by the Israel police as part of German investigations of war crimes cases.

TR.18 – Trial records in various countries.
Krakauer Zeitung, in Yad Vashem Library, Pfi 48.

United States Holocaust Memorial Museum Archive
RG-15.101M
RG 15.011M

Moreshet Archive
Record Groups:
A – Testimonies
D.1 – Documents
D.2 – Documents and testimonies

Massuah Archive
Video Testimonies:
Matla (Kleiner) Blender
Dov Finger
Zvi (Finger) Naor
Ruth Tatarko

Published Documents

Arad, Yitzhak, Yisrael Gutman, and Avraham Margaliot, eds., *Documents on the Holocaust* (Jerusalem: Yad Vashem, 1981).

Berenstein, Tatiana, Artur Eisenbach, Bernard Mark, and Adam Rutkowski, eds., *Faschismus - Getto - Massenmord; Dokumentation über Ausrottung und Widerstand der Juden in Polen während des zweiten Weltkrieges* (Berlin: Rutten und Loening und Jüdischen Historischen Institut, Warschau, 1961).

Berenstein, Tatiana, Artur Eisenbach, and Adam Rutkowski, eds., *Eksterminacja Żydów na ziemiach polskich w okresie okupacji hitlerowskiej; zbior dokumentów* (Warsaw: Jewish Historical Institute, 1957).

Blackbook of Localities Whose Jewish Population Was Destroyed by the Nazis (Jerusalem: Yad Vashem, 1965).

Blumental, Nachman, ed., *Documents from the Lublin Ghetto: Judenrat Without Direction* (Hebrew) (Jerusalem: Yad Vashem, 1967).

Blumental, Nachman, and Józef Kermisz, eds., *Dokumenty i Materiały do Dziejów Okupacji Niemieckiej w Polsce* 3 vols. (Lodz: Centralna Żydowska Komisja Historyczna, 1946).

Dawidowicz, Lucy S., ed., *A Holocaust Reader* (New York: Behrman House, 1976).

"Documents and Materials by District: 3. The Lublin District," (Yiddish) *Bleter far Geschichte*, XVII (1969), pp. 96–136.

"Documents and Materials: Materials Regarding the Labor Camps in the Lublin District during the German Occupation (1940–1941)," (Yiddish) *Bleter far Geschichte*, II:1–4 (January–December 1949), pp. 242–272.

Friedman, Tuvia, ed., *The Persecutor of the Jews, Globocnik, SS- und Polizeiführer in the Lublin District, the German Wehrmacht and the Annihilation of the Jews in the Generalgouvernement in Poland, A Documentary Collection* (Hebrew) (Haifa: The Documentation Institute, 1977).

Friedrich, Klaus-Peter, ed., *Die Verfolgung und Ermordung der europäischen Juden durch das nationalsozialistische Deutschland 1933–1945, Band 4, Polen September 1939—Juli 1941* (Munich: R. Oldenbourg, 2011).

Halder, Franz, *Generaloberst Halder, Kriegstagebuch*, edited by Hans-Adolf Jacobsen (Stuttgart: W. Kohlhammer Verlag, 1962).

Hilberg, Raul, ed., *Documents of Destruction; Germany and Jewry, 1939–1945*, (Chicago: Quadrangle, 1971).

International Military Tribunal (IMT), *Trial of the Major War Criminals Before the International Military Tribunal*, 42 vols. (Nuremberg: IMT, 1947-1949). (Blue Series)

Kermish, Joseph, ed., *To Live With Honor and Die With Honor; Selected Documents from the Warsaw Ghetto Underground Archives "O.S."* (Oneg Shabbath) (Yad Vashem: Jerusalem, 1986).

Lehnstaedt, Stephan and Jochen Böhler, eds., *Die Berichte der Einsatzgruppen aus Polen 1939: Vollständige Edition* (Berlin: Metropol, 2013).

Mallmann, Klaus-Michael, Jochen Böhler, and Jürgen Matthäus, eds., *Einsatzgruppen in Polen: Darstellung und Dokumentation* (Darmstadt: Wissenschaftliche Buchgesellschaft with Deutsche Historische Institut Warschau and Forschungsstelle Ludwigsburg der Universität Stuttgart, 2008).

Sakowska, Ruta, ed., *Archiwum Ringelbluma: Listy o Zagładzie* (Warsaw: Wydawnictwo Naukowe PWN, 1997).

Präg, Werner and Wolfgang Jacobmeyer, eds., *Das Diensttagebuch das deutschen Generalgouverneurs in Polen, 1939-1945* (Stuttgart: Deutsche Verlags-Anstalt, 1975).

Tafet, Gershon, ed., *The Destruction of Polish Jewry, Photographic Album* (Warsaw: Central Jewish Historical Committee, 1946).

The Trial of Adolf Eichmann: Record of the Proceedings in the District Court of Jerusalem, vol. 3 (Jerusalem: Ministry of Justice, 1993).

Trials of War Criminals Before the Nuernberg Military Tribunals, volume V, Case 4, The Pohl Case, Nuernberg, October 1946–April 1949 (Washington, D.C.: United States Government Printing Office, 1950) (Green Series).

Witte, Peter, et al., *Der Dienstkalender Heinrich Himmlers 1941/42* (Hamburg: Christians, 1999).

Zariz, Ruth, ed., *Letters from Haluzim in Occupied Poland, 1940–1944* (Hebrew) (Tel Aviv: Yad Tabenkin and Beit Lohamei Hagetaot, 1994).

Diaries and Memoirs

Ackerman, Notek, *Lublin Memories* (Yiddish) (Tel Aviv: Yisrael Buch, 1990).

Adler, Stanislaw, *In the Warsaw Ghetto 1940–1943; An Account of a Witness* (Jerusalem: Yad Vashem, 1982).

Bachrich, Jan, Testimony, manuscript (Hebrew) (in the collection of the late Dr. Leopold Laufer).

Blits, Mirjam, *Auschwitz 13917; Hoe ik de Duitse concentratiekampen overleefde* (Amsterdam and Brussels: Elsevier, 1961).

Bubis, Ignatz, *Ich bin ein deutscher Staatsbürger jüdischen Glaubens; Ein autobiographisches Gespräch mit Edith Kohn* (Köln: Kiepenheuer and Witsch, 1993).

Czerniakow, Adam, *The Warsaw Diary of Adam Czerniakow*, edited by Raul Hilberg, Stanislaw Staron, and Josef Kermisz (New York: Stein and Day, Scarborough edition, 1982).

Dziadosz, Edward, ed., *Juden Massen Exekutionen, 3. November 1943, Majdanek, Poniatowa, Trawniki; Erinnerungen* (Lublin: Państwowe Muzeum na Majdanku and Uniwersytet Marii Curie-Sklodkowskiej, 1990 [c1988]).

Edelman, David, *There Was Once a Jewish Lublin* (Hebrew) (Tel Aviv: Hechalot, 1979).

Erlichman-Bank, Sarah (Sojka), *In Impure Hands: Letters to My Sister from the Vale of Tears* (Hebrew) (Tel Aviv: Ghetto Fighters' House, 1976).

Frank, Moshe, *To Survive and Testify* (Hebrew) (Tel Aviv: Ghetto Fighters House and Hakibbutz Hameuhad, 1993).

Freiberg, Daniel, *Darkness Covered the Earth* (Hebrew) (Tel Aviv: Ghetto Fighters' House, 1970).

Freiberg, Dov, *To Survive Sobibor* (Jerusalem and New York: Gefen, 2007).

The Goebbels Diaries 1942–1943, trans. and ed. by Louis Lochner (Garden City, NY: Doubleday, 1948).

Gruber, Sam (Mietek), *I Chose Life* (New York: Shengold, 1978).

Gruber, Shmuel (Mietek), "Jewish Partisans in the Lublin District," (Hebrew) *Yalkut Moreshet*, 18 (November 1974), pp. 113–148.

Hindls, Arnold, *Einer kehrte zurück; Bericht eines Deportierten* (Stuttgart: Deutsche Verlags Anstalt, 1965).

Hochman, Stanley, *Mr. Fate: My Personal World War II Memoirs* (unpublished 1998 manuscript in Yad Vashem Library).

Höss, Rudolf, *The Commandant of Auschwitz* (New York: Popular Library, 1959).

Hurwitz, Cipora, *Forbidden Strawberries* (New Rochelle, NY: Multi Educator, 2010).

Kaplan, Chaim, *The Warsaw Diary of Chaim A. Kaplan* (New York: Collier, 1973, c1965).

Karski, Jan, *The Story of the Secret State* (Boston: Houghton Miflin, 1944).

Klukowski, Zygmunt, *Diary from the Years of Occupation 1939–1944* (Urbana and Chicago: University of Illinois Press, 1993).

Laks, Yehoshua, *I Was There* (Hebrew) (Bnai Brak: privately published, 1993).

Lewin, Abraham, *A Cup of Tears: A Diary of the Warsaw Ghetto* (Oxford: Blackwell, 1989).

Lewis, Mark and Frank, Jacob, *Himmler's Jewish Tailor: The Story of Holocaust Survivor Jacob Frank* (Syracuse: Syracuse University Press, 2000).

Modrzewska, Krystyna, "Pamiętnik z Okresu Okupacji," *Biuletyn Żydowski Institut Historycznego*, nr. 31 (1959).

Novitch, Miriam, ed., *Sobibor: Martyrdom and Revolt* (New York: Holocaust Library, 1980).

Orenstein, Henry, *I Shall Live; Surviving Against All Odds, 1939–1945* (New York: Beaufort Books, 1987).

Jan Osers, *Under Swastika and Hammer and Sickle: Persecutions in Two Dictatorships* (Prague: unpublished manuscript, 2005; available in Yad Vashem Library).

Pechersky, Alexander, "Revolt in Sobibor," in Yuri Suhl, ed., *They Fought Back; The Story of Jewish Resistance in Nazi Europe* (New York: Schocken, 1975, c1967), pp. 7–44.

Pinkus, Oscar, *The House of Ashes* (Cleveland and New York: World Publishing Co., 1964)

Reder, Rudolf, *Bełżec* (Kraków: Drukarnia Uniwersytetu Jagiellonskiego, 1999, c1946).

Ringelblum, Emmanuel, *Diary and Notes from the Warsaw Ghetto: September 1939—December 1942*, 2 vols. (Hebrew) (Jerusalem: Yad Vashem and Ghetto Fighters' House, 1992).

Ringelblum, Emmanuel, *Notes from the Warsaw Ghetto* (New York: Schocken, 1974).

Rós, Jerzy, "The Poniatowa Labor Camp," (Hebrew) *Yalkut Moreshet*, 13 (June 1971), pp. 17–27.

Rosenfeld, Else und Luckner, Gertrud, eds., *Lebenszeichen aus Piaski; Briefe Deportierter aus dem Distrikt Lublin 1940-1943* (Munich: Biederstein, 1968).

Schelvis, Jules, *Inside the Gates* (Tricht: Elzenhorst Tricht, 1990).

Schupack, Joseph, *The Dead Years* (New York: Holocaust Library, 1986).

Silberklang, Boruch, "Memoir" (Yiddish) (unpublished manuscript in author's possession).

Stahlhammer, Semmy, *Codename Barber: My Father's Story* (Stockholm: Semmy Stahlhammer Music and Violin Atelier, 2007).

Szifman, Nusia and Inia, *"My Life Is Still Before Me..."* (Yiddish) (Tel Aviv and Jerusalem: I.L. Peretz Verlag and Yad Vashem, 1962), edited by Nachman Blumental.

Waks, Shlomo, *Shlomo: The Holocaust Story of an Optimist* (Tel Aviv: Kotarim International Publishing, 2009).

Wdowinski, David, *And We Are Not Saved* (New York: Philosophical Library, 1963).

Weichert, Michael, *Jewish Mutual Assistance 1939–1945* (Yiddish) (Tel Aviv: Menora, 1962).

Wenkart, Hermann, *Befehlsnotstand Anders Gesehen; Tatsachenbericht eines jüdischen Lagerfunktionärs* (Vienna: Privately published, 1969).

Werner, Harold, *Fighting Back; A Memoir of Jewish Resistance in World War II* (New York: Columbia University Press, 1992).

Wiernik, Yankel, *A Year in Treblinka* (New York: American Representation of the General Jewish Workers' Union of Poland, 1944).

Wyszogrod, Morris, *A Brush with Death; An Artist in the Death Camps* (Albany: State University of New York Press, 1999).

Zuckerman, Yitzhak ("Antek"), *A Surplus of Memory: Chronicle of the Warsaw Ghetto Uprising* (Berkeley: University of California Press, 1993).

Zuckerman, Yitzchak and Moshe Basok, eds., *The Wars of the Ghettos: Behind the Walls, in the Camps, in the Forests* (Hebrew) (Tel Aviv: Hakibbutz Hameuhad, 1954).

Research (and other publications)

Adler, H. G., *Der verwaltete Mensch. Studien zur Deportation der Juden aus Deutschland* (Tübingen: Mohr, 1974).

Allen, Michael Thad, *The Business of Genocide; The SS, Slave Labor, and the Concentration Camps* (Chapel Hill; University of North Carolina Press, 2002).

Aly, Götz and Heim, Susanne, "The Economics of the 'Final Solution': A Case Study from the General Government," *Simon Wiesenthal Center Annual,* volume 5 (1988), pp. 3-48.

Idem, "The Holocaust and Population Policy: Remarks on the Decision on the 'Final Solution,'" *Yad Vashem Studies,* 24 (1994), pp. 45–70.

Aly, Götz, "Erwiderung auf Dan Diner," *Vierteljahrshefte für Zeitgeschichte,* 41:4 (October 1993), pp. 621–635.

Idem, "'Jewish Resettlement': Reflections on the Political Prehistory of the Holocaust," in Ulrich Herbert, ed., *National Socialist Extermination Policies: Contemporary German Perspectives and Controversies* (New York: Berghahn, 2000), pp. 53–82.

Idem, "*Final Solution*"; *Nazi Population Policy and the Murder of the European Jews* (London: Arnold, 1999).

Andraschko, Gustav, "Die 'Lehranstalt der Weisen Lublins,'" *Krakauer Zeitung,* May 31, 1942.

Arad, Yitzhak, *Belzec, Sobibor, Treblinka: The Operation Reinhard Death Camps* (Bloomington: Indiana University Press, 1983).

Arad, Yitzhak, "'Operation Reinhard': Extermination Camps of Belzec, Sobibor and Treblinka," *Yad Vashem Studies,* 16 (1984), pp. 205-240.

Balaban, Meir, *Die Yidn-Stadt Lublin* (Yiddish) (Buenos Aires: Union Central Israelita Polaca en la Argentina, 1946).

Bankier, David, "On Modernization and the Rationality of Extermination," *Yad Vashem Studies,* 24 (1994), pp. 109–129.

Bauer, Yehuda, *American Jewry and the Holocaust: The American Jewish Joint Distribution Committee, 1939–1945* (Detroit: Wayne State University Press, 1981).

Idem, *Rethinking the Holocaust* (New Haven and London: Yale University Press, 2001).

Idem, "When Did They Know?" *Midstream* (April 1968), pp. 51–58.

Idem, "Who Was Responsible and When? Some Well-known Documents Revisited," *Holocaust and Genocide Studies*, 6:2 (1991), pp. 129–149.

Birn, Ruth Bettina, *Die Höhere SS- und Polizeiführer: Himmlers Vertreter im Reich und in den besetzten Gebieten* (Düsseldorf: Droste, 1986).

Black, Peter, "Foot Soldiers of the Final Solution: The Trawniki Training Camp and Operation Reinhard," *Holocaust and Genocide Studies*, 25:1 (Spring 2011), pp. 1–99.

Idem, "Odilo Globocnik – Himmlers Vorposten im Osten," in Ronald Smelser, Enrico Syring, and Rainer Zittelmann, eds., *Die Braune Elite II* (Darmstadt: Wissenschaftliche Buchgesellschaft, 1994), pp. 103–115.

Idem, "Rehearsal for 'Reinhard'?: Odilo Globocnik and the Lublin *Selbstschutz*," *Central European History*, vol. 25, no. 2 (1992), pp. 204–226.

Idem, "Die Trawniki Männer und die 'Aktion Reinhard'," in Bogdan Musial, ed., *"Aktion Reinhardt": Der Völkermord an den Juden im Generalgouvernement 1941–1944* (Osnabrück: Fibre Verlag, 2004), pp. 309–352.

Blaschek, Dr., "Reisebericht über meine Dienstreise zur Regierung nach Krakau vom 21 bis 26.VIII.1942," *Biuletyn Głównej Komisji do Badania Zbrodnii Hitlerowskich*, vol. 15 (1965), pp. 129–163.

Breitman, Richard, *The Architect of Genocide: Himmler and the Final Solution* (New York: Alfred A. Knopf, 1991).

Idem, "Himmler's Police Auxiliaries in the Occupied Soviet Territories," *Simon Wiesenthal Center Annual*, 7 (1990), pp. 23–39.

Broszat, Martin, Buchheim, Hans, Krausnick, Helmut, Jacobsen, Hans Adolf, *Anatomy of the SS-State* (London: Collins, 1968).

Broszat, Martin, *Nationalsozialistische Polenpolitik in 1939–1945* (Stuttgart: Deutsche Verlags Anstalt, 1961).

Browning, Christopher R., *Fateful Months: Essays on the Emergence of the Final Solution* (New York: Holmes & Meier, 1985).

Idem, "A Final Hitler Decision for the 'Final Solution'? The Riegner Telegram Reconsidered," *Holocaust and Genocide Studies,* 10:1 (1996), pp. 3–10.

Idem, "Genocide and Public Health: German Doctors and Polish Jews, 1939–1941," *Holocaust and Genocide Studies* 3:1 (1988), pp. 21–36.

Idem, "German Technocrats, Jewish Labor, and the Final Solution: A Reply to Götz Aly and Susanne Heim," *Remembering for the Future; The Impact of the Holocaust on the Contemporary World* (Oxford: Pergamon Press, 1988), II:2199–2208 and in revised form in idem, *The Path to Genocide,* (Cambridge: Cambridge University Press, 1992), pp. 59–76.

Idem, "Nazi Ghettoization Policy in Poland, 1939–41," *Central European History,* XIX (1986), pp. 343–386.

Idem, *Nazi Policy, Jewish Workers, German Killers* (Cambridge and New York: Cambridge University Press, 2000).

Idem, "Nazi Resettlement Policy and the Search for a Solution to the Jewish Question, 1939–1941," in Michael Marrus, ed., *The Nazi Holocaust* (Westport, CT and London: Meckler, 1989), *3. The "Final Solution": The Implementation of Mass Murder,* Volume 2, pp. 760–782.

Idem, *Ordinary Men: Reserve Police Battalion 101 and the Final Solution in Poland* (New York: HarperCollins, 1992).

Idem, *The Origins of the Final Solution: The Evolution of Nazi Jewish Policy, September 1939—March 1942* (Jerusalem and Lincoln: Yad Vashem and University of Nebraska Press, 2004).

Idem, *Remembering Survival: Inside a Nazi Slave-Labor Camp* (New York and London: W.W. Norton & Co., 2010).

Brustin-Berenstein, Tatiana, "Deportations as a Stage in the German Annihilation Politics Regarding the Jewish Population," (Yiddish) *Bleter far Geschichte,* vol. 3, nos. 1–2 (January-June 1950), pp. 51–77.

Idem, "Martyrologia, opór i zagłada ludności żydowski w dystrykcie lubelskim," *Biuletin Żydowski Institut Historycznego,* 21 (1957), pp. 22–92.

Idem, "Obozy pracy przymusowej dla Żydów w dystrykcie lubelskim," *Biuletin Żydowski Institut Historycznego,* 24 (1957), pp. 3–20.

Idem, "O Podolozu Gospodarczym Sporów Między Władzami Administracyjnymi A Policyjnymi w Generalne Guberni (1939–44)," *Biuletyn Żydowski Instytut Historycznego*, no. 53 (Jan.–Mar. 1965), pp. 33–79.

Büchler, Yehoshua, "The Deportation of Slovakian Jews to the Lublin District of Poland in 1942," *Holocaust and Genocide Studies,* 6:2 (1991), pp. 151–166.

Idem, "*Kommandostab Reichsführer-SS*: Himmler's Personal Murder Brigades in 1941," *Holocaust and Genocide Studies,* 1:1 (1986), pp. 11–25.

Idem, "Document: A Preparatory Document for the Wannsee Conference," with additional remarks by Richard Breitman, *Holocaust and Genocide Studies,* 9:1 (Spring 1995), pp. 121–129.

Bühler, Josef, ed., *Das Generalgouvernement - Seine Verwaltung und seine Wirtschaft* (Krakow: Burgverlag G.M.B.H., 1943).

Calvocoressi, Peter, Guy Wint, and John Pritchard, *Total War: The Causes and Courses of the Second World War,* Revised second edition. (London: Penguin, 1989).

Central Commission for the Investigation of German Crimes in Poland (Główna Komisja), *German Crimes in Poland* (Warsaw: Główna Komisja, 1946-47), 2 vols., reprinted in one vol.: (New York: Howard Fertig, 1982).

Curilla, Wolfgang, *Der Judenmord in Polen und die deutschen Ordnungspolizei 1933–1945* (Paderborn: Ferdinand Schönnningh, 2011).

Cüppers, Martin, *Wegbereiter der Shoah: Die Waffen-SS, der Kommandostab Reichsführer-SS, und die Judenvernichtung 1939–1945* (Darmstadt: Wissenschaftliche Buchgesellschaft, 2005).

Dallin, Alexander, *German Rule in Russia, 1941–1945: A Study of Occupation Policies* (New York and London: Macmillan, 1957).

Dean, Martin, *Collaboration in the Holocaust: Crimes of the Local Police in Belorussia and Ukraine* (New York: Saint Martin's Press, 2000).

Idem, ed., *The United States Holocaust Memorial Museum*

Encyclopedia of Camps and Ghettos, 1933–1945, Volume II, Ghettos in German-Occupied Eastern Europe (Bloomington and Indianapolis: Indiana University Press with the United States Holocaust Memorial Museum, 2012).

Diner, Dan, "Rationalization and Method: Critique of a New Approach in Understanding the 'Final Solution,'" *Yad Vashem Studies*, 24 (1994), pp. 71–108.

Du Prel, Max Freiherr, *Das Deutsche Generalgouvernement Polen; Ein Überblick über Gebiet Gestaltung und Geschichte* (Krakow: Buchverlag Ost, 1940).

Idem, *Das Generalgouvernement* (Würzburg: Konrad Triltsch Verlag, 1942).

Dworzecki, Meir, "The Day-to-Day Stand of the Jews," in *Jewish Resistance During the Holocaust*, edited by Aryeh Tartakower, et al. (Jerusalem: Yad Vashem, 1971), pp. 152–181, and the discussion on pp. 181–190.

Dziadosz, Eduard and Józef Marszalek, "Więzienia i obozy w dystrykcie lubelskim w latach 1939–1944," *Zeszyty Majdanka*, III (1969), pp. 59–122.

Eisenbach, Artur, "Operation Reinhard: Mass Extermination of the Jewish Population in Poland," *Polish Western Affairs*, III:1 (1962), pp. 80–124.

Engel, David, *In the Shadow of Auschwitz: The Polish Government-In Exile and the Jews, 1939–1942*, (Chapel Hill and London: University of North Carolina Press, 1987).

Engelking, Barbara, *"Jest taki piękny słoneczny dzień... Losy Żydów szukających ratunku na wsi polskiej 1942–1945"* (Warsaw: Centrum Badań nad Zagłada Żydów, 2011).

Evans, Jon, *The Nazi New Order in Poland* (London: Victor Gollancz, 1941).

Farbstein, Esther, "A Close-up View of a Judenrat: The Memoirs of Pnina Weiss — Wife of a Member of the First Judenrat in Warsaw," *Yad Vashem Studies*, 33 (2005), pp. 61–99.

Farkash, Talia, *The History of the Jews of Puławy District in the Province of Lublin during World War II and the Holocaust 1939–1944* (Hebrew), masters thesis, University of Haifa, February 2013.

Fatran, Gila, *Struggle for Surviving? The Leadership of Slovakian Jews in the Holocaust 1938–1944* (Hebrew) (Tel Aviv: Moreshet and Institute of Contemporary Jewry, 1992).

Friedländer, Saul, *Nazi Germany and the Jews: The Years of Extermination, 1939–1945* (New York: HarperCollins, 2007).

Friedman, Philip, "The Jewish Ghettos of the Nazi Era," in idem, *Roads to Extinction; Essays on the Holocaust* (Philadelphia: Jewish Publication Society of America, 1980), pp. 59–87.

Idem, "The Lublin Reservation and the Madagascar Plan: Two Aspects of Nazi Jewish Policy during the Second World War," in ibid., pp. 34–58.

Gerlach, Christian, "The Wannsee Conference, the Fate of German Jews, and Hitler's Decision in Principle to Exterminate All European Jews," *The Journal of Modern History*, 70 (December 1998), pp. 759–812.

Gilbert, Martin, *Atlas of the Holocaust* (London: Michael Joseph, 1982).

Idem, *Auschwitz and the Allies* (New York: Holt, 1981).

Idem, *The Holocaust: A History of the Jews of Europe During the Second World War* (New York: Henry Holt and Co., 1985).

Gicewicz, Ryszard, "Obóz Pracy w Poniatowej (1941-1943)," *Zeszyty Majdanka,* X (1980), pp. 88-104.

Gingerich, Mark Philip, *Toward a Brotherhood of Arms: Waffen-SS Recruitment of Germanic Volunteers, 1940–1945* (PhD dissertation, University of Wisconsin-Madison, 1991)

Goldhagen, Daniel J., *Hitler's Willing Executioners: Ordinary Germans and the Holocaust* (New York: Alfred Knopf, 1996).

Goshen, Seev, "Eichmann und die Nisko-Aktion im Oktober 1939," *Vierteljahrshefte für Zeitgeschichte,* 10 (1981), pp. 74–96.

Idem, "The Nisko Operation (1939–1940)" (Hebrew), *Dapim L'Heker Ha-Shoah,* 2 (1981), pp. 177–195

Gottwaldt, Alfred, and Diana Schulle, *Die "Judendeportationen" aus dem Deutsche Reich 1941–1945* (Wiesbaden: Marix Verlag, 2005).

Grabitz, Helga and Wolfgang Scheffler, eds., *Letzte Spuren; Ghetto Warsachau, SS-Arbeitslager Trawniki, Aktion Erntefest, Fotos und Dokumente über Opfer des Endlösungswahns in Spiegel der historischen Ereignisse* (Berlin: Editons Hentrich, 1988).

Grabowski, Jan, *Hunt for the Jews: Betrayal and Murder in German-Occupied Poland* (Bloomington and Indianapolis: Indiana University Press, 2013).

Idem, "Rural Society and the Jews in Hiding: Elders, Night Watches, Firefighters, Hostages and Manhunts," *Yad Vashem Studies,* 40:1 (2012), pp. 49–74.

Gross, Jan Tomasz, *Neighbors: The Destruction of the Jewish Community in Jedwabne, Poland* (Princeton: Princeton University Press, 2001).

Idem, *Polish Society under German Occupation; The Generalgouvernement 1939–1944* (Princeton: Princeton University Press, 1979).

Gruner, Wolf, *Jewish Forced Labor under the Nazis: Economic Needs and Racial Aims, 1938–1944* (Cambridge: Cambridge University Press, 2006).

Gushee, David, "Many Paths to Righteousness: An Assessment of Research on Why Righteous Gentiles Helped Jews," *Holocaust and Genocide Studies,* 7:3 (1993), pp. 372–401.

Gutman, Israel, ed., *Encyclopedia of the Holocaust* (London and New York: Macmillan and Yad Vashem, 1990).

Idem, *The Jews of Warsaw, 1939*–1943 (Bloomington: Indiana University Press, 1982).

Idem, ed., *Patterns of Jewish Leadership in Nazi Europe, 1933–1945* (Jerusalem: Yad Vashem, 1979).

Idem and Shmuel Krakowski, *Unequal Victims: Poles and Jews During World War Two* (New York: Holocaust Library, 1986).

Herbert, Ulrich, "Racism and Rational Calculation: The Role of 'Utilitarian' Strategies of Legitimation in the National Socialist 'Weltanschauung,'" *Yad Vashem Studies,* 24 (1994), pp. 131–145.

Hilberg, Raul, *The Destruction of the European Jews,* Third Edition (New Haven and London: Yale University Press, 2003).

Idem, "The Kommandostab Revisited," *Yad Vashem Studies,* 34 (2006), pp. 355–367.

Höhne, Heinz, *The Order of the Death's Head: The Story of Hitler's S.S.* (New York: Ballantine, 1977, c1969).

Hurwitz, Ariel, "The Death March of the Jews of Chełm and

Hrubieszów to the Bug River, December 1939," M.A. seminar paper, The Hebrew University of Jerusalem, 1984.

Jäckel, Eberhard, "From Barbarossa to Wannsee: The Role of Reinhard Heydrich," in Shmuel Almog, et al., eds., *The Holocaust, History and Memory: Essays Presented in Honor of Israel Gutman* (Jerusalem: Yad Vashem and Avraham Harman Institute of Contemporary Jewry, Hebrew University, 2001), pp. 1–9.

Karay, Felicja, "The Confrontation among the German Authorities Regarding the Forced Labor Camps for Jews in the Generalgouvernement" (Hebrew), *Yalkut Moreshet,* 52 (April 1992), pp. 107–122.

Idem, *Death Comes in Yellow: Skarżysko-Kamienna Slave Labor Camp* (Amsterdam: Harwood, 1996).

Karski, Jan, *The Story of the Secret State* (Boston: Houghton Miflin, 1944).

Kasparek, Józef, "The Situation and Extermination of Jewish Population in Lublin during the Nazi Occupation (1939-1942)," paper presented before the *International Scientific Session on Nazi Genocide in Poland and in Europe 1939-1945,* April 14-17, 1983.

Idem, "Wysiedlenia w Lublinie w Okresie Okupacji Hitlerowskiej (1939-1944)," *Zeszyty Majdanka,* X (1980), pp. 108–130.

Kassow, Samuel D., *Who Will Write Our History: Rediscovering a Hidden Archive from the Warsaw Ghetto* (New York: Vintage Books, 2009, c2007).

Kielboń, Janina, *Migracje Ludności w Dystrykcie Lubelskim w Latach 1939–1944* (Lublin: Towarzystwo Opieki nad Majdankiem Państwowe Muzeum na Majdanku, 1995).

Idem, "Deportacje Żydów do Dystrykta Lubelskiego (1939–1943)," *Zeszyty Majdanka,* XIV (1992), pp. 61–92.

Koehl, Robert L., *RKFDV: German Resettlement and Population Policy 1939-1945* (Cambridge, MA: Harvard University Press, 1957).

Kopciowski, Adam, "Demographic Structure of the Jewish Population of Zamość," in *Everlasting Name: Zamość Ghetto Population List — 1940* (Tel Aviv: The Israeli Organization of Zamość Jewry, vicinity & their descendants, 2001), pp. 4–10.

Kossoy, Edward, *Handbuch zum Entschadigungsverfahren* (Munich: Oldenburg, 1958).

Krakowski, Shmuel, "The Fate of Jewish Prisoners of War in the September 1939 Campaign," *Yad Vashem Studies*, 12 (1977), pp. 315–318.

Idem, *Chełmno, A Small Village in Europe: the First Nazi Extermination Camp* (Jerusalem: Yad Vashem, 2009).

Idem, *The War of the Doomed* (New York: Holmes and Meier, 1984).

Kranz, Tomasz, "Das KL Lublin – zwischen Plannung und Realisierung," in Ulrich Herbert et al., eds., *Die Nationalsozialistischen Konzentrationslager – Entwicklung und Struktur*, vol. 1 (Göttingen: Wallstein Verlag, 1998), pp. 363–389.

Idem, "Das Konzentrationslager Majdanek und die 'Aktion Reinhardt'," in Bogdan Musial, ed., *"Aktion Reinhardt': Der Völkermord an den Juden im Generalgouvernement 1941–1944* (Osnabrück: Fibre Verlag, 2004), pp. 233–255.

Idem, *Extermination of Jews at the Majdanek Concentration Camp* (Lublin: Państwowe Muzeum na Majdanku, 2007).

Kroll, Bogdan, *Rada Główna Opiekuńcza 1939–1945* (Warsaw: Książka I Wiedza, 1985).

Kuwałek, Robert, "Das Durchgangsghetto in Izbica," *Theresienstädter Studien und Dokumente*, vol. (2003), pp. 321–351.

Idem, "Die Durchgangsghettos im Distrikt Lublin (u.a. Izbica, Piaski, Rejowiec, und Tawniki)," in Musial, ed., *"Aktion Reinhardt,"* pp. 197–232.

Kryl, Miroslav, "Deportationen von Theresienstadt nach Majdanek," *Thersienstädter Studien und Dokumente*, vol. 1 (1994), pp. 74–89.

Idem, "Deportacja Więźniów Terezinskiego Getta do Obozu Koncentracynego na Majdanku w 1942 roku," *Zeszyty Majdanka*, XI (1983), pp. 23–45.

Lenarczyk, Wojciech and Dariusz Libionka, eds., *Erntefest: Zapomniany epizod Zagłady, 3–4 Listpad 1943* (Lublin: Państwowe Muzeum na Majdanku, 2009).

Leociak, Jacek, "Censorship Keeping Guard over the Church.

Krystyna Modrzewska's Censored Memoir," *Holocaust: Studies and Materials*, 2 (2010), pp. 289–311.

Libionka, Dariusz, ed., *Akcja Reinhardt: Zagłada Żydów w Generalnym Gubernatorstwie* (Warsaw: Instytut Pamięci Narodowej, 2004).

Idem, "The Life Story of Chaim, Hirszman: Remembrance of the Holocaust and Reflections on Postwar Polish-Jewish Relations," *Yad Vashem Studies*, 34 (2006), pp. 219–247.

Idem and Laurence Weinbaum, "A New Look at the Betar 'Idyll' in Hrubieszów," *Yad Vashem Studies*, 37:1 (2009), pp. 85–108.

Idem, "Polska Ludność chrześcijańska wobec eksterminacji Żydów – dystrykt lubelski," in idem, ed., *Akcja Reinhardt: Zagłada Żydów w Generalnym Gubernatorstwie* (Warsaw: Instytut Pamięci Narodowej, 2004), pp. 306–333.

Lozowick, Yaacov, *Hitler's Bureaucrats: The Nazi Security Police and the Banality of Evil* (New York: Continuum, 2002).

Idem, *Malicious Clerks: The Nazi Security Police and the Banality of Evil* (Hebrew) (doctoral dissertation, The Hebrew University of Jerusalem, November 1995).

Lukas, Richard, *The Forgotten Holocaust; The Poles under German Occupation 1939-1944* (Lexington, KY: University of Kentucky Press, 1986).

Madajczyk, Czesław, *Die Okkupationspolitik Nazideutschlands in Polen 1939-1945* (Köln: Pahl-Rugenstein Verlag, 1988).

Marszałek, Józef, "Centralny Zarząd Budowlany SS i policji w Lublinie," *Zeszyty Majdanka*, IV (1972), pp. 11–35.

Idem, *Majdanek: The Concentration Camp in Lublin* (Warsaw: Interpress, 1986).

Idem, *Obozy Pracy w Generalnym Gubernatorstwie w Latach 1939–1945* (Lublin: Państwowe Muzeum na Majdanku, 1998).

Idem, "System obozów śmierci w Generalnym Gubernatorstwie i jego funkcje (1942–1943)," *Zeszyty Majdanka*, XVII (1996), pp. 17–38.

Matthäus, Jürgen, "What About the 'Ordinary Men'? The German Order Police and the Holocaust in the Occupied Soviet Union," *Holocaust and Genocide Studies*, 10:2 (1996), pp. 134–150.

Megargee, Geoffrey P., ed., *The United States Holocaust Memorial*

Museum Encyclopedia of Camps and Ghettos, 1933–1945, Volume I, Early Camps, Youth Camps, and Concentration Camps and Subcamps under the SS-Business Administration Main Office (WVHA) (Bloomington and Indianapolis: Indiana University Press with the United States Holocaust Memorial Museum, 2012).

Meirtchak, Benjamin, ed., *Jewish Prisoners-of-War Murdered by Germans in the Lublin District 1939–1943* (Tel Aviv: Association of Jewish Veterans of Polish Armies in Israel, 1996).

Michman, Dan, *The Emergence of Jewish Ghettos during the Holocaust* (Cambridge: Cambridge University Press and Yad Vashem, 2011).

Idem, *Holocaust Historiography: A Jewish Perspective: Conceptualizations, Terminology, Approaches and Fundamental Issues* (London: Vallentine Mitchell, 2003).

Milgram, Stanley, *Obedience to Authority* (New York: HarperCollins, 1974).

Miron, Guy and Shlomit Shulhani, eds., *The Yad Vashem Encyclopedia of the Ghettos in the Holocaust* (Jerusalem: Yad Vashem, 2009).

Moser, Jonny, "Nisko: The First Experiment in Deportation," *Simon Wiesenthal Center Annual,* 2 (1985), pp. 1–30.

Musial, Bogdan, ed., *„Aktion Reinhardt". Der Völkermord an den Juden im Generalgouvernement 1941–1944* (Osnabrück: Fibre Verlag and Deutsche Historishces Institut Warschau, 2004).

Idem, *Deutsche Zivilverwaltung und Judenverfolgung in Generalgouvernement; Eine Fallstudie zum Distrikt Lublin 1939–1943* (Wiesbaden: Harrassowitz Verlag, 1999).

Idem, "Ursprünge der 'Aktion Reinhardt'. Planung des Massenmordes an den Juden im Generalgouvernement," in idem, ed., *"Aktion Reinhardt': Der Völkermord an den Juden im Generalgouvernement 1941–1944* (Osnabrück: Fibre Verlag, 2004), pp. 49–85.

Idem, "The Origins of 'Operation Reinhard': The Decision-Making Process for the Mass Murder of the Jews in the *Generalgouvernement,*" *Yad Vashem Studies,* 28 (2000), pp. 113–153.

Neshamit, Sarah, "The Expulsion of the Jews of Suwalki and the Area, October–November 1939 and the Efforts to Save Them" (Hebrew), *Dapim L'Heker Ha-Shoah,* B (1981), pp. 202–216.

Oliner, Samuel and Pearl, *The Altruistic Personality* (New York: Free Press, 1988).

O'Neil, Robin, "Belzec: A Reassessment: Resettlement Transports to Belzec, March-December 1942," (December 6, 1999), www.jewishgen.org/Yizkor/belzec/belzec.html.

Paldiel, Mordecai, "The Altruism of the Righteous Gentiles," *Holocaust and Genocide Studies,* 3:2 (1988), pp. 187–196.

Idem, *The Path of the Righteous: Gentile Rescuers of Jews during the Holocaust* (Hoboken, NJ: KTAV, 1993).

Pilichowski, Czesław, *Obozy hitlerowskie na ziemiach polskich 1939–1945: Informator encyklopedyczny* (Warsaw: Państwowe Wydawnictwo Naukowe, 1979).

Pinkas Hakehillot: Encyclopedia of Jewish Communities, Poland, vol. 3, Western Galicia and Silesia, edited by Avraham Wein and Aharon Weiss (Hebrew) (Jerusalem: Yad Vashem, 1984).

Pinkas Hakehillot: Encyclopedia of Jewish Communities, Poland, vol. 4 — Warsaw and Its Region, edited by Abraham Wein (Hebrew) (Jerusalem: Yad Vashem, 1989).

Pinkas Hakehillot: Encyclopedia of Jewish Communities, Poland, vol. 7, Districts Lublin.Kielce, edited by Abraham Wein (Hebrew) (Jerusalem: Yad Vashem, 1999).

Piotrowski, Stanislaw, *Misja Odyla Globocnika: Sprawozdania o wynikach finansowych zagłady żydow w Polsce* (Warsaw: Państwowy Instytut Wydawniczy, 1949).

Pohl, Dieter, "Die Grossen Zwangsarbeitslager der SS- und Polizeiführer für Juden im Generalgouvernement 1942–1945," in Ulrich Herbert et al., eds., *Die Nationalsozialistischen Konzentrationslager — Entwicklung und Struktur,* vol. 1 (Wallstein Verlag, 1998), pp. 415–438.

Idem, "Hans Krüger and the Murder of the Jews in the Stanisławów Region," *Yad Vashem Studies,* 26 (1998), pp. 239–264.

Idem, "Rola dystryktu lubelskiego 'ostatecznym rozwiązaniu kwestii żydowskiej'," *Zeszyty Majdanka,* XVIII (1997), pp. 7–25.

Idem, *Von der «Judenpolitik» zum Judenmord; Der Distrikt Lublin des Generalgouvernements 1939–1944* (Frankfurt am Main: Peter Lang, 1993).

Polen, Nehemiah, *Holy Fire: The Teachings of Rabbi Kalonymos Kalman Shapiro, the Rebbe of the Warsaw Ghetto* (Northvale, NJ: Jason Aronson, 1994).

Poprzeczny, Joseph, *Odilo Globocnik: Hitler's Man in the East* (Jefferson, NC and London: McFarland, 2004).

Proudfoot, Malcolm J., *European Refugees: 1939–52; A Study in Forced Population Movement* (Evanston: Northwestern University Press, 1956).

Rich, Norman, *Hitler's War Aims; vol. 2, The Establishment of the New Order* (New York: W. W. Norton and Co., 1974).

Ringelblum, Emanuel, *Polish-Jewish Relations During the Second World War*, edited by Joseph Kermish and Shmuel Krakowski (Jerusalem: Yad Vashem, 1974).

Rohde, Horst, "Hitler's First Blitzkrieg and its Consequences for North-eastern Europe," in Klaus Maier, et al., *Germany and the Second World War; volume II, Germany's Initial Conquests in Europe*, (Oxford: Clarendon Press, 1991).

Rossino, Alexander, *Hitler Strikes Poland: Blitzkrieg, Ideology, and Atrocity* (Lawrence: University of Kansas Press, 2003).

Rothkirchen, Livia, *The Destruction of Slovak Jewry: A Documentary History* (Hebrew and English) (Jerusalem: Yad Vashem, 1961).

Rozett, Robert, "Jewish Armed Resistance in Hungary: A Comparative View," in David Cesarani, ed., *Genocide and Rescue, The Holocaust in Hungary 1944* (Oxford: Berg, 1997), pp. 135–146.

Rubin, Arnon, *The Rise and Fall of the Jewish Communities in Poland and Their Relics Today, vol. 2, Lublin* (Tel Aviv: privately published, 2005).

Rückerl, Adalbert, ed., *Nationalsozialistische Vernichtungslager im Spiegel deutscher Strafprozesse; Belzec, Sobibor, Treblinka, Chelmno,* (Munich: Deutsche Taschenbuch Verlag, 1977).

Saidel, Rochelle G., *Mielec, Poland: The Shtetl That Became a Nazi Concentration Camp* (Jerusalem and New York: Gefen, 2012).

Sakowska, Ruta, "Two Forms of Resistance in the Warsaw Ghetto – Two Functions of the Ringelblum Archives," *Yad Vashem Studies*, 21 (1991), pp. 189–219.

Schechtman, Joseph B., *European Population Transfers, 1939–1945* (New York: Oxford University Press, 1946).

Scheffler, Wolfgang, "The Forgotten Part of the 'Final Solution'; The Liquidation of the Ghettos," *Simon Wiesenthal Center Annual*, vol. 2 (1985), pp. 31–51.

Schelvis, Jules, *Vernichtungslager Sobibór* (Berlin: Metropol, 1998).

Idem, *Sobibor: A History of a Nazi Death Camp* (Oxford and New York: Berg, in association with the United States Holocaust Memorial Museum, 2007).

Schulte, Jan Erik, *Zwangsarbeit und Vernichtung: Das Wirtschaftsimperium der SS; Oswald Pohl und das SS-Wirtschafts-Verwaltungshauptamt 1933–1945* (Paderborn: Ferdinand Schöningh Verlag, 2001).

Schwindt, Barbara, *Das Konzentrations- und Vernichtungslager Madanek. Funktionswandel im Kontext der "Endlösung"* (Würzburg: Köningshausen & Neumann, 2005).

Seifert, Hermann Erich, *Der Jude an der Ostgrenze* (Berlin: Zentralverlag der NSDAP, 1941).

Seifert, Hermann Erich, *Der Jude an der Ostgrenze* (Berlin: Zentralverlag der NSDAP, Franz Eher Nachfolger, 1942).

Segal, Simon, *The New Order in Poland* (New York: Alfred A. Knopf, Feb. 1942).

Seraphim, Peter-Heinz, "Die Judenfrage im GG als brennendes Problem," *Die Burg*, X (1940).

Skibińska, Alina and Jakub Petelewicz, "The Participation of Poles in Crimes against Jews in the Świętokrzyskie Region," *Yad Vashem Studies*, 35:1 (2007), pp. 5–48.

Silberklang, David, "A Step Towards Death: The Bełżec Forced Labor Camps in 1940" (Hebrew), in *Dapim Studies on the Shoah*, 19 (2005), pp. 57–80.

Idem, "Defining the Ghettos: Jewish Perspectives and German Perspectives in the Lublin Ghetto," in Jonathan Petropolous, Lynn Rapaport, and John Roth, eds., *Lessons and Legacies*

Volume IX (Evanston: Northwestern University Press, 2010), pp. 106–123.

Idem, "Die Juden und die ersten Deportationen aus dem Distrikt Lublin," in Bogdan Musial, ed., *"Aktion Reinhardt": Der Völkermord an den Juden im Generalgouvernement 1942–1944* (Osnabrück: Fibre Verlag, 2004), pp. 141–164.

Idem, "Refleksje na temat losu Żydów w okupowanej Polsce 1939–1945," in *Pamięć i Sprawiedliwość,* no. 1(12) (2008), pp. 113–126.

Idem, "Willful Murder in the Lublin District of Poland," in Michael L. Morgan and Benjamin Pollock, eds., *The Philosopher as Witness: Emil Fackenheim and Responses to the Holocaust* (Albany: State University of New York Press, 2008), pp. 185–205.

Idem, "Working for Their Lives? The Last Jews in the Lublin District, 1943–1944," in Eduard Nižňansky, ed., *Z Dejín Holokaustu a Jeho Popiernia* (Bratislava: Stimul and Univerzita Komenského v Bratislave, 2007), pp. 54–88.

Idem, "Żydzi i pierwsze deportacje z dystryktu lubelskiego," in Dariusz Libionka, ed., *Akcje Reinhardt: Zagłada Żydów w Generalnym Gubernatorstwie* (Warsaw: Instytut Pamieci Narodowej, 2004), pp. 54–68.

Statistischen Amt des Generalgouvernement, *Amtliches Gemeinde- und Dorfverzeichnis fur das Generalgouvernement auf Grund der Summarischen Bevölkerungsbestandsaufnahme am 1. Marz 1943,* 2 vols. (Krakow: Burgverlag, 1943).

Steinhardt, Eric C., "The Chameleon of Trawniki: Jack Reimer, Soviet Volksdeutsche, and the Holocaust," *Holocaust and Genocide Studies,* 23:2 (2009), pp. 239–262.

Streim, Alfred, *Die Behandlung sowjetischer Kriegsgefangner im "Fall Barbarossa"* (Heidelberg: C. F. Müller Juristischer Verlag, 1981).

Streit, Christian, *Keine Kameraden: Die Wehrmacht und die sowjetishcen Kriegsgefangenen 1941–1945* (Stuttgart: Deutsche Verlags-Anstalt, 1978).

Sydnor, Charles Jr., "Executive Instinct; Reinhard Heydrich and the Planning for the Final Solution," in Michael Berenbaum and Abraham J. Peck, eds., *The Holocaust and History; The Known, the Unknown, the Disputed, and the Reexamined* (Bloomington: Indiana University Press and the United States Holocaust Memorial Museum, 1999), pp. 159–186.

Szyndler, Artur, "It's high time that the emigration problem will be solved finally": Leon Schönker and His Plan for Jewish Emigration from the Katowice District," *Yad Vashem Studies*, 39:1 (2011), pp. 71–115.

Tec, Nechama, *When Light Pierced the Darkness* (New York: Oxford University Press, 1986).

Tessin, Georg, Hans-Joachim Neufeldt, Jurgen Huck, *Zur Geschichte der Ordnungspolizei, 1936-1943, "Teil II - Die Sztabe und Truppeneinheiten der Ordnungspolizei"* (Koblenz: Bundesarchiv Koblenz, 1957).

Tregenza, Michael, "Belzec Death Camp," *Weiner Library Bulletin*, vol. XXX (1977), New Series, nos. 41/42, pp. 8–25.

Idem, "Bełżec — Okres Eksperymentalny, Listopad 1941 — Kwiecien 1942," *Zeszyty Majdanka*, XXI (2001), pp. 165–206.

Idem, "Christian Wirth a Pierwsza Faza 'Akcji Reinhard'," *Zeszyty Majdanka*, XIV (1992), pp. 7–37.

Idem, "Christian Wirth: Inspekteur der SS-Sonderkommandos 'Aktion Reinhard'," *Zeszyty Majdanka*, XV (1993), pp. 7–57.

Idem, "Report on the Archeological Investigation at the Site of the Former Nazi Extermination Camp in Belzec, Poland, 1997–98," (Lublin, 1998), www.jewishgen.org/Yizkor/belzec/belzec.html.

Trunk, Isaiah, "The Beginnings of the Deportation Methods: The Nisko Operation" (Hebrew), *Dapim L'Heker Tekufat HaShoah*, B (1982), pp. 196–201.

Idem, *Judenrat: The Jewish Councils in Eastern Europe under Nazi Occupation* (New York and London: Macmillan, 1972).

Umbreit, Hans, *Deutsche Militärverwaltungen 1938/39; Die militärische Besetzung der Tschechoslowakei und Polens* (Stuttgart: Deutsche Verlags-Anstalt, 1977).

Uziel, Daniel, *Arming the Luftwaffe: The German Aviation Industry in World War II* (Jefferson, NC: McFarland, 2011).

Weiss, Aharon, "Jewish Leadership in Occupied Poland - Postures and Attitudes," *Yad Vashem Studies*, 12 (1977), pp. 335-365.

Idem, *The Jewish Police in the Generalgouvernement and Upper Silesia during the Holocaust* (Hebrew) (doctoral dissertation, Hebrew University of Jerusalem, 1973).

Idem, "On the Policies of the 'Judenräte' in Eastern Poland" (Hebrew), *Yalkut Moreshet*, 15 (November 1972), pp. 59–122.

Idem, "Towards an Assessment of the Judenräte" (Hebrew), *Yalkut Moreshet*, 11 (November 1969), pp. 108–112.

Weitbrecht, Dorothee, "Ermächtigng zur Vernichtung: Die Einsatzgruppen in Polen im Herbst 1939," in Klaus-Michael Mallmann and Bogdan Musial, eds., *Genesis des Genozids: Polen 1939–1941* (Darmstadt: Wissenschaftliche Buchgesellschaft with Deutsche Historische Institut Warschau and Forschungsstelle Ludwigsburg der Universität Stuttgart, 2004), pp. 57–70.

White, Elizabeth B., "Majdanek: Cornerstone of Himmler's SS Empire in the East," *Simon Wiesenthal Center Annual*, 7 (1990), pp. 3–21.

Witte, Peter, "Functioning of the Death Camps in Belzec and Sobibor," paper presented at the conference "'Aktion Reinhardt': Extermination of the Jews in the General Government," Lublin, November 7, 2002.

Idem, "Letzte Nachrichten aus Siedliszcze: Der Transport Ax aus Theresienstadt in den Distrikt Lublin," *Theresienstädter Studien und Dokumente*, III (1996), pp. 98–113.

Idem and Stephen Tyas, "A New Document on the Deportation and Murder of Jews during 'Einsatz Reinhardt' 1942," *Holocaust and Genocide Studies*, 15:3 (Winter 2001), pp. 468–486.

Yahil, Leni, *The Holocaust: The Fate of European Jewry, 1932–1945* (Oxford and New York: Oxford University Press, 1990).

Idem, "Madagascar — Phantom Solution for the Jewish Question," in Bela Vago and George Mosse, eds., *Jews and Non-Jews in Eastern Europe 1918–1945* (Toronto & Jerusalem: John Wiley & Sons and Israel Universities Press/Keter, 1974), pp. 315–334.

Żbikowski, Andrzej, "Texts Buried in Oblivion. Testimonies of Two Refugees from the Mass Grave in Poniatowa," *Holocaust: Studies and Materials*, 1 (2008), pp. 76–102.

Yizkor Books

Barnea, Aryeh, ed., *The Jews of Lubartów: Life, Holocaust, Remnants* (Hebrew) (Tel Aviv: Lubartów Immigrants Committee, 1987).

Bernstein, ed., Mordechai W., *Puławy Yizkor Book* (Yiddish) (New York: Pulawer Yizkor Book Committee, 1964).

Bychawa Memorial Book, edited by Yaakov Adani (Hebrew) (Tel Aviv: Bychawa Immigrants Association in Israel, 1969).

Chełm Yizkor Book, edited by Melech Bakalczuk-Felin (Yiddish) (Johannesburg: Chełm Landsmannschaft, 1954).

Częstochower Yidn, edited by Raphael Mahler (Yiddish) (New York, 1947).

Dęblin-Modzitz Book, edited by David Shtockfish (Yiddish) (Tel Aviv: Dęblin-Modzitz Immigrants Association, 1969).

Destruction and Heroism from the Town Markuszów, edited by David Shtokfish (Yiddish) (Tel Aviv: Markuszów Immigrants Association, 1955).

Dos Buch fun Lublin: Memories, Testimonies. and Materials on the the Struggle for Life and the Martyrdom of the Jewish Community of Lublin (Yiddish) (Paris: C.A.P.N. Press, 1952).

Encyclopedia of the Jewish Diaspora, vol. 5, Lublin, edited by Nachman Blumental and Meir Korzen (Hebrew) (Jerusalem, Tel Aviv: Encyclopedia of the Jewish Diaspora, 1957).

Feigenbaum, Moshe Yosef, ed., *The Biała-Podlaska Book* (Hebrew) (Tel Aviv: Charity Fund in Honor of the Biała-Podlaska Community, 1961).

Feigenbojm, Mosze Yosef, *Podlosie in Its Downfall: Notes from the Destruction* (Yiddish) (Munich: Commission of the Liberated Jews in the American Zone in Germany, 1948); Hebrew edition – (Tel Aviv: Association of Immigrants from Międzyrzec-Podlaski in Israel, 2002).

Hurban Częstochow, edited by Shlomo Waga (Yiddish) (Buenos Aires, 1949).

In Memory of the Destroyed Jewish Community of Ryki, edited by Shimon Kanc (Yiddish) (Tel Aviv: Ryki Immigrants Association in Israel, 1973).

Jewish Radom in Its Destruction (Yiddish) (Stuttgart: Radom Jews Committee, 1948).

Kaplinski, Baruch, ed., *Pinkas Hrubieszów* (Hebrew) (Tel Aviv: Hrubieszów Immigrants Association, 1969).

Kehillat Horodło: Memorial Book to the Horodło Martyrs and the Martyrs of the Nearby Villages, edited by Yosef Haim Zawidoeicz (Yiddish and Hebrew) (Tel Aviv: Horodło Immigrants Committee in Israel, 1960).

Lublin: City of Torah, Rabbinics, and Hassidut, edited by Nahman Shemen (Yiddish) (Toronto: Gershon Pomerantz Essay Library, 1951).

Memorial Book for the Grabowiec Kehilla, edited by Shimon Kanc (Hebrew) (Tel Aviv: Grabowiec Immigrants Association in Israel, 1975).

Memorial Book for Włodawa and the Sobibór Area, edited by Shimon Kanc (Hebrew) (Tel Aviv: Włodawa Immigrants Association in Israel, 1974).

Memorial Book to Kehillat Rawa-Ruska and the Area (Yiddish and Hebrew) (Tel Aviv: Rawa Ruska Immigrants Society, 1973).

Memorial Book to the Kehilla of Siedliszcze and the Area, edited by Benjamin Haruvi (Hebrew) (Siedliszcze Immigrants Association in Israel, 1970).

Memorial Book to the Szczebrzeszyn Kehilla (Hebrew) (Haifa: Szczebrzeszyn Immigrants Association in Israel and the Diaspora, 1984)

Mezericz: Scrapbook in Honored Memory of a Fallen Jewish Community, Our Hometown (Yiddish) (Buenos Aires: Mezericz Landsleit Association, 1952).

Opole-Lubelski Yizkor Book, edited by David Shtokfish (Yiddish and Hebrew) (Tel Aviv: Association of Opole Immigrants in Israel and the Diaspora, 1977).

Ostrów-Lubelski Book, edited by David Stokfisch (Yiddish and Hebrew) (Tel Aviv: Organization of Ostrów-Lubelski Immigrants in Israel, 1987).

Pinkas Kuzmir, David Shtokfish (Hebrew and Yiddish) (Tel Aviv: Kuzmir Immigrants Association in Israel, 1970).

Pinkas Tyszowiec, edited by Yaakov Zifer (Hebrew) (Tel Aviv: Tyszowiec Immigrants Association, 1971).

Pinkas Zamość: Yizkor Book, edited by Mordechai Bernstein (Yiddish) (Buenos Aires: Central Committee for Pinkas Zamość, 1957).

Radzyn 1939–1943, by Yehoshua Rosenkrantz (Hebrew) (Tel Aviv: Radzyn-Podlaski Immigrants Committee in Eretz-Israel, 1944).

Sefer Częstochow (Hebrew) (Jerusalem: Encyclopedia of the Jewish Diaspora, 1967).

Sefer Frampol, edited by David Shtokfish (Hebrew) (Tel Aviv: Orly Press, 1966).

Sefer Kraśnik, edited by David Shtockfish (Yiddish and Hebrew) (Tel Aviv: Society of Kraśnik Jews in Israel, 1973).

Sefer Łuków: Honoring the Destroyed Community (Yiddish) (Tel Aviv: Łuków Immigrants Association in Israel, 1968).

Sefer Mezericz: In Memory of Our City's Martyrs, edited by Yitzhak Ronkin (Hebrew) (Tel Aviv: The Mezericz Center in Israel and Landsmannschaften in the Diaspora, 1978).

Sefer Radom, edited by Yitzhak Perlow (Hebrew) (Tel Aviv: Radom Immigrants Association, 1961).

Sefer Radzyn; Yizkor Book, edited by Yitzhak Zeligman (Yiddish and Hebrew) (Tel Aviv: Radzyn Immigrants Committee in Israel, 1957).

Sefer Tarnogrod: In Memory of a Destroyed Jewish Community, edited by Shimon Kanc (Hebrew) (Tel Aviv: Tarnogrod Immigrants Association in Israel, 1966).

Sefer Turobin, Memorial Volume (Hebrew) (Tel Aviv: Turobin Immigrants Association in Israel, 1967).

Shimon Kanc, ed., *Memorial Book for the Chełm Community* (Hebrew) (Tel Aviv: Chełm Immigrants Association, 1981).

The Book of the Piaski Community in Its life and Destruction, edited by Yisrael Dayan (Hebrew) (Haifa: Piaski Immigrants Association in Israel, 1988).

The Destruction of Biłgoraj, edited by Avraham Kronenberg (Yiddish and Hebrew) (Tel Aviv, 1957).

The Jewish City Mezericz, from Its Beginning until the Eve of the

War (Yiddish) (Buenos Aires: Mezericz Landsleit Association, 1957).

The Rachów/Annopol Book: Testimonies and Memoirs, edited by Shmuel Nitzan (Yiddish and Hebrew) (Tel Aviv: Rachów Annopol Immigrants Association, 1978).

Tomaszow Yizkor Book (Yiddish) (Brooklyn: Tomashover Relief Committee New York, 1965).

Włodawa Memorial Candle: Documentary Book and General Survey, edited by David Rowner (Hebrew) (Jerusalem: National Library, 1968).

Yizkor Book for the Destroyed Wojsławice Kehilla, edited by Shimon Kanc (Yiddish) (Tel Aviv: Wojsławice Immigrants Association in Israel, 1970).

Yizkor Book in Memory of the Krasnystaw Martyrs, edited by Aryeh Schtutzinger (Yiddish) (Munich: Befreiung, 1948).

Zamość in its Agony and Destruction, edited by Ze'ev Tamari (Hebrew) (Tel Aviv: The Committee of Zamość Immigrants in Israel, 1953).

Index

People

Places